Russia
and History's
Turning Point

Russia
and History's
Turning Point

by

ALEXANDER KERENSKY

DUELL, SLOAN AND PEARCE

New York

First Edition

DUELL, SLOAN & PEARCE
AFFILIATE OF
MEREDITH PRESS

Library of Congress Catalog Card Number: 65-24855

MANUFACTURED IN THE UNITED STATES OF AMERICA FOR MEREDITH PRESS

VAN REES PRESS   •   NEW YORK

Acknowledgments

Grateful acknowledgment for assistance in translation and research is made to: Tatiana Dirugina, Max Hayward, Mrs. Ellen Powers, George Reavey, and John Richardson.

My special thanks are offered to the Warden of St. Antony's College, Oxford, and the members of the College; and to Mrs. Kenneth F. Simpson and Countess Fira Ilinska.

Unless otherwise indicated, all dates prior to February 1, 1918 are Old Style (13 days earlier than New Style). All dates after February 1, 1918, are New Style.

Contents

Historical Prelude

ON August 30, 1880, Fyodor Dostoyevsky wrote in his *Diary of a Writer:* " . . . I have a presentiment of sorts that the lots are drawn. Accounts may have to be settled far sooner than one might imagine in one's wildest dreams. The symptoms are terrible. The age-old, unnatural situation of the European states may suffice to set things in motion. Indeed, how could this situation be natural when age-old artificiality lies at its very root. No longer can one part of mankind enslave all the rest. Now, *all* the civil institutions (which long ago ceased to be Christian) of Europe (which is now completely pagan) have been set up to do just this. . . . This unnatural state of affairs and these insoluble political problems (which, let it be said, are today known to all) cannot but lead to a huge, final political war, involving everyone, that will break out in this century, and perhaps, even in this decade . . ."

There was nothing clairvoyant about Dostoyevsky's prophecy. From a close study of the activities of Bismarck and other contemporary politicians and statesmen, Dostoyevsky had come to the logical conclusion that the struggle of the great powers for world domination was bound to lead to war. His prediction came true in the early part of the twentieth century.

By the early 1890's the possibility of an all-European war was being taken very seriously by all who observed the deteriorating relations between the great powers and their ever-growing military budgets, which they justified on the principle that "if you want peace, prepare for war." A movement for disarmament was gaining popularity, and military experts and economists were pointing out the disastrous social and political implications of a European war with new weapons and modern armies. The eminent historian I. S. Bliokh, for instance, summed up as follows the prevailing mood among experts at the turn of the century:

Any future war will give rise to new economic phenomena. The great European powers have split into two hostile camps and war would no longer be localized but would spread throughout the entire continent. Military and naval blockades were unknown in earlier wars. Vital changes have taken place since 1870; first of all, there is tremendous industrial development combined with the expansion of communications and of international financial and trade relations; and secondly, there is the economic pressure exerted by the vast North American republic upon Europe. The giant industrial development of North America represents a potential threat for the European market, which, in the case of war, would be paralyzed. . . . If the armaments race continues at the rate of the past thirty years, the culture of many generations will be destroyed.[1]

In the same vein Field Marshal von Moltke said at the end of the century:

War will obliterate war. It is fairly obvious that the armaments race and the resulting equal preparedness of all countries for war are based on the illusion that belligerent ambitions can be realized with the same ease as in the past.
Hardly anyone in European ruling circles would venture to deny that means of mass destruction may become so powerful as to make war an impossibility. It is up to us to determine whether we have reached the stage at which war has become not only destructive but politically futile.

In the spring of 1899, an attempt was made to halt the race toward the brink. On Russia's initiative the First International Peace Conference met at the Hague, attended by all the great powers, including the newly emerging United States and Japan. This conference proved as futile as all subsequent peace talks, for it only revealed the unwillingness of all imperialist governments to cut down their armed forces. This was particularly true of the expanding sea powers, which were now frantically vying with one another and with England.

But in that age of vehement expansionism, no stigma was attached to the concept of imperialism, which was regarded by the great powers

[1] See I. S. Bliokh, *Economic Difficulties in Case of War*, Vol. IV (St. Petersburg, 1898), pp. 163, 169, 170, 175, 195, personal library of Tsar Nicholas II.

as a mission to be fulfilled for the benefit of mankind. This concept was embodied in the person of that outstanding advocate of imperialism and sea power, Alfred Thayer Mahan (1840–1914), of whom his biographer William E. Livezey writes: [2]

As an ardent navalist, forthright imperialist and frank nationalist, Mahan interpreted his age to itself; and that age of competitive navalism, rampant imperialism, virulent nationalism and lawless militarism acclaimed him seer and champion ... He was an expansionist who believed the greatest good to the greatest number of people came from a policy of beneficent imperialism ... he claimed that the ever-increasing armaments of Europe not only preserved the peace but prevented the demoralization of the European peoples by preventing a flood of socialist measures which would follow the release of the sums then spent on armaments. ...

France, an ally of Russia, obsessed by the idea of "revenge" for the disaster of 1871, was no less persistent than Germany in trying to undermine the work of the Peace Conference at The Hague. The futility of negotiating on a reduction of armaments in a world filled with gunpowder and mutual distrust was further demonstrated in October, 1899, when England declared war on the Boers. This unfortunate venture lasted almost three years, until May, 1902. Then, finally coming to sense the hostility of all continental Europe, Britain abandoned her policy of "splendid isolation." This was the signal for a dramatic change in international policy.

Britain resolutely set about preparing an agreement with such traditional enemies as France and Russia. In April, 1904, after Russia had declared war on Britain's ally, Japan, the Entente Cordiale was signed between Britain and France. Then, as soon as the Russo-Japanese War ended, secret overtures were made to Russia, which culminated, in September, 1907, in the inclusion of Russia in the entente.

Europe was now split into two irreconcilable blocs of almost equal strength. The outbreak of World War I on August 1, 1914, was a turning point in man's destiny, the full consequences of which were not apparent until after World War II.

In terms of long-range historical developments, the effects of World

2 See William E. Livezey, *Mahan on Sea Power* (University of Oklahoma Press, 1957), pp. 271, 272, 293.

War I, described at the time by the leaders of the great democratic powers as "the war to end all wars," in fact led our century into a series of international conflicts, revolutions, and uprisings; it brought about a state of permanent warfare.

The war that was supposed to abolish all vestiges of absolutism and to set up a new democratic order gave birth instead to an unprecedented totalitarian ideology, which was first put into practice in 1917 by the Russian Bolsheviks. This new form of dictatorship was not a purely Russian phenomenon. On December 10, 1918, after the capitulation of Germany, the "Spartacists" made their first attempt to take over the government in Germany. In the beginning of January, 1919, in league with a group of independent leftist socialists in Berlin, they tried again to organize a revolt. Further Communist uprisings in Munich and Berlin followed in February and March. The Communist movement was rapidly growing in Germany. The Third International was founded in Moscow on March 4, 1919. In Hungary Bela Kun's savage Communist dictatorship raged for several months, only to be replaced by Admiral Horthy's rightist dictatorship, which lasted until the end of World War II. In December, 1920, when, at a congress in Tours, a majority of the French Socialist Party adopted the program of the Third International, the unity of the Socialist Party was disrupted once and for all. At a party congress held in 1921 in Leghorn, the Italian Socialist Party was also irrevocably split.

On June 28, 1919, Germany, which had become a democratic republic after the collapse of the Empire founded in 1871 by Bismarck, signed the Peace Treaty of Versailles dictated by Russia's former allies. It was a punitive and unrealistic agreement. In the spring of 1920, Adolf Hitler, in collaboration with General Ludendorff (the *de facto* dictator of Germany during the last two years of World War I), launched a "national-socialist" movement which, like Communism, was totalitarian and antidemocratic, but, unlike Communism, extremely nationalist in spirit. Armed clashes between Mussolini's Fascists and Communists throughout Italy marked the month of April, 1921. On October 28, 1922, armed Fascists occupied Rome without meeting any resistance, and their "Duce" became the dictator of Italy. The "beer-hall putsch" in Munich and Hitler's abortive attempt to take over Bavaria occurred in the early part of November, 1923. In the late 1920's Western Europe was the arena of a struggle for ideological and political hegemony between two fundamentally irreconcilable totalitarian movements.

On January 30, 1933, Hitler was officially appointed chancellor, while remaining the unofficial ruler of Germany—its *Führer*. He tore up the "Versailles Dictate" and furiously started to rearm Germany. The contrived structure that was the Versailles concept of Europe collapsed. Fascist and semifascist dictators, puppets of the *Führer*, seized power all over Europe, from the Urals to Spain.[3]

As Marshal Foch had predicted, the Versailles Peace Treaty was in reality a temporary truce, which was only the prelude to an even more disastrous war. Britain and France declared war on the Third Reich on September 1, 1939. By the end of 1941, all continental Europe was occupied by the Nazis. France capitulated on June 22, 1940. Great Britain, isolated on her island, valiantly continued to wage a war in the air and on the sea for what seemed to be a lost cause. Paradoxically, it was Germany and Japan that gave the British Empire a respite. First, on June 22, 1941, German tanks invaded Russia. Then the Japanese made a surprise attack on Pearl Harbor on December 7, just as they had attacked the Russian fleet at Port Arthur 37 years earlier. In both cases they completely changed the balance of forces between themselves and their enemies.

Great Britain, Russia, and the United States crushed Germany, Italy, and Japan only after six long years of war. At the end of this apocalyptic war, continental Western Europe was materially and spiritually exhausted. It had disappeared from the map of the world as the arbiter of world politics.

The reins of power were held by the leaders of Great Britain, the USSR, and the United States. Ostensibly in harmony, "The Big Three," Roosevelt, Stalin, and Churchill, set about rebuilding the structure of the world community on a basis of freedom, peace, and social justice.

But the war had scarcely ended before the omnipotent triumvirate split up. This schism marked the final stage in the turning point of history: The world entered an era of "cold" or psychological warfare.

Now another factor has been added to the situation: The national liberation movement for racial and political equality and social justice has developed into a struggle against foreign oppression and colonial-

---

[3] England, France, Belgium, the Netherlands, Scandinavia, Switzerland, and Czechoslovakia remained untouched, however.

ism. The wind of freedom has become a hurricane sweeping through the boundless spaces of Africa and Asia. In April, 1955, the representatives of the Afro-Asian liberation movement met in Bandung to proclaim the inalienable right of their countries to independence and to participation in the building of a new political, social, and economic order. Within an incredibly short period of time many young nations in Africa and Asia won independence, and their birth marked the dawn of a new era.

Thus, the dominance of a great civilization came to a sudden and tragic end, engulfed by the bloody orgy of a two-stage war (1914–1945).

The struggle of the imperialist powers for world leadership, for colonies, protectorates, spheres of influence, and trusteeship territories was launched in 1914, only to end in 1955 with the destruction of the colonial and imperialist system.

Henceforth, the destiny of mankind is in the hands of the representatives of all peoples and not only of a minority nurtured in the very Hellenist-Christian ideals that it has betrayed. A great world cataclysm has run its course and we are on the threshold of an unknown era.

History Versus Autobiography

In describing the changing tide of world events, it has not been my purpose to write "objective history." Such an endeavor, I believe, would be premature. So I have only tried to set down my record of that period in the history of my country to which I was a witness or in which I was a participant. I am frequently approached by representatives of the postwar generation, including Soviet students, with questions about the extraordinary course of events in Russia from its depths of degradation in November, 1917 to its present elevation to a position of world power. I have found my own answers to these questions, but I would not wish to impose them upon others. For I have arrived at these conclusions, not as a historian, but as an eyewitness.

It is commonly said that the historian writes objectively, while the eyewitness gives a biased testimony that must be carefully scrutinized by the historian. From both the historian and the eyewitness, however, all that one can reasonably expect is objectivity with regard to the facts. For both, their interpretation of the facts and the conclusions they draw from them are subjective and cannot be anything else; everything external, whether past or present, is perceived by historian and eyewitness alike through an "ego" that is unique in every person. The truth of this may be tested by reading about an event as described by two different historians. There is, for example, the *History of the Great French Revolution,* written by an admirer, Jules Michelet, and by a critic, Hippolyte Taine.[4] In both writings the events described are the same; their evaluation, however, is diametrically opposed. By analogy, the accounts of two eyewitnesses who live through the same experiences may differ greatly according to their points of view.

Nevertheless, the "ego" does not occupy a central place in the historian's account—nor should it do so—in the sense that the historian does not write in the first person, although in evaluating events and the persons they involve he does express thoughts and pass judgments conditioned by his particular view of the world.

In the writings of an eyewitness, on the other hand, the "ego" occupies a dominant place. For in recounting the feelings and actions of others, he cannot avoid discussion of himself. He has no right to be self-effacing. He must write in the first person, since willy-nilly his story is largely an autobiography.

The personality of an adult is, of course, deeply rooted in his childhood. From the moment a man is born he is exposed to a great flood of impressions and sensations. Contrary to what Jean Jacques Rousseau would have us believe, however, a child's mind is not a *tabula rasa* on which anything at all can be written. A child is not just a bundle of conditioned reflexes. Apart from his animal instincts and neurophysiological responses, he has a spiritual essence or substance—a unique "self"—which strives to express and assert itself externally. From the moment he is born man does not merely react passively to the flow of external impressions and sensations, but distinguishes between them, selecting what is most congenial to and compatible with his "ego."

Man's spiritual essence, of which he is unaware at the beginning

---

[4] P. Milyukov, the well-known historian-turned-statesman, used to say that before the Russian Revolution he used to be in favor of Michelet, but that after 1917 he came to prefer Taine.

of his life, becomes by adolescence a self-aware and autonomous "personality."

That is why man's life is not determined by the law of causality of the material world, but rather by the *free* intuitive choice of his "ego," which expresses itself in deliberate acts of the will.

When faced with a new set of external circumstances, an adult is free to respond in his own way and to choose between the several courses of action open to him. And the higher up on the political and social scale he is, the greater his influence on those around him, the greater is his responsibility for the path along which others follow him to their chosen goal.

In stable and peaceful times people hardly feel their ties with history, and they are unaware of their part in creating it. They are content with the thought that the particular social and political system under which they live has little connection with their everyday activities, interests, and ambitions. They imagine that politics does not concern them. In such times materialist ideologies gain ground, and it becomes fashionable to belittle the importance of man's role in history and to consider him a mere cog in the huge machine of "objective" progress.

During my youth any belief in the independent "role of personality" in history was regarded in intellectual circles as the hallmark of cultural backwardness and even of political reaction. But later, in the period of violent and radical changes on the world scene, the role of personality in history became increasingly difficult to deny.

I have been led to my firm belief in its supreme importance by the experience of my own life.

Alexander Kerensky

New York,
May 4, 1965

The Roots
of My Weltanschauung

1

The Formative Years

SIMBIRSK,[1] a town on the middle Volga, was one of the most backward of Russian provincial capitals under the reign of Alexander III. There was no railway at all. Steamers plied the river during the navigable period, but only horses could be used during the long winter months when the only highway was the endless frozen river. The town was built in 1648 on a hill on the higher bank. At the top of the hill stood the cathedral, the governor's mansion, the grammar school, a nunnery, and the public library. The hillside, right down to the water's edge, was covered with luxuriant apple and cherry orchards. In the spring it was white with fragrant blossoms and breathless with the songs of nightingales at night. A broad tree-lined boulevard, popularly known as Venets (Crown), ran down steeply from the top of the hill to the waterfront, and the view across the river over miles of meadowland was magnificent. Each year with the melting of the snow, the river left its bed and flooded the low-lying lands on the left bank, stretching like a boundless sea over the fields. Later, in the heat of summer, those fields would be enlivened by the songs of the peasants who came to mow the rich grass and build it into tall haystacks, and by the games of picnicking townspeople. All around the town, on the steep banks of the river, stood the country manors of the gentry.

Politically, the town reproduced in miniature the full gamut of the emotions that were rocking the foundations of the country. For although Simbirsk was predominantly a town of conservative landowners hostile to the great liberal reforms of Alexander II, there was also a small elite of teachers, doctors, judges and lawyers that ardently

[1] Now Ulyanovsk, after Vladimir Ilyich Ulyanov, better known as Lenin, who was born there in 1870.

3

supported these reforms and introduced new, liberal ideas into the everyday life of the town. And at the bottom of the social hierarchy, there was a third group, the radicals, or "nihilists," as the young revolutionary firebrands were called by the conservative upper class.

St. Petersburg was reminded of the existence of Simbirsk in a rather unpleasant way with the uncovering of a plot to assassinate Alexander III. It was to have been carried out on March 1, 1887, and one of the conspirators was Alexander Ulyanov, son of the director of primary education in Simbirsk and elder brother of Vladimir Ulyanov (Lenin). Without so much as a railway or a daily postal service, our obscure town had managed to interlace its life with that of the mighty Empire.[2]

Although Alexander Ulyanov entered my life only fleetingly, he left an indelible impression, not as a person but as an ominous threat that played upon my childish imagination. The mere mention of his name evoked the picture of a mysterious carriage with drawn green blinds driving through the town at night to take people away into the unknown at the behest of Sonya's stern father. Sonya was a little girl who was occasionally brought to dance with us, and her father was chief of the gendarmerie of Simbirsk Province. The discovery of the assassination conspiracy in St. Petersburg and the arrest of the son of a prominent Simbirsk civil servant led to reprisals and arrests in the town, and it was usual for them to be carried out at night. The frightened talk of the grown-ups about these dreadful events penetrated into our nursery, and owing to the close connection between our parents and the Ulyanovs we soon learned of the execution of their talented son. Such was my initial contact with the revolutionary movement.

I was born on April 22, 1881. My father, Fyodor Mikhailovich Kerensky, was at that time director of a grammar school (gymnasium) for boys and of a secondary school for girls. His career was not altogether commonplace. He was born in 1842 into the family of a poor parish priest of the Kerensky[3] District of the Penza Province.

---

[2] By a curious whim of history the three men most immediately connected with the crucial years of Russian history—the universally despised last Tsarist minister of the interior, A. D. Protopopov (b. 1864), Vladimir Lenin, and myself—were all natives of Simbirsk.

[3] Our name and that of the town were derived from the river Kerenka. The stress is on the first syllable (Kérensky), not on the second, as my name is commonly mispronounced by Russians and foreigners alike.

In those days the clergy was an estate in itself, with its own age-old traditions and customs. The children of clergymen even attended special schools. My father graduated from such a school and then studied at the theological seminary in Penza. After the 1848 revolution in Western Europe, admission to the universities had been barred to all but the children of the gentry, but under Alexander II this social discrimination had been abolished, and my father's great ambition of enrolling in a university had eventually been fulfilled. Because of his poverty he was forced to work for a time as an ordinary district school teacher, but when he had earned enough money by this drudgery, he entered the University of Kazan, which at the time was one of the best in Russia. Like many would-be priests of his generation, he had no genuine vocation for the ministry, and instead of following in the footsteps of his father, he now devoted himself wholeheartedly to the study of history and classical philology. His outstanding talent for teaching was soon recognized and appreciated. At the age of 30 he was appointed to the post of inspector of a grammar school, and at 37 he became school principal in Vyatka. Two years later he took over two schools for boys and girls in Simbirsk.[4]

My parents met in Kazan, where my father held his first teaching post after leaving the university. My mother was one of his pupils. She was the daughter of the chief of the Topographical Section of the staff of the Kazan Military District, and the granddaughter, on her mother's side, of a serf who had bought his own freedom and had become a prosperous Moscow merchant. My mother inherited a considerable sum of money from him.

My earliest memories merge into a general picture of happy days spent in the family home. A long corridor divided our home into the world of the grown-ups and the world of the children. My two elder sisters, who attended school, were cared for by a French governess. But the young children were the responsibility of the *nyanya,* whose name was Yekaterina Sergeyevna Suchkova. She was illiterate and had been a serf in her youth. Her duties were those of any *nyanya:* She woke us up in the morning, dressed us, gave us breakfast, took us for walks, and played with us. At night when she put us to bed, she took particular care that the collars of our long shirts were unbuttoned "to let the evil spirit out," as she put it. Before bedtime she told us folk

4 See Note at end of chapter.

tales, and when we grew older she sometimes reminisced about the days of serfdom. She shared our spacious nursery. Her own corner was lovingly adorned with icons, and at night the oil lamp that she always lit threw a soft light on the ascetic faces of her favorite saints. In the winter she went to bed with us; then, through half-closed eyes, I would watch her as she knelt before the icons, fervently whispering her prayers. There was really nothing remarkable about her. She had neither a keen mind nor profound wisdom. But to us children she meant everything.

In our daily childish preoccupations and joys Mother was closer to us than Father. Father never interfered with the routine of the nursery. In our childish minds he stood apart, a superior being to whom *nyanya* and Mother reported only in emergencies. Usually, order could be restored by the threat: "Father will teach you a lesson, just you see," although Father never used physical punishment, but talked to us and tried to make us understand how we had been wrong. Mother liked to sit with us while we had our milk in the morning. She asked about our doings, and scolded us gently whenever necessary. At night, she came into the nursery to make the sign of the cross over our heads and kiss us goodnight. From earliest childhood we said our prayers in the morning and at bedtime.

After our morning walk with the *nyanya*, Mother often called us into her room. We did not have to be asked twice. We knew that we would be allowed to sit snugly next to her while she read to us or told stories. She read not only fairy tales but also poems, epics about Russian heroes and books about Russian history. These mornings stimulated us not only to listen but also to read by ourselves. I cannot recall when it was that Mother first read from the Gospel to us. It was not like the usual sort of religious instruction, because Mother never tried to drum religious dogmas into our heads. She simply read and talked about the life and words of Jesus.

The practice of Christianity, however, was taught to us by our *nyanya*. I shall never forget, for example, one fine spring morning when we went for our regular walk. After a long, hard winter the first ships were moving down the Volga. A party of convicts condemned to exile in Siberia was being led through the town from the local prison to the wharf. The grim procession, guarded by a convoy of soldiers, was followed by a wagon crowded with women and children. To us children the convicts were frightening with their half-shaven heads and their clanking chains, and when we saw them my brother and I started to run away. "What's the matter with you?" our *nyanya* called after us. "Do you really think they're going to hurt you? These poor wretches, you'd better take pity on them. Who are we to judge and condemn them? Let's be kind to them in the name of Christ." And turning to me, she said, "Now, Sasha, I'll buy a *kalach*,[5] and you must ask the soldier in front to let you give it to the poor men. Not only will they enjoy it, but it'll make you feel good, too." Thus it was *nyanya* who brought Christianity into the practical sphere of our daily life. When we fought with each other, my brother Fedya and I, she used to shame us by saying: "Aren't you horrid little boys! Jesus wants us to forgive each other and this is how you obey Him."

It is with a deep feeling of satisfaction that I think back to my childhood in a Russia where everyday life had its roots in religious feelings nurtured by a thousand years of Christianity.

My brother Fedya and I loved the religious festivals of the year. On Annunciation Day we waited impatiently for the caged birds to be brought in and set free, in recognition of the spiritual brotherhood of all creation. For, according to an old Russian adage, "even birds rest on that holy day and do not build a nest." In Lent a solemn silence fell upon the town, in strong contrast to the merrymaking of the carnival just ended. At the age of seven we were allowed to attend the magnificent midnight mass at Easter. I remember one solemn service in particular, the priest coming out to administer Holy Communion to the children, and my brother and I, dressed in white piqué with red ties under our stiff white collars, being brought up to him. Behind us there was an orderly row of schoolboys in tight-fitting blue uniforms with silver buttons, and among them must have been the model pupil Vladimir Ulyanov (Lenin). I remember too an occasion when I stopped, deeply struck, before an image of the resurrected Christ which was so illuminated as to appear transparent and seemed to me to be alive. As a boy, Vladimir Ulyanov must have also looked at that image and, perhaps, laughed heartily to himself while keeping up a devout appearance—if we are to believe his own story that he threw

---

[5] When convicts were driven through the streets, the people in their compassion gave them alms or bought them bread—a special kind called *kalach;* there were always several *kalach* vendors walking alongside the convict parties.

his baptismal cross into the dustbin at about the age of fourteen. There was no duplicity, however, about my own feelings, and in a childish way I was deeply religious. I remember the old archpresbyter of our cathedral, who came for tea on Sundays and gave me popular religious leaflets which explained the meaning of the major church holidays. Religion was part of our everyday activities and entered our lives intimately and forever. These early impressions, and the image of the marvelous Man who had given His life for others and had taught but one thing—love—were the source of the youthful faith I later acquired in the idea of personal sacrifice for the people. This was the source of my revolutionary fervor and of that of many young men and women of my time. Of course, this kind of faith was not the only kind; there was also the official government orthodoxy of the Holy Synod—a heartless, bureaucratic institution which persecuted all dissenters and inculcated atheism in many people by its indifference to human needs. But we children were unaware of this other aspect of the Church.

At the age of six my carefree childhood came to an abrupt end. My parents, *nyanya,* my elder sisters, and all our friends suddenly became very solicitous and affectionate. I could sense the change around me but did not know the reason. Somewhat puzzled, I enjoyed an unexpected flow of gifts. I was constantly urged to take things easy and rest. On several occasions a doctor came to the house to examine my hip and my leg. Finally, Mother came to the nursery one night, sat down quietly on my bed and announced that we should soon be going to Kazan in a troika with jingling bells. I was delighted at the idea. In the winter, the only way to travel to Kazan was on the frozen surface of the Volga. We left for Kazan in a closed sleigh (*vozok*) with a brazier inside to keep us warm. Upon our arrival I was given a few days' rest and then Mother took me to Professor Studensky, a leading bone specialist. After a thorough examination he diagnosed my illness as tuberculosis of the hip. When he came to see us the next morning, he was accompanied by a pleasant-looking young man. They looked at my right leg and, like a bootmaker, the young man took measurements. The next day, the young man returned. He took my right leg and fitted it into a bootlike metal object which covered my knee so that I was unable to bend my leg. I let out a howl, but the young man merely said, "Perfect." Finally, Mother spoke up: "You don't want to be lame for the rest of your life, do you?" Fear must have shown in my eyes. "Well, I see that you don't; be reasonable now, and stay in bed when we get home. It won't be too long before you can run and play as much as you want to." Her grave voice was reassuring. Two days later we set out on our journey back to Simbirsk. We returned before Christmas, and I still remember how I was rolled out in my special bed to look at the tree. I stayed in bed for six months and was allowed to sit up only in my iron boot with weights attached to its heel.

I had always been a lively, energetic boy, and it was hard to be out of things for six months. My eldest sister told me years later that I was quite unbearable during my illness. "But your tantrums never lasted," she added. "It was reading that saved you—and us from you." I had always liked books, but had not so far been an avid reader. During my illness, however, tired one day of just lying and sulking, I took a book from the bedside table. That marked the end of my boredom. The title and the author of the book escape me now, but it launched me on a lifelong habit of reading. I forgot my surroundings and the loathsome iron boot. I devoured books and magazines, historical novels, travel and science books, stories about American Indians, and lives of Saints. I fell under the spell of Pushkin, Lermontov, and Tolstoy; I could not put down *Dombey and Son* and I shed bitter tears over *Uncle Tom's Cabin*.

By the summer of 1887 I must have been well again, for I remember the exhilaration of roaming the countryside where we spent our holidays. I had recovered completely and was again a happy-go-lucky boy. Yet something had changed. I had outgrown my nursery, and the company of my brother Fedya was no longer enough for me. Hitherto all my feelings and impressions had merged into one harmonious but vague entity for which I could find no word. Now I knew that its name was Russia. In the very depth of my heart, everything that surrounded me and everything that happened was intimately linked with Russia: the beauty of the Volga, the chimes of evening bells, the bishop sitting solemnly in a carriage drawn by four horses, the convicts with heavy chains, the pretty little girls with whom I went to dancing lessons, the ragged, barefoot village boys with whom I played in the summer, my parents, the nursery and *nyanya,* the Russian epic heroes, and Peter the Great. I began to ponder, to ask questions, and to try to understand some of the things I had always taken for granted.

Outwardly life was the same as ever. Only our children's parties and boisterous Christmas celebrations broke the calm routine of our everyday life. I discovered the beauty of music and would listen to my mother's mellow contralto for hours as she accompanied herself on the piano. Sometimes she held musical soirees, and I never tired of crouching behind the closed doors to hear a concert, long after I was supposed to have been in bed. The next morning I would sneak into the ballroom, pick up the scattered sheets of music, and try to read the music and sing to myself the lovely songs I had heard the night before. Occasionally we were taken for a stroll on the boulevard which led down from the center of town to the bank of the Volga. About halfway down to the river there was a modest parish church with a small, neat cemetery and a rich orchard. The priest of this church was our father's eldest brother. We were taken there in the spring when the apple and cherry trees were in full blossom, or in the autumn after our return from the country, when the apples and pears had been made into delicious jam. In our uncle's immaculate cottage, which was gay with geranium plants and all sorts of cacti and greenery, we were lovingly pampered and fed on homemade jam and other goodies.

We always accepted our aunt's tender concern for us as our due. It goes without saying that we had never been told that there was any difference in status between the two brothers. But the unassuming church house was such a contrast to our own spacious quarters that we children could not help noticing the difference and drawing our own conclusions.

In the early part of 1889 we learned that we were to leave Simbirsk for good and move to a remote city called Tashkent, the capital of Turkestan.[6] We had never heard of Tashkent and we were very much excited about the move. We were told that we would travel down the Volga, board another ship in the Caspian Sea, get into a train on the other side, and make the last leg of our journey by horse-drawn carriage. After the spring term, hectic preparations for our departure began. The house was in turmoil, but we children loved every minute of it. The morning of our departure, our closest friends came to bid us farewell and sit down with us in silent prayer, as is customary in Russia before any departure. Then we all got up, made the sign of the

[6] My father was transferred to Turkestan as the chief inspector of schools.

cross, embraced each other, and set out for the boat landing. There were tears of sorrow, and through our excitement we children sensed that something had gone irrevocably. At the landing a crowd of well-wishers was waiting for us. Finally, the last sharp whistle pierced the air, the last desperate goodbyes were said, and the gangplank was hauled aboard. The wheels were set into motion and churned up the water, and the crowd on the pier shouted and waved white handkerchiefs. One more whistle and Simbirsk, where I had spent the happiest years of my life, gradually receded to become part of a distant past.

As I write these words, I am once more under the spell of a certain unique moment of my life in Simbirsk. It happened one day in early May. The Volga, seemingly boundless, had freed herself from her icy yoke and in a joyous outburst flooded the meadows on the left bank. From the top of the hill down to the waterfront Simbirsk was dressed like a bride in the pink and white attire of her cherry and apple blossoms. This breathtaking beauty shimmered and quivered shyly in the sunlight. The distant roar of the spring waters filled the air, the hillside was alive with the twittering and singing of birds, the humming of bees, and the buzzing of May bugs and God only knows what sounds of other creatures, wide awake after their winter sleep. On that memorable day my heart was not in our games, and I ran off to gaze at the river. Spellbound by the beauty of the scene, I experienced a sense of elation that grew almost to the point of spiritual transfiguration. Then, suddenly overcome by an unaccountable feeling of terror, I ran away. For me that moment was decisive in choosing the spiritual path that I was to follow throughout my life.

I have only a dim recollection of Astrakhan and the SS *Caspian*, which we boarded after leaving the Volga. Nor do I remember how long it took us to reach Fort Aleksandrovsk [7] on the northeastern shore of the Caspian Sea, where the ship anchored briefly. One morning we were told, "Today, we are landing, children." We dressed rapidly and ran up on deck. All the passengers were waiting impatiently for a glimpse of the far-off land that was to be our destination. Finally we sighted a strip of barren red land and the outlines of remote mountains; small houses and huge storage tanks appeared along the shore.

[7] Now Port Shevchenko, after the famous Ukrainian poet who spent years of exile there.

The ship dropped anchor and we landed in Uzun-Ada, a miserable port on the Transcaspian shore—the only one at that time. Even at sea the scorching sun had been merciless, but now we suddenly found ourselves in a furnace and there was nothing in the view to please the eye or bring relief. Only parched sands stretched out on every side to merge with the horizon. A single-track railroad line ran from Uzun-Ada to Samarkand through the desert and its oases. (It was hailed at that time as a great achievement of military and civil engineering.)

After our numerous trunks and crates had been transferred from the ship to the train, we children set out on our first railroad trip. There were many new impressions, the most memorable one being the crossing of the Amu Darya (the ancient Oxus) over a wooden bridge. The river is swift-flowing and the long bridge trembled and shook under the impact of its turbulent waters. The train moved at a snail's pace. Water barrels were lined up along the bridge in case of fire, and a sentry paced up and down, keeping an eye on the sparks from the engine.

In Samarkand the railroad track ended abruptly. After the peaceful charm of our native Volga shores, the quiet tree-lined streets and the native town with its remarkable fifteenth-century mosaics and ancient mosques were as much of a novelty as the ominous sands of the dead Transcaspian Desert. We stayed in Samarkand for three days and then set out for Tashkent in horse-drawn carriages. At the end of another three days, we reached a handsome house that stood at the corner of two wide streets. There I was to pass my school years from 1890 to 1899, and there also I was to encounter a new social environment very unlike that of European Russia.

Tashkent was not on top of a hill, like Simbirsk with its breathtaking view of the boundless Volga. It stood in a flat plain, and the snow-capped tops of the Pamirs could just be made out, like phantoms, in the distance. The streets were a colorful mixture of Europe and Asia. Like Samarkand, Tashkent was divided into two dissimilar but closely linked cities. The new city, founded after the occupation of Tashkent by Russian troops in 1865, was one vast garden. The city had been laid out on a generous scale, and poplars and acacias graced the wide streets. Houses of all sizes were hidden by the lush green of trees and shrubs. The old city, with a Moslem population of about 100,000, dated back many centuries and was a maze of narrow alleys and lanes. The tall, windowless mud walls of the houses concealed the life within from prying eyes. The heart of the city was a large covered marketplace where all trade and public activities were carried on.

As a boy of nine I was, of course, unable to understand the peculiarities of the political and social life of Tashkent and of Turkestan as a whole. Unlike Simbirsk, Turkestan had no gentry longing for the days of serfdom, nor had its development been influenced by an impoverished peasantry. Turkestan had not experienced the absurd government campaign against literacy in rural areas, the pernicious policies of barring the children of the "lower classes" from school and of suppressing any expression of independent thought in colleges, the press, and civic organizations. Turkestan was too remote to be the target of the reactionary officials who were trying to turn the empire, with its many different peoples, into a Muscovite kingdom.

As already mentioned, Tashkent was conquered in 1865 and made into the capital of Turkestan. In 1867, General K. P. Kaufman, a hero of the Caucasian wars, became the first governor general of the newly conquered country. An outstanding administrator, he went down in the history of Turkestan (after his death in 1882) as the organizer of this new territory. In this task he was guided by the Statute on the Administration of Turkestan, which had been drafted by Alexander II. The statute does credit to the most enlightened years of the reign of Alexander II, when Russia was being transformed in accordance with the highest ideals of personal freedom and equality.

The Russian empire of Central Asia extended from the eastern shore of the Caspian Sea to the frontiers of Persia, China, and Afghanistan. Having reached its natural limits, Russia's *Drang nach Osten* had come to a standstill. The creative energies of the Russians were now directed toward cultural and economic endeavor and toward the civilizing of outlying areas. Russian expansion into Asia was viewed with suspicion by Great Britain. Historical tradition dies hard, and long after Russia had taken over her share of Central Asia Great Britain continued to look upon her as a hostile rival. But the Russians did not display excessive confidence in England, either. The advance of Russian troops toward Kushka on the Afghan frontier in the 1880's nearly developed into an Anglo-Russian war. And during my school days, Lord Curzon caused a certain amount of uneasiness in the military circles of Tashkent, which died down only after the Anglo-Russian Commission drew a final demarcation line in the Pamirs.

It is a widely accepted view in the West that, in its ruthless attempt to Russify the Muslim population, Russia destroyed a great native civilization in Central Asia. I have seen the effects of Russian rule in Turkestan and they seem to me to reflect nothing but credit on Russia. When we arrived in Turkestan, only six years had passed since General Skobelev's pacifying expedition to Geok-Tepe (1881), a Turkmen oasis in the Transcaspian Desert, and only 24 years since the conquest of Tashkent itself. Yet during our preparations for the long journey from Simbirsk we never for a moment thought of ourselves as going to live in an "occupied" country. Tashkent was simply a far-off corner of Russia. Actually, the ability of the Russian invaders to mix with the native population and to win their respect and friendship was amazing. The same peaceful Russian life went on everywhere, whether in Samara on the Volga, or near the grave of Tamerlane. Throughout his years in Turkestan, my father traveled constantly on official duty, and in his capacity as chief inspector of schools he had to visit the most isolated districts. He never took so much as a walking cane with him, let alone a firearm. During the 20 years he remained there, he covered the whole of Turkestan, mostly by horse-drawn carriage, without ever running into the least bit of trouble from the native population. The success of Russian colonial policy in Asia was based on tolerance toward the local mode of life. Of course, there were overbearing and ignorant officials in Turkestan, just as in any province of Central Russia; and there may well have been occasional attempts at interference with national customs or religious observances. But from the outset it was clear to the population that these cases were the exception and not the rule. Russian towns grew and prospered side by side with the native settlements. Along with the traditional system of Muslim education, Russian schools were open to everyone, without religious or national discrimination. The local judicial system based on the Koran coexisted with the open jury trial introduced by the Russians. Railways, banks, industrial enterprises, the development of cotton-growing and agriculture, irrigation projects, and other economic improvements favorably impressed the Muslim population. Turkestan, once the site of a splendid vanished civilization, was brought back to life and prosperity after about 30 years of Russian domination.

For me, life in Tashkent continued to be carefree, and it also became more varied and exciting. Things had changed at home. The barrier between the grown-ups and the children had broken down. Our nurse no longer ruled over us. We younger ones participated in the life of our parents and elder sisters. Our French governess was replaced by a young Russian girl, who was more of a friend to my sisters than an educator to us. My room was next to my father's study, where he spent most of his time. He rarely went to his office, for he worked and received his colleagues and visitors at home. As time went on, he became an essential part of my life. It was reassuring to hear him move about in his room as I waited for him to come and look at my homework. He took a great interest in my Russian compositions, discussed history and literature with me, and urged me to develop a clear and concise style, frequently repeating his favorite adage, *non multa sed multum,* which, freely translated, means "fewer words, more thoughts." I began to listen to adult conversation a great deal. I frequently listened to conversations between my father and other high-ranking Turkestan officials, in which they discussed important issues. They always spoke in terms of the state or the country as a whole. To them the state was a living body and they placed the satisfaction of its needs above all other considerations.

My father frequently spoke of Sergey Yulyevich Witte, whom he greatly admired. Witte was a true and dedicated statesman and a man of considerable vision, but he had a hard time holding his own against the reactionary St. Petersburg officials. Once, during a visit to Tashkent, Witte came to see my father. His genial, courteous manner caused my father to comment later: "If all the bigwigs in St. Petersburg were like Witte, Russia would be a different place to live in."

Another experience contributed no little to my way of thinking. After the conclusion of the Franco-Russian Alliance (1892), Leo Tolstoy voiced his indignation in an open letter. To him, as to all progressive Russians, an alliance between a republic and an autocracy was a flagrant violation of the principles of right and freedom. His forceful pamphlet, a bitter attack on Alexander III, could not be published in Russia. But mimeographed copies were circulated secretly, and a copy reached Tashkent. From bits of conversation and other hints at the dinner table I gathered that my parents were going to read Tolstoy's pamphlet after dinner. It was their custom to spend an hour together in my mother's study discussing current affairs or reading aloud to each other. After dinner we children were supposed to stay in our rooms, but I sneaked back and concealed myself behind a curtain. I listened breathlessly to Tolstoy's accusing words, each of them as sharp as a razor's edge. I did not hear my parents' comments, having retreated hastily as soon as the reading was over. But the emotion in my father's voice and some of his remarks as he read made it clear to me that my father agreed with him to a certain extent. I was too young to understand the full import of Tolstoy's accusations, but I sensed that Russia was in the throes of some terrible affliction.

My monarchism and youthful adoration of the Tsar, however, were in no way impaired by what I had heard. And on October 20, 1894, when Alexander III died, I wept long and copiously as I read the official obituaries eulogizing the services he had rendered to Europe and to our country. I fervently attended every requiem mass held for the Tsar and assiduously collected small contributions in my class for a wreath to the Tsar's memory. The grown-ups, on the other hand, did not mourn him. They were full of hope that the new tsar, the youthful Nicholas II, might make some bold move toward granting a constitution. But Nicholas II scornfully rejected the very idea as a "meaningless fancy."

I shall not dwell on my school years in Tashkent. I was gregarious, fond of social life and girls, and an enthusiastic partner in games and dances. I attended and participated in literary and musical soirees. There were frequent outings on horseback, Tashkent being a center of the military. My sisters were never short of suitors and life treated us all very well indeed. However, somewhere inside I was withdrawn and reserved. At the age of 13 I had a fairly clear idea of the world I lived in, but at times I felt the urge to be alone and think matters over. Later in life, even at the height of my political career, this inner loneliness never left me.

In the decade between 1880 and 1890 most Russian children were bored by school or hated it, but this was not true in Turkestan. We were not stifled by the indifferent formalism of schools in European Russia, and we rather liked our teachers and our classes. By the time we left school we had established solid bonds of friendship with some of the teachers, and they, in turn, treated us almost as equals. The knowledge imparted by them often went far beyond the limits of the official school curriculum. We talked a great deal about our future plans and had endless conversations about the merits of various universities. I decided to study two major subjects: history and classical philology (which were taught together), and jurisprudence. My childhood dream of becoming an actor or musician gave way to a decision to serve my people, Russia and the state, as my father had done all his life.

Neither I nor my classmates were aware of the problems that were exciting the young people of our age in other parts of Russia, leading many of them to join clandestine societies while still at school. I now believe that both the peculiar social, political, and psychological aspects of life in Tashkent, and our isolation from young people in the European parts of Russia, were instrumental in shaping my thinking. Years later, in the course of my political activities, I met a number of people of my own generation who had participated in the events of 1905 and 1917. It was obvious that their attitudes and ideas had been formed by the social and political dogmas which they had absorbed during their school years in European Russia, and the result was that they looked at Russian reality in the light of obsolete and rigid concepts. With rare exceptions, we who went to school in Tashkent saw life in a less prejudiced way. We had no ready-made beliefs imposed upon us, and we were free to draw our own conclusions from events. It was under these conditions that I gradually changed my views about the supposedly benevolent rule of the Tsar.

In the summer of 1899 I made final preparations for my departure to St. Petersburg. My sister Anna was coming with me to enroll at the St. Petersburg Conservatory of Music, and we were both looking forward eagerly to our years in the university, although we knew that student disorders were a daily occurrence in the capital. My sister Yelena, who had come from St. Petersburg, where she attended the new Medical Institute for Women, had told us about the student riots of the spring of 1898. Our parents were profoundly worried, but Nyeta (Anna) and I were not in the least perturbed. Yelena's stories only increased our desire to get to St. Petersburg as soon as possible.

NOTE

The following description of my father is taken from A. N. Naumov, *Utselevshiye vospominaniya,* Vol. II, pp. 26–28. Naumov, a minister at the time when I was a member of the Duma, was one of my fiercest political opponents.

... The change of school turned out to be a memorable experience. First of all, the more than modest building of the new school contrasted sharply with the splendid premises of my former military academy. The teaching staff was a far cry from what I had been used to. ... Instead of a general ... there stood before me a middle-aged man in a loose dark blue coat (*vitsmundir*), tall and broad-shouldered with an enormous head and close-cropped hair. He had prominent cheek-bones and small intelligent eyes which peered from under a massive forehead. This was Fyodor Mikhailovich Kerensky who ... had replaced the former principal. The latter had left the administrative part of his work in a rather chaotic state. Thanks to his exceptional energy Fyodor Mikhailovich soon began to improve matters and tighten things up. He was an energetic principal and a sensitive person who had a thorough understanding of the problems at stake and who attended to everything himself. Educated and intelligent, he was also an outstanding teacher.

I had the good fortune of attending the two top classes in which ... he taught literature and Latin. He had an excellent command of spoken Russian and loved Russian literature. His method of teaching was utterly novel in those times. Thanks to his inherent talent he turned our literature lessons into fascinating hours during which the pupils listened attentively to their teacher, who employed neither a formal curriculum nor textbooks with the usual routine assignments. ... This method of teaching awoke in us a vivid interest in Russian literature ... and in our free time we read books recommended by him. ... His dictum was *non multa sed multum!* He expected this in oral answers and he looked for it also in written work, about which he was particularly strict as to form and content. In this way, he trained his pupils to think a great deal, but to write down only the gist of their thoughts in a clear and concise literary form.

... Unfortunately, he taught Latin only in the fifth and sixth form. I say "unfortunately" because in this subject, too, he excelled as a teacher. Strange as it may seem, we waited eagerly even for our Latin lessons, which were enlivened by his outstanding personality and his unorthodox approach to the subject. ... Instead of having to learn by rote the rules and exceptions of Latin grammar, we assimilated them through the reading of texts. The reading was carried out under his guidance in a way vastly different from that generally practiced in schools. He was not in the habit of asking us to prepare lessons, but on coming into the classroom he would take something by Ovid, Sallust or Julius Caesar, etc. and ask one of us to read out the Latin text in Russian, all the while helping and encouraging the pupil; at the same time, his explanations of the text were so lively and vivid that we all used to volunteer to read. Latin was no longer drudgery, but a fascinating way of getting to know the history and literature of Ancient Rome. . . . By the end of the sixth form we were reading Latin classics without difficulty. . . .

Fyodor Mikhailovich was very well disposed to me personally. He appreciated my progress and during the last years of school made me take his place in reading aloud to the class, which, I confess, flattered me not a little.

2

The University Years

IN my youth, most of the University of St. Petersburg students used to live in the modest and shabby boarding houses on Vasilyevsky Island. At that time the student dormitories were not very popular with the students because they were suspicious of possible supervision. As a matter of fact their suspicions were totally unjustified, for the dormitory residents enjoyed complete freedom.

At first I had intended to room, like the majority of the students, in one of the boarding houses, but I changed my mind when I discovered that living in the dormitory would enable me to meet young people of my own age from all over Russia. This proved correct, and I soon had a good many friends.

We engaged in lively discussions on a variety of subjects—I still remember our heated arguments about the Boer War. And after the Boxer revolt, in 1900, our attention was focused on the Far East, but our own national affairs were always of great interest to all of us.

Another advantage of the dormitory was its location. The building, a gift of an admirer of Alexander II, was in the courtyard of the university and stood at the head of an alley that led to the Neva Embankment. The beauty of the Embankment never ceased to enchant me. It was the majestic heart of the Russian Empire. On the left bank, right in front of my eyes, were the Admiralty and the Senate, on the historic square where the Decembrist Revolt took place; the equestrian statue of Peter the Great (Pushkin's "Bronze Horseman"), silhouetted against St. Isaac's Cathedral; and, to the left of the "Admiralty Spire," the Winter Palace and the Peter and Paul Fortress, all of them familiar and all of them symbolizing the history of our time. The Island was the site of the Academy of Science, founded as the *Kunstkammera* (museum) by Peter the Great. The vast university buildings were built in the harmonious and dignified style of the early eighteenth century. The former Menshikov Palace, in our time a military school, was next to the university. To the right of the palace was Rumyantsev Square, a small park where students were beaten up in 1899; farther on, the Academy of Fine Arts and the famous sphinxes could be seen. St. Petersburg, to me, was not only the splendid city of Peter the Great, but also the place immortalized by Pushkin and Dostoyevsky. His tragic heroes lived in the remote, poverty-ridden district around Sennaya marketplace, but all the same, one felt the presence of Dostoyevsky all over the city.

We newcomers experienced an exhilarating sense of freedom. Most of us had been living at home and were now for the first time at liberty to do as we liked. We were thrown into the whirlpool of life, where the only restraints were those we imposed upon ourselves. One of the most delightful aspects of the new freedom was embodied in the so-called "Corridor," a long hallway that connected six of the university buildings. Here we gathered after lectures and crowded around the more popular teachers. Others we pointedly ignored, and they passed us by, feigning indifference.

By the time I entered the university, the student strikes were over, but the vestiges of former unrest that remained were a constant source of amusement. We gleefully boycotted professors who came to replace the teachers dismissed for sympathizing with the striking students in the preceding academic year. I remember that we particularly enjoyed making things unpleasant for Professor Erwin Grimm, a young lecturer from Kazan who had been appointed to replace the popular professor of medieval history, Grevs. As soon as the object of our scorn appeared in the Corridor we would break into jeers and follow him into the lecture hall, where his words would be drowned in pandemonium. Eventually, the supervisor would come, and a few culprits would be ejected from the lecture hall. The campaign was carried on until the fun began to wear off, and then peace was restored.

During my first year in St. Petersburg I had no friends outside the university except my parents' acquaintances, whose social position set them quite apart from my student life. Somehow, I felt that they were shocked to discover that the modest young man they had known had suddenly been transformed into a young madman who bubbled over with excitement as he talked about the theater, the opera, music, and modern literature, and who hinted at certain new friends from the Institute of Higher Learning for Women.

In the fall of 1900, however, after returning from my first student vacation in Tashkent, I made the acquaintance of the Baranovsky family. Mrs. Baranovsky, the divorced wife of L. S. Baranovsky, a colonel of the General Staff, was the daughter of the eminent sinologist, V. P. Vasilyev, who was a member of the Russian Academy of Science, as well as of a number of foreign ones. She had two daughters, Olga and Yelena, and a son, Vladimir, who was in the Guards artillery. The charming 17-year-old Olga attended the Bestuzhev-Ryumin Courses of Higher Learning for Girls, which were enjoying great popularity at the time. A circle of students had formed around Olga, and we were soon joined by Olga's cousin Sergey Vasilyev, a very gifted and enterprising young man of my own age. These young people were much more my own kind than my society friends, and we had a great deal in common. We had a wide range of interests. We discussed modern Russia and foreign literature and endlessly recited the poetry of Pushkin, Merezhkovsky, Lermontov, Tyutchev, Baudelaire, and Bryusov to each other. We were ardent theatergoers, and the brilliant performances of the Moscow Art Theater under Stanislavsky and Nemirovich-Danchenko during the spring season left us spellbound for weeks. We had heated debates about current political developments in Russia and abroad, for like most young people of our time, we were fiercely opposed to the official political line. Almost unanimously we were in sympathy with the *narodnik* movement, or rather the socialist revolutionaries, but as far as I recall there were no Marxists among us. Many of us, needless to say, participated in student demonstrations.

After the Baranovskys moved from their home on Vasilyevsky Island to a street near the Tauride Garden, our circle broke up. We had grown up by then, and the carefree life of our student years was over. I was not unduly distressed, however, for Olga Baranovsky became my bride.

The university charter of 1884 had denied the student body the right to set up corporate organizations and had outlawed even the most innocent nonpolitical student associations and clubs. With such outlets for collective activity blocked, the urge for public service was driven underground. The largest student groups were the Zemlia-chestvos, which were fraternal societies open to students from the same area. They were the main centers of student activity and could never be suppressed. During my first years as an undergraduate, the fraternity for students from Turkestan was like home to me, and I was elected to its council. The main purpose of the fraternity and others like it was to give aid to poorer students and to maintain contact between students from the same locality. Among other things, we organized benefit concerts in which famous actors and singers frequently participated. Once a year I had to approach such stars as Maria Savina, Vera Kommisarzhevskaya, and Khodotov, and they never refused to help the student body.

My sister, a medical student, lived in a well-run dormitory for women that also sponsored benefit concerts. They invited the participation of artists and writers in other activities as well. The first literary soiree I ever attended was one organized by my sister's group at which eminent writers like Merezhkovsky and his wife Zinaida Hippius read from their works. Each fraternity also engaged in education work, established libraries and book exchanges, and so on.

V. A. Maklakov was one of the founders of the Moscow student movement in 1887. The Moscow fraternity was the center for the "fight against the lawlessness and arbitrary conduct" of the specially appointed university inspectors. The central organ, known as the United Council, also led the students at large. Most students had *narodniki* (populist) leanings, but political parties had not as yet crystallized and undergraduates tended to be vaguely in sympathy with not always clearly formulated ideas of freedom. We were united, however, in our opposition to absolutism.

The Marxists (Social Democrats) propagated their "economic" doctrine, which demanded alienation from the bourgeois and petty bourgeois student body and called for the marshaling of all efforts to achieve the victory of the industrial proletariat. Very few of the students sympathized with this idea, however. To most of us in Russia the exclusive regard for the industrial proletariat and the contemptuous disregard for the peasantry was utterly absurd. Even apart from its attitude toward the peasants, Marxism repelled me because of its

innate materialism and its approach to socialism as a one-class proletarian doctrine. In Marxism the class has swallowed the human
being. Yet without man, without the living human personality and its
individual worth, without the liberation of man as the ethical and
philosophic aim of the process of history—without these concepts
there is nothing left of Russian thought. The tradition of our literature
must then be deleted from memory.

Even so, the powerful "central fund" (*tsentral'naya kassa*) was in
the hands of Marxists.

The Social Democrat leaders in the student body were G. S. Khru-
stalev-Nosar, future president of Workers' Deputies (in 1905) and
Nicholas Iordansky, future editor of *Mir Bozhiy* (*God's World*).
Assisted by a few other students, Iordansky carried on all negotiations with General P. S. Vannovsky, the head of a committee that
investigated the causes of unrest among students. Iordansky was one
of the first Social Democrats to oppose the "economic" trend, as he
himself told me later. As a matter of fact, Lenin was also opposed to it.

The contest between the socialist groups within the university during the early years of the century was a reflection of the sharp clash
of two social and economic schools of thought among the radical
intelligentsia. Later it played a tremendously important part in the
1917 revolution.

The Student Movement

Following the famine of 1891–1892 and the resultant cholera
epidemic, there had been an appreciable revival of political activity,
largely inspired by Leo Tolstoy. Faced with an emergency, the government had been compelled to allow the *zemstva* [1] to participate in relief
work, and it had grudgingly encouraged public initiative. It was under
these conditions that a student movement was formed whose purpose
was to effect the restoration of the liberal university charter of 1863.
In 1897, Vera Vietrova, a student imprisoned in the Peter and Paul
Fortress, burnt herself alive after soaking her clothes in lamp oil. The
student body was deeply shaken. A wave of meetings swept over every
university in the country. A vast gathering at the Kazan Cathedral in
St. Petersburg, where a requiem mass for Vietrova was to be held,
had to be dispersed by the police. On February 8, 1899, the Annual

[1] Local self-government organizations.

Celebration Day of the University of St. Petersburg, a political demonstration broke out during the solemn official ceremony, and the students walked out. In the Rumyantsev Square the demonstrators were set upon by mounted police and flogged unmercifully. It was this event that laid the foundation of a *political* student movement. N. P. Bogolepov, a good professor of Roman law but a ruthless minister of education, requested and obtained an imperial order decreeing the immediate military conscription of all students suspended for their participation in the disturbances. This measure was rigorously applied, much as it would have been in the days of Nicholas I, and scores of students were deported to Siberia. The Government was obviously hoping to terrorize the students into submission, but in Siberia the exiled students showed their defiance by circulating a letter in which they pointed out that the purpose of the student movement was to stimulate political activity among the older generation and urged them to tread the path of freedom according to the English pattern.

I remember Bogolepov's visit to our dormitory shortly before his death—we had been told that the minister was coming to see for himself how the students lived. Bogolepov, a tall, stern, impeccably dressed man, was accompanied by the rector. Without any hostile intentions toward him personally, but largely on account of the general mood, none of the students greeted him in the corridors. In the library, where a large group had gathered, he was completely ignored. It was a silent but eloquent protest. Some students just sat there sullenly, some pretended to be absorbed in their books, and others looked at newspapers. Bogolepov was left in no doubt as to the students' frame of mind.

Shortly afterward, on February 14, 1901, Peter Karpovich, an ex-student who had twice been expelled from the university, requested an audience with the minister. No political assassinations having occurred for many years, the minister calmly allowed the young man to approach. A shot rang out, and Bogolepov fell, mortally wounded.

By his individual action—he was not backed by any political or party organization—Karpovich had taken us back to the revolutionary terrorism of the days of Alexander II, although surprisingly enough, he was not executed. His deed made an indelible impression on many people, including myself: We looked upon this willingness to die in the name of justice as an act of great moral heroism.

The Tsar himself seemed to confirm our faith in the political efficacy of terror when he replaced the assassinated official by the elderly General P. S. Vannovsky, known in the past as a reactionary minister of war, who surprised everyone by his fairness to the students. Conscription was dropped, and students exiled to Siberia were allowed to return in the fall of 1902.

Vannovsky did not last long in his post. After a series of clashes with the minister of interior, D. S. Sipyagin, an out-and-out reactionary, Vannovsky was replaced. The new minister of education was G. A. Zenger (1902–1904), whom I knew personally. A professor of philology at Warsaw University and an enthusiastic classicist, he was the author of a Latin version of Pushkin's *Eugene Onegin*. He was a handsome, pleasant man, but he lacked a forceful personality and was content simply to continue Vannovsky's liberal policy. Eventually he was replaced by General Glazov, whose appointment gave rise to fresh outbursts among the students.

During this time most of the professors behaved with discretion and tried to remain neutral, and only a few spoke out openly against the arbitrary conduct of the police. Nevertheless, there were about 350 signatures on a professors' petition in 1903 in defense of the students and of academic freedom. The petition was rejected.

My First Political Speech

I cannot recall the occasion of my first political speech, but I know that it was at the end of my second year, at a student meeting. A crowd of students was gathered on the main staircase, and I made my way through the crowd to the top of the stairs and launched into an impassioned speech. I was not a member of any political group, and I still do not know what prompted me to speak. My speech was deeply felt, nonetheless, and in it I urged the students to help the nation in the liberation struggle. It was greeted with loud applause.

Up to now my record had been impeccable, but the next day I was summoned by the rector. He greeted me with the words: "Young man, I should expel you from the University were it not for your honorable father and his service to the country. May I suggest that you take a vacation and stay with your family for a while." This was a very lenient sentence, and I was not altogether displeased to become an "exiled student." It was my first distinction earned in the struggle for liberty.

To the youth of Tashkent I was a hero, and I basked in their admiration. Unfortunately, however, my homecoming was marred by my first serious clash with my father, who was greatly upset by the whole affair. He was probably worried that I might go the same way as the Ulyanov brothers. His argument was that if I wanted to do something for my country I should think of the future, study hard, and keep out of trouble. "Believe me," he said, "you are still too young to know the country and to understand what is going on. Do as you like when you are older, but now you must listen to me." He extracted a promise from me to be reasonable and keep out of all political movements until after my graduation.

My father's words made a great impression on me. He was quite right in saying that I knew very little about life in Russia; but even as I gave him my promise I knew that my thoughts, if not my actions, would still be turned toward politics.

I had originally planned to finish my studies in two faculties, history and law; but just at the end of my first year at the university Bogolepov published an order forbidding students to study in two faculties simultaneously. I therefore transferred to the law faculty, and my graduation was delayed a year.

During my third and fourth terms at the law faculty my academic work proceeded satisfactorily, but political events in Russia, which were becoming increasingly turbulent, pulled me in a different direction. I was preparing for an academic career, hoping to take up postgraduate study in criminal law. But somewhere deep inside I already felt that this was not to be, and that my place was among the active opponents of the autocracy, because I realized that for the salvation of the country a constitution had to be established as quickly as possible. The revolutionary movement in the country did not spring from sociological doctrines. We did not join the ranks of the revolutionaries as a result of a clandestine study of forbidden doctrines. The regime itself forced us into revolutionary activity.

The more I thought about Russia, the more clearly I saw that it was the supreme power that was to blame and not the government. After the Revolution a great many documents, memoirs, and reports by high officials and friends of the imperial family were published abroad and in Russia, all of which confirm the opinion I held at the time. These documents were not available then, of course, and I had to rely on my own judgment and intuition to discover the source of the evil. But events were taking place which made this a cruelly simple task.

The unwarranted curtailment of Finland's liberties embittered and antagonized the law-abiding and loyal Finns. It was the right and responsibility of the supreme power to take care of all the peoples that constituted the Empire. The head of the great, heterogeneous Empire should have been concerned with unity and solidarity instead of with a policy of Russification of the non-Russian population.

In the Caucasus, the folly of Russian policy was typified by the attempt to confiscate all the property of the Armenian Church in Echmiadzin, the spiritual center of the Armenians. The Tsar turned a deaf ear to the pleas of the Catholicos,[2] who appealed to him twice to stop the destruction of the Armenian people. This was not done.

In the government, Vyacheslav Plehve, a militant and ruthless reactionary hated even in government circles, was appointed minister of the interior to succeed the murdered Sipyagin. Soon after his appointment on Easter Day (April 6, 1902), a wholesale massacre of Jews took place in Kishinev. In a personal letter to the Tsar, Witte wrote: "God help us should a Tsar appear in Russia who would represent only one estate." Nicholas II disregarded Witte's warning.

In the aftermath of the poor harvest of 1901, the administration sent several punitive expeditions into the Poltava and Kharkov provinces, and hundreds of peasants were flogged because, driven by the famine, they had helped themselves to grain from the local estates, which were immensely rich. At first, crowds of peasants had made the rounds of the manors asking for a free distribution of grain and fodder, which was refused. A few weeks later the peasants had gone to the great estates with long lines of carts, broken the locks on the barns and carted away the badly needed fodder and grain. Unrest seized other rural areas also. Soon after the peasant disturbances the Tsar attended maneuvers and the unveiling of a monument to Alexander III in Kursk. An open-air reception was held by the Tsar, attended by the marshals of nobility of all the southern provinces, the *zemstvo* representatives, and the township (*volost*) and village elders. First, addressing the members of the landed gentry, the Tsar said approvingly: "My unforgettable father, implementing the fine deeds

2 The head of the Armenian Church.

of my grandfather, called upon you to lead the peasantry. You have served me faithfully. Let me thank you for your services." And turning to the *zemstvo* guests, he admonished them: "Remember, your task is concerned with the *local* organization in the area of agricultural needs." When he came to the peasants, his voice rose: "This spring the peasants have pillaged estates in the Poltava and Kharkov provinces. The guilty will be punished, and the authorities will not, I hope, tolerate any more of these disturbances. Let me remind you of the words of my late father when he addressed the township elders in Moscow on the occasion of his coronation: 'Listen to your Marshals of Nobility and do not believe in stupid rumors.' Remember now that you cannot get rich by grabbing what does not belong to you, but only by honest toil, thriftiness and by living according to the Lord's commandments. Tell your people in the townships what I have told you and that I shall look after them."

In the beginning of the twentieth century it was extraordinarily naïve to urge the peasants to obey only the marshals of nobility. It shows how little the Tsar knew the country that he was called upon to rule. To the Tsar the nobility was the repository of all political strength and economic power, although by this time it no longer played an independent role in the economic or political life of the country. His attitude explains why he sided with Plehve, the advocate of privileges for the nobility, and why he appointed Plehve to succeed Witte.

I had now come to the realization that Russia was embarking upon the path of great hardships and disaster through the fault of the supreme power.

The Professors

A university education is important not only because it teaches—indeed forces—the student to think independently, but also because it makes him revise his judgments in accordance with knowledge acquired from primary sources. But the result is that some people modify their outlook on the world, not by abandoning their former views, but by adopting whatever available doctrine will serve as a suitable framework for their ideas. This is precisely what my studies in the faculty of history and philology did for me. I sought out and found professors who confirmed for me *my own* instinctive feelings about the world.

S. F. Platonov was stern in both looks and manner. Always impeccably attired, he never permitted his students the slightest familiarity. In some respects I considered him a better historian than Klyuchevsky, for Klyuchevsky always embellished his descriptions of historic events and personalities with what I felt to be superfluous sarcastic comments. Platonov, on the other hand, always spoke clearly and to the point. He was very popular among the students, but he was never the object of hero worship as Klyuchevsky was in Moscow. Platonov took us on a series of excursions, first to Pskov and then to Novgorod, where he explained the organization of the ancient Russian democracy that had flourished there.

Tadeusz Zelinsky, a professor of Greek, was a tall, good-looking man whose curly hair made him resemble one of his beloved Greek statues. Whenever he spoke of Socrates and Plato, or of the essence of Greek culture, the Beautiful and the Good, he confirmed my own opinion that the ideas embodied in Christianity came from a much earlier tradition.

Professor Michael I. Rostovtsev, who was still very young at the time, gave us a good understanding of Roman history. He also thrilled us with his accounts of the Greek towns that flourished on the Black Sea before the birth of Rus (Ancient Russia). His lectures on this pre-Russian world in the south of Russia clearly demonstrated that the roots of democracy in Ancient Rus went back much farther than had been thought, and that there was some connection between early Russian statecraft and the ancient Greek republics.

Another remarkable teacher was the philosopher Nicholas Lossky. His teaching derived from the proposition that man, as an independent spiritual being, should develop the voice of his conscience and act in accordance with its promptings, disregarding any dogmas that are incompatible with his spiritual self. He was a small, unassuming man with bright, innocent eyes, who lived in a world of his own and was painfully shy even in front of the students. Although he is well over 90 now, he remains unchanged, eternally young and eternally creative. When I transferred to the law faculty I continued to attend Platonov's and Lossky's lectures whenever I could.

In the law faculty I was tremendously impressed by Professor Lev Petrazhitsky's lectures on the philosophy of law. At that time he was between 35 and 40.[3] He used to begin his lecture courses by saying: "You will have difficulty in understanding me because I think in Polish, write in German and will be speaking to you in Russian." Later he mastered Russian so well that he became a brilliant speaker in the first Duma. Like Zelinsky, he was one of those Poles who later became so unpopular in Pilsudski's Poland for their belief that relations between the peoples of Russia and Poland should be based on fraternal rather than on purely political ties. They understood, of course, that all liberal-minded and cultivated Russians favored an independent Poland. Men of their kind were disliked in Poland for recognizing the value of Russian culture and Russian social thought.

Petrazhitsky was an outstanding person. He was the first to differentiate accurately between law (*pravo*) and morality, and between law *per se* and the laws as instituted by a state. His psychological approach to law and his theory of political science based on the idea of natural law, which he was one of the first to revive, would have been universally accepted had the Russia of that time not ceased to exist. Even so, there is a tendency nowadays to return to his teachings.

The important thing for me was that, on the basis of experimental psychology, Petrazhitsky defined law and morality as two principles coexisting in man's mind and guiding his inner life. True morality is an innate sense of duty, a duty that man must fulfill in his lifetime, though he is aware that he is under no outside compulsion to do so. According to Petrazhitsky, law is an innate sense of what a human being can ask of others and of what is expected of him in return. Petrazhitsky proved his theory in experiments with children. Later I tried them out myself on my sons, and I found them utterly convincing. Petrazhitsky was to law and jurisprudence what Galileo was to astronomy.

Another extremely important idea of Petrazhitsky's was his recognition of the superpersonal organic nature of the state; he declared that the state must go beyond the simple function of maintaining law and order and must also seek to guide the economic and social struggle that takes place in society. He rejected, however, the Marxist idea that the authority of the state is merely a tool to be used by the ruling class for the exploitation and suppression of its opponents in a classless society.

3 He subsequently committed suicide in Poland.

According to the Marxist creed the state authority is destined to become a "dictatorship of the proletariat" once the proletariat has seized power. But since this class will be the final and idealogically perfect one, the need for a dictatorship will disappear and the age of freedom begin. History offers examples, Petrazhitsky used to say, when the laws in force lag behind the requirements of everyday life, when there is a younger generation whose concept of law or *pravo* is completely different. By way of example he mentioned how the emergence of the working class changed the labor laws and affected social legislation throughout Europe. In this particular case the change was legitimate and inevitable.

Petrazhitsky was also an expert in Roman law, and he took part in the preparation of the German Civil Code. He believed that Roman law should not be blindly copied by modern societies, since it was extremely formal and had scant regard for justice and the human personality. A new era had begun with the coming of Christ, and he felt that all creative endeavor emanated from the feeling of Christian love.

Petrazhitsky was a slight man with sandy hair, of quite undistinguished appearance, yet at the same time he was a man of enormous moral and spiritual strength. Such was his influence that it was almost impossible, after him, to revert to any earlier theories on law and morality. For students used to the usual hackneyed arguments on law and morality, his theories were so fresh and stimulating that his lectures had to be held in the large assembly hall that seated at least 1,000 students.

Later on, when I was in the government, he frequently came to see me, and he made many useful suggestions on law and politics as a means of improving social relations. Alas, in the conditions of 1917 it was hardly possible to act on his excellent advice.

Also of great value to me in further strengthening my convictions were the lectures on the history of Russian law given by Professor Sergeyevich, a former rector of the university, who had to leave, unfortunately, after the events of 1899. Whenever he spoke of ancient law he used to stress the point that both the eleventh-century *Russian Law* of Yaroslav the Wise and Vladimir Monomakh's *Testament* to his children (twelfth century) contain a rejection of capital punishment.

He also described the legal relationships in Rus in his lectures, emphasizing the fact that the concept of the Divine Right of Kings did not exist in Rus, and explaining in depth the relationship between the ruling prince and the popular assembly (*veche*). Platonov, of course, stressed the political aspect of the conflict between them, while Sergeyevich considered it more from the juridical point of view.

Korkunov was no longer at the university when I arrived, but his works, in particular his course in state law and his dissertation, *Laws and Edicts,* were read by us all. Korkunov was a stern critic of all authoritarian regimes, but he tried to show that absolutism in Russia was not equivalent to arbitrary police rule, because of the existence of a universally binding law, with which edicts (*ukasy*) issued by the supreme authority must conform.

Unfortunately, this was true only in theory. To a considerable extent, Alexander III did observe this rule; but Nicholas II completely disregarded it, in the belief that his will, no matter how much it went against the laws in force, was binding on all his subjects.

Lossky and Petrazhitsky provided me with a systematic rational framework for my intuitive views. By nature I was never a positivist. Nietzsche, Spencer, and Marx all arrived, by different paths, at a sort of faith based on materialism. I could never adopt any such faith for myself. Material progress is the progress of things, the transformation of a wheeled cart into an aeroplane. But this does not mean, as 90 percent of educated people in both Russia and the West believed in the nineteenth century, that human nature may progress in the same way. The absurdity of this belief has been shown by two terrible wars, by the experience of Bolshevism and Fascism. The ideas of goodness, beauty, love, and hate are the eternal elements of human nature, and the Christian ethic is, to my mind, the one most relevant to them. It is a difficult, almost unattainable ideal. It appears absurd and unrealistic to many people, because loving one's enemy is contrary to human nature. Some people even regard it as something that only weakens man's will.

As a student I was very much interested in this problem, and I read a great deal about primitive people. I was looking for proof that there is some sort of progression from primitive society to modern man, but I found no evidence for it. On the contrary, I learned that the ideals of primitive societies were not basically different from those of contemporary mankind. Society, then as now, based its life on some idea shared by all—for example, on faith in certain deities. This may have been idolatry, but it was nevertheless the expression of a common idea. Furthermore, I found that in every society there was always some sort of universal ethical code.

A man's particular view of the world is not a matter of logic alone. Just as there are people incapable of appreciating music or painting, there are also those who live in a three-dimensional "scientific" world and who do not feel the presence of any "irrational" element in life. A good friend of mine once told me that he could neither sense nor understand God. I replied: "Then *that* is your religion." Man is a religious being. He always tries to reshape the world in accordance with what he feels inside him. This is a religious instinct; it does not follow from any science.

At school I was tremendously impressed by Vladimir Soloviev's statement that materialist theories turn human beings into tiny cogs of a monstrous machine. And I always sympathized with the social revolutionaries—and the Populists as well—because of their belief that they were working for the total emancipation of man, not for his transformation into a weapon of class warfare.

I also read the critical essays of the young Marxist economist, Peter Struve. But when I came to the passage where he says that the individual does not exist and is a negligible quantity, I knew that Marxism was not for me. My feeling was confirmed by the *Communist Manifesto* of Marx and Engels, which depicts human morality as a tool in the class struggle and asserts that the morality of the working class has nothing in common with the morality of the capitalist world.

Russia Before
World War I

3

The Liberation Movement

The 1905 Revolution and the Constitutional Manifesto

My Russia

IT is my belief that everyone who gives thought to his country sees it in his own way and carries in his mind a vision of how he would like it to be. As a young man I, too, had my own vision of a Russia that did not exist, and had never existed, but that must, I was convinced by the logic of history, inevitably arise in the future. This conviction, like others I have mentioned, was one that I had always held instinctively, and it, too, received the confirmation I sought for during my years at the university from such men as Platonov and Sergeyevich.

While still a schoolboy in Tashkent, I read the English historian Buckle, and I realized then that the historical development of a country depends not only on what its people aspire to, but also on its geography and its history. I saw that the people of Britain—which, cut off from the rest of Europe, had not been successfully invaded for almost a thousand years—had been given an opportunity for relatively free development. Russia, I perceived, was the antithesis of Britain, and as a result her history had been a tragic one. She had been the victim of continual attack, first from the nomads of Asia, then from Lithuania, the Teutonic Knights, Poland, Sweden, and Turkey. But although this had slowed down the country's political development, it had also strengthened the feeling of national unity. Despite warring among princes of the Rurik dynasty, this feeling had survived, and that is why the people of the various principalities had instinctively been drawn toward Moscow.

The Church played a tremendous part in the development of Russian national consciousness. When Russia had been deprived of all possibility of building up a secular culture such as the West had achieved, she had turned instead to the culture of the Church, to the gospels and their interpretation. It is highly significant that the Russians adopted Christianity from the outset in a language they understood. As a result, ideas that had long been abandoned in the West took firm root in Russia. One could draw a parallel between Theodosius of Pechersk, a boy from a leading boyar family who renounced all his social advantages and went off to live with and serve the poor and needy, and the "going to the people" of the nineteenth century; or between the Russian saints Boris and Gleb, who, in the name of Christ, refused to defend themselves against the murderers sent by their brother, Prince Svyatopolk, and Tolstoy, who preached passive resistance to evil; or, finally, between Vladimir Monomakh's outright condemnation of capital punishment in the twelfth century and Vladimir Solovyev's public appeal to Alexander III not to execute the assassins of Alexander II—not because he felt any sympathy for them, but because he felt that the new Tsar ought to show the perfection of Orthodoxy and the greatness of a Christian monarch who, having the power to punish, chose instead to forgive.

But this attitude had its bad as well as its good side. The disadvantage was that Russia did not develop a sense of law (*pravo*), but only a sense of fraternity and equality.

In fact, the adverse attitude toward state authority and formal law of a large portion of the Russian intelligentsia of the nineteenth century (particularly the Slavophiles and Populists) springs from this spiritual tradition.

To understand the history of Russia it is essential to bear in mind the words of Dostoyevsky: "Those who judge Russia should not do so by the villainy committed in her name, but by the ideals and goals for which the Russian people strive."

The Russians have always striven to take part in the running of their country. It is a well-known fact that ancient Rus, the Russia of Kiev, Pskov, and Novgorod, had a system, fairly free for that time, in which the popular assembly or *veche* played a vital part. A. K. Tolstoy, the great poet and friend of Alexander II, described in one of his stylized epics the fall of the Novgorod republic. Recalling that the bell that used to be rung to summon the people to the *veche* was taken away to Moscow, he makes Prince Vladimir, the saint of Kiev, propose the following toast: "To the ancient Russian *veche!* To freedom, to the honest Slavonic people! I drink to the bell of Novgorod. And even if it falls into the dust, may it ring on in the hearts of our descendants!"

Another example is the first assembly of the land (Zemsky Sobor) under Ivan the Terrible,[1] who in his youth fiercely denounced his own government and social system and granted the rural and urban communities the right to govern themselves.

The idea of democracy continued to develop in the Time of Troubles and during the eighteenth century. It was the main line of development because it was desired by the people.

During the Time of Troubles the boyars suggested to the Polish pretender to the Moscow throne that he should sign a charter granting the fundamental rights of freedom from arbitrary arrest and torture, execution without trial, and other acts of violence, and that the boyars should be allowed to have a say in the running of the country. The same thing had been suggested to Prince Shuysky some time before, on his election to the throne after the fall of the Godunov dynasty.

Whereas in France the States-General was not convened between the infancy of Louis XIII and the outbreak of the French Revolution (between 1614 and 1789), in Muscovy the tsars ruled in conjunction with the Assembly of the Land right up to the death of the father of Peter the Great. After his journey through Europe Peter introduced into Russia the same regime of enlightened absolutism that had spread throughout Europe, but only five years after Peter's death the Empress Anna, on ascending the throne, acceded to the demand of the Supreme Privy Council that she adopt certain constitutional "points."

The Struggle for the Constitution

The ideas of the French Revolution had an immediate and far-reaching effect on Russian public opinion. A movement sprang up for the adoption of a constitutional system in Russia, and the result

[1] The Russian name *Grozny* does not mean terrible. It derives from the Russian word *groza*—thunderstorm. People called him *Grozny* because he was terrifying to the enemy after the victory over the Kazan and Astrakhan khanates. Moreover, the view commonly held in the West, that Russia is a totally benighted country lacking any idea of freedom in the Western sense, is often supported by reference to Ivan the "Terrible." It is certainly true that he committed some terrible crimes, but at that time crimes of the same sort were being committed all over Europe—Philip II of Spain, Henry VIII and Bloody Mary of England, Louis XI of France, Eric of Sweden, and the Duke of Alba were all equally guilty in this respect.

was the first uprising against autocracy, which took place on December 14, 1825, and was engineered by young officers of the guards ("Decembrists").

Both Alexander I and Nicholas I were conscious of the need to emancipate the serfs, but neither of them had been able to bring himself to take the step, fearing open resistance on the part of the gentry. Alexander II was more politically astute, and his emancipation of the serfs and other reforms laid the foundations of the Russia which, despite attempts to turn back the clock during the reign of Alexander III, was now mature enough for outdated absolutism to be replaced by a constitutional system.

The emancipation of the serfs heralded a new stage in the development of Russia, the stage of industrial progress, which led, in turn, to the creation of private banks similar to those in the Western countries and to the development of the railroads. In the 1890's the pace began to quicken, as the statistics for industrial programs, construction projects, railroads, and so on all attest. This was, to some extent, the result of the famine after the poor harvest of 1891 and the utter economic exhaustion of both peasants and landed gentry. It was this economic decline that finally brought the public to the realization that it was time to take action to stop the stifling of the economic and spiritual life of the country by reactionary ministers in the government.

There was, however, another factor: the appearance on the scene of Sergey Yu Witte. This exceptionally talented man was given the task of reorganizing the country's economic life. He also played a leading part in shaping both foreign and general domestic policy. His removal from office and replacement, in 1903, by Plehve, an intolerable reactionary who immediately set about destroying the foundations of the political life of the Empire, marks the beginning of a period in Russian history that can be regarded as the prologue to the 1905 revolution. So destructive was Plehve that not only the most progressive of the zemstvo officials and intellectuals, but also the workers—and later on the peasants, too—were gradually drawn into this revolutionary movement.

Absolutism, at that time nothing more than a historical relic in Russia, was already doomed. But Nicholas II, instead of completing the reforms begun by his grandfather and granting a constitution, stubbornly sought, with the aid of men such as Plehve, to return to the darkest ages of bureaucratic absolutism. The ill-fated reign of Nicholas II is further proof that it is impossible to turn back the clock of history. By the turn of the century discontent with the existing situation and the hope of something better was shared by ever larger sections of the population.

A particular bone of contention was the absurd policy of Russification in the non-Russian regions. This was not because the Russian provinces cared more for the freedom of others than for their own, but because the authorities in the non-Russian areas were showing a complete disregard for the people's sense of freedom.

This and other issues became acute at the beginning of the century, while I was still a student at the university. There was now a nation-wide movement for the abolition of autocracy.

One day in the fall of 1902, someone brought into the university the second issue of the weekly publication *Osvobozhdeniye* (*Liberation*), which had first been published in Stuttgart the year before and was edited by the young Marxist, Peter Struve. We were amazed and excited, because until that moment we had been completely unaware of the secret work that had been going on since the mid-1890's to organize the movement of which this journal was the official organ, a movement which combined *zemstvo* liberalism with the ideas of intellectual, liberal, radical, and socialist circles. Naturally, the articles in this underground publication were left unsigned; but from the style of writing and from the apparent knowledge of what was going on in Russia, it was quite clear that the authors were in close contact with prominent and influential members of liberal and radical circles. The journal's aim was to campaign among educated people for the adoption of a constitution in Russia, and it soon became so popular that it was read even by the authorities, from provincial governors to ministers in the capital. We students used to scout around for copies, and whenever we found one we would read it aloud to one another until it literally fell to pieces, for it always contained a wealth of information not to be found in the legal press.

By the beginning of 1904, a large-scale underground organization called the Union of Liberation had sprung up around the journal. It was run by a group of *zemstvo* members, together with members of the liberal and socialist urban intelligentsia, led by Petrunkevich, Prince Shakhovskoy, Prince Dolgoruky, Rodichev, and a number of others. Obviously, I could not be a member of the Union itself, because of my youth, for its members were all distinguished public figures. I was, however, one of the young people who helped on the technical side of the Union's activity—distributing copies of the journal, and so on.

A few months before I took my final examinations, the Russo-Japanese war broke out. The war started with an attack by Japanese destroyers on the Russian fleet, which was laid up at Port Arthur. But there was no sign at all of the patriotic fervor that later swept over Russia when war was declared by Germany in 1914. It is true that the mobilization of troops to be sent to the Russian Far East went off smoothly enough, but the patriotic demonstrations held in the capital and other places were formal and lacking in enthusiasm. Knowing that Witte, and with him the entire Cabinet—with the exception of Plehve—was opposed to the war, most people foresaw difficult times and a disastrous outcome for Russia. In fact, Witte had done his best to oppose the pro-war policy of the Tsar's new favorite, State Secretary Bezobrazov. At the end of 1901, the famous Japanese statesman Marquis Ito had visited St. Petersburg in the hope of settling the impending conflict by peaceful means. Despite Witte's urgings, the Tsar gave the marquis a very frigid welcome, and the visitor went on to London, where Hayashi, the Japanese ambassador, was openly advocating war with Russia. Hayashi made full use of the failure of Ito's negotiations with Witte, as a result of which Britain and Japan signed a treaty of alliance (January, 1902) which was directed at Russia. In the summer of 1903, Witte was transferred to an honorary post and thereby removed from direct participation in state affairs—a triumph for Plehve. At the last moment, however, Tsar Nicholas suddenly came to his senses and tried to avert the war. The episode is described by the young Russian historian Andrew Malozemov, who writes:

Even before Bezobrazov arrived at Port Arthur, Admiral Abaza telegraphed him while en route the following instructions:

"The Emperor orders you to keep in mind that His Majesty has definitely decided to allow the Japanese complete possession of Korea, maybe even as far as the boundary of our concession on the Tumen in the north and on the Yalu in the west. A more exact demarcation of Japanese Korea is a matter for the future and must depend on Russia. This may not be communicated to Japan until after the arrival of troops (two brigades) sent from Russia to the Transbaikal region, so as not to appear a concession. The Emperor believes that by yielding to Japan on the Korean question we avert the risk of coming into conflict with her."

Bezobrazov was ordered to pass on this directive to Alekseyev,[2] who in turn was to inform Lessar, Pavlov and Rosen [3] of its content. However, on his own initiative Bezobrazov decided not to pass it on.[4]

Some people consider that the 1905 revolution was brought on by the Japanese war and Russia's defeat. That I think this is untrue can be seen from my account of the events in Russia from 1901 onward. The Japanese war did not bring about the 1905 revolution. It merely distorted and disfigured it.

On leaving the university in June of 1904, I went to my future uncle-in-law's estate, which was near the village of Kainki, in the province of Kazan. There Olga Baranovsky and I were married, and there we stayed until the fall. Even during those troubled times the newspapers were only delivered once or twice a week, so we looked forward to getting them and to reading the latest news from the theater of war.

One day in July my wife and I went for a stroll by the edge of a wood, taking the newly arrived newspapers with us. When we opened them the first thing that caught our eyes was a report that in St. Petersburg on July 15, while on his way along the Zabalkansky Avenue to see the Tsar, Minister of the Interior Plehve had been killed by a bomb thrown by a former university student named Igor Sazonov.

It is difficult to describe the mixture of feelings that the news aroused in me, and, I think, in a tremendous number of other people as well: a combination of joy, relief, and the expectation of a great change. When I returned to St. Petersburg in the fall, the city was scarcely recognizable because of the change in atmosphere. There was tremendous enthusiasm and excitement at the new situation created by Plehve's death. The man appointed in his place was Prince Svyatopolk-Mirsky, the governor general of Vilna, who was highly regarded by all who knew him. He was a cultured, educated man with a much more modern outlook than his predecessor. He began his ministerial career

[2] Admiral Alekseyev was viceroy of the Russian Far East.
[3] Baron Rosen was the Russian ambassador in Tokyo, and Lessar and Pavlov were Russian representatives in Peking and Seoul respectively.
[4] *Russian Far Eastern Policy* (University of California Press, 1958), p. 220.

with the statement that he would pursue his policy in tune with public opinion, which he would always take into consideration. Later on his era became known as a "political springtime."

Back in St. Petersburg I made great haste to register as a member of the bar so that I could work with those barristers who defended political cases, and thus embark on my political and professional work. My career as a barrister began rather curiously. To be called to the bar one had to give names of three references who knew the applicant well and would vouch for his integrity. I put down a former governor, a former prosecutor of the Tashkent Court of Appeals, and Senator Koni, a member of the State Council and a man greatly respected by the public and by the legal profession. But I had made a mistake. It seems that these highly placed references were unacceptable to the Board of Junior Barristers, whose decision determined whether or not I would be called to the bar. I was rejected on the grounds that my references were from higher bureaucratic circles. At first I was furious and was ready to give up the whole idea of the bar. But my friends persuaded me to change my mind, and I finally found references politically acceptable to the young barristers on the board. And so I became a junior barrister. I had no intention whatsoever of dealing with any but political cases, and I went straight into the legal aid organization.[5] In St. Petersburg, Moscow, and certain other cities, there were a number of legal aid groups who gave free advice to the poorer people, especially in the working-class districts and outlying areas of the city. It was there that I became acquainted with the lowest strata of the urban population, in particular the working class.

I began working at the office located in the People's Club (Narodni Dom),[6] an organization founded by that wonderful social worker, Countess Sofia Panin. The work soon engrossed me completely. The people who used to come to us for advice, above all the women, would talk for hours, complaining of all sorts of things and pouring out their troubles. As time went on there grew up a group of young, capable barristers with whom I worked for many years; one of them subsequently became the head of my private office when I was in the government.

[5] The Russian word used was *konsultatsiya,* because legal aid was given in the form of consultations held in the evening, when the workers were free.
[6] The People's Club was an institution which provided cultural and educational facilities for the poorer people.

At this point the Union of Liberation was organizing its so-called banquet campaign. The banquets were held in St. Petersburg, Moscow, and a number of other places to mark the fortieth anniversary of Alexander II's judicial reforms. They were in effect a parade of the political forces current among the intelligentsia and in the professions. There were always seats for workers at these banquets, although few of them were ever filled. The younger people, such as I, were not officially invited because of our youth, but we acted as secretaries, calling up people to tell them when the banquet would be held, sending around invitations, and so on. The banquets made a tremendous impression because the keynote of all of them was the demand for a constitution.

With the exception of Svyatopolk-Mirsky, all the government officials were angered by the banquets. But on November 11, the officially banned congress of *zemstvo* members held a secret meeting to adopt a resolution appealing to the Tsar to establish a constitutional government in Russia.

The widespread hope that the Svyatopolk-Mirsky "spring" would bring changes that would satisfy, at least to some extent, the nationwide desire for a new order seemed to be coming true. On December 12, 1904, an imperial rescript introducing a substantial number of changes was made public. It dealt first with religious tolerance; second, with freedom of speech and a reform of the press laws; and third, with a review of labor legislation. Committees were set up immediately, under the chairmanship of members of the State Council and other dignitaries, to look into these questions and to work out recommendations.

Shortly thereafter, the Synod, which at that time was presided over by the greatly esteemed Metropolitan Anthony of St. Petersburg, adopted a resolution calling for complete autonomy in matters affecting the Church. The synodal administration was recognized to be uncanonical, and a meeting of the Ecclesiastical Council (Sobor) to elect a patriarch was proposed. The resolution was a remarkable document, and it amazed people at the time, since neither the Synod nor any other church body had raised its voice in dissent since the time of Muscovy, when the metropolitans had spoken up for the rights of the people. Within a short time the church set up a so-called "preparatory committee" to draft a decree on the autonomy of the Orthodox Church. After the Tsar's rescript, steps were taken to recognize the Old Believers Church, and from that time on all persecution of the Old Believers was stopped. The Protestant sects, such as the Baptists and Quakers, did not fare quite so well, although things were made somewhat easier for them, too.

The other committees were not quite as successful, because shortly thereafter, on January 9, the climate at the top changed abruptly.

1905

The events that led up to January 9, or Bloody Sunday as it came to be called, began in Moscow in 1901, and may to some extent be laid at the door of Grand Duke Sergey, the uncle of the Tsar, at that time governor general. He advocated the idea that there should be labor unions, patronized by the authorities, which would campaign for improved standards for the working class. These unions offered the additional advantage, not outwardly apparent, of helping the authorities to restrain the industrialists, who were becoming more and more progressive, to the extent that they had come to share with the *zemstva* the aim of replacing absolutism with a constitutional monarchy.

The police labor unions were set up by Zubatov, head of the Moscow Secret Police, an intelligent man who had had a university education. He evidently tried to imitate Bismarck's experiment in Germany, modified to fit the situation in Russia, by pursuing an apparently pro-working-class policy while simultaneously attempting to stem the political influence of the socialist parties among the workers.

In 1903, Zubatov was removed from his post. The new movement had become too "successful," inasmuch as some of his agents had taken part in, or even organized, general strikes. In Odessa, for example, the chief instigator of a strike was a key agent called Shayevich. But despite Zubatov's dismissal, his plan had an extraordinary and totally unexpected result: his police unions grew into genuine trade unions. The leader of this movement in St. Petersburg in 1903 was a young and gifted priest by the name of Father George Gapon, who had only recently been ordained. Gapon's story, which everyone knows, ended tragically, but I still cannot believe that he was from the very outset merely a police agent. I think that the young priest was genuinely carried away by the idea of working for the workers. It may well be that later on he was ensnared in political traps, but I submit that he did not join the workers from the outset as a deliberate *agent provocateur*. Be that as it may, he was very able in his dealings with the workers. His father had been a simple village priest, and Gapon understood people and knew how to talk to them. His influence on the masses was staggering, and in St. Petersburg the Gaponist movement assumed huge proportions. The priest's speeches, in which he always urged the workers to go directly to the Tsar, appealed to his listeners, and the idea of marching to the palace and voicing their grievances in a mass demonstration quickly gained their support. There can be no doubt that at that stage Gapon had far more influence on the workers than all the underground organizations and socialist parties put together.

In the beginning the socialist parties had taken little interest in the Gaponist movement. By the time they woke up, it was too late to counter Gapon's influence. By early January, the workers were growing impatient, and they completed their plans to march to the palace and present the Tsar with a petition. The petition itself had actually been drafted, but the police did nothing to restrain the workers or to stop Gapon's activities.

Of course, Svyatopolk-Mirsky was unable to do very much himself, since he was no longer in charge of the police department of the Ministry of the Interior. His duties had been handed over to his assistant, General Trepov, formerly chief of police of Moscow and currently a rising star on the palace horizon. The general enjoyed the patronage of the Grand Duchess Elizabeth, who had recommended him to her sister the Tsarina, and to the Tsar. He soon became a great favorite at court.

On the eve of the march, the organizers learned that the police and a number of guard units had been alerted to stand by, and by Saturday night there was tremendous tension in the air. The tension was increased by news of the arrest and subsequent release of politicians who had gone to see the minister of the interior in the hope of averting a disastrous clash. On Sunday morning I went down to the Nevsky Prospect with a student friend of mine, Alexander Ovsyannikov, to watch the demonstration.

It was an amazing sight. Along the Nevsky Prospect from the direction of the working-class districts came row upon row of orderly and solemn-faced workers, all dressed in their best clothes. Gapon, marching in front of the procession, was carrying a cross, and a number of the workers were holding icons and portraits of the Tsar. The huge procession was moving fairly slowly, so we walked along with it from the Liteyny down the whole length of the Nevsky Prospect. A crowd of people lined the streets to see the columns of workers, and everyone felt a sense of a great excitement.

We had already reached the Alexander Garden, on the other side of which lay the Winter Palace Square, when we heard the sound of bugles, the signal for the cavalry to charge. The marchers came to a halt, uncertain as to what the bugles meant and unable to see what was happening. In front on the right was a detachment of police, but since they showed no signs of hostility, the procession began moving again. Just then, however, a detachment of cavalry rode out from the direction of the St. Petersburg Military District Headquarters, and the first volley of shots rang out. Another body of troops, which had apparently been formed on the other side of the square opposite the Admiralty, also began shooting. The first volley was fired in the air, but the second was aimed at the crowd, and a number of people fell to the ground. Panic-stricken, the crowd turned around and began running in every direction. They were now being fired on from behind, and we bystanders took to our heels along with the rest. I cannot describe the horror we felt at that moment. It was quite clear that the authorities had made a terrible mistake; they had totally misunderstood the intentions of the crowd. Whatever the plans of the organizers of the march may have been, the workers were marching to the palace without any evil intent. They sincerely believed that when they got there they would kneel down, and that the Tsar would come out to meet them, or at least appear on the balcony. But all they got was bullets. It was a historic error for which both the monarchy and Russia paid very dearly.

The first estimates showed the number of casualties to be at least two or three hundred killed and wounded. Ambulances were quickly called, and those who had not been hurt helped to carry the wounded men, women, and children. Everything broke up in confusion, and the crowd eventually dispersed into the neighboring streets. Gapon himself was rescued by well-wishers, who shaved off his beard, dressed him in civilian clothes, and got him out of the city. From his hiding place he sent a message to the workers in which he heaped curses on the monarchy and the Tsar.

The events of Bloody Sunday brought about a radical change in the mentality of the masses of workers, who up to that time had been little affected by the propaganda directed at them. The spiritual bond between the Tsar and the masses of ordinary workers was severed by General Trepov and by all those who had allowed this insane act to be perpetrated.

Soon afterward the Bar Council set up a special committee for assistance to the victims of the tragedy. People were needed to visit the working-class areas and find out how the families involved in the events had been affected. I took part in this work eagerly. My job was to visit workers' homes in all parts of the city. It was then that I began to see what enormous differences there were in the living conditions of individual working-class families, for some lived in comparatively well-furnished tenements, while others lived in awful hovels. The wives of the workers who had been killed were shocked and bewildered by the whole affair, and they could not understand how it had happened. After all, they said, the men had set off with the best of intentions. They had only wanted to present a petition, but they had been met with bullets. These women had no feelings of resentment or hatred; they simply felt that something had happened that would change the whole course of their lives.

Naturally, Bloody Sunday provided ample grist for the mill of left-wing propaganda. My work as a legal consultant among the workers and my visits to working-class homes after January 9 convinced me that much of this propaganda was based on false premises, and that the notion of a "conscious" worker was pure wishful thinking.

What I saw on that Sunday made a tremendous impression on me. At a time when the country was at war and the Russian Army was in retreat, the pick of the imperial guards regiments had blindly obeyed an absurd and monstrous order to fire on the workers! To me the state of the army and the morale of the troops seemed of paramount importance. I was well aware there had to be a strong and healthy bond between the people and the army.

When I reached home and had calmed down a little, I wrote a letter to the officers of the guards. I cannot recall exactly what words I used, but I stated my feelings in no uncertain terms. I reminded them that at a time when the army was fighting for Russia, they at home, with all Europe looking on, had shot down defenseless workers and had thereby greatly harmed the country's prestige abroad. I knew several guards officers, among them my wife's brother, who was an officer in the First Brigade of Guards Artillery. I signed the letter with my own name and sent copies to a number of them. There were no unpleasant consequences. The men to whom I had written were gentlemen, after all, and not one of them betrayed me or passed on my letter to the police. But from that time on, I broke off relations with all my friends and acquaintances in bureaucratic circles, so intolerable to me was any reminder of that Sunday morning on the Nevsky Prospect.

February 28, 1905, was a day to remember. On that day, by sheer coincidence, three extremely important documents were published. No one, as far as I know, has ever been able to suggest a plausible reason why all three came to be published at the same time. The first document was a manifesto from Nicholas II appealing to all "true Russians" to rally around the throne and defend from sedition the ancient autocracy without which Russia could not exist. The second was a rescript instructing Bulygin, the new minister of the interior,[7] to draft the outline of a "consultative" state Duma. The third document was a ukase ordering the ruling senate to accept petitions sent in or handed in by representatives of the various sections of the population.

These three imperial decrees were a puzzle to everyone, but the one that gained most attention was the rescript on the proposal to create a consultative state Duma. The ukase on petitions was also of major importance, in that it gave to everyone the right to hold meetings and to draw up petitions and send them to the ruling senate. But the ukase was later to assume a different significance. After the dissolution of the first Duma in July, 1906, there were numerous reprisals against those who had organized or collected signatures for petitions of this kind.

Few people realized that the document of greatest significance to the authorities was the first—the manifesto aimed at rallying "true Russians" round the throne. It breathed life into the extreme right-wing movement, which had long been embryonic and which emerged

[7] Svyatopolk-Mirsky had resigned after Bloody Sunday.

eight months later, on October 17, 1905, as the Union of the Russian People.

The assumption by Trepov of virtually dictatorial powers, in conjunction with the three government decrees of February 28—simultaneous measures that seemed to meet the demands of the people while actually preparing countermeasures to oppose these demands—showed that the government was fast losing its grip. After Witte's disappearance from the scene there was no one left who could govern competently.

For several months, while the law on the new "consultative" Duma was being drafted, the burning question among all sections of the population was whether or not to take part in the forthcoming elections. Naturally, the subject was discussed with particular vehemence by the group that was molding public opinion at the time, that is, the Union of Liberation.

The meetings held for the purpose of compiling petitions served as a basis for the formation of countless new unions. In effect, the entire country became "unionized." There were unions of university professors, unions of teachers, unions of lawyers, doctors, engineers, architects, actors, postal workers, railroad men, and many others. A prominent part was played by the Union of Railroad Employees, one of the first to be established. Its members were highly disciplined, and they had great *esprit de corps*. In fact, this union made an enormous contribution to the Revolution of October 17, 1905. The postal and telegraph workers were also a highly disciplined group with well-developed team spirit. Both of these unions did much to establish communications between groups of the population which until then had been disorganized and out of contact with one another.

All of the unions (including the Peasants' Union) were merged into a federation called the Union of Unions, and this body was the focus for the entire liberation movement. It included many members of the Union of Liberation as well as numerous representatives of the working class. The newly elected president was the well-known historian and prominent political figure, Professor P. N. Milyukov.

Meanwhile the war was drawing to a close, and after the Battle of Mukden it was clear that Russia had been defeated. Actually, the battle of Mukden, which lasted for two weeks and which was, in terms of the number of soldiers involved, the greatest battle in military history up to that time, ended in much the same way as had the Battle of Borodino in 1812. For although the Japanese were the nominal victors, their losses were so great that they were unable to continue fighting. Shortly thereafter they began negotiations for peace, at first through the mediation of the French. After the Battle of Tsushima on May 14, in which the Baltic Fleet was lost, it became imperative for Russia to end the war.

I will not say much about the international aspect of the peace talks, except to note that the French foreign minister, Théophile Delcassé, played an important part in them. France considered it essential to halt the Russo-Japanese War in view of the increasing German threat to both France and England. The English had already realized that there was no longer any need to protect India from the "northern colossus," which was not planning an invasion, and that they would do better to turn their attention to the real pretender to world domination.

It was decided to hold the peace talks in the United States, since President Theodore Roosevelt had agreed to undertake the mediation. The mediation, incidentally, was of a rather curious kind. The President was wholly on the side of Japan, and during the negotiations at Portsmouth he was at times more Japanese than the Japanese themselves. It was not until after the peace talks in 1908 that he realized his mistake, but from then on he took a totally different view of both Japan and Russia.

It was an extremely difficult time for Russia to be conducting peace talks, in view of the complete isolation resulting from her internal policies, and the fact that the whole of Europe sympathized with Japan. Witte, who had been instructed to conduct the talks for the Russian side, despite the Tsar's intense dislike for him, showed himself to be an exceptionally shrewd diplomat. The settlement that he obtained for Russia was in no way degrading, and involved no major concession other than the cession to Japan of half the island of Sakhalin. In fact, even this concession was made against his better judgment, as the result of pressure from the Tsar. Witte wanted to prolong the talks, knowing that the Japanese were so weak that, given a little time, they would be forced to abandon all their claims.

The revolution of October 17 was precipitated by the demoralization of the army, which was probably due mainly to a feeling, not always conscious, of wounded national pride.

Numerous efforts were made to prevent the authorities from heading straight for disaster, but there was little that could be done, for the simple reason that the regime had outlived its place in history. By 1905 there was not a single section of the population that was not aware that life under these conditions was intolerable.

The appeal to the Tsar that the *zemstva* and towns had presented in May had been a last desperate attempt to persuade the Tsar that his course was suicidal; but the Tsar would not listen, and the country continued to move toward the goal that the Russian people had always sought to attain.

Toward the fall of 1905, the normal life of the country began to slow down; strikes broke out in a number of places, and there were frequent cases of rioting and mutiny among peasants and soldiers. Anyone who lived in St. Petersburg at that time was aware that Russia had reached the limits of her endurance.

During the last two or three weeks prior to October 17, a strike took place that was, perhaps, historically unique. For this strike brought the entire life of the country to a halt. Railroads, post offices, law courts, schools, and universities—all came gradually to a standstill. I remember the last few days: all the cabs had disappeared, the street lamps were dark, and everywhere there was an uncanny silence. This silence was felt in the palace at Peterhof, too, where the Tsar and his family were living at the time.

Constitutional Manifesto

During the last few days before the Revolution, Peterhof was completely cut off from the outside world. Communication by road was no longer possible. The Tsar's ministers either communicated with him by military telegraph or sent couriers by naval launch. Failing this, they went in person. Two destroyers were standing by in Peterhof Harbor in case it became necessary to send the Tsar's family to England. This was the atmosphere in which the Tsar sent for Witte, just back from the Portsmouth peace talks, to ask him to prepare a memorandum on the situation. Witte went to see the Tsar on October 9 and gave him the memorandum, the contents of which were not published until much later, when the Bolsheviks inserted it in the *Red Archives*. Among other things, the memorandum said:

The principal slogan of the present movement is freedom. The present liberation movement was not born yesterday. Its roots lie deep in the past—in Novgorod and Pskov, in the Zaporozhye Cossacks, in the freemen of the Volga region, in the Church schism, the protest against Peter's reforms, in the revolt of the Decembrists, in the Petrashevsky case.[8]

Man always strives for freedom. Civilized man strives for freedom and law; freedom controlled by law and by law ensured.

. . . leadership first requires a clearly set goal. A goal that is informed by an ideal, supreme and recognized by all.

This is the goal set by society; its importance is great and overwhelming, for in this goal is the truth.

The government must therefore accept it. The slogan "freedom" must become the slogan of the government. There is no other way to save the country.

The march of history cannot be held up. The idea of civil liberty will prevail, if not through reform, then through revolution. But in the second case it will rise from the ashes of a thousand-year-old past. A Russian revolt, meaningless and merciless, would sweep all before it and turn everything to dust. How Russia would emerge from such an ordeal the mind dare not think; the horrors of a Russian revolt could exceed anything in the past. Intervention by other countries would dismember the country. Attempts to practice theoretical socialism would not be successful, but would undoubtedly destroy the family, freedom of religious worship, private ownership, all the fundamentals of right and law.

Just as in the 1860's the government came out for the emancipation of the peasants, so at this infinitely more perilous moment the authorities have no choice: they must boldly and openly take the lead in the liberation movement.

The notion of civil liberty contains nothing that would threaten the existence of the State. . . .

---

[8] The Petrashevsky case concerned a conspiratorial group of young intellectuals who met in St. Petersburg from 1845 to 1848 to study the revolutionary ideas of the French socialist Fourier. Their program for Russia was the emancipation of the serfs and the introduction of trial by jury and freedom of the press. Some of the members of this circle, notably F. M. Dostoyevsky, were not satisfied with the "moderate" tendencies of the majority, and they discussed among themselves plans for some immediate revolutionary acts. It is well known that Dostoyevsky and some of his associates were sentenced to death for their activity, but that at the last moment their sentence was commuted to a term of imprisonment in Siberia. Dostoyevsky based *The House of Death* on this experience.

The liberation movement will, admittedly, break with the past, but was not the emancipation of the peasants also a renunciation of many centuries? . . .

. . . The authorities must further be ready to adopt a constitutional course. The word need not frighten them or be a forbidden one. The authorities must strive sincerely and openly for the good of the country, and not for the retention of any particular form [of government]. Let it be proved that the good of the country is the Constitution; a sovereign monarch whose interests cannot be separate from the good of the people would undoubtedly pursue such a policy. There cannot be any place here for apprehension, and you must bear in mind and be prepared to accept this solution.[9]

Witte's proposal for a constitution was accepted. The Tsar decided to publish a manifesto in which, without mentioning the word "constitution," he would establish a new order that would in effect be a constitutional system.

On the night of October 16 I heard someone urgently ringing my doorbell. I thought it was the police (at that time they were searching houses and making political arrests), but it turned out to be my friend Ovsyannikov, in a state of great excitement. I asked what had happened, and he showed me the manifesto, just published in a special supplement to the official newspaper *Government Messenger*.

The manifesto pledged:

(1) To grant the people the unshakable fundamentals of civil liberty based on principles of true inviolability of the individual, freedom of conscience and speech, and the right of assembly and union.

(2) Without halting the forthcoming elections to the Duma, to encourage forthwith those classes that at present have no electoral rights whatsoever to participate in the work of the Duma, as far as is possible in the time left before the convocation of the Duma, after which further development of the principle of universal suffrage is to be left to the newly constituted legislative system.

(3) To make it an *unbreakable* rule that no law shall be put into force without the approval of the Duma and that those elected by the people are

[9] *Red Archives,* Vols. 4–5 (Moscow, 1925). On the eve of the Manifesto of October 17 it was not generally known in the capital that Count Witte had urged the Tsar to choose between the institution of an unlimited dictatorship or the granting of a constitution. The Tsar decided to grant a constitution after Grand Duke Nicholas Nikolaevich had refused to serve as a dictator. See Count S. Yu. Witte, *Memoirs,* 2d ed., Vol. II (Berlin, 1922), pp. 20–21, memorandum by Prince N. D. Obolensky.

given the opportunity of genuine participation in the work of ensuring that the actions of the authorities established by us conform to the law.[10]

The fundamental principle of any constitution is that the supreme authority may not pass any laws without the consent of the representatives of the people. With this manifesto, absolute power became a thing of the past.

[10] In the *Code of Laws of the Russian Empire* (1829), Vol. I, Part I, Sec. I, Art. 1: The Emperor of all the Russias is a monarch sovereign and absolute.

In the *Code of Laws of the Russian Empire* (1906), Vol. I, Part I, Art. 4: The Emperor of all the Russias possesses *supreme sovereign power*. The word "absolute" had been deleted.

4

Revolutionary Romanticism

I SPENT the rest of that night in a state of elation. The age-long bitter struggle of the people for freedom and for the right to participate in the affairs of state seemed to be over. "Constitution" was no longer an empty slogan of the revolutionary movement. The Constitution had become a reality, the cornerstone of a new Russia. Accepting Witte's wise judgment, the Tsar had found the inner strength to heed his people's just demand that he renounce absolutism, which he had hitherto considered his by divine right. From the beginning of his reign, his policy had reflected a stubborn unwillingness to follow the path of constitutional reform. Now I felt almost guilty for having considered him an irreconcilable enemy of freedom. A wave of warmth and gratitude went through my whole being, and my childhood adoration for the Tsar revived. The night seemed endless. I could not wait to run to the Nevsky Prospect in the morning and join the enthusiastic crowds of intellectuals, factory workers, students, and ordinary citizens who would be pouring out into the streets to celebrate this great victory of the people.

But when I went to the Nevsky Prospect in the morning, I found the wide avenue strangely deserted. Bewildered, I walked on toward the Admiralty and the Winter Palace, thinking to find the jubilant crowds on the palace square. A handful of people were standing in the middle of the street holding black banners inscribed "Long Live Anarchy" in red letters.

There was nothing to do but to return home. I rang my friends on the telephone and learned that no manifestations were planned. The Soviet of Workers' Deputies, which had formed in the beginning of

October, was issuing appeals to the workers to continue their unrelenting struggle against "tsarist autocracy."

The next day news from Moscow showed that the Soviet of Workers' Deputies was not alone in its attitude to the manifesto of October 17. A conference of the Union of Liberation was being held in Moscow at the time. It proved to be the last meeting of that organization, because then and there the majority of the delegates founded the liberal Constitutional Democratic Party (the "Cadets").

On the evening of October 17, while P. N. Milyukov was giving a speech, the manifesto was handed to him, and he stopped to read aloud its contents. Then he resumed his speech with the words: *"Nothing has changed; the struggle continues."*

I did not know what to think. The goal of the liberation movement, under the leadership of the Union of Liberation, had been that very constitution which they now, in forming the Constitutional Democratic Party, resoundingly rejected.

The day after the manifesto brought also a number of "patriotic" demonstrations, mostly in southern cities, instigated by the Union of the Russian People, an organization that Witte scathingly described as "a mob of thugs and scoundrels." In St. Petersburg hysterical crowds carrying portraits of Nicholas II and marching to the strains of the national anthem, "God Save the Tsar," shouted threats and vile accusations against Jews, revolutionaries, and intellectuals, thus spreading panic among the population at large. Pogroms were started, and the opportunity for looting attracted the dregs of society. Cruel indignities were inflicted upon thousands of innocent people, but the police condoned the pogroms and looked the other way.

In the early part of November the press announced that the Tsar had accepted an honorary membership badge of the Union of the Russian People from its head, Dr. A. I. Dubrovin.

This dismaying event revealed the true meaning of the manifesto of February 28, 1905, which had called upon all "true Russians" to rally around the throne and defend Russian autocracy against sedition. Now, I suddenly understood that this manifesto had consciously invited the formation of the Dubrovin movement and of similar "patriotic" organizations. It soon leaked out that the notorious Dr. Dubrovin had originally been introduced to the Tsar by none other than Grand Duke Nikolai Nikolayevich. It was not in itself surprising that extreme rightist organizations had formed and were disturbing public peace and order. They are the natural concomitants everywhere of revolution and social upheaval. What mattered, however, was the fact that Nicholas II was officially patronizing Dubrovin's organization. It was this that now led me to the inescapable conclusion that for the salvation of Russia and her future the reigning monarch must be removed.

How was this task to be accomplished? I did not yet know the answer, but I decided to give up all my former plans and devote myself to the work of ridding the country of this monarch.

Among other things, the manifesto of October 17 proclaimed the freedom of the press, and almost at once the Organization of Armed Rebellion, founded by N. D. Mironov, took advantage of this to begin publication of *Burevestnik* (*Stormy Petrel*), a revolutionary socialist bulletin. When I was invited to write for this paper I accepted readily, since it accorded well with my desire to work for the revolution. I was anxious to voice my views on the Tsar's real attitude toward the constitution he himself had promulgated. Furthermore, I had made up my mind to combat the absurd decision of both the Social Democrats and the Socialist Revolutionaries to boycott the elections to the first Duma. I felt very strongly that this policy only played into the hands of the enemies of democracy and was, moreover, contrary to the mood of the people.

Backed by the young Sanskrit scholar N. D. Mironov, son of a wealthy St. Petersburg merchant, the journal was first published on November 15, and its sixteen pages of closely set type thereafter appeared twice a week. The articles in *Burevestnik* were signed by our pen names, but the identities of the authors were known, of course, to the Central Committee of the Socialist Revolutionary Party. The bulletin was a great success from the very first issue, and in the fifth issue, published on December 4, the editors announced that *Burevestnik* had been recognized as a press organ of the Socialist Revolutionary Party.

After the Revolution of 1905, the students, too, had plunged head over heels into political work. A vast number of Menshevik, Bolshevik, and social-revolutionary groups sprang up, some affiliated with party centers and some independent. The autonomy unexpectedly granted to the universities in August, 1905 turned the lecture halls into public forums where freedom of speech and assembly blossomed, immune from police intervention, since the police now had no right to enter the university. The professors were unable to stem the revolutionary oratory that flowed from the rostrums.

My wife's cousin Sergey Vasilyev, who was in his final year at the Institute of Means of Transportation, joined the institute's student committee of the Socialist Revolutionary Party. Together with A. A. Ovsyannikov, and N. D. Mironov, he founded a socialist revolutionary group, which engaged in propaganda and the distribution of mimeographed leaflets. My wife and I allowed them to store their material in our apartment, a good deed which was later to cost us dear.

I did not take all these improvised political groups too seriously. I thought their activities were just a temporary craze, which I dubbed "revolutionary romanticism." What, for instance, was the point of Sergey's proclamations, which were signed in the name of a formidable sounding "Organization of Armed Rebellion"? I knew only too well that none of the members possessed firearms and that no insurrection in St. Petersburg was even so much as contemplated by the group.

Yevgeniya N. Moiseyenko, a student at the Courses of Higher Learning for Women, was a close friend of my wife and a frequent visitor to our house. Her brother Boris was a member of a special terrorist unit at the headquarters abroad of the Central Committee of the Socialist Revolutionary Party, and I knew that he occasionally came to Russia. His comings and goings were, of course, kept strictly secret, but on his clandestine visits to St. Petersburg he always managed to meet with his sister. One day in early December of 1905, when my wife was out of the room, I asked Yevgeniya Nikolayevna to meet me somewhere away from our house—but not in the apartment that she shared with a friend. She was surprised at my secretiveness, and I explained that I wanted to have a word with her about a very serious matter without alarming my wife.

When we met a few days later in a quiet restaurant off the Nevsky Prospect, I asked her to arrange a meeting for me with her brother, for I wanted to ask him to allow me to participate in their plot against the Tsar. We argued for a long time in hushed, agitated voices. At first she refused outright and even got up to leave, but I managed to make her stay. I must have been unusually persuasive, because she finally gave in, her eyes filled with tears.

Scarcely two weeks later, as she was leaving our apartment one day, she asked me with a smile to see her to the streetcar. When we were alone she told me that the next afternoon at five o'clock sharp I was to walk along Nevsky Prospect to the corner of Liteyny in the direction of the Anichkov Bridge, and then turn right into Fontanka. I would be approached by a clean-shaven man in an overcoat and an Astrakhan hat who would ask for a light. "Take a box of matches with you. He will take a cigarette out of a silver case, and while he is lighting it, tell him briefly what you want. He will give you his answer and walk away briskly. You are to slow down and turn back, unless you notice someone following you."

Everything happened exactly the way she had told me. Moiseyenko was brief: "In a few days you will hear from me directly or through my sister." A few days later we met at the same hour and at the same corner, and as he passed me he said without turning his head: "Nothing doing."

Soon after this Yevgeniya Nikolayevna told me that her brother had asked her to explain that my request had been turned down because I had no experience as a revolutionary and could not, therefore, be relied upon. I had to laugh at the thought that I, too, had turned out to be just another revolutionary dreamer.

Twelve years later I was to meet with Boris Moiseyenko again. After the proclamation of a general amnesty he returned to Russia and became one of my best commissars at the front. Recalling our two clandestine meetings in the winter of 1905, I asked him how he had been able to get an answer from his party center abroad in such a short time. "I didn't ask our people abroad. Azev [1] was in the city just then, and he personally vetoed you." It turned out that a police agent within the leadership of the party itself had been deliberately discouraging people who were willing to sacrifice themselves for the cause. By the time of this second meeting with Moiseyenko I had met Boris Savinkov, the famous terrorist and second-in-command to Azev, and I was struck by his amazing resemblance to Moiseyenko. However, the resemblance was purely physical. There was hardly a more honest, devoted, and modest person than Moiseyenko. Sometimes he stood

[1] Evno Azev was the famous double agent who managed to become head of the Socialist Revolutionary terrorist organization while simultaneously working for the Okhrana (Tsarist secret police).

in for Savinkov under dangerous circumstances, and he did it willingly, without a thought for his own safety, or for his "career" as a revolutionary.

It is a disaster when revolutionary terrorist activities become part of a party program and are devised in seclusion by people who are neither directly involved nor risk their own lives.

Those who live in normal conditions under the rule of law are unable to understand what it means, psychologically, to commit a terrorist act. "How can you be indignant about Communist or Nazi terrorism when you yourself once condoned terror?" I am occasionally asked by political Pharisees. "After all," they argue, "murder is murder."

It is quite true that a government system of terror and individual acts of revolutionary terrorism both deprive human beings of life. But the similarity ends there. Essentially, the two types of terrorism are diametrically opposed.

In times when people could still distinguish between right and wrong the public conscience never failed to accord moral approval to tyrannicides such as Brutus, Charlotte Corday, or, in Russia, Yegor Sazonov.

When a group of courtiers and officers of the guards assassinated the nearly insane Emperor Paul I on March 11, 1801, the whole of St. Petersburg rejoiced and strangers kissed each other in the streets, as they do at Easter.

At his trial for the assassination of V. K. Plehve, Sazonov said: "We took up the sword, which we were not the first to raise, after a terrible struggle and agony. Yes, I am guilty before God. I await His judgment calmly for I know He will not judge me as I have been judged here. How could I do otherwise when my Teacher said: *Take up thy cross and follow Me.* It was not in me to refuse my cross."

By 1905 I had come to the conclusion that individual terrorism was inevitable. I was quite willing if need be, to take upon myself the mortal sin of killing the incumbent of supreme power who was ruining the country. Much later, in 1915, at a secret meeting of the liberal and moderately conservative majority of the Duma and the State Council, V. A. Maklakov, a highly conservative liberal and monarchist said, in discussing the policy of the Crown, that disaster could only be avoided and Russia saved if the event of March 11, 1801, were repeated. The difference in our views was only a matter of timing, as I had come to that conclusion a decade earlier. Furthermore, Maklakov and his followers expected others to do the job. I had felt that in accepting the idea, I must also be willing to accept the responsibility for it by acting myself.

Prison

By the end of December the authorities had recovered from their confusion, and life seemed to be returning to its "pre-October" confines. Witte judged the time ripe for strong measures. The disaffection among the troops returning from Siberia after the disastrous Japanese war was suppressed by two harsh disciplinarians, generals Meller-Zakomelsky and Rennenkampf.[2] The leaders of the St. Petersburg Soviet of Workers' Deputies, who had overestimated their influence and popularity, were arrested, tried, and deported to Siberia (whence they quickly escaped abroad). The serious uprising attempted in December in the Presna district of Moscow by the Social Revolutionaries and Social Democrats was crushed by local troops and a regiment of light guards sent from St. Petersburg. Dubrovin's thugs (known as "Black Hundreds") were running amok all over the country, and even in St. Petersburg there was some fear that a pogrom of the intelligentsia might take place. Police roved the town, making sporadic arrests of "unreliable" workers, students, and intellectuals. The free press that had arisen after the manifesto was losing ground, but nevertheless maintained a precarious existence. Police broke up meetings, which continued nonetheless. Meanwhile, however, the electoral campaign for the first Duma had begun under the provisions of the liberal electoral law of December 11, which had been drafted under Witte's supervision. The police could no longer have their way so easily with well-organized social forces now conscious of their strength. A new era in the life of Russia had started, and the public, recognizing that a return to the past was no longer possible, was full of scorn for the antics of the police.

Our paper *Burevestnik* was one of the victims of police oppression. They were watching for a chance to confiscate an issue, but we used to rush each issue from the press before the police had time to pounce. It was a kind of game. But they caught us on the eighth or ninth issue,

[2] Later responsible for the Russian debacle in East Prussia in 1915.

which, unfortunately, ran a particularly outspoken article by me. This issue was destined to be the last.

When I heard the news about the confiscation of *Burevestnik* I was not unduly upset. With Christmas drawing close I welcomed the opportunity to rest from my hectic journalistic activities and spend the holidays quietly with my family. But late on the night of December 21, while my wife and I were decorating a Christmas tree for our eight-month-old son, the front doorbell rang. At the same moment someone knocked on the back door. It could only be the police. I went immediately to answer the doorbell so as not to arouse any suspicions that we were trying to hide something. At the front door was the local police inspector, a stout, good-natured man who happened to be a near neighbor of ours. We knew each other by sight and had often exchanged neighborly remarks about the weather or something equally trivial. His bearing was extremely courteous as he requested permission to enter, but he was accompanied by a gendarme captain (*rotmistr*), three or four gendarmes, and a regular policeman. At the same time another group of policemen, accompanied by a handyman and several witnesses, entered through the back door. Like an enemy bastion, our apartment had been occupied by the minions of the law. The captain handed me a search warrant and asked me to read it over. The search that followed lasted for hours, but the captain and his subordinates behaved at all times with complete correctness. When the policemen entered the nursery, the captain, at my wife's request, ordered his men to stay away from the cradle of our son Oleg and to be quiet so as not to disturb the child. The search was nearly over when one of the gendarmes discovered a bundle under a pile of newspapers in one corner of the sitting-room. It contained the appeals of the Organization of Armed Rebellion, which we had long ago forgotten. After the October Manifesto these childish leaflets had become quite obsolete. The discovery seemed to be significant to our good neighbor, however. Looking calm and impassive, he wrote out his deposition on the evidence of criminal activity found in my apartment. He handed me the paper for signature and then had it countersigned by the two witnesses. While this formality was taking place, the captain signed a warrant for my arrest and told me what things I was entitled to take with me. Despite her deep concern, my wife accepted the turn of events with outward calm and even offered a cup of tea to the tired police inspector and captain. They were bleary-eyed with fatigue and drank the hot steaming tea with obvious pleasure. An outsider would never have guessed that this peaceful "tea party" was made up of representatives—albeit minor ones—of forces at war with each other.

It did not take me long to get my belongings together, and my wife and I spent even less time saying goodbye, as if we feared to break down and show our true feelings. The Christmas tree was lit without me that year.

There was no carriage with drawn green blinds such as I remembered from my childhood awaiting me outside. There was only an ordinary droshky drawn by a miserable nag. It was a tight squeeze sitting next to the fat inspector, especially as a sturdy policeman was perched precariously on the tiny seat opposite me. As we jogged along through the deserted streets I could see the sky growing lighter in the east. It was almost dawn. No one told me where we were going, but as we crossed the Neva and turned to the right on the other side of the bridge I saw the notorious Kresty [3] Prison looming up ahead. The formalities in the office were brief, and almost at once I was led to my cell. Perfunctorily, the prison regulations were explained to me. Then the lock snapped behind me and I was alone.

My cell was six paces long and three paces wide, and the only daylight came from a small window set high in the outer wall. It was furnished with a bed, a table and chair, and, of course, a chamberpot. There was a dim light in the middle which was never turned off. The heavy door was equipped with a peephole shuttered on the outside with a metal disk. I never knew when the disk would be moved aside and the warder's eye appear in the opening. During the first days this unceremonious observation was most disquieting, but eventually I came to disregard it.

When I had finished taking stock of my surroundings, I found myself overwhelmed by a dreadful feeling of fatigue, and I slumped down on the narrow cot. Mercifully, I was asleep within seconds.

About three hours later I was awakened from a deep slumber by the sound of a key in the lock. It was the warder, who told me that it was time to wash. Hastily I took a toothbrush, soap, and a towel from

---

[3] It was called the *Kresty* (Cross) Prison because it was built in the form of a cross, with a central tower from which all four wings could be guarded.

my overnight case and followed him outside to the gallery, where a group of prisoners was waiting. I joined them and we were marched off to a common washroom. To a newcomer like me the whole procedure was revolting. We were given five or at the most ten minutes to wash. There were no individual washbasins, only a long zinc trough with dozens of faucets. Clumsily I tried to put the cake of soap and the toothbrush into the narrow space under the faucet. Seeing that I was a novice, my neighbor gave me all sorts of useful information, and asked my name and cell number. Among other things, he told me that the prison held very few criminals, the majority being political offenders. I felt a little better after talking to him. It was good to know that there was some sort of underground, unofficial life in the prison. A few days later, returning from the washbasin, I found that, without my knowledge, a thin, tightly rolled sheet of paper had been slipped into my pocket. It was a table with six rows of letters in alphabetical order, the rows being numbered one to six. A note at the bottom explained how to use the letters to communicate with other prisoners by knocking against the wall or on the central heating pipes. It was a special prison code not unlike the Morse system. When I had sufficiently acquainted myself with the code, I started to knock on the wall. My neighbor responded immediately, and one of the first things he told me was that Sergey Vasilyev was imprisoned on the floor above me.

By this time I had settled in the cell. The rules were not especially strict. For example, the families of political prisoners were permitted to send food and candy, as well as an unlimited number of books. Books could also be borrowed from the excellent prison library. Strangely enough, I almost enjoyed this solitary confinement, which gave me leisure to think, to look back at my life, and to read to my heart's content. There was the additional pleasure of exchanging news with Sergey Vasilyev by means of our code. Two weeks went by in this way.

According to law, no prisoner could be held for more than two weeks without informing him of the reason for his arrest. So far I had not been informed of the charge against me. This I was particularly anxious to learn because of the curious behavior of the police inspector at the time of my arrest. Instead of questioning me about Sergey Vasilyev or his group, the captain had shown each member of my family—except me—a photograph of a young girl, apparently in an attempt to detect some sign of recognition. Of course no one had been able to identify her, since she had never been to our house. The captain had shown as little interest in my copies of *Burevestnik* as he had in Sergey Vasilyev. What was all this about a girl? Turning the matter over in my mind, I decided that he had had some reason for coming which was quite unconnected with the pamphlets for which I had been arrested. But I could think of no explanation.

We were not allowed to write ordinary letters, but we did enjoy the privilege of writing to the prison authorities. For that purpose official writing materials were provided upon request. As soon as the legal period of detention had expired, I wrote to the assistant prosecutor of the St. Petersburg District Court that I would go on a hunger strike unless I was informed of the charges against me within five days. When five days had elapsed and I had received no answer to my request, I started my hunger strike. The smell of the food which was left by the side of my bed each day was almost unbearable. I was greatly plagued by thirst as well, and I sometimes broke down and sipped some water. Then, all of a sudden, it became easier. By the fourth day I felt quite numb, and I fell into a state of semiconsciousness. I began to experience hallucinations. I felt almost blissful. On the seventh or eighth day the deputy chief of the prison and some warders came into the cell, got me out of bed, dressed me, and took me to the prosecutor. Two warders had to support me, for I was so weak that I could scarcely move my legs. In the warden's office I found a colonel of the gendarmes and the assistant public prosecutor of the District Court. After a long talk, the prosecutor charged me, under paragraphs 101 and 102 of Part Two of the Criminal Code, with complicity in the preparation of armed rebellion and membership in an organization that had as its aim the overthrow of the existing state system. I did not hear the end of the indictment; I had fainted from weakness. When I had regained consciousness I signed the charges, as was required. Then I was led back to my cell, where the prison doctor was waiting for me. Under the doctor's care I soon recovered completely, and I returned to my normal prison routine.

My hunger strike had been motivated by the desire to draw to the attention of the public the fact that the law continued to be violated despite the October Manifesto. My friends, who knew of my intention through my "angel" (in prison terminology angels were warders who sympathized with the political prisoners and acted as messengers for them), had not transmitted the information to the press, for fear of causing anxiety to my wife. Little did they know her. Had I been able to send news of my hunger strike directly to her, she would have had it published immediately.

My interview with the colonel and the assistant public prosecutor threw no light on the enigma of the young girl. Much later I discovered that my arrest was prompted by "reliable information" that a certain Serafima K. had visited our flat frequently in the winter of 1905. For participation in a terrorist socialist revolutionary organization she had been deported to Archangelsk in 1903 or 1904, but she had managed to escape in the fall of 1905. Since then she had been living illegally in St. Petersburg, and the police had been trying in vain to locate her. The leaflets discovered in my apartment had only been a ridiculous pretext for my arrest.

Looking back on it, I have always been grateful for the absurd chance that resulted in my imprisonment. Just as the long months of enforced idleness during my early illness had decisively influenced my inner development in childhood, so this four months' seclusion at government expense broadened my views and contributed to my understanding of what was going on in the country. Now entirely free of my youthful romanticism, I knew that Russia would never achieve genuine democracy unless her people consciously strove for unity in pursuit of the common goal. I made up my mind that once I was free again, I would devote all my efforts to the cause of unifying all democratic parties in Russia. I did not have to wait long for my freedom.

The political preparations for the elections to the first Duma had begun in the early spring of 1906. Count Witte was instrumental in preventing the administration from interfering with the electoral campaign or tampering with the votes. While the rightist organizations and the reactionary circles of officialdom were fighting the Duma in impotent rage, both the Social Democratic and Socialist Revolutionary parties were advocating a boycott of the Duma and attacking Witte and the liberals, thus playing into the hands of the court clique. My friends and I considered this policy of the left-wing parties to be nonsensical and even criminal. Fortunately, the people as a whole were unflinching in their determination to participate in the elections. The peasantry in particular were unshakable in their conviction that this would enable them to bring their grievances directly to the Tsar. They were equally certain that he would help them.

We political prisoners in the Kresty Prison participated in the electoral campaign in spirit, and we kept abreast of all developments. In the middle of April the results of the elections were made public. Not a single extreme or even moderate rightist had been elected. The conservative Constitutionalists [4] (led by A. I. Guchkov, who was not elected) won 12 seats. The moderate liberals (Union of Democratic Reforms), won 75. Eighteen Social Democrats were elected. The Constitutional Democratic Party ("Cadets") dominated the assembly with 179 members. Of the 200 peasants elected, over 100 organized a Toiler Group with a simplified Narodnik (Socialist Revolutionary) program. The national groups, comprising 35 Poles and 25 representatives of other minorities, merged into the Union of Federalists.

These freely elected deputies represented a new Russia born from the struggle for a constitution. In prison we were delighted, and many of us again indulged in futile dreams that now, at last, the sovereign would make his peace with the people, particularly as there were no "wild men" of either Left or Right among the people's elect. For Witte, who, despite certain mistakes during the brief months of his rule, had become one of the greatest statesmen in Russian history, these free elections were a swan song. Just before the opening of the Duma he was thrown out of the government, the reforms he was planning were scrapped, and he was replaced by that classic example of St. Petersburg bureaucracy, I. L. Goremykin. The latter, backed by the monarch, had no intention of cooperating with this kind of Duma. As though to ridicule it, he introduced a bill on "The Modernization of the Greenhouse at Derpt University." But nobody paid any attention to this calculated affront. Everyone was waiting for the first encounter between the Tsar and the elected representatives of his people.

On April 27, 1906, the new legislature was inaugurated with an imperial reception in the Winter Palace for the members of the Duma and Council of State. In a setting of the greatest splendor, surrounded by courtiers and grand dukes, the Tsar read his address from the throne. The whole of St. Petersburg and the country at large expected

[4] "Octobrists."

him to end his address by proclaiming an amnesty. But their expectations were not fulfilled.

The windows of the prison wing that housed my cell gave on to the Neva, and the Duma members would have to walk along the embankment on the other side to get from the Tauride Palace to the reception at the Winter Palace. We knew this, and, violating the prison regulations, we jumped on our tables and craned our necks to catch sight of the procession through our tiny windows. As hundreds of deputies passed by in the direction of the Winter Palace, we waved whatever came to hand—handkerchiefs, towels, or pillow cases—and yelled "Long live the amnesty, amnesty!" It is unlikely that the deputies actually heard us, but they did see us, and some of them waved and shouted back.

I shall not dwell on the history of the first Duma, which became known as the "Duma of Popular Wrath." Enough has been written about it already. I saw it from my prison window and learned about its short-lived activities only from the press.

The first Duma was dissolved by imperial decree. A bill on the partial expropriation of estates introduced by the Constitutional Democratic Party and the Toiler Group proved "totally unacceptable" to Nicholas II. In fact, the bill provided for the completion of the agrarian reform of Alexander II. If the bill had been passed, the peasants would have had the opportunity of obtaining from the landowners any land which the latter had not themselves farmed for a certain number of years. Under the old system the land was leased to the peasants at inflated prices. Under the provisions of the bill, landowners would receive compensation from the Treasury.

The "Bloody Sunday" of January 9, 1905, had destroyed the bonds between the workers and the Crown. On July 8, 1906, a fatal blow was dealt to the Russian peasantry's faith in the Tsar as a just and impartial defender of the people's interests.

The Duma was dissolved on July 8, 1906. On July 24, a well-known statesman and philosopher, Prince Yevgeny Trubetskoy, sent a prophetic letter to the Tsar. The following excerpt needs no comment:

It is with a feeling of profound alarm that I observe the deep changes which occur daily and hourly in the attitude and the moods of the people. Feelings were quite different even at the time of the elections to the Duma;

the people sent their deputies to tell the Tsar of their grievances and wishes. Then, the slogan was "Unity of the Crown with the People"; and that contrary to the propaganda calling for a boycott of the Duma. What propaganda failed to accomplish has been done now by the worst enemies of Your Majesty—by your advisers . . . When you refused to receive the Duma delegation, the ministers, by their actions, implanted the idea among the people at large that the Emperor is unwilling to see their deputies. In taking your place, Sir, the ministers made use of a language which is the prerogative of the supreme power. Usurping your power they rejected the amnesty bill and vetoed the agrarian program. They compromised the Crown . . . whenever they spoke in its name. They linked all that is abominable to the people with the Crown: the refusal to grant additional land by means of expropriation and the failure to proclaim an amnesty for political prisoners . . . The dissolution of the Duma has driven me to despair. A terrible blow has been dealt to the monarchist idea. The Duma enjoys vast sympathy among the population. All hopes were pinned on it . . . Your Majesty, believe me that the hunger of the peasantry for land is an irrepressible force. Anyone who opposes compulsory expropriation will be wiped off the face of the earth. Now the peasantry is convinced that the dissolution of the Duma was caused by the refusal to give them land. Your advisers shifted all responsibility to the Crown . . . I see the situation deteriorating by the joint efforts of your cabinet. The Crown is being isolated and you are deprived of support. The vacuum that is gradually forming around you and the abyss before you are a terrifying sight. The government may succeed in suppressing the revolutionary movement by reprisals, but it will merely go underground. However, such temporary achievements should not blind you, Sir. The more terrible the final explosion which will eliminate the present order and level Russian culture to the ground . . . Sire, that bureaucratic system which you have condemned is in any event doomed. But if you are slow in abolishing it, if you do not make haste to remove the advisers, trained in its traditions, you yourself will be buried under its ruins. And together with you will perish also our better future, our hope for the peaceful regeneration of our Fatherland.[5]

Even though the Tsar and the people had not come to terms during the first Duma, the political climate had eased somewhat while it lasted. Although an amnesty was not proclaimed, many political prisoners who had been arrested by mistake or who were not considered dangerous were quietly released. Among them were Sergey Vasilyev and his friends, and myself. Sergey was allowed to stay in the capital, but I was

[5] *Red Archives.*

banned for some years—I've forgotten the number—from St. Petersburg, Moscow, and several other large towns. Evidently the mysterious motives behind my arrest were responsible for this decision too. All the other members of the Organization of Armed Rebellion returned to a normal existence and to political work, but I, who had done nothing but store some of their pamphlets in my apartment, was to have my whole life distorted.

I spoke to Madame Troynitskaya, an old friend of my parents. Her family belonged to "middle-upper society"—an expression coined by Leo Tolstoy for that part of the aristocracy which did not belong to the intimate court circles. She was greatly upset at my predicament and immediately telephoned Senator Zvolyansky, the director of the Police Department, whose daughters I had met at her house. He agreed to see me in his office. During our conversation he tried to console me, explaining that it was a minor matter. He urged me in a fatherly way to be patient just for a little while until the excitement had died down. But with the recklessness of despair I said that I could not submit to an arbitrary police decision and that, if it could not be annulled, I would demand to be arrested, returned to prison, and given a new charge. Eventually we arrived at a compromise. The order would be withdrawn, but I would have to leave for a "vacation" with my father in Tashkent and stay away from St. Petersburg until the fall. A few days after this conversation I took the train to far-off Turkestan in the company of my wife and infant son.

Political Work

AFTER my exile in Tashkent I returned to St. Petersburg. My return coincided with the attempt to assassinate Stolypin on August 12, 1906. The Maximalists [1] blew up his summer residence on Aprekarsky Island, and the explosion killed 32 persons, including the perpetrators of the crime, and wounded 22 others, among them Stolypin's son and daughter. Stolypin himself escaped unhurt.

By this time I had given up all hope of a rapprochement between the Tsar and the people, although it had seemed so close after the October Manifesto.

After the dissolution of the first Duma and the "Vyborg appeal" of the former Duma members urging the population to offer "passive resistance" by refusing to pay taxes or comply with army drafts, there was a new wave of revolutionary unrest in rural and urban areas and in the army. Peasant disorders flared up in Russia and were ruthlessly suppressed. In the non-Russian areas, particularly in Finland, the Baltic provinces, and Poland, anti-Russian feeling had become very strong. Punitive expeditions were sent out all over the country. There were clashes with soldiers and strikes in the cities. Anti-Semitic pogroms, perpetrated by the notorious Union of the Russian People, broke out with unprecedented violence. In a word, Russia seemed to have regressed to the darkest period before the 1905 Manifesto.

For my part, I was tired of sitting and waiting for the day when I could get down to work as a defense lawyer in political cases. I wanted the opportunity this would give me to travel through Russia and study the mood of the population at first hand. In view of political developments, this task was becoming increasingly urgent. And it was no

[1] A newly formed extreme Socialist Revolutionary group.

longer just a matter of gaining insight into the minds of the people; they needed active help. But my prospects seemed cheerless. I was refusing all criminal and civil cases, waiting for a political case to turn up. My spirits were low. How could someone as anxious as I was to help people be denied the opportunity of doing so?

My gloom was dispelled quite suddenly. About the end of October, N. D. Sokolov, an eminent attorney, rang me on the telephone: "Your chance to take a brief in a political trial has come." I was delighted. "When, where?" was all I asked. Sokolov replied: "Our group of lawyers has to leave for a major trial in Kronstadt in connection with the mutiny on board the cruiser *Pamyat Azova* (*The Memory of Azov*). Fundaminsky-Bunakov, a socialist revolutionary leader, is involved, and we are going to defend him and the sailors. Unfortunately, another trial opens on the same day, October 30th, in Reval— some peasants who sacked a baronial estate. You must go to Reval and handle this trial for us."

"But surely that is impossible! I have never handled a political case," I objected. "Well, that's up to you. This is your big chance. Take it or leave it."

I barely hesitated. "All right, I'll go." That same night I took the midnight train to Reval.

All that night and the following day, drinking black coffee so as not to fall asleep, I studied the case page by page. Before me, I felt, was a genuine piece of history. The file was heavy with the depositions of witnesses, official and medical reports, statements of the accused. The two days before the trial were spent in a thorough study of the case and its social and political implications. The position of the Baltic peasants was particularly difficult. Liberated by Alexander II, they had not been given land, but had become the tenants of the local landowners, mostly German barons, who retained some feudal rights over them. In the current wave of punitive expeditions, some of the landowners in the areas of unrest had been appointed honorary "deputy district chiefs" and had been vested with police power, which they ruthlessly applied against their own peasants.

In this case an estate and a castle had been looted, and much had been destroyed. But the crimes of the peasants paled before the criminal methods of reprisal. Instead of being arrested and held for trial in the normal way, the defendants had been flogged and many had even been shot on the spot. Several scapegoats had then been selected at random, flogged, and dragged before the judges' bench. The court then announced that the main culprits were not available for trial as they had either escaped or been killed.

On the opening day of the trial I went to the local district court where the hearings were to take place. The local defense attorneys, headed by I. I. Poska, the future president of the Estonian Republic, were clearly embarrassed. Instead of an experienced St. Petersburg lawyer, they were confronted by an unknown young man. (I have always looked younger than my years, and I was only 25 at that time.) Nevertheless, they were all very friendly. I asked Poska to take over the lead since the only cases I had ever handled had been a few criminal ones for my bar examination. Poska amiably declined the offer, and I was on my own. Despite my inexperience, it all went very well. I not only defended the peasants but also pointed an accusing finger at those who had inspired or participated in the punitive expeditions. We won the case, and most of the accused peasants were acquitted. After I had finished my speech there was a moment of silence and then a storm of applause. The presiding judge, Muromtsev, who displayed great impartiality, called the public to order and threatened to clear the court unless the clamor stopped. After the verdict was read, the lawyers and the relatives of the accused crowded round me to congratulate me warmly and shake my hand. I was becoming rather embarrassed. Poska said to me: "Why did you tell us that you have never handled a case before? Why haven't you been here before?" They couldn't believe it was my first case.

Two days later, when I returned to St. Petersburg and went to the Lawyers' Division in the Court Establishment (a kind of lawyers' club) my colleagues greeted me with the words: "Remarkable, indeed," and "Congratulations."

I asked, "What is so remarkable?"

"Don't pretend you don't know. The telephone calls that we have been getting and the reports in the local press about your speech in Reval!"

This was my debut as a lawyer and a political speaker. Without false modesty I can say that my effectiveness as a public speaker was generally recognized. I may add that I never wrote my speeches down or rehearsed them.

After the Reval trial the cases started pouring in. Until my election to the Duma in the fall of 1912 I spent little time in St. Petersburg. My work took me to the provinces, and I got to know the whole country, from Irkutsk to Riga, from St. Petersburg to Margelan in Turkestan, as well as the Caucasus, the Volga, and Siberia.

Not all political cases were handled by attorneys belonging to organized groups of political lawyers, for sometimes the accused could afford to choose their own defense. Some of the most brilliant criminal lawyers of the day, including Andriyevsky, Karabchevsky, and Gruzenberg from St. Petersburg, and Maklakov, Muravyev, Lednitsky, and Teslenko from Moscow, accepted political cases. But there were special groups of political lawyers like the one I belonged to in all major Russian cities, and they gave legal aid in cases involving peasants, factory workers, etc., who could not afford to pay legal expenses. We had no rules or membership list. According to an informal agreement, our fees were limited to the cost of a second-class round trip ticket and a daily allowance of 10 rubles. The older, well-established lawyers among us did not take on these charity cases as often as the younger ones. The work called for a profound sympathy with the accused and a keen awareness of the political significance of these trials. It was exactly the type of work I had been longing to do.

Reprisals in the aftermath of the 1905 Revolution went on from late 1906 to the early part of 1909. After peasant and other uprisings had been crushed by punitive expeditions, it was a question of hunting out the remnants of revolutionary organizations—gangs, as they were called. The victims were handed over to military tribunals. It was a campaign of systematic judicial terror. Not only was this morally wrong, but it was also unnecessary, since the revolutionary tide had receded and people were returning to their normal everyday life. The trouble was that the authorities could not forget what had happened in 1905–1906 and were unwilling to let the public forget it either.

Judicial guarantees of the rights of the defendants were not provided by the specially constituted military courts introduced by Stolypin on August 19, 1906. [2] Their institution set off such a storm of indignation in the country that Stolypin did not even present it to the Duma, as he was supposed to by law, within the prescribed two months after its convocation.

[2] See Chapter 6.

Many political cases were judged by district military tribunals. General Pavlov, the chief military prosecutor at that time, was a merciless man who expected the judges to fulfill their "duty" without paying any attention to the arguments of the defense. Pavlov did not last long. Expecting attempts on his life, he took every precaution. He never left the Main Military Court building, where he had an apartment with a garden surrounded by a tall fence. He was assassinated by political terrorists in that very garden.

One of the special military judges in the Baltic provinces was a certain General Koshelev whose brutality and abnormality were quite notorious. He was a sadist, and he had a habit of studying pornographic photographs in court during the hearing of cases in which the accused could be sentenced to death. At the end of 1906 and the beginning of 1907 he presided at the so-called "Tukum Republic" trial in Riga, for which I was one of the defense counsels. Fifteen dragoons had been killed during an uprising in Tukum in 1905. At the trial it soon became obvious that Koshelev was not interested in trying to establish the truth, but only in selecting fifteen of the defendants to be hanged as a retaliation for the dead dragoons. The fifteen were hanged.

According to the rules, the judge in a military court was always assisted by four colonels with whom he consulted. The colonels were supposed to be independent jurors chosen by rota from a local military unit. In the Baltic provinces the military authorities had violated the spirit and the letter of this rule by selecting two very compliant colonels to be permanently attached to the presiding judge and accompany him to every trial he conducted in the Baltic area.

Of course, not all the military judges were like Koshelev. In the Baltic provinces there were two other judges, Arbuzov and Nikiforov, and Nikiforov was the antithesis of Koshelev. A very devout man, he used to go to church before pronouncing a death sentence. In the fall of 1908 he heard the case of the so-called "Northern Fighting Unit" of the Social Revolutionists, an autonomous terrorist unit. The group was led by the Estonian Trauberg, who suspected that there was a high-level *agent provocateur* in the leadership of the Socialist Revolutionary Party. Trauberg's dignified behavior at the trial impressed everyone, and it was obvious that he was telling the truth. At one point, when the assistant prosecutor, Ilyin, a highly ambitious man, tried to browbeat the defendant, he was sharply reprimanded by Nikiforov with the words: "If Trauberg says this, we take his word for it."

There were other decent judges, such as General Kirilin of the St. Petersburg Military District, whose conduct of trials, despite all pressure from above, was impeccable.

I preferred to work in provincial military courts, where the judges did not have to yield so much to such pressure from above. I remember the case of the expropriation of the Miass Treasury in the Southern Urals. The case was tried before a military court in Zlatoust. As usual, the presiding judge was a general with a law degree from the Judicial Military Academy, assisted by four colonels—but in this case there was no outside pressure on them. The accused were all very young men, members of a group of Social Democrat Bolsheviks led by Alekseyev, the son of a wealthy merchant family in Ufa. We succeeded in proving false evidence and the judge acquitted some of the defendants.

Afterwards Alekseyev told me about the expropriations carried out by his group. Officially, Lenin and the Bolshevik press condemned the expropriations as *"petit-bourgeois* practice" on the part of the leftist Socialist Revolutionaries and the Maximalists. "How is it," I asked Alekseyev, "that you carry out these expropriations despite the views of your Party?"

"It's quite simple," he replied. "We have a special arrangement about them in the Party. Before an expropriation is carried out—about two weeks beforehand—we resign from the Party saying that we disagree with its policy. Then we are free to go ahead with an expropriation. The money is channeled to Maxim Gorky in Capri, who finances his school with it.[3] Two weeks later we apply for readmission to the Party ranks, 'deploring' our errors, and we are immediately readmitted."

In the special division for political cases at the civil Courts of Appeal, the sentences were passed by majority vote of the judges appointed on the recommendation of I. G. Shcheglovitov, minister of justice. The attitude of these judges was eloquently described by the president of the St. Petersburg Court of Appeal, N. S. Krasheninnikov, in a private conversation with me. "I hope you realize that these political trials do not even claim to administer justice. This is a fierce political struggle. What your clients consider just is a criminal offense to me." Prior to the Revolution of 1905, Krasheninnikov had been one

[3] The school trained and indoctrinated future rebel leaders.

of the most impartial judges, but the excesses of the revolution had embittered him and driven him to the Right.

My experiences in Russia and my later observations during my exile abroad have confirmed my belief that impartiality is impossible when politics is involved. No judge could humanly remain indifferent while a bitter political struggle is being waged.

Shcheglovitov was encouraged in his attitude by the Tsar, who was irreconcilable in political matters. His policy in the pogrom trials involving members of the Union of the Russian People was revealing. Among the documents of the Extraordinary Commission of Inquiry into the Activities of Former Ministers and Dignitaries set up by the Provisional Government is a statement made by Lyadov, department head at the Ministry of Justice. Lyadov asserted that among the appeals for pardon that were considered in his department, the Tsar invariably approved those submitted by members of the Union of the Russian People and rejected those submitted by revolutionaries.

In the early years of my career I handled the case of the Teachers' Union in the Province of St. Petersburg. The case came before the Court of Appeals in November, 1907. The defendants were charged with antigovernment statements made in petitions to the Senate. But originally these petitions had been solicited under the provisions of the imperial edict of February 28, 1905.[4] The edict had urged all groups, organizations, and private individuals to propose reforms and point out any inadequacies of the government. Now, years later, these petitions were being carefully studied and used against the petitioners. Many rural teachers were involved in the case. During the period of relaxation, when people had dared to voice their opinions freely, schoolteachers had often been delegated to speak up for the peasants at meetings and discussions. Local officials, such as the superintendents of elementary schools, testified on behalf of the defense to the good faith of the teachers and praised their useful activities at village commune meetings or at meetings of cooperatives, pointing out that teachers often managed to curb violent passions. The verdict was lenient and many teachers were acquitted, but none were reinstated in their jobs. The result of this trial was a terrible blow to the educated rural class in the Province of St. Petersburg. The edict on petitions, it now appeared, had been nothing but a trap for those who had taken

[4] See pp. 50–52.

the word of the Tsar at its face value. There were many other such cases. In 1908 or 1909, for example, several postal and telegraph office clerks in Vilna were accused of instigating a general strike in 1905 prior to the October 17 Manifesto—long after many of the accused themselves had forgotten all about it.

Once I defended a Peasants' Brotherhood group in the province of Tver. The leader, a young peasant, was about 25 or 30 years old. I had an interesting and highly instructive conversation with him. He had a keen mind and analyzed the situation from the viewpoint of his village and the peasantry in general. He talked at length about the brotherhood and its significance. Although persecuted, the brotherhood groups took a definite stand on the agrarian issue and promoted the development of the peasantry. The members were aware of the value of education, read books and the local newspapers, and participated in the organization of cooperatives and in many other useful endeavors. Russia had indeed grown politically since 1905.

In military trials soldiers cooperated willingly with the defense lawyers and spoke frankly of the reasons for their actions. At the trial of military clerks of the First Guards Artillery Brigade in St. Petersburg, for example, the authorities claimed that the agitators incited hatred of the officers among the soldiers, although, the charge read, they did not, in fact, know what they were talking about. On the contrary, the accused were intelligent and knew very well what they were doing. They did not object to discipline as long as they were treated fairly by the officers.

One of my major trials was that of the Armenian Dashnaktsutyun Party in 1912. The case was an epilogue to the deplorable activity of Prince Golitsyn [5] at the beginning of the century, which had turned even such faithful friends of Russia as the Armenians into a revolutionary force. The entire Armenian intelligentsia, including writers, physicians, lawyers, bankers, and even merchants (the latter for allegedly giving funds to the revolutionaries) stood trial. The inquiry lasted for several years. Throughout Russia people were arrested, and finally a special Senate Court was instituted in St. Petersburg. Some of the accused were held in prison for up to four years before the case came to trial. The hearings opened in January, 1912, and lasted until the latter part of March. Six hundred witnesses were summoned. The

[5] Chief administrator of the Caucasus from 1898 to 1900.

government expected disturbances, and special precautionary measures were taken by the police. The case was heard behind closed doors, and even relatives of the accused were barred from the hearings. The atmosphere was forbidding. At the beginning of the trial one of the accused pleaded not guilty. The presiding judge, Senator Krivtsov, ruled that a totally incriminating pretrial deposition be read. I intervened and requested the judge to appoint an expert to examine the testimony, which I knew to contain perjury.

Krivtsov was taken aback by my request and asked: "Do you know what you are implying? And what will happen to you if you are mistaken?"

I did not hesitate. "Yes, I do."

An expert examination was ordered and much of the evidence proved false. The defense also succeeded in proving false evidence in other depositions. Finally, whenever I rose to object, the judge would wave his hand and mutter: "Request granted, Counsellor." Of the 146 defendants, 95 were acquitted, 47 sentenced to prison or exile in Siberia, and only 3 to hard labor. The outcome of the trial raised Russia's prestige abroad, particularly among the Armenians in Turkey. The examining magistrate Lyzhin was accused of perjury, but the case against him was eventually dismissed when a panel of psychiatrists pronounced him insane.

The Lena Massacre

The trial of the Armenians ended in the middle of March. I did not have much time to rest on my laurels. On April 4, 1912, the Lena Massacre occurred. The event was a landmark in the history of the struggle against the reactionary forces in Russia, and I shall, therefore, describe it briefly.

The powerful Anglo-Russian Lena Gold Mining Company had mines in the northeastern part of the Province of Irkutsk in the Bodaybo River area. Irkutsk, the nearest railroad station, was about 1,400 miles away. The goldfields covered a desolate mountain plateau crossed by barren valleys and turbulent streams. The mountains were capped by snow until the end of June, and winter set in at the end of September. The miners lived and worked in this desolate area in unspeakable poverty. They were virtually imprisoned by the lack of transportation, which put them completely at the mercy of the company—it owned the only railway line and controlled all river traffic. In 1911 the governor of Irkutsk, Colonel Bantysh, visited the Lena gold-fields, and, appalled by the working and living conditions of the miners, he urged the administration to take drastic measures lest the workers force the issue. His warning went unheeded.

The pretext of the strike was trivial—the workmen refused to work because of bad meat in their rations—but it was the straw that broke the camel's back. The workers were quite peaceful, but they had decided to see it through to the bitter end. The company management adamantly refused to negotiate with the miners. Fearing serious disturbances and determined not to give in to the legitimate requests of the workers, the management asked for help from the capital. Captain Treshchenkov of the Gendarmerie was promptly sent by the Department of Police in St. Petersburg to establish order in the troubled area. But his methods of intimidation only strengthened the will of the workers to fight for their rights. On April 4, the workers, accompanied by their wives, were walking toward the company's head office to demand better conditions. They were met by a barrage of fire, killing about 200 persons and wounding many more. A priest who was hastily summoned to attend to the dying men has left us a description of the scene, preserved in the records of the local church:

In the first ward I saw wounded workers carelessly dumped on the floor and on the bunks . . . The air was filled with the moaning of the victims. I had to kneel down among huge pools of blood to administer the last rites, and I hardly had time to finish with one man before I was summoned to the next. All the dying men swore that their intentions had been peaceful and that they had simply wanted to submit a petition. I believed them. A dying man does not lie.

The Lena Massacre of April 4, 1912 was the signal for a new burst of public activity and revolutionary agitation. There were protests everywhere, in the factories, in the press, at party meetings, in the universities, and in the Duma. The government had to appoint a commission with full powers to investigate the circumstances of the massacre on the spot. The commission was headed by the former minister of justice in Witte's cabinet, S. S. Manukhin, a man universally respected, and he went to the goldfields in person. Nevertheless, public opinion was not satisfied; the Duma opposition (liberals, Social

Democrats, and Trudoviks) decided to send its own commission of inquiry to the Lena. I was appointed to head the commission, and I invited the participation of two Moscow lawyers, S. A. Kobyakov and A. M. Nikitin. The journey was exceptionally interesting. We traveled by train, by troika, by steamboat, and, on the last leg of the journey, by *shitik*.[6] The beauty that surrounded us on the Lena defies description. We saw houses on one bank and virgin woods on the other. At sunrise whole families of bears would come down to the river to drink.

All the way down the Lena we kept meeting political exiles, and I spent memorable hours with the famous "Grandmother of the Russian Revolution," Catherine Breshkovska, whom I met there for the first time.

At the goldfields the situation was rather awkward. The government commission under Senator Manukhin sat in one house, and our headquarters were in another house across the street. Both commissions were summoning and crossexamining witnesses. Both were recording the testimony of the employees and preparing reports. Senator Manukhin was sending his reports in code to the ministry and to the Tsar, and we were dispatching wires to the Duma and to the press. Needless to say, the goldfield administration greatly resented our intrusion, but neither the senator nor the local officials interfered with our work. On the contrary, the governor general of East Siberia, Knyazev, sympathized with our cause, and the Irkutsk governor, Bantysh, and his special assistant, A. Maysh, proved of great help. As a result of the public inquiry the monopoly of the company was abolished and its administration completely reorganized. The slums in which the workers and their families had lived were torn down and replaced by new buildings. Wages were increased and working conditions greatly improved. We had every reason to be pleased with the outcome of our joint endeavor.

Election to the State Duma

I had never given much thought to the future, and I had had no political plans. My only desire, since the beginning of my political life, had been to serve my country. As a result, I had been taken unawares when, during a trial in St. Petersburg in the fall of 1910, I was approached by L. M. Bramson, Duma leader of the Trudoviks (labor

[6] Similar to a Venetian gondola.

group) in the first Duma, and S. Znamensky, a member of the Central Committee, who asked me to consent to stand for election to the fourth Duma as a Trudovik candidate.The possibility of entering the Duma had never occurred to me, and the request came as a complete surprise. I learned that the Trudovik faction in the Duma was to be expanded by the inclusion of other Populist groups. I was also told that property ownership was a requirement, and they urged me, therefore, to buy property. I had always sympathized with the Populist movement, so I accepted the offer without hesitation.

Since I had no party connections I was given the most difficult campaigning area—the Province of Saratov, where the gentry was steadily gaining ground as a result of Stolypin's electoral law. Other candidates were assigned to "democratic" provinces such as Vyatka and Perm. As it turned out, however, all the other candidates were disqualified, and in the fall of 1912 I was the only one left of the 15 new candidates of the labor group.

Upon my return from the Lena goldfields I left for Volsk, the district capital in the Province of Saratov, where I was to start my campaign. I had visited the town only once before, when I had signed the title to a property which qualified me as a candidate for the elections. Volsk on the Volga was a colorful old Russian town. The freedom-loving tradition and the fierce spirit of independence of the townspeople could be traced back to the time of Pugachev's peasant revolts in the latter part of the eighteenth century.

In Volsk I made immediate contact with a fine group of professional people, including judges, physicians, and officials. At preelectoral meetings I was able to speak freely, for here my ideas were understood, and there was no need to resort to revolutionary clichés.

The new electoral law was complex, and it violated every canon of democratic procedure. Deputies were elected by provincial colleges consisting of delegates chosen separately by four groups (curias): landowners, the urban population, peasants, and, in a few districts, factory workers. One mandatory delegate to the Duma was elected by each curia, and the rest of the deputies were elected by the provincial college as a whole. At an electoral meeting of the urban group, I was nominated as the mandatory candidate. No one ran against me. In the peasant group no such unanimity would have been possible, because there was always some wealthy peasant or village elder who agreed to accept the nomination. That is how I became a member of the fourth Duma.

The Mendel Beylis Affair

In the years 1912–1913 the international situation in Europe had become critical, and it was in the vital interests of the Russian Empire to follow a benevolent and cautious policy toward the non-Russian nationalities living in the border areas.

At a time when relations with Germany, Austria-Hungary, and Turkey were rapidly deteriorating, the illegal abolition of the constitutional regime in Finland turned this hitherto loyal country into a future base for German defeatist propaganda in Russia. Shcheglovitov's attempt to take advantage of the Dashnaktsutyun trial to unleash a wave of animosity against the Armenians living on the Turkish border had failed. But these attempts to stir up trouble were not enough for the reactionaries, who were quite oblivious of their responsibilities as the leaders of an immense empire, inhabited by many different peoples, on the eve of a general European crisis. The Balkan Wars of 1912–1913 were a prelude to World War I. The saber-rattling of both coalitions of the Great Powers was beginning to acquire an ominous ring.

It was at about that time that the Mendel Beylis trial opened in Kiev. This simple and innocent man was accused of having committed the ritual murder of a little Christian boy, Andrey Yuschinsky. I would be doing Russia and her people a great injustice, were I to fail to impress upon my readers that a tremendous wave of indignation swept the country. Not only did free public opinion voice its protest in no uncertain terms, but the entire body of public servants, including the officials of the Ministry of Justice, considered the trial a personal disgrace. The top hierarchy of the Russian Church categorically refused to make a pronouncement that the ritual murder of Christian boys by Jews was part of the Jewish faith.

The legal profession is a constituent part of the judicial system of a country and its primary function is the defense of truth, justice, and civil liberties. We, the members of the bar, were an autonomous body. It was our duty to present the truth openly to Shcheglovitov and to all other corruptors of the Russian judicial system. The barristers of St. Petersburg had to take a firm stand. On October 23, 1913, five days before the jury pronounced Mendel Beylis innocent of the crime, a plenary meeting of members of the bar of St. Petersburg unanimously adopted the following resolution:

The plenary meeting of members of the bar of the District of St. Petersburg considers it a professional and civic duty to raise its voice in protest against the distortion of the very fundamentals of justice reflected in the instigation of the Beylis trial, against the slanderous attack on the Jewish people launched within the framework of judicial order and condemned by all civilized society, and against the imposition upon the court of a task that is alien to it, namely the propagation of racial hatred and national hostility.

This outrage against the fundamentals of the community of man humiliates and disgraces Russia before the world, and we raise our voices in defense of the honor and dignity of Russia.

The resolution had a tremendous impact in Russia and, what was even more important at the time, made a profound impression abroad. In Europe and the United States, the Beylis trial greatly intensified anti-Russian feeling and vividly illustrated the antipatriotic activities in top government circles on the eve of World War I. President Woodrow Wilson had no understanding of or sympathy for Russia and her problems. The Beylis Affair was the last straw. When the war broke out the policy of the U.S. government was hostile toward Russia, and it was decided not to give Russia any assistance, financial or otherwise.

The instigators of the trial were infuriated by the reaction of the people at large, and 25 eminent lawyers who had sponsored the resolution were brought to trial. I was one of those lawyers. Our trial opened at the St. Petersburg District Court on June 3 and lasted until June 6, 1914, less than eight weeks before the outbreak of the war. We were wholeheartedly supported by the press and the public at large, regardless of political opinion. Somewhat earlier, V. Shulgin, a right-wing leader in the Duma, made a scathing attack on the whole affair in the conservative publication *Kievlyanin*. Politically, Shulgin was known as an anti-Semite, but in the face of the shameful Beylis trial he could not remain silent. Subsequently he, too, was sentenced to eight months of detention.

Since the new Criminal Code of 1903 contained no provisions applicable to our "crime," we were convicted under Article 279 of a law dating back to the time of Catherine II, as "slanderers" disseminating anonymous letters. Twenty-three of my colleagues were sentenced to six months' detention in the fortress. N. D. Sokolov, as the first sponsor, and I, as mover of the resolution, were sentenced to eight months' imprisonment and deprived of our right to run for elections.

The Freemasons

Tolstoy's description of the role and activities of the Freemasons in *War and Peace* is substantially correct. In the eighteenth and early nineteenth centuries, this organization played a leading part in the spiritual and political development of Russia, particularly after N. I. Novikov and many other outstanding political figures and statesmen had joined the lodges. There were believers as well as freethinkers among the members. At first, Catherine II tolerated the lodges. A Voltairian and a freethinker, the Tsarina was not burdened with "religious prejudices." The advancement of education by the Freemasons took the form of such projects as the setting up of printing houses and the promotion of liberal ideas. There is little truth in the sadly distorted picture of Freemasonry that had been generally accepted, even by an enlightened section of Russian public opinion, since the reign of Nicholas I.

Novikov was subsequently persecuted because the future Tsar, Paul I, had come under the influence of Freemasons in his immediate entourage, and Catherine II had reason to believe that the Freemasons were planning to make the Grand Duke their tool. This persecution dealt a blow to Russian Freemasonry from which it never fully recovered. After the ascension of Paul I to the throne, Novikov was recalled from exile to the imperial residence in Gatchina, where he soon realized that the policies of the martinet in Gatchina, Paul I, had nothing in common with his ideas.

The beginning of the reign of Alexander I was dominated by men who were members of Masonic lodges. The main concern of the "society" was the unification of the cultural elite of Russia for the purpose of abolishing absolutism and emancipating the serfs, an idea favored by Tsar Alexander I himself, who patronized the order. Outstanding statesmen like the liberal Speransky and the hero of the Napoleonic wars, General Kutuzov, participated in the order. Many of the Decembrists were affiliated with the lodges. After the Decembrist insurrection under the reactionary reign of Nicholas I, the lodges were outlawed, but they probably went underground. At the beginning of the twentieth century, the revived Masonic societies helped to strengthen the ties between the enlightened *zemstvo* leaders and the urban intelligentsia. In my time the Freemasons in Russia carried on their work in secret, not only because until 1905 all social and political work had to be carried on clandestinely, but also because public opinion frowned upon any association that united for a common goal members of different political parties.

Originally, I had not intended to write about Russian Freemasonry. But certain "revelations" that have appeared in the Russian and non-Russian press in recent years have attributed the fall of the monarchy and the formation of the Provisional Government to the secret activity of the lodges. I feel it to be my duty to refute this absurd interpretation of the great and tragic events that led to the greatest turning point of Russian history. For the sake of historical truth, therefore, I shall dwell briefly on the subject.[7]

Upon my departure from Russia in the summer of 1918, I was instructed to reveal the essence of our work, without mentioning any names, so that, should a distorted version ever appear in the press, the true facts might be made known. The time has now come to do so, for Y. D. Kuskova, a Freemason of long standing and a prominent political figure, mentioned my name in secret letters to two friends and told another political leader about my membership in the lodge.[8]

My participation was solicited in 1912, just after my election to the fourth Duma. After serious consideration, I came to the conclusion that my own aims coincided with those of the society, and I accepted the proposal to join. I should like to stress that our society was an irregular Masonic organization. First of all, it was unusual in that it had severed ties with all foreign societies and accepted women for membership. Furthermore, the complex ritual and the Masonic system of degrees were abolished, and only that essential inner discipline was maintained which would ensure the moral qualifications of the members and their ability to maintain secrecy. No written records or membership lists were kept, and this maintenance of secrecy is reflected in the lack of information on the aims and structure of the society.

[7] In discussing the political composition, the work, and the aims of the Masonic society of which I was a member, I should like to emphasize that I am bound by the solemn oath made by me at the time of my admission, not to reveal the names of any other members.

[8] The letters were posthumously published in Gregory Aronson, *Rossiya nakanune revolutsii* (New York 1962).

While studying the circular letters of the Department of Police at the Hoover Institute, I found no evidence of the existence of our society, even in the two circulars dealing directly with me.[9] The local lodge was the basic unit of the society. In addition to territorial lodges, the Supreme Council had the right of forming special lodges. Thus there was a lodge in the Duma, another for writers, and so on. At its inception each lodge became an autonomous unit. Other organs had no right to interfere with the work or election of members. At annual conventions the delegates of the lodges discussed their work and elected members to the Supreme Council. At the conventions, the Supreme Council submitted a progress report through the secretary general, assessed the political situation, and proposed the program for the year ahead. Sharp clashes of opinion sometimes occurred among members of the same party on such vital problems as the nationalities question, the form of government, and agrarian reform. But we never allowed these disagreements to affect our solidarity.

This nonpartisan policy produced remarkable results, notably the program of a future democracy in Russia, which was implemented on a broad base by the Provisional Government. There is a myth, which has been accepted as fact by the detractors of the Provisional Government, that a mysterious troika of Freemasons foisted its program upon the government in defiance of public opinion. In fact, the situation in Russia and the needs of our country were discussed at the conventions by people who were not vying with each other to impose their own political programs, but were guided only by their consciences in their quest for the best solution. We felt the pulse of national life, and we were always trying to embody the aspirations of the people in our work.

During the fourth Duma the idea of unification for a common goal enjoyed even greater success. Let me repeat that all our efforts were directed toward the establishment in Russia of a democracy based on broad social reforms and on a federal state order. During the last, fateful years of Rasputin's power, most members of the "society" felt that the monarchy was doomed, but this feeling did not prevent mon-

[9] Circular letter 171902 signed by Brune de St. Hyppolite, director of the Department of Police, is the only document dealing with the Masonic Rosenkreutz Society, which was known to us as the "Barbara Ovchinnikova Organization" and which led to the formation of a society under the auspices of Grand Duke Alexander Mikhailovich that included courtiers and members of the aristocracy.

archists from participating in the common endeavor, since the problem of the future form of government was subservient to more urgent tasks.

With the outbreak of World War I our program had to be revised. It was the first total war that not only involved the army but also affected the civilian population at large. If final victory was to be achieved, it was essential to effect a reconciliation between all classes of society, and between the people and the supreme power. My attempt to compel the Tsar to make a gesture toward the people [10] was, of course, naïve, but in all other respects the new wartime program was implemented. The unconditional defense of our country remained the basis for our work until the end. After the February Revolution, however, political passions flared up, and nonpartisan cooperation became quite impossible.

Police Surveillance

Secret
For circulation

M.V.D.
Police Department
Sixth division.
May 30, 1915

    To Heads of provincial, regional and urban Security Police Administrations, Internal Security Sections, and Officers of the Special Security Police Corps in charge of criminal investigation. . . .

Second section

    Reports reaching the Police Department from Heads of the Imperial criminal investigations organs, which have been keeping observation on Alexander Fedorov *KERENSKY,* Barrister and member of the Trudovik Group of the Duma, mentioned in this Department's Circular No. 165377 dated January 16, during his travels through Russia in the current year, indicate that the antigovernment activities of the said person, referred to in the above Circular,[11] have been confirmed through both completely secret and open surveillance on the spot of his activities and associations; the surveillance has revealed that during his constant trips through the country Kerensky has had repeated meetings with many party officials

---

[10] See Chapter 8.

[11] The circular referred to was an earlier version, similar in content.

and very prominent members of civic and political organizations known for their political unreliability, at the places visited and has organized conferences attended by these persons in certain towns.

Attaching major importance, in view of the foregoing, to Kerensky's travels to the provinces, the Police Department requests you, further to Circular No. 165377, to step up your investigation into the activities of the said person through normal channels, and also by insinuating the secret agents at your disposal into the confidence of Kerensky and his closest contacts, already registered by the criminal investigation organ in your charge, and also by placing him under unflagging open observation.

All information received thereby which might throw light on Kerensky's antigovernment activities, as well as all his movements, should be reported to the department.

Signed: Acting Deputy Director Vasilyev
Compiled by: Section Head Dyachenko
Checked by: Lt. Col. . . . . [illegible signature]

During my travels as a political defense attorney, I never limited myself to my professional work, but always attempted also to sound out the mood of the people and to establish contact with the local representatives of the various liberal and democratic movements.

Since my election to the Duma and my initiation as a Freemason, the broadened scope and increased importance of my work had prompted the security police to take a correspondingly increased interest in my activities.

In 1915, the police surveillance of my activities had not yet become quite as close in the provinces as in St. Petersburg, and I was hardly aware of it at all. In the capital, however, I was surrounded by both overt and covert agents, whose surveillance of me was steadily tightening.

I was not worried by the idea of being arrested, although I probably would have been arrested early in 1916 if I had not suddenly become very ill and ceased all political activities for seven months. It was not difficult to see it coming—it was, in fact, an inevitable risk in the life I was leading. But the constant presence of the policemen who dogged my footsteps day and night soon got on my nerves.

One day in the autumn of 1915, during a Budget Committee discussion of appropriations for the Ministry of Internal Affairs, I sud-

denly decided to poke a little fun at the Minister [12] by telling a story
that I knew would amuse the members of the Duma and, at the same
time, would show them the conditions under which members of the
opposition were forced to work.

When we began discussing the estimates for the Police Department
I rose and said to the Minister, "Sir, I feel that this department of yours
is wasting far too much money. I am most grateful, of course, to the
Director of the Police Department for his regard for my safety. I live
in a cul-de-sac and whenever I got out into the street, there are two—
sometimes even three—men standing there on either side. And it is
not difficult to recognize who they are, because summer and winter
alike they wear galoshes, overcoats, and carry umbrellas. Near them,
one on either side of the street, are cabs just in case I should need to
drive anywhere. But for some reason or other I don't like these cabs
and I always walk instead. I walk along slowly and behind me come
two escorts. When I walk quickly, these traveling companions begin
to pant. On occasion, having turned a corner, I stop and wait, and they
come flying round the corner and bump into me, look embarrassed,
turn quickly back, and leave me without a bodyguard. Whenever I
take a cab, having walked a little way from my apartment house, one
of those standing at the corner immediately comes trotting along behind me. In the hallway of the house there are often some charming
people talking together, also dressed in galoshes and carrying umbrellas. It seems to me, sir, that there must be from 15 to 20 men
assigned to look after my precious person, since they are often changed
in the course of the day and night. You are yourself aware that these
people are of little help to you. Why don't you tell the Director of the
Police Department to put an official chauffeur-driven car at my disposal? Then he will know everything—where, when and with whom
I go—and it will be an advantage to me as well, because I won't have
to spend so much time running around the city, and I won't get quite
so tired."

My remarks greatly amused the Budget Committee, and Khvostov
replied with a laugh, "If I give you a car, I'll have to give all your
colleagues one, too, and that will put the treasury to great expense."

Both these statements were greeted with delighted applause.

---

[12] A. N. Khvostov.

6

Russia on the Road to Democracy

THE brief period between the dissolution of the Duma in 1906 and the beginning of World War I in 1914 was one of exceptional importance for Russia and for Europe.

The Western view of this period, however, is a distorted one. When Russia, exhausted and ravished by the war, suddenly became a totalitarian dictatorship, nearly everyone in the West saw in this violent upheaval a normal return to "tsarism," except that this time it was the "red" instead of the "white" variety. In actual fact, however, during the last few decades before the outbreak of World War I, there was a tumultuous advance in the economic, cultural, and political life of our country.

During the first Duma a bitter struggle had been fought in court and government circles between two distinct currents of opinion. One group, which based its hopes on the natural aversion of the Tsar and his wife to a constitution, pressed for a return to unlimited monarchy. To bring this about, the Union of the Russian People performed the part of the "dissatisfied populace," and, operating from a number of provincial towns and cities, sent in a barrage of demands for the suppression of the Duma and the annulment of the Manifesto of October 17, 1905. The second group, which consisted of those who had not entirely lost their sense of reality, sought to show that it would be madness to go back to unlimited autocracy, and that abolition of popular representation would send even the most loyal and moderate sections of the population running to join the revolutionary camp. And anyway, they argued, Russia's international position at that time was not compatible with a swing to the extreme right.

The second group won the day. Instead of abolishing popular representation and the constitution, it was decided to amend the electoral law so as to form in the Duma a working government majority of upper-class, bourgeois, conservative, and moderately progressive elements. At the same time it was decided to put a fundamental land reform into immediate effect. The aim was to create a new "third estate" of moderately prosperous farmers to replace the waning upper class, following the example of the French and Germans. These steps were to be accompanied by strongly repressive measures against the clearly weakening revolutionary movement, which was disintegrating from within.

Just before the first Duma was due to meet, a new minister of the interior was appointed in St. Petersburg. This was the governor of Saratov, Peter A. Stolypin, who was hardly known to anyone at the time of the appointment. In less than three months, just after the dissolution of the Duma on July 8, 1906, he was appointed chairman of the Council of Ministers, with instructions to put into effect the plan I have just described.

Stolypin's magical rise to fame was in itself a sign of the times. Of provincial upper-class origin, he was not a member of the St. Petersburg court set and had never been employed in any of the higher government establishments of the capital. The whole of his career had been spent in the provinces, where he had no lack of connections among prominent public and *zemstvo* figures.

Stolypin had a thorough knowledge of the work of the *zemstva*, and he recognized their value. In Saratov, where I was later elected a deputy to the fourth Duma, he was considered a governor of liberal views. He was a very effective public speaker, and his adventurous and ambitious temperament made the idea of a high-level political career particularly attractive to him. He did not share the view of his predecessor Goremykin that the Duma was merely an idle "talking-shop." On the contrary, unlike the hidebound and soulless bureaucrat, Goremykin, he was strongly attracted by the role of a constitutional minister. The idea of making speeches in parliament, openly debating vital issues with the opposition, and governing the country on the basis of his government majority appealed to him greatly.

The fighting spirit lacked by the St. Petersburg officials was more than compensated for by Stolypin. The Tsar liked Stolypin for his youth, self-confidence, devotion to the throne, and readiness to carry out the Tsar's plan for illegal changes in the electoral law. The heads of the Council of United Gentry saw in him one of their own kind who would save the system of upper-class land proprietorship from destruction. The Octobrists and various other moderate constitutionalists, frightened by the excesses of the revolution, clutched at him as a drowning man clutches at a straw. They welcomed his program, which was intended to unify the government with the moderately liberal and conservative public, thus strengthening the constitutional monarchy and eliminating for good the revolutionary movement. They thought of him as a Russian Thiers (the man who consolidated the bourgeois Third Republic in France after the defeat of the Commune in 1871).

Thiers, however, had based his plans on a strong French peasantry well endowed with the acquisitive instinct. In Russia, a peasantry of this kind had not yet been created, and it would have taken many decades to do so.

I was always opposed to Stolypin and to those who supported him. Together with the rest of the opposition, I felt that Stolypin's basic tactical slogan, "First pacify the country, then make reforms," was not just misguided, but actually dangerous to the country's future. The Russian ambassador to London, Count Benkendorf, wrote to St. Petersburg that only timely reforms could really appease the country.

Nevertheless, whatever errors—or even crimes—the Stolypin government may have committed, the fact remains that Stolypin's intentions were neither to restore absolutism, nor to abolish popular representation, but to establish in Russia a conservative but strictly constitutional monarchy.

His dream was a powerful, centralized empire, economically sound and culturally advanced. "You want great changes," said Stolypin to the left-wing, half-socialist majority in the second Duma, "I want a great Russia."

It was this utopian dream that cast the country into a fresh sea of troubles. For Stolypin's fatal mistake was his failure to realize that in the Russia of that time the upper class had already degenerated as a political force, while the middle classes, which were only beginning to emerge as a single unit, could not possibly act as an intermediary between the ruling few and the working masses.

Admittedly, the rapid development of the towns and of industry meant that an urban "third estate" was now starting to play a part in the country's social and political life. But in the countryside there was no such stratum. The elections of the first Duma had shown that the peasants, who for the most part farmed on a subsistence rather than on a capitalist basis, could not play the role of a socially conservative class.

At the same time, private ownership of the land by the gentry was clearly on the way out. The system had become so economically inefficient that its contribution to production was less than 10 percent of the total. Whether they liked it or not, the government and the conservatives were finally being forced to accept the fact of the natural decline of the landowning gentry. Their only hope was that they could keep the system alive by gaining support for it from the new class of "peasant-farmers."

As we know, a great number of peasants in Russia proper farmed on the basis of communal land tenure. The owner of the land was not the peasant, but the commune (*mir*). This system was first championed by the Slavophiles, and later by the Narodniks, or Populists. Both of these schools of thought held that the poorly developed sense of private ownership among the peasants would enable Russia to move on to more equitable forms of national economy without having experienced the horrors of Western capitalism. In demanding the "nationalization" or "socialization" of the land, the Narodniks had been certain that the peasants would easily shift from the communal to the cooperative system of land tenure. In actual fact, however, the peasant commune of that time had very little in common with the ideal commune as imagined by the Slavophiles and Narodniks. From the administrative standpoint, the commune was very convenient for police control—as Witte put it, for keeping the peasants under surveillance like little children—and also for collecting taxes, since defaulters were paid for by the rest of the commune on a pro rata basis. The authorities turned the commune into a bulwark of economic backwardness and gradually drained it of its vitality. Furthermore, compulsory membership in the commune was always a sore point among the peasants themselves.

After the agrarian riots of 1905–1906, everyone realized that the compulsory commune had to be abolished. It was thought that free land-owning communes would then break up, some becoming private holdings and some becoming cooperative land organizations, according to what the peasants themselves decided. The first Duma's agrarian reform bill, which was intended to settle the land problem by buying up the privately owned estates and handing them over to the peasants, would have allowed the peasants to decide the fate of the communal system of ownership. This was a sensible and democratic way of dealing with Russia's oldest and most fundamental social-political problem.

If the bill had taken effect, the social stratification of the countryside would have occurred spontaneously, and there is no doubt that there would have emerged from the peasant masses a "bourgeois" minority that would have introduced a farming system along French or German lines.

After the dissolution of the first Duma, the problem of the land passed into the hands of Stolypin. On November 9, 1906, about three months before the opening of the second Duma, he took advantage of Article 87 of the Fundamental Laws (which gave the government the right, in cases of emergency, to pass laws between sessions of the Duma and State Soviet and submit them later for ratification), and announced a land reform. In proclaiming this reform law, Stolypin proved that his strong character was not equalled by political acumen.

In his hands, or to be more exact, in the hands of the Council of United Gentry which was backing him, the land reform, basically a sound idea, merely became a weapon for further class oppression. Instead of doing away with the compulsory nature of the communal system and the laws specifically restricting the civil rights of the peasants, so as to develop the free farming economy advocated by Witte, Stolypin's law forcibly broke up the commune to the advantage of the "bourgeois" minority in the peasantry.

The reform was put into effect with tremendous energy, but also with gross disregard for the most elementary tenets of law and justice. The government, which was "backing the strongest," expropriated the land belonging to the commune and gave it to those well-to-do peasants who opted to withdraw from it. They were given the best plots of land, in complete violation of the commune's right to tenure. And the new owners of this land were given loans, amounting to 90 percent of cost, with which to set up their farms.

Stolypin was very proud of his role as an agrarian reformer. He even invited foreign experts in the agrarian problem to study the work that he and his government had done in the countryside.

In the course of five years—1907 to 1911—the peasant land tenure system underwent a tremendous transformation. With what result?

Making a speech in the fourth Duma, in which I sharply criticized the political and economic aftermath of the Stolypin reform, I quoted the words of the well-known German agrarian expert, Professor Auf-hagen. After inspecting a large number of Russian villages, he had written: "By his land reform Stolypin has thrown the brand of civil war into the Russian countryside."

And as Milyukov tells us, Professor Prior, another foreign scholar and sympathizer of Stolypin's who also made a close study of the land reform, came to the conclusion that the aim of the reform had not been attained.

Indeed, in spite of all the benefits and privileges offered them, by the first day of January, 1915, only 2,719,000 peasant households could say that their holdings had become their private property (about 22 or 24 percent of the total amount of available peasant land).

For the most part the peasants took an unfavorable or even hostile view of the Stolypin land reform for two reasons. First, and most important, the peasant did not want to go against the commune, and Stolypin's idea of "backing the strongest" ran counter to the peasant's outlook on life. He had no wish to become a semilandowner at the expense of his neighbors.

Second, the freer political atmosphere created by the Manifesto of October 17 provided the peasantry with an opportunity for new economic progress which was more in keeping with the peasant mentality through the cooperative system.

In accepting power Stolypin had undertaken to suppress the revolutionary movement and pacify the country. In this respect, too, just as in his agrarian reform, he showed great character, but a lack of political acumen.

Russia was already settling down again by this time. The revolutionary movement was dying a natural death. The Manifesto of October 17 paved the way for freedom and fruitful political activity. The so-called "excesses" of the upheaval, that is to say, the bank robberies for the "needs" of the revolutionaries, the murder of petty officials as "enemies of the people," and so forth, had first caused perplexity among the public, and then resentment and strong condemnation. Instead of taking advantage of this mood of the people in order to finish what remained of the revolutionary outbreak by ending the state of tension and returning the country to normal life, Stolypin went on dealing harshly with those who had already been rendered quite harmless by the very development of events. The measures originally intended to protect the country from the brief popular storm were soon being used by the victors for purposes of personal revenge. The more peaceful the country became, the greater the number of people arrested, convicted, and exiled or executed.

Stolypin counted on winning over the majority of the population by the firmness of his "pacification" policy. He achieved the exact opposite; the more resolute and firm his policy became, the more resolute were the protests against it. The first two or three years following the dissolution of the first Duma were often called the era of "White Terror." Nowadays this definition of Stolypin's policy seems rather odd to us. After the experience of the totalitarian regimes suffered by Europe and Russia, to call Stolypin a terrorist ruler would be just as absurd as to compare the performance of an amateur singer with the consummate artistry of a Chaliapin. This is amply demonstrated by the fact that in the course of the day following the attempt on Lenin's life by Dora Kaplan in 1918, the number of innocent hostages shot in Russia greatly exceeded the number sentenced to be hanged by Stolypin's so-called "quick-firing" field courts-martial over the whole of the eight months they lasted. Furthermore, Stolypin's repressions were aimed against one relatively small section of the population which was actively resisting the government.

But even so, the whole of educated Russian society, regardless of class or creed, was outraged by the news of every fresh execution. Russian public opinion did not object so vehemently to the hangings because it sympathized with the revolutionary terror, which had by now degenerated into futile acts of violence, but because of its traditional aversion to capital punishment. It is highly significant that Russia was one of the very few countries in which capital punishment for criminal offenses had been abolished.

The Russia of that time did not wish to see the government resort to bloodshed and violence in dealing with its political opponents. That is why, after the institution of Stolypin's summary courts-martial, Tolstoy wrote his deeply touching appeal ("I cannot be silent") to the government to end the executions. That is why one of the greatest parliamentary orators of that time, the moderate liberal Rodichev, denounced Stolypin before all Russia from the speaker's stand in the Duma, referring to the hangman's noose as "Stolypin's necktie." That is why, immediately after the fall of the monarchy in 1917, the government of the democratic revolution, carrying out one of the most cherished and sacred aims of the Russian liberation movement, abolished capital punishment for all crimes without exception, to the explicit approval of all. That is why, in the spiritual atmosphere that Russia breathed just before World War I, Stolypin's "pacification" policy failed in the same miserable way as his land reform, and, what is more, brought about his own tragic end.

On September 1, 1911, during a special performance at the City Theater in Kiev, Stolypin was shot and mortally wounded by a former anarchist and police agent, only a few feet from the royal box where the Tsar was sitting with his daughters. By this time the Tsar could hardly stand the sight of his erstwhile favorite. It was established by a special investigation that while in Kiev Stolypin had not had the usual police agents guarding him. There was talk of criminal proceedings against the assistant minister of the interior, General Kurlov, who was in charge of the police. But the preliminary investigation was stopped by the personal intervention of the Tsar.

There was something very curious about the circumstances of Stolypin's death. The assassin was executed posthaste, and was kept strictly incommunicado beforehand. People who were aware of the finer points of the struggle between Stolypin and Rasputin and those around him were convinced that the secret police had connived at the crime, wishing to please Stolypin's highly influential enemies. A few months after Stolypin's death, the chief military prosecutor sent for Stolypin's son-in-law, B. L. von Bock, and told him that the main responsibility for his father-in-law's death lay with Kurlov, and that the deed had been carried out at his instigation. At the same time, the prosecutor told von Bock that the case against Kurlov had been dropped on the Tsar's instructions.[1]

[1] A V. Zenkovsky, *The Truth About Stolypin* (New York, 1956).

Stolypin himself once told Guchkov in the Duma that he felt he would be killed by a police agent.

And so it seemed that the all-powerful "pacifier" of Russia was powerless to muzzle the "dark forces" which had the support of the coterie around the young Tsarina. Stolypin had been much too upright and independent a man for the likes of Rasputin. And he had also split with the leading party in the third Duma—the Octobrists—a situation which had been set up under his own conservative electoral law of June 3, 1907.

Professor Bernard Pares, the British historian, who made many long visits to Russia during both the Duma period and the ensuing World War, aptly notes with regard to the third Duma in his book *The Fall of the Russian Monarchy* that, given the public feeling prevalent at that time, even a Duma composed of former ministers would have been in the opposition.

The electoral law of June, 1907, practically eliminated the participation of peasants and workers from the towns and villages. In the provinces the elections were virtually handed over to the moribund gentry, and in the larger towns the right of quasi-universal suffrage was also suppressed; the number of deputies was cut down, and half the seats were assigned under a curial system to an insignificant minority of the property-owning bourgeoisie. Representation of the non-Russian nationalities was reduced. Poland, for example, was allowed to send only 18 deputies to the third Duma (and the fourth), as opposed to the 53 representatives sent to the first and second Dumas, and the Muslim population of Turkestan was excluded entirely.

The people's representatives elected under Stolypin's law were rightly called Russia's "distorting mirror." The left-wing parties making up the majority in the first and second Dumas practically vanished in the third Duma of 1907–1912, which, moreover, contained only 13 members of the Labor Group (Trudoviks) and 20 Social Democrats. The Social Revolutionaries boycotted the elections. The Cadets, the party of the liberal intellectuals, had dropped from their dominant position to the role of "His Majesty's loyal opposition," with 54 seats.

Fifty seats were taken by the reactionary Union of the Russian People, which was subsidized from special funds available to the secret police and was patronized by the Tsar and Grand Duke Nicholas. These deputies, under the guidance of three very able men—Markov,

Purishkevich, and Zamyslovsky—tried to sabotage the Duma from within by incessantly causing trouble. Along with these, 89 seats were given to a completely new party called the Nationalists. They were returned by and large from the western and southwestern provinces, which had been torn by feuding between the Russian, Polish, Lithuanian, and Jewish sections of the population as far back as could be remembered. The gap between the Cadets and the right wing was filled by the 153 Octobrist deputies, of whom there had hardly been any at all in the first two Dumas. They thus comprised slightly more than a third of the total membership of the Duma.

I have given these details regarding the composition of the third Duma since the distribution of seats in the fourth Duma (1912–1917) was for all intents and purposes the same, and the latter played a role of tremendous significance in the conflict between the monarch and the people in the last few years before the revolution. But even the third Duma, despite its conservative makeup—socially speaking—and despite the presence of the right wing, with all its influence in government circles, proved from the very first day of its existence to be just as much the defender of the constitutional system and of the political rights of the people as the first Duma. The only difference was in methods and mood.

The first Duma expressed the heart and soul of Russia. Its aim was the merciless exposure of the seamy sides of the old regime. It was relentless; it would stand for no compromise. It demanded unconditional surrender from the supreme ruler—the handing over of complete power to the representatives of the people. Its principal demand was well expressed by V. Nabokov, the eloquent son of the minister of justice under Alexander III, who said, "Let the executive power be subordinate to the legislative power." But the first Duma had no time to make any laws for the country, since it was dissolved before regular work could be begun.

The third Duma started out without any glamor. It made no demands for capitulation on the part of the rulers. Its slogan was compromise, loyal collaboration with the authorities on the basis of the Tsar's October Manifesto. This manifesto, which was the banner of the predominant party in the Duma, the Octobrists, invested the people's representatives with legislative power, budget rights, and the right to debate all issues openly. In amending the electoral law illegally, the government had solemnly reaffirmed the inviolability of the rights of the Duma. The Octobrist leaders were determined to make use of these rights to consolidate popular representation so as to make the Duma the real deciding force in the Russian state system.

Neither the Tsar and his courtiers, nor the democratic and left-wing sectors of public opinion could understand the point of this compromise. After the *Sturm und Drang* of the first two Dumas, the Tsar was at first quite happy with the third Duma. He imagined that the Tauride Palace was now full of people from all parts of the country, well versed in local affairs and needs, who would advise his ministers in the drafting of suitable laws without encroaching in any way upon the royal prerogative. That was also how most of the public understood the third Duma's loyalist stand, and that is why public opinion was so violently opposed to this "reactionary parliament" and called its leaders "lackeys of reaction."

These leaders, however, were far from reactionary. Socially, the Octobrists represented the middle and upper classes of Russian society. They included members of the gentry, the local administration, and the liberal professions, as well as artisans and petty officials at both metropolitan and provincial levels. There were few experts among them, but there were many who had gone through the good school of practical experience in their various occupations. And their experience led them to the firm conclusion that Russia, having now outgrown her swaddling clothes, no longer needed bureaucratic tutelage—and moreover, that the Russo-Japanese War had finally shown the inability of this bureaucratic system to cope with the needs of a growing empire.

The first president of the third Duma was N. A. Khomayakov. Formerly a prominent St. Petersburg administrator, he was from a distinguished family and was the son of one of the founders of the Slavophile movement. The founder of the Octobrist Party and its leader in the third Duma, A. I. Guchkov, was from a very different background. The grandson of a serf, he was an intellectual from Moscow merchant stock. He was proud of his background, despised class privileges, and strongly distrusted bureaucracy. Nevertheless, these two representatives of two such different social classes were drawn together into one party. For both of them the consolidation of a constitutional system was the main aim. They both realized that without popular representation and a radical renovation of the whole structure of the ship of state, Russia was threatened by disaster at the very first clash with the outside world.

Europe was living on top of a volcano at that time. The question was no longer whether or not there would be a war between the great powers, but when was it going to start. The experience of Tsushima and Port Arthur had opened the eyes of all patriots to the truth. And the entire process by which the loyal conservative majority was converted within seven or eight years came about through increasing patriotic alarm, which eventually turned into patriotic indignation.

I knew Guchkov well. We spent some time together in the Provisional Government and later we met frequently abroad as émigrés. He told me that from the very beginning of the activity of the third Duma he and the other Octobrist leaders had been in a hurry to consolidate Russia from within so as to be able to deal with the external clash when it finally came. The economic and industrial development of Germany at that moment was proceeding apace. The Germans were feverishly building up their navy, and the technical strength of their army was growing all the time. To anyone with any understanding at all of international relations, it was obvious that the temporary weakness of Russia in the wake of the Russo-Japanese war was considered in Berlin to be a trump card in the race for world domination.

Guchkov, Khomyakov, Shidlovsky, and the other leaders of the Octobrist Party knew full well the danger to the country of the morbid atmosphere surrounding the Tsar. Well aware that they could not rely on the weak-willed Tsar, they firmly rejected all of Stolypin's tempting invitations to join the government. They preferred to keep watch on the activity of the official government by applying the statutory rights of the Duma Budget Commission, to support it in the struggle against the irresponsible and powerful influence of the Rasputin clique in court circles, and to try to improve the country's military and economic position through regular legislation.

The idyllic relationship between the Tsar and the third Duma was very short-lived. Under the Code of Fundamental Laws of the Russian Empire, foreign policy and the army and navy came under the direct control of the Tsar. Officially, the Duma was not in a position to interfere in the affairs of the relevant ministries or to seek in any way to influence their activities. But the estimates for these government departments passed through the hands of the Budget Commission, as a result of which, as in all parliaments, the latter became the dominant and most influential body. All the ministers began to take it very much into account. Before they were submitted to the Budget Commission, the estimates for the various ministries were scrutinized by special departmental committees. Through this system—that is, through the financial control exercised by the Budget Commission—the War Ministry and the Admiralty virtually came under the control of the Duma. After the Russo-Japanese war, the navy had to be built up almost from scratch, and the army had to be radically reorganized, enlarged, and rearmed in accordance with the technical requirements of the day.

There was no firm direction of the army and navy. The higher military and naval establishments were constantly being reorganized. A great many individual military administrations were headed by completely irresponsible grand dukes, who generally pursued their own private aims without regard for anyone. In both the army and the navy there were many capable and energetic military experts who worked enthusiastically on plans for reform, but who were completely powerless to have them put into effect.

When Guchkov became the president of the Duma Defense Commission he made immediate contact with such men in the War Ministry and the Admiralty as were in favor of an ambitious reorganization of the services. In this way the Duma became the focal point for all the work of reorganizing Russia's defenses.

There is no doubt that the third and fourth Dumas played a very significant part in Russia's military preparations for the 1914–1918 war. The sober-minded, enterprising elements in the army and navy felt the firm backing of the Duma, and the Duma, in turn, now had their support in its struggle with the court camarilla.

This rapprochement, however, was viewed with immediate apprehension by those close to the Tsar who favored a return to absolutism.

In the spring of 1908, during discussion of the War Ministry budget in the Duma, Guchkov made a speech in which he called upon the grand dukes to make a "patriotic sacrifice," pointing out that the Duma had already asked the people to submit to great privations in the interests of defending the country. Guchkov was in fact asking the grand dukes to relinquish their administrative jobs in the army, for which they were hardly suited anyway, and in which they had shown great irresponsibility. He made his request with the full knowledge of the military administration. The speech naturally caused great indignation in court circles. The Tsarina immediately interpreted it, just as she interpreted the Duma's intervention in military matters in general, as an attack on the royal prerogative.

These suspicions were confirmed in her mind by the coup d'état that occurred the next year in Constantinople, where the sultan was deposed by the Young Turks. The court promptly nicknamed Guchkov the "Young Turk," and from then on regarded him as Public Enemy No. 1.

The minister of war, Rediger, an expert on military affairs who had established an atmosphere of great harmony in his work with the Duma, was dismissed. He was replaced by the commander of the Kiev Military District, General Sukhomlinov, a second-rate soldier with little knowledge of modern warfare, who, in obedience to the desire of the Tsar, refused to cooperate with the Duma.

The Tsarina was right in sensing that the leader of constitutionalism was her most dangerous opponent in the realization of her insane dream of restoring absolute autocracy in Russia. The Octobrist movement, with all its satellite groups, was certainly in the rear guard of those forces in the country which were striving for true democracy. On the other hand, it was in the vanguard of those forces at the highest level, that is, in leading military, administrative, and high-society circles. In leading the revolt against reaction, it was, willy-nilly, clearing the way for an extensive revival of the revolutionary movement, which had been given greater impetus in the spring of 1912 by the notorious massacre at the Lena goldfields.[2] Although the Octobrists had no intention of further democratizing Russia, they did want to raise the country to the higher economic and cultural level appropriate to a great power. They gained support for this end from the moderate opposition and from the more enlightened of the men occupying the higher administrative posts. Hence the third and fourth Dumas, despite their counterrevolutionary origin, played a progressive role in the history of Russia. Some of the laws they passed, by virtue of their very existence, promoted the economic and cultural boom which Russia experienced during the last decade prior to World War I.

For instance, during the Duma period, education developed at such

[2] See Chapter 5.

a headlong rate that when war broke out Russia was just on the point of introducing compulsory universal education. The absurd and criminal campaign waged against public education by reactionary ministers toward the end of the nineteenth century had been discontinued by the beginning of the twentieth century. By 1900, 42 percent of all children of school age were going to school. In the third Duma the minister of education, Kaufmann-Turkestansky, introduced a bill on universal education which was adopted by a majority. Unfortunately, however, it was rejected by the State Council, one half of whose members were personally chosen by the Tsar, and the bill was returned to the Duma for revision. It was eventually passed by the fourth Duma. By that time the minister of education, then Count P. N. Ignatiev, considered that the standard of literacy among the young was sufficiently advanced to introduce a system of compulsory primary education. Had the war not broken out, this would have been put into effect in its entirety by 1922. Even before the war, the only children not attending school were, in most cases, those whose parents did not want them to do so.

In 1929, the Carnegie Endowment published a book entitled *Russian Schools and Universities in the World War*.[3] It was written by two professors specializing in the field of Russian education, Odinets and Pokrovsky, and it included a preface by Ignatiev, the former minister of education. This book should have dispelled the myth that until the coming of the Bolsheviks only about 10 percent of the people were literate, or that the ruling classes did their best to prevent the children of peasants and workers from receiving education. The higher and secondary educational establishments in Russia were the most democratic in the world as regards the social background of their students. Even before the Duma period the *zemstva* had been spending 25 percent of their budget on education, but now they began spending up to a third. Over the period between 1900 and 1910 alone, educational grants to the *zemstva* from the government were increased twelvefold. In 1906 there were 76,000 schools, attended by about 4 million pupils. In 1915, there were already more than 122,000 schools with 8 million pupils. Over this period the minimum school-leaving age was raised, and the curricula were broadened so as to enable the most gifted peasant children to go on to attend secondary schools. The state schools not only catered to children, they became centers of

[3] Yale University Press.

instruction for adult peasants, too. The schools organized libraries, arranged lectures, held evening and Sunday classes for adults, and even gave theatrical performances. For the teachers themselves the *zemstva* arranged special courses. Every year there were free trips abroad for men and women teachers. Thousands of state school teachers visited Italy, France, and Germany before the First World War.

To sum up, as Odinets and Pokrovsky wrote: "The conclusion to be drawn from the general state of primary and secondary education in Russia in the years immediately preceding the war is that throughout the history of Russian civilization never was the spread of education so rapid as during the period in question."

In addition to the rapid improvement in literacy, the *zemstva,* together with the Duma and the cooperative organizations, forged ahead in the field of agriculture. From 1906 to 1913, the area of land under cultivation was increased by 16 percent and the yield of produce by 41 percent. Over this period there was a six-fold increase in the local *zemstvo* funds issued to the peasant population for agronomic aid. The central government also assigned large sums of money for this purpose. Throughout European Russia the *zemstva* energetically assisted the peasants to switch to mechanized farming, and in Siberia, where there were no *zemstva,* the government did the same.

The Peasant Land Bank bought up millions of acres of land from the private landowners and resold them to the peasants. The credit cooperative associations and the *zemstva* supplied the peasants with the agricultural implements they needed. By the start of the war 89.3 percent of the arable land reserves were in the hands of the peasants. The average peasant holding ranged from 30 to 75 acres. During the economic boom in Russia just prior to World War I, the export of Russian agricultural produce increased by 150 percent. The peasants dominated both the foreign and home markets, since they supplied three quarters of the grain and flax and practically all the butter, eggs, and meat.

The transfer of the land to the peasants and the tremendous increase in the proportion of peasant farming (by this time the amount of farming done by private landowners was almost nil) was accompanied by a period of great migration and resettlement among the peasants with the active assistance of the government, the *zemstva,* and the cooperatives. It was at this time that Siberia began to enter a stage of American-type economic and cultural development. Between the Russo-Japanese War and World War I, the population of this region doubled, and the area of land under cultivation trebled. Agricultural output rose more than threefold, and agricultural export rose tenfold. Prior to World War I, all the butter imported by Britain from Russia was produced by the Siberian and Ural peasant cooperatives. Whereas in 1899 hardly any butter had been exported from Siberia at all, by 1915 the cooperatives were exporting thousands of tons.

Indeed, it was the cooperative movement, freely developed in constitutional Russia, that enabled the Russian people, above all the peasantry, to show their natural initiative and talent for organization. Before World War I about half the peasants' households had joined the cooperative movement, making it the largest movement in Europe, except for Britain's.

In 1905, the peasant credit cooperatives had a membership of 7,290,000, and by 1916, the figure had risen to 10,500,000. In 1905, the total subscriptions amounted to 375,000,000 gold rubles, whereas by 1916 they amounted to 682,500,000. The cooperative movement in the towns grew just as rapidly. The federation of consumers' cooperatives, headed by the Moscow Central Union, became one of the most influential social and political bodies in Russia.

The general improvement in the welfare of the people was shown by the marked increase in the consumption of such consumer goods as sugar, butter, kerosene, and footwear, as well as by the increased deposits in the savings banks. This is admitted by the Soviet economist Lyashchenko.

According to the calculations of one of the greatest experts on the Russian economy, Professor S. Prokopovich, Russia's national income, despite the war with Japan and the accompanying depression, which lasted until 1909, increased by 79.4 percent over this period (in the 50 provinces to which the figures relate).

Even Communist writers sometimes bear witness to the rapidity of Russia's industrial development during the constitutional "five-year plan" prior to the outbreak of World War I: "Russia was rapidly advancing along capitalist lines, overtaking the older capitalist countries which had gone ahead." [4]

The gross output of industry increased by 44.9 percent between the

[4] *Outlines of History of the October Revolution* (Moscow, Ispart, 1927).

years 1900 and 1905, and by 1913, had increased by 219 percent. Individual industries showed an even greater increase. Technically speaking, industry was greatly expanded and modernized as a whole. A very incomplete summary gives a total of 537.3 million gold rubles as the investment in industrial equipment for the years 1910–1912. During this period of prosperity the increase in the capital stock of our industry was three times as rapid as that of America. In concentration of industry, Russia became one of the foremost countries in the world. The concentration of her industry was greater than that of America, for instance. The production of Russian industry for the years 1908, 1911, and 1916, was 1.5, 5.5, and 8.5 billion rubles, respectively.

The building of the Turkestan-Siberian railroad, the "Turksib," was begun just before the war and completed during the Soviet period. Over these years an ambitious program was launched for the reorganization of the entire national economy. Completion of this program was halted by the 1914 war.

This superconcentration of Russian industry had two important consequences. First, it resulted in the concentration of large numbers of workers in the cities and created more favorable conditions for organizing them. And second, it strengthened not so much the middle classes as the power of bank capital. Hence, neither in the towns nor in the countryside did Russia's economic boom alter the social structure in such a way as to create a solid foundation for a constitutional-monarchist system.

The life of a normally operating country is based on the principle of fair play. Both the authorities and the populace are supposed to obey certain rules in their mutual dealings. Whenever the authorities, who are usually in possession of superior physical force, break the rules, they abuse their power. The people must then make a choice: They can either meekly submit to the arbitrary rule of the authorities, or they can fight for their fundamental rights by resorting to extreme methods.

During the years I traveled around the country I gained a thorough knowledge of the feelings, hopes, and aspirations of democratically-minded people. Later, as a member of the Duma, I soon became aware of the whole system by which the country was run, and I began to realize the tragic complexity of the relationship between the government, which was formally responsible for the country's welfare, and the supreme authority, then in the hands of an irresponsible clique of ignorant and dishonest advisers. My eyes were suddenly opened to the complete unwillingness of the ruling and privileged sections of Russian society to take an independent stand and to hand over the power to sober and sensible men.

At the same time, everyone realized that Rasputinism had become a disgrace to Russia and that the Tsar's helplessness in the face of it was forcing the country toward another major crisis. Everyone saw that the coming clash would deprive not only the Tsar of power, but also those conservative groups that had forced their way into the Duma under the Stolypin law of June, 1907, since that law would immediately be replaced by universal suffrage. And Russia was the only great power in the world in which such suffrage could have democratized the country both politically and socially without any armed uprising or revolution.

Eighty percent of the peasants, possessing virtually 90 percent of the land under cultivation; the moribund gentry; the factory proletariat, concentrated in the towns and rapidly growing in strength; the still politically and socially weak middle class; the huge army of bureaucrats, mainly composed of educated people from the middle classes completely uninterested in defending the capitalist system; and last but not least, the intelligentsia, traditionally imbued with the spirit of Russian culture with its classless principles of justice and the sacred inviolability of the individual—all these elements threw their weight into the battle that was now approaching its climax between the privileged majority in the Duma and the crown.

Having learned the lessons of the fight for popular representation in the third Duma, the Octobrists entered the fourth Duma, in the autumn of 1912, as the opposition.

Before the opening of the new Duma, Guchkov had a new slogan ready for his supporters: *"Against* the participation of irresponsible people in affairs of state; *for* a government responsible to the nation's representatives."

And so, in the autumn of 1912, Guchkov voiced the same appeal that Milyukov's Cadets had made in the spring of 1906, in the first Duma. Another crucial moment in the history of Russia was approaching, and a rapprochement between political enemies, until very recently irreconcilable, had become inevitable.

It was their common goal to preserve the monarchy as a symbol of the unity of the state, while effecting a complete transfer of power to a government enjoying the confidence of the people's elected representatives. But it was an impossible goal. The monarch, who hated the very thought of the constitution and was scheming to bring back outmoded absolutism, could not tolerate parliamentary democracy. To do so he would have had to change his very nature and side with the people. The hand of fate offered him a chance. . . .

At midnight, on July 31, 1914, the German ambassador handed the Russian foreign minister an ultimatum. Russia was at war once more.

War

7

The Origins and the Beginning of the War

The Year of Silence

WORLD WAR I, which had been brewing in the heart of Europe for some years, hit Russia like a whirlwind. No other great power in Europe needed and wanted peace as much as Russia after her war with Japan. Objectively, Russia was not ready for war with Germany in 1914; subjectively, the Russian people had no thought of war. They were completely engrossed in internal political, cultural, and economic problems. Indeed, Russia in 1914 was nearing a new and decisive internal crisis and hardly noticed the menacing international situation so rapidly developing around her.

Russia's tragic position on the eve of World War I is shown very clearly in two letters from the private correspondence between Premier Stolypin and A. P. Izvolsky, who was leaving his post as foreign minister to become ambassador to Paris.

The two short extracts given below forcefully illustrate my contention that the Great War was absolutely contrary to the national interests and aims of Russia in 1914.

On July 21, 1911, Izvolsky wrote to Stolypin:

... You know that during the five years of my ministry I was continually beset by the nightmare of a sudden war. There was no possibility of modifying the convention; to weaken it would have meant an immediate all-European war, or definite and complete enslavement by Germany. In either case, this would have been *finis Rossiae* [the end of Russia] as a great and independent power.

To this Stolypin replied:

Kolnoberge, July 28.

I am extremely grateful for your interesting letter. I must admit I was most confused concerning all that was going on. You know my point of view. We need peace: a war during the approaching year, and especially in the name of a cause the people would not understand, would be fatal to Russia and to the dynasty. Conversely, every year of peace fortifies Russia not only from the military and naval point of view, but also from the economic and financial one. Besides, and this is more important, Russia is growing from year to year; self-knowledge and public opinion are developing in our land. One must not scoff at our parliamentary institutions. However imperfect, their influence has brought about a radical change in Russia, and when this country's time shall come, it will meet its enemy in full awareness. Russia will hold out and emerge victorious only in a popular war. I am conveying these thoughts to you myself, as it is impossible to form an idea of Russia through the newspapers.

Izvolsky was beset by the nightmare of a sudden war, not because he was imagining things, or because he was a timid statesman, as Lord Grey has said of him. If he was a cautious, possibly an unduly cautious diplomat, it was because it was becoming more and more difficult for Russia to tread the path of peace in a Europe on the brink of war. In his memoirs Lord Grey himself tells us that Europe, steadily and rapidly arming herself, was moving toward war with fateful inevitability and that all the governments were suspicious of each other and saw a trap behind every diplomatic move, however innocent.

Unable to establish a new international balance of power, and incapable of curbing the monstrous dynamism of the German economy and military machine without force, the Entente concentrated more and more on building up and perfecting its armaments. These armies and navies were automatically pushing Europe further and further toward an armed clash, for in every arms race there eventually comes a psychological moment when war seems to be the only way to relieve the unbearable strain of waiting for a catastrophe. From 1909 on it was only a question of time. The demarcation line between the jobs of the diplomat and the staff officer began to disappear.

There were three main problems in Europe just before the First World War. These were, first, the Anglo-German struggle for naval supremacy; second, the Austro-German-Russian disagreement over the Balkans and Turkey; and third, the Franco-German rivalry in Alsace-Lorraine and the African colonies. The task of settling these problems was left to the diplomats. As is clear from documents now published, most of them tried to do their job conscientiously. But despite all the good intentions of "secret diplomacy," the three diplomatic problems became more and more entangled and intertwined. The time was approaching when the task of unraveling them would pass from the diplomats to the warriors.

There is no doubt that the Anglo-German feud was the crux of the international situation.

When did the German government finally decide to precipitate the outbreak of the European war?

While still in Russia, and for some time after my departure, I used to share the commonly held opinion that Germany had decided on a preventive war after the grand military program for the radical reorganization of the defense system on Russia's western frontier, which was actually in progress, had been officially approved at the very end of the 1914 spring session of the Duma, at a secret conference of the majority leaders ("progressive bloc").

But now, having reexamined Germany's entire policy during the Balkan wars, I have come to the conclusion—and this is now my profound conviction—that the plan for a preventive war was adopted by the German Command as early as the summer of 1912. Preparations for it were methodically and swiftly carried out both during and after the Balkan Conference.

In February, 1912, the British Government made a final attempt to reach agreement with Germany to halt the naval buildup in both countries. Lord Haldane, an influential member of the Cabinet and an advocate of friendly relations with Germany, was sent to negotiate the matter in Berlin, where he had many important contacts in political and government circles. Lord Haldane's mission, as might have been expected, was a complete failure, and he returned to London empty-handed. The Berlin government had no intention of concluding a naval agreement unless certain changes it demanded in British foreign policy were put into effect. Britain, on the other hand, had no intention whatsoever of making concessions in her foreign policy—and could not afford to do so in 1912, anyway.

Lord Haldane's departure from Berlin was followed almost immediately by more appropriations for the German navy. On March 8, the Reichstag passed Admiral Tirpitz's second navy bill.

Haldane's mission was Britain's last attempt to try to avert an armed clash with Germany. When it had failed, as he himself told me in London in 1918, it became clear that war was inevitable. And it was in the summer of 1912 that all the European powers began busily making preparations for it.

On the initiative of the British Admiralty, the British and French cabinets concluded a top-secret agreement, of which no official record was made, regarding the disposition of their naval forces. The whole of the British Navy was to be concentrated in the English Channel and the North Sea, and Britain undertook to defend France's northern shores; the French Navy was to be massed in the Mediterranean.

By undertaking to guard the northern shores of France in the event of war with Germany, the British Cabinet of Asquith and Grey made certain Britain's participation in a war in which Russia was also bound to become involved by her alliance with France. And in Berlin this Anglo-French agreement on naval spheres of action, which did not escape the notice of German intelligence, extinguished Germany's last hope of destroying the Anglo-French-Russian Entente through diplomatic channels.

The French Cabinet, in turn, sure of Britain's support, completely reversed its attitude toward the Russian situation in the Balkans. On October 25, 1912, A. P. Izvolsky, Russian ambassador to Paris, informed Foreign Minister Sazonov of the following statement of policy adopted by the French Cabinet: "France now recognizes that Austria's territorial ambitions involve the over-all balance of power in Europe and consequently France's own interests."

In short, France was encouraging Russia to take a stronger stand in the Balkans. At about the same time France began pressing Russia to strengthen and reorganize her armed forces as soon as possible and to complete the construction of strategically important railroads without delay.

France herself had been taking steps to improve her artillery situation since 1911 and now possessed an adequate number of heavy field guns. In August, 1913, the army underwent modernization, and a three-year period of national service was introduced, although the law was passed only after long and stubborn resistance on the part of the trade unions, the Socialist Party, and left-wing radicals. All expenditures on rearming and enlarging the armed forces had met with the strongest opposition in the Chamber before the law was finally approved.

Generally speaking, public opinion in the countries of the Entente —Britain, France and Russia—was far removed from the militaristic and chauvinistic feelings reigning among official circles of all shades of opinion in Germany.

At their congresses, all the socialist parties in Europe (including Germany), as well as the worker's organizations, voted against war and for a general strike if the "capitalists" started one. In Russia public opinion was by and large against any kind of war. The country during these prewar years was too preoccupied with the struggle against the "Rasputin regime."

The Germans took their cue from information on the military, political and psychological position in the potentially enemy countries, which all went to show that an Austro-German victory was more than likely. But the likelihood would lessen with every year of waiting, since the military and psychological preparedness of the Entente powers was certain to increase as time went on.

By the end of 1913 everything was ready for the first blow. All that was needed was the right moment. The moment came on June 15, 1914.

That day, during a visit to the province of Bosnia, the Archduke Franz Ferdinand and his morganatic wife were driving without any police protection along the streets of Sarajevo in an open coach. As they were turning a corner a young man ran up to the coach and fired several shots from a revolver, killing them both. The assassin, Gavrilo Princip, belonged to the Black Hand, an ultranationalist terrorist organization in Serbia.[1]

The whole of Europe was shocked and outraged by this tragic event. All government and political circles were greatly alarmed that the Balkan fire, only just extinguished by the joint efforts of the Great Powers at the London Conference, might now easily flare up again and renew the tension between them.

[1] Bosnia was a Slav province of Austria, only officially annexed in 1908, though since the Berlin Congress of 1878 it had been occupied and administered by the Austrians under a secret pact reached by the emperors of Austria-Hungary, Germany, and Russia.

Their alarm was short-lived. The Austrian government hastened to assure St. Petersburg that it had no intention of taking any military action. And about a week after the Archduke's death, Kaiser Wilhelm II went off on a summer "vacation" to the Norwegian fjords. The German Emperor's departure finally convinced Europe that peace would be preserved.

The usual political lull of the summer season began. Ministers, members of parliament, high-ranking military and government officials all began leaving on vacation. In Russia nobody bothered much about the tragedy in Sarajevo; most politically minded people were too engrossed in internal affairs.

Even in the light of our present knowledge, it is hard to imagine how it happened that no one among the European ruling set, except the conspirators in Germany and Austria, realized that this blissful summer was merely the calm before the terrible storm.

In July, taking advantage of the parliamentary recess, Raymond Poincaré, president of the French Republic, and Viviani, premier and foreign minister, made an official visit to Tsar Nicholas II, traveling there aboard a French battleship. On the way back from Russia they were scheduled to visit the Scandinavian countries.

The meeting (July 7–10) was held in Peterhof, the Tsar's summer residence. Early in the morning of July 7 the French guests were transferred from the battleship, anchored at Kronstadt, to the Tsar's yacht, which took them to Peterhof. After three days of discussions, banquets, and receptions, interspersed with trips to watch the regular summer maneuvers of the guards regiments and troops from the St. Petersburg Military District, the French visitors returned to their battleship on July 10 and sailed for Scandinavia. A little later, on that same day, Paris, St. Petersburg, and London received notification that the Austrian government had handed the Serbian Government an ultimatum, the terms of which were to be carried out within 48 hours.

It is clearly no coincidence that the ultimatum was presented on the very day that Poincaré sailed from Russia. France was thus left for several days without a president, a head of the Cabinet and a foreign minister; there was only a deputy minister who was unversed in foreign affairs. At this crucial moment, speedy, concerted action on the part of France and Russia was well nigh impossible.

The demands contained in the ultimatum were clearly unacceptable to any government. No self-respecting country would consent to the dismissal of its officials at the demand of a foreign power; no government would allow foreigners to take charge of its administrative and legal institutions under threat of armed force; no government would apologize for criminal actions in which it was not an accomplice, that is, falsely admit to collusion or connivance. Even the Austrian Baron von Wiesner, sent to Sarajevo to investigate the assassination, had told the Austrian government on July 2 that he had not discovered any indication of the complicity of the Serbian government in the assassination.

As soon as the Russian government heard about the ultimatum, it suggested that Serbia accede to all demands other than those violating the fundamental rights of a sovereign state. And that is what the Serbian government did in its reply to the note of July 10.

The note from Belgrade was considered unsatisfactory by the Viennese government, and from that moment Austria and Serbia were in a state of war. On July 15 the Austrians shelled Belgrade.

The same day Lord Grey called for an immediate conference of the great powers, but the Austrians objected to Grey's discussing the question of Austro-Serbian relations, a question that involved their national honor. Berlin supported their contention.

All attempts by the Russian government in its direct negotiations with the Austrians to persuade them to find a peaceful solution and to modify the terms of the ultimatum were sharply rebuffed. Meanwhile German agents in Western Europe sought to convince public opinion that the Serbian government had refused Austria's just demands under pressure from an aggressive St. Petersburg. This news was readily accepted by pacifist and pro-German circles in Britain and France, which were certain that Russia was the chief culprit in all international intrigues jeopardizing the peace of Europe.

Nowadays there is no point in repudiating this ridiculous idea or in proving that World War I was not caused by the provocative "premature mobilization" of the Russian armies. Even in the summer of 1917, at the height of the fighting on the Russian front, Haase, an independent left-wing social democrat, made an official announcement in the Reichstag for which, had it been false, he would have been tried for high treason. Haase stated that on June 22, 1914, a week after the murder of the Archduke, Kaiser Wilhelm called a secret meeting of highly-placed officials in the Austrian and German governments and armed forces. At the meeting it was decided to use the Sarajevo tragedy as an excuse for a preventive war against the Triple Entente, and a general plan of action was accordingly worked out. The first part of the plan, obviously enough, was to be put into effect by Austria alone, without any association with Germany, so as not to arouse British or Russian suspicions. It should be said that this strategic ruse—the Kaiser's departure on "vacation"—worked rather well. Unsuspected by her future adversaries, Germany now had three weeks' grace to prepare for the initial onslaught.

Knowing that an all-European war between the two groups of powers was inevitable; knowing that Britain had a navy, but—for the moment—no army; knowing that Britain's continental allies were rapidly reorganizing and rearming their forces, but were not yet ready for war; knowing that in 1914 Russia was not the Russia of 1904, but was now a country with a well-developed heavy industrial production, including a war industry; and knowing that in two or three years France and Russia would be fully prepared and that their military might would then surpass that of Germany; the Germans took what they thought was the only possible course—they took their ill-prepared enemy unawares.

Could Russia, so completely unready for a clash with Germany, and knowing from the experience of 1908 that Austria was backed by Germany, really have provoked the Kaiser into a war? Obviously not. The documents on the origins of the war published in the White Book of 1915 by the St. Petersburg government rule out this possibility completely. At the first military council on the Austro-Serbian conflict, held by the Tsar a day before the bombardment of Belgrade, it was decided to announce precautionary measures the next day, July 13, and, if the situation deteriorated, to proclaim *partial* mobilization; thirteen corps were to stand by in four military districts not bordering on Germany. Foreign Minister Sazonov immediately informed the German ambassador in St. Petersburg, Count Pourtalès, of this decision, pointing out that the measures were not directed against Germany and that no action against Austria was envisaged.

The European crisis was developing at such lightning speed that there could be no question of merely partial mobilization against Austria, for both technical and political reasons. Partial mobilization was not a stage in the program for general Russian mobilization in the event of war, and by remaining in force it could only endanger Russia at the crucial moment. Hurrying back to St. Petersburg from the Caucasus, General Danilov, the first quartermaster general on the general staff, urged General Yanushkevich, who had just been appointed chief of general staff but who had not had time to familiarize himself with the mobilization plans, to reconsider the order. Two separate drafts, one for partial and one for general mobilization, were sent to the Tsar for his decision.

On the morning of July 16 the plan for general mobilization, already signed by the Tsar, was taken from Tsarskoye Selo; it was to be put into effect at midnight. At that moment the military authorities received reliable and accurate information on the concentration of German forces in the vicinity of the French and Russian frontiers.

On the morning of the sixteenth, Pourtalès called on Sazonov and told him rather sharply that the continuation of the Russian mobilization measures against Austria would force Germany to take corresponding measures. However, the same day, July 16, Nicholas II was in constant communication by telegraph with the Kaiser, who was now back from his "sightseeing trip" to the Norwegian fjords. Mistakenly believing from one of the messages that the Kaiser really wanted peace, the Tsar sent him a telegram in reply that evening, thanking him for his message and pointing out that it differed sharply from the tone in which the German Ambassador had discussed the same matter that day with Sazonov.

That evening the Tsar canceled his order for general mobilization and substituted an order for partial mobilization effective from the same date—July 17.

The next day, when it was already known that on July 18 Austria was going to announce a general stand-by and that military preparations in Germany were now being carried on quite openly, the Tsar received another telegram from the Kaiser, now worded much more sharply. The German Emperor made it quite clear that Pourtalès' statement was in complete accordance with his instructions and that if Russia did not cancel the mobilization, the Tsar would have only himself to blame for the consequences. It was at that point that the Tsar, after agonizing vacillation, finally canceled partial mobilization for the second time and gave the order for general mobilization, setting midnight on July 18 as zero hour.

Furthermore, wishing to avoid aggravating the Germans, the Tsar forbade the navy to lay minefields in Baltic waters without first asking his consent. On July 17, the Admiralty received a report that the German fleet had left Kiel and set sail for Danzig. Aware of the Tsar's orders, Admiral Essen, commander of the Baltic Fleet, telegraphed the chief of naval staff, Admiral Rusin, urging him to ask the Tsar for permission to lay mines at once. The telegram was received at about midnight on July 17. The chief of staff, accompanied by his closest aides, went to the minister of the marine, despite the lateness of the hour, and asked him to wake up the Tsar and request his permission to lay the minefields. The minister of the marine flatly refused to do so. Attempts to secure the assistance of the Grand Duke Nicholas were also a failure. It was only at about 4:00 A.M., when the officers sent by Rusin to see General Yanushkevich, a regimental comrade of the Tsar, had not returned, that the Admiral decided to go against the imperial command and to order the mines to be laid. Several minutes later permission was received from General Yanushkevich.

At 11:30 A.M. on the morning of July 18, Admiral Essen reported to the chiefs of staff in a radio telegram that the minefields had been laid.

Late that evening Count Pourtalès called on Foreign Minister Sazonov and informed him with tears in his eyes that with effect from midnight, July 18, Germany was at war with Russia.

8

The Monarchy's Road to Ruin

THE spring session of the fourth Duma came to a close on May 28, 1914. The meetings had been extremely lively and at times even stormy. Members of all the factions, from Social Democrats to Octobrists, severely criticised Goremykin's disastrous policy and insisted on the resignation of the three ministers most fanatically opposed to popular representation—Maklakov (interior), Shcheglovitov (justice) and Sukhomlinov (war). Their desire to see the end of Goremykin's cabinet was motivated, in the case of the extremely moderate deputies, not so much by the government's home policy as by the highly alarming situation in Europe.

The Russian army was passing through a critical phase at that moment because of the implementation of the major armament program devised by the French and Russian general staffs in retaliation for the military buildup in Germany and Austria.

It was at the end of the spring session that the government decided to brief some of the more influential members of the Duma Armed Services Commission on the progress of the defense measures. Accordingly Rodzyanko held a top secret meeting in his office, at which the Minister of War was supposed to explain the purpose and aims of the radical reorganization of Russia's defense system along her western borders.

Being a representative of the left-wing opposition, I was not invited to attend this extremely important meeting, and so I can only quote from the evidence that was given by Milyukov, the leader of the Cadet Party, at a special inquiry held in August, 1917, to investigate the activities of former Tsarist ministers and officials: "At the private conference on the war program, Sukhomlinov revealed total ignorance of military matters. We were not great experts ourselves, but we could see that he had no idea what was being done, and knew as much about the 'reform' he was supposed to explain to us as the man in the moon. And anyway, it was not a question of 'reforming' the armed forces, but of regrouping and reorganizing them under a contingency plan for a major war, which was expected to break out in 1916."

What was to be done? I had no answer, but one thing I did know: A war with Germany would not be a relatively marginal conflict, like the Russo-Japanese War, but a struggle in which the whole nation would have to fight, just as in 1812.

Naturally, not everything that was discussed and done behind the solid walls of government offices reached the ears of even the more politically-minded members of the public. But now that I knew that theoretical arguments and discussions as to whether or not there was going to be a war were meaningless and that the clash was inevitable, I sincerely felt that I could not—dared not—withhold my knowledge from certain prominent members of the left-wing and radical groups. I also felt it was essential to sound out the views of these people before setting out on my annual tour of the country.

I finally managed to organize a conference, although it was rather sparsely attended since most people were already away on their summer vacations. There were heated arguments—not everyone believed that war was imminent—but on one point we were in complete agreement: If war were to break out, everyone would have to do his bit to defend the country.

At long last, after days of tedious argument, I managed to get away from St. Petersburg and breathe the fresh country air of the unsophisticated Russian provinces. During the summer recess it was my custom to travel around the country giving talks on Duma affairs and helping with the organization of local political work. My itinerary took me through the Urals to the Volga. Looking back now, the political freedom that Russia enjoyed at that time seems like a fairy tale. Russia had become a totally different country from what it had been before the Russo-Japanese War. By the summer of 1914, Russia was already a politically organized country, and it would have taken only two or three years more for the remaining traces of autocracy and Rasputinism to have been swept from the face of the land, leaving a new and democratic Russia.

At the beginning of July, I left Ekaterinburg,[1] where I had gone to attend an elementary schoolteachers' congress, and went to spend a few days in Samara. The town showed a keen interest in political affairs. When I gave my talk, the municipal theater was packed, and crowds of people had to stand in the square outside.

The evening was a lively one, although as usual no one asked me any questions about the international situation; they were much more concerned with current internal issues. The talk was followed by a reception attended by the vice-president of the Duma, Nekrasov, myself, and a small group of local people prominent in politics. There, however, the chief topic of conversation was the tense international situation.

The next day, July 10, we went down to the jetty, accompanied by our friends. Nekrasov was going to the Black Sea coast to see his family, and I was heading for Saratov, where I was to give another talk. As we stood on the jetty, a newsboy suddenly ran by, shouting frenziedly, "Latest news! Austria sends Serbia ultimatum!" It was a wonderful summer morning. The Volga glistened in the sunlight and the decks of the large river steamer alongside the jetty were crowded with happy, excited people. Few of them paid much attention to the newsboy, but in our small group everyone suddenly stopped talking. Our good spirits—engendered by our very rewarding visit to Samara —vanished in a flash. We saw only too clearly what the ultimatum meant: It meant war throughout Europe.

After a brief discussion, we decided that I should go straight back to St. Petersburg and that Nekrasov would cut short his trip to the Black Sea.

There are moments in a man's life when he does not need to reason or ponder; he is instantly aware of the significance of what is happening. At that moment I saw clearly that all of the Russian people would be involved in the coming war, and that they would all do their duty.

It was at the end of June, 1914, that unrest had broken out among the workers (numbering about 200,000) in the capital, and barricades began to appear in the Vyborg area, a working-class section of the city. A few days before the actual outbreak of the war, Pourtalès had

[1] Renamed Sverdlovsk in 1924.

cabled Berlin that the psychological moment to declare war had arrived since Russia would not be able to fight, so ridden was she with internal strife.

His Excellency made a fatal error of judgment. The day war was declared, the revolutionary strikers of the evening before marched in their thousands to the Allied embassies in an impressive demonstration of their solidarity. And on the square in front of the Winter Palace, the same square that had been witness to the tragedy of January, 1905, huge crowds of people from all walks of life enthusiastically cheered their sovereign and sang *God Save the Tsar.*

The whole nation, in the cities, in the towns, and in the country villages, knew instinctively that the war with Germany would decide the political destiny of Russia for many years to come. Proof of this was in the way people responded to the mobilization. Throughout the vast expanses of Russia the whole operation went off remarkably well considering its scale; only 4 percent of the drafted men failed to report for duty on time. Further proof was in the sudden change in the mood of the industrial proletariat. To the astonishment and indignation of the Marxists and other armchair socialists, the Russian worker, like his French and German counterpart, showed himself just as much a patriot as his "class enemies."

"During the initial period of the war," wrote a Communist historian later on, "the numerically weak party forces, finding themselves in an apathetic and even hostile atmosphere, took the only course open to them—they slowly but surely recruited allies. This painstaking work resulted in the gradual correction and elimination of this subjective failing [2] manifested by the party ranks at the beginning of the war. As it recovered and became ideologically firm, this party stratum began a relentless struggle against the patriotic feelings of the revolutionary masses." [3]

I felt that the battle we had been waging against the remnants of absolutism could now be postponed. We were fighting a powerful enemy that was technically far superior to us. Now we had to concentrate all our efforts and the will of the people on a single aim. The unity of the country depended not only on the people's patriotism;

[2] I.e., patriotism.
[3] *Essays on the History of the October Revolution,* ed. by M. N. Pokrovsky (Moscow, Ispart, 1927), p. 203.

it also depended very much on the internal policy of the government. The masses had shown that they were willing to let bygones be bygones. It was up to the monarchy to do the same.

On my way back to St. Petersburg I worked on a plan of action for the war, based on a reconciliation between the Tsar and the people.

This was, perhaps, a hopeless dream, but there are times, both in the history of countries and in the lives of men, when only the irrational and illogical can save them. This second war for national survival (the first was in 1812) gave the Tsar a unique opportunity to extend the hand of friendship to the people, thereby ensuring victory and consolidating the monarchy for many years to come.

There was no lack of noble, patriotic, and human sentiment in the Tsar's manifesto on the war with Germany, but what we needed was not reconciliation in word, but in deed.

An emergency session of the Duma was fixed for July 26. In the time immediately preceding this historic session, the representatives of the various parties held daily meetings of the Council of Elders in Rodzyanko's office. There was no doubt that the Duma would unanimously affirm the determination of all classes and national groups to defend their homeland and emerge victorious from the battle. The crucial question was whether or not the Tsar would meet the people halfway.

Rodzyanko was due to report to the Tsar before the Duma opened on July 26. At one of the meetings I urged him to say on behalf of the Council of Elders that the Duma considered it absolutely essential to the outcome of the war that the Tsar take the following steps: (1) modify his home policy; (2) proclaim a general amnesty for political prisoners; (3) restore the Finnish Constitution; (4) declare the autonomy of Poland; (5) give the non-Russian minorities cultural freedom; (6) abolish the restrictions against the Jews; (7) end religious intolerance; and (8) stop obstructing the legitimate working-class organizations and trade unions.

All these points were contained in the Constitutional Manifesto of October 17, 1905, but the authorities had studiously avoided putting any of them into effect. I advised the Elders not to ask the Tsar for any new reforms, but merely to insist on the implementation of the promised ones. My request was supported by the Progressives, Mensheviks, and left-wing Cadets.

The next person to speak was Milyukov. He was actually a historian and was considered an expert on international relations. Citing Britain as an example, he asserted that the Duma must show complete confidence in the government, no matter what its failings, and must make no stipulations. His reference to Britain seemed totally irrelevant to me, since every British government is under the close scrutiny of public opinion, and is, moreover, an expression of the will of the party that has won the elections. In Russia, however, there had never been a truly democratic parliamentary system. In fact, Goremykin's Cabinet merely followed the dictates of Rasputin and his clique and paid absolutely no attention to public opinion.

Furthermore, the example of Britain was particularly inapposite in that the British Conservative opposition had not given the Liberals their confidence until the leaders of both parties had reached a private agreement on wartime policy.

Nevertheless, my proposal was outvoted.

But even if my points had been adopted, I doubt whether the demands made by the Council of Elders would have influenced the Tsar's state of mind any more than had the enthusiasm of the people.

Just before Rodzyanko was due to leave for Tsarskoye Selo, I had a long talk with him. He wrote down my views on a piece of paper and promised to mention them to the Tsar. On his return, he told me that he had done what I asked, but that the Tsar had merely glanced at the piece of paper and put it down on the table without comment.

In his last report to the Tsar, dated February 10, 1917, Rodzyanko reminded him of those first few months of the war, when everything had been possible, but nothing had been done. The report said:

We have seen how the governments of our Allies were organized in accordance with the demands of the moment, and we have seen the brilliant results that were obtained. And what were we doing at that time? The whole nation was striving for unity, but our government had no general policy and was frightened by the unity of the people. The Government not only refuses to make any change in its methods of administration, it even seeks justification by reference to time-honored practices long since cast aside. Arrests, deportations, and the persecution of the press have reached extremes. Even people on whose support the Government could at one time rely are now considered suspicious. The whole country is under suspicion.

There was no point in Rodzyanko's recalling, when it was already too late, what might have been possible at the beginning of the war. He should have joined me in 1914 in trying to convince the Council of Elders that we had to do our duty as representatives of the people by showing the Tsar that the only way to unite the country was to unite the supreme authority with the people in the common struggle for Russia.

The objection may be made that this advice would not have been taken. Possibly not. But at least the majority of the Duma would not then have been condemned by the people for its obedient silence during the first year of the war and its acceptance of the ruthless and uncontrolled actions of the Tsar's ministers.

Any possibility of victory now depended solely on the grim determination of the people to defend their country to the last man. I put my trust in this; I was certain that the obstacles placed by the monarch in the way of victory would be swept aside. In fact, that is what I said at the historic sitting of the Duma on July 26.

The moments before the meeting opened were very depressing ones for me. The Trudoviks and Social Democrats had originally decided to make a statement in which both parties expressed the determination of the people to defend the country (as had been agreed at the conference), despite the antipopular and obstructionist policy of the government.

The joint statement had been formulated in general outline the night before, and I had been given the job of drafting the final version and bringing it with me to the Duma the next day. When I arrived, however, a bitter disappointment awaited me.

Chkheidze, chairman of the Social Democrats, came over to me in the Catherine Hall and told me rather sheepishly that a joint statement was unfortunately no longer possible. I was dumbfounded. When I asked why, he made the excuse that a telegram had been received during the night from a certain agency, which reported that the Social Democrats in Germany had organized a demonstration against war, and that he had to support them. I objected that it could not be true, pointing out that German Social Democrats are Germans first, and that the Germans were far too pig-headed to do that. Chkheidze waved his hand rather vaguely. I asked to see the text of his party's statement. I read it and gave it back saying, "Do as you wish, but you must cross out this passage at all events. Otherwise you may have to pay heavily . . ." [4]

At the meeting which opened soon afterward, a Bolshevik named Khaustov read out a statement on behalf of the whole Social Democratic faction. It was worded in typical Marxist jargon and merely said that the "proletariat, the eternal defender of the liberty and interests of the people, will at all times defend the cultural welfare of the people against all attacks, no matter what their source," and hoped that the present wave of barbarism [5] would be the last.

The same evening official reports came through that there had been no action at all on the part of the German Social Democrats. The trick had only partially succeeded, however, since the most crucial passage in Chkheidze's statement had been taken out.

As soon as the ministers had completed their explanation of the government policy, the president of the Duma called on me to take the floor. The concluding lines in my brief statement on behalf of the Trudoviks were as follows:

. . . We are absolutely convinced that the great elemental and innate force of Russian democracy, together with all the other forces of the Russian people, will rebuff the aggressors and defend the homeland and cultural heritage created by the blood and sweat of generations. We believe that the brotherhood of all Russian people will be strengthened by suffering on the battlefields and that there will be born the single aim of freeing the country from its terrible shackles.

However, the authorities refuse to halt internal strife, even at this fearful hour; they do not wish to grant amnesty to those who have struggled for the freedom and happiness of our land, nor do they wish to come to terms with the non-Russian minorities, who have forgiven all and are fighting hard beside us for Russia. Instead of easing the burden of the working classes, the authorities are forcing them to bear the brunt of war expenditure by increasing the burden of indirect taxation.

Peasants, workers and all of you who desire the happiness and well-being

---

[4] The passage contained an appeal for the sabotaging of military supply trains.
[5] I.e., the war.

of the country, steel yourselves for the great trials ahead of us, gather your strength, and, *having defended the country, you will free it . . .*

These brief sentences sum up the wartime political program of the groups with which I was associated, whose will I obeyed and whose aims I sought to express.

Milyukov was in complete sympathy with the feelings of the conservative and right-wing parties making up the majority in the Duma, and he firmly stated that "we demand nothing and impose no conditions; we will simply place our indomitable will to victory on the scales of war."

And so, for the duration of the war, the majority of the Duma put Russia at the mercy of an arbitrary and self-willed government, thereby dooming itself to inaction and silence at a time crucial to the destiny of the country.

How did the monarchy and the reactionary ministers explain to themselves this unexpected outburst of patriotism and the even more unexpected vote of confidence in the government by the Duma? Exactly as might have been expected from men who still dreamed of a return to absolute power in Russia. They told themselves that the would-be politicians in the Duma who were playing the game of representing the people and trying to meddle in affairs of state had been forced to capitulate in the face of the powerful wave of feeling among the "true people," who were rallying around the Tsar and helping him to save the country from enemy invaders as they had done countless times before. And now that the people had sided with the Tsar, the ministers, the defenders of traditional absolutism, had no further need of the Duma and no longer feared its criticism. That is probably how they rationalized the situation!

But did the Duma really want the abolition of the monarchy? No. Russia, like all the other countries of Europe at that time except for France, was a monarchy. And at that moment, with the future of Russia at stake, even the Republicans—and for that matter, myself as well—were willing to forget the past for the sake of national unity. After all, had the Tsar not said in his declaration of October 17, 1905, that from then on no law could be passed without ratification by the Duma? Was this not, in fact, already a constitutional monarchy, even if a rather rough and ready one?

The destruction of the patriotic feelings of the workers, who were going all out to strengthen the country's defenses, was now being carried out on two fronts. The government authorities were sabotaging the hospitalization funds and other workers' welfare organizations, and sending many of the most experienced and popular workers and expert trade unionists to the front. Most of the people working in these organizations were Social Democrats and Mensheviks completely unsympathetic to Lenin's defeatist propaganda. Finding themselves in a small minority, the Leninists took advantage of this fact to further their own ends.

Since the beginning of the war, the hope of the working class for unification of the numerous parties and settlement of their inter-factional squabbles had grown stronger. If this hope had been realized, the patriotic mood of the workers might have been considerably strengthened. Lenin saw this quite clearly, and he was, therefore, vehemently opposed to any association with the Mensheviks.

On December 16, 1914, the director of the Police Department issued the following circular (No. 190791) to all secret police sections:

In view of the extreme gravity of the present plan (to unite the parties) and the desirability of thwarting it, the Police Department feels obliged to advise all security section heads to impress upon agents in their charge that when attending any party meetings they should persistently advocate and convincingly defend the idea of the utter impossibility of any organized merging of these currents of opinion, especially between the Bolsheviks and Mensheviks.

The deeper the dissension among the workers, and the more relentlessly the authorities sabotaged the activity of the working-class welfare organizations, the easier it would become for the Bolshevik minority to dampen the patriotic spirit of the proletariat.

At the beginning of December Lenin's theses—later known as his "defeatist theses"—reached Russia from Switzerland. The Central Committee of the Bolshevik Party held a secret meeting in the outskirts of Petrograd [6] to discuss them, attended, naturally, by the "Five"—that is, the entire Bolshevik faction in the Duma. Also present was the famous Kamenev (Rosenfeld), who had returned from exile abroad not long before and was living in Russia legally at the

[6] The name of St. Petersburg was changed to Petrograd in August, 1914.

time. Through their agents, one of whom was the editor of *Pravda*, the secret police found out exactly when and where the meeting was to be held, and how many people were going to attend it. The meeting had hardly begun before the police came in and took the "Five," and Kamenev, into custody. They were tried immediately, and on February 14 they were exiled to Siberia.

Few workers knew the contents of Lenin's theses. They only knew one thing—their spokesmen in the Duma had been thrown out. But the Bolsheviks were delighted to have gained five martyrs, and the fate of the "Five" became the dominant theme in the destructive operations carried out by Lenin's followers among the workers. Oddly enough, this did not seem to worry Maklakov and Shcheglovitov at all.

It was agonizing to watch the way those in power sought to suppress every expression of patriotic feeling among the people, and to frustrate every attempt to assist the government and the Russian soldiers at the front, who were heroically fighting a well-armed foe under conditions of extreme hardship.

All individual attempts, including my own, to stop the decay were to no avail. The once-free press, now muzzled by wartime censorship and used by Goremykin as a weapon against public opinion, was unable to speak the truth. The Duma, which could and should have done so, was silent of its own accord for many months to come.

In February, 1915, a session of the Duma was held to consider the budget. It lasted only two days. During this time the Progressive Bloc remained faithful to its promise and was silent; no criticism was voiced of the ministers' activities. The consequences of this "patriotic" silence were fatal.

9

The Break with the Crown

Plots and Counterplots

THE terrible ordeal of the Russian armies during the great retreat in the spring and summer of 1915 finally roused the liberal and conservative leaders in the Duma from their apathy. It had taken a whole year of unrestrained mismanagement by reactionary ministers to make people prominent in various walks of life realize their unforgivable mistake. Finally, however, backed by public opinion throughout the country, they demanded reorganization of the government and an immediate meeting of the Duma, and they insisted that independent organizations should be allowed to participate in the work of supplying the army.

In May, on the initiative of leading Moscow industrialists and businessmen, an All-Russian Trade and Industry Convention was held, without prior notification to the government. The main business of this meeting was the establishment of a Central War Industry Committee with a number of subsections. All industry was now being mobilized for the immediate dispatch of munitions, clothing, and equipment to the front. Everyone of importance in Russia became active in the cause. The Committee included a group of "defensist" workers,[1] who, from the end of 1916 right up to the Revolution, valiantly strove to counteract the defeatist propaganda spread by the agents of Protopopov, Lenin, and Ludendorff.

The Committee worked hand in hand with two powerful public bodies—The Union of Zemstvos and the Union of Towns. It was

[1] I.e. those who supported the defense of the country against Germany, as opposed to the "defeatists."

presided over by Prince Lvov, Chairman of the Union of Zemstvos and later, first president of the Provisional Government. The Union of Cooperatives also worked with the Committee.

All of these bodies had the full support of all political parties (with the exception of the Bolsheviks and the extreme right wing), as well as the Supreme Command at the front, the Duma, and all of the genuinely patriotic ministers.

Later on, while living abroad as an émigré, Prince Lvov wrote:

There was probably no other country during the war faced with as difficult a problem as Russia. She not only had to fight an enemy infinitely superior in arms and overall fighting-fitness, she also had to form new and powerful defence organizations. These were set up in the face of government opposition and drew their support from forces whose potential had been unknown up to that time. It was native talent and inborn ability to organize, based on the initiative of the Russian people, that alone saved the situation in Russia at that time.[2]

In June the four most hated ministers in the country, Sukhomlinov, Shcheglovitov, Maklakov, and Sabler were dropped from the government, and General Polivanov, Samarin (Marshal of the Moscow Nobility), Prince Shcherbatov, and Senator Khvostov were appointed in their place. These were honest men who had the confidence of the Duma.

The first question to come up in the "new" government (still headed by that aged and cunning courtier, Goremykin) was the problem of the highly strained relations between the government and the supreme commander, Grand Duke Nicholas. The trouble was that the statute on the rights and duties of the supreme commander, approved just before the beginning of the war, invested him with unlimited power both at the front and at home, and also on all matters concerning the actual conduct of the war. This had come about because Tsar Nicholas had intended, in the event of war with Germany, to assume the function of supreme commander. It was only at the last minute that he heeded Goremykin's plea and changed his mind.

The Grand Duke Nicholas, who was very popular in both social and military circles at the time—I could never understand why—had

---

[2] *Russian Local Governments During the War and the Union of Zemstvos* (Carnegie Endowment for International Peace, Yale University Press, 1930). Papers of Prince G. E. Lvov.

been appointed in his stead. The rights with which the supreme commander was officially invested, however, were not modified.

A paradoxical situation arose. The supreme commander, although not the ruler of the country, found himself with virtually unlimited power, for he was not even responsible to the government.

At the very beginning of the war Goremykin had told the president of the Duma: "The Government will rule the home front. I am not concerned with problems of war." [3] In actual fact, therefore, there were two rulers of the country at this point.

Neither the exuberant Grand Duke Nicholas, nor his chief of staff, General Yanushkevich, understood anything about Russia's internal politics or economics. They were acting within their rights, however, when they completely ignored the government in St. Petersburg and sent instructions directly to the provincial authorities without bothering to inform the capital. The provincial officials, receiving orders from two sources, were at a loss to know whom they should obey.

During the great retreat of 1915, the High Command had caused veritable chaos within the country by forcibly evicting every Jewish member of the population from the area near the front—not hesitating to include some of the other local people as well.

On the supreme commander's staff General Danilov was the only real strategist trained for war. In fact, in his letters to the minister of war, Yanushkevich frankly admitted that he was not trained for the post he held.

Hence it can easily be seen that the situation at the front and within the country necessitated a radical change in the relationship between the High Command and the government. The new Council of Ministers was almost unanimously of the opinion that it could not possibly run the country while this abnormal division of power continued.

While tactfully evading the issue of the activity of the headquarters at the front, the majority of the ministers, both new and old, fiercely criticized the existing situation. Goremykin begged the ministers not to exacerbate the matter, since their criticism might make the Tsar assume the duties of supreme commander himself.

This is in fact what happened. Tsar Nicholas became the supreme commander and sent the popular Grand Duke Nicholas to be his viceroy in the Caucasus. Naturally, this decision was widely regarded

[3] *The Fall of the Tsarist Regime,* Vol. 7, p. 119.

as a great misfortune, heralding fresh disasters at the front. But this fear was unjustified.

All who had followed the developments at the front during the German advance in the spring and summer of 1915 knew that, despite their enormous superiority in armaments and their brilliant tactical successes, and despite even the confusion among Grand Duke Nicholas' generals, the German High Command had suffered a strategic defeat. The planned pincer movement, which was to have encircled the entire Russian army and annihilated it as a military force, had not succeeded. The Russian army had recovered from the blows inflicted on it and had taken up a position along a new defense line, where it remained until the October Revolution. Observers were aware, also, that this excellent strategy had been successful chiefly through the efforts of General Alekseyev, whom the Tsar now appointed as his chief of staff, thereby handing over the leadership of the Russian army to the best strategist in Europe. Indeed, by the autumn the position at the front had greatly improved, since the new supreme commander made a point of not interfering in General Alekseyev's operational decisions.

Nevertheless, the Tsar's decision to become supreme commander was a fatal one for Russia. He began visiting the general staff more often and staying there longer, thus neglecting the internal affairs of the country. Having become supreme commander, he made the Tsarina co-ruler with him, although he advised her to consult the ministers fairly frequently and to give them instructions, and also instructed them to keep the Tsarina informed of events in his absence. It did not take long for the effects of this strange new dual leadership to become apparent.

The Duma was called on July 19. A new majority of liberal and moderately conservative elements had gradually begun to form. By the middle of August this majority had turned into the so-called Progressive Bloc with a program consonant with my own ideas about the future of the country. The Bloc aimed at the formation of a government "enjoying the confidence of the country" and willing to govern it in accordance with the program drawn up by the Bloc, which included members of the State Council as well as the Duma.

The Bloc, led by Milyukov, Shidlovsky, and Shulgin, hoped that they would be able to persuade the Tsar, without having to demand the creation of a ministry directly responsible to the people's representatives, to appoint as chairman of the Council of Ministers a man who, although conservative, would nevertheless not be as hostile as Goremykin to the very existence of the Duma. The Tsar consented to the setting-up of "Emergency Consultative Committees" on defense, transport, fuel, and food in all ministries concerned with the conduct of the war. They were to include representatives of the majority of the Duma, the State Council, the Zemstvo and Town Unions, and the cooperatives. The fact that these committees were created on the initiative of the Duma seemed to indicate a new-found willingness on the part of the Tsar to govern the country in accordance with the wishes of the Duma.

On August 23, the Tsar, as supreme commander, went to visit his Headquarters. Three days later, on August 26, the Progressive Bloc announced its program at a meeting of the Duma. The next evening those ministers most favorably disposed toward collaborating with the Duma, Kharitonov, Prince Shcherbatov, and Khvostov, and Prince Shakhovskoy, a stooge of Rasputin's, discussed the program with the leaders of the Bloc.

This attempt to get the Tsar to collaborate with the Duma and form a ministry independent of Rasputin's influence was of paramount importance in the destiny of the Russian monarchy. That is why I think that instead of relying on my own recollection of this episode I should quote some relevant extracts from notes taken by Milyukov during the Bloc's conferences. These notes were published many years later in the *Red Archives* and their accuracy has been confirmed by Milyukov in writing.[4]

On the evening of August 27, at the request of the Council of Ministers, the four ministers Kharitonov (State Controller), Shcherbatov (Acting Minister of the Interior), Khvostov (Justice) and Shakhovskoy (Trade), had talks with the following representatives of the Progressive Bloc—Shulgin (Central Party), VI. Lvov (same), Krupensky (Nationalist), Dmitryukov (Octobrist), Shidlovsky (left-wing Octobrist and President of the Bloc), Yefremov (President of the Progressive Party), Milyukov (leader of the Cadets), Grimm (Academic group), Meller-Zakomelsky (Octobrist—the last two were also members of the State Council). . . .

The proceedings developed as follows:

Yefremov noted that the Bloc's program, apparently by mistake, had left

4 P. N. Milyukov, *Memoirs,* Vol. II (New York, Chekhov Press, 1955), p. 217.

out the section on amnesty for the five Social Democrat deputies and their reinstatement.

Milyukov confirmed that the point had been left out by mistake.

Khvostov reported that Kerensky had been to see him and had threatened that if he (Khvostov) had not settled the matter in the deputies' favor within three days, he would cause a scandal in the Duma. Together with Kerensky he went through his rough notes and examined the case more thoroughly. His impression was that the court had not made a mistake. He was nevertheless ready to appeal for a pardon and only asked Kerensky that the convicted men should issue a statement condemning "defeatism." Kerensky rejected this.

Milyukov pointed out the difficult moral position in which the minister had put the deputies by demanding in return for a pardon a statement in which they officially retracted their views. It was not possible politically. It would be tantamount to political suicide for them; and in any case, a pardon was not in fact a revision of the sentence in the light of changed circumstances but complete remission.

Krupensky gave his opinion on point five, dealing with "abolition of the restrictive laws on Jews." Although he was a born anti-Semite, he had decided that a concession should now be made for the good of the whole country. The country needed the support of its allies. There was no doubt the Jews were a major international force, and a hostile policy towards them might jeopardize Russian credit abroad. Now that Bark (Minister of Finance) had gone abroad to secure a loan, his chances of success should be made easier. Relations with America would also improve if the policy on the Jewish question were changed. He therefore renounced his former view and supported the Cadets' demands.

Shcherbatov said the Government had already begun considering abolition of the Jewish Pale, but realized from this example how difficult it would be for it to go any further.

Kharitonov stated with regard to the fourth point that Goremykin had already announced the autonomy of Poland and that abolition of restrictions of rights (concerning State posts and gentry's organizations) was possible. But what did the Bloc mean by "review" of the laws on ownership of land in Poland? The transfer of land had already been made easier. He then began reading a report given him by Krzyzanovski, the Head of the Chancellery of the Council of Ministers. At the words "formation of a united government of persons enjoying the confidence of the country" he broke off.

Milyukov drew his attention to the fact that the Bloc considered that point the fundamental one and everything else in the program was contingent upon it. Thus the question of the "agreement with the legislative bodies" related to implementation of the program and should be discussed by a government enjoying the confidence of the people.

Kharitonov considered that the point was beyond the competence of the Cabinet. The Bloc obviously meant that its opinion should be relayed to the Supreme Authority.

Yefremov and *Milyukov* confirmed that this was exactly what they thought.

This was the first and last meeting between representatives of the Progressive Bloc and members of the government. It had an unexpected outcome for the former.

On September 3, further meetings of the Duma were postponed until November. The ministers in Goremykin's cabinet, who had joined it after the summer debacle at the front, began disappearing one after the other (with the exception of Polivanov, the war minister), and with them went those of the older ministers, such as Krivoshein, who had urged the Tsar not to take over the Supreme Command.

At the beginning of October Shcherbatov was dismissed from his post as acting minister of the interior and replaced by the extreme right-wing Alexei N. Khvostov. This clever and highly ambitious young man had already been picked out by Rasputin in 1911, before Stolypin was murdered, as a possible deputy minister or even minister of the interior.

The Tsar's co-ruler, the Tsarina, was thus giving notice to the entire nation that there was to be no more vacillation in the defense of the time-honored principles of Russian autocracy.

All hopes for an agreement with the Crown were crushed—that much the leaders of the Progressive Bloc now realized. What were they to do next?

This was the question raised at the next conference on October 25, 1915. It was attended, in addition to the Bloc members, by Prince Lvov and Chelnokov, representing the Zemstvo and Town Unions, and Guchkov, representing the War Industry Committee. The conference took place just after Khvostov had been appointed minister of the interior.

In order to bring home the dramatic quality of this extremely important discussion I quote again from Milyukov's notes. First to speak was M. M. Fyodorov, a nonparty liberal.

Fyodorov: There can be no doubt of the mood of depression and it's quite natural. There was a widespread hope that the Tsar would grant an interview to a delegation from the Progressive Bloc [5] and that this would yield some result, as previous steps had done. Its failure (the request for an interview with the Tsar had been flatly refused) cannot but cause a reaction. For the majority it means the need for direct action. . . . There have been attempts to sway public opinion against the majority of the Congresses. Tatischev has been put forward for the Trade and Industry Committee. Grand Duke Michael has been told about the situation through a person close to his wife. He has spoken to the Tsar, (and says) the Tsarina, Goremykin and Rasputin are even prepared to go as far as closing the Duma. "The threat to the dynasty now comes from the Army. The Army is now the People." (To the question of whether or not he would be prepared to succeed to the throne the Grand Duke replied: "May this cup pass me by. Of course, if this were, unfortunately, to come about, I sympathize with the British system. I cannot understand why the Tsar won't take it calmly.")

Shingarev: The Tsar's refusal to receive the delegation has given the very impression I foretold in Moscow at the Zemstvo Congress. In Moscow I felt it was the last chance. The talking is over, now it's time for action . . .

Meller-Zakomelsky: It is not right to take such a facile view of the mood prevalent in Russia. It's not a mood of depression but rather of political decay. All hope is lost. The best-intentioned elements say that we must do this and that to achieve victory, and the Tsar does the opposite. Everyone concludes that there is now no point in replacing Goremykin, that what we need is revolution. We cannot allow Goremykin to make peace. So what should we do? All the public organizations have shot their bolts and there is nothing to be gained from pursuing that course any further. The battle between the Tsar and Russia will have to be waged on another plane. The Congresses of Zemstvos and Towns have already tried and failed. We must wait until the Duma is called again, and then there may be new platforms in the legislative chambers. The Congresses will be extra support for parliament. We should wait until then before deciding on future tactics.

Milyukov: There is no need to be afraid of the leftist elements. We have their respect as long as the Duma is open. We must stand firm and not give way; we must prepare our self-defense, material with which to justify ourselves. We must keep the public organizations up to scratch.

Guchkov: There is a risk in every struggle, but it need not be exaggerated in this case. We are exhausted, but we have also made a gain—the situation

[5] The Tsar refused to meet the delegation of the Progressive Bloc on the question of the reorganization of the ministry.

has been clarified. All illusions have been shattered and all agree on the diagnosis. Public opinion seems apathetic, but that is because it has reached the limit of despair. The patient is seen to be moribund. People are dead quiet because they expect an event of vital importance. With our new platform we shall find unheard-of unity both in the army at the front and here, in the rear. For my part, I would challenge the regime to open battle. Circumstances are leading us towards a conflict anyway. Inaction will be interpreted as reconciliation. Never before have we seen such a crowd of irresponsible people—a regime of favorites, conjurers and clowns. That is a new note which has to be struck. And it means the breaking off of peaceful relations with the authorities. I would be willing to wait until the end of the war if there were any guarantee of a favorable outcome. But we are being led toward complete defeat abroad and total collapse within. Our government is a defeatist one. Will mere words have any effect? They may, since the regime is withered and rotten to the core. There is no one at the top of sufficient strength or conviction to admit its weakness.

Maklakov (a leading Cadet): The congress [6] cannot confine itself to its own business. It would have to drop its own agenda and deal with matters of high-level policy. The congress must first speak on behalf of the country. The only possible platform is a showdown with the Crown. We cannot go on with the former fiction. Should we hand over the task to the Congresses rather than the Duma, which really ought to do it? Milyukov demands the former. He is an optimist and not at all nervous. Telegrams to the Tsar only aggravate the people. We cannot continue to be loyal. Perhaps the Congresses won't go that far, in which case they will be finished and you will have queered the Duma's pitch. The towns do not have sufficient authority for that. The stand taken by the leftists is to wait for capitulation. But the appeal to the Tsar was a failure. From the moment you are prepared to do it, that is, break with the Crown, I am no longer afraid of the leftists. Are we ready for this break? Should we say that we no longer need to keep the peace? To call strikes and cause unrest throughout the country is a course of action which we all fear. I am hoping for a *deus ex machina,* another March 11.[7] I understand Milyukov and Shingarev, but I think the recalled Duma should be the first to announce the clash with the Crown. Let us think it out—either the eleventh of March or a strike. *At that time* we did not think it out. Milyukov, you were certain that the Tsar would not dare refuse to see your delegation . . . I do not know whether the Duma will want to go as far as a clash with the Crown, but it will have to.

[6] I.e., of Zemstvo and Town Unions.

[7] On March 11, 1801, Paul I was assassinated by conspiring guards officers and court officials.

Shingarev: Guchkov has asked what is holding the regime together. A lot of things—inertia, groups with personal interests at stake, the state machinery and lack of courage and even understanding. It is not the job of a congress to arrange another March 11. I question our readiness for such direct action. Especially among the Zemstvo members. I would prefer the Congresses, not the Duma, to announce the break with the Crown, since the disappearance of the Duma would pulverize society . . .

Guchkov: The clash with the Crown does not need to be created but only to be put on record. Each group will find its own terms in which to express the conflict, even the right wing . . .

Not all those down on the list to speak were able to do so at that meeting and the discussion was resumed on October 28. First to take the floor that day was Count Olsufyev, a member of the State Council:

Olsufyev: At first the country showed sympathy for the Progressive Bloc, but there has been a great change since then. We took a tragic view of the transfer of the Supreme Command and were certain it would be disastrous. We were all wrong. The Tsar had more foresight. The change was for the better. The idol [8] proved to be merely an idol. Both the Bloc and the public were wrong on a fundamental issue, and we came to grief. Next, we suggested replacing ministers for the sake of the war. The most undesirable one, Goremykin, was left, and the war situation improved. The flow of refugees diminished. Moscow cannot be taken now. It is up to us to change our tactics of "armed neutrality."

Shulgin: The war situation improved because Yanushkevich was dismissed. The new Chief of Staff, Alekseyev, was after all a Duma choice.

Prince Lvov: Criticise if you like, but be fair . . . What has happened is lunatic. The Bloc was not wrong. Russia is suspended in mid-air. The replacement of the Council of Ministers and the Crown's direct intervention have set the whole country against the Crown . . .

Bobrinskoy (Duma member and Nationalist): The Government is now worse. What will happen if the Government and the Duma meet? It does not matter about Kerensky's speeches, the point is what will *we* say? On September 3, we thought that the Duma could not be called with Goremykin. What is to be done now? We cannot say it is none of our business. I cannot find any answer, and the idea of convening the Duma scares me.

Kovalevsky (Academic group): Rumor has it that Goremykin has said "they curse me up hill and down dale, but I am guided by the highest motives; when I go, peace will be concluded."

[8] Grand Duke Nicholas.

Gurko (member of the State Council and former Minister of the Interior):
It is not a question of past mistakes, but of whether or not we have attained
our goal of ensuring victory. We decided that was out of the question with
the present government. Has the situation changed? The answer can only
be no. If we continue to do nothing, then even Grishka (Rasputin) may
become prime minister.

But Grishka was a peasant with a lot of common sense. He knew
full well that it was better to be the power in Tsarskoye Selo than to be
prime minister in Petrograd and responsible to Tsarskoye Selo.

The meeting of the Bloc leaders went on. But the irony of it all was
that as they argued and debated about how to deal with Goremykin
if he were to turn up at the November session of the Duma, it had
already been decided in Tsarskoye Selo that there was not going to be
any autumn session of the Duma at all, nor any meeting of the legislative bodies until Goremykin's chair had been filled by someone ready
to carry out unreservedly the plans for a decisive battle with the people.

Plots and Conspiracies

In 1905 the spiritual bond between the Throne and the urban working class, the industrial proletariat, was severed.

On July 8, 1906, the faith of the peasantry in the Tsar as the
"bearer of the people's truth" had been destroyed by the dissolution
and dispersal of the first Duma over the question of land reforms.

Now, following the break with the modern conservative-liberal
majority in the legislative chambers, the throne became completely
isolated from the people, supported only by right-wing reactionaries
and unscrupulous careerists, who were all controlled by Rasputin.

Everyone could see that the root of the evil lay not in the government, nor in the ministers, nor in chance mistakes, but in the reluc-
tance of the Tsar himself to give up his *ideé fixe* that Russia could
only exist and be strong if governed by an autocrat. This realization
underlay all the private discussions and plans formulated within the
Progressive Bloc, and it had also penetrated to the very core of the
people and the army.

It posed for every patriot one inevitable and fateful question: Was he
for Russia or for the Tsar? The first person to speak out was Nikolai N.
Lvov, a monarchist and moderate liberal. His reply was, "For Russia."

And the same answer echoed through the country, both at the front and at home.

In 1915 a series of completely infantile plots to rid Russia of the Tsar were devised by various officers in the army. One, for example, involved the well-known fighter pilot, Captain Kostenko, who intended to nosedive his plane onto the imperial car while it was at the front, thus killing both himself and the Tsar. And there were the two officers (one was a captain in the Engineering Corps named Muravyov, later a "hero" of the civil war), who came to see me to obtain approval for a plan to ambush the Tsar while he was inspecting the front and to take him prisoner. Even General Denikin writes in his memoirs that the fall of the monarchy was regarded favorably by the soldiers, who had long felt that the cause of all their misfortunes was the *Nemka* (German woman) at Tsarskoye Selo.

In the fall of the same year, 1915, I was visited by an old friend, Count Paul Tolstoy, the son of one of the Tsar's equerries. He was a close friend of the Tsar's brother, Grand Duke Michael, whom he had known since childhood. He told me that he had come at the request of the Grand Duke, who knew that I had connections with the working-class and left-wing parties and who wanted to know how the workers would react if he took over from his brother, the Tsar.

These incidents were symptomatic of the profound change in thinking that was in progress in the country. The people had been driven beyond endurance. Moreover, an ever-growing number of people felt that all of Russia's troubles stemmed from Rasputin and that the government's policy would change if he could be eliminated. Even A. N. Khvostov, who was a militant leader of the Union of Russian People in the Duma, had evolved a plan for Rasputin's murder.[9]

It was finally the Tsar's favorite cousin, Grand Duke Dimitri, who, together with Prince Yusupov and Purishkevich, a right-wing Duma member, took it upon himself to try to save the dynasty and the monarchy by killing Rasputin.

I have mentioned all this in order to give the reader a better under-

[9] The plan fell through. A man called Beletsky, the deputy minister and chief of police, deliberately gave the game away. Khvostov was dismissed and on returning to the Duma as a deputy described the plot in detail; he said he had planned to do away with Rasputin not only because of the latter's influence at Tsarskoye Selo, but also because he was in constant contact with German agents, which he, Khvostov, had found out for certain in his capacity as minister of the interior.

standing of the mood prevailing in Russia at that time and of the mental agony that people went through before embarking on the sort of course taken by the Progressive Bloc.

In restrospect, I can firmly refute those who say that the opposition to the throne by the leaders of the Progressive Bloc was motivated by self-seeking and ambitious aims which led to Russia's collapse. It is necessary only to recall the backgrounds of most of the deputies in the third and fourth Dumas. They were people closely associated by tradition, social status, and personal interests with the regime and the government, and they were loyal subjects of the Tsar. In the fourth Duma this majority was conscious of a great sense of tragedy because it was forced to abandon its traditional concept of the monarchy and its place in Russia. It had all been considered and thought out; after all, it was no longer a handful, but the majority in the Duma who now asked themselves the same question asked of Lvov—"For the Tsar or for Russia?" And their answer was, "For Russia."

At the end of 1915 I became gravely ill and had to spend several months in a sanatorium in Finland, where I underwent a serious operation. As a result, seven months passed before I was able to return to Petrograd. I did not remain long in the capital, however, since almost immediately I had to go to Turkestan to investigate the first major native uprising. This mutiny had been sparked by Stürmer's absurd order for the conscription of 200,000 natives to dig trenches at the front. The Muslim population was not even subject to military conscription, much less to forced labor. Furthermore, the directive was put into effect just at the time when the cotton picking was at its peak. Worst of all, the junior administrative officials abused their authority in return for bribes, by exempting the sons of the wealthier beys. German and Turkish agents, whose center of activity was Bukhara, took full advantage of the resentment of the local populace to foment trouble.

I returned to Petrograd during the third week in September. A new minister of the interior had just been appointed, and the choice had fallen on Alexander Protopopov, former vice-president of the Duma. In the course of a few months this man, who was in fact the last minister of the interior of the Russian Empire, managed to incur the wrath and hatred of the whole nation.

Shortly after my return the leaders of the Progressive Bloc held a secret meeting at which they agreed on a plan to depose the reigning monarch by a palace revolution and to replace him by Alexis, the twelve-year-old heir apparent, with Grand Duke Michael as regent.

The story of this little-known conspiracy has been told in the memoirs of its ringleader, Alexander Guchkov, which were published soon after his death in 1936.[10] I knew about the plan from the very start, and I would say that Guchkov's account is somewhat watered down. During the month of September he was invited to a secret meeting of some of the Progressive Bloc leaders at the apartment of a prominent nonparty liberal, Michael Fyodorov. Among the people present were Rodzyanko, Nekrasov and Milyukov. The purpose of the meeting was to discuss what action to take now that it was clear that Russia was on the brink of a nationwide uprising. They all agreed that the Progressive Bloc must act at once to stop the revolution from below. The most interesting comments were made by Milyukov, who considered it the Bloc's duty not to take part in an uprising, but to await its results. He foresaw two possible results: either the supreme authority would come to its senses in time and ask the Bloc to form a government; or the revolution would be victorious, and the victors, being unskilled in governing, would ask the Bloc to form a government on its behalf. In support of his argument he cited the French Revolution of 1848.

In reply to this rather academic thesis, Guchkov said that he did not think that the people who accomplished a revolution would then hand over power to someone else. In his opinion, a revolutionary could not possibly think along those lines. With that in mind, the Bloc had to make the first move by replacing the present ruler themselves. According to Guchkov, the meeting ended at this point. Milyukov adds that from this meeting it became clear that Guchkov intended to organize a coup d'état and that for this reason the leaders of the Progressive Bloc began arguing among themselves about who should be in the new government. Many of those earmarked for posts in a revolutionary government under a regent subsequently found their way into the Provisional Government.

Guchkov goes on to say in his memoirs that he then began to suffer

---

[10] *Poslednie Novosti* (September 9 and 13, 1936, Paris). The others were: Shidlovsky, Shingarev, Godnev, Lvov (the brother of N. Lvov), and Tereshchenko.

from heart trouble and was forced to take to his bed. During his illness, Nekrasov, the Duma vice-president, came to see him and asked if he was really plotting a coup d'état. Guchkov replied that he had been considering the idea, and there and then they decided to form a "cell" in which they included Tereshchenko, then vice-chairman of the Central War Industry Committee, and also Prince Vyazemsky. Guchkov shouldered entire responsibility for devising and executing the plan so that the other Bloc leaders who had been present at the meeting, especially Rodzyanko, should not be implicated. According to my own information, however, the decision to put the coup into effect was not made by Guchkov alone, but in concert with the other Bloc leaders.

In the meantime another plot was afoot, which was scheduled to take place at the Tsar's headquarters on November 15–16. It was a private arrangement between Prince Lvov and General Alekseyev. They had made up their minds that the Tsarina's hold on the Tsar must be broken in order to end the pressure being exerted on him, through her, by the Rasputin clique. At the appointed hour Alekseyev and Lvov hoped to persuade the Tsar to send the Empress away to the Crimea or to England.

I think this would have been the best solution to the problem, since all those who had observed the Tsar at headquarters noticed that he was much more relaxed and sensible when the Empress was not nearby. Had the plan worked, and had the Tsar remained at the headquarters under the good influence of General Alekseyev, he might have become a completely different person. Unfortunately, Alekseyev fell ill during the first two weeks in November and was sent to the Crimea to convalesce. He did not return until a few days before the monarchy was overthrown. I was told this story by a friend of mine, V. Vyrubov, a relative and close collaborator of Lvov's, who went to see Alekseyev at the beginning of November to learn the date fixed for the operation. General Alekseyev, who also knew him very well, was a cautious man, as I was later to find for myself. Without saying a word he got up from his desk, walked over to the calendar on the wall, and began tearing off the days until he arrived at November 16. But by that day he was convalescing in the Crimea. During his convalescence he was visited by some of the members of the Guchkov conspiracy who were anxious for his consent to the coup, but he absolutely refused to give it. Naturally, the preparations for the coup were known only to those directly involved; after all, the guiding principle in any conspiracy is that no conspirator should know more than his own part in the plan. The Progressive Bloc leaders knew only that the plan was underway, and made their own preparations accordingly. We leaders of the Masonic organization also knew about it, although we did not know all the details, and we, too, made preparations for the decisive moment. These preparations were concluded with the setting up of an information office of the left-wing parties for the purpose of preparing the people to receive the results of the coup d'état, step by step, and to encourage them to give it their support, or in any event to take no action against it.

To gain a better understanding of the atmosphere of the final session of the Duma, which lasted from November 1, 1916 to February 26, 1917, it must be realized that the expectation of a palace revolution was uppermost in everyone's mind. Rank-and-file members of the political parties, of course, had no precise knowledge of the coming coup, but there were veiled allusions to it in the speeches of those who did know of it and who could see where the policy of the Tsar's cabinet, in which Protopopov played no mean part, was leading the country.

At the beginning of January, 1917, A. M. Krymov, the well-known general who commanded the Third Cavalry on the southwest front, arrived in Petrograd with a group of his officers. Rodzyanko made arrangements for them to present a report at his apartment, and the leaders of the Progressive Bloc were invited to be present.

At the gathering General Krymov urged the Duma on behalf of the army to carry out a coup d'état without delay, asserting that otherwise there was no chance of winning the war. It was a blunt and very convincing statement. All those present endorsed Krymov's point of view, and some of them began speaking of the reigning monarch in such terms that Rodzyanko had to ask them not to use such language in the house of the Duma president.

The actual execution of the planned coup d'état kept being put off, since it was a really difficult task in the form in which it had been planned. First of all, the ringleaders wanted to have as few people in it as possible—and only officers, so as not to implicate any ordinary soldiers. Secondly, they had decided that it could not be carried out at headquarters, let alone in Tsarskoye Selo, since this might involve bloodshed. The idea of the conspirators was to stop the Tsar's train somewhere between headquarters and Petrograd, in an area where the railroad line was guarded by Life Guard Cavalry units, whose officers would then board the Tsar's private coach and demand his abdication. In his memoirs Guchkov wrote that the conspirators had had no intention of using physical force, or of killing the Tsar. "We were not going to carry out a coup," he wrote, "in which a brother and a son would have had to step over the body of a brother and father." Preparations were now nearing an end, though at an agonizingly slow pace. The coup was fixed for the middle of March. But the end came in a completely different way on February 27.

On May 4, at a private meeting of the Duma members, Maklakov sharply attacked the Provisional Government as follows:

Gentlemen, I want to tell you the whole truth. No, we did not want a revolution in wartime. We were afraid that it was beyond the capability of any nation to change both the state system and the social system linked to it, to cause an upheaval and still end the war successfully. But there came a moment when it was clear to all that it was impossible to bring the war to a victorious end under the old system. And for those who believed a revolution would be disastrous, it was a duty and a mission to save Russia from revolution by a coup d'état from above. That was the mission which faced us and which we did not carry out. And if posterity curses the revolution, it will also curse those who did not see in time the means by which it could have been prevented.[11]

On August 2, Guchkov reaffirmed what Maklakov had said, without admitting the leading part he had played in the plot to depose the Tsar. He told the Special Investigating Committee:

The course of action required was a coup d'état. The fault, if one can speak of the historical fault of Russian society, lies in the fact that this society, represented by its leading circles, was not sufficiently aware of the need for the coup and did not undertake it, thereby leaving it to blind, spontaneous forces to carry out this painful operation.[12]

[11] The newspaper *Rech,* May 5, 1917.
[12] *Padenie Tsarskoyo rezhima,* ed. by Shchegolev (Moscow, 1926).

10

The Reign of Folly in the Palace

ON November 1, 1906 Nicholas II wrote in his diary: "... we met the man of God Gregory from the Province of Tobolsk. ..." That year marked the beginning of Gregory Rasputin's ascendancy at the imperial court and of the fateful path that inexorably led the Tsar and his family to the basement of the Yepatyev house in Ekaterinburg to be killed by the bullets of the Cheka.

It is not easy to comprehend the astounding power held by the illiterate peasant from the remote Siberian village of Pokrovskoye. Rasputin's leap from the personal chronicles of the imperial family into the arena of Russian history was one of those historical absurdities, a case of an intimate family drama moving into the limelight of world politics. This only supports my belief that history is not ruled by "objective" laws, and that man's personality is instrumental in determining its course.

The future emperor Nicholas II met and fell in love with Alice of Hesse-Darmstadt at Windsor Castle. Queen Victoria was not displeased with the budding romance between her favorite granddaughter and the young heir apparent. Aware that hemophilia was hereditary in the house of Hesse, Tsar Alexander III was opposed to any marital plans, but he finally had to give in. Princess Alice knew scarcely anything about Russia, which she had visited only once before, when she spent a few weeks with her sister, the wife of Grand Duke Sergey Aleksandrovich.[1] She had no time to prepare for her august duties. Her betrothal to the heir apparent was announced in April, 1894, and the marriage was celebrated in November of that same year, shortly after the death of Alexander III.

[1] Governor general of Moscow and youngest brother of Alexander III.

Princess Alice had been brought up at Windsor Castle, but in every other respect she was a typical English girl of the Victorian era. No one could have foreseen the gloomy and fanatically orthodox future Tsarina in the radiant princess, the "Sunshine of Windsor," as Nicholas II fondly called her. But the seeds of disaster were hidden in this lovely princess: She had inherited her mother's mysticism along with the capacity to transmit hemophilia to a male heir. At first, providence seemed kind to her in denying her a son. The birth of four daughters impaired her health, but she had so far failed to provide a successor to the throne. Her longing for an heir made the Tsarina seek the aid of charlatans, adventurers, and "miracle workers." At the time, Europe abounded in them, and several tried their luck in Russia. Dr. Encausse, a Frenchman known as Papus, was the first to appear at the Russian court. He was introduced to Nicholas II in 1901 by the Grand Duke Nicholas in Paris. Subsequently, Papus visited Russia in 1901, 1905, and 1906, and he remained a lifelong friend of the imperial family. As the president of the Supreme Council of the Martinist Order he founded a Masonic lodge in St. Petersburg of which the Tsar was rumored to be the "Superior Stranger." The lodge counted among its members many of the most prominent men of the capital. Papus held séances at which he used to summon the spirit of Alexander III for conversations with his son Nicholas II. The Tsar's unswerving loyalty to his alliance with France, which he was unwilling to sever despite outside pressure, was frequently attributed to his ties with the Martinist Order. [2] Papus was the predecessor and spiritual father of Philippe Vachod, another "miracle worker," who was quite a remarkable man. A native of Lyon, he was introduced to the imperial couple in Compiègne during their visit to France, and such was his hold on the Tsarina that in 1916 she wrote to her husband about him as "one of the two friends sent to us by God," the second being, of course, Gregory Rasputin. Philippe Vachod enjoyed great prestige and had a large following in France. The Tsarina followed all his instructions religiously, but still there was no heir. Finally, the Frenchman had to leave Russia. Bishop Theophanes, the confessor of the Tsarina, had denounced him as possessing "the evil spirit."

[2] Cf. Dr. Philippe Encausse, *Sciences occultes* (*Papus, sa vie, son oeuvre;* Éditions Ocia, Paris, 1949), p. 283.

At long last, on July 30, 1904, after ten years of marriage, a son was born to the Tsarina. His birth caused a transformation in Alexandra Fyodorovna. Hitherto, she had confined her interests mainly to the family circle. In the alien and hostile court atmosphere she had lived in constant dread of acts of terrorism against the Tsar. Sickly, painfully shy and ill at ease at public functions, the Tsarina had made only rare appearances in St. Petersburg society and had seen few people outside a small group of mystically inclined friends. After the birth of the heir apparent, however, she began to turn her attention to affairs of state, since the autocracy now stood not only for her husband's power but also for her son's future. Alexis was to be a true autocrat. In her exalted mind orthodoxy and absolutism were inseparable. She believed in a mystical union between the Crown and the people and dreaded the very idea of any limitation to the power of autocracy. In this she was encouraged by both Philippe Vachod and Rasputin. As she wrote in a letter to the Emperor: [3] ". . . Monsieur Philippe himself said that granting a constitution would be your loss and Russia's." She urged the Tsar to be a true autocrat, reminding him that "they must learn to tremble before you, remember Monsieur Philippe and Gregory say the same thing, too . . ." Monsieur Philippe's name also appears in a letter written in 1915 when the Emperor assumed the supreme command of the army under pressure from her: ". . . our first friend [4] gave me that image with the bell to warn me against those who are not right, and it will keep them from approaching. I shall feel it and thus guard you from them." And further: ". . . be another Peter the Great, show them your power . . . it is essential that the ministers should fear you."

But over the throne there lay the shadow of death. The Tsarina's son Alexis was a hemophiliac, and the boy's illness was incurable. Alexandra Fyodorovna was not a woman to yield without struggle, however. She was convinced that faith could move mountains. She was obsessed with the idea of finding a holy man to pray for herself and her son. And now, from the very depths of the people, from amongst the lowest of the low, appeared Gregory Rasputin.

The life of this amazing man is well known, and I shall confine myself to recalling the main facts.

[3] December 14, 1916.
[4] I.e., Philippe.

In his youth Rasputin, an illiterate peasant, excelled in debauchery,[5] drunkenness, and rowdy behavior. He was a ne'er-do-well, and, like his father, who trafficked in stolen horses, he was not adverse to thieving. Like many Siberian peasants, Gregory occasionally worked as a coachman, making trips to the farthest corners of the Province of Tobolsk. As the story goes, he once had to take a priest to a remote monastery, and along the way they fell into conversation. The priest must have touched some hitherto silent chord in the heart of the village rowdy. Quite unexpectedly Rasputin was seized by repentance. He now directed the full force of his violent nature to prayer, fasting, and church-going. Leaving his home and family, he set out on foot across the wide open spaces of Russia, wandering from monastery to monastery. He became a wandering preacher of a type that was common in Russia. Soon, he found himself surrounded by women disciples whom he called his "balm bearers." His ideas about sin and repentance were an inextricable mixture of religious frenzy and eroticism.

Before long, stories about Rasputin—strange tales of depravity and orgies, holiness, and divine inspiration—spread all over Russia and quickly reached St. Petersburg. In the hectic year of 1905 Rasputin was already in the capital. His star was rising rapidly. He was a welcome guest of church dignitaries and a darling of society, where mysticism, along with spiritualist sessions, had become very fashionable. Women were the mainstay of his influence and success.

Gregory could pass from the most depraved orgies to the highest religious ecstasy. Endowed with a keen mind, remarkable intuition, and inexplicable magnetism, he also knew what role to cast himself in. Eventually he gained access to Bishop Theophanes, rector of the St. Petersburg Theological Academy and confessor to the Tsarina, a monk of holy life and a true ascetic. He was easily swayed by Rasputin's "gift for Prayer," the contagious fervor of his faith, and the innate wisdom of his hazy interpretation of the Gospel. The blessing of the highly respected bishop firmly sealed Rasputin's reputation as a saint and prophet.

Rasputin also profited greatly from the patronage of the two daughters of the king of Montenegro, "the Montenegrins" as they were called. Militsa was married to Grand Duke Peter Nikolaevich and Anastasia to his brother, Grand Duke Nicholas Nikolaevich. Anastasia

---

[5] Hence his nickname, which means "the licentious one" in Russian.

was an ardent believer in spiritualism and mysticism. At the time, the sisters, who were generally ostracized by high society, were friendly with Tsarina Alexandra. Through the Grand Duke Nicholas Nikolaevich they introduced Rasputin to the imperial couple. It did not take Bishop Theophanes long to realize that Rasputin was neither a saint nor a "holy devil," as he was affectionately called in the capital, but simply a devil. However, by then even the good bishop was unable to curb Rasputin's power. Instead, it was Bishop Theophanes who had to leave the capital and go to the Crimea.

When Rasputin gradually edged the Montenegrin princesses out of the Tsarina's intimate circle, Grand Duke Nicholas turned against him. In 1914, when the Grand Duke was appointed supreme commander, he received a wire with a request to let Rasputin visit him. His reply was brief: "Welcome. Will hang him."

In the palace Rasputin was thought to be a saint and a healer endowed with supernatural power. Credible witnesses like the Tsar's devoted valet Chemodurov and D. Derevenko, the family physician, told me that on several occasions Rasputin stopped the bleeding of the sick boy. They noticed, however, that Rasputin always seemed to arrive at the bedside of the child just before the crisis was over, when the bleeding would have stopped anyway. But it was from the faithful old lady-in-waiting Elizabeth Alekseyevna Naryshkina ("Zizi") that I learned the most revealing facts. She had known and loved the Tsar, whom she always called "Niki," from his birth. She attributed a great deal of his insecure and shifty nature to the environment of his formative years and to the heavy hand of his stern father. Alexander III, she told me, had crushed the will of his sensitive eldest son, making him insincere, secretive, and even treacherous. But it was the Tsarina whom she blamed most of all—though not on account of the fact, so commonly held against her during the war, that she was a German by origin. Mme. Naryshkina approached the royal tragedy quite differently, looking at it from an intimate, family point of view. She utterly rejected the idea taken for granted by most people—even by those quite close to the throne—that the Tsarina was devoted only to the interests of Nicholas II. To Naryshkina, it seemed that "Niki" and his daughters were one group, from which Alexandra Fyodorovna and her son remained aloof. "It's all because of him"—meaning the Tsarevich—she said to me with a curious sort of irritation. She also hinted that the Dowager Tsarina, who was intimately acquainted with the life of the imperial couple, regarded her daughter-in-law as the source of all their troubles. It became clear to me that the origin of the Tsarina's mental affliction and the tragedy not only of the Tsar but of the whole Empire was somehow linked with the birth of the heir. The true story of the Tsarina's private life has not come to light and probably never will. But unless we assume that some personal, intimate circumstances so affected Alexandra Fyodorovna as to change her completely, there is no way of explaining the morbid drama that went on in Tsarskoye Selo during those years. Her friend and confidante, Anna Vyrubova, knew the whole story, but she chose to disclose nothing in her fictionalized memoirs. After the murder of the royal family, the Tsar's head valet Chemodurov let slip some ominous words about "punishment for a terrible sin."

Rasputin fitted perfectly into the Tsarina's image of Russia. He was the embodiment of the "sacred union" between the Crown and the peasants, and hence was an instrument of Providence. Reports about Rasputin's loose morals were simply dismissed as calumny. The Tsarevich's nurse Vishnyakova was seduced by Rasputin. When the burden of the secret became too heavy to carry, she confessed the misdeed to the Tsarina, but such was Rasputin's standing that Alexandra Fyodorovna took it as an attempt to slander the holy man. Sophie Ivanovna Tyutcheva, a lady-in-waiting and member of the inner court circle, by family tradition was charged with the upbringing of the royal princesses. She found Rasputin's habit of entering the private apartments of her charges unannounced at any time of day and night most objectionable. But the Tsarina was equally deaf to Mme. Tyutcheva's indignation, and the lady-in-waiting had to resign. In the end, the Tsar intervened, and Rasputin was asked to refrain from surprise visits to the young princesses.

It is unlikely that the Tsar disbelieved the reports on Rasputin's activities outside the palace walls, particularly when they came from such loyal and trustworthy servants of the Crown as Kokovtsev, his prime minister; Rodzyanko, president of the Duma; Samarin, chief procurator of the Holy Synod; and General Dzhunkovksy, undersecretary of the interior and chief of police, who was, moreover, the Tsar's personal friend.

By the outbreak of the war, to which he was fiercely opposed, Rasputin had quite a following at Tsarskoye Selo, and the group around him met frequently at what was known as "the little house" of Anna Vyrubova. The Tsarina's blind faith in Rasputin led her to seek his counsel not only in personal matters but also on questions of state policy. General Alekseyev, held in high esteem by Nicholas II, tried to talk to the Tsarina about Rasputin, but only succeeded in making an implacable enemy of her. General Alekseyev told me later about his profound concern on learning that a secret map of military operations had found its way into the Tsarina's hands. But like many others, he was powerless to take any action. Alexandra Fyodorovna staunchly believed that no minister ought to be allowed to disobey Rasputin. We read in one of her letters: ". . . I don't like the choice of the Minister of War [General Polivanov]. . . . He is our Friend's enemy, and that brings bad luck . . ." Rasputin's advice was accepted even in strategic matters: "I shall anxiously follow your journey [along the front] . . . remember what *he* said about Riga . . ." And again: "Our Friend, whom we [the Empress and Anna Vyrubova] saw yesterday . . . was afraid that if we had not a big army to pass through Roumania we might be caught in a trap from behind . . ." A little later she wrote: ". . . Sweet Angel, I long to ask heaps about your plans concerning Roumania, our Friend is so anxious to know . . ."

Rasputin's house was watched and guarded from outside by the secret police, and huge sums were spent by successive ministers of the interior to have a reliable informant inside the "Man of God's" abode. The Extraordinary Commission of Inquiry which I set up on behalf of the Provisional Government revealed a truly monstrous picture of the activities of Rasputin and his camarilla. The Tsarina and Vyrubova were also surrounded by the most unconscionable courtiers and the most unscrupulous ministers, as well as by common charlatans. Many of the latter were connected with the German secret service, which surrounded Rasputin with a ring of informants and "advisers."

There can be no doubt that Rasputin was the pivot around which revolved the work, not only of the pro-Germans, but also of outright German agents. The evidence is overwhelming. Khvostov, who was appointed minister of the interior during the war on Rasputin's advice made his decision to kill Rasputin after he learned the contents of the secret files of his ministry.

Khvostov told me later that he had found out with absolute certainty that the Germans were receiving the most secret General Headquarters information through Rasputin, and that it was quite impossible to keep him away from the palace. Rasputin was a godsend for any intelligence service; the German Government would have been mad not to exploit him. He had three invaluable qualities: He was against the war and mixed with people who shared his views; he was not fussy as to his choice of friends, particularly if they could find him women to his taste; and finally, he was inordinately fond of boasting about his complete hold over "papa and mama," as he called his imperial sponsors, and would brook no expression of doubt from anyone as to his position at Court. Thus, with a little skill, Rasputin could be made to absorb the necessary information, which would then be squeezed from him like water from a sponge.

The High Command also had good reason to suspect Alexandra Fyodorovna's despicable entourage. For this reason there was always a great deal of uneasiness at Headquarters when the Tsarina came to visit her husband. An experiment initiated by Minister of the Navy Admiral Grigorovich showed beyond any doubt how well-founded these misgivings were.

The Admiral was devoted to the Tsar, but he was so beset by doubts and suspicions that he could stand it no longer and decided that his patriotic duty made it incumbent upon him to check the rumors about the infiltration of Tsarskoye Selo by German spies. In reply to persistent questions from Tsarskoye Selo about the date of a certain naval operation, he supplied them with fictitious information about the sailing orders of some Russian cruisers. Sure enough, a German naval squadron appeared at the exact hour and at the very spot where he had said the Russian cruisers would be.

Gradually, all state business was taken over by the Tsarina, who held almost daily consultations with Rasputin and Anna Vyrubova. At the same time, it was rumored that Rasputin was pressing the Tsarina to oust the Tsar altogether and proclaim herself as the regent of the Empire. Clearly, the Tsar was beginning to be a nuisance, a dangerous obstacle to the plans of the Rasputin clique. It was essential for Rasputin to keep the Tsar well under his control and supervision. In this he was helped by his friend, the Tibetan wizard Badmayev. The most influential person in the Rasputin clique, the Tibetan doctor treated his patients with herbs, roots, and balms; he claimed to know the ancient healing secrets of the land of the Dalai Lama, and he had many patients in Petrograd, whose faith in him was implicit. In a moment of indiscretion Rasputin told Yusupov that some of Badmayev's herbs and roots could "cause mental paralysis and either stop or aggravate hemorrhage." What more suggestive example could there be of the effect of Badmayev's treatment than the Tsar with his wandering eyes and helpless smile? At about this time the Tsarina repeatedly reminded the Tsar in her letters to take "the drops prescribed by Badmayev."

But what was the attitude of the Tsar to all this? What was his part in the unfolding drama? It is usually assumed that the Tsar was as convinced of the holiness and wisdom of the "Friend," as was the Tsarina. It is true that the imperial couple shared a dislike of people of their own circle and preferred "simple people." To get close to the people outside the intelligentsia, professional politicians, and statesmen was a dream cherished by Nicholas II, and one which he was fond of discussing with his mother, Dowager Tsarina Marya Fyodorovna.

It was Rasputin's master stroke that he had come to the Imperial Palace in the garb of a *muzhik* and that he behaved accordingly. Endowed with an almost uncanny intuition, the "holy devil" was quick to understand the imperial couple. He never flattered them. In his cunning he never gave up his sleeveless coat, belted shirt, greased boots, and unkempt beard, knowing their great appeal for the imperial family. The Tsar and Tsarina saw the true people of Russia speaking to them through one of her illiterate sons. Rasputin had no political program. He simply advocated the mystical belief in the Tsar as a person anointed by God. He persuaded the imperial couple that through him they were dealing with the Russian people at large, whereas the peasant representatives in the Duma were fakes and puppets of the gentry. In fact, however, the further away Russia moved from the Tsar's dream of an autocratic, orthodox, Muscovite Tsardom, the greater and more profound became the breach between the monarch and the nation. Finally, the coexistence of Russia and Nicholas II became quite impossible, as the Tsar persisted in using the power of the Crown to destroy the living body of the Empire for the sake of his absurd fantasy. The Tsar firmly believed that he had to remain true to the oath he had given Alexander III on his deathbed, "to bear loyally the burden of absolute monarchy."

There was a striking difference between the Tsar and the Tsarina in their attitude toward power. Alexandra Fyodorovna was ambitious and fully conscious of her right to rule. Nicholas II bore the burden of power with resignation. He always remembered that he was "born on the feast day of the long-suffering Job." Kokovtsev, who knew the Emperor intimately, claimed that Nicholas II would have been an excellent constitutional monarch by nature. But owing to his obstinacy he persisted in behaving like an autocrat, even after he had granted Russia a constitution. Perhaps the very reason for his impassiveness when he was at last forced to abdicate lies in the fact that he considered it a divine release from the burden of power, which he could not throw off voluntarily because he was bound by his oath as "the Lord's anointed." He found the daily routine of a monarch intolerably boring. And he had no desire to fight for his lost power. This I am qualified to assert, because the imperial family was in my custody after the fall of the monarchy and I had an opportunity to observe the behavior of both Alexandra Fyodorovna and Nicholas II.

Although Nicholas II must have been fully aware of Rasputin's antics, he did not realize that outside the palace they had a damaging effect on the Crown that was far more serious than any revolutionary propaganda, and that the very groups that had been the pillars of the monarchy for centuries were profoundly shocked and alienated. But the Tsar had no way of removing Rasputin from the bedside of the sick Tsarevich. The source of Rasputin's influence lay in the intimate relations between the Tsar and the Tsarina. For reasons which I am not free to disclose, the Tsar felt that he had to give in to Alexandra Fyodorovna with regard to the heir apparent. Even if the Tsar had had the good sense to want to entrust the life of the child to the care of competent doctors, the Empress, with her faith in Rasputin's healing power, would still have had her way.

Needless to say, Rasputin's residence in the palace and his general behavior were too good a story to be overlooked by the public. Rumors spread like wildfire, and the press began to take notice. The imperial couple were not pleased by this interest in their private affairs. Meanwhile, Rasputin's sphere of influence grew ever larger. Bearers of illiterate notes scribbled in pencil by Rasputin turned up to ask for

favors at various official places. Rasputin's orgies and drunken es-
capades could not be hushed up. Despite the Tsarina's efforts to keep
Rasputin's name out of the public eye, scandals in the church administration involving him were given wide publicity. His name recurred
in the deliberations of the Duma. Rasputin approached ministers and
top-ranking officials with increasing arrogance and insolence. Infuriated at the slightest display of disrespect, he terrorized the Tsarina
by threatening to return to his native village.

Kokovtsev, who took over the post of premier after Stolypin's death,
was forced to resign on account of Rasputin. In his memoirs, in which
he defends the Tsar, he tells of the "reign of folly" at the imperial
palace and of its tragic consequences. Early in his premiership Kokovtsev enjoyed the favor of the Tsarina because she considered him quite
incapable of any independent action. But like most responsible civil
servants, he could not tolerate Rasputin's presence in the palace and
his growing power. In February, 1912, when Rasputin's position at
court became the subject of heated discussions in the third Duma,
Kokovtsev received an invitation from the Dowager Tsarina. "The
talk, which took place on the 13th of February and lasted an hour and
a half, was devoted exclusively to the subject of Rasputin," he wrote
in his memoirs. "I answered all the questions raised by the old Tsarina
and told her frankly all I knew, without concealing anything and without making any attempt to minimize the dangers of the situation which
had exposed the private life of the imperial family to the public gaze
and had made its most intimate details the subject of merciless slander
and idle gossip for people in every walk of life. The Tsarina wept bitterly and promised to speak to her son, but she added: 'My unhappy
daughter-in-law cannot understand that she is bringing ruin upon herself and the dynasty. She has deep faith in the holiness of this shady
character, and the rest of us are powerless to forestall the disaster.' "
Her words proved to be prophetic. The Dowager Tsarina implored
Kokovtsev to tell the Tsar the truth. In April, with evidence in hand,
Kokovtsev reported to Nicholas II. The Tsar made no comment.
Here is what Kokovtsev writes about the outcome of that audience:
". . . Everything changed suddenly after Rasputin's visit to me on the
15th of April, 1912,[6] and my subsequent report to the Tsar. From
that moment my dismissal became inevitable. His Majesty remained

6 Evidently Kokovtsev refers to an attempt by Rasputin to win his sympathy.

outwardly gracious for two years longer, but the Tsarina changed toward me almost from the very day that I reported Rasputin's visit to the Tsar . . . My disapproval of the former's presence in the palace was the deciding factor."

On January 29, 1914, Kokovtsev was created a count and was suddenly dismissed without any apparent reason. Dowager Tsarina Marya Fyodorovna, who was much perturbed by his dismissal, had a talk with Kokovtsev immediately afterward. "On hearing my explanation," says Kokovtsev in his memoirs, ". . . the Tsarina was silent for a long time, then began to weep and said to me: 'I know you are an honest man and wish my son no evil. You will understand, therefore, how much I fear for the future, what dark forebodings I have. My daughter-in-law dislikes me and always thinks that I am jealously guarding my prerogatives. She can't understand that my only thought is for my son's happiness and that I can see we are heading straight for disaster while the Tsar lends an ear only to flatterers. Now that you are free, why should you not dare to tell the Tsar all you think and warn him before it is too late?' "

Kokovtsev's dismissal was a personal triumph for Rasputin, since there were no reasons, apart from Rasputin's opposition to him, for the dismissal of this dedicated civil servant who had always loyally supported the Duma.

The Duma took an irreconcilable stand against Rasputin, and quite naturally, therefore, the Tsarina and her coterie did their best to undermine the prestige of the Duma.

There is no doubt that the pathological absurdity of the Rasputin affair would not ordinarily have provided any impediment to Russia's rapid economic and political development, but the country could ill afford it in wartime.

I have already said that Rasputin was fiercely opposed to the war. But in the crucial days of July, 1914, Rasputin was not at the side of his imperial patrons.

My friend Sukhanov, a member of the Duma from the Province of Tobolsk (Rasputin's home province), showed me a copy of a telegram which Rasputin had sent by direct wire to the Tsar: "Don't declare war," it read, "dismiss Nikolashka . . . if you declare war . . . evil will befall you and the Tsarevich." During the investigation of the murder of the imperial family conducted in 1918, Rasputin's daughter Matryona testified to the same effect:

My father was fiercely opposed to war with Germany. When the war broke out he was lying wounded [7] in Tyumen. His Majesty sent him many telegrams asking for counsel . . . Father strongly advised him to "stand firm" and not to declare war. I was by his side at that time and saw both the Tsar's telegrams and my father's replies. He was so upset by this business that his wound began bleeding again.

We are taken a step further by the testimony of the police official who kept watch over Rasputin: "I had occasion to hear him say in about the middle of 1916: 'If only that hussy hadn't poked me with a knife there would never have been any war at all, I should not have permitted it.' He also declared openly that it was time to put an end to the war: 'I should think enough blood has been shed, the Germans are no longer a danger, they are weak now.' His idea was that we should conclude peace with Germany."

The Tsar himself was torn by indecision in the crucial days before the declaration of the war, and he spared no effort to prevent what seemed inevitable. In one respect he remained above reproach: This tragic man loved his country with boundless devotion, and he did not try to purchase a reprieve by surrendering to the Kaiser. Had Nicholas II been concerned with his own well-being rather than with the dignity and honor of Russia, he could have come to terms with the Kaiser. In 1915, a year of particular hardship for Russia, the Tsar was approached by Germany with favorable peace terms which would have given him the much-disputed Dardanelles and the highly desirable Bosporus. But the Russian Tsar did not even deign to answer.

It seems to me that the Tsarina made an honest effort to love Russia, but it was a Russia of her own imagination, in which her son was to reign as an autocrat. For the sake of her myth she bitterly opposed the real Russia.

There is much evidence that by the fall of November, 1916, the Tsar had grown weary of Rasputin and his protegés. Rasputin's behavior was increasingly insolent, and on various occasions he openly flouted the Tsar's wishes. It did not require a profound knowledge of the Tsar to see that he no longer trusted Rasputin.

[7] He had been stabbed by a certain Guseva.

In December, 1916, ten years after his first meeting with the imperial couple, Rasputin was killed by a group of conspirators consisting of Grand Duke Dmitri Pavlovich, Prince Felix Yusupov,[8] and Purishkevich, a reactionary Duma deputy. But the deed came too late. Nothing was essentially changed in the palace, because the Tsar himself was the central figure in the drama now nearing its tragic climax.

[8] Husband of the Tsar's niece.

11

The Emperor's Plan

DURING the first days of the February Revolution, a special commission of inquiry found an anonymous memorandum among the personal papers of Nicholas II, outlining a fantastic plan which had been submitted to the Tsar in November of 1916. The memorandum provides a key to the policy of the government in the months before the fall of the monarchy and to certain actions of Protopopov's—all initiated by the Tsar. The following is an excerpt from this illuminating document:

Memorandum Drafted in the Rimsky-Korsakov Circle and Submitted to Nicholas II by Prince Golitsyn in November 1916:

There is no longer any doubt that the Duma, backed by the so-called civic organizations, has embarked upon a clearly revolutionary path. The immediate result is the enlistment of the rebellious masses at its resumed session and a number of active measures for a revolution, and possibly an overthrow of the dynasty. We must therefore prepare and implement, when necessary, a number of decisive actions to crush a revolt. These are as follows:

1. The appointment of persons to such posts as ministers, commanders-in-chief and top military administrators away from the front (chief of district, military governor general) whose unswerving loyalty and dedication to the indivisible Tsarist autocratic rule has been proven, and who are capable of combating the forthcoming rebellion resolutely and without hesitation.

2. Immediate dissolution of the Duma *sine die* by manifesto of the Tsar . . .

3. In both capitals [1] and in large cities where the revolutionary crowds

[1] I.e., Petrograd and Moscow.

are expected to be particularly violent, martial law should be immediately introduced (if necessary even a state of siege), including such extreme measures as courts-martial.

4. Although the military forces available in Petrograd, such as reserve battalions of guards infantry regiments, are sufficiently strong to suppress a rebellion, they must be provided with machine guns and artillery in good time.

5. The immediate suspension of all leftwing and revolutionary press organs and utmost support for rightwing publications . . .

6. Militarization of all factories, workshops, and enterprises working on defense projects and a change in the status of deferred workers by considering them as called up for military service.

7. Appointment of government commissars to all central and local unions of zemstvos and cities away from the front, and commandants from among evacuated officers at the front to supervise the spending of treasury funds, and put an end to revolutionary propaganda among the lower ranks . . .

8. All governors-general, governors, and representatives of the higher provincial administration to be given the right to dismiss any official, regardless of rank or position, who participates in antigovernment actions.

9. The State Council to remain pending a general revision of basic and electoral laws and the end of the war, but all bills to be submitted for the Tsar's consideration together with majority and minority views. Its composition should be changed so as to eliminate any members of the so-called Progressive Bloc, including even those appointed by order of the Emperor.[2]

The above memorandum contained no reference to a separate peace treaty as a means of saving Russia. But an explanatory note to the second item of the memorandum, written by Govorukho-Otrok and approved by Maklakov, stressed that it was a patriotic duty to restore the "Crown's unlimited autocracy" because, in addition to the "abominations . . . inevitably engendered by a constitutional order," Russia was threatened by "enemy invasion and partition among her neighbors."

The origin of the anonymous memorandum was revealed to the members of the Provisional Government's Special Commission of Inquiry by S. P. Beletsky, a deputy minister who had wormed himself into Rasputin's favor and was associated with extreme reactionaries.

[2] *Arkhiv Russkoy Revolyutsii,* Vol. V (Moscow, Gosizdat, 1925), pp. 337–338.

In addition to oral statements, Beletsky bombarded the Special Commission with explanatory notes written in the Peter and Paul Fortress. In one of his written statements to the Commission he detailed the nature and composition of the "Rimsky-Korsakov circle," which consisted, he claimed, mainly of senators and members of the State Council.[3]

The members of the Special Commission summoned Maklakov for additional testimony. In a brief statement dated August 23, 1917, he cautiously admitted that the memorandum had had his approval and he gave an account of a letter he wrote to the Tsar on December 19 or 20, 1916, which contained similar ideas. Furthermore, he said: "... there was another letter I wrote with a *draft Manifesto* [italics mine]. I cannot remember the wording and the details of all these documents." [4] The manifesto in question was undoubtedly the one on the dissolution of the Duma recommended in the second item of the memorandum.

It would be altogether unrealistic to assume that a small group of extreme rightists from the State Council and the Union of the Russian People could have compelled the Tsar to initiate a coup d'état. Both groups were entirely dependent on the Tsar, and it is obvious that the "Rimsky-Korsakov circle" drafted the memorandum at his request. The circle was approached with this request by Maklakov, whom the Tsar had received in a secret audience which was not recorded in the Court Circular. However, the news leaked out to Rodzyanko and several other Duma members.

In the middle of September, 1916, Protopopov, deputy chairman of the Duma, was unexpectedly appointed minister of the interior. At the time of the appointment, I was in Turkestan, where I was investigating the serious unrest among the native population. On my way back I stopped in Saratov on the Volga, the capital of my electoral district, where I gave a talk and met many political and civic leaders.

[3] In addition to senators and members of the State Council, N. Y. Markov the Second and Zamyslovsky participated in the group. Markov the Second was an outstanding and active leader of the Union of the Russian People. *Arkhiv Russkoy Revolyutsii,* Vol. V, pp. 337–343.

[4] In this connection see: A. Blok, *Collected Works,* Vol. VI (1962), pp. 218–219: "On February 11 or 12 (1917), M. Maklakov saw the Tsar. Maklakov had been asked by Protopopov to prepare a draft manifesto at the Tsar's request in case the Tsar decided in favor of dissolving the Duma. ..."

There Protopopov's appointment had come as a surprise to everyone. It was interpreted, however, as an indication of the Tsar's desire to come to terms with the Duma, for the close ties between Protopopov and Rasputin were not generally known. (Protopopov was in theory a moderate Liberal and a representative of the Progressive Bloc.) It is reported that Rasputin bragged that he had been instrumental in Protopopov's appointment; showing the palm of his hand Rasputin said: "That's where the power is now."

On my return to Petrograd I found a telegram from Saratov on my desk informing me that many of the civic leaders who had met me had been arrested after my departure. Both Protopopov and I came from Simbirsk, and we were on good terms, so I telephoned him immediately to ask for an appointment. "You may come right now, my door is always open for you," was his answer.

The new minister, dressed in the uniform of chief of the Gendarmerie, welcomed me cordially at the door of his spacious office. He looked extremely handsome in the uniform, but I could think of no reason why he should wear it. As soon as I walked in, he started to tell me what a great responsibility he had shouldered and about his plans and projects for the future. At the first opportunity, I handed him the telegram and started to go into the details of my visit to Saratov. He interrupted me, pushed a button, and exclaimed: "We shall settle everything immediately!" A young aide appeared at his side. Handing him the telegram, Protopopov said: "Send a wire immediately to release the persons mentioned in this telegram."

On the left-hand side of the Minister's desk I had noticed an easel with a reproduction of a famous painting by Guido. It was a picture of Christ's head with remarkable eyes, which seemed to be closed at a distance and open when one looked more closely. Facing me again Protopopov remarked: "I see you are surprised, aren't you? You have been looking at Him intently all the time. I never part with Him. Whenever there is a decision to make, He shows me the right way."

I began to suspect that there was something uncanny going on. Protopopov continued to talk, but I no longer listened to him. I was aghast. Was I dealing with a mental case or with a charlatan who had adapted himself too thoroughly to the unwholesome atmosphere of the Tsarina's suite and of Anna Vyrubova's "little house"?

I had known Protopopov as a normal, elegant, and well-bred man, and the change in him was mystifying. Meanwhile, Protopopov continued talking about his plans to save Russia, but I could stand it no longer. Without letting him finish I got up, smiled, thanked him, and almost ran out of his office.

I went directly to the Duma at the Tauride Palace and burst into Rodzyanko's office, where several Duma members had gathered. Unable to control myself, I almost shouted: "He is a lunatic, gentlemen!"

"Who is a lunatic?"

I related what I had just experienced with Protopopov. When I mentioned his uniform Rodzyanko burst out laughing and said good-naturedly: "You said yourself that he is crazy; that's why he wears the uniform of chief of the Gendarmerie—he even came to see us here in it."

Then he told me the story of Protopopov's appointment. A delegation comprising the most distinguished members of the State Council and the Duma had visited Paris, London, and Rome that summer. The delegates, all either members or sympathizers of the Progressive Bloc, had been sent to strengthen the friendly ties among the Allies. Protopopov, as deputy speaker of the Duma and an excellent linguist, was the head of the delegation, and according to Milyukov and Shingarev, who were also members of the delegation, he displayed great tact and skill in fulfilling his mission.

On his return journey he spent a few days in Stockholm, where he met a German banker named Warburg, a close associate of Lucius, the German ambassador to Sweden. It was known to the Russian authorities that Lucius was in charge of defeatist propaganda and the entire German intelligence network in Russia. As a result, when news of this meeting leaked out there was a storm of indignation in the Duma and in the country at large.

Protopopov then tried to prove that the meeting had been arranged with the approval of Neklyudov, the Russian ambassador to Sweden. A man of high moral caliber, Neklyudov had been waging an extremely difficult but very successful struggle against German attempts to involve Sweden in the war with Russia. On learning that Protopopov had used his name to justify the secret meeting, Neklyudov advised the Ministry of Foreign Affairs that he had found out about the sensational encounter *post factum* and had warned Protopopov of the possible consequences.[5]

Nevertheless, Protopopov was promoted to the post of minister of the interior immediately after this scandalous Stockholm affair. Soon afterward the whole story came out.

Evidently, Protopopov was suffering from an incurable venereal disease, for which he had been under the care of Dr. Badmayev for many years. It was in Badmayev's house that he had met Rasputin, who had had no difficulty in subjugating a man with a disturbed mind, although Protopopov did do his best to conceal his friendship with Rasputin. The friendship seems to have blossomed, however, and at Anna Vyrubova's "little house" Rasputin introduced him to the Tsarina, whom he charmed. It was she who subsequently suggested him for the post of minister of the interior. As far as I know, few members of the Duma were aware of all this, and those who were preferred to keep silent.

Protopopov was not the first minister to get his post through Rasputin. But he was the first member of the Duma to accept his nomination without first informing his colleagues. A few days after his appointment he tried to convince Rodzyanko and other members of the Progressive Bloc of his good intentions, but they were not persuaded. In the early part of October the rift became final, and the doors of the Duma remained closed forever to the new minister of the interior.

The Duma knew of a pending imperial decree appointing General Kurlov to the post of deputy minister of the interior. General Kurlov was none other than "the main culprit in Stolypin's assassination," to use the expression used by the military procurator-general in conversation with Stolypin's son-in-law. In that same conversation the military

---

[5] In a memorandum published in *Golos Minuvshego* (Berlin, No. 2, 1926), Protopopov stated that "the question of a separate peace" had not come up for discussion in the conversation during the secret Stockholm meeting. P. Ryss, to whom Protopopov gave this memorandum, remarked: "According to Protopopov, Russia should have advised the Allies several months earlier . . . that, being unable to carry on the war, the government has decided to end it. In the course of these months the Allies and Russia should negotiate with Germany. . . . Should the Allies refuse to negotiate, Russia could still withdraw at the time mentioned after concluding peace with Germany. Russia would then become a neutral country. In December, 1916 . . . Protopopov expounded his plan to the Tsar, who, according to Protopopov, approved it." The Tsar could have approved the plan of crushing Petrograd, but certainly not the plan of a separate peace.

procurator-general had also said that "on the order of the Crown the investigation of the Kurlov affair was broken off." It is not surprising, therefore, that the proposed appointment of the general provoked a storm of indignation in the Duma. On behalf of all Duma members, with the exception of the extreme rightists, Rodzyanko warned Protopopov that Kurlov's appointment would be countered by the publication of all the details of Stolypin's assassination, including Kurlov's own role in it. Shulgin, a highly respected man of great integrity, would confirm the story. The decree was withdrawn, but Kurlov remained Protopopov's "secret" deputy and was placed unofficially in charge of the police department. Having met at the house of the Tibetan doctor, they knew each other well.

Kurlov's appointment, albeit unofficial, was soon to have its effect. Around the middle of November, at about the time when the Tsar was considering Maklakov as Protopopov's successor, my friend Professor V. N. Speransky came to see me on confidential business. He asked me whether I would be interested in meeting Senator S. N. Tregubov, who had just arrived from Supreme Headquarters in Mogilev. The meeting was to be held in complete privacy at the apartment of his father, Dr. Speransky, the head of the Medical Department at the Ministry of the Court. I had known Tregubov during my schooldays in Tashkent, where he had been the procurator of the district court. I had always respected him for carrying out his duties according to the dictates of his conscience instead of following Shcheglovitov's directives. The meeting was held a few days later. When we were alone in the room Tregubov said that there was great concern at Supreme Headquarters about information received from military intelligence on the intensified activity of German agents among the Petrograd workers. "We know," he added, "that you have contacts among the representatives of the workers through your political work, and we should like to have your views on the matter." I told him that although I had no definite information on the work of German agents, I was pleased to discuss the matter with him. I was also anxious, I said, to share with him my concern over the attitude of the Department of Police toward the violent conflict within the working population on questions of war propaganda.

"What exactly do you mean?" he asked.

"From personal observation and from talks with workers I have come to realize that for some reason the Department of Police is ignoring the subversive activity among factory workers of defeatists who are operating along the lines of the notorious 'theses on war,' which Lenin has been sending to Russia. I would suggest that you start investigating the Department of Police as soon as possible. Perhaps it could best be done by setting up a Senate Commission." In substantiation of my suspicion I told him of several cases in which the Okhrana had arrested the wrong speakers after a political meeting. The defeatist agitators had made their escape, after having urged the workers to strike in protest against the imperialist war, while those who had spoken in favor of working for the defense of the country had been arrested. It was quite obvious that the agents of the Okhrana, undoubtedly acting on instructions from higher levels, were displaying no interest whatsoever in defeatist agitators. This incomprehensible behavior lent veracity to the rumors that were spreading among the workers about "treason at the top."

When we had concluded our confidential talk we returned to the drawing room, where our host was waiting for us. After a few general remarks I left with a heavy heart. There was no doubt in my mind that Tregubov would transmit the gist of our conversation to the right people. I am sorry to say, however, that nothing came of it, and Kurlov remained in his responsible post.

"In the second half of November," wrote Protopopov shortly before his death, "the workers' movement began to crystallize. Strikes broke out sporadically in different areas of the city . . . We had to plan a campaign that would suppress the workers' movement should it flare up violently and begin to spread." As a first step in this direction he consulted General Balk, the governor (*gradonachalnik*) of Petrograd, and asked to be briefed on the situation in the city. To his surprise, Protopopov learned that a military commission under General Khabalov had been appointed, to include representatives of the Police Department, for the purpose of planning the joint action of army and police detachments should disorder break out in the capital. Although the Governor's Office was subordinate to the Ministry of the Interior, the minister had been completely unaware of this development. While a detailed plan was being worked out to bring in troops with machine guns to assist the Petrograd police, the minister of the interior was intensifying his campaign against the Union of Zemstvos and Union of Towns as well as against cooperative and civic organizations. On the other hand, the Police Department was almost openly supporting the propaganda of Bolshevik defeatist organizations that incited the workers to strike. With the appointment of Shcheglovitov as chairman of the State Council on January 1, 1917, Protopopov took an overt and irreconcilable stand against the Duma.

It is clear that item 2 of the Rimsky-Korsakov memorandum was an expression of the Tsar's own policy, of which Protopopov was the main instrument. I must stress that it was the Tsar's personal policy and not that of the government as such. All cabinet members, including their chairman Prince Golitsyn, opposed the line followed by the deranged Protopopov, and all attempted to maintain proper if not amicable relations with the Duma and the civic organizations working for national defense. In order to prevent a head-on clash between Protopopov and the Duma, Prince Golitsyn postponed the reopening of the Duma session from January to February and pleaded with the Tsar on three different occasions to dismiss Protopopov. He pointed out that Protopopov was "completely uninformed about the business of his ministry and that he lacked experience in handling the complex setup of the Ministry of the Interior . . ."; that he "did harm without even being aware of it." [6] The Tsar's answer was evasive, but under pressure from Golitsyn he finally said: ". . . I have been thinking it over very carefully and have decided against a dismissal for the time being." [7] The Tsar's indecision about Protopopov seems to contradict his earlier desire to appoint Maklakov in his place. The only logical conclusion is that the Tsar must have considered Protopopov "harmless" after Rasputin's death and hence unable to pursue a policy of separate peace. Although the Emperor must have been fully aware that Shcheglovitov and Protopopov did advocate such a policy, it did not greatly concern him, as long as they both continued, in the spirit of his own grand design, to oppose the Duma and all the civic organizations.

In January of 1917 the plan for the transfer of troops and police to St. Petersburg was completed. All troops and police detachments, as well as squadrons of gendarme forces, were placed under the com-

---

[6] *Padeniye Tsarskogo Regima* (Leningrad, Gosizdat, 1925), pp. 253–254.
[7] *Ibid.*

mand of specially appointed staff officers in each of the six offices of the Chief of City Police. In the event of disorders, the police were to act first on their own; Cossacks were to follow; and if the situation called for it, troops with machine guns would then be brought into action. A shipment of machine guns sent by Great Britain via Petrograd for use at the front was diverted by special order and placed at the disposal of the governor of the city.

This plan to deal with the capital as if it were an occupied city was absurd, and it was doomed to failure from the start. The Tsar, alarmed after a talk with Protopopov in which the latter expressed doubts as to the reliability of the reserve troops in Petrograd, summoned General Khabalov for consultation. As a result of Khabalov's report, he promptly ordered General Gurko [8] to send two cavalry regiments of the guards and a regiment of the Ural Cossacks back to their barracks in Petrograd on the pretext of giving them a rest. Protopopov was delighted with the Tsar's decision.

Meanwhile, with the help of an *agent provocateur,* General Kurlov found a pretext for a raid on the Central War Industry Committee. On January 26, 1917, every member of the "workers' group" was arrested, with the exception of the police agent Abrosimov. The center of the patriotic "defensist" movement among the workers was thus destroyed.

The same fate befell the groups of "defensist" workers in Moscow and the provinces. On January 31, mass demonstrations and strikes broke out throughout the capital, and it was judged that the time was now ripe to launch the military operations against the population called for in the Rimsky-Korsakov memorandum. But the attempt to destroy the "defensist" movement among the workers had given rise to an unprecedented burst of indignation among the people, who saw in it a sure sign that the Crown was secretly working for a separate peace with the Germans. Even the hastily summoned cavalry regiments would have been unable to save the situation.

During his last talk with Protopopov on February 22, the Tsar motioned to the minister to leave the Empress' drawing room for a tête-a-tête discussion. His voice betraying his alarm, Nicholas II told Protopopov that General Gurko had flagrantly disobeyed his orders and had dispatched naval guards to Petrograd, instead of the regiments

[8] General Y. Gurko had temporarily replaced General Alekseyev as chief of staff.

of the Life Guards he had asked for. The sailors were commanded by Grand Duke Cyril, who, like most of the grand dukes, was a sworn enemy of the Tsarina.[9] The Emperor told Protopopov he had decided to leave immediately for Supreme Headquarters, in order to supervise the dispatch of the necessary regiments to the capital and to take disciplinary action in connection with General Gurko's behavior. Protopopov pleaded with the Tsar not to stay away any longer than absolutely necessary, and obtained from him a promise to be back within eight days.

Before he left, the Tsar signed one decree on the prorogation of the Duma, and another on its dissolution, but left the dates open on both and entrusted the documents to Prince Golitsyn and Protopopov.[10]

This was the final move in the Tsar's plan to restore absolute rule and to assure victory under his own leadership.

[9] See preceding chapter.
[10] *The Russian Provisional Government* (Stanford, Calif., Stanford Univ. Press, 1961), p. 41.

12

The Final Session of the Duma

AT long last, the right man, a man "ready for anything," was found. On January 18, 1917, Goremykin, who had now lost the last vestiges of restraining influence in Tsarskoye Selo, was dismissed.

On January 19, he was replaced by Stürmer, an extreme reactionary who hated the very idea of any form of popular representation or local self-government. Even more important, he was undoubtedly a believer in the need for an immediate cessation of the war with Germany.

Goremykin's ominous prediction had come true—"When I go they will make peace." Preparations for a peace settlement were soon in full swing.

During his first few months in office, Stürmer was also minister of the interior, but the post of minister of foreign affairs was still held by Sazonov, who firmly advocated honoring the alliance with Britain and France and carrying on the war to the bitter end, and who recognized the Cabinet's obligation to pursue a policy in tune with the sentiments of the majority in the Duma.

On August 9, however, Sazonov was suddenly dismissed. His portfolio was taken over by Stürmer, and on September 16, Protopopov was appointed acting minister of the interior. The official government of the Russian Empire was now entirely in the hands of the Tsarina and her advisers.

It was now all too clear where this band of irresponsible reactionaries, adventurers, and neurotics was leading Russia. Erzberger, the German minister of propaganda, and a very influential member of the Reichstag, wrote in his memoirs:

In September 1916 one was impressed by the fact that news concerning the possibility of peace with Russia was on the increase. On September 20, 1916, someone communicated his impressions to me in the following words:

"When I visualize the political situation, which I find so disturbing as a whole, I think I have the right to conclude that Russia is the only country of the quadruple alliance with which one could start negotiations, and that Russia, if she made gains which would save her military prestige abroad, would be the first to conclude peace. The key to the situation lies in the personality of Stürmer—he has ideas different from those of Sazonov. . . ."

On the same day I learned from Petrograd that Russian high officials had said that they were tired of war and would gladly conclude peace with Germany. Naturally this fact was brought to the notice of Stürmer's adversaries. The appointment of Protopopov as minister of the interior, which was the work of Stürmer, and publications regarding the meeting with Dr. Warburg [1] provoked extremely blunt speeches from Milyukov and Shulgin in the Duma in December, 1916. They brought about the downfall of Stürmer, the "Prime Minister of Peace." [2]

It now became equally clear that all chance of avoiding a clash between the people and the monarchy was gone.

On the first day of the fifth and last session of the Duma, on November 1, Milyukov made a violent speech denouncing Stürmer. In his tirade he referred to the young Tsarina, who was nominally immune from criticism, and hinted that she was indirectly a party to the German intrigues, ending his charge with the words, "What is all this —stupidity or treachery?"

To this rhetorical question there was but one answer from the army and the people—"treachery." Although Milyukov asserted later that in asking the question he had meant to indicate stupidity and not treachery, few ever believed him, especially since all the other representatives of the Progressive Bloc and the left-wing groups had long been saying exactly the same thing, except that they had never mentioned the Tsarina by name.

During this meeting members of the Duma were surprised by a totally unexpected speech from the extreme right-wing leader, Purishkevich, who was later to be an accomplice in the murder of Rasputin. Purishkevich described the machinations of the Rasputin clique in no uncertain terms, and ended his speech with an appeal to all Duma

[1] See Chapter 11.
[2] *Souvenirs de guerre de M. Erzberger* (Paris, Fayot, 1921), p. 271.

members loyal to Russia and the Monarchy to go to Tsarskoye Selo and implore the Tsar "on their knees" to save Russia and the throne from the perfidious "forces of darkness."

Stürmer was relieved of his office on November 10. His successor was Trepov, an extreme rightist member of the State Council and a man close to the Tsar.

The Bloc was delighted; they thought they had gained a brilliant and unexpected victory. But the Trudoviks and the Social Democrats used obstructive tactics to prevent the new prime minister from addressing the Duma, because he had retained Protopopov as minister of the interior in his cabinet. A motion of censure against us was passed unanimously, and we were excluded from the fifteen subsequent meetings of the Duma.

Meanwhile, the government's campaign against the voluntary public organizations supporting the war effort continued with increasing intensity.

On December 8 and 9, on orders from Protopopov, the congresses in Moscow of the Zemstvo Union and the Union of Towns were broken up by the police. The congresses dealing with cooperatives and food supplies were prohibited. On December 13, just before a major debate in the Duma on Protopopov's action, the chairman of the Duma announced that, in accordance with the rules of procedure, the government had requested that the debate be held behind closed doors.

Immediately I took the floor and read aloud in *open session* the motions passed by the two congresses before they were broken up. The one unanimously adopted by the Union of Towns read, in part, as follows:

In Russia all levels of the population, all classes of society and all organizations of honest men are fully aware that the irresponsible criminals and hysterical fanatics who so blasphemously utter words of love for Russia are making ready her defeat, dishonor and enslavement. Russia has finally awakened and has seen the terrible reality before her. The life of the country has been shaken to the core, and the government measures have plunged the country into economic ruin, while the latest action only worsens the upheaval and makes way for social chaos. There is only one way out of this disastrous situation—a change of regime and the formation of a responsible ministry. The Duma must continue its struggle against this shameful regime to the bitter end. In this struggle the Duma will be backed by the entire nation. The Congress calls upon the Duma to do its duty and remain in session until the main aim—the setting up of a responsible ministry—is attained . . . The Congress calls upon all organized groups among the population—the towns, the zemstvos, agriculture, trade, industry, the cooperatives, and all workers, to unite their efforts—to work first and foremost for the organization of food supplies, the disruption of which is a threat to the country and the army.

On the same day, the Congress of the Union of Zemstvos, headed by Prince Lvov, had stated its motion even more bluntly and clearly:

The historical regime of the country stands on the brink of an abyss. The disruption of the home front is growing worse every day, and each day it is becoming harder and harder to organize the country so as to meet the demands imposed by war. Our only salvation—which is our patriotism—lies in our unity and responsibility to our own land. When the regime places obstacles in the way of its salvation, it is up to the country as a whole to make itself responsible for the future. The government, which is being used as a tool by the forces of darkness, is leading Russia along the path of ruin and shaking the foundations of the throne. We must set up a government worthy of a great people at one of the greatest moments in its history, a government which is strong and responsible to the people and the Duma. Let the Duma, in this resolute struggle which has begun, remember its great responsibility and justify the faith which the whole country is showing it. There is no time to be lost. The time limit given us by history has run out.

Having read aloud both of these historic resolutions, I emphasized that I was quoting a motion adopted not by peasants and workers but by Town and Zemstvo officials.[3] I went on to say that we would stand with all those who openly denounced the old regime in the name of the entire country.

My proposal that the matter should be discussed at an open meeting was not put to the vote; in refusing to do so Rodzyanko was acting in accordance with the procedural statute.[4]

I am quite certain that if my proposal had been adopted on December 13, this "revolutionary" act on the part of the Duma would not have brought any reprisals in its wake. The Rasputin clique was not

[3] I.e., people of a liberal rather than a revolutionary cast of mind.
[4] Verbatim record of the fourth Duma, fifth session, fifteenth meeting on December 13, 1916, pp. 1095–1098.

quite ready at that moment for its final moves, and the Duma might well have become not only the focal point of the hopes of the people, but also the country's leader at the turning point in its history.

The murder of Gregory Rasputin on December 17 did not cause the slightest change in the policy of the Court.

A few days later, just before Christmas, the Duma was adjourned for one and a half months, and a week after that, on December 27, Trepov, the chairman of the Council of Ministers, was replaced by Prince Golitsyn, a high-ranking court official who was the Tsarina's aide in matters relating to charity. This appointment was rather curious in view of the fact that the new head of the government, who was supposed to take charge of all home and foreign policy at the crucial hour, beseeched the Tsar with tears in his eyes not to appoint him to such a responsible post, least of all in wartime! But all his pleas went unheeded. Actually, he was appointed precisely because he had had no experience in affairs of state, and lacked a will of his own.

All power was now concentrated in the hands of Protopopov and his backstairs associates.

On January 1, 1917, one of the most influential figures behind the throne, the former minister of justice Shcheglovitov, was appointed chairman of the State Council. This post, like that of the chairman of the Duma, carried with it the right of making personal reports to the Tsar. The appointment of a man who only six months before had been ousted from office by popular demand was an indication that the monarch had broken finally and irrevocably with all elements of consequence in the country. It was just at this moment, too, that Protopopov and his cronies finally took the bit between their teeth and went all out to attain their goal.

Their war on the *zemstva,* the Union of Towns, the cooperatives, and all the voluntary organizations working for national defense, was growing more and more insensate. It became known in the Duma that the government intended to take over direct control of all these organizations, which meant, among other things, that Protopopov had been put in charge of food supplies for the citizens of Petrograd.

In January unrest among the workers of the capital greatly increased. During 1916, there had been 243 political strikes all over the country, but in the first two months of 1917, there were 1,140.

By the middle of January a special committee under the presidency of General Khabalov, commander of the Petersburg Military District until February 27, had drafted a detailed plan for the deployment of troops to be used in conjunction with the police in the event of riots in the capital. Simultaneously, the government began a campaign against the Central War Industry Committee because of its Workers' Group. This independent working-class group, which functioned as part of the Committee (consisting of leading representatives of industry), was anathema to Protopopov for one very simple reason: Guided by Marxist ideology and working-class principles, the group successfully protected the material interests of the industrial proletariat and forced the industrialists to make concessions to it. It thus averted strikes at the factories engaged in defense production.

On January 31, the entire Workers' Group was arrested and charged with participation in a "criminal association striving for the overthrow of the present state system and the establishment of a socialist republic." A letter addressed by the arrested leaders of the group to the workers of Petrograd, urging them to continue their defense work and not to hold demonstrations or go on strike because of their arrest, was kept out of the newspapers on the orders of General Khabalov. Only one of the group managed to "evade" arrest; this was Abrosimov, the extreme left-wing member of the group, who had continually come forward, though not with much success, with all sorts of "revolutionary" proposals.

During the first few weeks after the fall of the Monarchy, when the records of the secret police came into the hands of the new government, it was revealed that Abrosimov was a prominent police agent. But even without this irrefutable proof, the whole story of the Protopopov-Kurlov campaign to demoralize the "defensist" working class in the capital is evidence enough of his assistance to the "defeatists."

On February 8, at the orders of the Tsar himself, the Petrograd military district was detached from the Northern Front, and the district commander, General Khabalov, was given special powers. The Duma was the only remaining independent institution that Protopopov had not yet dared to touch. This body of popular representatives, although far from perfect, was Russia's only hope during those black months. The army at the front had faith in it, and the factory workers in the capital believed in its power. But the weeks went by, the forces of disruption grew bolder and bolder, and still the Duma did not reassemble.

Rumors quickly began to spread that Tsarskoye Selo had decided to do away with the Duma. The rumors grew louder and caused increasing unrest. Everyone knew that if the Duma were abolished public opinion would no longer count for anything. All classes of society, from commanders at the front to ordinary factory workers in Petrograd, believed in the Duma's power to save the situation.

When a meeting of the Duma was finally fixed for February 14, a delegation of workers from the Putilov Factory, which had taken the lead in the working-class movement of the capital, came to see Chkheidze and myself and told us that on the day the Duma opened the workers were planning to stage a mass demonstration in its support. The demonstration was called off because the Bloc decided, for tactical reasons, not to give its support to the plan. This was announced in a letter which Milyukov wrote to the press.

Just before the opening of the Duma, Rodzyanko went as usual to make a personal report to the Tsar.

"The Government," he said, "persists in widening the gulf between itself and the representatives of the people. The ministers are doing everything they can to prevent the Tsar from learning the truth. Responsible critics have been accused of treason. Censorship, arrests, and even a show of force have been employed to suppress justified anxiety and questioning. The Duma has been threatened with prorogation, and the government has urged the president of the Duma to take 'heroic measures' to silence its members." In view of the prevailing circumstances such action was patently impossible. "Furthermore," Rodzyanko continued, "the president would hardly be doing his duty to the popular representatives and to the country were he to take any measures to achieve such an end. The Duma would lose the confidence of the country, with the probable result that the country, exhausted from the hardships of life and impatient of the disorder existing in the administration, might itself take a stand in defense of its lawful rights. This must be prevented at all costs, and this is our basic task." [5]

The Tsar, obviously annoyed at Rodzyanko's repeated importu-

[5] The Russian Provisional Government, 1917, documents selected and edited by Robert Paul Browder and Alexander F. Kerensky, Vol. I (Stanford, Calif., Stanford Univ. Press, 1961), p. 3.

nities, warned him that the Duma would be allowed to continue in session only if there were no further "indecent outbursts against the government," and refused to comment on Rodzyanko's request that the most objectionable ministers be removed. To Rodzyanko's apprehensive allusion to the state of public opinion and his hints at the possibility of violent action from below, Nicholas responded that the information reaching him was "directly to the contrary." Yielding to despair, Rodzyanko expressed his "profound foreboding . . . and conviction" that this would be his last report, "because the Duma will be dissolved, and the course the government is taking bodes no good. There is still time; it is still possible to change everything and to grant a responsible ministry. That, apparently, is not to be. You, Your Majesty, disagree with me, and everything will remain as it is. The consequence of this, in my opinion, will be revolution and a state of anarchy which no one will be able to control." Rodzyanko's prophecy was soon to be fulfilled.

This attitude of defiance toward Rodzyanko's report was a clear indication that the Tsar approved of Protopopov's actions and that he had absolutely no intention of making any changes.

When the Duma met on February 14, the subject discussed was its role in the clash, now nearing its climax, between government and country. Milyukov said that he thought the country had quite outstripped the government, but that the will of the people was only able to express itself through the abhorred channels of dead bureaucratic machinery. Hence, it was to the Duma that people everywhere now looked for action. At the same time, he felt embarrassed by such appeals for action since, as he put it, "our only deeds are our words!" [6]

This was perfectly true. Words are the deeds of poets, philosophers and writers, but for statesmen and politicians words are not enough. Their words, no matter how inspiring and profound, are useless unless followed up by deeds. As Milyukov so rightly said, at that time the entire nation believed in the Duma, but Russia was appealing to it for action and not just for speeches. Whether or not their faith in the Duma was justified, the people wanted it to take the lead and become its spokesman. And it was not only the "dead bureaucratic machinery" that had brought the country such suffering and prevented the people

[6] Fourth Duma, fifth session, twentieth meeting on February 14, 1917.

from exercising their creative ability. After all, there is some form of bureaucratic machinery in every country; no modern state could be run without it. In any case, the Russian bureaucratic machinery was far from dead, for a large number of sensible and dedicated officials still served it. But they had been completely disabled; they only carried out the orders of the ministers. But who appointed the ministers? Who dismissed the honest ones and replaced them by Rasputin's cronies?

Replying to Milyukov's remark about the dead bureaucratic machinery, I said exactly what everyone was thinking but no one had dared to say outright in the Duma. I said that it was not the bureaucracy, nor even the "forces of darkness" which was responsible for what was happening, but the Crown. The root of the evil, I said, was in those who now sat on the throne.

Addressing the members of the Progressive Bloc, I went on to say:

We are told that the government—meaning the high administrative officials—is guilty; but they come and go like shadows. Have you thought for a moment who the people are who put these shadows there...? If you recall the history of the regime over the past three years, you will remember what a lot of talk there has been in this assembly about the "forces of darkness." And the talk gave rise to an alliance of young, naïve dreamers and political adventurers; [7] and this "dark force" is now gone! Rasputin is gone! But have we entered a new phase in the life of Russia? Has the system changed? No, it has not; it is still exactly the same. . . .

And so I ask you, gentlemen, and all the people you represent, have not the past three years led you to the same conviction, and is it not the only thing that can unite you with us, the revolutionary democrats? Have you not realized that . . . the historic task . . . is the immediate overthrow of the medieval regime at all costs . . . How can this view be reconciled with the oft-repeated fact that you only want to fight by "legal methods"? [At this point Milyukov interrupted me to say that the expression meant the Duma.] How can we use legal methods against those who have turned the law into an instrument for their own use against the people? . . . The only way to deal with those who violate the law in this way is to remove them by force. . . .

The acting president of the Duma then asked me what I meant. I replied, "I was referring to what Brutus did in the days of Rome."

[7] The reference is to Rasputin's assassins, Prince Yusupov, Purishkevich, and others.

The President of the Duma afterward gave orders for my statement justifying the overthrow of tyrants to be omitted from the verbatim record of the meeting. When the Tsarina was later told what I had said, she exclaimed: "Kerensky should be hanged."

The next day, or possibly the day after, the president of the Duma received a note from the minister of justice requesting that I be deprived of my parliamentary immunity, as a man impeachable for a grave crime against the state.

As soon as he had received the note, Rodzyanko called me into his room, read me its contents and said: "Don't worry, the Duma will never surrender you."

The next meeting of the Duma, on February 17, discussed the question of the Workers' Group of the War Industry Committee, and the arrest and trial of its members. (The question had been put on the agenda by the decision of a large majority that very day.)

The first person to take the floor was Konovalov, a member of the Progressive Party and vice-president of this committee. He gave a detailed report on the raid made on the headquarters of the "defensist" workers' movement by the police. Konovalov's speech aroused great indignation throughout the Duma—except among the extreme rightists, of course. People were particularly outraged by two things: The first was the order forbidding publication by the press of the letter from the arrested workers in which they appealed to all workers to continue working and to refrain from staging any mass protests; the second was the fact that the worker Abrosimov, the only one in the group who had not been arrested, clearly showed by his behavior after the arrests that he was a police agent.

The factual evidence contained in Konovalov's report gave every honest member of the Duma a clue as to who was behind the "wildcat" strikes in the factories and the lockout policy which the managers of factories engaged in war production were being encouraged to pursue.

On February 18, a series of strikes broke out as a result of a steep rise in prices. The forging shop at the Putilov Metal Works made a demand to the management for a 50-percent wage increase. The manager flatly refused, and the workers laid down tools but stayed on the premises. Meetings were held in all the other shops of the factory.

Three days later the management, anxious to rid itself of the "undesirable elements," closed the forging shop on the pretext that the supply of coal had run out, and discharged the personnel concerned. Other sections of the metal works followed suit, and strike meetings were held that evening all over the factory.

The next day, February 22, the management of the Putilov Works retaliated by declaring a lockout, which meant that about 40,000 workers were literally thrown into the street. The workers decided to make an appeal for the support of all the other workers of Petrograd, and a strike committee was elected for liaison purposes. On this same day, the Tsar, who had been living in Tsarskoye Selo since the death of Rasputin, left for the front, promising Protopopov that he would be back in a week.

This was a time of increasing food shortages. A few days before, on February 19, people had been milling around the food stores the whole day long, demanding bread. On February 21, at several places, the wives of workers broke into and looted shops selling bread and dairy products.

The critical food situation was discussed in the Duma on February 23, with particular reference to Petrograd. In my speech I said, among other things:

Yesterday afternoon representatives of the Putilov factory came to see me and asked me to tell you on their behalf that they did everything to stop the works being closed, and had even agreed . . . to return to work on the same terms as before. But just when the leaders of the working masses were in this mood, they read about the lockout and the fact that 40,000 of the poorest and neediest citizens of Petrograd had been thrown out on the street. They read it just after there had been a series of workshop meetings at which the workers themselves felt that it was the wrong time to promote the working-class movement. They asked me to tell you that. I told them I doubted whether the majority of the Duma would understand them, since you and they did not speak the same language (voices from the left and center: "Wrong!"). But I promised I would convey their message to you. And if I'm wrong, then do the civic duty that the present moment demands of you!

And they did—they debated the problem!

At the end of the meeting Milyukov, on behalf of the Progressive Bloc, proposed the following motion:

Considering it essential that (a) the government should take immediate steps to provide food for the population of the capital and other towns and cities; (b) the workers employed in factories of the defense industry should be supplied with food immediately; and (c) town administrations and public bodies should be enlisted straight away in the distribution of food, and food committees should be set up, the State Duma now proceeds with the regular agenda.

On behalf of the Trudovik Group I proposed that the following item be added to the Progressive Bloc's motion: ". . . that the jobless workers from the Putilov Works should be taken back and that the factory should resume operations immediately."

My paragraph was put to a vote and my amendment was adopted.

Unfortunately, the Duma's attempt to put an end to the provocative behavior of the factory management and the government came too late. A general strike of workers began on February 23.

Meetings were held and work was stopped at dozens of factories. As soon as the meetings were over, the workers marched into the streets singing revolutionary songs. By midday the Samsonovsky Prospekt was thronged with workers, and reinforced units of mounted and foot police were unable to hold back the crowds. At two o'clock the task of suppressing the riots passed from General Balk, the chief administrator of the city, to the military.

The next day the Duma continued its debate on the critical situation, and an emergency bill was tabled for the transfer of the organization of food supplies to the town and *zemstvo* councils. Rodzyanko urged Prince Golitsyn to take the matter out of Protopopov's hands and hand it over to the municipal administration.

In the meantime, thousands of workers had pushed their way through to the Liteyny Prospekt, and crowds began gathering in other parts of the city. Barricades were set up across bridges so as to divide the city into two halves, in accordance with General Khabalov's plan for the deployment of troops for the suppression of riots by force of arms. But the general's orders came too late.

On February 25, the Cossack detachments and infantry went over to the people. The Nevsky Prospekt and adjoining streets were invaded by milling crowds. A meeting attended by thousands of people was held at the Nicholayevsky Station near the statue of Alexander III, but the Cossack troops made no attempt to interfere and even fraternized with the crowds. Suddenly a detachment of mounted police arrived, led by an officer. He gave orders for the warning bugle to be sounded, but at that very moment there was a shot from a Cossack rifle and the police officer fell dead. The police immediately fired a salvo into the crowd and people fled into the adjoining streets.

That day the Duma assembled for its last and shortest meeting. Anxious to send the bill on reorganizing food supplies to joint town and *zemstvo* commissions as soon as possible, the members met at 11 A.M. and broke up by 12:50, having fixed the next meeting for 11 o'clock on February 28.

It was clear to all that the life of the Duma hung by a thread and that either dissolution or prorogation was certain. To avoid being caught unawares it would have to stay in session at all costs. The left-wing opposition insisted that the next meeting be held on Monday, February 27, rather than on Tuesday, February 28.

Our insistence was useless against the determination of the majority, and the proposal was rejected. But they made one concession—it was agreed at a private meeting of the Council of Elders in Rodzyanko's office that a closed meeting of the members of the Duma would be held on Monday at two o'clock.

On Sunday a large number of Duma members from different factions tried in vain to persuade the president to hold an official meeting on Monday.

At midnight on February 26–27, the spring session of the Duma was suspended by a decree signed by the Tsar and antedated February 25 by Prince Golitsyn.

With the decree of prorogation of the Duma, the execution of the Tsar's plan came to an end. On the morning of February 27 began the revolt of the reserve battalions of the guards regiments. The cavalry, which had been summoned from the front, failed to arrive in the capital. That same morning the government headed by Prince Golitsyn ceased to exist.

The Turning Point
in Russia's History

The February Revolution

13

The Days of Destiny

A T about 8 A.M. on Monday, February 27, 1917, my wife awakened me with the news that Nekrasov had telephoned to say that the Duma had been suspended, the Volyn Regiment had mutinied, and that I was wanted immediately at the Duma. Despite the fact that the political situation had grown ominously stormy during the last few days, it was several moments before I grasped the full significance of Nekrasov's news. The stage had long been set for the final showdown, but as often happens in such cases no one had expected it to come when it did.

It did not take me long, however, to realize that the hour had struck at last.

I dressed quickly and set off at once for the Duma building, which was about five minutes' walk from my home. My first thought was that the Duma must be kept in session at all costs and that close contact between the armed forces and the Duma must be established.

As soon as I reached the Duma I went straight to Catherine Hall, where I found Nekrasov, Yefremov, Vershinin, Chkheidze, and several other deputies of the opposition. They agreed with my suggestion that the Duma should hold an official sitting. Nekrasov told me that Rodzyanko had sent telegrams to the Tsar at headquarters in Mogilev and to the commanders of the army fronts, informing them that the riots in Petrograd were spreading.

On the preceding day, the president of the State Duma had sent the following telegram to the Tsar at Supreme Headquarters:

The situation is serious. The capital is in a state of anarchy. The government is paralyzed. Transport service and the supply of food and fuel have become completely disrupted. General discontent is growing. There is wild shooting in the streets. In places troops are firing at each other. It is necessary that some person who enjoys the confidence of the country be entrusted at once with the formation of a new government. There must be no delay. And procrastination is tantamount to death. I pray to God that at this hour the responsibility may not fall upon the Monarch.

On February 27, Rodzyanko sent the following telegram to the Tsar:

By Your Majesty's Ukase the session of the State Duma has been suspended until April. The last bulwark of order has been eliminated. The government is absolutely powerless to suppress disorders. Nothing can be hoped from the troops of the garrison. The reserve battalions of the guard regiments are in rebellion. Officers are being killed. Having joined the crowds and the popular movement, they are proceeding in the direction of the Ministry of the Interior and of the State Duma. Civil war has started and is waxing hotter and hotter. Order the immediate calling of a new government according to the principles reported by me to Your Majesty in my telegram of yesterday. Cancel Your Imperial Ukase, and order the reconvening of the legislative chambers. Make these measures known without delay through an Imperial Manifesto. Sire, do not delay. If the movement spreads to the army, the Germans will triumph, and the ruin of Russia, and with her the Dynasty, will become inevitable. On behalf of all Russia I beg Your Majesty to fulfill the foregoing. The hour which will decide the fate of Yourself and of the homeland has come. Tomorrow it may already be too late.

Rodzyanko,
President of the State Duma

Before I left my apartment that morning, I had called some of my friends and urged them to go to the barracks of the insurgent regiments to try to persuade the troops to come to the Duma.

During the few days before the Revolution, the deputies had come to regard the Duma's left wing as the only group that knew the mood of the masses and that was in contact with developments in the city. In fact, we had been fairly successful in organizing an intelligence and news-gathering service all over the capital, and every ten or fifteen minutes reports were telephoned in to us. As soon as I appeared in the hall, I was surrounded by people and bombarded with questions. I told them that there were riots all over the city, that the insurgent troops were on their way to the Duma and that I knew the Revolution had begun. I said that as representatives of the people it was our duty to welcome them and to make common cause with them.

The news that the soldiers were heading toward the Duma at first caused some alarm among the deputies, but this feeling was soon forgotten in the excitement at the prospect of their arrival.

In the meantime, the soldiers of one regiment after another began pouring into the streets without their officers. Some of the officers had been placed under arrest, and there were a few cases of assassination. Others had slipped away, deserting their units in face of the obvious hostility and distrust of the enlisted men. Civilians were joining the troops everywhere. Great crowds of workers came pouring into the city from the suburbs, and there were lively exchanges of gun fire in a number of areas. Clashes with the police were soon reported. Police machine-gunners were firing at the crowds from rooftops and belfries.[1] For the moment the throngs of people in the streets did not seem to have any particular aim, and it was difficult to see at that stage how things would develop. One thing was clear, however: The government intended to take advantage of the growing disorder for its own nefarious purposes. Everyone thought that the hunger riots, the disintegration of the military, and the "disloyalty" of the Duma would be used as an excuse by the Protopopov clique to make an open move toward the conclusion of a separate peace treaty with Germany.

Nekrasov, Yefremov, Chkheidze, and I, as representatives of the left-wing opposition, proposed in the Council of Elders an immediate official session of the Duma and suggested that the Tsar's decree be ignored. The majority, including Rodzyanko, and, rather surprisingly, Milyukov, were against this move. No arguments were of any avail. Despite all the crimes and follies of the government, the majority of the deputies were still living in the past. The Council overruled our proposal and decided on an "unofficial session," as originally planned. Both politically and psychologically, this meant a closed meeting of a private group, a group that included many men of great influence and

---

[1] It has been claimed that this did not actually happen. I refer all those interested to "Order No. 2 to the City of Petrograd," signed by Karaulov, an officer of the Kuban Cossacks and member of the Temporary Military Committee, which stated, *inter alia,* that those found harboring machine-gunners would be court-martialed. I have personal knowledge of two houses where machine guns were set up on the rooftops: at Moyka Quai and Sergiyevskaya Street. Both streets were strictly residential.

standing but that was, nevertheless, only a private group. The meeting could not, therefore, claim official recognition.

The Duma's failure to announce an official session was tantamount to committing political suicide at the very moment when its authority was at its height in the country and the army, and when it could have been of far-reaching benefit. This demonstrated the weakness of a Duma largely based on a narrow upper-class franchise, which had inevitably restricted its capacity to reflect the mood of the nation as a whole. By failing to take the initiative, the Duma became a private body on a par with the Soviet of Workers' Deputies, which was then just beginning to emerge. The next day, realizing his mistake, Rodzyanko made an attempt to revive the Duma as an official institution. But it was too late. By then there were already two centers of authority in the capital, both of which owed their existence to the Revolution. They were the Duma in unofficial session, with its Provisional Committee appointed as a temporary guiding body, and the Soviet of Workers' Deputies, guided by its Executive Committee.

I cannot recall all the topics discussed on that Monday morning in the Council of Elders, and later at the unofficial session which met from 12:00 to 2:00; but the decision was made to form a Provisional Committee with unrestricted powers. It was to consist of Rodzyanko, Shulgin, Milyukov, Lvov, Chkheidze, Nekrasov, Karaulov, Dmitryukov, Rzhevsky, Shidlovsky, Engelhardt, Shingarev, and myself. All parties except the extreme rightists were represented. These rightist members, who had behaved so arrogantly until a short while before, suddenly vanished from the scene.

At 1:00 P.M., the soldiers still had not arrived, and when someone at last shouted to me from the main entrance that they were in sight, I raced toward the window hardly believing it could be true.

From the window I saw the soldiers, surrounded by civilians, lining up on the opposite side of the street. It was clear that they felt awkward in these unusual circumstances, and they looked lost without their officers.

Without stopping to put on a coat, I ran out through the main entrance to greet those for whom we had been waiting so long. I hurried to the center gate and shouted some words of welcome on behalf of the Duma. As a detachment of the Preobrazhensky Regiment surged around me in a confused throng, Chkheidze, Skobelev, and several other deputies reached the gate behind me. When Chkheidze had spoken a few words of greeting, I urged the soldiers to follow me into the Duma building in order to disarm the guard and defend the building in case of attack by troops loyal to the government. At once the soldiers lined up in orderly ranks and marched in after me. We went straight to the guardroom through the main entrance to the Palace. I was afraid that it might be necessary to use force to remove the guard, but they had apparently fled some time before we got there. I gave the command of the post to a noncommissioned officer and explained to him where sentries should be posted.

Back in Catherine Hall I addressed the crowd that had now filled the building. These people, who had come from all parts of the city, no longer had the least doubt as to the reality of the Revolution. They wanted to know what we intended to do with the supporters of the Tsarist regime, and they demanded harsh treatment for them. I said that the most dangerous of them would be kept in custody, but that under no circumstances was the crowd to take the law into its own hands. I insisted that bloodshed be avoided. They asked me who would be arrested first, and I told them it would be Shcheglovitov, former minister of justice and president of the Imperial Council. I gave orders for him to be brought directly to me. It appeared that some soldiers from the Preobrazhensky and Volyn regiments had themselves gone to arrest Protopopov, but that he had managed to slip away. At four o'clock, however, I received word that Shcheglovitov had been arrested and brought to the Duma. The deputies were greatly distressed, and the moderates urged Rodzyanko to have him released, since, as the president of a legislative body, he enjoyed personal immunity.

I went to see Shcheglovitov and found him in the custody of a hastily improvised guard and surrounded by a crowd of people. Rodzyanko and some of the deputies were already there, and I saw Rodzyanko greet him amiably and invite him into his office as a "guest." I quickly interposed myself between the two and said to Rodzyanko, "No, Shcheglovitov is not a guest and I refuse to have him released."

Turning to Shcheglovitov, I said, "Are you Ivan Grigoryevich Shcheglovitov?"

"Yes."

"I must ask you to follow me. You are under arrest. Your safety will be guaranteed." Everyone fell back, and Rodzyanko and his friends, somewhat embarrassed, returned to their rooms, while I led the prisoner to the ministerial chambers known as the Government Pavilion.

This was a separate wing consisting of several comfortable rooms connected by a semicircular gallery with the main hall in the Duma. The rooms had been used by ministers when they came to speak before the Duma. Since it was not physically part of the Duma, the Pavilion came under the jurisdiction of the government. It had its own staff of servants, and deputies were not allowed to enter without permission. By using it as a temporary place of detention, we avoided turning the premises of the Duma into a prison, and the government officials could thus be kept in custody in their own quarters. Shcheglovitov was soon joined by Protopopov, Sukhomlinov, and a whole galaxy of luminaries of the old bureaucratic world.

By three o'clock that afternoon the Duma was unrecognizable. It was packed with civilians and soldiers. From every direction people approached us for instructions or advice. The Provisional Committee, which had only just been formed, was compelled to act as an executive power. We were like the general staff of an army during war operations: We could not see the battlefield, but we learned what was going on from reports, telephone messages, and eyewitness accounts. Although we did not have a detailed report of every single development, we had a good overall picture of events. The reports came in at a bewildering rate. Hundreds of people wanted attention, gave advice, and asked for work. There was a constant hubbub of excitement which sometimes bordered on hysteria. We had to keep our heads, for it would have been disastrous to waste precious time or to show any lack of self-confidence. We had to decide on the spot what answers to give, what orders to issue, when to encourage and when to discourage, where to send troops and reinforcements, how to find room for the hundreds of people being arrested, how best to utilize the services of competent people, and, last but not least, how to feed and house the thousands of people crowding the Duma. Apart from all that, we had to think about the formation of a new government and about drafting a program acceptable to all parties. At the same time we had to keep track of events outside Petrograd, particularly at Army Headquarters and in the Tsar's train.

I think it was approximately four o'clock when someone came to see about finding space in the Tauride Palace for the Soviet of Workers' Deputies, which had also just been formed. With Rodzyanko's consent Room 13 was turned over to them, and they convened their first meeting there without delay. Naturally, the representatives of the workers had been selected more or less at random, since it had been quite impossible to organize a proper election at such short notice. The Soviet elected a temporary Executive Committee with Chkheidze as chairman and Skobelev and myself as vice-chairmen. I only learned of my election later, as I was not present at the meeting. In fact, I seldom attended the meetings of the Soviet or its Executive Committee. From the very beginning my relations with the leaders of the Soviet were strained. They hated the way I continually opposed the theoretical socialism which they tried to impose on the Revolution. But I am speaking of the Executive Committee as it was during the first few weeks. Later on, both it and the Soviet as a whole changed for the better.

But the Duma was the only national center of power. The Committee had acted without any prompting from the extreme left wing; it had set the Revolution going simply because the time was ripe. In fact, the first news communicated to the front was an account of the Duma proceedings, and the Revolution was successful chiefly because all the soldiers in the field, with their commanding officers, welcomed the change from the very first. The men at the front saw the gravity of the country's plight, and they, more than anyone else, accepted the Duma's authority.

By sundown on February 27 the entire city of Petrograd was in the hands of insurgent troops. The former government machinery had ceased to operate, and some of the ministry buildings and government offices had been occupied by revolutionaries. Other buildings, such as the headquarters of the secret police, the police stations, and the law courts, had been set on fire. Inside the Duma we had by now set up a central body to control the troops and the insurgents. At times, the crowds had been so enormous that they seemed about to engulf us all, but then they would subside and give us a few moments' respite. The Tauride Palace had seemed to groan and sway under the pressure of the mighty human waves. From the outside it looked more like a military camp than a legislative institution. Boxes of ammunition,

hand grenades, stacks of rifles and machine guns lay about everywhere. Every available corner was taken up by soldiers, among whom,
unfortunately, there were very few officers.

Due to the impossibility of tackling the fundamental issues of government during the daytime, in the maelstrom of men, reports, and
events, we had been forced to wait for nightfall, when the crowd dispersed and the halls and lobbies emptied. As soon as calm was restored, endless discussions, conferences, and impassioned arguments
filled the rooms of the Provisional Committee. There, in the stillness
of the night, we began to sketch the outline of a new Russia.

We were confronted, first of all, with the problem of organizing
emergency defenses and with the task of taking over the Petrograd
garrison. On that first day, however, we had very few officers at our
disposal and few men with adequate technical knowledge. One of our
first actions that evening was to set up an *ad hoc* Military Commission,
which initially comprised civilians with some knowledge of military
affairs, a sprinkling of officers and enlisted men, and Rodzyanko
and myself. It was the task of this commission to direct operations
against Protopopov's police, who still offered armed resistance to the
revolution.

While the Commission was being organized, the First Infantry Reserve arrived at the Duma. It was the first regiment to arrive with its
personnel complete, headed by its colonel and officers.

However, despite this dearth of officers, we managed to improvise
the capital's defenses, although it was painfully clear that we could
never resist an all-out attack and that the enemy could gain complete
control of the city with two or three well-trained regiments. However,
the former government did not have a single soldier in Petrograd willing to turn against the people and the Duma.

We in the Duma knew that victory was ours, but we had no idea
what forces the former government had at its disposal outside the
capital. We did not even know the government's whereabouts or what
it was doing. Eventually a report came in that the officials were sitting
at the Mariinsky Palace. A detachment of troops with armored cars
was immediately dispatched to arrest all the members, but the soldiers
returned at midnight, having been unable to reach the Palace on account of gunfire. Later, the members of the former government were
said to be hiding in the Admiralty, which was guarded by troops and

artillery from Gatchina. Another report came in that Tsarist troops were approaching from Finland, and we hastily organized defenses in the Vyborg district of the city along the Russian-Finnish railroad line.

At the same time, the Provisional Committee sent Alexander Bublikov, who had been a member of the fourth Duma, with a detachment of soldiers to take over the central railroad telegraph administration. This well-timed step gave the Duma control of the entire railroad system, and henceforth no trains could leave without Bublikov's consent. It was Bublikov, acting upon instructions from the Provisional Committee, who telegraphed the first news of the revolution to the rest of the country. The railroad workers welcomed the revolution with great enthusiasm. At the same time, they maintained excellent discipline, and it was entirely due to their efforts that military trains ran to the front on schedule.

By now, we had made such headway that a return to the past was no longer possible. The rift between the old and new regime was final; the Provisional Committee had virtually wrested power from the Tsarist authorities.

All through the night we talked and argued in the Duma President's office, and every item of news or vague rumor was subjected to intense scrutiny. The formation of the Soviet earlier in the day was regarded as a critical event, since there was now a danger that unless we formed a provisional government at once, the Soviet would proclaim itself the supreme authority of the Revolution. Rodzyanko was one of those who wavered longest. Finally, just before midnight, he announced his decision to accept the post of president of the Provisional Committee, which would now assume supreme power, pending the formation of a new government. When the clock struck midnight on February 27–28, Russia possessed the nucleus of a new national government.

The first night of the Revolution had passed, and an eternity seemed to separate us from the day before. That morning, February 28, the military academies [2] and most of the guards regiments came to express their solidarity with the Duma. Reports came in that civilians and soldiers in the neighboring towns were also joining us. Rodzyanko received telegrams from the commander-in-chief and many commanding officers which dispelled all anxiety regarding the feelings

[2] In Russia military academies were institutions of higher learning for officers.

of the army in the field. The people of Tsarskoye Selo declared their allegiance to the Revolution the very same day that Nicholas II left headquarters for Tsarskoye Selo.

In Petrograd, despite all the chaos, new organizations were beginning to emerge. Resistance to our authority was negligible, and we were now only worried about a possible last stand by the former government in some other part of the country. However, the situation in Tsarskoye Selo encouraged us to believe that this was very unlikely. Then we learned that the Tsar had ordered General N. Ya. Ivanov, hero of the first Galician campaign (1914), from the front with a body of special troops to take Petrograd and restore order. The troops arrived at Tsarskoye Selo at dawn on March 1, where they completely vanished. The General himself escaped and made his way back to Mogilev.

Meanwhile we were receiving so many welcome expressions of support from the local garrison that we soon established a routine for greeting them. A body of troops, such as the Semyonov Guards Regiment, would arrive at the Duma, rush excitedly into the Catherine Hall, and form in the middle. Then Rodzyanko would deliver a speech urging them to trust the men in power, to maintain a high standard of discipline, and so on. His speech would invariably be drowned out by wild cheering. Then the commanding officer would reply, and there would be more jubilant cheering. The soldiers usually asked to hear other speakers such as Milyukov, Chkheidze, or myself. I found it an exhilarating experience to be able to speak freely at last to a free people. The arrival of these troops, including the sensational appearance of the Tsar's Cossack bodyguard, greatly strengthened our status at the Tauride Palace.

At the same time, however, these troops presented us with a number of acute problems. For one thing, the soldiers were becoming restless and unmanageable, not least because they suspected that the officers were hatching a counterrevolutionary plot with the High Command. When rumors began circulating that at some barracks officers were confiscating the soldiers' arms, Colonel Engelhardt, a staff officer, conservative deputy of the Duma, and chairman of the Military Commission, immediately issued an order, promulgated early on the morning of March 1, saying that "the rumors, which have been checked in two regiments, are totally devoid of foundation. The Commander of the Petrograd Garrison hereby announces that the most rigorous measures, *including the death penalty,* will be applied against such acts by officers."

In addition, the shortage of officers made it easier for the Soviet to infiltrate the barracks. Its leaders were quick to see the advantage of gaining control of the 150,000 men of the Petrograd Garrison, and, once they had obtained it, they utilized this advantage to the full. The Executive Committee of the Soviet formed its own so-called Military Section on the night of February 27. The Section soon established close contact with all parts of the city, and during the two months in which Guchkov was minister of war and Kornilov was military commander of the Petrograd Military District, it competed on an equal footing with the official military authority. That same evening, a delegation from the newly-formed Military Section of the Soviet called on Colonel Engelhardt. The members of the delegation asked him to issue an order to the thousands of soldiers who were without commanders and had no idea what they should do.

Engelhardt refused to have anything to do with the order. He said that the first order relating to the Petrograd Military District should come from the new minister of war, Guchkov, who would probably take up office within a few days.

The soldiers' delegation of the Soviet was greatly disappointed by the Colonel's refusal. In parting, they told Engelhardt that, in view of his unwillingness to help, they would have to issue the order themselves. They returned to the Soviet and there drew up their famous "Order No. 1."

The passage pertaining to officers suspected of counterrevolutionary activities was couched in terms much milder than Engelhardt had employed. It contained no threat of capital punishment. Contrary to assertions, no mention was made of the election of officers to the soldiers' committees, and strict discipline in the ranks was demanded. Furthermore, the order instituted soldiers' committees in all units of the Petrograd Garrison to supervise the economic, cultural, and political affairs of the soldiers. The order also stated that arms were not to be issued to officers, but were to be kept under lock and key by the committees.

Some individual or group, whose identity still remains a mystery, malevolently broadcasted this order, intended only for the Petrograd Garrison, to the entire front. Although this action caused a great deal of trouble, it was not, as many members of Russian and foreign military circles absurdly believed, the source of the "disintegration of the Russian army." Nor is it true, as these people maintained, that the order was drafted and issued, if not directly by the Provisional Government, then at least with its connivance. The simple fact is that the order was promulgated two days before the formation of the Provisional Government. Moreover, the first step taken by this government was to make it clear to the soldiers at the front that the order had been issued for the Petrograd Garrison alone and was not applicable to them.

There is no doubt that the receipt of the order at the front was a misfortune, and it speeded up the formation of the soldiers' committees, but it was not a decisive factor, since committees had already been formed, before its publication, aboard ships of the Black Sea Fleet and in certain units at the Northern Front. Furthermore, shortly after the collapse of the monarchy, General Tsurikov, commander of the Fourth Army on the Rumanian Front, reported to headquarters that in view of the emergency he had organized committees in the armies under his command and that he considered it advisable for all the other armies to follow the same procedure as soon as possible.

Although German agents were trying to stir up trouble among the sailors and soldiers by inciting them against their officers, most people in responsible positions, including the Soviet Executive Committee, condemned the mistreatment or lynching of officers and did their best to prevent insubordination. Chkheidze and I published a message to the Petrograd Garrison, pointing out that a certain proclamation against the officers purportedly issued by the committees of the Social Democrat and Social Revolutionary parties was a deliberate forgery, perpetrated by *agents provocateurs*. Soon after this the officers of the garrison pledged their allegiance to the revolution and the Duma, and the tension eased. Their statement, signed by Milyukov, Karaulov, and myself, was widely circulated, and the first speech I made as minister of justice ended with a call for obedience to the officers and for the maintenance of discipline.

From the very beginning of the Revolution, a host of police spies, German agents, and extreme leftists tried to incite hatred toward us. To understand how dangerous and how effective this propaganda was, it must be realized that the secret police (Okhrana) of the old regime still had several thousand agents, spies, agitators, and informers operating among all segments of the population. In addition, there were many enemy agents at work, who printed and circulated leaflets which urged the crowds to commit murder, and who aggravated misunderstandings and spread false news, which, despite obvious spuriousness, had an inflammatory effect on the gullible populace.

By the morning of March 1 the framework of the new government and its program had been drawn up, and it was at this point that representatives of the Provisional Committee opened talks with the Soviet. A Provisional Government was projected, to be composed almost entirely of members of the Progressive Bloc. At the last moment, a portfolio was offered to Chkheidze as minister of labor and to myself as minister of justice.

The Provisional Committee invited the Executive Committee of the Soviet to send two representatives as members of the Provisional Government, but the Executive Committee decided to refrain from participation in the Provisional Government because the Revolution was a "bourgeois" one.

This decision presented me with a major problem: Should I remain in the Soviet and reject a post in the Provisional Government or should I accept the latter and withdraw from the Soviet? Both alternatives seemed unacceptable. Unable to come to a conclusion, I was forced to put the problem aside for the time being, for events were taking place which demanded my full attention.

That day, March 1, the general situation seemed to grow even more alarming. Vague rumors were circulating about disorders at the Kronstadt Naval Base. In Petrograd itself hoodlums attacked the Astoria, an officers' hotel, broke into some of the rooms, and molested several women. At about the same time news of the arrival of General Ivanov and his troops at Tsarskoye Selo spread rapidly through the city. Although there was no cause for alarm, the crowds in the Duma building were nervous and agitated by the uncertainty of the situation.

Order was gradually restored. At eleven o'clock Grand Duke Cyril came to pledge his allegiance at the head of a detachment of Navy Guards. In Petrograd the troops continued to fraternize with the people, and the firing slackened off. A city police force, the militia, was formed, and a new chief of police was appointed. People were working hard to restore discipline in the garrison, and Guchkov, who became minister of war the next day, took an active part in this work.

Meanwhile, the Revolution was spreading to the provinces. Good news came in from Moscow, where, as one eyewitness put it, "everything was going like clockwork."

News of the spread of the Revolution came pouring in from hundreds of towns all over the country; the movement was now nationwide. This made it all the more urgent to speed the formation of a new government. By the evening of March 1, the Provisional Committee was busily putting the finishing touches to the Provisional Government's manifesto, which was due to be published the next day. For the moment we were only concerned with the organization of ministries. The question of a supreme executive authority was not on the agenda, since at that time the majority of the Provisional Committee of the Duma still took it for granted that Grand Duke Michael would be regent until the heir Alexis came of age.

But by the night of March 1–2, it had been agreed almost unanimously that the future state order would be decided upon by a constituent assembly. Thus the monarchy was discarded forever and relegated to the archives of history.

The first official statement made by the Provisional Government was a subject of heated discussion. On certain items there was complete disagreement. The representatives of the Provisional Committee and the Soviet were at loggerheads over the rights of the soldiers, and this item of the original Soviet draft had to be changed. Every paragraph gave rise to sharp dissension, although there was no mention of the war in it.

It is extraordinary that an issue as painful and crucial as the war was not even considered in discussing the draft statute of the government. The government was given a completely free hand with regard to war aims and undertook no formal obligations. Later on, however, no other issue was the cause of such bitter attacks on the Provisional Government from the Left.

It may seem even more extraordinary that this inaugural document did not make any mention of the urgent need for agrarian reforms. In fact, it was couched in such general terms that I could feel little enthusiasm for it. Nevertheless, despite the fact that from its inception the government met all its obligations, and even launched an ambitious program for agrarian and labor reform, the Left continued to accuse us of neglecting our duty to the peasants and workers, and thereby of sowing the seeds of distrust among the masses.

The cabinet lists were ready. Among the Duma members it was considered essential that I have a government post, and I learned later that some of the ministerial nominees had made their acceptance conditional upon my participation.

The night of March 1, which was perhaps the climax of those incredible days, found me near collapse. The excessive strain of the previous two days was beginning to tell on me, but I had to find a way out of my difficult dilemma. Even in the Soviet it was generally considered wise to include me in the government, and I realized that unless a representative of the Soviet was included, the government would not enjoy full popular support. I remained firm in my determination, therefore, even when Chkheidze flatly refused a post and I found myself isolated in the Cabinet.

Finally, unable to come to any conclusion, I decided just before daybreak to go home. It was strange to walk the familiar street without the familiar escort of secret police, to pass the sentries and see the smoke and flames still rising from the Gendarmerie, where I had been questioned in 1905.

It was not until I reached home that the full impact of recent events hit me. For two or three hours I lay in a semidelirious state. Then suddenly the answer to my problem came to me in a flash. I must telephone my immediate acceptance of the government post and fight it out later at a general meeting of the Soviet. Then the Executive Committee and members of the Soviet could argue it out among themselves. Oddly enough, my decision to go against the ruling of the Executive Committee was strongly influenced by the thought of the prisoners in the Government Pavilion. If any minister from the Progressive Bloc could succeed in protecting them from the fury of the mob and so keep the Revolution free from bloodshed, it was I.

I telephoned the Provisional Committee and told Milyukov of my decision. He, at least, seemed pleased and offered his congratulations, but I was not so certain of the Soviet's reaction to it.

When I returned to the Duma, I found my decision the subject of lively discussion, for everyone was uncertain as to the Soviet's reaction. I went straight to the Executive Committee, where I was met by grim faces. A plenary meeting was in progress, and I announced that I would go in and explain my move at once. The members of the Executive Committee tried to dissuade me, but I refused, for I was unwilling to delay the matter.

In the adjoining chamber I found Steklov, a member of the Executive Committee, reporting on his negotiations with the Provisional Committee about the formation of a government. As soon as he had finished, Chkheidze, who was in the chair, announced that I had asked for the floor. I climbed onto a table and launched into a speech. I soon saw that I was putting my point across. I only needed to look at the faces of the crowd and to watch their eyes to see that they were with me. I told them I had come there as minister of justice in the new government and that it had been impossible for me to wait any longer for the approval of the Soviet. I had now come, I told them, to ask for a vote of confidence. The rest of my speech was drowned in thunderous applause.

When I jumped down from the table, I was lifted on the shoulders of the Soviet delegates and carried across the Duma to the very door of the Provisional Committee. I was triumphant. I had led the way against the absurd veto of the Executive Committee, and I was confident that others would follow, so that eventually a coalition could be formed. But in the midst of the ovations I understood that the Soviet leaders would try to get their revenge, and sure enough, a fierce campaign was soon unleashed against me and against my influence and authority among the masses.

On the morning of March 2, Milyukov, speaking to the throng in Catherine Hall about the composition of the Provisional Government, declared that the Grand Duke Michael Alexandrovich would become regent and that we had decided to establish a constitutional monarchy in Russia. Milyukov's declaration aroused the ire of all the soldiers and workers in the Tauride Palace.

The Executive Committee hurriedly called a special meeting, at which I was subjected to hostile crossexamination. But I refused to be drawn into a dispute and merely replied: "Yes, that is the plan, but it will never be carried into effect. It is quite impossible, so there is no reason to be alarmed. I have not been consulted about the regency

Kerensky at the age of two, with his mother.

Kerensky at the age of twelve.

Soldiers and workers thronging the Duma in Catherine Hall during the first days of the Revolution.

Pictorial Parade

Prince Georgi Evgenievich Lvov, Minister-President of the first Provisional Government.

M. I. Tereshchenko, Minister of Finance in the first Provisional Government, and later Foreign Minister in Kerensky's cabinet.

Members of the first Provisional Government: counterclockwise, Prince G. E. Lvov, A. I. Konovalov, A. F. Kerensky, A. I. Guchkov, V. N. Lvov, P. N. Milyukov, M. I. Tereshchenko, F. I. Rodichev (not a member of the cabinet), N. V. Nekrasov, A. A. Manuilov, A. I. Shingarev, and I. V. Godnev.

Kerensky addressing the workers during a May visit to Helsinki.

Kerensky (center) greeting soldiers on the Northern Front.

Kerensky (+) among his men at the front, September, 1917.

Members of the second coalition government: left to right, seated, P. P. Yurenyev (Cadet), Transport; F. F. Kokoshkin (Cadet), State Comptroller; A. V. Peshekhonov (Popular Socialist), Food; N. V. Nekrasov (Cadet), Deputy Prime Minister and Minister of Finance; A. F. Kerensky (Socialist Revolutionary), Prime Minister and Minister of War and the Navy; N. D. A. V. Avksentiev (S.R.), Interior; V. M. Chernov (S.R.), Agriculture; A. M. Nikitin (Menshevik), Post and Telegraph; standing, A. V. Kartashov (no party), Religion; S. F. Oldenbourg (Cadet), Education; A. C. Zarudny (Popular Socialist), Justice; I. N. Yefremov (Progressive), Welfare; B. V. Savinkov (S.R.), Deputy Minister of War; M. I. Skobelev (Menshevik), Labor; S. N. Prokopovich (Menshevik), Industry and Commerce.

Last visit with Alekseyev at Headquarters.

Culver Pictures

Kerensky exhorting a regiment.

Kerensky (center) reviewing a regiment of Cossacks, during the funeral of fifteen Cossacks killed by the Bolsheviks in the July 4th uprising.

Historical Pictures Service, Chicago

Kerensky (second from right) and his aides de camp in the Kremlin.

Kerensky's supporters in the Winter Palace awaiting the attack of the Bolshevik forces. Note the machine guns in the foreground at left.

Russo-German fraternization in 1917—soldiers dancing the krakowiak in the snow after the Armistice.

Kerensky in Paris, 1918.

and I took no part in the discussion. As a last resort, I can ask the government to choose between abandoning this plan and accepting my resignation."

This question of a regency did not trouble me in the least, but it was difficult to transmit my own confidence to others, and the Executive Committee tried to interfere. It wanted to send its own delegates to the Tsar or, failing that, to prevent our delegates from getting a train. But in this they did not succeed, and the delegation of the Provisional Committee of the Duma, consisting of Guchkov and Shulgin, left for Pskov at about 4:00 P.M., to demand the Tsar's abdication.

While we were waiting for news from Guchkov and Shulgin, there were many things to be attended to. There was a special telegraph office in the Duma, and that evening I sent out my first orders as minister of justice. The first wire instructed public prosecutors throughout the country to liberate all political prisoners and to transmit to them the greetings of the new revolutionary government. The second wire went to Siberia, ordering that Catherine Breshkovska, "the grandmother of the Russian Revolution," be released at once from exile and conveyed with all due honors to Petrograd. I sent similar wires ordering the release of five Social Democrat members of the fourth Duma who had been condemned to exile in 1915.

Meanwhile, a very serious situation was developing in Helsinki: The destruction of the fleet and a massacre of the officers was expected at any moment. I was hurriedly summoned to the Admiralty to conduct a long-distance telephone conversation with a representative of the sailors. In response to my pleas the man promised to do everything he could to calm the sailors, and the massacre of the officers was averted. The same evening a delegation made up of representatives of all parties left for Helsinki to try to restore discipline. For a time we had no more trouble from that naval base. But on March 4, Admiral Nepenin was murdered by a civilian, who turned out to be a German agent.

The affair at Kronstadt, mentioned in Chapter 14, had actually occurred on February 27, but news of it did not reach us until later.

On the evening of March 2, the following statement from the Provisional Government was signed, and it was then issued on the following day:

FROM THE PROVISIONAL GOVERNMENT [3]

The Temporary Committee of the members of the State Duma, with the assistance and the sympathy of the army and the inhabitants of the capital, has now attained such a large measure of success over the dark forces of the old regime that it is possible for the Committee to undertake the organization of a more stable executive power.

With this end in mind, the Temporary Committee of the State Duma has appointed the following persons as ministers of the first cabinet representing the public; their past political and public activities assure them the confidence of the country:

Minister-President and Minister of the Interior—Prince G. E. Lvov
Minister of Foreign Affairs—P. N. Milyukov
Minister of War and Navy—A. I. Guchkov
Minister of Transport—N. V. Nekrasov
Minister of Trade and Industry—A. I. Konovalov
Minister of Finance—M. I. Tereshchenko
Minister of Education—A. A. Manuilov
Chief Procurator of the Holy Synod—V. Lvov
Minister of Agriculture—A. I. Shingarev
Minister of Justice—A. F. Kerensky

The actual work of the cabinet will be guided by the following principles:

1. An immediate and complete amnesty in all cases of a political and religious nature, including terrorist acts, millitary revolts and agrarian offenses, etc.

2. Freedom of speech, press, and assembly, and the right to unionize and strike with the extension of political freedom to persons serving in the armed forces as limited by the exigencies of military and technical circumstances.

3. The abolition of all restrictions based on class, religion, and nationality.

4. The immediate preparation for the convocation of the Constituent Assembly on the basis of universal, equal, direct suffrage and secret ballot, which will determine the form of government and the constitution of the country.

[3] *Izvestiia Revoliutsionnoi Nedeli*, No. 7, March 3, 1917, p. 1. See also *The Russian Provisional Government, 1917*, Vol. I, pp. 135–136.

5. The substitution of a people's militia for the police, with elective officers responsible to the organs of local self-government.

6. Elections to the organs of local self-government are to be held on the basis of universal, direct, equal suffrage and secret ballot.

7. Those military units which took part in the revolutionary movement shall be neither disarmed nor withdrawn from Petrograd.[4]

8. While preserving strict military discipline on duty and during military service, the soldiers are to be freed from all restrictions in the exercise of those civil rights to which all other citizens are entitled.

The Provisional Government considers it its duty to add that it has not the slightest intention of taking advantage of the military situation to delay in any way the realization of the reforms and the measures outlined above.

President of the State Duma, M. RODZYANKO
Minister-President of the Council of Ministers, PRINCE LVOV
Ministers: MILYUKOV, NEKRASOV, MANUILOV, KONO-
VALOV, TERESHCHENKO, V. LVOV, SHINGAREV,
KERENSKY

When night fell on March 2, the members of the Provisional Government met to talk over other basic issues. We were still impatiently waiting for news from Guchkov and Shulgin. We knew that any attempt to transfer the power to a regent would have grave consequences, and I learned from private conversations with my colleagues that nearly all of them had come to accept the fact with equanimity. Milyukov was the only one there who still held out, and Guchkov and Shulgin were not present to give their views. But everyone agreed that the crucial moment was approaching.

The Tsar's Abdication

The first news of the Revolution of February 27 was received calmly by the Tsar. The inevitable disorders resulting from a showdown with the Duma had been provided for in his plan for the restoration of absolute power, and he had been assured by General Khabalov, com-

---

[4] This clause was the most controversial one. Milyukov wrote in his *Vospominaniia*, II, 307, that he could not oppose point 7 because "after all, we did not know at that moment whether or not they (the insurgent troops) would have to engage in further combat with the 'loyal' units that would be sent to the capital."

mander of the Special St. Petersburg Army, that "the troops will do their duty." Several guard cavalry regiments had already been recalled from the front, as the Tsar had promised Protopopov before leaving for headquarters on February 22, and were now moving in the direction of the capital.

On the morning of February 27, the Tsar received a frantic appeal from his brother, Grand Duke Michael, urging him to halt the disorder by appointing a prime minister who had the confidence of the Duma and the public. But the Tsar curtly told the Grand Duke to mind his own business and instructed General Khabalov to use every means at his disposal to crush the incipient revolt. The same day, the Tsar ordered General Ivanov to Tsarskoye Selo.

The next day, the Tsar himself left for Tsarskoye Selo.

At the orders of Bublikov, commissar for transport, the imperial train and a second train carrying his suite were to be halted at Dno, a junction through which they must pass on their way to Tsarskoye Selo.

Finding the line blocked at Dno, the Tsar consulted hastily with his closest aides, and then ordered the train to proceed to the headquarters of General Ruzsky, commander of the Northern Front, in Pskov. The line in that direction was still open. And so at 7:30 P.M., on March 1, the Tsar reached Pskov, where he was met by General Ruzsky and his staff.

According to the eyewitness accounts of his aides, the Tsar showed no sign of nervousness or irritation during this difficult journey. Actually, there is nothing surprising about this, for the Tsar had always shown a strange lack of response to external events. But I am certain that beneath this unnatural outward calm Nicholas II was undergoing profound mental stress; he must have realized by now that his plans had collapsed and that he had lost all his authority.

The man who reached Pskov was a very different person from the Tsar who only the day before had sallied forth from Mogilev to put an end to "sedition." All his supporters had melted away. Now he was ready to make any concession to save Russia's fighting strength on the eve of the decisive spring offensive against the armies of Wilhelm II, whom he so despised and hated.

That evening, in his private train, the Tsar listened to reports from General Ruzsky and his chief of staff on what had been happening during the journey. The reports had no effect on his resolve.

At 11:30 that night General Ruzsky brought him a telegram just received from General Alekseyev, in which the general spoke of the "steadily growing danger that anarchy will spread throughout the entire country, the further demoralization of the army, and the impossibility of continuing the war in the present situation." The telegram went on to demand the publication of an official statement offering the people some sort of reassurance, preferably in the form of a manifesto announcing the formation of a "responsible ministry" and entrusting this task to the Duma President. Alekseyev implored the Tsar to publish the manifesto without delay and went on to suggest a suitable draft for the contents of it. Having read the telegram and listened to Ruzsky's arguments, the Tsar agreed to publish a manifesto the very next day.

Immediately after this decision the Tsar sent General Ivanov the following message: "Hope you arrived safely. Please don't take any action until I arrive and you report to me. Nicholas. March 2. 00.20 hours."

Then the Tsar ordered the return to the front of all the units that had been moved to Petrograd to crush the revolt by force.

At two o'clock in the morning, General Ruzsky tells us, Nicholas signed a manifesto appointing a government responsible to the legislature. This manifesto was never published.

The spontaneous revolutionary movement had spread from St. Petersburg to the front, and at 10:00 on March 2 General Alekseyev contacted the commanders of all the fronts and of the Baltic and Black Sea Fleets and proposed to them that in view of the catastrophic situation they should implore the Tsar to preserve the monarchy by abdicating in favor of his heir, Alexis, and appointing Grand Duke Michael as regent. The commanders, with Grand Duke Nicholas Nicholaevich at their head, complied with astonishing promptness.

At 2:30 P.M. Alekseyev passed these messages on to the Tsar, who announced his abdication almost at once. But the Tsar abdicated not only on behalf of himself, but also on behalf of his son, naming his brother Michael his successor. At the same time he appointed Prince Lvov as president of the Council of Ministers and Grand Duke Nicholas Nicholaevich as commander-in-chief of the Russian armies. But apart from his closest aides, no one in Russia knew anything about the decision of Nicholas II.

In fact, it was at a meeting of the new government and the members of the Provisional Committee on the night of March 3 that the first news of the Tsar's unexpected step was received from Guchkov and Shulgin. When the announcement was made there was a momentary hush, and then Rodzyanko said: "Grand Duke Michael's accession is impossible." None of the Provisional Committee raised any objection. The whole gathering seemed unanimous.

First Rodzyanko and then many of the others put forward arguments as to why the Grand Duke could not be Tsar. They claimed, for example, that he had never been interested in affairs of state, that he was married morganatically to a woman well known for her political intrigues, and that, at the crucial moment when he could have saved the situation,[5] he had shown himself to lack the power of decision, and so on.

As I listened to these irrelevant arguments, I realized that it was not the arguments themselves that mattered. What mattered was the speakers' intuitive realization that at this stage of the revolution *any* new tsar was absolutely out of the question. Suddenly Milyukov, silent until then, began to speak.

With his usual doggedness he argued that what mattered was not *who* was to be the new tsar but that there should be a tsar. The Duma was not seeking to establish a republic, but merely wanted a new figure on the throne. He went on to say that he thought the Duma, in close collaboration with the new tsar, should quell the raging storm. Russia could not be without a monarch at this crucial moment in her history. He insisted that all the necessary steps should be taken to accept the new tsar without further complication.

Shingarev made an attempt to support him, prompted by his close friendship with his party leader, but his arguments were feeble and unconvincing.

By now time was running out; it was already getting light, and a solution had yet to be found. The first essential was to stop the publi-

[5] On the morning of February 27, there had been a meeting between the Grand Duke, Rodzyanko, Nekrasov, Dmitryukov, and Prince Golitsyn in the Mariinsky Palace. The members of the Duma Presidium and the Chairman of the Council of Ministers had insisted that the Grand Duke take charge of the Petrograd Garrison cavalry and act at once to restore order. But the Grand Duke had tried to avoid an independent decision and had said that he would have to talk it over with his brother and ask him to appoint a new chairman of the Council of Ministers.

cation of the act of abdication in favor of the Tsar's brother until the conference could reach some final decision.

By general consent the meeting was temporarily adjourned. Rodzyanko drove to the War Ministry, which had a direct wire to Headquarters, and got in touch with General Alekseyev, who told him that the Act was already being distributed to the troops. Rodzyanko instructed him to stop the distribution immediately. This order was given, but in certain sectors of the front the soldiers had already received the announcement and were swearing their allegiance to the new sovereign. I refer to this episode because it led to some unpleasant complications in one or two of the units, where the soldiers suspected the generals of intrigue.

When Rodzyanko came back from the telephone, we decided to contact the Grand Duke at the apartment of Princess Putyatin at No. 12 Millionny Street, where he had been staying since his return from Gatchina, and inform him of the night's events. It was six o'clock in the morning and no one wanted to disturb him at such an early hour. At that moment, however, there seemed to be little point in observing the rules of etiquette, so I rang up the Princess' apartment myself. Everyone must have been up, for the phone was immediately answered by the Grand Duke's close friend and private secretary, an Englishman named Johnson. I explained the situation and asked if the Grand Duke would be prepared to meet us between eleven and twelve that morning. An affirmative answer was given a few minutes later.

During our discussion of the attitude we were to adopt at our meeting with the Duke, most speakers advocated Rodzyanko and Prince Lvov as spokesmen for our side, with the others present as observers.

However, as I had expected, Milyukov disagreed, saying that he had the right, both as a statesman and as a person, to make his view known to the Grand Duke at that vital moment in Russian history. After some argument it was decided, on the basis of a proposal I myself had put forward, that Milyukov should be given as much time as he felt he needed to state his opinion to the Grand Duke.

At 11:00 A.M. on March 4 we held our meeting with Grand Duke Michael. Rodzyanko and Lvov opened the meeting with a brief exposition of the majority opinion. Then Milyukov, speaking at great length and with all the force of his personal conviction, tried to prove to the Duke that he should accept the throne. Milyukov was stalling for time—to the obvious embarrassment of the Duke—in the hope that Guchkov and Shulgin, who held similar views, would return from Pskov in time to support him. His ploy was successful, for they did indeed arrive toward the end of his speech. But when called upon, Guchkov, a man of few words, merely said, "I fully support Milyukov's views." Shulgin said nothing at all.[6]

There was a brief silence, and then the Grand Duke said he would like to confer in private with two of the people present. The Duma President was somewhat at a loss, and glancing at me, replied that it would not be possible in view of the fact that we had decided to hold the meeting as a body. I felt that since the Tsar's brother was about to make such a momentous decision, we should not refuse him this request, and I said so. That was how I "influenced" the Grand Duke's choice.

Again there was a silence. The identity of the men the Grand Duke chose would be an indication of what his decision would be. He asked Lvov and Rodzyanko to accompany him into the next room.

When they returned, Grand Duke Michael announced that he would accept the throne only at the request of the Constituent Assembly, which the Provisional Government had undertaken to convene.

The question was settled: The monarchy and the dynasty were things of the past. Russia was virtually a republic from that moment, and the power—supreme, executive, and legislative—was now, pending the convocation of a Constituent Assembly, in the hands of the Provisional Government.

---

[6] The reason for their reticence soon became clear. It seems that at the Warsaw Station thousands of railroadmen had organized a welcome for them on their way back from Pskov, but as soon as Guchkov began reading the act of abdication and reached the point mentioning the handing over of power to Grand Duke Michael, the crowd became enraged, so much so that the two delegates had to be hustled out of a side door in order to save them from the most unpleasant consequences.

14

The First Months of the Revolution

> Blest is he who visits this earth
> at its moments of destiny:
> he has been summoned by the gods
> to partake with them at their feast.
>
> He is witness to their sublime spectacles,
> they make him privy to their councils,
> and, like a god himself, in his own lifetime,
> he drinks immortality from their cup.
> —Tyutchev.

ALTHOUGH I read these lines many times in my youth, it was not until after the fall of the Monarchy in Russia that I truly understood their meaning.

A man who lives through a fateful turning point in the history of the world is blest because he is given a chance to plumb the very depths of human history, to witness the destruction of an old world and the creation of a new one. He sees that the main course of human affairs is determined, not so much by economic "laws," as by a clash of human wills, of people pitting themselves against each other in the attempt to create a new way of life out of the wreck of the old one.

From the moment of the collapse of the Monarchy in February, 1917, until the downfall, in October of the same year, of the free Russia that briefly succeeded it, I found myself in the center of events. I was, in fact, their focal point, the center of the vortex of human passions and conflictive ambitions which raged around me in the titanic struggle to erect a new state built on political and social principles utterly different from those which had governed the life of the old imperial Russia.

The downfall of the Monarchy came quite unexpectedly for the population of the country, at a critical moment in Russia's total war with Germany, and it was accompanied by the equally unexpected collapse of the whole administrative machinery of the state. The task before us now was to build up the complete structure of a new state.

During the very first days of its existence, the Provisional Government began to receive from every corner of Russia, from large towns and remote villages, as well as from the Front, a stream of jubilant messages of support. But along with these telegrams came alarming reports from all over the country telling of the paralysis of local authority and of the total collapse of the administration and police forces. It looked as if Russia would be torn apart by riots, looting, and uncontrollable violence. If this had happened, the country would have suffered a swift defeat at the hands of the German and Austrian armies.

But this did not happen, mainly because the overwhelming majority of the population, irrespective of class, religion, or race, understood that the collapse of the Monarchy was the culmination of the long and difficult struggle for emancipation which had been the main theme of its history in modern times.

For a moment, therefore, all sectional, class, and personal interests were set aside, all differences forgotten. As Prince Yevgeny Trubetskoy wrote at the time, the February Revolution was unique in history in that all classes of society participated in it. It was a moment which brought into being "my" Russia—an ideal Russia which took the place of the Russia corrupted and defiled by Rasputin and by the universally hated Monarchy.

Unpopular officials were literally thrown out, and many were killed or wounded. Workers in the factories stopped working and got rid of unpopular managers and engineers by wheeling them out in barrows. In some places the peasants, remembering 1905–1906, began to solve the agrarian question in their own way by chasing away the landlords and seizing their land. In the towns, self-appointed "defenders of liberty" started arresting "counterrevolutionaries," or simply engaged in looting.

After three years of war the soldiers at the front were utterly weary.

They were no longer in a mood to obey their officers or to go on fighting the enemy.

The Provisional Government had four main tasks. These were, in order of priority:

(1) To continue the defense of the country; (2) to reestablish a working administrative apparatus throughout the country; (3) to carry out a number of basic political and social reforms; (4) to prepare the way for the transformation of Russia from a highly centralized state into a federal state.

In the spring of 1917, Russia's situation, both externally and internally, was so critical that it was vital, in the interests of the country's very existence, to carry out this program as quickly as possible. But it had to be carried out in a Russia which was politically and socially quite unlike the Russia in which the new government had been conceived and had come into being. This government, as Milyukov pointed out on the first day of the Revolution, was called upon to carry out the program of the Progressive Bloc. But the Progressive Bloc no longer existed. With the fall of the Monarchy the social structure of the country had changed beyond recognition. The overwhelming majority of the population, which had formerly been denied any part in the government of the country, had suddenly emerged at the forefront of political life. At the same time, the middle classes, which had hitherto played a positive and active part in the economic and political life of the country, receded into the background, while the landowning aristocracy, which had been so closely associated with the old regime, disappeared from the scene altogether. Under these conditions, the new Russia could only be ruled by men who possessed an immediate awareness of the fact that they were called upon to rule, not the Russia of yesterday, but a new Russia which was striving to attain the eternal goal of the Russian people: democratic government based on the rule of law and social justice. With scarcely a single exception, this understanding of the basic aim of the revolution was shared by all the members of the new government—these representatives of the "upper-middle classes" who were bound, according to the firm conviction of left-wing socialist doctrinaires, to rule in the name of the "bourgeoisie." In fact, in the opinion of the left wing, February 27, 1917, was merely the beginning of the "Girondist" phase of the Revolution. Utter nonsense as this idea was, it had unfortunate—indeed fatal—consequences for the future.

My memories of the first weeks of the Provisional Government are among the happiest of my political career. There were eleven of us in this government, of whom ten belonged to the liberal and moderate conservative parties. I was the only Socialist, and the left-wing press was soon ironically calling me "the hostage of democracy." Our President, Prince Lvov, was descended from Rurik and hence belonged to the ancient family which had ruled Russia for 700 years. Yet he had spent his whole life trying to improve the lot of the peasants, and he had long been an active participant in the struggle against the rapidly degenerating absolutist Monarchy. In the *zemstvo* he had fought stubbornly for the peasants' right to be represented in the political life of the country. He was one of the founders of the liberal movement in the *zemstvo* which, since the beginning of the century, had been in the forefront of the struggle for the Constitution, and had culminated in the Manifesto of October 17, 1905. He was by nature a shy, quiet man who did little talking and was a good listener. He had outstanding talent as an organizer, and his great moral authority showed itself in his creation of the all-Russian *zemstvo* union. Lvov had never been a party man, and after a short spell of collaboration with the People's Freedom Party in the first Duma he never again joined any party, or political or conspiratorial organization. He was a deeply religious man, and there was in him something of the Slavophile and the Tolstoyan. He preferred persuasion to giving orders, and at cabinet meetings he always tried to coax us into general agreement. He was often accused of lack of will power. This was completely untrue, as I discovered when I first met him in December of 1916. He believed "blindly," as Guchkov said of him, in the eventual triumph of democracy, in the capacity of the Russian people to play a constructive part in the affairs of state; and he was always saying, both in public and in private, "Do not lose heart, have faith in Russian freedom!"

I still find it difficult to understand how it was that from the very first cabinet meeting we talked with such complete and immediate agreement among ourselves about what had to be done. We all shared a feeling of duty which completely transcended our loyalty to any party. It is true that this feeling did not last, and that in the later life of the Provisional Government there was no longer such faith, solidarity, and mutual trust; but the fact remains that in the first month of the Revolution each of us was guided, rightly or wrongly, by only one consideration: the higher interests of the nation.

A number of my personal friends from the first days of the Provisional Government have since told me that all this was wishful thinking on my part and that we were never at any time as united as I had imagined. Be that as it may, the first weeks of the revolutionary transformation of Russia are engraved on my memory as being similar to the experience of a man who has seen a miracle taking place before his very eyes. And I think that even the most rationally minded of us must have had very similar feelings.

In an amazingly short time, we were able to lay the foundations, not only of a democratic government, but also of a whole new social system, which guaranteed a leading part in the affairs of the nation to the toiling masses of the population, and which, for the first time, established freedom from all political, social, and ethnic restrictions.

It could not be otherwise, if only for the simple reason that this whole new state of affairs was a direct expression of the will of the indisputable majority of the population.

In the library of the Hoover Institute there is an original set of the minutes of the meetings of the Provisional Government. Looking through these minutes a few years ago, I was myself astonished at the enormous amount of reforming legislation carried out in the first two months after the February Revolution. How were we able to accomplish so much in such a short time? After all, apart from passing legislation, the government also had to conduct the war and cope with innumerable day-to-day administrative questions. Moreover, there was an endless procession of visitors and delegations, representatives of the new local administrative bodies, and of the national minorities, constantly crowding the halls of the Mariinsky Palace and the offices of the individual ministers. It was an unbelievably hectic time of endless cabinet meetings by day and by night, and of all kinds of conferences and addresses to mass meetings. During the first weeks of the Revolution, it was impossible for a minister in the new government to avoid appearing at such meetings, for the simple reason that the populace, shaken and bewildered by the swift turn of events, wanted to get their bearings again by hearing a true account of what had happened directly from members of the new government, whom they felt they could trust. In this maelstrom of frantic activity we nevertheless managed to put through a tremendous amount of new legislation, not least because our previous experience in public life had made us well acquainted with the hopes and needs of all sections of the population. All of us, with the exception of Prince Lvov, Tereshchenko and Manuilov, had gained this experience as deputies of the Duma, in which capacity we had traveled the length and breadth of Russia. Prince Lvov, too, had an intimate knowledge of the problems of local government, through his long years of service in the *zemstvo*. Manuilov, a former rector of Moscow University and a member of the editorial board of the leading liberal newspaper, *Russkie Vedomosti*, was an expert on educational matters. Tereshchenko, the youngest member of the government, was a leading figure in the industrial world of the south of Russia, and during the war he had become deputy president, together with Konovalov, of the War Industry Committee presided over by Guchkov. He was, in addition, very well connected in military circles and in Petrograd society.

Apart from the wide experience of the members of the new government, a very important factor in accounting for the remarkable scope and pace of our legislative activity was that nearly all the senior officials of the old ministries and other government offices remained at their posts under the new government, and, with few exceptions, they served it with great enthusiasm.[1] Many of them frequently worked all night drafting new laws and proposals for reform. Their expert knowledge and training were of a very high order, and it was a great misfortune that later on in May some of the newly appointed ministers from the socialist parties began to replace experienced civil servants with party colleagues who were totally ignorant of the workings of a governmental department.

Despite all the difficulties caused by the war and the collapse of the old administration, the Provisional Government carried out its entire legislative program with the approval of the whole country and thus laid a firm foundation for Russia's transformation into an advanced state. Even Lenin, as he prepared to seize power in October, could not refrain from paying tribute in the following terms: "The

[1] Only the Ministry of the Interior had to be thoroughly purged by the new government. Nearly all of its senior officials were replaced.

[February] Revolution has managed in a few months to bring Russia, politically, up to the level of the advanced countries." [2]

Of course, Lenin also accused the Provisional Government of all the mortal sins of capitalism, and in the article from which the above quotation is taken he said nothing about the basic *social* reforms—the agrarian and labor legislation—it effected. To this very day, the younger generation in Russia is kept in ignorance of the fact that in the brief period following the February Revolution the Provisional Government placed within the grasp of the peoples of Russia not just political freedom but also a social system guaranteeing human dignity and material welfare.

For a full picture of the Provisional Government's legislative record readers may turn to my edition of the documents on this subject,[3] and here I shall only summarize the main points. Of primary importance, of course, were political and civil rights. The independence of the courts and judges was established. All "special" courts were abolished, and all "political" cases, or cases involving the security of the state, were now subject to trial by jury, like any ordinary criminal case. All religious, ethnic, and class restrictions were abolished.

Complete freedom of conscience was declared. The independence of the Orthodox Church was reestablished, and in March a special church council was called in order to prepare a convention (*sobor*) to confirm the autonomy of the church. The *sobor* itself was opened on August 15. All other churches, sects, and religions were given full freedom to proselytize.

Women were given the same political and civil rights as men.

With the participation of representatives of all parties, of all public organizations and all ethnic groups, an electoral law was drawn up for elections to a constituent assembly on the basis of universal suffrage and proportional representation. To my mind, however, the latter was a mistake. Town and rural self-government was also established on the same elective principles.

A law on cooperatives admitted the cooperative movement into the economic system of the country as one of its component parts. I

[2] *Collected Works*, 4th ed., Vol. 25, p. 338. Also quoted in *History of the CPSU* (1960), p. 228.

[3] *The Russian Provisional Government, 1917*, documents selected and edited by Robert Paul Browder and Alexander F. Kerensky (Stanford, Calif., Stanford Univ. Press, 1961).

should note in passing that this law on cooperatives, as well as the laws on trade unions and local government bodies, was actually drafted by representatives of these organizations. In general the Provisional Government tried to draw as many people as possible into the business of constructing the new order, thus instilling into the population a feeling of responsibility for the fate of the country as a whole.

In the field of economic and social reform, the main question was, of course, that of the land. The measures proposed by the Provisional Government were revolutionary, for they envisaged the total transfer of the land to those who worked on it. Only three weeks after the collapse of the Monarchy, the new government published a decree on agrarian reform. It had been drafted by the new minister of agriculture, A. Shingaryev, a member of the liberal Cadet Party. The Provisional Government sought to entrust the working out of the actual details to those most closely concerned. The Central Land Committee was set up, with local branches throughout the country whose members were elected under the new electoral law. While they were working out the details of the reform, these committees exercised interim supervision over local land matters.

On May 20 the Central Land Committee published a directive on the general principles which should underlie the reform: "In accordance with the new needs of our economy and with the frequently expressed wishes of the peasants and the programs of all the democratic parties of the country, the basic principle of the coming land reform must be the transfer of all agricultural land to the working agricultural population."

This unequivocal decision in favor of the peasants enraged the large landowners, and their determination to thwart this proposed land revolution was one of the basic motives behind the attempted overthrow of the Provisional Government in August. The Bolsheviks, for their part, were concerned only with creating the greatest possible anarchy and confusion among the peasants during this transitional period, in order to prevent peaceful reform. In the summer and autumn of 1917, acting on Lenin's instructions, they incited the most backward and ignorant elements in the countryside to take the law into their own hands by looting the houses of the landowners and destroying and expropriating the crops. Naturally the Provisional Government, with the support of all the democratic and socialist parties, tried to prevent, sometimes by armed force, the willful disruption of this, the greatest agrarian reform ever to be attempted in the history of Europe. Some influential members of the democratic and socialist parties, both inside Russia and abroad, were later to write that the Provisional Government had been "too slow" with the land reform. But they failed to explain how it could have been carried out any more quickly over the whole, vast expanse of Russia, at the height of a terrible war, and in the midst of a harvest upon which food supplies in the coming winter, for the army and indeed for the whole country, depended.

By autumn the preparatory work of the land committees would have been complete, and the government would have appeared before the Constituent Assembly with a draft bill ready for its approval. In the spring of 1918 the land would have been handed over in orderly fashion to the peasants, and they would not have become, as they later did, the helots of a single landlord—the state.

The labor legislation of the Provisional Government gave the workers unprecedented rights and independence. They were to lose these rights under the Bolshevik regime of "workers and peasants." Despite the war emergency, Guchkov immediately introduced the eight-hour working day—unheard of as yet anywhere else in the world—in all government armament factories. As a result of his initiative, it also became the rule throughout privately owned industry. Upon the suggestion of A. Konovalov, minister of industry and trade, private industrialists came to an agreement with the Petrograd Soviet on an eight-hour working day. Arbitration courts were set up; factory committees [4] and trade unions were given the fullest possible autonomy. In general, the Provisional Government did everything possible to

[4] On September 5, 1915, an international conference of European Socialists opened at Zimmerwald in Switzerland. The task of this conference was to unite those political parties and groups which had split up after the disintegration of the Second International at the beginning of the war of 1914. In its resolution, the conference stopped halfway. The position of the Zimmerwaldists may be summed up in one sentence: "We stand for neither defeat nor defense; we are neutral in an imperialist war waged by capitalist states." Their aim was to organize the working class for the rapid conclusion of the war without any conquerors or conquered. After the February Revolution the majority of the Russian Zimmerwaldists recognized the necessity of defending Russia, but many of them were psychologically unprepared to collaborate with the "bourgeois democracy." I. G. Tsereteli and V. M. Chernov, both of them party leaders, until the revolution were stubborn adherents of the Zimmerwald program.

ensure the emergence of organized labor as a force co-equal with that of the industrial management.

Finally, I should like to say a few words on the record of the Provisional Government with regard to the difficult question of the national minorities. The Provisional Government recognized that a free democratic Russia could not remain a centralized state, and it immediately took practical measures to reverse the whole oppressive policy of the old regime toward the non-Russian peoples of the empire. In the very first days after the fall of the Monarchy it proclaimed the independence of Poland and restored the complete autonomy of Finland. In the summer the Ukraine was also granted autonomy. Earlier, in March, representatives of the various nationalities within the Empire had been invited to participate in the new administration in the Caucasus, in Turkestan, and in the Baltic provinces. Early in July a commission was set up to draft the necessary laws for the reorganization of Russia along federal lines.

From this brief sketch of the internal policies of the Provisional Government during its short life, it will be seen that in Russia the establishment of political democracy led simultaneously to the triumph of social democracy. On his return to Russia in 1917, Lenin said: "Russia is now, among the belligerent powers, the freest country in Europe, and there is no oppression of the masses."

The Problem of Power

If all the work of internal reform which I have outlined above eventually came to nothing, this is in large measure due to the fact that the Provisional Government was unable to solve the problem of organizing a stable democratic regime to implement and sustain these reforms.

In this connection, I vividly recall the third session of the Provisional Government, on the afternoon of March 4. This was the first time we had met outside the Tauride Palace, away from the hectic revolutionary excitement surrounding the Duma building. We met instead in the building of the Ministry of the Interior, where Prince Lvov had taken up residence.[5]

I remember the solemn silence as we sat there in the vast confer-

[5] As well as being prime minister, Lvov had also taken the portfolio of Internal Affairs.

ence room under the stern gaze of the dozens of former ministers and officials of the old regime, whose portraits lined the walls. I think it was here, surrounded by these portraits of previous rulers instead of by the exalted revolutionary crowd in the Duma, that each of us suddenly realized for the first time the full implications of what had happened in Russia during the preceding few days and what a terrible burden of responsibility now lay upon us.

Prince Lvov had not yet arrived, but there was none of the usual conversation, for none of us were in the mood for it. At last Lvov appeared from the inner rooms with a sheaf of telegrams in his hand. Not greeting each of us individually as he usually did, he went straight to his chair, placed the telegrams in front of him and said: "Look what is happening, gentlemen. Since yesterday telegrams like these have been pouring in from all parts of European Russia. These are no longer the messages of support that you have all been reading. These are official reports from all the provincial capitals and from many smaller towns. They all say more or less the same thing: that at the first news of the fall of the Monarchy, the local administration has fled, beginning with the governor and ending with the lowliest policeman, and those higher officials, particularly in the police, who either would not or could not get away in time have been arrested by all kinds of self-appointed revolutionary authorities and public committees."

There was dead silence in the room as each of us wondered what to do. Here we were in the middle of a war, and large areas of the country had passed into the hands of completely unknown people!

I do not remember who broke the silence with the words: "But the same thing is going on here in Petrograd, and yet we are already restoring some kind of authority." This broke the spell, and everybody began to talk excitedly. I have forgotten now the details of what was said, but I clearly remember Prince Lvov's summing up. Speaking with extraordinary confidence, he said: "We must forget all about the old administration—any return to it is psychologically quite impossible. But Russia will not go under without it. The administration is gone, but the people remain. The people have survived this sort of trouble more than once in the past. Look at Moscow for example . . . we have information that things have already been remarkably well organized there by the democratic parties with the help of members of the municipal Duma and the cooperatives ... It is no use for us, as the central government, to give orders where there are no local authorities to carry out such orders ... Gentlemen, we must be patient! We must have faith in the good sense, statesmanship, and loyalty of the peoples of Russia." Listening to this, I realized for the first time that Lvov's great strength was his faith in ordinary people—it was rather like Kutuzov's faith in the common soldier. And indeed we had nothing at all except this faith in the people, patience, and a quite unheroic awareness that there was no turning back for us. With the best will in the world, we could not hand over power to anybody else —for the simple reason that there was nobody to hand it over to!

By the end of this meeting, we had decided that our first step toward setting up a new administrative apparatus would be to make contact with reliable people in the provinces and give them full powers to take the place of the former provincial governors in order to reconstitute the machinery of local government. In cases where no local people could be found to do this job, responsible men were to be sent out from Petrograd. Two weeks later, after the dispatch of "commissars" from Petrograd and the transfer of the functions of the former provincial governors to the chairmen of *zemstvo* boards had proved a failure, it was decided to appoint as the commissars of the Provisional Government people on the spot who had been elected or recommended by the most authoritative local public committees. These were generally organized on the Moscow model to include representatives of all relevant local bodies and organizations. Prince Lvov was subsequently much criticized for this method of appointing the local representatives of the new government, and he was accused of "softness" and of a lack of administrative ability. But none of his critics, either inside or outside the Government, were able to propose any other way of establishing local administrative machinery at a time when the central government in Russia had no means whatsoever of effectively enforcing its authority. It was easy at this time for demagogues to incite workers and soldiers, who had lost their sense of discipline, to all kinds of excesses, and in these first weeks after the Revolution the forces of disruption very often outpaced the growth of a new governmental and social structure.

How was it possible to fight these disruptive forces without the machine guns dreamed of by Shulgin, the most intelligent of the conservative members of the Duma to join the Progressive Bloc? How was it possible to stem the tide of blind hatred for anything remotely reminiscent of the old Tsarist regime, a hatred which was now indiscriminately directed against any kind of authority? The new government had no physical means of imposing its will, and the only instrument of persuasion at its disposal was the spoken word. As Milton once pointed out, words are a great force which can be used for either creative or destructive purposes. During the early days of the Revolution, the spoken word played a quite extraordinary part, both for good and for evil.

For the new government trying to create order out of chaos, it was vital to take account of this potent weapon and exploit it for constructive purposes. It was not enough to write and publish high-minded manifestos and articles in the press. It was not enough to build up a new administrative machinery. It was also necessary, by constant use of the spoken word, to counter the forces of destruction and to instill in people a sense of their individual responsibility to the nation as a whole.

Because circumstances had put me at the apex of power during the Revolution and because my name had become a kind of symbol to the people of the new life of freedom, it fell chiefly to me to wage this verbal battle among the masses of the population. But I had many allies. Hundreds of thousands of people from all walks of life, from humble village schoolteachers to Moscow professors, fought this same verbal battle.

In the first few days after the Revolution I was sent by the Government to the naval base at Kronstadt. An enraged mob of sailors had literally torn to pieces the commander of the Kronstadt fortress, Admiral Wiren, killed a number of their officers, and thrown hundreds of others into prison after savagely beating them up. My mission was to try to obtain the release of these officers, who had suffered quite unjustly at the hands of the sailors. I had no means of persuasion except the spoken word.

I arrived there with two adjutants and, ignoring all warnings, went directly to the main square in Kronstadt, which was the meeting place for the insurgent sailors. I was met by an ominous silence, which gave way to an angry roar as soon as I began to speak. It was clear that the sailors' leaders wanted to keep me from getting a hearing. When the noise had died down a little, I said that I had come on behalf of the Provisional Government to get an explanation of what had happened. One of the leaders immediately stood up and started talking about the "atrocities" committed against the sailors in Kronstadt.

I knew that Admiral Wiren had been something of a martinet and had perhaps been too strict in his treatment of his officers and men, but I also knew that he had never allowed any physical brutality and had certainly committed no atrocities. This is what I said in my answering speech, and it had some effect. By the use of words alone I managed to calm down the angry crowd, and although I was not able to obtain the release of all the arrested officers, 10 or 20 of them were allowed to go to Petrograd.[6]

Prince Lvov was always asking me to go to trouble spots to quell anarchic moods with the spoken word, and to give moral support to more healthy and constructive elements. From my own experience and from the reports of others who traveled around the country on similar missions, I can say without any exaggeration that the vast majority of the population in the towns and villages in those first months after the February Revolution was very little influenced by demagogues and rabble rousers. Most people went about the work of creating a new life with enormous enthusiasm. Throughout that summer of 1917 there were innumerable meetings and conferences of representatives of all groups of society, who met to work out their own proposals for fundamental reform in all branches of the economic, social, and cultural life of the country. They bombarded the government with countless resolutions and suggestions of every kind. The peoples of Russia were rapidly learning to participate in the construction of a new way of life. They did so in harmony with the government and not against it.

The Soviet

I now come to the thorny question of relations between the Provisional Government and the Petrograd Soviet of Workers' and Sol-

[6] The struggle for the release of the officers went on until July, when the last of them were allowed to come to Petrograd. I should say in this connection that Kronstadt was a hotbed of both German and Bolshevik activity, as were also Helsinki, Sveaborg, Riga, and Petrograd itself. Among ourselves in the government we used to call the triangle formed by these places "the rotten corner" of Russia.

diers' Deputies. This was in some ways the most important aspect of the whole problem of power after the Revolution.

There was general agreement among the members of the government that it was essential to include representatives of the socialist parties in the government as soon as possible, since their strong political and moral authority within the army and the working-class civilian population would greatly increase the stability of the new government. We felt it to be imperative to erase the false impression that the forces of Russian democracy were divided into two camps— "revolutionary" and "bourgeois."

The leaders of the Petrograd Soviet had themselves created this impression, in accordance with their respective party ideologies rather than in response to the real mood of the people as a whole. Their attitude toward the "bourgeois" Provisional Government was demonstrated in one of the first resolutions of the Executive Committee, which expressed readiness to support the new government only "insofar as it does not encroach on the rights of the workers won by the Revolution." This reserved attitude of the Petrograd Soviet created a paradoxical and intolerable situation in that the new national government was to some extent at the mercy of, or at least dependent upon, the goodwill of a local institution which, by virtue of the authority it enjoyed among certain sections of the population, could jeopardize the very existence of the legally constituted government authority.

The most important circumstance was that on the morning of February 27, the 200,000 soldiers of the Petrograd Garrison, completely bewildered by events, suddenly found themselves without officers. The Soviet had not yet come into being, and the city was in complete turmoil. It was only natural that the insurgent soldiers should turn for leadership to the one existing institution which had any moral authority, the Duma. But there was not a single officer in the Duma who at this moment had the courage and good sense to take charge of the entire garrison, as Lieutenant Colonel Gruzinov [7] did in Moscow. The municipal Duma in Petrograd had no prestige whatsoever, and the various public organizations were not able, on the first day of the Revolution, to create some authoritative focal point in the city representing the democratic parties and organizations. The Provisional Committee of the Duma also hesitated to take this task upon

[7] President of the Moscow Province Zemstvo.

itself, even though all the political and public figures of note rushed to the Duma to place themselves at its disposal for the work of restoring order in the city.

In the afternoon the few representatives of the socialist parties who happened to be in Petrograd at the moment of the Revolution also flocked to the Duma building. Their thoughts had turned automatically to the Soviet which had sprung up in St. Petersburg in the autumn of 1905 to play such a fatal part in the revolutionary events of that year.

I remember vividly being approached by Rodzyanko in one of the corridors of the Tauride Palace at about three o'clock that same afternoon. He told me that Skobelev, the Menshevik member of the Duma, had asked him for a room in the building for the purpose of organizing a soviet of workers' deputies, and thus maintain order in the factories. "What do you think?" Rodzyanko asked me, "wouldn't that be dangerous?"

"What's dangerous about it?" I replied. "After all, somebody must take charge of the workers."

"I suppose you're right," Rodzyanko said. "God knows what's happened to the city, all work has come to a halt—and we are supposed to be fighting a war!"

The people who had taken the initiative in establishing the Soviet got the room they wanted—the large hall of the Budget Committee, together with the adjoining office, formerly occupied by the chairman of this committee. In a matter of hours a small group of people well versed in the techniques of organization and underground work had set up a provisional executive committee of the Soviet. It was joined by Gvozdev and some of his comrades just out of prison. Also fresh from prison was the veteran Nosar-Khrustalyov, who had won fame as the chairman of the Soviet in 1905, but who had in the meantime been virtually forgotten. He did not get on with the people in this new Soviet and soon retired to the provinces.

Toward evening all the Petrograd factories were asked to elect delegates and send them at once to a session of the Soviet in the Duma building.

This is not the place for a detailed account of how the Soviet was organized, but I should like to emphasize that its first Executive Committee was not elected, but was simply formed by a process of cooption. By evening it had grown to include, in addition to the original

Socialist Revolutionaries and Mensheviks, representatives of the Popular Socialists and the Trudoviks. The Bolsheviks played no part whatsoever in the actual creation of the Soviet and were even hostile toward it, because it evidently formed no part of their plans. However, by the evening, they too had changed their minds, and Molotov, Shlyapnikov, and one or two others joined the Executive Committee.

With the appearance of the Bolsheviks, the very nature of the Soviet suddenly changed. At Molotov's suggestion, it was decided to invite all the military units of the Petrograd Garrison to send deputies, despite the protests of the Mensheviks and some of the Socialist Revolutionaries. The result was a workers' organization in which the total membership of 3,000 was made up of 2,000 soldiers and only 1,000 workers.

In retrospect, I cannot help feeling that the Bolsheviks' abrupt change of attitude toward the Soviet was the result of their success in creating an imbalance in favor of the military; the soldiers in the Soviet gave them direct access to the barracks and the Front. Of course it also gave the Bolsheviks and other Soviet leaders such as Steklov, who sympathized with them, a powerful military weapon for the political struggle—particularly in the capital, where the garrison was especially large. It is highly significant that Steklov insisted upon the inclusion in the constitution of the Provisional Government of a clause forbidding the withdrawal from Petrograd of any of those military units which had supposedly participated in the struggle against the Monarchy.

Another important advantage which the Soviet possessed was the considerable psychological effect of its location in the Tauride Palace. In the eyes of politically ignorant people, its close physical association with the new government made it appear to be an institution somehow on a par with the government, and thus to possess powers over the whole country. Furthermore, the reserved, conditional nature of the support offered by the Soviet inevitably made our impeccably democratic government somewhat suspect in the eyes of the workers and soldiers, as being essentially "bourgeois" in its acts.

This was brought home to me on March 7 during an official visit to Moscow on behalf of the Provisional Government. When I appeared at the Moscow Soviet of Workers' Deputies, its chairman said to me, "We greet you as a deputy chairman of the Petrograd Soviet of Workers' Deputies. The workers do not allow their representatives to join the new Cabinet. But we know that while you are in it, there will be no treachery. We trust you." [8] This expression of trust in one member of the government, rather than in the government as a whole, was quite inadmissible and gave ample demonstration of the danger implicit in the Soviet's qualified support. From a "benevolent opposition" the Soviet had turned into a vehicle of irresponsible criticism of the new government, which was accused of all kinds of "bourgeois" sins.

I do not wish to be one-sided or to deny the positive aspects of the Soviet's work. Apart from restoring discipline, not only in the factories but in the barracks, it made an enormous contribution to the organization of regular food supplies for Petrograd, and it also played a highly fruitful part in the preparation of reform measures in all spheres. Its representatives were also helpful—though not always successful—in their attempts to reestablish normal relations between the soldiers and their officers. At the Front, both the Petrograd and Moscow Soviets provided many courageous and loyal men who acted as commissars and leaders of the various front-line committees. The daily criticism directed against the government by the Soviet newspaper *Izvestiya* was often both useful and necessary, and the government neither feared nor resented it. Such criticism, which now came from all sides—from the Duma Executive Committee as well as the right-wing press—was an inevitable concomitant of democracy. What was harmful was the deliberate use of lies to incite the masses. Insinuations were made that the government wished to revive various aspects of the hated past. Fortunately, with unlimited freedom of the press, public opinion—particularly the more responsible sections of the democratic and socialist press—was generally quick to take issue with such extreme demagogy.

The main difficulty with the Soviet was that the leaders of the socialist parties who headed it were not content with reasonable criticism of the government's actions, but actually tried to intervene in matters of policy. Though they denied any intention of interfering, they often forgot in practice the boundary between criticism and intervention. They frequently behaved as though they had governmental power, and they even tried to pursue a foreign policy of their own, since they suspected the government of "imperialist" designs.

[8] As quoted in the newspaper *Russkoye Slovo* (Moscow), March 8, 1917.

I can best illustrate this high-handedness on the part of the Executive Committee by describing in some detail its attempt to interfere in our handling of the ex-Tsar and his family.

Shortly after midnight on March 3, having signed the Act of Abdication, Nicholas II left Pskov for headquarters in Mogilev to take leave of the subordinates who had worked under him there for nearly two years. Although he traveled in his private train and was accompanied by his usual suite, this journey caused neither the government nor the Duma the slightest alarm, since the ex-Tsar was now totally isolated and helpless.

On the evening of March 3, the government was holding its second meeting in the Tauride Palace. At one point—I no longer remember what time it was—I was suddenly called out of the meeting by Zenzinov, a member of the Soviet Executive Committee. He had come in some alarm to warn me that there was considerable indignation among the members of the Soviet about the government's failure to prevent the ex-Tsar's journey to Headquarters. He told me that, at the instigation of one of the Bolshevik members (Molotov, I think), they had passed a resolution that the ex-Tsar, his family, and other members of the dynasty were to be arrested; that the government was to be invited to carry out this arrest jointly with the Soviet; and that Prince Lvov was to be asked to indicate what attitude the government would take if the Soviet were to make the arrest in case the government refused to do so. Zenzinov warned me that Chkheidze and Skobelev, who had been delegated by the Soviet to handle the negotiations with the government, might appear at any moment.

I went back to the government meeting at once and reported my conversation with Zenzinov. Someone—I think it was Guchkov—said that in view of all the pent-up hatred for the old regime, there was nothing surprising in this alarm among the soldiers and workers about the ex-Tsar's journey, but that nevertheless we must firmly oppose any attempt on the part of the Petrograd Soviet to assume governmental functions. Since we all agreed with this, we asked Prince Lvov to explain to the delegates from the Soviet that the government was completely certain that the ex-Tsar had no designs on the new regime, and that a decision regarding his future would be taken in the next few days. He was also to tell them that in the meantime there were no grounds whatsoever for taking any action against other members of the dynasty, since they had all thoroughly disapproved of everything that had gone on at the court in the last few years. As he told us later, Prince Lvov's conversation with Chkheidze and Skobelev passed off amicably.

The whole question of the deposed Tsar's future was extremely sensitive. During the first two months following the collapse of the Monarchy, the so-called yellow press conducted a vicious campaign of defamation against the ex-Tsar and his wife, aimed at stirring up feelings of hatred and vengeance among the workers, soldiers, and ordinary citizens. Fantastic and often obscene accounts of life at the palace began to appear, even in some of the press organs that up to the very last day of the former regime had been "semiofficial" voices of government opinion and had made great play of their loyalty to the Crown. The liberal and democratic press avoided any sensationalism in its critical comments on the deposed monarch, but here, too, there sometimes appeared articles by sober-minded writers that were in questionable taste. We were only too well aware, however, that the reign of Nicholas II provided abundant material for this campaign of hatred. The tragedy of Kronstadt and the excesses of the Baltic Fleet and at the Front had already been sufficient warning. I was better acquainted than other members of the government with the dominant mood in extreme left-wing circles, and I made a firm resolve to do everything in my power to prevent any move toward a Jacobin terror.

On March 4, the day after this attempted intervention by the Soviet, the government's moderate policy toward the ex-Tsar was suddenly justified in an unexpected and historically unprecedented way.

That morning General Alekseyev called Prince Lvov on the direct line from Headquarters to inform him that on the previous evening Nicholas II had handed him a sheet of paper on which he had scribbled a message for transmission to Prince Lvov. It began abruptly without any form of address, and in Alekseyev's words, the gist of it was as follows:

The abdicated Tsar asks me to communicate to you the following requests. First, that you permit unobstructed passage for him and his suite to Tsarskoye Selo in order to join his ailing family there. Second, that you guarantee the safe sojourn in Tsarskoye Selo of himself, his family, and his suite until the children recover their health. Third, that you grant and guarantee unobstructed passage to Romanov [Murmansk] [9] for himself, his family, and his suite.

Informing Your Excellency of the request made of me, I urgently solicit the earliest possible decision of the Government on the aforesaid matters, which are of particular importance to Headquarters as well as to the abdicated Tsar *himself*.

Nicholas' note included a fourth request: "To return to Russia, after the end of the war, for permanent residence in the Crimea-Livadia." [10] General Alekseyev did not read out this fourth point over the telephone, evidently considering it to be impossibly naïve.

The point is, however, that this document went a long way toward solving our problem. A solution worthy of the government of free Russia had been suggested by the Tsar himself.

On March 5, General Alekseyev telegraphed Lvov and Rodzyanko asking them to speed up the ex-Tsar's departure from Headquarters and to send representatives to escort him to Tsarskoye Selo, saying that the sooner this happened the better it would be for Headquarters as well as for the ex-Tsar himself.

It was quite clear that from now on the former Tsar could remain in Russia only under guard. On the evening of March 7, a four-man delegation consisting of representatives of different parties in the Duma was sent to Mogilev with instructions to take the ex-Tsar into custody and to transfer him to Tsarskoye Selo. On March 8 the government published its decree ordering the ex-Tsar to be put under guard and specifying as his place of residence the Alexander Palace in Tsarskoye Selo. All the arrangements for the ex-Tsar's detention were entrusted to General Kornilov, who had been recalled from the front and appointed commander-in-chief of the Petrograd Military District.

When I addressed the Moscow Soviet on March 7, I was questioned rather aggressively by the workers, who asked such questions as: "Why has Nikolai Nikolaevich been appointed commander-in-chief, and why is Nicholas II allowed to travel freely around Russia?" The questions were clearly inspired by hostility to the government, and I was disturbed at this evidence of the extent to which the mood of the Petrograd Soviet had spread to Moscow. I realized that my answer to

[9] I.e., as a port of embarkation for England.
[10] See *The Russian Provisional Government, 1917,* ed. by Robert P. Browder and Alexander F. Kerensky, Vol. I, p. 177.

the workers had to be clear, unequivocal, and firm: "The Grand Duke Nikolai Nikolaevich was appointed by Nicholas II just before his abdication, but he will not remain supreme commander. The ex-Tsar himself is in my hands as prosecutor general. Let me tell you, comrades, that until now the Russian Revolution has been bloodless, and I do not want it to be sullied. I will never be the Marat of the Russian Revolution. Nicholas II will shortly, under my personal supervision, be put on a boat and sent to England."

This announcement of mine (and a similar statement by Prince Lvov to Chkheidze) of the government's decision to ask the British Government to give asylum to Nicholas II [11] provoked a storm of indignation against the government in the Executive Committee of the Petrograd Soviet.

If the leaders of the Soviet had been concerned to find a reasonable and nonviolent solution of the ex-Tsar's future, they would, of course, have supported the government's decision, but the majority of them had completely different designs. They wanted to throw him into the Peter and Paul Fortress and then reenact the drama of the French Revolution by having the tyrant publicly executed. This is clear from the furious statement issued by the Executive Committee on March 9 "decreeing" a number of measures which by their very nature could only be carried out on the authority of the government: that all key railway stations on the ex-Tsar's route be occupied by troops, that a warrant for the arrest of the ex-Tsar be telegraphed to all towns, and that on his arrest he be incarcerated in the Trubetskoy Bastion of the Peter and Paul Fortress, and so on.

At 11:30 A.M. on March 9, the ex-Tsar, accompanied by the four delegates of the Duma, arrived at the station at Tsarskoye Selo. He was met by the commandants of the palace and the town, and transferred to their charge to be conveyed to the Alexander Palace, where he was awaited by his wife and his children, who were sick with measles.

Later in the evening of the same day a representative of the Executive Committee also arrived in Tsarskoye Selo, bringing with him an armed detachment in armored cars. The representative, whose name

[11] Milyukov had been to see the British ambassador, Buchanan, about the matter on March 6 or 7, and on March 10. Buchanan had a telegram from London giving a positive reply.

was S. Maslovsky, had been instructed to arrest Nicholas II and bring him to Petrograd—whether to the Soviet or straight to the Peter and Paul Fortress never became clear. Fortunately, this dangerous move to usurp the government's authority was a total failure. The military units and their officers in Tsarskoye Selo categorically refused to hand over the ex-Tsar to Maslovsky unless he could produce a warrant signed by General Kornilov, who was responsible to the government for the security of the ex-Tsar and his family. Maslovsky tried to get out of his embarrassing predicament by asserting that he had only come to test the reliability of the guard, but in his official report to the Soviet Executive Committee on March 10 he contradicted this by saying that the ex-Tsar "had not been handed over to him."

This open attempt by the Petrograd Soviet to usurp the government's authority was the only episode which gives any real support to the legend of "dual power," the legend put forth by the government's enemies on both the Right and the Left—i.e., that it shared its authority with the Soviet. For me, however, this affair offered the best possible proof that such attempts at interference were not a threat to the moral authority of the new government. Maslovsky's expedition to Tsarskoye Selo had ended in a fiasco because it had received no popular backing, because the Soviet's threats to break off relations with the government had had no effect. We now felt that the country was with us and that we should be able to overcome the inevitable tendency to lack of discipline and toward anarchy. We felt that all the healthy and constructive elements in the country were instinctively drawn to one single focus of state authority. It was surely significant that during these hectic days between March 8 and 10, even the population of Petrograd had shown no sympathy for the absurd antics of the self-appointed leaders of the still very poorly organized Soviet.

My feeling that our government was basically in harmony with the people was reinforced during the day I spent in Moscow on March 7. As I addressed the various public bodies there on the policies of our government, I could plainly see that these policies were complementary to the spontaneous efforts of the people themselves to elaborate a new political and social framework based on the highest aspirations of the long Russian struggle for freedom. When I spoke, for instance, before the Committee for Public Organizations and told them that, in the near future, the government would publish a decree abolishing the

death penalty for political offenses, and that all such cases would
henceforth be tried by jury, my words were met by extraordinary
and unanimous enthusiasm.[12]

The moment I got back to Petrograd from this unforgettable visit
to Moscow and before I had had time to report on it to the government, my adjutant came into my office and told me that Steklov was
waiting to see me. At that time he was one of the most influential
members of the Soviet Executive Committee as well as being editor-
in-chief of *Izvestiya*. He was a brash and rather crude person. Without
any preliminaries he told me that the Executive Committee was extremely dissatisfied with my Moscow statement about the proposed
abolition of the death penalty, and he advised us to think again about
this decision if we wished to avoid a serious misunderstanding with
the Soviet. This visit of Steklov's took place on March 8, if my memory
serves me correctly, but at any rate it was before Maslovsky's journey
to Tsarskoye Selo. I was very much taken aback by Steklov's words,
since all educated Russians, including the Mensheviks and Socialist
Revolutionaries, had always been against the death penalty. At the
time of the so-called Stolypin terror, for instance, they had joined
their voices to the nationwide protest against it. However, I was in no
mood to enter into a discussion of the matter with my visitor. I
thanked him for his warning and told him that I would inform the
government. That was the end of our conversation. The next day I
told Skobelev and Zenzinov about Steklov's visit and asked them to
dissuade the Soviet Executive Committee from protesting against the
abolition of the death penalty, a measure which was being greeted
with universal enthusiasm. To my astonishment, they told me that
they had no knowledge of what Steklov had said to me. "All the more
important to find out what's going on!" I urged them. "Do so as
quickly as you can. For my part I will delay the publication of the
decree so as not to embarrass the Soviet." Evidently some members of
the Executive Committee had visions of a Jacobin terror and meant
to act behind the backs of their colleagues in this matter of the death
penalty. I was soon informed that there would be no protest from the
Soviet.

---

[12] In Moscow I visited the Polish democratic club and announced there that in a
few days the government would make a declaration restoring the independence of
Poland.

There is no mention at all of the question of the death penalty in the minutes of the Executive Committee's meetings. It is obvious that after the failure of the attempt to arrest the Tsar and imprison him in the Peter and Paul Fortress, the question of the death penalty was no longer such a burning issue for Steklov and his friends.

As I have said, this episode involving the Tsar was the only serious attempt on the part of the Soviet to act in place of the government. After the failure of the Maslovsky mission, the leaders of the Soviet realized that direct encroachments upon the authority of the "bourgeois" government were futile, and that under current conditions its best policy was to try to influence events simply by "supervising" as closely as possible the activities of the new government. This policy found expression in the so-called liaison committee (*kontaktnaya kommissiya*), ostensibly for the purpose of exchanging information and maintaining proper liaison between the Soviet and the government. I do not now remember who in the Executive Committee of the Soviet was responsible for this idea, but I have no doubt that it sprang from an awareness that they were badly informed about what was going on in the country. I myself was wholeheartedly in favor of this plan, because it seemed to me to be an admirable stepping stone to the fulfillment of my hope of including representatives of the socialist parties in the government. The minutes of the meeting of the cabinet on March 10 record my proposal that Prince Lvov, Tereshchenko (minister of finance) and Nekrasov (minister of transport) represent the government in the proposed liaison committee. This proposal was the result of an earlier discussion of the question at a closed session of the Cabinet on the previous day.[13]

The Soviet members of the liaison committee were the Mensheviks Chkheidze, Skobelev, Steklov, and Sukhanov, and the Socialist Revolutionary Fillipovski.[14]

---

[13] I should note that we established a rule right at the beginning that all basic matters of home and foreign policy should be discussed in closed sessions of the Cabinet, that is, without the usual secretaries recording the proceedings as in ordinary "open" sessions. In closed sessions the minutes recorded only *who* made this or that proposal, without giving any summary of the discussion about it. Thus in the records for March 10 there is only a bare note that my proposal was carried.

[14] They were later joined by Tsereteli, one of the leaders of the Social Democrat faction in the second Duma who had been sent to forced labor in 1907 and got back to Petrograd from exile in the middle of March, 1917. He belonged to the so-called Siberian faction of the Zimmerwald group which took up the strange attitude toward

Partly because I was so often absent on trips around the country, but also because of the behavior of the Soviet delegates—particularly Steklov, whom Prince Lvov suffered with great patience—I very rarely took part in the meetings of the liaison committee.

Prince Lvov's patience was rewarded in that these talks averted a number of potentially unpleasant conflicts, and caused the leaders of the Soviet to take a more responsible approach to the course of events and to the policies of the government, of which they now had a much better understanding.

The situation became more and more intolerable, and all the members of the government understood only too well that the growing political tension in the country could only be lessened by changing the composition of the Provisional Government so as to reflect more closely the real disposition of forces in the country by bringing in representatives of the socialist parties. Only Milyukov stuck obstinately to his theory that all power must belong exclusively to representatives of the Progressive Bloc. Oddly enough, his views on foreign policy were to precipitate a crisis which in fact led to a change in the government's composition.

By nature Milyukov was a scholar rather than a politician. Had it not been for his combative temperament, which led him into the political arena, he would probably have had a distinguished career as a scholar. Because of his natural bent as a historian, Milyukov tended to look at political events in rather too much perspective, as one looks at them through books or historical documents. Such a lack of real political insight would not have mattered much under more stable conditions, but at the critical moment of the nation's history through which we were then living, it was little short of disastrous.

The unfortunate fact is that Milyukov had come to his post as minister of foreign affairs determined to continue in all essentials the imperialist policy of Sazonov, his predecessor under the old regime. In the autumn of 1916 this policy had been quite acceptable to some members of the Progressive Bloc, but by March of 1917 it was already hopelessly out of date—to put it mildly.

---

the war summed up in the formula: "We are neither defeatists nor defensists, we are neutral in the struggle between the two imperialist camps." Tsereteli was a gifted, energetic, and courageous man who soon became one of the main leaders of the "revolutionary democracy," in which capacity he recognized the need to defend the country.

It soon became apparent that there was a sharp difference of opinion on the question of war aims between Milyukov and the rest of the Provisional Government. I well remember a closed session of the Cabinet in the very early days of the government, at which this became only too clear. Milyukov was reporting to us on the secret treaties which had been concluded in the first years of the war between the Russian imperial government and England, France, and Italy. These treaties provided for a grandiose redistribution of the spoils of war between France, England, and Russia. Under the secret treaties, Russia was to be given not only the long-coveted Bosporus and Dardanelles, but also vast territories in Asia Minor.

We were shaken enough by this, but we were utterly flabbergasted when Milyukov told us about the agreement of 1915 with Italy, under which, as a reward for her entry into the war on the side of the Entente, she was promised sovereignty over the whole Slav coast of the Adriatic Sea. Vladimir Lvov, a man of a conservative cast of mind, leaped from his chair, waving his arms excitedly and shouting: "We can never, never accept these treaties." During this outburst only Milyukov remained calm and composed. After a stormy debate it was finally agreed that we should somehow or other persuade our Western allies to revise these agreements, and that in any event we must at least bring our own policy into line with the new mood of our own public opinion, a mood which was quite unsympathetic to the diplomatic formulas of the old ruling circles and the policy of Sazonov, the former minister of foreign affairs.

Someone reminded Milyukov of a significant incident in our own very recent past. It was during the second meeting of the Cabinet, when we were still in the Duma building. A telegram had been received from the French Government on February 22 agreeing to Russian annexation of the Austrian and German provinces of Poland in return for the Tsarist Government's agreement to French annexation of the left bank of the Rhine. We had decided to ignore this suggestion and to enter into immediate negotiations with the representatives of the Polish people, with a view to restoring that country's independence.

But Milyukov was impervious to any argument. Shortly afterward, a sharp exchange took place between Milyukov and Guchkov during one of the closed sessions of the Cabinet, at a time when Milyukov's speeches in the Sazonov style about the Dardanelles were beginning to have a dangerous effect because of the sharp reaction they provoked in democratic circles. In defense of his attitude Milyukov said: "Victory is Constantinople, and Constantinople is victory—for this reason it is necessary to remind people all the time of Constantinople." To this Guchkov retorted sharply, "If victory is Constantinople, then talk about victory, since victory is possible without Constantinople, but Constantinople is not possible without victory . . . think what you like and how you like, but speak only of things which raise morale at the front."

This obstinacy of Milyukov's in harping on the theme of the Dardanelles was very puzzling. He knew as well as Guchkov and I did that General Alekseyev was opposed on military grounds to any adventures in the Straits. Furthermore, as a historian, he must have been well acquainted with what General Kuropatkin had said as early as 1909 in his book, *The Tasks of the Russian Army:* "Not only would it be harmful for Russia to annex Constantinople and the Dardanelles, but such an annexation would inevitably give rise to the danger of a long-drawn-out armed struggle for the retention of this hazardous acquisition."

On March 24 we had arranged to hold a meeting of the liaison committee in order to discuss the whole question of war aims with representatives of the Soviet, but this had not prevented Milyukov from giving an interview to journalists on the previous day in order to tell them his views on the subject. On my instructions a statement appeared in the newspapers the next morning to the effect that Milyukov had voiced only his personal views and not those of the Provisional Government.

As a result of this action of mine, the delegates from the Soviet realized in advance of the meeting that they would not be able to lay Milyukov's views at the door of the government as a whole. The Soviet leaders were therefore able to accept *in toto* the solemn declaration on war aims which the government published on March 27. The essential principle underlying our war aims was now expressed as follows:

Leaving to the will of the people, in close union with our allies, the final solution of all problems connected with the World War and its conclusion, the Provisional Government considers it to be its right and its duty to declare at this time that the aim of free Russia is not domination over other nations, or seizure of their national possessions, or forcible occupation of

foreign territories, but the establishment of a stable peace on the basis
of self-determination of peoples. The Russian people do not intend to increase their world power at the expense of other nations. They have no
desire to enslave or degrade anyone.

It is interesting to note that this text was entirely the work of the government except for the phrase "or forcible occupation of foreign territories," which was inserted at the instance of the Soviet leaders. This
phrase adds nothing whatsoever of substance to the declaration, but
its insertion enabled the Soviet representatives in the liaison committee
to declare later in the Soviet that, by insisting on it, they had made it
impossible for "bourgeois imperialists" (and in particular Guchkov)
subsequently to distort or misinterpret the sense of the document. As
a matter of fact, neither Guchkov nor the conservative circles which
he represented had the slightest desire at this time to pursue any "imperialist" aims.

Unfortunately, Milyukov did not share the government's desire not
to exacerbate differences over war aims. On the appearance of the
government's declaration he let it be known that he did not regard
it as binding on him as minister of foreign affairs. This bombshell produced a flood of recriminations, as a result of which the authority of
the government suffered badly, despite its success in reaching an understanding with the Soviet.

The outburst of hatred for Milyukov which now took place in left-
wing circles revealed the precarious nature of the government's position. The stubbornness of the Minister of Foreign Affairs created a
crisis of confidence which had been inevitable since the very first day
of the Revolution, owing to the contradiction between the composition
of the government and the disposition of forces in the country. If the
country was not to go through a new and even more dangerous crisis,
it was essential to overcome this contradiction.

Milyukov's repeated public statements of his personal views were
already being accepted in all revolutionary, democratic, and socialist circles as evidence of bad faith on the part of the Provisional
Government.

However much we valued the unity in which the government had
been born, and despite the great importance we attached to retaining
all the original members of the Cabinet until the Constituent Assem-

bly could be called, it was increasingly evident that Milyukov's continuance as minister of foreign affairs was now a grave threat to the unity of the nation. Moreover, it was no longer possible to tolerate a situation in which the leaders of the Soviet, with their great influence and prestige, did not share direct responsibility for the conduct of the country's affairs. At this time I was probably in closer touch with the mood of the people than any other member of the Provisional Government, and I felt it to be imperative that we bring the whole matter to a head. Late in the evening of April 12, I informed the press that the government was about to consider the question of dispatching a note to the Allies informing them of Russia's revised war aims.

For some reason my statement appeared the next day in a garbled form. Anticipating events, the newspapers announced that the government was already discussing a note to the Allies about our new war aims. In fact, though some members of the government had given notice that they intended to bring this question up at a cabinet meeting, no such discussion by the Cabinet as a whole had yet taken place.

On formal grounds, therefore, Milyukov was quite justified in demanding that the government publish an official denial. Thus, on April 14 the newspapers reported that "the government has not discussed and is not preparing any note on the question of war aims." This denial provoked a storm of indignation, and, as had been foreseen, Milyukov was forced to agree to the immediate dispatch to the Allies of a note about war aims. Unfortunately, this was misinterpreted by the general public, which imagined that the government's hand had been forced by the Soviet and, even worse, by the Petrograd Garrison.

Because of the delicacy of the situation, the note to the Allies was drafted by the entire cabinet. Theoretically, the resulting text published on April 19 should have satisfied even the most extreme critics of Milyukov, but things had by now gone so far, and hostility to Milyukov in the Soviet and in left-wing circles in general was so great, that they were no longer capable of making a rational judgment, or even of understanding the sense of our note. The atmosphere became hysterical.

The Executive Committee of the Soviet published a sharp protest against the "imperialist" note of the Provisional Government.

Lenin, who had recently arrived from Switzerland, immediately dispatched his lieutenants to the barracks. On April 4 the Finnish

Guard Regiment, fully armed, marched to the Mariinsky Palace carrying red banners and placards denouncing, in particular, Milyukov and Guchkov.[15]

General Kornilov, the commander of the Petrograd Military District, sought the government's permission to call out troops for its protection, but we unanimously declined the offer. We were confident that the people would not permit any acts of violence against the government.

Our faith was amply justified. That same day immense throngs appeared on the street to demonstrate in support of the Provisional Government, and shortly afterward the Executive Committee of the Soviet issued a statement disassociating itself from the antigovernment demonstration by the troops. They also agreed to publish a statement explaining the foreign minister's note, which had precipitated all the fuss.

As a matter of fact, no explanation was really necessary, for there was nothing to explain. Thus the statement merely tried to calm public opinion by emphasizing that the note represented the unanimous views of all the members of the government.

The First Ministerial Crisis

We all agreed now that the Ministry of Foreign Affairs must go to someone who would be able to conduct the nation's foreign policy with greater flexibility.

On April 24 I myself threatened to resign from the Cabinet unless Milyukov was transferred to the Ministry of Education. At the same time I insisted upon the immediate entry into the government of representatives of the socialist parties.

The crisis in the Cabinet came to a head on April 25, when Milyukov refused to accept the Portfolio of Education and resigned from the Cabinet. On the same day I sent a statement to the Provisional Committee of the Duma, the Soviet, and the Central Committee of the Socialist Revolutionary and Trudovik groups, in which

---

15 At the time it was thought that this demonstration by the troops had started more or less spontaneously and that if anybody was to blame it was a certain Lieutenant Linde, a fanatical pacifist, and that Lenin and the Bolsheviks certainly had had nothing whatsoever to do with it. Looking through the secret German archives during my work in the Hoover Institute a few years ago, I came across clear documentary evidence that the whole thing was in fact engineered by Lenin (see Chapter 18).

I declared that henceforth the Provisional Government must consist not merely of individual representatives of democracy, but of men "chosen formally and directly by the organizations they represent." I made my continued participation in the government contingent upon their compliance with this demand.

The next day (April 26) Prince Lvov sent a formal letter to Chkheidze asking him to send representatives of the various parties concerned to negotiate on their entry into the Cabinet.

This was easier said than done. Not only were some liberals firmly opposed to the entry of socialists into the government, but several Mensheviks and Socialist Revolutionaries (particularly Chernov and Tsereteli) were equally reluctant to be associated with the Provisional Government.

On the evening of April 29, a stormy debate took place in the Executive Committee of the Soviet as to whether the Soviet was to be represented in the Provisional Government. The vote was negative, but only by the very narrow margin of 23 to 22. There were 8 abstentions. With individual exceptions, the Socialist Revolutionaries, the Mensheviks, the Popular Socialists, and the Trudoviks voted affirmatively.

The negative vote proved very unpopular in democratic circles, and it was also unacceptable to the majority of the Soviet Executive Committee. The Bolsheviks and the other uncompromising opponents of collaboration with the government had succeeded in winning the ballot by one vote only because those in favor of joining the government had failed to mobilize all their forces at the session of April 29. They now insisted that the question be put to the vote again.

The second vote was taken on the night of May 1–2. I was summoned to attend this session in order to outline the views of the government on the situation as it had developed. My statements, which were followed by the sudden news of Guchkov's resignation, helped to dissipate the misunderstanding and to clear the atmosphere in the Soviet (see Chapter 15). By a majority of 25 (44 in favor, 19 against) it was decided to participate in the government. Of the 19 negative votes, 12 were Bolshevik, 3, Menshevik-Internationalist, and 4, extreme left Socialist-Revolutionary.

The way was now open to broaden the base of the government.

With the resignation of War Minister Guchkov, the first Cabinet of the Provisional Government had ceased to exist, and the first period of the Provisional Government was at an end.

At its dissolution, the first Cabinet of the Provisional Government addressed to the nation a political testament that still stirs the mind and heart. In drawing the balance sheet of its short but extremely difficult and intense life, the government spoke the following words of warning, which proved to be a terrible prophecy:

.... The primordial tendency to fulfill the desires and solicitations of individual groups and strata of the population by means of seizures and by direct action, bypassing legal avenues, and the accompanying transition to the less conscious and less organized strata of the population, threaten to destroy internal civil cohesion and discipline; they are paving the way (on the one hand) for violent acts, thus sowing bitterness and enmity among the victims toward the new order, and (on the other hand) for the development of private ambitions and interests at the expense of the common interest and for the evasion of civic duties.

The Provisional Government considers it its duty to make a forthright and definite declaration that such a state of affairs renders the governing of the state difficult and that a further continuation in the same direction threatens to bring the country to internal disintegration and to defeat at the Front. Before Russia rises the terrible apparition of civil war and anarchy, carrying destruction to freedom. There is a somber and grievous course of peoples, a course well known in history, leading from freedom through civil war and anarchy to reaction and the return of despotism. This course must not be the course of the Russian people.[16]

[16] See *The Russian Provisional Government, 1917,* ed. by Robert P. Browder and Alexander F. Kerensky, Vol. III, pp. 1250–1251.

On the Russian Front

15

The Spring of Great Changes

General Nivelle's Fateful Decision

THE third year of the war (1917) was to have been the year of final victory over the Central Powers. Such was the decision of the military leaders of the Entente at the Chantilly Conference on November 3, 1916.

At the Inter-allied Conference in Petrograd in January, which was attended by delegates from Britain, Italy, Russia, and France, the minutes of the Chantilly Conference were approved. The meeting also planned the 1917 campaign which was to be launched on all the Allied fronts; it was agreed that a vigorous joint offensive by Russian and Rumanian troops in the north and by Entente forces in the south should rapidly compel Bulgaria to withdraw from the war.

The Russo-Rumanian offensive was planned for the first week of May.

On December 12, 1916, General Nivelle replaced Marshal Joffre as the French commander-in-chief. Nivelle had gained fame through his successful offensive operations at Verdun in the fall of 1916, and he was a national hero in the eyes of the French populace.

Preparations for the general offensive proceeded at top speed, but the collapse of the Russian monarchy on February 27 brought sudden disaster to Russia and to the Russian front. General Nivelle must have received reports on the situation from General Janin, head of the French mission attached to the Russian General Staff.

This sudden and profound upheaval in an allied country with a front stretching over 1,250 miles should have been reason enough for the new commander-in-chief of the Allied Forces in the West to reconsider his plan or at least to postpone its implementation.

But even if he chose to disregard the turmoil in Russia, General Nivelle must have known that in the November battles of the preceding year the Rumanian Army in Transylvania had been thoroughly routed by the German and Bulgarian forces and that Rumania had been occupied by the Germans since the beginning of December!

Nevertheless, without even having conferred with the Russian High Command, General Nivelle decided that military operations on the Russo-Rumanian front must be launched at the end of March or the beginning of April, instead of in May. The fate of General Nivelle's offensive had such importance for the subsequent development of World War I that I shall quote the relevant documents more or less in full.

On March 8, General Janin transmitted the following memorandum from Nivelle to General Alekseyev:

Headquarters,
March 8, 1917

. . . General Janin . . . has the honor to transmit to him [General Alekseyev] the following telegram just received from General Nivelle . . .

"I request you to inform General Alekseyev of the following: In agreement with the British High Command, I decided on April 8 [N. S.] as the date for beginning of the joint offensive on the Western Front. This date cannot be postponed.

The enemy has begun to withdraw along part of the British front and is actively preparing a further withdrawal along part of our front, thereby indicating the intention to avoid combat by means of a maneuver that will enable him to amass new and considerable forces.

It is therefore essential for us to begin our offensive as soon as possible, not only in order to clarify the situation, but also because to postpone it would mean playing into the hands of the enemy and taking the risk of the enemy outstripping us.

On November 15 and 16, 1916, at the Chantilly Conference it was resolved that in 1917, the Allied Armies would endeavor to crush the enemy by a simultaneous offensive on all fronts, using all the means at the disposal of the respective armies.

I intend to make use of all the forces of the French Army on the Western Front for the offensive since I am *aiming at decisive results* [italics mine] the attainment of which cannot be postponed at this stage of the war.

I would, therefore, ask you to launch the Russian offensive around the beginning or middle of April. It is essential that our joint operation be begun simultaneously (within a few days of each other), otherwise the enemy will be free to utilize their reserves, which are large enough to enable them to halt the offensive at the very outset.

I should add that the situation has never been as favorable as now for (Russian) troops in that nearly all available German forces are fighting on our front, and the number is increasing from day to day!"

Commander-in-Chief

In another cable received, General Nivelle draws my attention to the fact that this request is entirely in accordance with the agreement reached by the Allies on the fourth item discussed at the last conference in St. Petersburg, and requests me to urge Your Excellency to comply with his request on the basis of that agreement.

Janin [1]

Replying to General Janin with a short note in which he pointed out that it would be impossible to carry out the proposal of the French Commander-in-Chief, General Alekseyev wrote a memorandum to Nivelle in answer to his communication, which sounded more like an instruction to a subordinate than a letter to an equal. In a very restrained and calm manner, General Alekseyev explained to Nivelle the danger to all the Allies presented by his reckless and unduly hasty plan for a general offensive. With astonishing accuracy he predicted the consequences of an offensive by the Allies without support from the Russian Front. The memorandum stated:

Further to my letter of March 9, No. 2095, . . . I deem it my moral duty to express a frank opinion and avoid the painful consequences which may be incurred by my failure to do so.

(1) A letter received from the War Minister shows that the political upheaval inside Russia has had a very bad effect on the morale of our reserve units (at the depots) in all districts. The morale of these units has fallen and it will not be possible to use them as replacements for three or four months, say June or July.

(2) The same situation applies basically to the supply of horses for the entire army.

(3) We are therefore forced to face facts and state openly that we would be even unable to launch an offensive at the beginning of May, and cannot

---

[1] No. 812, copy of memorandum from General Janin, head of French Military Mission, to General Alekseyev, conveying Nivelle's request for the launching of an offensive. *The Russian Provisional Government, 1917,* Vol. II, p. 926.

be counted on to take an extensive part in the operation until June or July.

(4) This situation will enable the enemy either to concentrate his entire reserves on the Anglo-French Front, or else attack us in full force and take advantage of our temporary weakness.

(5) I think that this fact should be instrumental in a reappraisal of operations in the near future and should influence the decisions of the French High Command. (In this connection) General Nivelle's message of March 3, stating that he intends to use all French forces for his offensive on the Western Front and to aim at decisive results, merits special attention. In my opinion, the forced standstill of the Russian Army during the next few months—necessary so as to conserve its strength for the future—makes it essential that the French Army should not exhaust itself until the right moment and should keep its reserves until such time as we are able to attack the enemy on all fronts in a joint operation.

(6) Given the relative inactivity forced upon us at present, I consider it more expedient for the Anglo-French Army to continue a slow and cautious advance in the wake of the enemy withdrawal and to set up new and strong defense lines.

(7) It is my opinion that the aforesaid makes an Anglo-French general offensive inadvisable against an enemy who is undoubtedly withdrawing to strongly fortified defense lines and who may intend to carry out . . . extensive field maneuvers . . . in which free maneuvering of the reserves might offer good opportunities to both sides. But in any such operation the enemy, by relying on fortified positions prepared (in advance) would enjoy undoubted advantage . . .

General Alekseyev,
March 13, 1917.

In reply to this memorandum, on March 15, General Nivelle wrote that the British operations had already begun, and he insisted once again that the Russians launch an immediate offensive, adding rather sententiously that "in view of the overall state of morale of the Russian Army the best possible solution to the problem would be to resume offensive operations."

This new demand, and the impertinent suggestion about the psychological state of the Russian Army it contained, enraged General Alekseyev. His reply, dated March 20, stated bluntly:

. . . If things settle down soon, *and there are signs that they will;* if it proves possible to restore the fighting capacity of the Baltic Fleet, whoever is Commander-in-Chief will do everything possible under any circumstances to tie down the enemy forces which at present are on our front . . . It is not possible for us to launch even sporadic attacks before the early part of May, with spring just beginning; there is a tremendous amount of snow and the thaw will be one of the worst." [2]

But the "general offensive" had already begun. To stop the British advance on the Arras-Soisson sector was out of the question. Henceforth, things developed much as Alekseyev had predicted. The impetuous General Nivelle had miscalculated, and the British and French armies were caught in a trap.

In the north, the British were unable to penetrate the German defense installations and, having advanced only a few miles, were halted with heavy casualties.

In Champagne, the French Army also suffered a crushing defeat with a tremendous loss of life.

The psychological consequences were perhaps even more disastrous. The rank-and-file troops in a number of corps displayed growing dissatisfaction with their officers; antiwar propaganda started to take hold, and there was talk of demanding immediate peace. Finally, the situation reached a peak when two corps mutinied and started to march on Paris. On May 15, General Nivelle was relieved of his command and replaced by General Pétain, who had organized the defense of Verdun and enjoyed tremendous respect and prestige in the army.

Having halted the march of the mutinous soldiers, and having restored law and order at the front almost entirely without recourse to tough repressive measures, General Pétain extricated the Allied armies from a situation of extreme danger. Cautiously retreating to new positions which he himself had selected, the General remained on the defensive throughout that summer and fall.

Thus Nivelle's reckless attempt to bring the whole French Army into play and gain decisive results without the support of the Russian Front ended in defeat, and not only destroyed all chance of a combined attack from East and West but also deprived the Entente powers of almost all hope of ending the war in 1917.

It was also the disagreement among the Allied Powers that gave the German Government and Supreme Command a chance to adopt the notorious "master plan."

[2] *Red Archives,* vol. 30 (1929), p. 34.

The plan was clever and concise: First, end all operations on the Russian Front, and instead, launch a "peace offensive" accompanied by defeatist propaganda, thereby paralyzing the Russian fighting spirit; second, switch all regular divisions from the Russian to the Western Front, concentrating in that area the whole force of the German Army; and, third, stage a decisive battle in Western Europe before the United States could give real and effective support to the Allies.

The only possible way to thwart this cunning plan was to prevent the disintegration of the Russian Front, to restore discipline among the troops, and to resume action, since an idle and demoralized front would make Russia an easy prey to corrosive propaganda. Indeed, it was the resumption of military operations on the Russian Front that eventually made victory for the Germans impossible in World War I.

Later, General Hindenburg confirmed in his memoirs [3] that in 1917 the Russian High Command saw the purpose of the German "peace policy" on the Russian Front, chose the right strategic plan of action for the Russian Army, and pursued it to the hilt.

The Russian Front

The demoralization of the Russian troops in the fall and winter of 1916 had led the Tsar to extreme measures in a futile attempt to prepare for the spring offensive. Acting at the instigation of General Gurko, the acting chief of staff, the Tsar had decided upon a major reorganization of the army.

Despite the objections of the commanders-in-chief of the Northern, Western, and Southwestern fronts, as a result of the Tsar's explicit wish and General Gurko's firm opinion, it was decided to transfer another 20 divisions from the above-mentioned fronts to the Rumanian Front. By the summer, 21 divisions would have been formed for the European fronts. Following the German model, it was decided to reorganize the two-division corps into three-division corps. Seventy heavy artillery batteries were being formed. The offensive on the Russian Front was planned for the early part of May, by which time the railroad lines toward Rumania would be ready.

Had General Alekseyev been at Supreme Headquarters at this time, this plan would never have seen the light of day, for it was absolutely

[3] From *My Life,* by Marshal Paul von Hindenburg, tr. by F. A. Holt, Vol. II (New York, Harper & Bros.), pp. 65–66.

unthinkable, from a military point of view, to effect any radical re-organization of the army and the transportation system—even at the Tsar's "explicit wish"—in the few months before the beginning of the offensive.

It was in the midst of this hasty and chaotic reorganization of the army that news of the Tsar's abdication was received from the capital. The masses of soldiers and many of the officers were highly enthusiastic at the news of the coup d'état in Petrograd. The high commanders, who, with the Duma and Supreme Headquarters, had originally demanded the Tsar's abdication in favor of his heir as the price of saving the Monarchy, were taken aback by what had happened. But they had no thought of making any attempt to restore the dynasty. In short, the psychological reaction at the Front was just the same as in the rest of the country, which was only to be expected.

The collapse of the Monarchy and the resultant disintegration of the entire governmental and administrative apparatus seemed at first not even to have affected the Front. The structure of the army in the field, including the chain of command, from the commanders of the individual fronts down to the rank-and-file soldiers in the trenches, appeared to remain intact.

But that was only on the surface. The distrust of the High Command which had been growing among the lower ranks over the few months prior to the final collapse came to a head during the first weeks of the Revolution and broke out with elemental force, wrecking the very foundation of discipline—the soldier's trust in his officers.

Now that their daily routine at the front had been disrupted, the soldiers took to discussing matters among themselves, they held numerous meetings, argued continuously about when they would return home, and refused to carry out orders. Sensing their loss of authority and thoroughly confused by the new situation, the officers were hesitant to issue orders.

The whole country passed through a crisis during the few weeks following the fall of the Monarchy, but it was at the Front that the crisis was most profound and dangerous. For an army without discipline inevitably disintegrates and loses its fighting power.

It was during this initial period of disintegration that committees first began to be elected in the fighting units. At the same time, the Duma and the Petrograd Soviet both began sending their own delegates to the front to give an account of what had happened and to calm the troops.

However, the Duma's tremendous authority among the soldiers began to wane after the first few weeks, and its delegates rapidly vanished from the Front. This was because on the first day of the Revolution the Duma had refused to take the lead in the nationwide revolutionary movement.

On the other hand, the Soviet delegates, acting in the name of the workers and peasants, rapidly gained authority among the troops and were chosen to act as commissars in charge of all the activities of the elected committees, and also as mediators between the latter and the officers. The same thing happened in the navy.

Taking advantage of the situation, Bolshevik agents in the guise of delegates and commissars infiltrated the army; this was easily done during the initial weeks of the Revolution, when "commissar mandates" were issued to all and sundry without a proper check being made as to an applicant's motives for visiting the front.

The German Government had long dreamed of breaking the ring of steel with which the Entente had encircled Germany and now at last they saw a way of implementing their "master plan."

On instructions from the German High Command, Crown Prince Leopold of Bavaria, supreme commander-in-chief of the Eastern Front, abruptly ceased all hostilities against the Russians, and a deathly silence fell over the German lines. Prince Leopold had suddenly become an apostle of peace, a friend of Russian soldiers and a fierce foe of the imperialist warmongers.

All along the front the Russian lines were showered with leaflets signed by him. In them he called upon the Russian soldiers to make peace with their German brothers on the other side and promised not to attack them. He also demanded publication of the secret treaties between Russia, Britain, and France, encouraged distrust of the Russian officers, and referred to the members of the Provisional Government as hirelings of Franco-British bankers.

The war-weary Russian soldiers, mostly peasant youths who had been hastily trained and put in uniform,[4] were easy prey to this trickery, and many of them genuinely believed that the Germans wanted

---

[4] Two-thirds of the regular infantry had been killed or wounded during the preceding years, and, as Brusilov put it, the army had turned into a "militia."

peace, while their own officers, the Russian upper class, were against it.

The German High Command was well aware of the situation on the Russian side and took full advantage of it. German soldiers crawled out of their trenches to visit their Russian "comrades" and fraternize with them. After a while the Germans grew bolder and began to send officers with white flags to the Russian lines to ask permission to visit headquarters with offers for a cease-fire. Some of the Russian batteries tried to drive the unwanted guests away with gunfire, but this action aroused a wave of indignation, particularly in the "Third Division," the hapless invention of General Gurko.

An enthusiastic participant in the staging of these incidents was a German lieutenant named Wollenberg, who was subsequently commissioned by his German superiors to assist in the organization of the international battalions for Lenin in 1918. In the 1930's Wollenberg became a political émigré, and he called on me in Paris. He told me in great detail about the German plans to engineer the collapse of the Russian front. This subversive activity was rated by the German government as a vital "technical-military" mission, and it was carried out by special teams of officers and soldiers.

The Russian officers and members of the regimental committees tried hard to counteract the effect of German propaganda, but their efforts were futile; fraternization had assumed the proportions of an epidemic, the trenches and dugouts were left unattended, and military routine at the front gradually collapsed. Meanwhile, the regular German divisions were being transferred, one by one, to the Western Front.

These poisonous propaganda "attacks" were a crowning success for Berlin, and in Russia there was ever-increasing concern for the fate of the front.

Not long before Lenin's arrival in Petrograd, an article by none other than Joseph Stalin appeared in *Pravda* on March 15, 1917, shortly after his return from exile:

> The war goes on. The great Russian Revolution has failed to put an end to it, and there is no hope that it will end tomorrow or the day after. The soldiers, peasants and workers of Russia who went to war at the call of the deposed Tsar, and who shed their blood under his banners, have freed themselves, and the Tsarist idols have been replaced by the red banners of the Revolution. But the war will continue, because the German troops have

not followed the example of the Russian Army and are still obeying their Emperor, who avidly seeks his prey on the battlefield of death.

When one army confronts another, the most absurd policy would be to propose that one of them lay down its arms and go home. This policy would not be a policy of peace but a policy of slavery, a policy which free people would reject with indignation. No, the free people will stand firmly at their posts, will reply bullet for bullet and shell for shell. This is inevitable.

The revolutionary soldiers and officers who have overthrown the yoke of tsarism will not leave their trenches so as to make room for the German or Austrian soldiers and officers, who as yet have not had the courage to free themselves from the yoke of their own governments. We cannot permit any disorganization of the military forces of the Revolution! War must be ended in an orderly way by a pact among the liberated peoples, and not by subordination to the will of the imperialist conqueror.

Within the army itself every effort was made to counter this pernicious German propaganda, but the soldiers in the trenches continued to fraternize enthusiastically.

But the standstill at the front was too much of a strain on Prince Leopold and his chief of staff, General Hoffmann. They finally gave way to temptation.

Without any warning the German troops launched an attack on the River Stokhod in the region assigned to the Special Army. The attack was opened on March 21, when the river was in flood, and a Russian corps under the command of General Leshch was wiped out.

The German authorities in Berlin were extremely irritated by General Hoffmann's arbitrary and unauthorized operations, which might easily have undermined their plans for subverting the Russian army by peaceful means. The General was ordered to cease all hostilities, and it was suggested that the victory on the River Stokhod be played down as much as possible in the official communiqué.[5]

[5] "After the unsuccessful fighting on March 21 for the bridgehead on the River Stokhod in the region of Tabol-Gelenin, our forces took up positions on the right bank of the river. According to our reports from those in command of the operation, Russian forces defending the bridgehead on the German side suffered severe casualties; out of two regiments of the fifth rifle division only a handful of men reached the right bank of the river. Both regimental commanders were killed. The third regiment of this division was reduced to half its original number. Out of two regiments of two other field divisions only a few hundred men survived. Other regiments suffered to a lesser extent."

A. V. Gorbatov, "Years and Wars," *Novy Mir* (Moscow), No. 3, 1964, p. 134.

However, the German Government was unable to hide the truth from the Russian public or the Russian Army, since an exact account of what had happened was published immediately in the Russian press. The news of the defeat on the River Stokhod stunned Russia and gave rise to profound alarm at the overall situation on the front. This grave concern was only increased by the publication of a statement of the German Supreme Command, unprecedented in the history of warfare. The statement, signed by Hindenburg, referred to the attack on the River Stokhod as an accidental "misunderstanding" which would not occur again. This promise was frequently repeated, and it was indeed kept.

It was at this point (April 3) that Lenin arrived in Petrograd to help carry out General Hoffmann's plans. He abruptly changed the Bolshevik policy reflected in Stalin's *Pravda* article, and all his articles, statements, and slogans served the propaganda campaign unleashed by Prince Leopold and his subordinates.

The ends desired by Lenin and the German "peacemakers" were diametrically opposed and certainly irreconcilable, but their means were identical—the destruction of Russia's fighting spirit. Fostered by the Bolsheviks, the germs of demoralization spread rapidly through the body of the army. All attempts to resume preparations for military action met with vigorous opposition from the soldiers all along the front. There were companies, regiments, and even whole divisions in which the committees were dominated by Bolshevik defeatists and German-paid agents. The committees subjected the officers and commissars in these units to incessant badgering. Orders were not obeyed, and commanders whom the committees disliked were replaced by expert demagogues or by ignoble opportunists.

Obviously all this greatly increased the difficulties of restoring the fighting fitness of the Russian Army, but after Stokhod, and the defeat of General Nivelle's armies, the German-Bolshevik coalition was nevertheless unable, for the time being, to achieve its aim of totally paralyzing the Russian war effort.

The Fighting Spirit Returns

There was a growing feeling at the front that it was the army's duty to defend the country.

In his last letter to General Nivelle (March 20), General Alekseyev wrote that "the first signs of a return to normal are in evidence" and that the situation had been aided by the "proximity of the enemy."

Indeed, at the beginning of April the congresses of the various committees began sending delegations to Petrograd urging an immediate return to full-scale production at defense plants and appealing to the nation to give wholehearted support to the defenders of the country.

At the first congress of front-line delegates on April 22, at which both Guchkov and I spoke frankly and explicitly, there was hardly anyone who supported Lenin's defeatist views. The resolution adopted by the majority was an accurate reflection of the new mood of the soldiers in the trenches.

But at the end of April German divisions were still being transferred from the Russian Front to the West.

This calm reaction on the part of the German High Command to the surge of patriotism in the committees and among the troops was quite natural and understandable, because Guchkov and his colleagues had taken no measures other than verbal persuasion to restore discipline in the theater of war. Instead, they had ceded more and more to the demands of the military section of the Petrograd Soviet.

At the end of April, a commission for the revision of the laws and regulations relating to military service [6] submitted a draft on the "rights of servicemen" to the War Minister. The draft was an almost exact reproduction of the notorious "Declaration of Soldiers' Rights" published by the military section of the Petrograd Soviet on March 9, which had been widely distributed at the front.

Polivanov's draft deprived the officers of all disciplinary power, even during actual operation, and permitted intervention on the part of the committees in the appointment, dismissal, and transfer of commanding officers. In other words, it directly contravened the declared policy of the Provisional Government, whose first message to the country on basic policy had stated:

... The extension of political freedom to persons serving in the armed forces is limited by the exigencies of military and technical circumstances. ... (point 2)

and

[6] Headed by General Polivanov, War Minister 1915–1916.

... The soldiers are to be freed from all restrictions in the exercise of those civil rights . . . while preserving strict military discipline on duty and during military service. . . . (point 8).

Guchkov released General Polivanov from his chairmanship of the Commission and appointed in his place a close colleague and deputy minister, General Novitsky, giving him instructions to alter the text of the draft. Two or three days later Novitsky told Guchkov that the declaration had been adopted unanimously without amendments.

At that point, when the army was again in a fighting mood, instead of stopping this game between the generals and civilians ignorant of military matters, Guchkov decided to resign from the Provisional Government. He made his decision known in the following letter to Prince Lvov:

May 1, 1917

In view of the situation in which the Government, particularly the War Minister, now finds itself, a situation which I am unable to alter and which jeopardizes the defense, freedom and even the existence of Russia, I can no longer conscientiously continue as Minister of War, nor share responsibility for the grievous harm that is being done to my country. I therefore request the Provisional Government to release me from these duties.[7]

This letter, which was published on May 2, heaped indiscriminate blame upon all the members of the Provisional Government with the exception of its author.

By breaking, in a rather ungentlemanly fashion, with the Provisional Government and with the democratic elements in Russia whose support he had enjoyed, Guchkov counted on rallying around him all the officers who, through the collapse of the Monarchy, had been put in a difficult and sometimes intolerable position at the front. But this was a miscalculation. As minister of war Guchkov had lost the confidence of the Supreme Command because of his association with the Polivanov Commission, but he had not won popularity among the soldiers and sailors. He thus found himself in complete isolation.

Upon receiving Guchkov's letter, Prince Lvov called a meeting of the government, which drew up an official statement regarding Guch-

[7] *The Russian Provisional Government, 1917,* ed. by Browder and Kerensky, Vol. III, p. 1267.

kov's resignation.[8] Then the question of a successor was raised. Since Guchkov's resignation had undoubtedly been motivated not only by his own opposition to the government's policy, but also by that of many senior officers, Lvov proposed that General Alekseyev, as the Supreme Commander, should be consulted as to his views in this matter. The proposal was adopted unanimously, and Prince Lvov instructed V. V. Vyrubov [9] to deliver a message to Alekseyev asking him to name his own candidate.

The next afternoon, before the meeting of the government, Lvov invited me into his office. Vyrubov had telephoned directly from Mogilev to say that, after conferring with the commanders-in-chief of all the fronts, General Alekseyev had given him a sheet of paper with two names—(1) Kerensky,[10] and (2) Palchinsky.[11]

"Palchinsky's name," Lvov added as an afterthought, "only stresses the fact that, in the view of all the commanders-in-chief, you are the only possible candidate, since they realize that although Palchinsky is an excellent organizer, he is not well known to the public and is largely unknown at the front. They know that we need a man of your stature who enjoys the confidence of the country and army as you do. It is your duty to accept the post, and you must not refuse."

I must admit in all sincerity that since the very beginning of the Guchkov crisis I had had a premonition that I would have to bear the heavy burden of his legacy. It was probably on account of this feeling

---

[8] Ibid., p. 1268.

[9] Chairman of the Committee of the All-Russian Union of Zemstvos on the Western Front at Minsk.

[10] In a personal letter to me dated January 10, 1958, Vyrubov gives the following account, taken from his unpublished memoirs, of his conversation with General Alekseyev:

"I conveyed the message from Prince Lvov. General Alekseyev replied: 'The question is so important that I want to confer with the commanders-in-chief. Just wait a moment.' I waited for half an hour. General Alekseyev came back and handed me a sheet of paper on which he had written in his small though remarkably clear handwriting: (1) Kerensky; (2) Palchinsky; and then he said: 'This is not only my opinion, it is also that of the other commanders-in-chief.' I must confess I hadn't expected this answer and asked the General: 'Don't you have a military candidate?' He answered: 'We feel that at the present time a general should not be minister of war.'"

[11] P. Palchinsky—mining engineer and nonpartisan political figure. Excellent organizer, active member of special governmental council for defense, organized in 1915. He was, in the beginning, member of the Executive Committee of the Petrograd Soviet, and acted as intermediary between the Executive Committee and General Kornilov, commander of the Petrograd Military District. By order of the Provisional Government he became chairman of the Special Council for Defense.

that I had tried so hard on April 29 to dissuade him from resigning, pledging my support and trying to convince him that the psychological climate at the front was improving. The idea of shouldering such tremendous responsibility was terrifying, and I was unable to give an immediate answer. I left the meeting, promising to return when I had made up my mind. At first, thinking things over in the solitude of my office at the Ministry of Justice, it seemed out of the question to divorce myself for any length of time from the general political leadership in the government. The political coalition in the Cabinet was still too unstable to be left to its own fate. With this in mind, I was reaching for the telephone to refuse the nomination when I was struck with the sudden realization of what would happen to my work, to the government, and to Russia if the "truce" were allowed to drag on. In two or three months the Russian front would disintegrate completely, the Hindenburg-Ludendorff master plan would succeed in the West, and Russia would be at the mercy of the German aspirants to world rule.

This had to be prevented at all cost! No one in Russia was going to conclude a separate peace with Germany. Russia could not permit the defeat of her Allies, for she was linked to them by a common destiny. Hindenburg's plan had to be foiled, and for that purpose military operations must be resumed on the Russian Front.

After several hours of agonizing inner struggle I finally realized that there was no alternative for the government, the Supreme Command, or myself, and I telephoned Lvov that I would accept the post.

16

The Offensive

By the morning of May 2 the government crisis was over, after a tense five-day battle within the socialist parties over Prince Lvov's invitation to contribute representatives to the cabinet.

The Germans, who were being grossly misinformed by their agents about Russian internal affairs and the balance of political forces, had been making preparations during the April Bolshevik uprising for some form of peace talks. They thought that the resignations of Milyukov and Guchkov would be a decisive step toward concluding a separate peace. But they were mistaken.

On May 5 the new Cabinet,[1] which now included the Socialists, published a declaration. The first item in the declaration stated that the government, "rejecting, along with the whole nation, any idea of a separate peace," would hold talks with the Allies as soon as possible on ways and means of modifying the war aims so as to achieve a general democratic peace along the lines laid down in the Government Manifesto of March 27.

The second item, which defined the role of Russia's own armed forces, ran: "Convinced that the defeat of Russia and her allies would not only be a source of great misfortunes for the people, but would also delay, or render impossible, the conclusion of a general peace on the basis mentioned above, the Provisional Government firmly be-

---

[1] The new members of the Provisional Government were: representing the Socialist Revolutionaries—V. M. Chernov, minister of agriculture, and P. M. Pereverzev, minister of justice; representing the Social Democrat Mensheviks—I. G. Tsereteli, minister of post and telegraph, and M. I. Skobelev, minister of labor; representing the Popular Socialists—A. V. Peshekhonov, minister of foods; representing the Cadets—Prince Dimitri Shakhovskoi, minister of welfare. M. I. Tereshchenko, minister of finance, became minister of foreign affairs; A. I. Shingarev, minister of agriculture, became minister of finance; and A. F. Kerensky became minister of war and the navy.

lieves that Russia's Revolutionary Army will not allow the German forces to overwhelm the Allies in the West, thus enabling them to turn the entire might of their weapons against us. Consolidation of democratic principles in the army and the organization and strengthening of its fighting fitness both in defensive and offensive operations will be the Provisional Government's most important task." [2]

How could the Russian army prevent the complete and utter destruction of the Western Front, with all its ruinous consequences for Russia? Hindenburg's plan, as I explained earlier, was to paralyze the Russian Front by means of peace propaganda and fraternization, to concentrate the whole might of the German army on the Western Front, and to deliver a crushing blow there by the end of the summer, before the Americans arrived. There was only one way Russia could scotch this strategic plan, and that was to take the initiative and resume hostilities. There was nothing else we could do. My duty as minister of war and the navy was to see that this was done with the least possible delay.

I took up my new office on May 2, and that same day I had a long talk with General Manikovsky, the deputy minister of war, who was in charge of the technical side of the ministry—war production supplies and so on. I knew him from his work in the Duma. During the first few days following the collapse of the Monarchy he had been able to restore order among the workers at the arsenal and other military establishments. After consultations with Konovalov, minister of trade and industry, Manikovsky had introduced an eight-hour working day in the factories under his control.

Konovalov had advised me to sound him out on how the top men in the War Ministry and the High Command felt about Guchkov's resignation. Without mentioning names, Manikovsky told me in detail of a secret meeting between Guchkov and the High Command, headed by General Alekseyev, about which some alarming rumors had reached the ears of the government. He told me that the meeting had been arranged on his, Manikovsky's, initiative, in order to discuss the Declaration of Soldiers' Rights drafted by General Polivanov and his successor, General Novitsky.[3]

[2] *Provisional Government Herald,* No. 49, May 6, 1917, p. 1.
[3] See Chapter 15.

The original draft of the declaration, drawn up by the Petrograd Soviet and published in *Izvestiya* on March 9, had not been passed over lightly by Polivanov's commission at the beginning of the discussion. On the contrary, spokesmen for the military department, headed by Polivanov, had systematically pursued a policy of "nonresistance to evil," and had merely sought to delay its publication by making various excuses. Considering all this, Manikovsky proposed at the generals' conference that they should review the text of the document, take out the more unacceptable points, and publish it straight away. If this was not done, he said, and the draft declaration was simply shelved, the top men in the War Ministry, and along with them the whole of the government, would appear as cowards and cheats in the eyes of the military. Manikovsky's proposal met with a rather curt reply—"Publish it if you wish, but we don't want it in that form." The meeting was adjourned.

When I heard this dramatic account, I realized that Guchkov's maliciously intentioned resignation might be followed by other resignations, a possibility that had to be prevented at once.

On May 3, there was a meeting of the Commission for the Revision of Army Laws and Regulations (known as the Polivanov Commission). I attended the meeting and asked Novitsky, who was in the chair, to allow me to address the meeting right away. My speech was brief. Pointing out the gravity of Russia's position as a belligerent power with an inactive front, I told them that the growing demoralization of the troops was attributable not only to German propaganda, but also to the overzealous legislative activity of all types of committees and subcommittees. I said that the situation was intolerable, and that if we went on like this we could only expect the disintegration of the army and total defeat by the enemy. To drive home my point, I told them about a delegation of Russian Poles that had just returned from Stockholm, where they had gone for talks with the Poles from German-occupied Poland. A. Lednitsky, a leading Polish politician, had bitterly told me the following story:

When the "German" Poles went to see Zimmerman, the German foreign minister, to ask him for permission to go to Stockholm, Zimmerman had replied with studied courtesy: "You may certainly go to Stockholm and conclude any agreement you like with the Russian

Poles. For us the Russian state no longer exists as an international force."

I told the meeting that, if Russia's present inactivity at the front and the collapse of the army's strength—its discipline—continued, the Germans as well as the Allies would lose all respect for us and would completely disregard our legitimate interests in the future. It was our duty to Russia, I said, not only to stop the decay in the army, but also to weld it together again into an efficient fighting force.

For the work that lay ahead of me in the army, at the front, and at home, I had no use for people who could not genuinely accept the *fait accompli* of the Revolution, or who doubted that we could rebuild the army's morale in the new psychological atmosphere. People like that might outwardly adapt themselves to the new situation, but inwardly they would be incapable of devoting themselves wholeheartedly to this work. For my work in the army I needed as my closest associates men with independent minds, men who were ready to serve a cause rather than a person. I needed men who had lived through the utter folly of the years of war under the old regime and who fully understood the upheaval that had occurred. I needed men who believed that the Russian army was not ruined, who were convinced that healthy political forces at the front and at home would eventually overcome the influence of demoralizing propaganda, and who realized that the army committees and commissars had not appeared at the front through the evil designs of Russia's internal and external foes, but as the inevitable result of the collapse of traditional relationships between officers and men during the period immediately following the collapse of the Monarchy.

After several days of hectic talks and conferences, control of the War Ministry finally passed into the hands of men who answered these needs, men who were young, energetic, and fully conversant with the situation with which we were faced. Lt. General Manikovsky and Colonels Yakubovich and Tumanov from the General Staff were made deputy ministers of war. I recalled Colonel Baranovsky (my brother-in-law) from the front, where he had been since the beginning of the war,[4] and made him head of my personal secretariat, in which

---

[4] He was at that moment on the staff of General Lukomsky, commander of the First Corps.

there was now a special department to look after political matters in the armed forces.

Colonel Baranovsky made daily reports to me on all current matters, carried out assignments at Headquarters, and kept me briefed on what was happening in Petrograd during my frequent tours of the front. I may say that I never had cause to regret the choice of my closest aide. Throughout my service in the War Ministry we worked in complete harmony.

Later, on May 25, I reorganized the top administration of the Navy Ministry. Captain B. P. Dudourov became first deputy minister for strategic and political questions, and Captain Kukel, second deputy minister for technical operations.

On the day the new composition of the Provisional Government was made public, I issued my first order. I quote it here since it testifies to the fact that the surrender to anarchy implicit in the recommendations of the Polivanov Commission was now a thing of the past:

Having taken upon myself the military authority of the country, I declare that:

(1) The homeland is in danger and everyone must help to avert this danger to the best of his strength and ability, despite all hardships. No letters of resignation from senior commanding personnel motivated by a desire to shirk responsibility at this moment will therefore be accepted by me;

(2) All soldiers who have willfully deserted their ranks and sailors who have deserted their ships must return by May 15;

(3) All those disobeying this order will be punished with the full severity of the law." [5]

When they read this order those who had attended Guchkov's secret meeting would realize that it would be a risky venture to follow his example. The order was also intended to assure the people who were becoming alarmed at the increasing acts of violence by deserters, that a serious campaign was now being waged against this evil.

In talks with the new Menshevik ministers, Skobelev and Tsereteli, who were also members of the Petrograd Soviet Executive Committee, it was decided that in the future the commissars attached to army

[5] *Provisional Government Herald*, No. 49, May 6, 1917.

units would be appointed and dismissed only by the War Minister, and that those already appointed by the Executive Committee would come under his jurisdiction. At the same time we withdrew from the Petrograd Military District Staff the representatives of the Soviet, who had been acting as observers.

Like Guchkov, the commander of the Petrograd Military District, General Kornilov, had not been able to win the confidence of the soldiers and the Soviet officials. I therefore replaced him with a young officer, General P. A. Polovtsev, who had recently returned from the front, and had been in the Duma Military Commission at the outbreak of the Revolution. His relations with the soldiers were friendly. At his own request I appointed as his assistant, chiefly for propaganda work among the men, a certain lieutenant, A. Kuzmin,[6] a man I knew to be devoted to his country.

In taking these preliminary steps, my colleagues and I were looking for a way out of the difficulties Guchkov had created by refusing to sign the Declaration of Soldiers' Rights. We could not cancel the declaration entirely, since most of it had been incorporated in Guchkov's Order No. 114 of March 5 (Abolition of Certain Practices and Restrictions Formerly Imposed on Enlisted Men). We soon found an answer, however. While being careful not to encroach on the new personal and political rights proclaimed by the Provisional Government, we reinstated the rights of commanding officers, without which the army could not possibly function.

On May 11, I signed Order No. 8 "On the Rights of Servicemen." Section 14 stated that officers were reinvested with the power to take disciplinary action, including the use of force in cases of insubordination, during operations at the front. In addition, Section 18 placed the appointment, transfer and dismissal of army ranks under the sole jurisdiction of commanding officers.[7]

---

[6] Lieutenant Kuzmin had taken part in the Russo-Japanese War, and when the defeated Russian troops mutinied on their way back from Manchuria, and riots and lawlessness spread along the whole Trans-Siberian Railway, Kuzmin became chairman of the so-called "Krasnoyarsk Republic." He was later court-martialed for this and sentenced to a long period of convict labor, although his only complicity in the mutiny had been that he had stopped the looting of the towns by the mobs of rioting soldiers, and had been elected president of the "republic" as a result.

[7] Lenin was well aware of the significance of these two sections, and furiously attacked the order in an article in *Pravda* under the cunning title of "Declarations of

By May 12 the healthy mood of patriotism at the front had become a definite force from which the government and High Command could have drawn support. The endless succession of political meetings within the regiments came to a stop, and the rank-and-file soldiers, wearied by a long period of idleness, returned of their own accord to their normal duties. The junior officers regained the confidence of their men, and it was seldom that attempts to restore discipline were met with resistance. The army, the corps, and the lower-level committees were now solidly organized; they were composed, in the main, of men in favor of a renewal of hostilities, and they carried out a great deal of effective propaganda work among the young recruits who were being sent to the front with a bare minimum of military training. Acts of violence against officers, and the replacement of efficient commanders by faint-hearted upstarts, were now comparatively rare. The widespread fraternization with the Germans in the trenches came to a stop, and the demoralization of the infantry, which had spread like a disease, now became confined mainly to the newly formed "Third Divisions." These units had become havens for Bolshevik agitators, German agents, and former members of the security and civil police sent to the front following the Revolution. Defeatism was particularly rampant in units where the men were under the influence of Leninist officers such as Krylenko, Dzevaltovsky, Semashko, Sivers, and Dr. Sklyansky. Although such units were few and far between, by the second half of May reason was no longer of any use in dealing with them, and we had to resort to force.

Armed force was first used against mutinous troops by General Shcherbachev, the commander on the Rumanian Front. The Supreme Commander received the following telegram from him: "In view of impossibility of completing organization of Third Divisions in time for commencement of operations, former Commander in Chief [8] sanctioned disbandment of those which commanding officers consider unfit for combat at present time. Sixth Army Commander's orders to

---

Soldiers' Lack of Rights." Others, for example, General Romeiko-Gurko, in command of the Western Front, were completely baffled by it. On May 15, this general sent the Commander-in-Chief and the Prime Minister a message saying that Order No. 8 would make it impossible to control the men and that he was therefore resigning. The resignation was not accepted; the government relieved him of his duties, and the Commander-in-Chief was instructed to demote him to the rank of divisional commander.

[8] General Alekseyev.

regiments of 163 Division to disband and transfer to new area have been ignored by three regiments who demand division be left intact."

General Shcherbachev ordered the dispatch of a special detachment of infantry and artillery to put down the mutiny. The three regiments were surrounded, and General Biskupsky, who was in command of the detachment, told them that unless they obeyed orders to lay down their arms and disband, he would open fire. General Shcherbachev's report ended with the words: "Everything passed off without bloodshed." [9]

Under the new conditions at the front, commanding officers were often hesitant to exercise the disciplinary powers with which they had once again been invested, and some of the commissars from the War Ministry were slow in urging them to do so. For instance, when several regiments in the Twelfth and Thirteenth Divisions refused to take up advance positions, Boris Savinkov, a commissar attached to the Seventh Army, sent me an urgent message asking what he should do. Col. Yakubovich, who was temporarily in charge while I was away at the front, ordered him by telegram to disband the regiments in question and have the officers and men guilty of insubordination arrested and court-martialed. Yakubovich also ordered him to notify the Minister at once as to what action had been taken.

At this same time a law was passed establishing hard labor as the penalty for desertion, refusal to obey orders, and open mutiny, or for inciting others to commit these offenses.

According to the strategy decided upon at headquarters, the Russian armies had to launch the offensive not later than mid-June (N. S.).

Our men at the front had enough equipment and supplies for limited offensive operations, since the opening of a direct railroad line to the ice-free port of Murmansk at the end of November, 1916, had enabled the Western Allies to send us heavy artillery and other armaments for the full-scale offensive planned against the Central Powers.

We intended to launch the offensive with an attack by the Southwestern Army, commanded by General Brusilov. The fighting spirit of the men, and their understanding of the need to defend their country

[9] It should be noted that this decisiveness on the part of the command was implicitly endorsed by an article in the Soviet's *Izvestiya*.

at any price, were proof against the German propaganda spread among them. They were quite ready to do their duty in the event of a German offensive.

The idea that they should go over to the attack was not so readily accepted, however. In addition, there were officers of all ranks who were extremely skeptical about an offensive at this stage, even though the army's morale and the officers' authority among the men had improved considerably. I had every hope, however, that a personal visit to the front and direct contact with the officers and men would help to boost morale and facilitate preparations for battle. After a tour of inspection of the troops of the Petrograd garrison, I left for Helsinki and Sveaborg late on May 8. It was in the Finnish Gulf, not far from these two ports, that our "big" fleet (i.e., dreadnoughts, battleships, and cruisers) was anchored. I spent two days attending a variety of meetings and conferences, both private and public. At the public gatherings I was subjected to thinly veiled attacks by Bolsheviks, and at the private meetings I was sometimes forced to listen to very harsh criticism from spokesmen for the officers, whose lives under the watchful eye of the sailors' committees had become sheer misery. But the majority of my audiences, both officers and men, were friendly. An extreme left-wing speaker at one of these meetings declared that, in case of need, the Baltic Fleet could hold its own and prevent the enemy from reaching the capital. These were brave words, but in practice the situation was quite different. I went back to Helsinki with the sad realization that the Baltic Fleet was heavily infiltrated with German and Leninist agents.

Late on May 12 I set off for the Southwestern Front. At Kamenets-Podolsk, General Brusilov's headquarters, a congress of delegates from all parts of the front was in progress, and I addressed the meeting on May 14. The large hall in which the delegates met was filled to capacity. I was surrounded on all sides by haggard faces and feverish eyes. The atmosphere was extremely tense. I felt I was facing people who had suffered some frightful shock from which they had not quite yet recovered. I realized that they only wanted to know one thing—why they were still in the trenches. As I listened to the speeches of the delegates, the army committee members, and General Brusilov himself, I could sense the mood of the entire army. I had no doubt that at that moment the army was facing a temptation which it found difficult to resist. After three years of bitter suffering, millions of war-weary soldiers were asking themselves: "Why should I have to die now when at home a new, freer life is only just beginning?"

The very question paralyzed their will. Men under enemy fire can only endure it when there is no doubt as to the aim for which they are fighting—or rather, when they believe unquestionably in the necessity of sacrifice for a clearly defined and, to their minds, indisputable purpose.

No army can afford to start questioning the aim for which it is fighting. Everything that was happening in the army at that moment—insubordination, the mutinies, the conversion to Bolshevism of whole units, the endless political meetings, and the mass desertion—was the natural outcome of the terrible conflict in the mind of each soldier. The men had suddenly found a way of justifying their weakness, and they were overcome by an almost unconquerable urge to drop their weapons and flee from the trenches. To restore their fighting capacity we had to overcome their animal fear and answer their doubts with the clear and simple truth: You must make the sacrifice to save your country. People who did not understand the feelings of the soldiers in those crucial months in Russian history, or who spoke to them in patriotic platitudes couched in high-flown language, could not reach their hearts or have any influence on them.

The secret of Bolshevik propaganda among the working classes and the soldiers was that the Bolsheviks spoke to them in simple language and played on the deep-rooted instinct of self-preservation. The gist of Bolshevik propaganda can be summed up in Lenin's words: "We summon you to a social revolution. We appeal to you not to die for others, but to destroy others—to destroy your class enemies on the home front!"

My words to the soldiers were: "It's easy to appeal to exhausted men to throw down their arms and go home, where a new life has begun. But I summon you to battle, to feats of heroism—I summon you not to festivity, but to death; to sacrifice yourselves to save your country!"

It is not at all surprising that later on, after several months' hard fighting, the dregs of the proletariat and deserters in the rear followed the Bolsheviks along the path of murder and violence, having been promised unlimited freedom. The surprising thing is that in the summer of 1917 the front line troops displayed, though for only a fleeting moment, a powerful sense of patriotism.

By mid-May the German General Staff had already detected the change in the mood of the Russian Front, and German troops were gradually being moved eastward again.

The congress in Kamenets-Podolsk ended in an ovation for General Brusilov. Afterward I went with him on a tour of inspection of the units which would be the first to go into action in the offensive a month later. When the soldiers had marched past and the order to break ranks had been given, we climbed up onto an improvised platform to address the men.

Brusilov and the divisional commanders whom we were visiting spoke first, followed by the members of the local military committees. Finally it was my turn to address the men. They pressed around the platform still more closely and listened attentively. In what I said there was nothing but the bitter truth and a simple appeal to their sense of duty to their country. I find it hard to describe the impression that my words created. I can only say that they stirred the hearts of my listeners and filled them with fresh hope.

On numerous occasions of this kind the excited crowds of soldiers milling around us made it difficult to reach the cars waiting to drive us to the next stopping place.

Sometimes the soldiers pushed forward a Bolshevik agitator hiding among the crowd and made him say his piece to my face, for at that stage the open campaign against me had not yet been fully organized.

Of course, the change in mood after my visits was generally short-lived,[10] but in the units in which the commanders, commissars, and army committee members were able to grasp the psychological importance of what I told them, morale was strengthened and the men regained faith in their officers.

Brusilov and I returned from this tour of the Southwestern Front in a closed car, and we drove to Tarnopol through a violent storm. I do not know why, but with rain beating against the windows and light-

---

[10] Officers who were hostile to the February Revolution ironically dubbed me the "persuader-in-chief," a nickname which, incidentally, I did not find in the least insulting.

ning flashing overhead, we somehow felt closer to one another. Our conversation became informal and easy, as though we were old friends.

We discussed the things that were worrying all the civilian and military leaders responsible for the fate of the country. I spoke of the difficulty the government was having to cope with in left-wing political circles, and Brusilov told me of the harm done to the army by the obsolete bureaucratic system of administration, and the remoteness from reality of many of the higher-ranking officers.

Naturally, being an ambitious man, Brusilov was careful not to express views that differed too greatly from my own in speaking of his plans or giving me thumbnail sketches of some of the other generals. But basically we agreed on the principal problems facing Russia, and we both utterly rejected the idea prevalent among many men at the top that the "Russian Army was no more." We were both convinced that it was pointless just to analyze and criticize; it was necessary to be bold and take risks.

During that drive to Tarnopol we managed to settle a number of important matters concerning the forthcoming offensive, and I decided there and then that, in time for the opening of the offensive, Brusilov should be given charge of the entire army in place of Alekseyev. I did not give him any hint of my intentions, however, since I was not sure that Prince Lvov would agree.

From Tarnopol I went on to Odessa, which at that time was the rear base for the Rumanian-Black Sea Front. There I met General Shcherbachev, who had just come from Yassy, and representatives of the Rumanian Front Committee. Talking things over with Shcherbachev, I gained the impression that the front was in good hands and that the Russian and Rumanian troops would fight despite transport and logistic problems. A talk with the delegation from the Front Committee confirmed my opinion. I did not get a chance to visit the Front itself, for I had to accompany Admiral Kolchak and his chief of staff, Captain Smirnov, to Sebastopol, headquarters of the Black Sea Fleet, to try to settle a violent clash between the Admiral and the Central Executive Committee of the Black Sea Fleet and the local army garrisons.

Admiral Kolchak was one of the most competent admirals in the Russian Navy, and he had become a very popular figure among both officers and sailors. Not long before the Revolution he had been transferred from the Baltic Fleet to take command of the Black Sea Fleet. During the first few weeks following the collapse of the Monarchy he had established excellent relations with the ships' crews, and had even been instrumental in organizing the Central Committee of the Fleet. He had swiftly sized up the new situation and had thus been able to save the Black Sea Fleet from the horrors that the Baltic Fleet had had to endure.

The sailors were in a patriotic frame of mind and anxious to get to grips with the enemy, and when I arrived in Sebastopol both officers and men were hoping for landing operations in the Bosporus. A delegation of sailors had even been sent to the front to persuade soldiers to return to their duties. It might be thought that under these circumstances a clash between the Admiral and the Central Committee would have been most unlikely. But that is exactly what had happened.

The Central Committee had ordered the arrest of the assistant harbormaster, General Petrov, for refusing to obey orders from the Committee which had not been countersigned by the Fleet Commander. This was a serious breach of discipline, but on May 12 Kolchak had tendered his resignation to Prince Lvov on the grounds that he could not tolerate such conditions. But it was vital that the Admiral remain at his post, and Prince Lvov had asked me to go to Sebastopol and try to settle the dispute.

In a tiny cabin aboard the torpedo boat taking us to Sebastopol, I had a long private talk with Kolchak. I did my best to convince him that this incident was nothing compared to what had happened to the Commander of the Baltic Fleet, that he should not be unduly upset by it, and that his position was more secure than he imagined. Not finding any logical objections to my arguments, he finally exclaimed with tears in his eyes: "To them [11] the Central Committee means more than I do. I don't want anything more to do with them. I don't love them any more . . . !" There was nothing I could say in reply to this argument, which was dictated by the heart rather than the head.

The next day, after a great deal of talking and coaxing, peace was restored between Kolchak and the Committee. But their relations were never quite the same again, and exactly three weeks later there was another violent clash. This time, without a word to the government,

[11] I.e., the sailors.

Admiral Kolchak and his chief-of-staff caught a direct train to Petrograd the same evening, abandoning the Fleet forever.

After these difficult negotiations in Sebastopol I went straight on to Kiev, where relations with the Ukrainian Rada were getting strained. The Rada had begun a campaign for a separate Ukrainian Army, and even if the Rada had been much more autonomous than it actually was, this was quite out of the question in view of the coming offensive.

From Kiev I went on to see General Alekseyev in Mogilev. I wanted to give him a report on my trips to the front, and I also wanted to see whether my decision to appoint Brusilov in his place was justified. During our conversation Alekseyev first showed absolutely no interest at all in what I was saying and then began giving me a pessimistic analysis of the situation at the front.

After this I returned to Petrograd, where I had talks with Prince Lvov and Tereshchenko, our foreign minister. Then, at a meeting of the Cabinet, I proposed Brusilov's appointment as commander-in-chief. My proposal was adopted and General Alekseyev was given the post, specially created for him, of military adviser to the Provisional Government.

After two or three days in the capital, I toured the Northern Front, arriving in Riga on the morning of May 25. This major industrial port, with its mixed Russian, German, and Latvian population, had become dangerously close to the front line after the "great retreat" of 1915, as a result of which most of the industrial plants and academic establishments had been evacuated. The ancient fortress, which in peacetime had housed the chief city administration, was now headquarters for General Radko-Dmitriev, the commander of the Twelfth Army.[12]

I was met at the station by the General, his entire staff, a huge crowd of soldiers from the front, and thousands of local inhabitants. I had visited Riga fairly frequently during the first few years after the "pacification" of the Latvian peasants' agrarian movement in 1905,

[12] This dynamic soldier, who had led the Bulgarians to victory during the first Balkan war of 1912, quit the Bulgarian Army and came to Russia when King Ferdinand of Bulgaria went over to the Austro-Germans and turned against the Serbs and Greeks, his allies of the day before. As we know, this second Balkan war ended in total military and political disaster for Bulgaria.

and I knew the city well. I expressed a desire to walk along the boulevard from the hotel where I used to stay when I came to Riga on legal business, to the Schloss, where the military tribunals used to be held—the harshest tribunals of all those I had occasion to deal with during those difficult years. The General willingly agreed to accompany me, and we walked to the fortress at the head of a happy, excited crowd.

After a conference with the chief of staff at headquarters, we drove to the front lines. There were sporadic outbursts of firing from both sides, but the General paid no attention to them. On the way back from our inspection, he suggested we visit a regiment in which a Bolshevik agitator had recently appeared; the man was difficult to deal with, and had, in a sense, taken command of the regiment.

Selecting a hollow out of range of enemy fire, the General summoned all the soldiers who were off duty. It was very much a heart-to-heart talk. I was plied with all sorts of questions, some of them very outspoken. But there was one puny little lad who refrained from saying anything at all, a fact which seemed both to astonish and irritate his comrades. They kept pushing him forward and trying to make him speak. The General whispered in my ear that this was the Bolshevik agitator in question. At long last he began speaking in a nervous, high-pitched voice. "This is what I've got to say. You tell us we must fight the Germans so that the peasants can have land. But what's the use of peasants getting land if I'm killed and get no land?"

I could see he was not a Bolshevik agitator, but just a village lad who was voicing aloud what his comrades were thinking. That was his strength, and no logical argument would have won him over. Without really knowing what I was about to do, I slowly walked over to the lad, who began trembling from head to foot. I stopped a few feet away from him, half-turned to the General, and said, "Have this fellow sent back to his village at once. Let his fellow villagers know that we don't need cowards in the Russian Army." Then, most unexpectedly, the trembling soldier fell flat on his face in a dead faint.

Several days later I received a request from the regimental commander that the order be canceled, since the soldier in question had reformed and was now a paragon of discipline.

From the Twelfth Army positions I went on to Dvinsk to see General Iury Danilov, commander of the Fifth Army, at his Headquarters there.[13] Danilov was one of the first senior commanders to understand the change in mood at the front, and he rapidly established good working relations with the commissars and army committees. The committee in this army was already very well organized by the beginning of April, and it was the first to send a delegation to Petrograd to appeal to the workers in the rear to end the anarchy and resume normal support of the front.

I had no time to visit the soldiers in the trenches, but I addressed a gathering of representatives from all the unit committees in Dvinsk before going on to Moscow. In Moscow, as arranged, I took the salute at a march-past of the Moscow Garrison in Devichye Field, gave a talk to the cadets at the Alexander Military School, spoke at a number of crowded public meetings, and attended a congress of the Socialist Revolutionary Party.

The influence of Moscow on the country's political mood was very strong, and it was the government's duty to strengthen Moscow's support for our plans to resume offensive operations at the front. It was for that reason that Lvov had asked me to go there. I could not stay very long, however, since I was shortly due back in the Southwest, and had to return to Petrograd in time for the opening of the All-Russian Congress of Soviet and Front Line Organizations.

On June 1, after an absence of three weeks, I returned to Petrograd. The Congress opened two days later. It was attended by 822 voting delegates, of whom only 105 were Bolsheviks.

The feelings of a large number of the delegates were brought out by an incident that occurred soon after the meeting opened. Evidently hoping to rouse feeling against the government and its war policy, one of the Bolshevik delegates began reading out Prince Lvov's appeal to the population to oppose Bolshevik and anarchic propaganda in every way they could. Unexpectedly for the speaker, every sentence in the appeal was drowned by stormy applause. When he went on to read, without the least embarrassment, my Order No. 17 dealing with the treatment of deserters (which had just been published), the applause turned into a standing ovation. At that moment it was easy to spot the "neutral" elements in the hall and on the dais.

[13] For the first 18 months of the war he was quartermaster general on Grand Duke Nicholas' Staff and the only competent strategist there.

In view of this demonstration I thought a resolution in support of the government would be adopted at the outset by an overwhelming majority. But this did not happen, for two reasons: First, it became known that in fact more than 200 delegates were present who opposed the renewal of hostilities, since two other groups—the Menshevik Internationalists and a left-wing group from the Socialist Revolutionary Party—had aligned themselves with the Bolsheviks. Both these groups had great influence among the intellectuals at the Congress.

Second, the Congress was prevented from functioning normally by a Bolshevik attempt, devised by Lenin, to sabotage plans for the offensive by staging an armed demonstration by "indignant" soldiers and workers shouting, "All power to the Soviets!" and "Down with the ten capitalist ministers!" [14]

For a few days military matters took second place in our thoughts, and the leaders of the Congress devoted all their time and energy to countering the Leninist conspiracy. It was only when the immediate danger had been averted that a resolution was finally passed (June 12). However, apparently reluctant to antagonize the left-wing opposition in their own ranks, the Menshevik and Socialist Revolutionary bloc moved an ambiguous resolution which left out any direct endorsement of the coming offensive. Instead, it merely stated that Russia's armed forces must be ready for both defensive and offensive action, but that the latter should only be undertaken on strategic grounds.

Late on June 13, after the adoption of this totally useless resolution, I left for Supreme Headquarters at Mogilev. There we finally fixed the date of the offensive for June 18. It was to be preceded by a two-day bombardment with our heaviest artillery of the enemy positions at the sector where we planned the breakthrough.

On June 16, I went to Tarnopol, where the official order for the offensive was issued to the army and navy. It was drafted at Headquarters in consultation with Brusilov, and was signed by me.[15]

After a short stay in Tarnopol, I went with General Gutor, the new commander of the Southwestern Front, by train to the forward posi-

---

[14] See Chapter 18.

[15] On the third day of the offensive, June 20, an appeal was published from the Congress of Soviets calling upon the people of Russia to make every effort to ensure the success of the operation, since this would bring peace and strengthen the new democratic order.

tions of the Seventh Army. This army, together with the Eleventh, was due to begin an advance in the direction of Brzezany.

I spent the whole of that day—June 17—making the rounds of the regiments, which were preparing for their attack at dawn the next day.

On the morning of June 18, an air of tense excitement reigned all along the front. It was the kind of atmosphere you find in Russian villages just before the midnight service at Easter. We climbed up to an observation point at the top of a chain of hills running the length of our forward positions. There was a constant rumble of heavy artillery, and the shells whining overhead made a plaintive sound.

From the Seventh Army's observation point, the battlefield lay before us like a huge, deserted chessboard. The shelling continued. We all kept looking at our watches. The strain was unbearable.

Suddenly there was a deathly hush: It was zero hour. For a second we were gripped by a terrible fear that the soldiers might refuse to fight. Then we saw the first lines of infantry, with their rifles at the ready, charging toward the front lines of German trenches.

During the first two days of this offensive we were extremely successful. We took several thousand prisoners and captured scores of field guns. On the third day our advance came to a halt. The report submitted by General Erdeli, commander of the Eleventh Army, gave a good idea of what had happened: ". . . despite our gains on June 18 and 19, which ought to have raised the spirits of the men and encouraged them to press on, no such spirit was noticeable in the majority of regiments, while in some there was a predominant feeling that they had done their stint and there was no point in going on with the advance." The general might have added in reference to the defeatist attitude of the men that in some regiments the officers did not hide their satisfaction that the offensive had petered out.

But perhaps the main reason for the failure of the offensive was that General Brusilov, during his brilliant offensive of 1916, had been faced by Austrian regiments, many of which were composed of Slavs only too willing to surrender to the Russians. In July, 1917, however, the Russian army was opposed by first-class German troops with powerful artillery.

The first two days of the offensive also brought to light a number of difficulties of a technical and psychological nature, which we had to try to correct in the shortest possible time. On June 20 I telegraphed the following confidential message [16] to Tereshchenko:

Point out to respective ambassadors that heavy artillery delivered by their governments apparently comes from defective stock since 35 percent of it has not even survived two days of moderate firing. Urge extra shipment of aircraft engines and material to replace what is expended. Have Knox, who is causing trouble, recalled from front and expedite convocation of Allied conference. Quicker pace and greater clarity essential in Allied diplomacy. Operations at front should be exploited in every way in view of country's and army's position, of which you are well aware. Remember every move at front costs us tremendous effort. Only through coordinated and simultaneous action in diplomacy and in army can we consolidate our position and avoid collapse. Telegraph situation.

Kerensky

Colonel Knox, the British military attaché, who was at that time on a visit to the Southwestern Front, was loudly criticizing the Russian Army wherever he went and openly expressing his dislike of the new order. He was gradually becoming a center of opposition among the commissioned ranks.

I received a reply from Tereshchenko on June 22. It ran: "British and French told of defective artillery and they have cabled their governments today. British mission to look into matter being sent out tomorrow. Knox told to return to Petrograd early next week . . . Firmness only possible because of our activity at front."

A few days later we received a communication from the Allied governments agreeing to a conference to review the aims of the war.

Colonel Knox left for Petrograd and then went on to London. The Allies' willingness to hold a conference on war aims put an end to the propaganda spreading along the front and in left-wing circles that Brusilov and I were waging the war for "imperialistic and expansionist aims."

On the eve of our campaign on the left flank of the Southwestern Front, I was with the Eighth Army, commanded by General Kornilov. My reception at headquarters was more than cool, but in the lines the

[16] Collection of Secret Documents of Foreign Ministry, Book 3, No. 144, p. 113, December, 1917, Petrograd.

men greeted me with such enthusiasm and warmth that I returned in a very cheerful and confident frame of mind.

On June 23, the Eighth Army went into the attack. Breaking through the Austrian Front, the Russian forces penetrated deep into the enemy's positions, took the ancient town of Halicz on June 28, and pushed on toward Kalusz. The whole of Russia jubilantly followed the advance. The outstanding success of this operation was largely attributable to the fact that in this sector the enemy forces consisted mainly of Slavs.

Soon afterward, however, there was a radical change in the course of events; German reinforcements with heavy artillery were swiftly moved up to replace the Austrian soldiers. On July 5 German shock brigades commanded by General von Bothmer were ready for a counterattack.

Hostilities on General Denikin's Front were due to begin early in July, and I had to arrive there in time to witness them. I had not seen General Brusilov since June 15, and I went back to Supreme Headquarters to make a report and brief him on the situation on the Southwestern Front. Furthermore, I wanted to find out at first hand what was happening on the Allied fronts.

I believe it was on the second day of my stay at Headquarters that Brusilov told me that some members of the soldiers' committee at Headquarters had requested an interview with him, his chief of staff (Lukomsky), and myself. At the interview, the spokesman for the group told us that he and his comrades were deeply perturbed by the hostility felt by the Central Committee of the All-Russian Army and Navy Officers' Union toward the three of us. Brusilov and Lukomsky were greatly astonished at this and said they had observed no sign of it, and would certainly take immediate and resolute action if this were so. The committee members nervously tried to assure us that they were well informed and were certain of their facts. After a while they went away, somewhat reassured by what the General had told them. It did not occur to me that there was any more serious basis for their statement than a certain amount of that distrust of officers which still persisted after the Revolution. Unfortunately, we soon discovered that these men had spoken the truth.

On June 28 I went to Molodechno. Denikin was one of the most gifted officers on the General Staff. As a young man he had written a number of rather biting articles in an army newspaper on the old military bureaucracy, and in the war he had soon shown himself to be a first-class commanding officer, quickly ascending the ladder of promotion to the rank of Lieutenant General in command of a corps. He had served under Alekseyev as chief of staff. His attitude to me was rather ambivalent. On the one hand he needed my aid as an intermediary between himself and the soldiers for the forthcoming offensive, but on the other hand, he disliked both my personality and my policy as war minister and member of the Provisional Government.

I, however, felt no hostility toward him, or, for that matter, toward any of the other commanders. But now this severe critic of the old military establishment had unconsciously idealized the past. At the first mass meeting, which we both addressed, I was distressed by the brusque tone which he used to the men, while he was shocked by some of my expressions and by my "hysteria."

I was forced to interrupt my tour almost immediately after it began. Prince Lvov wanted me to go to Kiev without delay and settle the problem of the Ukrainian Army. Tereshchenko and Tsereteli were at that moment rounding off some very tricky talks with the Rada, which was demanding the impossible.

From there I planned to return to Petrograd to report to the Cabinet on the agreement with the Ukrainians.

On July 3 I again visited the Western Front, as promised, in time for the offensive. But by now the atmosphere had changed unrecognizably; events were moving at a breathtaking pace.

17

The Dual Counteroffensive

BY July 1, Tereshchenko, Tsereteli, and I were back in Petrograd. The text of an agreement with the Central Ukrainian Rada had already been communicated to Prince Lvov by direct wire, and he had informed the rest of the ministers of its contents. At a meeting of the government that evening the agreement was ratified by the majority, whereupon the ministers from the Cadet Party announced their immediate resignation from the Cabinet. The whole of political Petrograd was outraged, and we now had a new government crisis on our hands.

The next day, after a long unofficial meeting of ministers in Lvov's apartment, an agreement was made to postpone a decision on new appointments to the Cabinet. This meant that I could carry out my promise to General Denikin and leave at once for the Western Front. I left Petrograd in the early evening of July 2 and arrived there the next morning.

The first thing I did was to make an inspection tour, which helped to take my mind off the troubled situation in the capital. A visit to the front was almost like coming home. Complications and formalities were unknown there. People were concerned with the elementary and essential business of survival, of death and life, and they felt much closer to each other in the face of the common danger.

Early on July 4 we received the first official reports of the armed uprising of workers and soldiers in Petrograd organized by Lenin, which is known to history as the uprising of July 3.[1]

---

[1] The uprising really began on the evening of July 2. (I only learned what happened then on returning to Petrograd on July 6.) On that evening trucks with armed soldiers and sailors suddenly appeared in the streets of the capital. A red flag on one of the trucks bore the words, "The First Bullet is for Kerensky." The armed men intended

I was not unduly alarmed by this news—I felt that there were enough reliable troops in the capital—and I began my rounds of the divisions that would be the first to go into action on July 9. I was much more favorably impressed by what I saw than was Denikin.

At one point, as I was walking along the edge of a wood behind a line of trenches, I caught sight of a group of soldiers huddled together under a tree, absorbed in reading a pamphlet. As soon as they saw us, they threw it behind the nearest tree and ran off into the woods. "Go and fetch me that paper," I told one of my aides. I took a quick look at it and handed it to the officers in our group. It was the latest issue of *Tovarishch* (*Comrade*), a subversive weekly published for Russian soldiers by the German staff in Vilna. In an article entitled "Russia and the Offensive" dated Petrograd, July 3, the Petrograd Telegraph Agency, its alleged author, wrote with curious foresight: "According to information received from Russia, the offensive in Galicia has given rise to great indignation among the Russian people. In all major towns crowds of people are assembling in protest against the mass slaughters of Russia's sons. Anger at the British, who are considered by everyone to be responsible for prolonging the horrors of war, is steadily growing. Kerensky is quite openly being called a traitor to his country. In Moscow, where the Cossacks have been sent to control the outraged populace, there have been mass demonstrations. The present situation cannot last much longer. *Russkoye Slovo* reports that in the last few days the state of siege in Petrograd has grown worse. In the last few weeks a large number of extreme left-wing socialists have been arrested. The paper reports that the extreme left-wing leaders have had to leave Petrograd and go far inland."

Obviously, the editor of *Tovarishch* had advance knowledge of the Bolshevik rising on July 3. He was, in fact, trying to indoctrinate the front-line soldiers with the same ideas that Lenin's propagandists had been drumming into the heads of the Petrograd soldiers and Kronstadt sailors during the rising. The Germans and the Bolsheviks were at one in calling for the overthrow of the Provisional Government and in

---

to catch me in the building of the Ministry of the Interior, where I was attending a conference with other ministers. One of the janitors told the armed band that I had just left for the Tsarskoye Selo railway station. They immediately drove off there. As the railroad workers reported later, my pursuers were only in time to see the tail end of my departing train.

advocating disobedience to military orders. They both claimed that the Galician offensive had been started by Kerensky and the officers, who had been put up to it by foreign capitalists. The only thing missing in this issue of *Tovarishch* was the Bolshevik slogan "All power to the Soviets"—Lenin's German allies were little concerned with the kind of regime the Bolsheviks were proposing to establish. The Germans wanted to paralyze the Russian armies at the front and disrupt the administrative apparatus of the country, so that they could gain complete control of Russia and then smash the Allies in the West. According to our intelligence reports, German divisions were now being rushed to the Eastern Front. The picture was clear: the dual counteroffensive was underway. It had opened on July 3 with a stab in the back from Lenin, and now we could expect a frontal attack from Ludendorff.

On the evening of July 4 I received word of the arrival in Petrograd of a strong detachment of sailors from Kronstadt and an urgent request from Prince Lvov to return immediately. Promising General Denikin, who was greatly upset by my abrupt departure, that I would come back in time for the launching of the July 9 offensive, I left the next day for the capital. At a station just outside the city I was joined by Tereshchenko, who briefed me on the latest developments and warned me that Prince Lvov had finally made up his mind to resign from the Provisional Government. At Tsarskoye Selo Station in Petrograd we were met by Colonel Yakubovich, General Polovtsev, commander of the Petrograd Military District, and a guard of honor from the Preobrazhensky Regiment. The station platform and the square outside were thronged with people of all ages and from all walks of life who had come to give me an enthusiastic welcome.

The welcome was just as enthusiastic on the Winter Palace Square as I drove to the headquarters of the Petrograd Military District, where the government had been housed since the beginning of the uprising.

Without pausing to greet them, I went straight to Prince Lvov's room. But the excited crowds refused to disperse and shouted for me to appear. Several times I had to go out on the balcony and address a few words to the people gathered below, assuring them that the treacherous uprising had already been put down and that there was no further cause for worry.

The twenty-four hours I spent in Petrograd on this occasion, and particularly the sleepless night of July 7, will always remain vivid in my memory. I found Lvov in a state of terrible depression. He had only been waiting for my arrival to quit the government. That day I became minister-president. Furthermore, late that evening the first brief report was received from headquarters announcing that the Germans had broken through the front of the 11th Army at Kalush and that we were retreating in disorder.

On the afternoon of July 8 I returned to the front, as I had promised General Denikin. He and his staff already knew of the German offensive on the Galician Front, but the soldiers in the advance lines had not yet heard about it. In any event, as I toured the regiments due to go into action the next day, I saw that they were in fine spirits.

Late that evening, in a hollow behind the first line of trenches, I talked to the men and their officers. A large number of them were from the Second Caucasian Grenadiers division, a division that had been much affected by Bolshevik propaganda.

It was getting dark, the artillery preparation had started, and shells were flying overhead. All of this combined to create an atmosphere of great camaraderie. The officers, the soldiers, and I all seemed to be imbued with a common sense of purpose, a common desire to fulfill our duty.

The men of the Second Caucasian Grenadier Division told me with pride that they had rid themselves of all the traitors in their midst and now wanted to be the first to go over the top, which, indeed, they were. Never in the whole course of my experience at the front had I felt so strong an urge to spend the whole night in the trenches with the soldiers and to go into action with them the next day. Never before had I been so ashamed at not doing myself what I was asking others to do. I am sure that all men in positions of responsibility must experience such moments of profound self-contempt, but I, like the rest, had no choice; the battle was to begin the next day, and I had to return to Petrograd to take over from Lvov, who was no longer capable of bearing the burden of power after what he had gone through during the uprising of July 3.

The next day, when General Denikin's troops stormed the German positions, they acquitted themselves very well indeed. Here is what General Ludendorff himself wrote of this offensive:

"The most violent of the attacks against troops of the Commander in Chief on the East front took place at Krevo, south of Smorgon, on July 9 and the days following. Here the Russians broke through a division of the Landwehr occupying a very long front, though it defended itself with extraordinary courage.

"For a few days things looked extremely serious, until our reserves and artillery fire restored the situation. The Russians evacuated our trenches. They were no longer what they had been." [2]

If General Denikin had not given way to pessimism and left the front on July 10 to return to his headquarters in Minsk, the few days when "things looked serious" for the Germans might not have come to such an abrupt end.

There was nothing shameful in the failure of the Russian soldiers, among whom were many young recruits who had never been in action before, to hold their positions against the onslaught of German divisions using poison gas and heavy artillery. After all, the crack French and British armies, which had not been subjected to the shock of a revolution, had also been soundly defeated that spring, and had needed a whole summer to recover. But the French and British generals did not behave like the Russian generals, who used the calamities at the front for their own political ends, often deliberately misrepresenting the behavior of their troops. The following incident is a good example of this kind of treachery.

In the early days of July, a German task force from the army commanded by General von Bothmer was prepared for action against our Eleventh Army on the Southwestern Front between Zborov and the river Seret. To reinforce the local German and Austrian troops, six first-rate German divisions and an enormous concentration of heavy artillery were switched from the Western Front.

At dawn on July 6, General von Bothmer launched a violent attack and broke through the Russian Front. A brief communication to this effect received by the government late the same night was followed by an official communiqué from Southwestern Headquarters, which was published in all newspapers on July 8. The news was shattering, and the whole country went into a state of shock. The communiqué read:

[2] *My War Memoirs, 1914–1918* by General Ludendorff (London, Hutchinson & Co.), p. 439.

At 10 A.M., the 607th Mlynovsky Regiment abandoned the trenches on the Bankuf sector without orders and moved back, as a result of which the neighboring regiment also withdrew, and the enemy was able to consolidate his gains. Our failure is to a considerable extent attributable to the fact that under the influence of Bolshevik propaganda many units which had been given orders to support the sector under attack, first held meetings to discuss whether or not the orders should be obeyed. Several regiments actually refused to carry out their combat missions and abandoned their positions without enemy pressure. Officers were unable to induce them to obey orders.

In fact, however, nothing of that kind had happened.

In reality, as the inquiry ordered by the supreme commander, General Brusilov, established, the division was all but wiped out by enemy fire from several hundred field guns (the Russian division had only six) and suffered casualties numbering 95 officers, including 2 regimental commanders, and as many as 2,000 men out of its already depleted strength. It appeared that the officer who wrote the communiqué had acted either with deliberate malice or in complete panic.

This communiqué must have suggested to General von Bothmer that the state of discipline in the Russian army was even worse than it actually was.

I could cite other instances in which the enemy was aided by such incorrect reporting from the battlefield. For by some strange coincidence the official dispatches from the fronts always seemed to stress the gross breaches of discipline of enlisted men and the valiant behavior of the officers, and never mentioned the courage and self-sacrifice shown by the soldiers.

During the long years that have passed since the debacle of the Russian revolutionary army, I have often wondered how the Eleventh Army would have behaved under von Bothmer's artillery fire if the first reports of the enemy offensive had told the truth. One of the most serious consequences of these misleading reports was that they helped to undermine discipline even further. The soldiers did not have to wait for the results of the Mlynovsky inquiry to learn that the regiment had been maligned, and their distrust of their officers began to revive with a vengeance. The High Command, they thought, was trying to shift the blame for its blunders on them and was seeking a return to the old order. Whether or not the soldiers were justified in their suspicions is now of little importance. What is important is that official reports on the situation at the front gave far too much comfort to the enemy, and far too little to our own troops.

A parallel and even worse development was that one section of the Russian press, notably the *Russkoye Slovo* (a popular Moscow newspaper with a circulation of over a million) began printing dispatches from the army in the field which often contained information of great interest to the German High Command.

The reintroduction of military censorship for all press reports did not, unfortunately, solve this problem of leaks to the enemy. The war correspondent of the *Russkoye Slovo* was banned from the front, but it was impossible to ban all the staff officers responsible for the official dispatches.

When, years later, I read what Hindenburg, Ludendorff, and Hoffmann had to say in their memoirs about the Russian army in 1917 and compared their accounts with those of our own Russian generals, I found, to my surprise, that the German generals gave a more balanced and favorable picture of our military record at that time than did our own generals.

The explanation of this paradox is quite simple: The Germans never for a moment forgot that they were waging a war on two fronts and viewed Russian military operations in the framework of a single strategic plan covering both fronts, whereas the Russians, apparently forgetting that, in 1917, the Russian army was only carrying out part of an overall Allied plan, decided to exploit for their political campaign against the hated Provisional Government the psychological consequences of grave, tactical errors made by the Russian army.

Let me remind the reader once more, that after the severe defeat of the French and British armies on the Western Front in the spring of 1917, the Russian Government and the Supreme Command (generals Alekseyev and Denikin) had adopted the only possible strategy that could save the Allies and, ultimately, Russia—offensive operations by the Russian army to prevent the defeat of the Allied Forces on the Western Front.

This grand strategy of drawing the Germans' fire was scrupulously carried out by the Russians. Prior to the collapse of the Monarchy, by the end of the Brusilov offensive in October 1916, no fewer than

74 German divisions were concentrated on the Russian Front. By August 1917 there were 86 German divisions and all the heavy artillery that went with them.[3]

It was only after the abortive Kornilov conspiracy,[4] when Russia and the front were once again, as in March of 1917, thrown into utter confusion, that the Germans were able to switch a considerable number of divisions to the West. By January 1918, there were only 57 divisions left on the Russian Front, and in the autumn of 1918, only 26. But this transfer westward of men and matériel came too late to be of strategic advantage to the Germans, because even our "moderate advances"—Hindenburg's expression—had made it impossible for Ludendorff to deal a crushing blow in the West before the arrival of American troops.

At the end of July 1917, the Germans began to move troops from the Rumanian and Southwestern fronts to Riga, where preparations for an offensive were in full swing. At that stage, fighting had died down on these two fronts and also on the Western Front. Having disengaged themselves from the enemy, the Russians were entrenched in new positions. By hard work, the more level-headed commanders, commissars, and army committees managed to restore order of sorts.

On July 18 General Kornilov was appointed supreme commander, and on August 3, at a meeting of the Provisional Government, he gave a fairly optimistic report on the general military situation and declared he was planning to go over to the offensive fairly soon.[5]

Riga

In the meantime, something strange was going on at the front. The Supreme Commander announced earlier that he was planning an offensive and that he would as usual coordinate his activities with the commanding officers and the commissars and elected army committees. However, facts did not bear out this intention.

Early in August General Denikin made an appearance at the Southwestern Front. He had just been placed in command of it and his views approximated those of Kornilov very closely. From then on, their

---

[3] See E. A. L. Buat, *L'Armée allemande de 1914–1918* (Paris, 1920), pp. 42, 51.
[4] See Chapter 21.
[5] When the General mentioned the offensive, I interrupted his report and said quietly: "It is rather unusual to bring up specific strategic plans at a government meeting." At the time, I could not have foreseen the effects of my remark.

policy toward the commissars and army committees changed abruptly. Commanders who considered a collaboration with these organizations necessary were given the cold shoulder and were replaced by diehard advocates of the former regime.

On August 13, Kolchinsky, deputy chairman of the Front Executive Committee, sent a wire to the Minister of War and the All-Russian Central Committee of the Council of Workers' and Soldiers' Deputies, describing exactly what was going on and pointing out that this policy, which had not been coordinated with the central democratic organizations, would certainly provoke unrest among the troops.

His words are in effect a commentary on Order No. 177, dated August 10, from Savinkov, acting minister of war. *Inter alia,* the order states:

> In view of the latest developments at the front, a certain concern is observed in the army units for the fate of the army organizations. This concern can only be explained by the atmosphere of mutual distrust which has unfortunately arisen and still persists to all kinds of propaganda by suspect individuals striving to exploit the unstability of the army by causing dissension in the ranks. . . ."

Who were these "suspect individuals" left unnamed by Savinkov? If he referred to the Bolsheviks he would obviously have said so directly. But they were not, of course, Bolsheviks, or should one say, "inverted" Bolsheviks. The campaign against the elected army organizations and commissars was waged—and I know this for a fact—by these very officers' organizations and groups which shortly after became the nucleus of the military conspiracy.

While General Kornilov was having lunch with me on August 3, I asked him to take disciplinary action against certain persons on his staff, whose names I gave him. No action was, however, taken. The activities of certain persons known to General Kornilov not only continued as before, but were carried on even further, both at the front and in Petrograd and Moscow.

The sharp discrepancy between the new Supreme Commander's words and the actual behavior of Denikin and other like-minded frontline commanders was very puzzling at a time when his chief of staff, General Lukomsky, was doing everything he could to strengthen the Northern Front's fighting capacity. Denikin and all senior officers in sympathy with him, who were certainly loyal Russian patriots, were apparently doing their utmost to undermine the morale of the men and shake their now fairly strong sense of discipline and confidence in their officers.

How could they do this at a moment when both the Supreme Commander and the senior ranks knew perfectly well that the German High Command was preparing an offensive in the vicinity of Riga on the Northern Front?

Was there any truth in their systematic campaign of defamation against the commissars and committees, a campaign waged at public meetings and in the press, as well as through official releases from Headquarters?

And even if there had been a modicum of truth in it, should it really have been shouted from the rooftops within earshot of the enemy now preparing for the attack? Why was it that the Northern Front during those tragic weeks was knowingly jeopardized by the highest command of the Russian armed forces?

At the time I could find no answers to these agonizing questions, but now I know the whole monstrous truth.

On the day that Riga fell, Diamandi, the Rumanian envoy to the Provisional Government, happened to be at headquarters in Mogilev. Shocked by the news, he asked Kornilov how the town had been abandoned to the enemy and what was to be expected next. General Kornilov "told him that one should not attach importance to the loss of Riga. The general added that the troops have left Riga on his orders and have retreated because he preferred the loss of territory to the loss of the army. General Kornilov also reckoned on the impression which the taking of Riga would produce on public opinion, for the purpose of immediately restoring the discipline of the Russian army." [6]

I do not know whether or not these words calmed down the frightened Diamandi, but Kornilov had not told him the truth. He did not tell him that the Russian soldiers had fought stubbornly under a hail of heavy artillery shells and in clouds of Yellow Cross [7] gas. He could

[6] See *Izvestiya*, No. 241, December 1, 1917, which reprints the telegram sent on August 22 by Baron Faschiotti, counselor of the Italian Embassy in Petrograd, to Italian Foreign Minister Sonnino.

[7] Yellow cross gas was a new gas invented by Councillor Haber and first used on the Eastern Front in 1917. It was an extremely deadly gas—gas masks provided no pro-

not admit that he had shocked public opinion not by telling how the Russian soldiers really behaved at Riga, but by insinuating in false reports that, under the first few blows from the Germans, the Russians had taken to their heels like a pack of cowards.

These official reports were immediately reprinted in the metropolitan and provincial press, and they caused a wave of ill feeling against the troops. The effect was similar to that of the false announcement of the flight of the Mlynovsky Regiment and the Sixth Grenadier Division on the first day of the German offensive in the Southwest. Kornilov could not reveal, of course, that he needed these fictitious stories to ensure the success of his march on Petrograd, which began soon after the fall of Riga.

Since I was not present with the Russian forces at Riga, I cannot give a personal description of the fighting, in which whole regiments, allegedly "corrupted by the revolution," were wiped out. But there are several eyewitness accounts which bear witness to the brave stand put up by the Russian troops against hopeless odds. For example, Vladimir Voitinsky, the assistant commissar of the Northern Front, reported in *Izvestiya* of August 22, 1917:

On August 19, under cover of heavy artillery fire, the enemy succeeded in crossing over to the right bank of the Dvina. Our artillery could not prevent the crossing since most of the guns covering the area of the crossing had been put out of action by the enemy. Our positions were saturated with shells and poison gas bombs. The troops were compelled to move back three miles from the Dvina over a front extending about six miles. Reinforcements have been moved up to restore the position on the Dvina.

I testify before all Russia that the Army was in no way disgraced by this reversal. The troops honorably carried out the orders of their commanding officers, at times making bayonet charges and facing certain death. *There were no cases of desertion or treachery on the part of the troops.*

Representatives of the army committees are here with me in the area of the fighting.

Despite this and other testimony to the bravery of the troops, that section of the press which was hostile to the Provisional Government

---

tection against it, and the gas also ate into the clothes and the body. See General von Hoffmann, *The War of Lost Opportunities* (London, Kegan, Trench, Paul, Trubner & Co., 1924).

gave wide publicity after the fall of Riga to General Kornilov's prediction, made at the Moscow State Conference on August 14, about the inevitable loss of Riga because of the "disintegration" of the Russian army. It was easy for him to make that prediction, since he had begun withdrawing troops from the Northern Front in the early part of August, and the cavalry sent there by his chief of staff, Lukomsky, was redirected to Petrograd instead.

18

The Path of Treason

A FEW years ago, some of the secret archives of the German Foreign Ministry, captured during the last war, were made available to
the public. Among them were a good many documents dealing with
relations between the Germans and Lenin and other Bolsheviks during
World War I. The contents of these documents may be variously interpreted or even passed over in silence, but their existence can no longer
be denied. Yet today in the USSR, in Soviet newspapers, in academic
historical journals, in history books written by reputable scholars, not
to mention the latest edition of *The History of the C.P.S.U.* edited by
Khrushchev, the Communists continue to dismiss any reference to
Lenin's dealings with the Germans as "a vile slander against the founder
of the Soviet system by the government of the February Revolution."

Why do the Kremlin leaders persist in refusing to admit the validity
of the evidence of these relations? After all, Khrushchev exposed some
of Stalin's crimes, relaxed the harshness of the dictatorship, and made
the everyday life of the people a little easier. Under his successors,
Brezhnev and Kosygin, the situation so far has changed very little. The
truth is that in spite of all industrial progress, in spite of certain efforts
to improve the country's economy, especially in agriculture, everything is basically much the same as it was under Stalin. With few exceptions, the bulk of the population lives in the same poverty, with
the same lack of rights, with the same impossibility of devoting itself
to the spiritual and material construction of a free country. Why is
this? It is because the Communists cannot disclose the root of the evil.
They have unmasked Stalin, the most zealous champion of Lenin's
cause, but Lenin himself and his cause have been idealized and placed
beyond the bounds of criticism.

To tell the truth about Lenin would be tantamount to destroying the totalitarian dictatorship and allowing Russia to return to the path of democracy, from which she was forcibly turned aside by the Bolsheviks in October, 1917.

That is why the German secret documents are so anxiously concealed from the people of the USSR. But it is impossible to conceal them from the outside world, and I have written this chapter on the Bolshevik uprising of July 3, 1917 in the light of these documents, as it might be written by a historian in Russia if Lenin's heirs had not so much to fear from the truth.

By the end of the century, the working-class movement in Europe had grown into an immensely powerful political force. The socialist parties closely associated with it had begun to be represented in the parliaments of the West. One of the main concerns of these increasingly powerful socialist parties and trade unions was the threat to peace implied in the arms race between the leading countries. They believed that war was an integral part of the capitalist system and that labor should oppose any threat of war with every means at its disposal, resorting, if necessary, to a general strike. There was, however, a small section of the socialist movement—to which Lenin and his followers belonged—that welcomed the prospect of war as a harbinger of the proletarian revolution.

As soon as the First Balkan War broke out, Lenin wrote Gorky a letter in which he said that he hoped the emperors Franz Joseph of Austria and Nicholas II of Russia would "take a potshot at one another!"

This hope was realized with the outbreak of World War I. Lenin, who was living near Crakow at the time, was immediately arrested by the Austrian military police. Upon his release a short time later, he left at once for Switzerland, accompanied by Zinoviev and his wife Krupskaya. In Poland they had lived in dire poverty and had been forced to make frequent appeals to their party associates in Petrograd to send them money, even if only a hundred rubles, to continue their work. In Switzerland, their fortunes improved slightly, and by the end of 1914 Lenin's militant publication, *Social Democrat,* the organ of the proletarian revolution, began to appear.

With morbid interest Lenin followed the development of the war in the West. He watched the mobilization of almost the entire male population in the belligerent countries and the conversion of all factories and plants to the production of war materials, and he noted the tremendous military expenditure involved.

In Germany, the introduction of a planned economy, which subordinated all private interests to the requirements and control of the military authorities, created—or so it seemed to Lenin—all the conditions which Marx had said were necessary to spark a world proletarian revolution. The wealth of the country was concentrated in the hands of a small group of military men, leading bankers, and factory owners; the middle classes were impoverished, and their standard of living was approaching that of the working class. The whole continent was gorging on its own blood, and its old way of life was completely disintegrating. After the failure of the social revolution in 1848, Marx, trying to comfort the German workers, had written:

You must endure 15, 20, or 50 years of civil and international wars, not only in order to change the existing relations, but also in order that you yourselves may change and become capable of taking over the political power.

At long last, though not through class conflict, but through an imperialist war launched by the great powers, Marx's prediction had come true. But it was a prediction that the socialists had begun to forget during the long years of comparative prosperity and steady growth in political power of the working class.

It was now that Lenin issued his directive to all "true" leaders of the proletariat, calling upon them to turn the international imperialist war into a "civil war between classes." This historical mission was to be carried out by the industrial proletariat.

In Lenin's plans, Russia, as an industrially underdeveloped country with a large peasant population, was of much lesser importance than the West European countries which had strong urban proletariats. At the same time, he believed that the defeat of tsarist Russia would speed the advent of world revolution. Only Germany could defeat Russia; hence, it was the plain duty of "true" revolutionaries to help her to do so. The concomitant of this was that only "social-chauvinists" and "hirelings of the Bourgeoisie" would refuse to promote the defeat of their own country.

Lenin himself had absolutely no moral or spiritual objection to promoting the defeat of his own country. G. A. Solomon, an old friend of Lenin's, has written as follows:

My next interview was with Lenin . . . My conversation with Lenin made the most depressing impression on me. It was sheer maximalist delirium. —"Tell me, Vladimir Ilyich, as an old friend," I asked, "what is going on here? Are you really staking everything on Socialism, on the island of Utopia, only in colossal proportions? I don't understand anything! . . ." —"There's no island of Utopia here," he replied in a harsh authoritarian tone. "It's a question of creating a Socialist state . . . As from now Russia will be the first state to have an established Socialist order . . . Ah! you're shrugging your shoulders. You may well be surprised even more! It's not a matter of Russia, my good sirs, I spit on her. That is merely a stage through which we are passing on the way to World Revolution. . . ."

Puzzling over Lenin's attitude later, Solomon comments, "I remember that Lenin, long before his death, had suffered from *progressive paralysis*. And it occurs to me now that what he said then might have been a sporadic symptom of his disease. . . ." [1]

Lenin firmly believed in the Marxist creed set forth in the Communist Manifesto. To him anything that was useful and beneficial to the working class was ethical, and everything that was harmful to it was unethical. Such a doctrine of moral relativism, if followed through to its logical conclusion, inevitably leads to the sort of amoralism so succinctly formulated by Ivan in Dostoyevsky's *Brothers Karamazov:* "If there is no God, everything is permissible."

Indeed, it was this brief maxim of spiritual and moral nihilism that Lenin and his fellow thinkers used as a guiding principle in all their revolutionary activities.

One day in September, 1915, an Estonian by the name of Keskula,[2] a former party associate of Lenin's, had a meeting with the German minister in Berne, Herr Romberg. He told Romberg what the international policy of the Russian government would be, if the Bolsheviks

[1] G. A. Solomon, *Among the Red Leaders,* Vol. I (Paris, 1930).
[2] Keskula was also a member of an Estonian nationalist organization and was working with Steinwachs, one of the counterintelligence chiefs attached to the German General Staff who in 1916 was sent to Stockholm to work for the German envoy, Lucius.

came to power. On September 30, Romberg sent a dispatch to the Foreign Ministry in Berlin describing the conversation, and Keskula himself went to Berlin at the same time.

A few years ago, when I first read Romberg's dispatch,[3] I realized how mistaken I had been in thinking that Lenin's dealings with Berlin had begun only after the collapse of the Monarchy—which, incidentally, had come as just as much of a surprise to Lenin as to the Germans.

On January 15, 1915, Wagenheim, the German envoy in Constantinople, reported to Berlin that he had been approached by a Russian subject, Dr. Alexander Helfand, with draft plans for a revolution in Russia. Helfand (alias Parvus) was immediately summoned to Berlin. He arrived on March 6, and was at once received by Ritzler, confidential adviser to Chancellor Bethmann-Hollweg. After a short preliminary discussion, he handed Bethmann-Hollweg an 18-page memorandum entitled "Preparations for Mass Political Strikes in Russia." Parvus suggested to the Germans first, that they give him a large sum of money for the development of a separatist movement in Finland and Ukraine; and second, that they finance the Bolsheviks—the defeatist faction of the Russian Social Democratic Party—the leaders of which were then in Switzerland. Parvus' plan was accepted without hesitation. On orders from Kaiser Wilhelm himself, he was given German citizenship and the sum of 2 million deutsche marks.

In May of the same year Parvus went to see Lenin in Zurich. They had a long discussion, of which Parvus gives a highly condensed account in his pamphlet *The Truth Hurts,* published in Stockholm in 1918:

I explained to him my views on the social and revolutionary consequences of the war and at the same time warned him that over this period a revolution would be possible only in Russia and that it would only occur as a result of German victory at that . . . After the fall of the Monarchy, the German social democrats did everything they could to help the Russian émigrés to get back to Russia. But Scheidemann himself, head of the imperialist majority of the German Social Democratic Party and a member of the German Government, explained to the Bolsheviks with all due em-

[3] For the text of Romberg's dispatch, a key document in the whole question of German-Bolshevik relations, see Note at the end of this chapter.

phasis that a revolution in Germany, as long as the war went on, was *impossible* [Parvus' italics] and that, moreover, it should not be required of us to jeopardize the western front. This we will not do, for a victory by the Entente would not only be the ruin of Germany, but of the Russian Revolution as well. . . .

It is clear that although Lenin declined to give Parvus a straight answer to his proposals, it was agreed between them that their secret go-between should be Fürstenberg (alias Ganetsky). Lenin sent him to Copenhagen, where he worked with Parvus.

On August 15 of the same year, Count Brockdorff-Rantzau, the German envoy in Denmark, sent Berlin a sensational dispatch telling them that in collaboration with Dr. Helfand (Parvus)—whom he described as a most brilliant man—he had "worked out a *master plan* for the organization of a revolution in Russia," and adding at the end of it:

Victory and, in reward, world supremacy are ours, if Russia can be revolutionized in time and the coalition thereby broken up.[4]

The plan was approved by Kaiser Wilhelm II in Berlin.

It must be said that the description of Parvus by the German Count was no exaggeration. Not only was he the best organizer of espionage and subversive activity in Russia, but he also had much more political foresight than the creators of "The Great October Revolution."

The secret files of the German Foreign Ministry archives make it quite clear that Kaiser Wilhelm and his government started collaborating in earnest with the Bolsheviks only when all attempts had failed to lure Nicholas II into concluding a separate peace with Germany, so as to save the system of monarchy in Europe. This separate peace was to have been negotiated through a variety of channels (including relatives of Empress Alexandra) on terms not detrimental to the prestige of the Russian monarch. But all German peace offers were firmly and curtly rejected by Nicholas.

The Germans had experienced a brief revival of hope in the possibility of a separate peace with Russia in the fall of 1916 when

[4] As quoted by David Floyd in the *Daily Telegraph* and *Morning Post* (London), April 13, 1956.

Stürmer became minister of foreign affairs and Protopopov was made minister of the interior.[5] It was at just about this time that Lenin and Krupskaya again began complaining of lack of funds, but their financial embarrassment did not last long.

On December 3, 1917, Baron von Kühlmann, minister of foreign affairs, sent the following telegram to Kaiser Wilhelm II:

Berlin, December 3, 1917
Tel. N1771

The disruption of the Entente and the subsequent creation of political combinations agreeable to us constitute the most important war aim of our diplomacy. Russia appeared (to me) to be the weakest link in the enemy chain.

The task therefore was gradually to loosen it and, when possible, remove it. This was the purpose of the subversive activity we caused to be carried out in Russia behind the front—in the first place (vigorous) promotion of separatist tendencies and support of the Bolsheviks. It was not until the Bolsheviks had received from us a steady flow of funds through various channels and under varying labels that they were in a position to be able to build up their main organ, *Pravda,* to conduct energetic propaganda and appreciably to extend the originally narrow basis of their party. The Bolsheviks have now come into power. . . .

. . . Once cast out and cast off by her former Allies, and abandoned financially, Russia will be forced to seek our support. We shall be able to provide help for Russia in various ways; . . . This could take the form of an advance on the security of grain, raw materials, etc., to be provided by Russia and shipped under the control of the above-mentioned Commission. Aid on such a basis—the scope to be increased as and when necessary—would in my opinion bring about a growing rapprochement between the two countries. . . .[6]

The next day, December 4, 1917, Kühlmann received a telegram from Grunau, his representative at General Headquarters, informing him that "His Majesty the Kaiser has expressed his agreement with Your Excellency's outline of a possible rapprochement with Russia." [7]

[5] See Chapter 12.
[6] *International Affairs* (London), April, 1956, p. 189.
[7] *Ibid.*

The total sum of German money received by the Bolsheviks before and after their seizure of power has been established by Professor Fritz Fischer as being 80 million gold marks.[8]

The fall of the Monarchy on March 12 came as a total surprise to the Russian populace, to the German Government, and also to the inventors of the "master plan." A few weeks before, at a meeting of Swiss workers, Lenin had told his audience that there would be a revolution in Russia, but that his own generation was not likely to see it. When a comrade came running in early on the morning of February 28, to tell Lenin that the revolution in Petrograd had begun, he refused to believe it. For a while he was completely confused, but he soon recovered, and on March 3 he sent a letter to Alexandra Kollontai, his close collaborator in Norway. In it he wrote:

I have just received the second government communiqué regarding the revolution in Piter [9] on March 1. A week of bloody battles by the workers; Milyukov and Guchkov plus Kerensky in power. The "old" European model. Well, so what! ! This "first stage" of the first (of those brought about by the war) revolution will be neither the last nor only Russian. Naturally, we are still against defending the fatherland, against the imperialist war led by Shingarev and Kerensky & Co. All our slogans are the same. . . .[10]

In the wake of the letter to Kollontai he telegraphed instructions to his collaborators in Stockholm who were just leaving for Russia:

Our tactics are: absolute distrust; no support for new government. Be wary of Kerensky above all. Arming proletariat is a sure path. Immediate election of Petrograd Duma. No reconciliation with other parties.[11]

[8] Fritz Fischer, *Griff nach der Weltmacht—Die Kriegszielpolitik des Kaiserlichen Deutschland, 1914–1918* (Dusseldorf, 1961), p. 176, n. 127. The famous, often quoted "Kaiser's millions for Lenin" should be looked upon in the right perspective. In accordance with the accounting of January 30, 1918, Germany up to this date had assigned and spent a total of 382 million marks from the Special Fund for Propaganda and Special Expeditions (*Sonderexpeditionen*). The 40,580,997 marks represented around 10 percent of the total expenditure. On January 31, 1918 about 14.5 million marks were "not yet" spent, but up to July 1, 1918, the monthly expenditure for German propaganda in Russia amounted to about 3 million marks. Shortly before his murder, Ambassador Count Mirbach asked for a further 40 million marks in order to match a similar expenditure by the Entente. Of these 40 million up to the end of the war only 6 million, or at the outside, 9 million marks, in two or three monthly installments were sent and used.

[9] A popular name for St. Petersburg, or Petrograd.

[10] *Vladimir Ilyich zagranitsei, 1914–1917 godahl*, p. 142.

[11] *Ibid.*, p. 93.

From the very first day of the revolution he began his campaign against me: "the agent of the revolution," "the man of fine phrases," but also "the most dangerous man for the revolution at the initial stage." [12]

In a letter to Fürstenberg (Ganetsky), dated March 12, 1917, he elaborated on the same theme:

Dear Comrade!

From the depths of my heart I thank you for your trouble and assistance. I cannot, of course, make use of the services of people with access to the publisher of *Die Glocke*.[13] I cabled you today that my only hope of getting out of here is through an exchange of Swiss émigrés for interned Germans. The English would never let me or the internationalists as a whole, or Martov and his friends, or Natanson and his friends, pass through. Chernov was sent back to France by the English even though he had all the papers for transit. It is clear that the Russian proletarian revolution has no sworn enemy worse than the British imperialists. It is clear that the salesmen of Anglo-French imperialism and the Russian imperialists, Milyukov & Co. are capable of anything—deceit, treachery—anything so as to stop the internationalists from returning to Russia. The slightest trust in this sense in Milyukov or Kerensky (an empty windbag and an agent of the Russian imperialist bourgeoisie, if we are to see his role objectively) would be absolutely ruinous for the working class movement and for our party; it would border on betrayal of the international. We must send a reliable man to Russia to put pressure on the government via the Soviet. This is all the more necessary for reasons of principle. The latest news in the foreign newspapers makes it ever clearer that with Kerensky's help and through the unforgivable vacillation of Chkheidze the government is duping the workers, and duping them with some success, by pretending that the imperialist war is a "defensive" one. There is no doubt that in Piter the Soviet has many members and evidently contains a predominance of (1) supporters of Kerensky, the most dangerous agent of the imperialist bourgeoisie, and (2) supporters of Chkheidze. And I would not personally hesitate for one second to declare, and to declare in print, that I would even prefer a gradual split with someone in our party to concessions to Kerensky & Co.'s social-patriotism, or the social-pacifism and Kautskiism of Chkheidze & Co. Best of all would be if a reliable young fellow like Kuba [14] were sent (he would do a great

[12] *Ibid.*
[13] A journal published by Parvus, who was a prominent member of the Central Committee of the German Social Democratic Party.
[14] This was Ganetsky's cover name. Lenin uses it here for reasons of security.

service to the world working-class movement) to help our friends in Piter. Conditions in Piter are arch-difficult. They are trying to sling mud at our party (the Chernomazov [15] "affair"—I'm sending you the documents, etc. Don't spare any money on relations between Piter and Stockholm! Do please cable me, dear comrade, and acknowledge receipt of this letter.[16]

On the evening of April 3, Lenin arrived in Petrograd from Germany in an "extraterritorial coach" put at his disposal by the Germans.

Two weeks after his arrival, while armed demonstrations of soldiers and sailors, organized by his headquarters, flared up in the city, certain unidentified Russian negotiators approached the Germans under flag of truce at the front. I regard this incident, of which I knew nothing at the time, as yet further evidence that, prior to his return to Russia, Lenin had undertaken to secure a separate peace with Germany as soon as possible.

The reference to this odd incident, which I discovered in the German Secret Archives only a few years ago, comes in an exchange of telegrams between Hindenburg's headquarters and the Imperial Government.[17]

On April 25 the Foreign Ministry's representative attached to Hindenburg's headquarters wired Bethmann-Hollweg in Berlin that talks with "representatives of the Russian front" had progressed to the extent that the German representatives should be recalled so that they could offer the Russian truce-seekers more specific terms at the next parley. The following is the full text of the telegram:

G.H.Q. April 25, 1917

To the Imperial Counselor of Legation at Ministry of Foreign Affairs General Ludendorff telegraphs as follows:

The negotiations with representatives of the Russian Front have been outstripped by events. *The negotiations have now reached a more acute stage*

---

[15] A worker and an editor of *Pravda* who was also a secret police agent.

[16] *Vladimir Ilyich zagranitsei, 1914–1917 godahl.*

[17] Unfortunately the archives of the War Ministry and Intelligence Department of the German General Staff were entirely destroyed by fire, so that the functions of this institution can only be conjectured from correspondence with the government. This was a substantial loss for the history of Russia in 1917. I am sure that in the military archives I would have found references to certain people that would have confirmed my observations. But without these documents I feel I have no right to mention them by name.

in which the persons conducting the negotiations on our side must be re-
called in order if need be to give the Russians more positive data upon our
conditions of peace [italics mine].

The foundation, therefore, can only be established on the basis of agreements between the German and Austro-Hungarian high commands, together
with the respective foreign ministries. The Russian front is in a position of
watchful quiet. From the rear it is pressed by the English agitators permitted
by the Provisional Government, and from the front by our own agitation.
Both at present counterbalance each other. We could easily tip the scales,
if in the course of the conversations we could make concrete proposals to
the Russians concerning peace.

I concur in this view and beg Your Excellency to harmonize data on our
conditions of peace with Austria on the basis of the conversations at Kreuz-
nach of 23/4.

I shall in the meantime advise Obost to inform the Russian representatives
that they should (1) remove the English and French agitators from the war
area and (2) send us representatives of the separate armies with whom our
A.O.K. can negotiate in earnest.

(signed) Grunau [18]

No names of any Russian negotiators are mentioned in Grunau's report, nor could there have been any such parleys with representatives
of the Russian High Command. The following, rather more surprising,
communication from headquarters to the German Foreign Ministry,
dated May 7, 1917 (N. S.), mentions the appearance on May 4
(N. S.) of Russian negotiators under a flag of truce at the German
Eighth Army's advanced lines, commanded by General von Eichhorn.

Conversation with Russian representatives south of the Desna:

The two representatives stated that two couriers had been sent to Petrograd
on May 4 to induce Steklov, Chkheidze's chief collaborator, to come here
on behalf of Chkheidze, who is himself unable to do so; that Steklov is
inclined to work out a compromise, so that they considered it would be of
value if we, for our part, could also send party comrades [i.e., members of
the majority of the German Social Democratic Party]. In answer to a

[18] German Foreign Office Files in National Archives of U.S.A. in Washington. File
1499, Fr. D627679–680.

question regarding reaction to the chief points in our propaganda, the deputies declared that they would never recognize annexations on the part of the Germans. If the Germans agreed to this, the Russians had no need to consider the Entente, and would conclude a separate peace. Russia requested financial indemnity for the majority of her prisoners-of-war. . . .

. . . General Ludendorff begs Your Excellency to appoint a reliable Social Democrat and, for balance, a member of a national party (Free Conservative) to participate in the negotiations. On the army's side, the former military attaché in Paris, Colonel von Winterfeld (now chief quartermaster in Mitau) might be considered for the negotiations. Your Excellency may wish to attach to him a younger diplomat more conversant with the proceedings.

General Ludendorff considers a neutral locality out of the question. Mitau, Riga, or some place between the lines, where telegraph wires could be laid for the negotiations, would be suitable.

I told General Ludendorff of Your Excellency's views on the union of Lithuania and Courland under a duke. He will get in touch with the Commander-in-Chief, East, on the subject. The word "annexation" should be replaced by "frontier adjustment."

The General asks to be informed of Your Excellency's position.

(signed)   Lessner [19]

If the negotiators reported on May 4 that they were now getting in touch with Steklov in Petrograd, then clearly this was not their first appearance. Indeed, in his memoirs, Erzberger, the German minister of propaganda and an influential member of the Catholic Center in the Reichstag, wrote that two days earlier, on May 2, he was told by General Ludendorff that some Russian delegates had tried to initiate parleys on "their own peace terms."

If we convert these dates from new style into old, we see that the mysterious Russian "negotiators" at the front were trying to start peace talks *at exactly the time* (April 19 and 21) *when the armed demonstrations organized by the Bolsheviks occurred in the capital.*[20]

[19] German Foreign Office Files, Document No. D–627769.

[20] That the demonstrations were indeed organized by the Bolsheviks is proved by the following account given by Midshipman Ilyan Raskolnikov, leader of the Bolsheviks in Kronstadt:

Comrades returning from Petrograd on April 20, in the evening, told a meeting of the party committee that there was unrest in Piter. . . . The next day Podvoisky

But the demonstrations ended in confusion, and the envoys "from Steklov" were never seen near the front again.[21]

It is quite clear, however, from all the documents relating to this affair, that Hindenburg, Ludendorff, Bethmann-Hollweg, Zimmerman, and even the Kaiser himself, were preparing for serious talks on a separate peace with persons in Petrograd whom they considered powerful enough to be able to impose their will on the country. General Hoffmann, who was virtually in command of the Eastern Front, took a skeptical view of his orders to go with Erzberger to Stockholm for instructions, so much so that in his book, *The War of Lost Opportunities,* he came to the absurd conclusion that "Kerensky is sending us his own men supposedly for peace talks, so as to distract the attention of the German military authorities while they prepare the Russian armies for an offensive."

But the men behind the "master plan" (a group to which General Hoffmann did not belong) knew in advance who would be coming to sign the truce or peace treaty—Lenin.

Visiting Petrograd at that time was Hjalmar Branting, the Swedish Social Democrat leader and one of the few prominent men in Stockholm who opposed the attempts of the Swedish army and government hierarchy to enter the war on Germany's side. He and I became quite friendly, and one day in a discussion about the uninhibited behavior of our Bolsheviks in the Swedish capital, he suddenly said to me with a laugh: "But do you know that while Lenin was in Stockholm (April

---

(an important member of the Central Committee of the Bolshevik Party) rang through from Petrograd. Covering himself by saying that he could not speak freely over the telephone, comrade Podvoisky, on behalf of the Bolshevik military organization, insisted on the dispatch of a reliable detachment of Kronstadt sailors to Petrograd. . . . In a nervous, broken voice, Podvoisky said that the situation in the capital was serious. We immediately sent telegrams to all the ships and coastal units, inviting each of them to contribute a few armed comrades to go to Piter. . . . (*Krasnaia Letopis' No. 7,* 1923, p. 91.)

[21] In May the German government made two attempts to push Russia into separate peace talks under the pretext of a truce, and to thwart any revival of the fighting capacity of our armies. One of them was on the Northern Front, where General A. M. Dragomirov was in command; the other in Petrograd through the offices of Robert Grimm, the eminent leader of the Swiss Social Democrats and a member of the Swiss National Assembly. The attempt at the front received no answer, while Grimm was asked to leave Russia immediately after his telegraphic correspondence with Berlin (via the Swiss Legation) had been deciphered. See the *Russian Provisional Government,* vol. II, pp. 1158 and 1180–81. Also the following documents in the Public Records Office, London: GFM–2, D–965716, 965717, 965718, 965719.

2) on his way to Petrograd, he told a meeting of the extreme left wing of our party that within about two or three weeks he would be back in Stockholm for peace talks?"

Seeing the puzzled look on my face, he added: "I assure you I'm not joking. I was told about it by a member of the Social Democratic Party who was present, a man whom I know well and trust implicitly."

The veracity of Branting's story is confirmed by a telegram to Sir George Buchanan from Lord Balfour in the Hague:

I have heard over the last few days from four different sources, all originating in Copenhagen, of Germany's certainty that peace will be declared between Russia and Germany within two weeks. One of the reports says that Kuhlmann, rumored to be in that city, is authorized to hold the talks.

Balfour's telegram was sent on May 4 (N. S.), and on April 15 (N. S.) Lenin was at the meeting of Swedish Social Democrats mentioned by Branting.

I thought about what Branting had told me as I read through the German documents on the parleys, and having checked over all the cases of armed demonstrations in 1917, I finally came to the conclusion that Lenin's chief aim at the time was to overthrow the Provisional Government as an essential step toward the signing of a separate peace. It was equally essential to the German High Command and the fanatical believers in a world proletarian revolution.

In order to attain this end it was quite unnecessary, in the view of the Bolsheviks, to organize any direct armed revolt against the government. All that was needed, they thought, was a variety of "peaceful" pressures (mass demonstrations, etc.) to bring about the downfall of the government and give effect to the slogan, "All Power to the Soviets." Once the government was in the hands of the motley band of leaders of the various parties represented in the Petrograd Soviet "revolutionary democracy," it could easily be turned into a dictatorship of the Bolshevik Party.

But Lenin and the people backing him abroad overlooked one important factor in their calculations: Petrograd was not the whole country, the "revolutionary democracy" was by no means representative of Russian democracy in general, and its leaders, despite their pretensions, had no real power in the country.

Every time "peaceful" armed demonstrations occurred in the capital—at the end of April, and on June 9 and 18—they broke up in confusion. This was for the simple reason that the leaders of the "revolutionary democracy" were fully aware that, if they gained power, they would themselves speedily be ousted by Lenin, who openly despised them and scarcely concealed his intentions in this respect. Lenin was quick to learn the lesson that there could be no intermediate stage between the overthrow of a government based on the will of a free people and the seizure of power by an armed minority.

In mid-April the French minister of military supplies, Albert Thomas, arrived in Petrograd. He brought with him and passed on to Prince Lvov some extremely important information on the links between the Bolshevik group headed by Lenin and a number of German agents. The Frenchman stipulated, however, that only the ministers investigating this matter were to be told that he was the source of the information. At a secret conference a few days later, with the consent of Thomas, Prince Lvov entrusted Nekrasov, Tereshchenko, and myself with the investigation of this serious matter.

On May 17 (or it may have been the next day) I received from General Denikin's chief of staff a letter enclosing a copy of notes taken at the interrogation by the intelligence officers on his staff of Yermolenko, an ensign of the 16th Siberian Rifle Regiment. While a prisoner of the Germans, this young officer had consented to act as a German spy and had received the necessary instructions, money, and addresses from two German staff officers, Schiditski and Luebers (whose actual existence was established). According to Yermolenko, he had been given a similar assignment by a certain Skoropis-Ioltukhovsky, chairman of the Russian section of the Union for the Liberation of the Ukraine, which had been operating in Austria since 1914 on funds issued by Wilhelm II, and also by—Lenin.

In view of Thomas' stipulation, no one else in Russia, not even the other ministers or the supreme commander, was told anything about this.

Early in July, when our investigations, having produced fruitful results, were nearing completion, some relevant papers were given to Pereverzev, minister of justice, so that he could take steps to make the necessary arrests. The minister was instructed that the papers were not to be shown to anyone without special permission from Lvov, and that he was to be personally responsible for them.

On the evening of July 4, when the Tauride Palace was surrounded by a solid mass of heavily armed soldiers and sailors, taking part in a Bolshevik-organized mutiny, the situation suddenly looked so grave to Pereverzev and his aides that they panicked, and without first asking for permission from Lvov, issued a statement to the press on the link between the organizer of the demonstration and the Germans.

The statement began with a reference to the interrogation of Yermolenko, and then went on:

> ... *according to information just received* [italics mine] these confidential agents in Stockholm are the Bolshevik, Yakov Fürstenberg, known under the name of Ganetsky, and Parvus (Dr. Helfand), and in Petrograd the Bolshevik Kozlovsky, Mrs. Sumenson, a relative of Ganetsky, who is engaged in profiteering along with Ganetsky, and several others. Kozlovsky is the chief recipient of German money transferred from Berlin through the "Diskonto Gesellschaft" to the Nia Bank in Stockholm, and from there to the Siberian Bank in Petrograd, where at the present time there is more than 2,000,000 rubles in a current account.

> Military censorship has discovered a continuous exchange of telegrams on political and financial matters between German and Bolshevik agents.

It should be noted that these details were taken from the report of the top-secret investigation made by Tereshchenko, Nekrasov, and myself, and do not derive from the interrogation of Yermolenko at all.

On the same evening a brief conversation took place over the telephone between N. S. Karinsky, the chief prosecutor of the Petrograd Court of Appeals, and Bonch-Bruyevich, a close friend and collaborator of Lenin's.

> "I'm calling you," began Karinsky, "to warn you that all kinds of documents are being amassed here against Lenin so as to compromise him politically. I know that you're close to him. Draw any conclusions you wish from this, but understand that it's serious and that words will soon be translated into action."

> "What's wrong?" I [Bonch-Bruyevich] asked him.

> "He's charged with spying for the Germans."

> "But you must realize that this is the vilest possible slander."

"What I realize makes no difference in this particular case, but on the basis of these documents he and all his friends will be prosecuted. The prosecution will be begun at once. I say this in all seriousness and ask you to please take all the necessary steps," he added quickly in rather a hollow voice. "I'm telling you all this because of our long-standing friendship. I cannot tell you any more. Goodbye. All the best. Act now . . ." [22]

Bonch-Bruyevich acted immediately, and on the night of July 4 Lenin and his inseparable henchman Apfelbaum (Zinoviev) vanished without a trace. Lenin had wasted no time. He knew full well what was afoot.

The hitherto unknown Ensign Yermolenko suddenly became the talk of the town. Ignoring the other incriminating evidence quoted in Pereverzev's statement, the leaders of the Soviet asked indignantly how charges could be made against such men as Lenin on the basis of evidence produced by some dubious ensign who was sent to spy on Russia. And Lenin himself, needless to say, also tried to confuse the issue by concentrating attention on Yermolenko.

On July 6, *Pravda* issued a special bulletin (the *Pravda* offices had been wrecked by some soldiers and they could not, therefore, bring out a regular issue of the paper) containing an article by Lenin, which he had written before escaping to Finland, while hiding out in the apartments of various Bolshevik workers—mainly with a worker named Alliluyev whose daughter later became the wife of Stalin. In this article Lenin angrily dismissed the evidence as a "shameless slander" and, following the old military axiom that attack is the best form of defense, went on to say:

The absurdity of the slander stares you in the eye . . . A report on the "documents" was sent to Kerensky back on May 16. Kerensky is a member of the Provisional Government and the Soviet, that is, of both the authorities. May 16 through July 5 is a fairly long time. The authorities, if they are authorities, could have and should have personally examined the "documents," interrogated the witnesses and arrested the suspects.

On July 27, after a further summary of all the incriminating evidence had been published in the newspapers, Lenin wrote in *Worker*

---

[22] Vladimir Bonch-Bruyevich, *Na boevykh postakh fevral'skoi i oktiabrskoi revoliutsii,* 2d ed. (Moscow, Federatsiia, 1931), pp. 83f.

and Soldier that the charge against him was in the style of the "Beylis affair," [23] and went on:

The Prosecutor is exploiting the fact that Parvus is associated with Ganetsky, and Ganetsky is associated with Lenin. But this is simply a piece of trickery, for everybody knows that Ganetsky had financial dealings with Parvus, but that we had *none* with Ganetsky [italics are Lenin's].

Lenin had conveniently forgotten the statement in the indictment that when the investigators searched his headquarters at the home of Miss Kshesinsky, the famous ballerina, they found a wire from Ganetsky, addressed to Lenin, on the subject of funds. But Trotsky felt that a comparison of the Lenin affair with the Beylis affair was not sufficient. He wrote an article on "the greatest slander in the world" and "the new Dreyfusiada." This article, which was translated into a number of foreign languages, for a long time provided many people in the West with grounds for indignation at the Provisional Government's attempts to besmirch the honor of the great revolutionary and champion of the working class.

But facts, to quote Lenin himself, "are stubborn things," and when, in July, the foreign and home-grown enemies of Russian freedom had failed in their first attempt to destroy the newborn Russian democracy, Lenin tacitly admitted their truth by fleeing the country. Indeed, he had no choice once it became known in Russia what company he kept.

After the quelling of the July uprising, the influence of the Bolsheviks sharply declined. Scarcely anywhere in the country were the voices of Bolshevik defeatist agitators to be heard; Leninist party representatives disappeared from the presidiums of local Soviets, and at the front the soldiers themselves often arrested Bolshevik agents and expelled them from their ranks.

Lenin and his men were only too well aware of this decline in their influence. Trotsky, in a pamphlet entitled *The Russian Revolution of 1917,* freely admits it and states unequivocally that after the July revolt the Bolshevik Party had to go underground for a while.

As he bided his time in Finland, Lenin concluded from the experience of the four "peaceful" armed demonstrations that he would never overthrow the Provisional Government by tempting the Men-

[23] See Chapter 5.

sheviks and the social-revolutionary parties with the slogan "All Power to the Soviets!"

Always quick to cut his losses, he therefore wrote a new directive to the Bolshevik Party entitled "On Slogans," in which he declared that henceforth the seizure of power would only be possible through an armed assault by the proletariat, which would have to wait until the Russian "Cavaignacs,[24] headed by Kerensky," had annihilated the Soviets and both the socialist "appeaser" parties had finally capitulated without a struggle. In the meantime the proletariat, under Bolshevik leadership, was supposed to prepare patiently for the moment when it and the "Russian Cavaignacs" would stand face to face in a final and decisive trial of strength.

In seeking to conceal the extent of his capitulation from the Russian soldiers and workers, who knew little of politics and even less of European history, Lenin was unable to think of anything better than to label me a "Cavaignac" and to quote Karl Marx's famous letter to the German workers after the fiasco of the so-called "social revolution" of 1848. In his new directive he wrote:

... It happens only too often that, when history takes a sharp turn, even the most advanced parties cannot get used to the new situation for some time and repeat slogans that were valid the day before, but have no more meaning today, having lost it just as "suddenly" as the sharp turn in history had "suddenly" occurred. Something like this could happen in the case of the slogan "All power to the Soviets." This slogan was valid during a period of our revolution—say, between February 27 and July 4—which is now over once and for all. This slogan has obviously ceased to be valid at present. Without understanding this it is impossible to understand anything about the present moment. Every single slogan must be deduced from the sum total of the specific features of a given political situation. The political situation in Russia is now, after July 4, radically different from the situation of February 27–July 4. . . .[25]

Referring to acts of violence by the mob infuriated by the reports of Bolshevik treachery after the abortive uprising, and also to articles

[24] General Louis Cavaignac suppressed the workers' uprising in Paris in June, 1848.
[25] See Lenin's directive, entitled "On Slogans," written in the middle of July, 1917, and published as a pamphlet by the Kronstadt Committee of the Russian Social Democratic Workers Party.

in the extreme right-wing gutter press, Lenin tried to depict the Provisional Government as a band of savage reactionaries:

First of all, and most of all, the people must know the *truth*—in whose hands state power still really lies. We must tell the people the whole truth, namely, that power is in the hands of a military clique of Cavaignacs (Kerensky, some of the generals, and others) who are supported by the bourgeoisie as a class, with the Constitutional Democratic Party at its head, and with all the monarchists acting through the Black Hundred papers, through *Novoye Vremya, Zhivoye Slovo,* etc., etc.

This regime must be overthrown. Without this, all phrases about fighting the counterrevolution are empty phrases, "self-deception and deception of the people."

This regime is now supported by the Ministers Tsereteli and Chernov, and by their parties. We must make clear to the people that such a *finale* of those parties was inevitable after their "errors" of April 22, May 5, June 9, and July 4, after their approval of the policy of the offensive at the front, a policy which predetermined nine–tenths of the Cavaignac victory in July. . . .

The cycle of development of the class and party struggle in Russia from March 12 to July 17 is complete. A new cycle begins into which enter not the old classes, not the old Soviets, not the old parties, but such as have been revived in the fire of struggle, hardened, enriched with knowledge, and recreated in the course of the struggle. We must look forward, not backward. We must operate not with old, but with new, post-July class and party categories. We must proceed, at the beginning of the new cycle, from the bourgeois counterrevolution that is victorious, that has become victorious through the reconciliation of the Social-Revolutionaries and the Mensheviks, and which can be vanquished only by the revolutionary proletariat. Of course, there are still going to be many and various states in this new cycle, before the final defeat (without a struggle) of Social-Revolutionaries and Mensheviks and the new . . . revolution. All this, however, can be discussed later on as and when each of these stages is reached. . . .[26]

Needless to say Lenin's failure to seize power in July was a great setback for the Germans. Lenin had not procured a separate peace, a peace that, as Field Marshal Hindenburg had written to Chancellor

[26] *Ibid.*

Bethmann-Hollweg on April 5, was essential before the winter of 1917.[27]

In the desperate search for a solution, someone in the German Government or perhaps on the General Staff had the idea of trying to conclude peace with the Provisional Government.

One day toward the end of July, Dr. Runeberg from Finland came to see me in my office. I had known Dr. Runeberg both as an excellent physician and as an able and astute politician, and I listened attentively to what he had to say. An important person from Stockholm, whose name he did not divulge, had asked him to tell me that he had a message for me from the German Government and was therefore requesting an interview. Dr. Runeberg added that he knew my attitude to such overtures, but felt that at such a historic moment, when the fate of the countries fighting the war was hanging in the balance, he (Runeberg) would have done wrong not to convey the message. I was very angry at the very idea that the Germans had dared to approach me, and told my friend to inform the man from Stockholm that "he can come and see me if he likes, but I'll have him arrested on the spot." I mentioned this overture at the Moscow State Conference, though without giving any details.[28]

In the long run, of course, Lenin did manage to sign a separate peace, but it came too late to enable the Germans to smash the Anglo-French Front.

NOTE

Romberg's Dispatch to the German Chancellor [29]

> The Minister in Bern to the Chancellor
> Report No. 794
> A 28659
> Bern, September 30, 1915

The Estonian Keskula [30] has succeeded in finding out the conditions on which the Russian revolutionaries would be prepared to conclude peace

[27] See the German Secret Archives, microcopies T. 120, ii., No. 1498, A 627623.

[28] The Hoover Institute at Stanford University has an affidavit signed by me which contains some further details about this incident.

[29] Excerpt from Z. A. B. Zeman's *Germany and the Revolution in Russia, 1915–1918* (London, Oxford University Press, 1958). See pp. 6–7.

[30] Keskula was a member of the Estonian National Committee, working, in Switzerland and in Sweden, for the independence of his country from the Russian Empire. He was in contact with the German Legation in Bern from September, 1914. Later, he worked with Steinwachs, the German agent.

with us in the event of the revolution being successful. According to information from the well-known revolutionary Lenin, the programme contains the following points:

1. The establishment of a republic
2. The confiscation of large land holdings
3. The eight-hour working day
4. Full autonomy for all nationalities
5. An offer of peace without any consideration for France, but on condition that Germany renounces all annexations and war reparations

On Point 5, Keskula has observed that this condition does not exclude the possibility of separating those national states from Russia which would serve as buffer states.

6. The Russian armies to leave Turkey immediately—in other words, a renunciation of claims to Constantinople and the Dardanelles
7. Russian troops to move into India

I leave open the question as to whether great importance should in fact be attached to this programme, especially as Lenin himself is supposed to be rather sceptical of the prospects of the revolution. He seems to be extremely apprehensive of the counter-campaign recently launchd by the so-called Social Patriots. According to Keskula's sources, this counter-movement is headed by the Socialists Axelrod, Alexinsky, Deutsch, Dneveinski, Mark Kachel, Olgin, and Plekhanov. They are unleashing vigorous agitation, and are supposed to have large financial resources, which they appear to draw from the government, at their disposal. Their activities could be all the more dangerous to the revolution as they are themselves old revolutionaries, and are therefore perfectly familiar with the techniques of revolution. In Keskula's opinion, it is therefore essential that we should spring to the help of the revolutionaries of Lenin's movement in Russia at once. He will report on this matter in person in Berlin. According to his informants, the present moment should be favourable for overthrowing the government. More and more reports of workers' unrest are being received, and the dismissal of the Duma is said to have aroused universal excitement. However, we should have to act quickly, before the Social Patriots gain the upper hand.

. . . Lenin's programme must not, of course, be made public, first because its publication would reveal our source, but also because its discussion in the press would rob it of all its value. I feel that it should be put out in an aura of great secrecy, so that it creates a belief that an agreement with powerful Russian circles is already in preparation.

Quite apart from the French aspect, I would ask you first of all to discuss this information with Keskula, so that nothing may be spoiled by premature publication.

[Signed]　　Romberg

19

The Restoration of the State Order

State Conference in Moscow

R USSIA'S recovery after the fall of the Monarchy was extraordinarily rapid. She gained strength at a tremendous rate. The constructive forces in the country quickly asserted themselves, and once again Russia began to work, to fight, to give orders, and to obey them.

The strategic plan adopted by the Russian army in the spring of 1917 proved most successful. Relations between officers and men improved, and desertion from the front was halted.

Here and there, in the depths of the country, agrarian riots broke out, but at no point did they attain the scale of the riots of 1905–1906. Most of the factories had started to function again, and what problems remained were caused not so much by poor relations between workers and management as by the blockade.

The nation had been shaken out of its normal routine by the Revolution, but it was once more getting back to the daily routine in the land committees, the cooperatives, and the trade unions, and the whole country was seized by enthusiasm for cultural and educational activities.

By August a great many of the *zemstva* and urban councils had already been reorganized on the principle of universal suffrage. In the Soviets, especially those in the provinces, Bolshevik influence had virtually disappeared following the July 4 uprising. In fact, the Soviets themselves, having served their purpose during the collapse of the monarchy, were tending to break up. By the autumn of 1917, this tendency had become so marked that even *Izvestiya,* the official organ of the Soviet Central Committee, declared:

The Soviets of the Soldiers' and Workers' deputies . . . are passing through an obvious crisis. . . . Many of them no longer exist, still more exist on paper only. The network of Soviet institutions is broken in some places, weakened in others and decayed in still others.

The reasons for this decay were explained by *Izvestiya* as follows:

First and foremost, the Soviets have ceased to be an all-embracing democratic institution. They do not represent the whole of the democratic movement anywhere, and it is doubtful whether, in any one place, they represent its majority. Even in the major centers, in Moscow and Petrograd, where the Soviet organization is at its best, they do not by any means embrace all democratic elements. The numerous intellectual classes, and even some of the workers, take no part in them.

The Soviets have done their work but now that the local governments have been elected by universal suffrage, now that the workers have the best possible system of professional representation on a democratic basis, the Soviets are no longer necessary.

They were a splendid institution for fighting the old regime, but they are quite incapable of taking on the building of the new. They have no trained men, no experience, and, finally, none of the necessary organization.

At the same time, however, we in the government were acutely aware of the need to establish closer links with all sections of the population. For we recognized that without them we were extremely vulnerable to demagogic pressures, both in the event of any setback at the front (such as in the savage German offensive after Kalush and Tarnopol) and in the face of the existing disaffection in military and civilian circles. As soon, therefore, as the July crisis was over and a new government had been formed, I proposed that a national state conference be convened in Moscow at the earliest possible date.

Direct contact with representatives of all classes and groups would give us an opportunity to take the pulse of the nation, and at the same time it would enable us to explain both our policies and our problems.

The State Conference was held at the Bolshoi Theater in Moscow from August 12 to 15, and it was attended by representatives of all democratic organizations. The only groups not represented were the extreme right-wing Monarchists, who were lying low for the time being, and the Bolsheviks, who refused to accept the rules of procedure for speaking at the conference.

On the first day, the Bolsheviks tried—unsuccessfully—to bring the entire working population of Moscow out on strike. At the other extreme, the supporters of a military dictatorship organized a tremendous welcome at the railroad station for General Kornilov, who was also attending the conference. These two incidents, the unsuccessful strike and the welcome for Kornilov, only served to mark off the left- and right-wing champions of a dictatorship from the overwhelming majority of the Russian population, who were wholeheartedly democratic in their beliefs.

I do not wish to describe the Moscow State Conference in detail.[1]

It was less interesting for what was said than for the extraordinary sincerity and intense patriotism of the speakers. There were moments when political opponents clashed rather violently, but there were also moments when the thousands of people present expressed their unanimous sense of dedication to the new state and their devotion to the country. A most remarkable incident occurred after an impassioned debate between Tsereteli, spokesman for the socialist parties, and Bublikov, a representative of large commercial and industrial interests. The two men suddenly walked toward each other, and with a hearty handshake, concluded a class truce in the name of Russia.

An amazing unanimity was expressed in the enthusiastic way the conference greeted the demand for a republic voiced by speaker after speaker—from workers to capitalists, from generals to ordinary soldiers.

Looking back on these three days, I now realize that I made one great mistake. By this time I knew that a military plot was brewing, and I also knew who some of the ringleaders were.

What I did not realize, however, was that the Moscow Conference coincided with a crucial phase in the preparations being made by the conspirators. For although Colonel Verkhovsky, who was in command of the Moscow Military District, had reported to me that there had been troop movements from the Don and from Finland, and had urged me to arrest certain higher officers, my own information gave

---

[1] Strange as it may seem, the Soviet State Publishing House published the minutes of the meeting back in the 1920's. All the speeches are given in full and with impeccable accuracy.

me no reason to expect an immediate uprising in Moscow. However, in my closing address, instead of being explicit, I contented myself with conveying to the chief conspirators, who understood me very well, that any attempt to impose their will on the government or the people would be firmly crushed. Nine-tenths of those attending the conference did not understand the warning, but some of the newspapers, which knew what was going on, wrote somewhat ironically that I had given way to "hysteria" at the end of my final speech.

I now realize that, instead of speaking in riddles, I should have revealed exactly what I knew of the armed uprising then being prepared. I kept silent because I did not want to shock the army and the country as a whole by talking about a conspiracy which was still only in preparation. If I had known at the time that it was headed by the Supreme Commander, whom I had appointed myself and upon whom I was relying for help in the struggle against the conspirators, I would have spoken out at the conference and taken the necessary steps on the spot. But I did not know this, and Russia had to pay the price of my faith in him.

By a supreme irony the counterrevolutionary movement, which did not have any deep roots in the country or in the army outside of a handful of officers, was in effect plotting the destruction of the values it pretended to be trying to save.

This was well understood by the Grand Duke Nicholas Mikhailovich, an amateur historian with a great deal of political common sense, who used to visit me now and then at night at the Winter Palace and report on what was happening in the guards regiments and among high social circles, without, incidentally, ever mentioning any names. "These brainy fellows," he said to me one day, referring to the guards officers involved in the plot, "are totally unable to understand that you [i.e., the Provisional Government] are the last bulwark of order and civilization. They are trying to break it down and when they do, everything will be swept away by the uncontrollable mob."

I myself told General Kornilov that he had better stop the dangerous game going on in his entourage. "After all," I said, "if any general chooses to oppose openly the Provisional Government, he will suddenly find himself in a vacuum, without railroads and without any form of communication with his own troops." And that is exactly what happened! The attempt launched on the night of August 26–27 to seize power by means of a lightning coup in Petrograd was nipped in the bud, without a single shot being fired.

The Imperial Family

I clearly remember my first interview with the former Tsar, which took place in the middle of March at the Aleksandrovsky Palace. Upon my arrival in Tsarskoye Selo I inspected the entire palace thoroughly and inquired about the regulations of the guard and the general regime under which the imperial family was being kept. On the whole, I approved of the situation, making only a few suggestions for improvement to the commandant of the palace.

Then I asked Count Benkendorf, former marshal of the court, to inform the Tsar that I wished to see him and Alexandra Fyodorovna. The miniature court composed of a few retainers who had not deserted Nicholas II still kept up the ceremonial. The old count, who sported a monocle, listened to me gravely and answered: "I shall report to His Majesty." In a few moments he returned and announced solemnly: "His Majesty has graciously consented to receive you." This seemed a trifle ridiculous and out of place, but I did not want to destroy the count's last illusions. He still considered himself first marshal to His Majesty, the Tsar. It was all he had left. Most of the immediate attendants of the Tsar and his family had deserted them. Even the Tsar's children, who were ill with measles, were left without a nurse, and the Provisional Government had to provide the necessary medical assistance.

I had done all I could to bring about the downfall of Nicholas II when he was omnipotent, but I could not revenge myself on a defeated enemy. On the contrary, I wanted to impress upon him that the Revolution was, as Prince Lvov had pledged, magnanimous and humane to its enemies, not only in word but in deed. This was the only revenge worthy of the Great Revolution, a noble revenge worthy of a sovereign people.

Of course, if the judicial inquiry instituted by the government had found proof that Nicholas II had betrayed his country either before or during the War, he would have been immediately tried by jury and his trip abroad would have been prevented at all cost. But he was proved beyond doubt to be innocent of this crime.

I had been looking forward to the interview with the former Tsar with a certain anxiety, for fear of losing my temper when I came face to face with him.

All these thoughts occurred to me as we passed through a succession of apartments. At last we came to the children's room. Leaving me before the closed door leading into the inner apartments, the Count went in to announce my visit. Returning almost immediately, he said: "His Majesty invites you." He threw open the door, remaining himself on the threshold.

My first glimpse of the scene as I went up to the former Tsar changed my mood altogether. The whole family was standing huddled in confusion around a small table near a window in the adjoining room. A small man in uniform detached himself from the group and moved forward to meet me, hesitating and smiling weakly. It was Nicholas II. On the threshold of the room in which I awaited him, he stopped as if uncertain what to do next. He did not know what my attitude would be. Was he to receive me as a host or should he wait until I spoke to him? Should he hold out his hand or wait for me to greet him first? I sensed his embarrassment at once, as well as the confusion of the whole family left alone with a terrible revolutionary. I quickly went up to Nicholas II, held out my hand with a smile and said abruptly, "Kerensky," as I usually introduce myself. He shook my hand firmly, smiled, seemingly encouraged, and led me at once to his family. His son and daughters were obviously consumed with curiosity and gazed fixedly at me. Alexandra Fyodorovna, stiff, proud and haughty, extended her hand reluctantly, as if under compulsion. This was typical of the difference of character and temperament between the husband and wife. I felt at once that Alexandra Fyodorovna, a clever and handsome woman, though now broken and angry, had a strong will. In those few seconds I understood the whole tragedy that had been developing for many years behind the palace walls. My few subsequent interviews with the Tsar confirmed my first impression.

I inquired about the health of the members of the family, informed them that their relatives abroad were solicitous of their welfare and promised to transmit without delay any messages they might wish to send. I asked whether they had any complaints, how the guards were behaving, and whether they needed anything. I asked them not to worry but to rely on me. They thanked me and I began taking my leave. Nicholas II inquired about the military situation and wished me success in my new and burdensome office. Throughout the spring and summer he followed the military events, reading the newspapers carefully and interrogating his visitors.

This was my first meeting with Nicholas "the Bloody." After all the horrors of many years of Bolshevik rule this epithet has quite lost its force. The tyrants who succeeded Nicholas were all the more revolting because they came from the people, or from the intelligentsia, and were thus guilty of crimes against their own brethren.

I think that the experience of the Bolshevik regime has already made some people revise their judgment about the personal responsibility of Nicholas II for all the crimes of his reign. His mentality and his circumstances kept him wholly out of touch with the people. He heard of the blood and tears of thousands only through official documents, in which he was informed of "measures" taken by the authorities, "in the interest of the peace and the safety of the State." Such reports did not convey to him the pain and suffering of the victims, but only the "heroism" of the soldiers "faithful in the fullfillment of their duty to the Tsar and the Fatherland." From his youth he had been brought up to believe that his welfare and the welfare of the country were one and the same thing, so that "disloyal" workmen, peasants, and students who were shot down, executed or exiled, seemed to him mere monsters and outcasts of humanity who must be destroyed for the sake of the country and his "faithful subjects."

If he is compared with our modern blood-stained "friends of the people," it is clear that the former Tsar was a man by no means devoid of human feeling, whose nature was perverted by his surroundings and traditions.

When I left him after my first interview, I was very much worked up. What I had seen of the former Tsarina made her character quite clear to me and corresponded with what everyone who knew her had said about her. But Nicholas, with his fine blue eyes and his whole manner and appearance, was a puzzle to me. Was he deliberately exploiting the charm he had inherited from his grandfather, Alexander II? Was he an experienced actor, an artful hypocrite? Or was he a harmless innocent entirely under the thumb of his wife and easily dominated by others? It seemed incredible that this slow-moving modest man, who looked as if he were dressed in someone else's clothes, had been the Tsar of all Russia, Tsar of Poland, Grand Duke of Finland, etc., etc., and had ruled over an immense empire for 25 years! I do not know what impression Nicholas II would have made upon me if I had seen him when he was still the reigning monarch. However, meeting him after the Revolution, I was struck by the fact that nothing about him suggested that only a month before so much had depended on his word. I left him with the firm intention of trying to solve the riddle of this strange, awesome, and yet disarming personality.

After my first visit I determined to appoint a new commandant to the Aleksandrovsky Palace, a man I could trust. I could not leave the imperial family alone with the few faithful attendants who still clung to the old ceremonial [2] and the soldiers of the guard who kept close watch over them. Later, there were rumors of a "counterrevolutionary" plot in the palace simply because the "court" used to send a bottle of wine to the officer on duty for his dinner. It was necessary to have a faithful, intelligent, and tactful intermediary at the palace. I chose Colonel Korovichenko, a military lawyer and a veteran of the Japanese and European wars, whom I knew to be courageous and upright. I was justified in putting my trust in him, for he kept his prisoners strictly isolated and managed to inspire them with respect for the new authorities.

In the course of my occasional short visits to Tsarskoye Selo I tried to fathom the former Tsar's character. I found that he did not care for anything or anyone except, perhaps, his daughters. This indifference to all external things was almost unnatural. As I studied his face, I seemed to see behind his smile and his charming eyes a stiff, frozen mask of utter loneliness and desolation. He did not wish to fight for power, and it simply fell from his hands. He shed his authority as formerly he might have thrown off a dress uniform and put on a simpler one. It was a new experience for him to find himself a plain citizen without the burdens of state. His retirement into private life brought him nothing but relief. Old Madame Naryshkina told me that he had said to her: "How glad I am that I need no longer attend to those tiresome audiences and sign those everlasting documents! I shall read, walk, and spend my time with the children." And, she added, this was no pose on his part.

[2] Count Benkendorf, Elisabyeta Naryshkina, Prince Dolgoruky, Dr. Botkin, Countess Buzhoevken, Schneider, and others.

Indeed, all those who watched him in his captivity were unanimous in saying that Nicholas II seemed generally to be very good-tempered and appeared to enjoy his new manner of life. He chopped wood and piled up the logs in stacks in the park. He did a little gardening and rowed and played with the children.

His wife, however, felt keenly the loss of her authority and could not resign herself to her new status. She suffered from hysteria and was at times partly paralyzed. She depressed everyone around her by her languor, her misery, and her irreconcilable animosity. People like Alexandra Fyodorovna never forget or forgive. While the judicial inquiry into the conduct of her immediate circle was going on, I had to take certain measures to prevent her from acting in collusion with Nicholas II in case they should be called to give evidence. It would be more accurate to say I had to prevent her from exerting pressure on her husband. Thus, while the investigation was in progress, I ordered the couple to be separated, allowing them to meet only at mealtimes, when they were forbidden to allude to the past.

I must mention here one brief conversation I had with Alexandra Fyodorovna, while old Madame Naryshkina was waiting in an adjoining room. We carried on the conversation in Russian, which Alexandra Fyodorovna spoke haltingly and with a strong accent. Suddenly her face flushed and she flared up:

"I don't understand why people speak ill of me. I have always loved Russia from the time I first came here. I have always sympathized with Russia. Why do people think I am siding with Germany and our enemies? There is nothing German about me. I am English by education and English is my language." She became so excited that it was impossible to continue the conversation.

In her memoirs Naryshkina also throws an interesting sidelight on what was going on in Tsarskoye Selo. On April 16, she writes:

Kerensky is said to be coming here in order to crossexamine the Tsarina. I have been called in as witness to the conversation. I found her in an excited and in an irritable, nervous mood. She was prepared to say a number of silly things to him, but I succeeded in calming her, by telling her: "For the love of God, Your Majesty, don't say a word of all this . . . Kerensky is trying his utmost to save you from the Anarchist Party. By interceding for you he is risking his own popularity. He is your only prop. Please try to understand the situation as it is . . .

At this moment Kerensky entered . . . He begged me to withdraw and remained alone with the Tsarina. I stepped into the small salon with the commandant, and here we found Benkendorf and Vanya (Dolgaruki). A few minutes later the Tsar, returning from a walk, joined us there too . . . Then we joined the Tsarina while Kerensky withdrew into the Tsar's study.

The Tsarina has been pleasantly impressed by Kerensky—she finds him sympathetic and honest . . . One could arrive at an understanding with him, she thinks. I am hoping that he has received as favorable an impression of her." [3]

I explained my reasons for the separation to Nicholas II and asked his cooperation so that no one should become involved in this matter beyond those who knew of it already—Korovichenko, Naryshkina, and Count Benkendorf. They were very cooperative and carried out my injunction strictly. Everyone concerned told me what a remarkably good effect the separation had upon the former Tsar; it made him livelier and altogether more cheerful.

When I told him that there was to be an investigation and that Alexandra Fyodorovna might have to be tried, he merely remarked: "Well, I do not believe Alice had anything to do with it. Is there any proof?" To which I replied: "I do not yet know."

In our conversations we avoided using titles. Once he said: "Well, so now Albert Thomas is with you. Last year he dined with me. An interesting man. Remember me to him, please." I delivered the message.

The way he compared "last year" with "now" showed that Nicholas II may have at times brooded over the past, but we never really talked about it. He only touched upon the subject casually and superficially. He seemed to find it painful to mention these things and, especially, to speak of the men who had deserted and betrayed him so quickly. With all his contempt for mankind, he had not expected quite so much disloyalty. I gathered from the hints that slipped out in his conversation that he still hated Guchkov, that he considered Rodzyanko superficial, that he could not imagine what Milyukov was like, that he held Alekseyev in great esteem, and respected Prince Lvov.

[3] Elizabeth Naryskin-Kurakin, *Under Three Tsars.* Relevant passages from this book are reprinted in *The Russian Provisional Government,* Vol. I (Stanford, Calif., Stanford University Press, 1961), pp. 187–188.

Only once did I see Nicholas II lose his self-control. The Tsarskoye Selo Soviet had decided to follow the example of Petrograd and organize an official funeral for the victims of the Revolution. It was to be held on Good Friday, in one of the main avenues of the park at Tsarskoye Selo, at some distance from the palace but exactly opposite the windows of the rooms occupied by the imperial family. The former Tsar was to witness the ceremony from the windows of his gilded prison, to see his guard with red banners paying the last honors to the fallen fighters for freedom. It was an extraordinarily poignant and dramatic episode. The garrison was still well in hand at that time, and we were not afraid of any disorder. We even felt sure that the troops wished to display their self-control and sense of responsibility as, indeed, they did, when the funeral ceremony did take place.

The question of the imperial family had been attracting too much attention and giving us a great deal of anxiety. On March 4 the government had received a note from the ex-Tsar, in which he made the request for safe passage for him and his family to go to Murmansk on the way to England. On March 6–7, Milyukov had been to see the British ambassador, Sir George Buchanan, and had requested him to ask the British Government to offer hospitality to the imperial family. On March 10, Buchanan had informed Milyukov that the British Government had agreed to the request. But it had been impossible to organize immediately the departure of the imperial family. All the children were ill with chicken pox. It had also proved impossible in these first weeks of the Revolution to guarantee the safe conduct for the ex-Tsar on his journey to Murmansk.

As of March 9–10 the Provisional Government had entrusted me with the supervision of the ex-Tsar's stay, under arrest, at the Aleksandrovsky Palace, and also with the preparations for the journey to Murmansk. Nicholas could not remain much longer in Tsarskoye Selo in any case. We feared that, if there were any new political complications or disturbances in Petrograd, the Aleksandrovsky Palace would not be safe. In the meantime the situation in London had also changed. The British government had gone back on its offer of hospitality to these relatives of its own royal house while the war was still on. Unfortunately, Sir George Buchanan did not immediately inform the Provisional Government of this decision, and the government went on with its arrangements for Nicholas' departure to England. When these were complete, Tereshchenko asked Sir George to get in touch with his government to find out when a British cruiser could be expected to arrive in Murmansk to take on board the imperial family. Sir George, visibly shaken, informed us only at this juncture that the imperial family were no longer welcome in England.

In his memoirs Sir George Buchanan writes: [4] *"Our offer remained open and was never withdrawn"* [italics mine]. Unfortunately, Sir George was not at liberty to reveal the truth. In 1932, after Sir George's death, his daughter Meriel describes the shattering effect on her father of the instructions received from London canceling the invitation that had been extended to the imperial family on March 10. "On his retirement, my father wished to reveal the whole truth," Meriel writes, "but he was told by the Foreign Office that he would lose his pension if he did so." [5] Sir George, whose personal means were slender, decided not to go against the wishes of the government. Meriel Buchanan blames Lloyd George for this change in policy. However, Harold Nicolson, in his official biography of George V, has at last revealed the truth:

"At a meeting which took place at Downing Street on March 22 [N.S.] between the Prime Minister, Mr. Bonar Law, Lord Stamfordham, and Lord Hardinge, it was agreed that since the proposal had been initiated by the Russian Government, it could not possibly be refused . . ." Nicolson continues: ". . . By this time [April 2, N.S.] the suggestion that the Tsar and his family should be given asylum in this country had become publicly known. Much indignation was expressed in left-wing circles in the House of Commons and the press. The King, who was unjustly supposed to be the originator of the proposal, received many abusive letters. George V felt that these disadvantages had not been sufficiently considered by the Government. On April 10 [N.S.] he instructed Lord Stamfordham [6] to suggest to the Prime Minister that, since public opinion was evidently opposed to the proposal, the Russian Government might be informed that His

[4] Sir George Buchanan, *My Mission to Russia and Other Diplomatic Memories,* Vol. II (London, New York, Cassel & Co., 1923).

[5] Meriel Buchanan, *The Dissolution of an Empire,* pp. 192, 195–197.

[6] Personal secretary to George V.

Majesty's Government felt obliged to withdraw the consent which they had previously given." [7]

I had the thankless task of telling the former Tsar of this new development. Contrary to my expectations, he took the news calmly and expressed his wish to go to the Crimea instead. But a journey to the Crimea, which would have involved crossing very unsettled and turbulent parts of the country, seemed very unwise at the time. Instead, I chose Tobolsk, in Siberia, which was without railway communications. I knew that the governor's mansion at Tobolsk was fairly comfortable, and could provide decent accommodations for the imperial family.

The preparations for their departure were shrouded in utmost secrecy, since any publicity might have led to all kinds of complications. Not even all the members of the Provisional Government were informed of the arrangements made for the imperial family. In fact, only five or six persons in Petrograd knew what was going on. The ease and expediency of the departure showed how much the authority of the Provisional Government had been strengthened by August. In March or April it would not have been possible to move the former Tsar without endless consultations with the Soviets. But on August 14, Nicholas II and his family left for Tobolsk upon my personal order and with the consent of the Provisional Government. Neither the Soviet nor anyone else knew of it until afterward.

After setting the date for the departure, I explained the situation to Nicholas II and told him to prepare for a long journey. I did not tell him where he was going, but simply suggested that he and his family take as much warm clothing as possible. Nicholas II listened attentively, and when I told him that these arrangements were being made for the benefit of his family, and generally tried to reassure him, he looked straight at me and said: "I am not in the least worried. We believe you. If you say this is necessary, I am certain that it is." And he repeated: "We believe you."

About eleven in the evening, after a meeting of the Provisional Government, I went to Tsarskoye Selo to supervise the departure for Tobolsk. To begin with, I made the rounds of the barracks and inspected the guards, who had been picked by the regiments themselves

[7] Harold Nicolson, *King George V, His Life and Reign* (New York, Doubleday and Co., Inc., 1953), pp. 299–302.

to accompany the train and guard Nicholas II on his arrival at his destination. They were all ready and seemed cheerful. There had been vague rumors in the town that the ex-Tsar was leaving, and from early evening a curious crowd had begun to gather around the palace park. In the palace final preparations were underway. Luggage was being brought out and stored in motor cars. We were all rather on edge. Before his departure Nicholas II was allowed to see his brother, Grand Duke Michael. Naturally, I had to be present at this interview, much as I disliked intruding on their privacy. The brothers met in the Tsar's study at about midnight. Both seemed very agitated. They were evidently very oppressed by the painful memories of the recent past. For a long time they were silent, and then they began the sort of casual, inconsequential conversation which is characteristic of such brief interviews: "How is Alice?" asked the Grand Duke. They stood facing each other, fidgeting all the while, and sometimes one would take hold of the other's hand or of a button of his uniform.

"May I see the children?" the Grand Duke asked me.

"I am afraid I have to refuse," I answered. "I cannot prolong the interview."

"Very well," the Grand Duke said to his brother. "Embrace them for me."

They began to take leave of each other. Who could have thought that this was the last time they would ever meet?

As I sat in the room near the Tsar's study giving the final orders and awaiting news of the arrival of the train, I could hear the young heir apparent Alexis running about noisily in the corridor. Time was passing and still there was no sign of the train. The railroad workers had hesitated about making up the train. It was daylight by the time it arrived. We motored over to where it was waiting, just beyond the Aleksandrovsky Station. We had previously arranged for the order of seating in the cars, but everything became confused at the last moment.

For the first time I saw the former Tsarina simply as a mother, anxious and weeping. Her son and daughters did not seem to mind the departure so much, though they too were upset and nervous at the last moment. Finally, after the last farewell had been said, the cars moved with an escort of Cossacks in front and behind. The sun was already shining brightly when the convoy left the park, but fortunately the town was still asleep. When we reached the train we checked the list of those who were going. More farewells and the train moved off. They were leaving forever, and no one had any inkling of the end that awaited them.[8]

[8] The fall of the Provisional Government opened the road for bloody dictatorship and led the Tsar's family to the martyr death of July 16, 1918, plotted by Lenin, Sverdlov, and Trotsky. In this connection it is interesting to read Trotsky's own evaluation of the tragic death of the Romanovs: "... My next visit to Moscow took place after the fall of Ekaterinburg. Talking to Sverdlov, I asked in passing: 'O yes, and where is the Tsar?' 'It's all over,' he answered, 'he has been shot.' 'And where is the family?' 'And the family along with him.' 'All of them?' I asked, apparently with a touch of surprise. 'All of them!' replied Sverdlov, 'What about it?' He was waiting to see my reaction. I made no reply. 'And who made the decision?' I asked. 'We decided it here. Ilyich believed that we shouldn't leave the Whites a live banner to rally around, especially under the present difficult circumstances ...' I did not ask any further questions and considered the matter closed. Actually, the decision was not only expedient but necessary. The severity of this summary justice showed the world that we would continue to fight on mercilessly, stopping at nothing. The execution of the Tsar's family was needed not only in order to frighten, horrify, and dishearten the enemy but also in order to shake up our own ranks, to show them that there was no turning back, that ahead lay either complete victory or complete ruin." See *Trotsky's Diary in Exile, 1935* (Cambridge, Mass., Harvard Univ. Press, 1953), p. 81.

Prelude to the Civil War

20

The Ultimatum

AFTER the Moscow State Conference the Provisional Government was faced with two urgent problems, the reorganization of the Cabinet in accordance with the new balance of political power and the eradication of growing clandestine opposition in the officers' corps. Various "secret" army organizations had rapidly gained ground after Lenin's abortive uprising on July 3, his escape to Finland, and the ensuing disarray in the Bolshevik party apparatus both at the front and in the country as a whole. The launching of the German offensive on the Northern Front and the fall of Riga both accentuated the need for a new cabinet.

It somehow became known to the rightist opposition that, during the Conference, I had made discreet approaches to certain groups in order to enlist their aid in carrying out the immediate tasks of the government. Upon my return to the capital on August 16, I received a message from Prince Lvov informing me that A. N. Aladin [1] had asked the Prince to arrange an appointment with me. Aladin's activities in England had been of a rather questionable nature, and Lvov had therefore refused to arrange the meeting; but he wanted me to know that as Aladin left him, he had said meaningfully: "Tell Kerensky that any changes in the Cabinet must be approved by Supreme Headquarters." It was not difficult to guess the nature of Aladin's contacts at Headquarters: We knew of the existence of a secret anti-government cell in the Central Committee of the Army and Navy Officers' Union. I was not unduly alarmed by Aladin's warning, since it had already been decided to remove the Central Committee of the

[1] A member of the first Duma who had just returned to Russia in the uniform of a British lieutenant. He had been living in England for some time.

Officers' Union from Supreme Headquarters and to arrest some of its most active members.

On August 22, Vladimir Lvov came from Moscow to see me. Lvov had been chief procurator of the Holy Synod from the first days of the Provisional Government until the middle of July. Prior to that he had belonged to the conservative faction in the Duma known as "the Center." A genuinely devout man, Lvov had been outraged by Rasputin's influence in leading ecclesiastical circles. During our five years as members of the Duma we had become good friends, and despite his violent temper I liked him for his forthright sincerity. Nevertheless, when I became premier in July I did not invite Vladimir Lvov to remain in the Cabinet. A national ecclesiastical council was to meet in August to discuss a new statute on the autonomy of the Russian Orthodox Church. This called for tact and subtlety, as well as a profound knowledge of church history, on the part of the procurator. A. V. Kartashov, an eminent member of the St. Petersburg Academy, had seemed more suited to the post, and he was appointed. But Vladimir Lvov bore a grudge against me for a long time for what he called his "removal" from the work of healing the Russian Church of the paralysis from which it had suffered ever since Peter the Great had abolished the patriarchate and made himself head of the Church.

At our memorable meeting on August 22, Lvov began by emphasizing that this was not a social visit but that he was the bearer of a message. Then he proceeded to tell me that by losing the backing of influential circles and by relying on the Soviets, who, he said, would get rid of me in the long run, I had placed myself in a precarious, indeed dangerous, position.

I knew that Lvov and his brother, N. N. Lvov, belonged to liberal and moderate conservative circles in Moscow. I was aware of the fact that they had incited public opinion against the Provisional Government and against me personally at a special conference of "civic leaders" held in Moscow before the State Conference, and the pointedly warm reception they had given General Kornilov at the State Conference had not escaped my attention. Bearing all this in mind, I let him speak and contented myself with asking him when he had finished: "What do you want me to do now?"

He answered that there were "certain circles" who were willing to support me, but that it was up to me to come to terms with them.

I asked him point-blank to tell me on whose behalf he had come. He replied that he was not authorized to tell me, but that, if I agreed, he would relate our conversation to the people he represented.

"Of course you may," I told him. "You know I am interested in forming a solidly-based government, not in hanging onto power myself." Apparently, Vladimir Lvov was satisfied with our meeting. As he left, he told me he would come to see me again.

I did not attach any particular significance to Vladimir Lvov's visit, since at that time I was constantly being approached on similar business. Furthermore, Riga had fallen the day before, and I had to give my full attention to the critical military situation. My first action in this regard had been to transfer the Petrograd Military District, with the exception of the city itself, to the jurisdiction of the supreme commander, and I had asked the supreme commander to dispatch a force of Cavalry Corps to Petrograd to be at the disposal of the government.

On the very day of Lvov's visit, Boris Savinkov, the acting minister of war, and Colonel Baranovsky, the head of my military secretariat, left for Supreme Headquarters to discuss these measures with General Kornilov. I instructed Savinkov to see that General Krymov was not given command over the Cavalry Corps and to make sure that the Caucasian Cavalry Division, known as the "Wild Division," was not included in it. I knew that Krymov and the officers of the "Wild Division" were deeply involved with a conspiratorial group in the army.

Upon their return Savinkov and Baranovsky reported that my proposals had been accepted by General Kornilov. The area under the jurisdiction of the Provisional Government had been agreed upon, and the cavalry had been dispatched without General Krymov and the "Wild Division." They told me, furthermore, that General Kornilov himself had agreed to take action against the disaffected Central Committee of the Army and Navy Officers' Union.

On August 23, a meeting took place in the office of the British ambassador, of which I did not learn until many years later. Here is what Sir George Buchanan writes about it:

On Wednesday, August 23/September 5, 1917, a Russian friend of mine who was the director of one of the principal Petrograd banks, came to see me and said that he found himself in rather an embarrassing position, as he had been charged by certain persons, whose names he mentioned, with a message which he felt it was hardly proper for him to deliver. These persons, he then proceeded to say, wished me to know that their organization was backed by several important financiers and industrialists, that it could count on the support of Kornilov and an army corps, that it would begin operations on the following Saturday, August 26/September 8 and that the Government would then be arrested and the Soviet dissolved. They hoped that I would assist them by placing the British armoured cars at their disposal and by helping them to escape should their enterprise fail.

I replied that it was a very naïve proceeding on the part of those gentlemen to ask an Ambassador to conspire against the Government to which he was accredited and that if I did my duty I ought to denounce their plot. Though I would not betray their confidence, I would not give them either my countenance or support. I would, on the contrary, urge them to renounce an enterprise that was not only foredoomed to failure but that would be at once exploited by the Bolsheviks. If General Kornilov were wise he would wait for the Bolsheviks to make the first move and then come and put them down.[2]

It goes without saying that Sir George could not pledge his support to Putilov. Nevertheless, an agreement on the armored cars must have taken place. On August 28, 1917, when General Krymov's forces were rapidly advancing on Petrograd, Kornilov sent the following message to the general headquarters of the Seventh Army at the Southwestern Front:

Issue immediate orders to the Commander of the British Armoured Division to dispatch all army vehicles including the "Fiats" with officers and crew to Lieutenant Commander Soames in Brovary. Also dispatch the vehicles stationed at the Dubrovka estate.

On August 26, at about 5:00 P.M., I received a second visit from Vladimir Lvov. He appeared strangely agitated, and began speaking rather incoherently of the dangers of my situation, from which he offered to save me. In response to my repeated requests to be more explicit, he finally came to the point. General Kornilov had commissioned him to advise me that the government must not expect any help in the event of a Bolshevik rising and that he could not guarantee my personal safety unless I moved to Headquarters. The General had

---

[2] Sir George Buchanan, *My Mission to Russia*, Vol. II (1923), pp. 175–176. The ambassador's visitor was none other than the leading banker A. I. Putilov, as Sir George himself told me years later in London.

further instructed him to say that the continued existence of the present cabinet was impossible, and that I must propose to the Provisional Government the transfer of all power to Kornilov as supreme commander. Pending the organization of a new cabinet by Kornilov, the deputy ministers must take over state business. Martial law must be declared throughout Russia, and Savinkov and I must leave at once for army headquarters, where we would be appointed ministers of war and justice respectively. Lvov emphasized, however, that the latter arrangements had to be kept secret from the rest of the cabinet.

Neither Lvov nor Kornilov had ever been mentioned in the reports I had received of the military conspiracy, and I tried to dismiss the matter with a laugh: "You must be joking, Vladimir Nikolaevich."

He replied in a manner that left no doubt as to his seriousness: "I certainly am not. I wish you would realize how grave the situation is." He pleaded with me to give in to Kornilov, insisting that it was my only chance of survival.

By now, I had no doubt that Lvov was in deadly earnest. I paced up and down my office trying to collect myself and to understand the full import of the situation. I suddenly remembered that on his earlier visit Lvov had referred ominously to "real power." I remembered, too, Colonel Baranovsky's report on the hostility displayed toward me by the officers at headquarters as well as other information about a conspiracy undoubtedly connected with it. As soon as I had recovered from my initial shock, I decided to put Lvov to a test. I pretended that I was willing to comply with Kornilov's request, but said I could not lay the matter before the Provisional Government unless I had it in writing. Lvov immediately agreed to write down Kornilov's demands. The text read:

General Kornilov proposed (1) the declaration of martial law in the city of Petrograd; (2) the transfer of all military and civil power to the Supreme Commander; (3) the resignation of all ministers, including the prime minister, and the temporary transfer of all ministerial business to deputy ministers, pending the formation of a cabinet by the Supreme Commander. Petrograd. August 26, 1917. V. Lvov.[3]

The readiness with which Lvov had agreed to write this down was enough to dispel any lingering doubt in my mind, and as I watched

[3] The original document is preserved in the Soviet State Archives

him write, I had but one thought: to stop Kornilov and to prevent any repercussions at the front. First of all, I had to have enough incontrovertible evidence of the link between Lvov and Kornilov to enable the Provisional Government to take action that very night. I had to get Lvov to repeat what he had said in the presence of a third person. I was convinced that this was the only way to handle the matter.

As he handed me his memorandum, Lvov said: "This is very good. Everything will now be settled amicably. At Headquarters it is considered important to transfer power from the Provisional Government legally. And you yourself, will you go to Headquarters?"

The question had an odd ring to it, and when I replied: "Of course not. Do you really believe that I would accept the post of minister of justice under Kornilov?" Lvov's reaction was quite extraordinary. He jumped from his chair, smiled broadly, and exclaimed: "Of course, of course—you mustn't go! They have laid a trap for you there. They will arrest you. Get away quickly—as far away as you can from Petrograd." And even more excitedly he added: "They hate you there."

We agreed that I should advise General Kornilov of my resignation by wire, telling him at the same time that I would not come to Headquarters.

Once again I asked Lvov for an assurance that the whole thing was not some ghastly misunderstanding. "Tell me, Vladimir Nikolaevich, what if this turned out to be a practical joke? Where would you stand then? Do you realize the seriousness of what you have written down?"

Lvov replied heatedly that it was neither a joke nor an error; that the matter was very serious indeed; and that General Kornilov would never go back on his own statements. I decided to get in touch with the General by direct wire in order to hear him confirm his ultimatum. Lvov seemed pleased at the suggestion, and we agreed to meet at 8:30 at the home of the Minister of War, where direct communications with army headquarters were possible.

Unless my memory fails me, Lvov left me well after seven o'clock. As Lvov was leaving my office he ran into Vyrubov, who was coming to see me, and I asked Vyrubov to stay with me during the conversation with Kornilov. Then I sent my aide to set up the connection with army headquarters and to invite Sergey Balavinsky, the deputy chief of the Department of Militia (the police) and Captain Andrey Kosmin, deputy chief of the Military District, to be present as well.

At 8:30 P.M. exactly the connection was made, but Lvov had not yet arrived. We telephoned his flat, but there was no answer. Twenty-five minutes passed with Kornilov waiting at the other end of the line. Finally, after consulting with Vyrubov, we decided to go ahead with the conversation. In order to ensure Kornilov's full cooperation, we decided that I should give him the impression that Lvov was also taking part in the conversation.

Quite frankly, both Vyrubov and I had a faint hope that Kornilov would be puzzled, that he would say: "What do you want me to confirm? Who is Lvov anyway?" or something along that line. But we hoped in vain. Here is the full text of that conversation, which was recorded on tape: [4]

Kerensky: Prime Minister Kerensky on the line. We are waiting for General Kornilov.

Kornilov: This is General Kornilov.

Kerensky: How do you do, General. Vladimir Nikolaevich Lvov and Kerensky are speaking. May we ask you to confirm that Kerensky can proceed according to the information transmitted by Vladimir Nikolaevich.

Kornilov: Hello, Alexander Fyodorovich, hello, Vladimir Nikolaevich. I am reconfirming the message on the situation in the country and in the army as told to Vladimir Nikolaevich with the request to transmit it to you; let me reiterate that recent developments and the course of events make resolute and immediate action imperative.

Kerensky: This is Vladimir Nikolaevich asking you whether or not that certain decision I was to communicate to Alexander Fyodorovich personally has to be implemented? Without your final confirmation Alexander Fyodorovich is hesitant to trust me entirely.

Kornilov: Yes, this is to confirm that I have asked you to transmit to Alexander Fyodorovich my urgent request that he come to Mogilev.

Kerensky: This is Alexander Fyodorovich. Do I understand that you are confirming the message transmitted to me through Vladimir Nikolaevich? Today, it cannot be done and I cannot leave. I hope to be able to leave tomorrow. Do you need Savinkov?

Kornilov: I urgently request that Boris Viktorovich [Savinkov] accompany you. My message transmitted through Vladimir Nikolae-

---

[4] The tape is preserved in the Archives in Moscow.

vich applies in equal measure to Boris Viktorovich. Please don't delay your departure beyond tomorrow. Believe me that only awareness of the responsibility involved accounts for the urgency of my request.

Kerensky: Shall we come only in the case of events which are subject to current rumors or in any case?

Kornilov: In any case.

Kerensky: Goodbye, see you soon.

Kornilov: Goodbye.

The tape eliminates any possible misunderstanding.

The conversation was more revealing than I had imagined. Not only did the General confirm that he had authorized Vladimir Lvov to speak on his behalf but he went even further in corroborating every statement made by Lvov.

After the conversation, as Vyrubov and I were coming down the staircase, we met Lvov, who was hurrying upstairs. I let him see the tape of our conversation. He read it through and said happily: "You see, I didn't get anything wrong." He was pleased that we had talked with Kornilov without waiting for him. He did not explain why he was late, but many years later, in the course of reading Milyukov's *History of the Second Russian Revolution,* I learned that after our first meeting on August 26, Lvov had spent an hour with Milyukov telling him frankly about the events at Headquarters.

Vyrubov, Lvov, and I made our way back to the Winter Palace, and Lvov accompanied me to my office. There, in the presence of Balavinsky, who remained invisible in a corner of the vast room, Lvov again confirmed the accuracy of his memorandum and the contents of the tape.

At about 10:00 P.M. I had Vladimir Lvov arrested and placed under guard in one of the palace rooms.

I proceeded immediately to the Malachite Chambers, where the Cabinet was in session, reported on Lvov's approach to me, and read aloud his memorandum and the verbatim text of my conversation with Kornilov. Then I said that the mutiny must be crushed, and that, in my opinion, it could only be done if I were invested with full powers. I added that this might necessitate some changes in the Cabinet. After a brief discussion, it was resolved to "transfer all power to the Prime

Minister in order to put a speedy end to the antigovernment movement launched by General Kornilov, the Supreme Commander." [5]

With the exception of the Cadets Yurenyev and Kokoshkin, who resigned, all the ministers put their portfolios at my disposal. I asked them all to remain at their posts.

We had no information on the situation at Headquarters, and some of the cabinet members suggested waiting until morning. But I was resolved to act at once. There was no time to waste. I sent a brief radiogram to the Supreme Commander directing him to hand over his post to his chief-of-staff, General Lukomsky, and to come to the capital. In the early hours of the morning I instructed the acting minister of railroads, Liberovsky (whom I had appointed to replace P. Yurenyev), to stop the movement of military trains in the direction of Petrograd and to dismantle the Luga-Petrograd line.

There was no answer from General Kornilov. But in the early hours of August 27, the acting minister of war received a laconic wire dispatched at 2:40: "Urgent. The corps arrives in the Petrograd area on the evening of the 28th. Please declare martial law in Petrograd on August 29. Kornilov." General Kornilov had sent this wire immediately after our conversation and before receiving my message summoning him to the capital.

We soon learned that the corps referred to in the wire was *not* the cavalry corps requested by the Provisional Government, but the vanguard of a "special army" commanded by General Krymov. It consisted mainly of the "Wild Division."

The same day we received official information that these troops had concentrated near Luga. It was clear that Kornilov's wire had been deliberately misleading.

Savinkov, fearing that I suspected him of collusion with General Kornilov, was very much upset and begged me either to put him on trial or to authorize him to organize the defense of the capital. I appointed him to the post of Governor General of Petrograd and entrusted him with the defense of the city.

Later in the day my message to the country was published. I told the people what had happened and urged them to maintain law and order. Kornilov responded with an appeal in which he explained the reason underlying his action.

[5] *Journal of the Provisional Government,* August 26.

At 1:00 I received a telegram from General Lukomsky, in which he said:

"... without pursuing self-seeking, ambitious goals, and relying on the certainty of the sound elements of the army, a strong government must be set up at once to save our country and to preserve the achievements of the revolution. General Kornilov has thought it necessary to take resolute steps to bring about the restoration of order in the country. The visit of Savinkov and Lvov, who made a similar proposal on your behalf, has prompted General Kornilov to come to a final decision and to take measures that cannot now be revoked. Today's wire indicates that your original decision, which was transmitted to us by Savinkov and Lvov, has now been changed.

Always bearing in mind the welfare of our country, it is my duty to tell you that it is impossible to halt an action which was launched with your approval, that it would merely unleash civil war and lead to the final collapse of the army and to a humiliating separate peace treaty, which would not contribute to the consolidation of revolutionary achievements.

The salvation of Russia requires that we cooperate with General Kornilov instead of replacing him. General Kornilov's dismissal would entail unprecedented horrors.

Personally, I cannot assume even temporary responsibility for the army, and I deem it impossible to take over General Kornilov's post, because such a step would cause an explosion in the army and bring ruin on Russia.

Awaiting urgent instructions. Signed: Lukomsky.

In the early morning hours of August 28, the following wire was dispatched to the commander-in-chief of the Northern Front, General Klembovsky: "By order of the Provisional Government you are appointed Supreme Commander, to remain in Pskov and to retain the post of commander-in-chief of the Northern Front. Suggest you take over from General Kornilov immediately and report to me. Prime Minister Kerensky." As was customary, the order was transmitted through the staff of the Supreme Commander.

General Klembovsky's reply came a few hours later:

Received wire from Supreme Commander that I am to replace him. Though willing to serve my country to the very last, my loyalty and love for Russia compel me to reject the appointment, since I feel I have neither the strength nor the ability required to handle such a responsible task at this difficult and trying time. Believe change of Supreme Command extremely dangerous at a moment when our country is threatened by the enemy, and when the unity and freedom of our country demand speedy action to restore discipline and security in the army. Klembovsky, August 28.

Later on, we learned that General Klembovsky was one of the two commanders-in-chief (there were five in all) who had pledged support to General Kornilov. The other was General Denikin, commander-in-chief of the Southwestern Front. Without waiting for word from Petrograd, General Denikin sent me a wire at 2:00 on August 27, which began with the statement: "I am a soldier and am not used to playing hide-and-seek." It ended:

I have learned today that General Kornilov, whose demands could still save the country and the army, is being dismissed from his post as supreme commander. Since I believe this to indicate that the government has returned to a policy of systematic destruction of the army, and consequently of the whole country, it is my duty to advise the Provisional Government that I am unable to follow along this path. Signed, General Denikin, August 27.

But the shrewd and cautious General Klembovsky, sensing that he had backed the wrong horse, hastened to disassociate himself from the actions of his friends at Headquarters by sending a second wire that same day, both to me and to General Lukomsky, which read as follows:

Cavalry units being transferred are not under my command but belong to the Supreme Commander's reserves. Transfer being carried out on his orders, not on mine. August 28. Signed: Klembovsky.

The commanders of the Western, Caucasian and Rumanian fronts, as well as the commanders on the Northern Front, sent telegrams affirming their loyalty.

The transfer of cavalry troops from the Northern Front, which had begun even before the loss of Riga, took place at a time when the Germans were launching a fierce offensive, and reinforcements were being urgently requested by the commanders.

In the afternoon of August 28, in accordance with a decision of the Provisional Government, I asked General Alekseyev to go straight to Headquarters and take over the Supreme Command. Alekseyev asked for time to study the pertinent documents.

A little later that same afternoon, Tereshchenko showed me a telegram from the representative of the Ministry of Foreign Affairs at Headquarters, Prince Gregory Trubetskoy. It read:

A sound assessment of the situation leads to the conclusion that the entire commanding staff, the overwhelming majority of officers, and the best army units will follow Kornilov. In the rear, he will be supported by all Cossacks, most military schools, and also by the best military units. Apart from the factor of sheer physical force, it is necessary to take into account the superiority of their military organization to that of the weak civil authorities, the sympathy to their cause of all nonsocialist sections of the population, the growing dissatisfaction of the lower classes with the existing order, and the indifference of the majority of the rural and urban masses, who now react only to the whip. It is quite obvious that a large number of "March socialists" [6] will not hesitate to side with them. Moreover, the recent developments at the front and in the rear, particularly in Kazan, where an arsenal was blown up recently, have clearly shown the utter bankruptcy of the existing order and the inevitability of a disaster unless an immediate and radical change takes place. This consideration seems to be decisive for General Kornilov, who has come to realize that only firmness can prevent Russia from hurtling into the abyss at the edge of which she now stands. There is no point in arguing that Kornilov is preparing the way for the Kaiser's victory, since all the German armies have to do now is to occupy our territory.[7] It is up to the people who are in power to decide whether they will meet the inevitable change halfway, thereby defending the fundamentals of popular freedom, or offer resistance and assume the responsibility for innumerable new calamities. I am convinced that only the immediate arrival of the Minister-President, the acting Minister of War, and yourself for the establishment of the basis for a strong government jointly with the Supreme Commander can prevent the imminent threat of a civil war.

Subsequently, Prince Trubetskoy stated that he had sent this telegram, which largely coincided with the text of General Kornilov's appeal to the people, with Kornilov's consent.

The Provisional Government was now confronted with the urgent task of removing the leading military conspirators from Supreme Head-

---

[6] Those who joined the socialist parties after the fall of the monarchy.

[7] This was written at a moment when our armies were stubbornly resisting a fierce German attack.

quarters. I was determined to prevent a recurrence of the situation that had obtained at the front during the initial weeks of the February Revolution.

Meanwhile, rumors were circulating about an alleged misunder-standing, the result of a muddle on the part of Vladimir Lvov, between myself and General Kornilov. It was even whispered in certain circles that I had been in agreement with Kornilov all along, but had suddenly betrayed him for fear of the "Bolshevik Soviets," although the Soviets were not yet dominated by the Bolsheviks at that time. All day long on August 28, I and the other members of the cabinet received visit after visit from both military men and civilians, all offering to go to General Kornilov on my behalf in order to iron out the "misunderstanding." It goes without saying that I rejected all such offers of mediation.

Late that afternoon, after having read all the relevant papers, General Alekseyev, accompanied by Milyukov, came to see me. They both told me that it was still possible to clear up the "misunderstanding." Finally, the ambassadors of Great Britain, France, and Italy made a "friendly offer" through Tereshchenko "to mediate between Kerensky and the Supreme Commander, General Kornilov." But they received the same response I had given the others: I was not interested in any offer of mediation between the government and the rebellious general. The Provisional Government was quite adamant on this score.

This was a hectic time for the Cabinet. The nights of August 28 and 29 were particularly trying. We had no certain knowledge of the mood in the country and at the front, and we were under constant pressure from go-betweens of all political shades from Right to Left.

By the afternoon of August 29, everything was more or less settled. The mutinous generals found themselves without effective support in the army. Although General Kornilov continued to dispatch orders to seize the capital, his orders were quite meaningless and only contributed to the breakdown of discipline in the army. Without the knowledge of the Provisional Government, two "punitive detachments" were sent to Headquarters from the Western Front and from the Moscow Military District. General Denikin and his aides were arrested by the Front Committee, which wanted to court-martial them, and the telephones in all army headquarters were seized by representatives of the various committees.

All officers were now under suspicion. The officers of the Baltic Fleet, who had no connection with the Central Committee of the Union of Army and Navy Officers and had not participated in the conspiracy, were made to pledge their loyalty to the cause of the Revolution. On August 31, four young officers [8] were killed by the crew of the battleship *Petropavlovsk*. The armed forces were rapidly getting out of hand, and any delay in dealing with the conspirators would have been criminally negligent.

Early on August 30, Vyrubov and I paid a visit to General Alekseyev at his apartment. We were determined to persuade him to do his duty by arresting General Kornilov and his accomplices and by assuming the Supreme Command. Our arrival provoked the General to a fierce emotional outburst. Finally he began to calm down, and he leaned back in his armchair and closed his eyes.

I waited a few moments and then said quietly: "But what about Russia? We must save the country."

He hesitated, and then replied almost inaudibly: "I am at your disposal. I accept the post of chief of staff under your command."

I was at a loss for an answer, but Vyrubov whispered: "Agree." And so I became commander-in-chief.

General Alekseyev left for Headquarters the next day and carried out my instructions to the letter. The punitive detachments were stopped on their way to Headquarters, and the state of siege declared by the conspirators in Mogilev was lifted.

On September 1, the following order was issued: [9]

As a result of Kornilov's action the normal life of the army has been completely disorganized. To repair the situation I order:

(1) that all political struggle in the army cease and all efforts be devoted to building up our military power, on which the salvation of the country depends;

(2) that all military organizations and commissars keep their work free of political prejudice and suspicion, confining themselves to activities which do not involve interference in the performance by commanding officers of their military duties;

---

[8] Lieutenant Zhizenko and Warrant Officers Mikhailov, Kanonba, and Kondratiev.

[9] The last two paragraphs were drafted by me, and the rest of the text by General Alekseyev.

(3) that the unimpeded transfer of troops as ordered by commanding officers be resumed;

(4) that the arrest of officers cease immediately, since such action falls exclusively within the competence of investigating authorities, the public prosecutor, and the Extraordinary Committee of Investigation created by me, which has already started working;

(5) that the dismissal and removal of superiors from commanding posts be stopped immediately, this being the prerogative of the competent authorities and not falling within the scope of activities of public organizations;

(6) that the arbitrary formation of detachments under the pretext of a struggle against the counterrevolutionary uprising be stopped immediately;

(7) that the control of equipment [10] by army organizations cease immediately.

The army, which during these dark and troubled days has demonstrated its confidence in the Provisional Government and in me as its prime minister responsible for the destinies of the country, must in its great wisdom understand that the only salvation of the country lies in proper organization, maintenance of order, discipline, and unity. Enjoying the confidence of the army, I appeal to all to ensure this. Let each one of you be guided by your conscience and sense of duty to your country at this dark hour when her destiny is at stake.

As the Supreme Commander, I herewith demand that all commanding officers, commissars, and army organizations rigorously carry out this order, and I warn them that any failure to do so will be severely punished. Signed: Supreme Commander, A. Kerensky. Chief of Staff, General of the Infantry, M. Alekseyev.

Almost everyone recognized that the Kornilov revolt had had a disastrous effect on the country in general and the army in particular. Baron Peter Wrangel, who since the spring of 1917 had been involved in plots to replace the Provisional Government by a dictatorship, and who subsequently became leader of the White Armies in the Crimea, commented on the Kornilov mutiny as follows: "Recent events have profoundly shaken the army. The process of disintegration in the army, which had nearly been halted, has started again, threatening the complete collapse of the front and, consequently, of Russia."

In an interview published in *Russkie Vedomosti* on September 1 Yurenyev, one of the two members of the Provisional Govern-

[10] Telegraph lines.

ment who had resigned at the beginning of the crisis, spoke of the attempted coup in the following terms:

As to my view on the Kornilov affair, I must say that it is a terrible blow for those forces in the country making for stability. We had been moving steadily on the road to stronger rule, and Kornilov's action greatly jeopardized the common effort. My resignation on the night of the 27th enabled Kerensky to exercise his dictatorial rights directly in the Ministry (of Railroads) of which I was in charge. On August 27, I transferred the Ministry to my deputy and advised him to implement Kerensky's orders. As I know, these orders were carried out without fail.

Six months of hard work on the part of the government, the officers' corps, the commissars of the Ministry of War and the front-line committees, had not been altogether in vain. The army and the navy did not revert to the leaderless anarchy of the March days, and they valiantly resisted the fury of the German offensive until Lenin's October victory.

However, the conspirators and their champions did not give up after the Kornilov mutiny. They continued to push Russia toward the abyss, stubbornly opposing what they termed a "weak" government, in the hope of setting up a "strong national government" under a military dictator. Their campaign to discredit the Provisional Government continued by every sort of ignoble means. But damaging though their campaign was, it failed to achieve the desired result.

I should like to end this chapter by saying that I respect the moral right to rebellion in exceptional circumstances. In time of war, however, the responsibility moral rebellion carries is enormous. But when the military action of the Kornilov conspirators failed, passions ran so high that they were less than ever able to put their country first. They maintained the deception and even exploited it.

I feel it is important to the cause of freedom everywhere to ascribe the main reason for the defeat of Russian democracy to this attack from the right instead of to the foolish myth that Russian democracy was "soft" and blind to the Bolshevik danger.

NOTE I

Radiotelegram from Kerensky to the Nation

I hereby announce:

On August 26 General Kornilov sent to me Member of the State Duma Vladimir Lvov with a demand for the surrender by the Provisional Government of all civil and military power, so that he may form, at his personal discretion, a new government to administer the country. The authenticity of Deputy Lvov's authorization to make such a proposal to me was subsequently confirmed by General Kornilov in his conversation with me by direct wire. Perceiving in the presentation of such demands, addressed to the Provisional Government in my person, a desire of certain circles of Russian society to take advantage of the grave condition of the State for the purpose of establishing in the country a regime opposed to the conquests of the revolution, the Provisional Government has found it indispensable:

To authorize me, for the salvation of our motherland, of liberty, and of our republican order, to take prompt and resolute measures for the purpose of uprooting any attempt to encroach upon the Supreme Power in the State and upon the rights which the citizens have achieved by the revolution.

I am taking all necessary measures to protect the liberty and order of the country, and the population will be informed in due time with regard to such measures.

At the same time I order herewith:

1. General Kornilov to surrender the post of Supreme Commander to General Klembovsky, the Commander-in-Chief of the Northern Front, which is defending the approaches to Petrograd; and General Klembovsky to assume temporarily the post of Supreme Commander, while remaining at Pskov.

2. The city and district of Petrograd to come under martial law, extending to it the regulations applicable to regions under martial law . . .

I call upon all the citizens to preserve complete tranquillity and to maintain order, which is indispensable for the salvation of the country. I call upon all the ranks of the army and navy to carry on with calm and self-sacrifice their duty of defending the country against the external enemy.

A. F. Kerensky

Minister-President
Minister of War and Navy

August 27, 1917

NOTE II

Kornilov's Answer to Kerensky's Radiotelegram

The Minister-President's telegram No. 4163 in its entire first part is a lie throughout: it was not I who sent the Member of the State Duma, Vladimir Lvov, to the Provisional Government, but he came to me as the envoy of the Minister-President. Aleksei Aladin, Member of the State Duma, is a witness to this. A major act of provocation has thus taken place, which jeopardizes the fate of the motherland.

People of Russia: Our great motherland is dying. The hour of her death is near. Forced to speak openly, I, General Kornilov, declare that under the pressure from the Bolshevik majority of the Soviets, the Provisional Government acts in complete harmony with the plans of the German general staff, and simultaneously with the forthcoming landing of the enemy forces on the Riga shores; it is killing the army and undermining the very foundations of the country.

The heavy sense of the inevitable ruin of the country commands me in these ominous moments to call upon all Russian people to come to the aid of the dying motherland. All in whose breasts a Russian heart is beating, who believe in God, in Church, pray to the Lord for the greatest miracle, the saving of our native land:

I, General Kornilov, son of a Cossack peasant, declare to each and everyone that I want nothing for myself, except the preservation of a Great Russia, and I vow to bring the people through victory over the enemy to the Constituent Assembly, where they will themselves decide their fate and choose their new form of government. But it is quite impossible for me to betray Russia into the hands of her ancient enemy, the German race, and to turn the Russian people into German slaves. I prefer to die on the battlefield of honor rather than see the disgrace and infamy of the Russian land.

Russian people, the life of your motherland is in your hands!

General Kornilov

August 27, 1917

21

The Preparation of the Revolt

IN describing the final stages and collapse of the Kornilov mutiny, I have so far confined myself largely to the external course of events as they appeared *at the time* to me and to other members of the Provisional Government. In this chapter I shall describe the more complicated history of the preparation of the attempted coup, as I have been able to reconstruct it from the subsequent admissions of overt and covert participants in it. These admissions were in large part the result of a stubborn campaign waged by me over a 20-year period (1917–1937). It took all this time to force the truth from those concerned. I regarded this as an imperative task, not just because I wanted to clear myself of all the unfounded allegations made against me in connection with the plot, but also because I wished to establish beyond doubt the major part played by the Kornilov plotters in the demoralization of the Russian Army, and hence their responsibility for the debacle of Free Russia.

The plot to institute a military dictatorship originated in the early days of the February Revolution as a widespread but loosely organized movement involving certain officer circles as well as a number of leading Petrograd financiers. Many eminent men were involved in one way or other, and each had a separate role to play in the organization of the movement.

Of the financiers, Putilov and Vyshnegradski [1] were the most important. In April of 1917 Putilov founded a "Union for the Economic

[1] Putilov was the director of Russo-Asiatic Bank and had a continuing interest in the famous steel works named after him. Vyshnegradski was the son of a minister of finance under Alexander III and was a most influential person in banking and financial circles.

Revival of Russia," which the directors of all the banks and major insurance companies were quick to join. After his resignation from the Cabinet at the end of April, 1917, Guchkov was invited to be its chairman. The ostensible aim of the organization was to raise campaign funds for "moderate" candidates in the elections to the Constituent Assembly, and thereby to "counteract socialist influence at the front and in the country." In fact, however, Putilov and Guchkov have since admitted that the 4 million rubles raised for that purpose were to be handed over to General Kornilov, who had just been appointed commander of the Eighth Army at the Southwestern Front.

Another key figure in the movement was V. Zavoyko, whom Kornilov took with him as his "orderly." A former district marshal of nobility and also a financier, Zavoyko had worked for Lianozov, the well-known oil magnate. In view of his background, it was rather strange that General Kornilov should have chosen this elderly financier to accompany him to the front in a humble position that did not even carry officer rank. Kornilov always claimed that he gave the job to Zavoyko because he was impressed by his literary style.[2]

April 1917 also saw the arrival in Petrograd from the front of Baron Peter Wrangel, an officer of an aristocratic guards regiment, who had acquired fame early in the war in a cavalry attack upon a German battery. Baron Wrangel has given two reasons for his arrival in Petrograd: first, the preparation of officers for the struggle to set up a military dictatorship; and second, the search for a suitable general with a "democratic name" for the role of dictator.

At first the candidate most favored by Baron Wrangel and his two close friends, Counts Pahlen and Shuvalov, was General Lechitzsky. No final decision was made, but after some discussion with Zavoyko they established contact with Kornilov.

The conspiratorial activity of General Krymov also dates back to the spring of 1917. According to General Denikin, Krymov considered the army to be on the verge of collapse and had no hope of a successful outcome to the war. Accordingly, he began to enlist officers, mainly from among his own Third Cavalry Corps, to participate in a secret group that was to prepare the ground for a march from the south on Petrograd and Moscow.

In the early days of May an "Army and Navy Officers' Union" was

2 It is worthy of note that Zavoyko was Mrs. Putilov's nephew.

founded under the aegis of the then supreme commander, General Alekseyev. The Union was founded at a time when all professional bodies—doctors, teachers, engineers, etc.—were organizing unions to improve their status and to defend their interests. The rank and file of the army had their "soldiers' committees," but until then there had been no such professional organization for officers. In view of the officers' very difficult situation at that time, Prince Lvov and I gave our blessings to Alekseyev's organization and did our best to defend it from demagogic left-wing attacks.

Unfortunately, at its very inception, a secret, very militant political group was formed within the Central Committee of the Officers' Union. Undoubtedly acting under General Alekseyev's guidance, this secret cell set itself the task of coordinating the antigovernment groups of officers at the front, in Petrograd, and in Moscow. It also established close contact with the civilian wing of the movement to set up a dictatorship. Liaison with civilians was the particular responsibility of Colonel Novosiltsev, of the General Staff, who was elected chairman of the Union's Central Committee. Novosiltsev, who came from an aristocratic Moscow family, was a member of the Central Committee of the Cadet Party and had been elected to the fourth Duma, though he had soon given up his seat. An active member of the right wing of his party, he had good connections in the liberal and conservative circles of Moscow.

The political liaison between the Officers' Union at Headquarters and civilians in Moscow and Petrograd was carried on with great discretion: An incident involving Vladimir Lvov, who at that time was still the chief procurator of the Holy Synod, gives a good idea of how such political links were formed. Vladimir Lvov writes:

Some time in June, 1917, I was sitting at my office desk when the telephone rang. I picked up the receiver and was asked when I could be seen. I answered that I was through for the day with my work in the Holy Synod, that my car was waiting outside and that I could meet the man I was talking to within five minutes. "That's splendid," I was told.

I drove to the apartment where I was expected. In the dining room I found Duma Member V. Shulgin, whose apartment it was, and Colonel Novosiltsev. Before we had even exchanged greetings Shulgin astounded me by saying that a coup d'état was in preparation and that he wanted to warn me of it, so that I could resign (from the government). I did not attach much importance to Shulgin's words, thinking that he must have his own reasons for wanting my resignation. I told him that I was not in a position to resign before the forthcoming Church Council.

"When will the Council be held?" asked Shulgin.

"On the fifteenth of August," I said.

"Very well, but don't forget that you must resign after that date."

"All right," I replied. It would have been extremely awkward for me, a cabinet member, to pursue the topic, and I cut short the conversation by asking Shulgin to dinner.[3]

It was not until the end of 1936 that the part played by the Petrograd financiers in the preparation of Kornilov's mutiny was exposed. From various memoirs published at that time it is revealed that in April, 1917, after the Union for the Economic Revival of Russia had decided to turn over the sum of 4 million rubles to General Kornilov, Guchkov went to see him at Headquarters. It was then that preparations for the coup began in earnest. P. N. Finisov,[4] a prominent figure in the central organization of the conspirators in Petrograd, describes the next step as follows: "In the early part of May, 1917, General Kornilov, K. Nikolaevsky,[5] myself, and two or three others, met at the apartment of F. A. Lipsky, member of the Board of the Bank of Siberia. The Republican Center was founded at this meeting." At first the "Republican Center" appeared, on the surface, to be chiefly concerned with anti-Bolshevik propaganda at the front and throughout the country, and with subsidizing the numerous patriotic military organizations that had sprung up in Petrograd.

At the beginning of July, however, at the time of the German counteroffensive, the Bolshevik rising of July 4, and the breakthrough at Tarnopol, the Republican Center started the work for which it had really been created. Conspiratorial groups of officers had begun even earlier to prepare for the seizure of Petrograd "from within," which was to have coincided with the advance on the capital of General Krymov's troops. Colonel of the Guards Vinberg,[6] one of the officers concerned, has revealed that they were making plans to seize all

---

[3] This meeting was mentioned for the first time in Vladimir Lvov's frank reminiscences, published in the Paris *Poslednie Novosti,* November 27, 1920, about his part in the Kornilov movement.

[4] A business associate of Putilov.

[5] A banker.

[6] F. V. Vinberg, *V plenu u obezian* (*In Captivity Among the Apes;* Kiev, 1919).

armored vehicles in the capital, to arrest the members of the Provisional Government, and also to arrest and execute the most prominent Socialist Revolutionaries and Social Democrats. By the time General Krymov approached the capital, the leading revolutionary forces were to have been defeated and disarmed, thus reducing General Krymov's task to the simple restoration of law and order in the city.

It was not until July that the leaders of the Republican Center realized that the Center was a cover for the seditious activities of Putilov, Guchkov, Vyshnegradsky, and others. Even then they were totally unaware of the existence of the Union for Economic Revival, since financial assistance for the Center was provided through individual banks and business companies. But when its work began in earnest, and Colonels du Cimitière and Sidorin [7] were assigned by headquarters to the military section of the Center, the amount of this assistance had to be increased.

Finisov writes:

Shortly after the Bolshevik uprising in July, Lipsky, the vice-president of the Siberian Bank, received a wire (or letter) from N. K. Denisov [8] in Gursuf requesting that they send him a representative of the Center on an important matter. Neither Nikolaevsky nor Lipsky was able to leave St. Petersburg, so they sent me instead. In Denisov's office I was introduced to A. I. Putilov. When he had heard and approved my views, Putilov said: "Please tell Lipsky and Nikolaevsky that I have organized the Union for the Economic Revival of Russia, which will give you the assistance you need. I expect to be back in Petrograd at the end of July, and we'll talk matters over then." [9] ... When he departed from the capital at the beginning of August, Nikolaevsky left a note on the allocation of funds from the Union for Economic Revival to various military organizations for their counterintelligence agencies. At the same time, a message was sent to us from the headquarters of General Kornilov, first by direct line and then through Colonels Sidorin and Pronin, who were close friends of Colonel Novosiltsev, that another Bolshevik uprising was expected on September 2nd or 3rd. We were asked to be ready for an emergency. About half a million rubles were needed to take over the military units and radio sta-

---

[7] Both members of the conspiratorial cell inside the Central Committee of the Officers' Union.

[8] A financial and industrial magnate in the south of Russia.

[9] Finisov does not know what Putilov said to Nikolaevsky and Lipsky when he came to Petrograd.

tions in Tsarskoye Selo, to move Captain Orel's battalion toward Petrograd, and to block the Baltic Canal by means of a loaded barge in order to prevent the arrival of naval reinforcements from Kronstadt.[10]

These three consecutive developments—the meeting of a representative of the Center with Putilov, the allocation of funds to the Republican Center for military needs, and the message from Sidorin and Pronin—were undoubtedly the result of direct negotiations between the conspirators at headquarters and the leaders of the Union for Economic Revival.

The conspiratorial activities of Novosiltsev, Pronin, and Sidorin, and the other members of the Central Committee of the Officers' Union, were kept secret from the Supreme Commander, General Brusilov, and his chief of staff, General Lukomsky. However, that these activities were no secret to his successor, General Kornilov, was later admitted by Denikin, the most outspoken of the generals. In an article, Denikin made it quite clear that Kornilov was not only privy to the secrets of the conspirators, but actually headed the military plot to overthrow the Provisional Government.[11]

After General Kornilov's appointment to the Supreme Command, his post as commander of the Southwestern Front was filled by Denikin, who had previously commanded the Western Front.

At the end of July, on his way to his new post, Denikin stopped at Headquarters for a meeting with the new Supreme Commander, who was at that moment engaged in the preliminaries of a project for military reforms. Denikin took part in a conference on the project, the aftermath of which he describes as follows:

After the meeting was over Kornilov asked me to stay, and, when all had left, said to me, almost in a whisper: ". . . They have invited me to join the government . . . No, thank you! These gentlemen are far too close with the Soviets . . . I have told them that if authority is given me I shall launch a resolute struggle. We must lead Russia to a Constituent Assembly, and then let them do as they please . . . Now, General, may I rely on your support?"

"To the fullest extent."

We embraced heartily and parted.[12]

[10] *Poslednie Novosti* (Paris), February 27, 1937.
[11] In *Poslednie Novosti* (Paris), November 14, 1937.
[12] General A. I. Denikin, *The Russian Turmoil* (London, Hutchinson & Co.), p. 307.

In this passage from his memoirs, General Denikin is rather more guarded than he was in his article for *Poslednie Novosti,* but together they provide ample evidence that General Kornilov came to headquarters as a conspirator and set about implementing a prepared plan with the help of accomplices in the Officers' Union. Almost at once, General Denikin was called upon to honor his promise of support. At Kornilov's request he assigned to Headquarters General Krymov, whom he had previously recommended for the post of commander of the Eleventh Army. In doing this Denikin either chose to ignore or did not know that Kornilov's staff had already acted on his earlier recommendation. In my capacity as minister of war I had received the recommendation to assign General Krymov to the command of the Eleventh Army, had reported it to the Provisional Government, and had transmitted our approval to Headquarters.

This was evidently a feint, intended to circumvent my vigilance, for while the Ministry of War assumed that General Krymov had taken over his command at the front, he had actually gone to Headquarters in Mogilev shortly before the Moscow State Conference. At Headquarters Kornilov entrusted him with the task of planning the seizure of Petrograd, and we know from General Lukomsky's memoirs that Kornilov took Krymov with him to the Moscow State Conference.

At about this time Denikin was also making preparations to support the conspirators with the armies under his command. To quote his own words:

Finally, by about the 20th of August, the situation had been somewhat clarified. An officer arrived in Berdichev, the headquarters of the Southwestern Front, with a letter from Kornilov in which he asked me to listen to what the officer had to say. The officer told me that according to reliable sources a Bolshevik uprising was expected in Petrograd at the end of the month. By that time the Third Cavalry Corps under General Krymov would be outside the capital, ready to crush the Bolshevik rebellion and with the same stroke put an end to the Soviets. The Supreme Commander asked me only to send a few dozen reliable officers to headquarters, officially to study mortar and bombing techniques, but actually to join officer detachments which were being formed in Petrograd. The instructions were to be carried out with the discretion necessary to avoid any embarrassment for either the officers themselves or their commanders.[13]

[13] *Ibid.*

I surmise that the young officer who conveyed Kornilov's secret message to General Denikin actually did so a little earlier than August 20, before the fall of Riga, in fact, because on August 21, immediately after its fall, a wire went out to the headquarters of all the fronts from General Quartermaster Romanovsky, Kornilov's closest aide, with official instructions [14] concerning the posting of officers for the special "Mortar and Bombing" course. It is clear that by the time these instructions went out, all the headquarters must have been informed of the real nature of the "course."

The young officers selected for this special mission began to arrive in Petrograd about ten days before Kornilov's ultimatum. Some of them were later arrested, and they testified before the Special Commission set up to investigate the affair. The testimony of one young officer is preserved in the Soviet archives and is reproduced in a collection of documents on the Kornilov affair: [15]

On August 25, 1917, I was instructed to go to headquarters for the alleged purpose of "studying British mortar and machine-gun techniques." I arrived at headquarters on August 27 and was met at the station by Captain of the General Staff Rozhenko, who instructed me to report to the staff immediately to test British made mortar and bomb throwers. At the same time he gave me the following directive: a Bolshevik uprising was expected shortly in Petrograd. The Bolsheviks intended to arrest the Provisional Government and seize power. Therefore, we officers were being sent there to restore order. He then gave me names and addresses to contact in Petrograd for further instructions and orders, namely: (1) Sergievskaya Street, No. 46, General Federov; (2) Furshtadskaya No. 28, flat 3, Colonel Sidorenko or Cornet Kravchenko; (3) Fontanka No. 22, Colonel du Cimitière. As there were about forty-six of us, we were assigned a special coach. The train was filled with officers of different regiments of the Third and Tenth Armies. Captain Rozhenko told us that under various pretexts over three thousand officers were being sent to Petrograd from the regiments of various fronts.

Up to August 10, all preparations for the seizure of Petrograd, including the withdrawal of military units from the Northern Front at

---

[14] According to Romanovsky's fake instructions, the course was to be supervised by the "English officer Finlayston" and was to last ten days.

[15] *Razgrom Kornilskogo myatezha*, Akademii Nauk SSSR, Moscow, 1959.

the height of the German offensive and their transfer to Petrograd and Moscow, were carried out by Generals Kornilov, Krymov, and Romanovsky without the knowledge of General Lukomsky.

General Lukomsky has given a vivid description of his role in his memoirs: [16]

On August 6 or 7, if I remember correctly, General Romanovsky conveyed to me a request from General Kornilov to concentrate the 3rd Cavalry Corps, with the "Wild Division," in the area of Nevel-Novye Sokolniki-Velikiye Luki.

These units formed the reserve of the Rumanian Front. A few days before, I had had a conversation with General Kornilov, during which we had discussed the necessity of strengthening the Northern Front by moving considerable cavalry forces from the Rumanian front.

"But why move them to the area of Nevel-Novye Sokolniki-Velikiye Luki?" I asked General Romanovsky.

"I can not tell you why. I am only transmitting General Kornilov's order."

"When did you receive this order and through what channels?"

"Yesterday, after eleven o'clock at night, General Kornilov called me and told me to transmit this order to you this morning."

All this seemed very strange. Why had this order been sent to me through the intermediary of the Quarter-Master-General, Romanovsky, instead of being given to me directly, and why were the troops to be concentrated in this particular area? I went to Kornilov, told him that General Romanovsky had conveyed his order to me, and begged him to explain why he had chosen to concentrate the cavalry in this area.

General Kornilov replied that he wished to concentrate the cavalry on a point from which it would be easy to move it, in case of necessity, to either the Northern or the Western Front. The area in question was quite suitable for this purpose.

I said that we had no reason to fear for our Western Front, where there were sufficient reserves at hand, and that it would be far better to concentrate the cavalry in the neighborhood of Pskov.

Kornilov, however, kept to his decision.

"Very well," I said, "I shall make the necessary dispositions; but I have an impression that you are keeping something from me. The area you have chosen would be perfectly suitable for moving the cavalry to Petrograd or Moscow, but I do not consider it to be the right one if it is only a question

[16] *Memoirs of the Russian Revolution,* in *Arkhiv Russkoi Revolyutsii,* **Vol. I.**

of reinforcing the Northern Front. If I am not mistaken, and you are, indeed, keeping something back, I must beg you either to let me go to the Front, or else to inform me of all your plans and intentions. A chief of staff can only remain at his post if he enjoys the full confidence of his commander."

Kornilov thought for a moment, then replied:

"You are right, I do have other reasons, which I will discuss with you later. Please issue the orders at once and ask the commander of the Third Corps, General Krymov, to report to me immediately. I will discuss it more fully with you when I return from Petrograd."

Upon his return from Petrograd, General Kornilov brought up the subject again:

"As you well know," he said, "all the reports of our Intelligence show that a new Bolshevik uprising may be expected to take place on August 28 or 29. Germany urgently needs to sign a separate peace treaty with Russia, so that she can deploy the armies on our front against the French and the English. The German Bolshevik agents, both those who have already established themselves here and those who were sent to us in sealed railway carriages by the Germans, will do everything in their power to organize a coup d'état and take over the supreme authority in the country.

"I feel sure, when I think of the events of April 20 and July 3 and 4, that the spineless weaklings who form the Provisional Government will be swept away. If by some miracle they should remain in power, the leaders of the Bolsheviks and the Soviet will go unpunished through the connivance of such men as Chernov.

"It is time to put an end to all of this. It is time to hang the German agents and spies led by Lenin, to break up the Soviet, and break it up in such a way that it will never meet again anywhere!

"You were right. My chief object in moving the Cavalry Corps is to have it at hand in the vicinity of Petrograd, so that I can move it into the city at the end of August. Then, if this Bolshevik demonstration takes place, I can deal with the traitors appropriately.

"I intend to place General Krymov at the head of this operation. I know that if necessary he would not hesitate to hang all the members of the Soviet.

"As to the Provisional Government, I have no intention of going against them; I hope to come to terms with them at the last moment. But I cannot tell them about it beforehand, because men like Kerensky and Chernov will not agree, and they will try to wreck the whole operation. Unless I come to an agreement with Kerensky and Savinko, I may have to strike at the Bolsheviks without their consent. But afterwards they will be the first to thank me for this, and it will then be possible to form a strong government in Russia, free from all traitors.

"I have no personal ambitions; I only want the salvation of Russia. I will gladly submit to a strong Provisional Government when it has been purged of all undesirable elements.

"Do you believe me when I say that I want nothing for myself? Will you go with me all the way?"

Knowing General Kornilov to be absolutely honest and devoted to his country, I replied that I believed what he said, that I shared his views, and would follow him to the end. . . .

"I did not speak to you about it before," Kornilov continued, "because I assumed it was your desire to return to the front. Now I am asking you to remain with me as chief of staff. I have already made some preparations, and Colonel Lebedev and Captain Rozhenko are working out the details under my direction. You have too much on your hands as chief of staff and I do not ask you to help with the preparations. I shall look after everything myself, and everything will be done properly. My orderly, Zavoyko, and my aide-de-camp, Colonel Golitsyn, are privy to all my plans."

Unfortunately, I agreed to this but did not take part in working out the details of the operation. As became apparent later, General Kornilov, for lack of time, did not direct the preparations in person. Those who were called upon to execute the plan—including General Krymov—were more than careless in their handling of the operation, and that is one of the reasons why it subsequently failed.

General Krymov arrived at military headquarters on August 12, but General Kornilov had no time to talk things over with him before leaving for the State Conference in Moscow. He therefore asked General Krymov to accompany him to Moscow in order to discuss the matter on the way.

The final agreement between Generals Kornilov, Krymov, and Kaledin [17] was reached in Moscow, in the Supreme Commander's private train.

Because General Krymov's presence in Moscow was kept secret, Milyukov makes no mention of him in his *History of the Second Russian Revolution,* when he refers to his talks with Kornilov and Kaledin in Moscow, and expresses the opinion that it was during the State

[17] Hetman of the Don Cossacks.

Conference that they coordinated their plans for military action against the government.

On August 23, upon his return from his meeting with me in Petrograd, Vladimir Lvov visited Aladin in the National Hotel in Moscow, where he also found I. A. Dobryinsky.[18] Shortly after his arrival, an orderly delivered a letter from Headquarters, which Aladin opened and read. It was an order from the Supreme Commander for General Kaledin, instructing him to begin moving his Don Cossacks toward Moscow. The order was immediately transmitted to him.[19]

The plan to seize Petrograd and set up a military dictatorship had been worked out before the Moscow State Conference. By the second half of August, the deadline for Vladimir Lvov's resignation, suggested to him by Novosiltsev and Shulgin, was rapidly approaching. The time had come for the military conspirators to make closer contact with the civilian groups that knew of and approved the proposed coup d'état.

During the Moscow State Conference, "a group of young officers from Headquarters," writes S. I. Shidlovsky,[20] "expressed the desire to have a confidential talk with some of the more prominent Duma members. A small secret meeting was arranged, during which the officers announced that they had been delegated by Kornilov to inform the Duma that everything was ready at Headquarters and the front for the removal of Kerensky. Only the consent of the Duma was lacking for the plot to be carried out in its name and, so to speak, with its blessing.

"The Duma members met this proposal with great caution and wanted to know in detail what had been organized and how. After prolonged questioning, they arrived at the unanimous conclusion that the plot could not really be taken seriously. Therefore, they refused even to speak with Kornilov. Of all the Duma members, only Milyu-

---

[18] A rather mysterious figure, who had once worked in the Ministry of Agriculture and who now served as a courier between Kornilov and Kaledin.

[19] On August 27 General Kornilov sent the following telegram to Kaledin: "Kerensky has advised all railroads by wire of my dismissal as supreme commander and of the appointment of Klembovsky. I have refused to give up the Supreme Command. Denikin and Baluyev are with me [this was not true as regards Baluyev] and have protested to the Provisional Government about my dismissal. Klembovsky has decided to refuse the government's official appointment. If you and your Cossacks support me please inform the Provisional Government by telegram with copy to me."

[20] Chairman of the Progressive Bloc in the fourth Duma.

kov went to see Kornilov in his private train. The contents of their discussion are unknown to me." [21]

The Duma members, being politically mature, refused to discuss with General Kornilov a plot which they considered inept, but they did nothing to stop the conspiracy and did not even bother to inform the person most concerned—myself!

Milyukov did not disclose the substance of his long conversation with Kornilov and Kaledin until after Denikin and Finisov had partially admitted the truth about their role in the affair,[22] when he wrote that the conversation had indeed taken place during the Moscow State Conference and that he had mentioned it in the second part of his *History of the Second Russian Revolution:*

On the basis of Kornilov's own words I had said in my book that Kornilov was already quite clear in his mind about the timing of his open breach with the Kerensky government, and *had even set the date for it as August 27* [italics mine]. This puts a rather different complexion on recently published accounts which are not quite in accord with my testimony. I have also mentioned, and would like to recall now, another aspect of our conversation: I warned General Kornilov that in my view a breach with Kerensky was untimely, and he did not strongly dispute it. I said the same to Kaledin, whom I also met at about that time. This would seem to have been in line with Kornilov's intention, which only later became known, to retain Kerensky in the Cabinet.

I can add yet another point to what I have already said: General Kornilov did not go into any details about his proposed coup, but he expressed a desire for the backing of the Constitutional Democrats, if only by the reorganization of ministers at the crucial moment. I replied that we would be unable to support him if, as his tone seemed to indicate, his action was going to involve bloodshed or violence. He gave no definite answer to this. Finally, I pointed out to General Kornilov that it was unwise to surround himself with individuals such as Aladin, whom I had seen leaving his coach as I was being ushered in. . . .[23]

Thus, after his conversation with Kornilov, Milyukov was well aware of the date set for the coup, of the proposal to remove the Con-

21 S. I. Shidlovsky, *Vospominaniya,* Vol. II (Berlin, 1923).

22 The account was published in his *Poslednie Novosti,* March 6, 1937.

23 Despite this unflattering reference to Aladin, Milyukov was evidently unaware of the fact that Aladin had come to General Kornilov as an important secret envoy from England, and not in the capacity of a former Duma member.

stitutional Democrats from the Provisional Government, and of the planned use of violence. But he chose to remain silent.

Shidlovsky and the other leaders of the Progressive Bloc, who had talked with the young officers sent by General Kornilov, adopted the same attitude. If I had known of Kornilov's duplicity, and had been given two weeks' notice of his intention to attempt a coup d'état, I would have been able to put an end to his dangerous game with the destiny of Russia. But Milyukov and the other people whom Kornilov had made privy to his plans remained silent out of sympathy with his designs and willingness to give him at least passive support.

Before his return to headquarters Kornilov summoned to his coach Putilov, Vyshnegradsky, and Meshchersky,[24] the heads of the Union for the Economic Revival of Russia. Meshchersky was not in Moscow, so only Putilov and Vyshnegradsky attended the meeting. An account of this secret midnight meeting was eventually given by Putilov,[25] after the disclosures of Denikin, Milyukov, and others. The account does not present the whole truth, however, and it even contains a number of actual falsehoods, such as that Kornilov said he was acting "in full accord with Kerensky," that they had not seen the General before the Moscow State Conference, and that the Supreme Commander did not know of the funds raised by them, but had turned to them because of their wealth, and so forth.

But the main point of the meeting still emerges quite clearly from Putilov's account. The General told them that he was sending a corps to Petrograd to break up the Bolsheviks, but that it was not enough to break them up. They must also be arrested. To avoid street fighting and to prevent the Bolsheviks from escaping from their headquarters in the Smolny Institute, support had to be organized for General Krymov inside the city.[26] Kornilov also asked for money to accommodate and feed his men, and he was told that funds were already available and could be handed over to him any time. To this he replied that direct contact would have to be avoided in this matter, and went on: "I give you the names of four colonels of the General Staff: Sidorin, du Cimitière, Pronin, and . . . [Putilov suppressed the fourth name,

---

[24] A director of the "International" Bank.

[25] *Poslednie Novosti* (Paris), January 24, 1937.

[26] The funds given to the Republican Center by Putilov in July were intended precisely for this purpose.

that of Colonel Novosiltsev]. Should any one of the four contact you, you will know that he is from me."

In his memoirs, Vladimir Dmitrievich Nabokov,[27] a prominent member of the Cadet Central Committee, describes as follows the events
preceding August 27:

It was on Tuesday [August 22] of the week of Kornilov's march on
Petrograd that Vladimir Lvov phoned me in the morning to say that he
would like to see me on an important and urgent matter. He said that he
had wanted to discuss it with Milyukov, the chairman of the Cadet Central
Committee, and M. M. Vinaver, the vice-chairman, but that since he had
not been able to find either of them, he would like to talk with me instead.

I was somewhat late in coming home and found Lvov waiting in my
study. After greeting me with a mysterious and important air, he took out
a sheet of paper and handed it to me silently. I did not make a copy of the
text, but I remember it very vividly: "The General who sat across the table
from you requests that you warn the Constitutional Democrats in the Cabinet to resign on such and such a date in August [the 27th in the original
note] both to create added difficulties for the government and in the
interests of their personal safety."

The message bore no signature. I asked: "What does it mean, and what
am I supposed to do about it?"

"Just pass it on to the Constitutional Democratic ministers."

"But how can they possibly pay any attention to an anonymous warning
like this?"

"Don't question me, I have no right to disclose more," Lvov replied.

"In that case, let me repeat, I do not see how I can act upon it."

After a number of enigmatic hints Lvov finally said that he was going to
speak openly, but made me promise to keep the information to myself.
Otherwise, he warned, I ran the danger of being arrested. I replied that I
should like to reserve the right to relate our conversation to Milyukov and
Kokoshkin [a member of the Provisional Government], to which he
immediately agreed. Then he said: "I am going straight from here to Kerensky with an *ultimatum* [italics mine]. A coup d'état is being prepared,
and a program has been drafted for a new regime with dictatorial powers.
Kerensky will be asked to accept this program. If he refuses, there will
be a complete break with him, and since I am close to Kerensky and
well-disposed toward him, I can only try to save his life." Lvov refused to

[27] *Vremennoye pravitel'stvo,* ARR I (1921), pp. 43–44.

give any further details in answer to my questions, insisting that he had already said too much. As far as I can recollect, Kornilov's name never came up in the conversation, but Lvov definitely said something to the effect that the ultimatum originated with Headquarters. As soon as our conversation was over, Lvov hurried off to Kerensky.

As far as I can judge from subsequently published accounts, during his first meeting with Kerensky Vladimir Lvov did not fulfill the mission of which he had spoken to me. I must add that I related the conversation that same night to Kokoshkin and Yureniev and to our other ministers [i.e., those who were Constitutional Democrats], whom I saw almost daily. I remember asking them to observe Kerensky's behavior at this evening cabinet meeting. Later they told me that Kerensky was his usual self. There was no difference in his behavior.

If Vladimir Nabokov had done his duty by reporting Lvov's visit immediately to me, it would still have been possible to prevent disaster. Instead, my colleagues in the cabinet held their peace and confined themselves to observing my behavior that night.

Lvov had not in fact transmitted the ultimatum to me during his first visit, because he was not supposed to. He had learned from a talk with I. A. Dobrynsky in Moscow that the question of a military dictatorship was to be discussed at a secret conference at Headquarters, to which Dobrynsky had been invited. Since he believed this solution of the growing political crisis would be fatal for Russia, Lvov proposed a reorganization of the government to include Kornilov and myself. In his memoirs Lvov writes that Dobrynsky agreed to put forward this plan at the meeting at Headquarters. Here is how Lvov describes what followed: [28]

On August 20th, Dobrynsky came to see me again in my hotel room and jubilantly announced that my plan had been accepted at the secret conference. True, they were inclined toward a military dictatorship, but he (Dobrynsky) had delivered a speech in defense of my plan, and the conference had finally approved it. Then he added that late at night he had been taken to the office of the Supreme Commander, where Kornilov had told him confidentially that he had decided to become a military dictator but that no one was to know this. When he bade him farewell, Kornilov said:

[28] *Poslednie Novosti* (Paris), November 30, 1920.

"Remember that you did not see me and I did not see you." Dobrynsky admitted that he was worried about the situation at Headquarters. "Just the same, we must act in the spirit of my plan," I retorted. Dobrynsky agreed. I telephoned my brother, N. N. Lvov, to come over immediately. When he arrived I told him what was going on and suggested that he approach the Moscow political groups on the formation of a national cabinet. He promised to act promptly.

On the following day, August 21, Dobrynsky told me that Aladin wanted to meet me. Aladin arrived wearing the uniform of a British lieutenant. He began at once to complain about Kerensky, saying that the latter had refused to see him although he, Aladin, wanted to tell him the whole truth. Then Aladin told me that he had received a letter from Zavoyko at Headquarters.

"Who is Zavoyko?" I asked.

"Kornilov's orderly," answered Aladin. "The letter contains a message of paramount importance. I have spent two hours at Prince Lvov's waiting to speak to him confidentially, but there were so many people there that it proved impossible."

"Could you tell me what the message is about?" I inquired.

Aladin showed me a piece of paper which read: "At lunch the General who was sitting opposite me said: 'It would be a good idea to warn the Constitutional Democrats to resign from the Provisional Government by August 27th in order to place the Provisional Government in a difficult situation and to avoid trouble for themselves.' "

"Who was the general?" I asked.

"Lukomsky."

"And where did the lunch take place?"

"At the Supreme Commander's."

"Why would a letter from a common orderly have any weight at all?"

"The point is that Kornilov never writes letters himself," explained Dobrynsky, "everything goes through Zavoyko, and a letter from Zavoyko is equivalent to an order from Kornilov."

I gasped. I could see the importance of Zavoyko's warning.

"The warning is of such great importance," I said, "that I am willing to go to Petrograd and transmit the message to the Central Committee of the Constitutional Democrats."

Aladin agreed.

Then I told Aladin about my plan and sought his opinion on the advisability of my going to Kerensky and attempting to persuade him to reorganize the Cabinet so as to appease Headquarters. Aladin agreed that it would be very good to get Kerensky to enter into negotiations. "Perhaps you will succeed in preventing something that is being prepared for August 27th."

"What is being prepared?" I asked.

But Aladin said that he did not know.

After his departure I asked Dobrynsky again whether or not I should approach Kerensky with my plan. Dobrynsky eagerly supported a meeting with Kerensky, and added that the secret conference at Headquarters had authorized him to ask just that of me.

After consulting his brother, Vladimir Lvov decided to come to see me in Petrograd. That same night, August 21, he left for the capital to transmit Zavoyko's message to the Central Committee of the Constitutional Democrats and to seek an appointment with me. The next day he had the meeting with Nabokov which has already been described, after which he saw me and then returned at once to Moscow.

Back in Moscow on August 23 he told his brother that I had consented to the formation of a national cabinet. It turned out that his brother had already discussed the matter with some political leaders, including V. Maklakov.[29] "It is difficult for us to side with Kerensky," Nicholas Lvov said, "but we shall do so."

After his brother had left, Lvov went to Dobrynsky's room, where he found him in conversation with Aladin. According to Vladimir Lvov the two were pleased with "Kerensky's consent" to negotiate with other political leaders and with Headquarters.[30]

It was at that moment that the orderly from Headquarters handed Aladin the letter containing General Kornilov's order to Kaledin that caused Lvov to leave at once for Headquarters on his conciliatory mission. Dobrynsky approved, and the two of them left that very night for a meeting with General Kornilov.

But Vladimir Lvov was not able to get an interview with the Supreme Commander on August 24, nor was he able to obtain a return ticket to Moscow! General Kornilov was in no hurry to receive "Kerensky's envoy," partly because Zavoyko, his political mentor, was absent that day.

While Lvov was rushing back and forth between Petrograd, Mos-

---

[29] The leader of the right wing in the Cadet Party.

[30] In his evidence of September 14, 1917, before the Extraordinary Commission of Inquiry on the Kornilov affair, Vladimir Lvov said: "Although Kerensky did not especially authorize me to negotiate with Kornilov I felt that it was all right to speak on behalf of Kerensky in so far as on the whole he was willing to reorganize the government."

cow, and Mogilev from August 21 to August 24, the vital decisions were being made at Headquarters. In the words of Finisov:

"Everything was ready in Petrograd when a telegram was received from Headquarters on August 21 [the day Riga fell] summoning the leaders of the Republican Center to give our views. Nikolaevsky was out of town and Colonels Sidorin and du Cimitière were unable to leave the military organization, so Lipsky and I were asked to go to Headquarters. That same night a meeting took place with Colonel R. Raupakh, assistant prosecutor of the Petrograd Military District, at Lipsky's estate at Sablino, near Petrograd. Final plans were worked out with regard to the constitution of the new cabinet, agrarian reform, martial law in Petrograd, and so forth. With these draft plans we went to see General Kornilov at Headquarters.

At midnight Prince Trubetskoy ushered us into the study of the ex-Tsar [at Headquarters], where we were greeted by Generals Kornilov, Krymov, Romanovsky and Lukomsky, as well as another general and about four colonels.

General Kornilov informed us that he had just seen Savinkov and that he had agreed to everything. However, he said, the government was against General Krymov's appointment and the inclusion of the Wild Division in the corps that was being sent to the capital. General Kornilov also reported that Vladimir Lvov had arrived from Petrograd with a message, but that he had not as yet been able to talk with him.

Then we gave our detailed views, presenting among other things the new list of ministers. Kornilov made a few changes, for instance replacing Yureniev as minister of transport with E. Shubersky.[31]

We pointed out the extreme bitterness among the officers and asked that Kerensky be invited to Headquarters in order to protect him, since his assassination could be disastrous.

Kornilov approved the entire plan. He added that he would discuss the final constitution of the government with Kerensky. This meeting took place during the night of August 23rd.[32]

Personally, I do not believe that the participants in this decisive nocturnal meeting were taken in by Kornilov. They knew he was playing a double game. He could not have told them that Savinkov "had just seen him and that everything was coordinated," because the day

[31] Shubersky, deputy minister of transport, was attached to Headquarters and was a party to the conspiracy.
[32] *Poslednie Novosti* (Paris), March 6, 1937.

before he had definitely promised Savinkov and Baranovsky that he would place the Cavalry Corps at the disposal of the Provisional Government, that he would not appoint General Krymov to command it, nor include in it the "Wild Division."

Yet on August 25 General Krymov, in his capacity as commander-in-chief of a "special Petrograd army," issued a secret order, declaring martial law in Petrograd, Kronstadt, the Petrograd Military District, and Finland. At the same time, he sent a secret order to Lieutenant General Bagration, Commander of the "Wild Division," directing him to suppress the revolutionary workers and soldiers of Petrograd.

General Kornilov finally found time to see Vladimir Lvov late on August 24. Lvov expounded his plan for a compromise and proposed the formation of a national government. The General's reply was rather vague. He said that he had pledged his support to me in a private conversation during the Moscow State Conference, but that I was too dependent on the Soviets, and so forth. General Kornilov concluded: "Anyway, come and see me tomorrow morning at 10:00 for a final answer." Here is Lvov's own account [33] of this second meeting:

At 10:00 A.M. the next day I walked up the stairs of the Governor's Mansion (Kornilov's residence), and an elderly man in the uniform of a volunteer met me on the top step. He was tall and well built, and his dark hair was streaked with gray. He introduced himself as "Zavoyko." He apologized on behalf of the Supreme Commander for asking me to wait. We made ourselves comfortable in a room adjacent to Kornilov's study. . . .

"I am planning to convene a National Assembly (*Zemsky sobor*)," he told me. I stared at him in astonishment, wondering who on earth he was to convene a "national assembly." While Zavoyko was expounding his views on the "national assembly," I was called into Kornilov's study and sat down by his side at his desk. Kornilov spoke firmly and resolutely. The uncertainty of yesterday was gone.

"Tell Kerensky," Kornilov said, "that Riga fell because the proposals submitted by me to the Provisional Government are still waiting for approval. The army is indignant about the capture of Riga. We must not waste any more time. Regimental committees must not have the right to interfere with military orders, Petrograd must be included in the sphere of military operations and placed under martial law, all units at the front and in the rear must be subordinated to the Supreme Commander. According to intel-

[33] *Poslednie Novosti,* December 17, 1920.

ligence reports received by me, the Bolsheviks are planning to stage an uprising in Petrograd between August 28th and September 2nd. The aim of this uprising is to overthrow the Provisional Government, proclaim the transfer of power to the Soviet, conclude peace with Germany, and surrender the Baltic Fleet to Germany.... In the face of this terrible threat to Russia I see no other solution than the immediate transfer of power from the Provisional Government to the Supreme Commander."

I interrupted Kornilov. "Do you mean the transfer of military power only, or of civilian power as well?"

"Both!" Kornilov said.

"May I make a note of that?"

"Go ahead," said Kornilov, handing me paper and pencil.

"Perhaps it might be preferable to combine the office of Supreme Commander with that of President of the Council of Ministers," I suggested.

Kornilov was embarrassed. "Well, your suggestion is not impossible," he said. "Of course, it has to come before the Constituent Assembly."

He continued: "Warn Kerensky and Savinkov that I cannot guarantee their personal safety unless they come to Headquarters, where I shall personally see that they are well protected ... I don't care who is appointed Supreme Commander as long as power is transferred to him by the Provisional Government."

I said: "If it is a question of a military dictatorship, then you are the logical choice for dictator."

Kornilov nodded and said: "At any rate, the Romanovs will ascend to the throne only over my dead body. As soon as power is transferred, I shall form a cabinet. I no longer trust Kerensky, he does not do anything."

"How about Savinkov?" I asked.

"No, I don't trust Savinkov either. I don't really know whom he wants to stab in the back, Kerensky or me," Kornilov replied.

"If that is what you think of Savinkov, why didn't you arrest him yesterday when he was here?"

Kornilov did not answer. After a pause he remarked: "However, I don't mind offering Savinkov the portfolio of Minister of War and Kerensky the portfolio of Minister of Justice ..."

At this point, to my astonishment, Zavoyko entered the office unannounced and interrupted the Supreme Commander to say, "No, not Minister of Justice but Vice-President of the Council of Ministers."

I looked in amazement first at Kornilov and then at the orderly. "Do you want me to relay our conversation to Kerensky?"

My question was directed at Kornilov, but it was Zavoyko who answered: "Of course, of course! A legal assumption of power is important."

I bade farewell to Kornilov and left the office.

As I was leaving the Mansion, Zavoyko invited me to lunch. I found Dobrynsky and another gentleman waiting when we arrived at Zavoyko's. He was introduced as Professor Yakovlev. Zavoyko took out a sheet of paper and began reading aloud Kornilov's manifesto to the army, in which Kornilov, referring to himself as the son of a Cossack, said that he was assuming supreme power to save the country. Then Zavoyko started reading Kornilov's proclamation to the soldiers. Each soldier was promised eight dessiatines [34] of land upon discharge from the army. This, it turned out, was the agrarian reform drafted by Professor Yakovlev. Zavoyko gave me a copy of both documents. I put them in my pocket, wondering why he wanted me to have them.

Lvov goes on to relate that Zavoyko scribbled on a piece of paper "Kerensky Vice-President" and continued with a grotesque list of the future cabinet, which was to include himself, Aladin, and Filonenko.[35] Lvov, quite taken aback by this procedure, suggested it might be better to call various political leaders to Headquarters for consultations before the formation of a cabinet. Thereupon Zavoyko urged Lvov to invite anyone he wished to come to Headquarters and suggested that he do so on behalf of the Supreme Commander. The following telegram was accordingly dispatched: "General Kornilov invites outstanding party and civic leaders, particularly Rodzianko, to proceed immediately to Headquarters. Subject of discussion: the formation of a cabinet. Immediate response is of paramount importance. Advise Prince Golitsin at Headquarters as to number of persons coming and time of arrival. Signed: V. Lvov."

Then Zavoyko and Dobrynsky drove Lvov to the railway station, and Zavoyko repeated to him the contents of the ultimatum he was to present to me the next evening (August 26).

After handing over Kornilov's ultimatum, Lvov told me that he might be late for our conversation with Kornilov. Then, without informing me, he went to see Milyukov to warn him of the alleged Bolshevik uprising. But Milyukov assured him that there would be no such uprising. Lvov, bewildered to hear Milyukov confirm what I had told him, pulled out Kornilov's manifesto and proclamation and

[34] A dessiatine is about 2.7 acres.

[35] The Provisional Government's commissar at Headquarters, who joined the conspiracy.

showed them to Milyukov. Milyukov's reaction was: "I don't like it a bit."

In desperation, the conspirators were eventually driven to try to provoke a Bolshevik uprising. This grotesque episode is described by Finisov in *Poslednie Novosti* of March 6, 1937:

It had become known that the Bolsheviks had decided to postpone their uprising indefinitely. It was impossible for us to proceed with our plans without this pretext. The situation would have become very difficult for us, since General Krymov's regiments were already heading toward Petrograd. It would have been a crime not to take advantage of this. If there were no grounds for action, such grounds simply had to be created. A special group was instructed to incite a "Bolshevik uprising," i.e., to sack the Sennaya Ploshchad and thus to provoke street riots. In response to this, the operations of the officers' organizations and General Krymov's Cossack regiments were to be launched that same day. The task was entrusted to General Sidorin. He was given the sum of 100,000 rubles for this purpose, but he spent only 26,00 rubles [on the preparation of a "Bolshevik riot"] . . . We, that is, Colonel du Cimitière and I, were to signal the command to proceed with the "riot" by sending a coded message to Petrograd after meeting with General Krymov.

On August 28 at 4:00 P.M., Finisov and Colonel du Cimitière left Petrograd to contact General Krymov. They found him in Zaozerye, a small village near Luga, and told him about the sham Bolshevik riot. General Krymov was all for it, since his thoroughly indoctrinated Cossacks would not otherwise march on Petrograd. At 8:00 A.M. on August 29, a motorcyclist was dispatched via Gatchina with the coded message to General Sidorin: "Act at once according to instructions." However, Sidorin decided first to consult General Alekseyev, who vehemently objected to the operation and declared: "If you proceed with this plan I shall shoot myself. And before I die I shall leave an explanatory note." Sidorin gave in, called off all the arrangements, and returned the unspent 74,000 rubles to the Republican Center. Even so, an attempt was made to provoke an incident on the Sennaya Ploshchad.

Ataman Dutov later told Vladimir Lvov that he had tried to incite a "Bolshevik" uprising, urging the crowd to loot stores, but that nothing came of it.

There is no doubt that, after the conspiratorial organization in Petrograd had renounced the idea of a sham Bolshevik riot, General Alekseyev realized that a "shock attack" on the capital had failed and that further military operations should be immediately suspended.

On August 29, at 11:00 A.M., Colonel Baranovsky brought me a dispatch from Colonel Voronovich, commander of the Luga garrison, reporting that the Cossacks under General Krymov had refused to march on Petrograd and were threatening their commander. It was essential to prevent any arbitrary action against the General, and I sent Colonel Samarin of the General Staff, a friend of Krymov's, to Luga to bring Krymov to Petrograd and hand him over to me at the Winter Palace. After reporting to Colonel Voronovich in Luga, Samarin proceeded to Krymov's headquarters.

It was not until 1936 that I learned [36] that Samarin had stopped on the way at General Alekseyev's office for "instructions." General Alekseyev "sanctioned" my order to bring Krymov to Petrograd, but added that he wished to see Krymov first.

During the night of August 30, Krymov consulted with Alekseyev. He reported to me at 10:00 the next morning. My conversation with Krymov was witnessed by both deputy ministers of war, Colonels Yakubovich and Prince Tumanov as well as by I. Shablovsky, chairman of the Extraordinary Commission of Inquiry into the Kornilov Affair.

General Krymov, an honest and gallant soldier, began the conversation by saying that his corps had been moving on Petrograd to assist the Provisional Government and that no hostilities against the government had been planned. Evidently as a result of his nocturnal discussion with General Alekseyev, he was trying to camouflage the reason for the march on the capital by repeating the false version spread about by Kornilov's friends. However, it was not in Krymov's nature to tell lies. All at once he broke off and pulled out a folded sheet of paper with the remark: "That is the order, Sir."

I read Order No. 128 and then handed it to the chairman of the Commission. General Krymov proceeded to admit that he had stayed at Headquarters in the early part of August when the military arrange-

[36] See *Poslednie Novosti,* November 14, 1936.

ments for the march on the capital were being worked out. He also revealed that, according to the plan adopted at that time, the city was to be divided into military sectors, and that he had been appointed commander of a special "Petrograd Army" by General Kornilov.

I am sure that he was beginning to find his situation unbearable, for he had become hopelessly involved in falsehoods. In the first place, he had not made an open admission of his part in the affair, and in the second, Clause 4 of the order began with a false announcement about Bolshevik disorders in the capital.

I questioned him as to why he had resorted to this blatant invention. His answer was vague—evidently he did not want to compromise his accomplices in the capital, who had advised him that a Bolshevik riot would be staged to coincide with his arrival in Petrograd.

General Krymov left my office a free man. The only restriction imposed upon him was a summons by Shablovsky to testify at 5:00 P.M. that day before the Extraordinary Commission of Inquiry. But General Krymov never appeared. He went to the home of Captain Zhuravsky, an intimate family friend, and there he shot himself. He left an explanatory note which was handed over to the Extraordinary Commission on Inquiry and which is probably still preserved in the archives of the case.

The Krymov case helped to reveal the double game of the generals. Their original plan had been to seize the capital, taking the Provisional Government by surprise. And even though they soon realized that the Provisional Government could not be fooled, they persisted in their folly, even after the failure of the plot. Krymov was the only one who had the courage to face reality.

General Kornilov adamantly refused to admit the truth. An interview he had with the French correspondent Claude Anet [37] shows the extent of Kornilov's mendacity. Kornilov stated:

If I had been the conspirator that Kerensky made me out to be; if I had been plotting to overthrow the government, I would naturally have taken the necessary measures. At the appointed moment I would have been at the head of my troops, and I do not doubt that I could have entered Petrograd without firing a shot. But in actual fact I was *not* plotting anything

[37] The interview took place immediately after the coup, before Kornilov's arrest, and is described in Anet's book *La Révolution russe*, Vol. II.

and *not* preparing anything. When I unexpectedly received Kerensky's telegram sent on the night of August 26 [summoning him to Petrograd], I lost twenty-four hours. As you know, I assumed that the post office had garbled it, or that there had been a revolt in Petrograd, or that the Bolsheviks had captured the post office. So I waited for confirmation or denial [of the telegram]. In that way I wasted a whole day and night; I let Kerensky and Nekrasov get the advantage. . . . The railroad workers had been ordered to prevent me from getting a train to the outskirts of the city. I could have got a train to Mogilev, but I would have been arrested in Vitebsk. I could have used a car, but it is three hundred miles to Petrograd, over poor roads. Be that as it may, despite all difficulties, I could still have taken action by Monday, made up for lost time, and rectified all the mistakes. But I was sick, I had a bad attack of fever and lost my usual energy.

In this whole absurdly contradictory statement, there is only one point that is true: my night telegram summoning Kornilov to the capital led to a fatal hesitation on the part of the conspirators. They lost their heads and panicked.

It was then that Zavoyko's slanderous introductory passage was added to the text of Kornilov's reply.

The whole first part of the Prime Minister's telegram, No. 4163, is a set of lies; it was not I who sent Duma Member Lvov to Kerensky, but the Prime Minister who sent him to me as an envoy. A witness to this fact is Duma Member Alexis Aladin. We are thus dealing with a great *provocation* which endangers our country.

This invention of Zavoyko's was subsequently used by the wily General Alekseyev in his campaign of slander against the Provisional Government and me personally.

The revelations of Denikin and Sidorin, as well as Finisov's memoirs—all published in 1936 and 1937—leave no doubt as to General Alekseyev's central role in the Kornilov affair, which first came to light in the letter written to Milyukov on September 12, 1917. He was chief adviser to General Kornilov and to the other military leaders of the proposed coup d'état, including Sidorin and Krymov. He also prepared the political ground for Kornilov's seizure of power. In the crucial days of the affair he was in constant touch with General Kornilov through Captain Shapron, who was Kornilov's son-in-law.[38]

[38] Shapron later became a White Army general.

On the morning of August 28, after having ordered General Sidorin to discontinue his preparations for the sham Bolshevik uprising, Alekseyev called on me, accompanied by Milyukov, to offer his services as mediator between Kornilov and me. Both he and Milyukov thought that this would help Kornilov, in whose ultimate victory they firmly believed. Later in the day Alekseyev summoned Maklakov and asked him to leave immediately for Headquarters for a conference about the formation of a government under Kornilov. Maklakov writes as follows: [39]

. . . General Alekseyev invited me on the telephone to come to see him. I found him in his train. Unlike me, he thought the hours of the government were numbered. According to him, it was merely a matter of deciding what Kornilov would have to do after his victory. He asked for my opinion on the subject. I did not share his "optimism"; however—I had made up my mind about the political situation some time before. In my opinion, the key issue was not concerned with individuals, but with the nature of the regime. If one persisted in maintaining a state of "revolution," the [revolutionary] process would continue and the cup would have to be drained to the dregs. Therefore, if Kornilov wished to show himself stronger than the government, and if he were to succeed in stopping the revolution, he would have to revert to "legality." Legality ceased with the abdication of Grand Duke Michael, and it would therefore be necessary to go back to that point of departure. He should have been guided by the abdication manifesto of Emperor Nicholas II, which was the last legal act, and restored the monarchy, the constitution, and national representation; and he should have planned to govern in a truly constitutional spirit. . . . But if the new government which you wish to install instead of the present government will still be "revolutionary" in character it will not last long. Finally, I told him: "Is it not strange? Our roles seem to have reversed. You, a general, the Emperor's aide-de-camp, a member of his retinue, oppose monarchy. While I, a member of the opposition, demand it!" "You are right," said the general; "because I knew monarchy so well, I am against it." The remark impressed me. "That is possible," I answered in turn, "but I know our politicians better than you do, and that is why I don't expect anything from your venture. . . ."

In his book on the events in Russia of the autumn of 1917, Ferdinand Grenard, a French diplomat who was living in Russia at the

[39] V. A. Maklakov, *La Chute du regime tsariste: Interrogatoires* (*complètes rendus sténographiques,* p. 85).

time, and who knew the country well, had the following comment to make:

Russia's allies were blinded by their desire to keep Russia in the war at all costs. They were unable to see what was possible and what was impossible at that moment. Thus they only furthered Lenin's game by isolating the Prime Minister of the Provisional Government from the people to an even greater extent. They could not understand that in keeping Russia in the war, they had to accept the inevitable concomitant of internal strife and the instability of a transitional period. In badgering Kerensky with continual requests—almost demands—for the resumption of normal order in the country, they took no account of the circumstances in which he had to work, and in fact only contributed to the chaos with which he was trying to deal.[40] Bruce Lockhart, who served at the British Consulate in Moscow during the war, held the same opinion as to the policy of the Allies toward Russia.

The real intentions of the Allied powers toward the Provisional Government after the collapse of the monarchy will not become known until the secret files of the governments concerned are made public. One thing is already clear, however: After the fall of the Monarchy, the struggle on the Russian front against Germany gave rise to a bizarre alignment of forces which consisted not just of two opposing camps—Russia and the Allies versus Germany and Lenin—but of a triangle: Russia and the Provisional Government, Kornilov and Russia's allies, and Ludendorff and Lenin.

General Kornilov himself left the scene on August 30, but his sympathizers continued their attempts to undermine the Provisional Government.

There was one thing the Allies failed to take into account when they lent their support to Kornilov. It did not occur to them that, having seized power, the military dictator would not have had time for the imperialist war—all his efforts would have been directed toward civil war. Furthermore, they did not realize that some of Kornilov's Russian backers regarded the continuation of the war with Germany, after the "disintegration of the army by revolution," as utter madness. Indeed, by the autumn of 1917, not only the Bolsheviks, but a considerable section of the liberal and conservative opinion that had been favorable to Kornilov considered an Allied victory out of the ques-

[40] Ferdinand Grenard, *The Russian Revolution* (Paris, 1933).

tion. They regarded it, as Trotsky was to say just before Brest-Litovsk, as an "impossible assumption."

It seems that the Allies learned nothing from the Kornilov affair, and the ignominious failure of the plot did not cause them to modify their disloyal attitude to the Provisional Government. It was almost as though someone in Paris or London were actively encouraging the Ludendorff-Lenin cause and wished to bring about the collapse of a government that had continued to aid its "allies" on the battlefield under incredibly difficult circumstances.

On September 25, Tereshchenko gloomily informed me that the three Allied ambassadors wanted to deliver a verbal note. I arranged for an appointment the next day and invited two of my ministers, Konovalov and Tereshchenko, to be present.

The three-power note was read by the senior envoy, Sir George Buchanan. Only once before had I seen the Ambassador as nervous as he was on this occasion, and that was when he had had to report his government's decision to refuse the Tsar and his family residence on British territory in time of war. A true diplomat, Sir George was usually reserved and self-possessed. But if his fingers began to tremble slightly, if his cheeks acquired a delicate, almost girlish pinkness, if his voice became slightly strained, and a moist gleam came into his eyes, it meant that Sir George was under great emotional stress. All these signs were evident on this occasion.

Next to Sir George sat the new French ambassador, Noullens, who was the French Senate's expert on financial and agricultural affairs. Heaven knows how he came to be appointed to the post of ambassador! Unlike the British diplomat, Noullens was in fine form and was evidently delighted that the Allies had finally decided to be firm with the Provisional Government.

The Marchese Carlotti, the Italian ambassador, played the part of observer.

The collective note was very candid: It threatened to cut off all military aid to Russia [41] unless the Provisional Government took immediate steps, evidently in the spirit of the Kornilov program, to restore order at the front and in the country at large.

I was really incensed by this Allied ultimatum to restore the order

[41] It is interesting to note that Winston Churchill was the minister in charge of supplies in Britain at that time.

that had been disrupted by Kornilov's lunatic action. As I listened to the quavering, nervous voice of the British Ambassador, I raged with inward fury. I was sorely tempted to accept the note and make it public, together with a commentary on who had helped Kornilov, and when and how they had done it! But that would have been the end of the Alliance, and it would have meant placing guards around all the Allied embassies. I forced myself to keep calm.

I returned the note to Sir George and suggested that the ambassadors should pretend it had never existed; the Allies would not publish it in their respective countries and the Provisional Government would say nothing about it in Russia. My suggestion was promptly accepted, and they left, though hardly in the best of spirits.

Immediately afterwards, I went to see David Francis, the U. S. ambassador, and asked him to send President Wilson a cable thanking him for not associating the United States with this unfriendly act.

The next day Tereshchenko sent the following two messages in code to our representatives in Paris, London and Rome:

1.

The French, British, and Italian ambassadors asked for a joint meeting with the Prime Minister and made a statement in which they pointed out that recent events give cause for alarm regarding Russia's capacity for resistance and ability to continue the war, on account of which public opinion in the Allied countries might demand an explanation from their governments concerning the material aid given to Russia. In order to give the Allied governments an opportunity to reassure public opinion, the Russian government must prove by its actions its determination to restore discipline in the army and to reawaken its true fighting spirit, and must also ensure that the government apparatus continues to function smoothly both at the front and in the country at large. In conclusion, the Allied governments express their hope that the Russian government will carry out this task and thereby assure itself of full Allied support.

2.

In his reply to the three ambassadors the Prime Minister said that the Provisional Government will take steps to see that their move was not interpreted by the public in a way likely to cause ill feeling against the Allies. In so doing he noted that Russia's position at present was largely a legacy of the former regime, the government of which had been shown confidence, which it had perhaps not deserved, from abroad. He also drew attention to the consequences of the Allied delays in supplying munitions to our army; the results of such delays only made themselves felt at the front two or three months later. With regard to the war, A. F. K. pointed out that Russia always had regarded it as a nationwide issue and would continue to do so, and that it was therefore unnecessary to stress the sacrifices made by the Russian people. The imperialism of the Central Powers was the greatest danger to Russia, and the struggle against them must be waged in close collaboration with the Allies. Russia, which had suffered from the war more than anyone else, could not end it without a guarantee of her territorial immunity and independence, and would continue the struggle no matter how much international tension there was. As regards steps to restore the fighting fitness of our army, the Prime Minister noted that the visit today to Headquarters of the Ministers of War and Foreign Affairs was made in response to the need to draw up a suitable plan of action. In conclusion, A. F. K. pointed out with regard to the joint authorship of the note that Russia was still a great power.

These telegrams caused a great stir among the Allied governments. A few days later the Russian representatives cabled reports of meetings with the foreign ministers in the three Allied capitals. The most frank and informative of them was the telegram from Nabokov, our chargé d'affaires in London, describing his meeting with Lord Balfour, the British foreign secretary:

Referring to your telegram No. 4461, I have informed Balfour of its contents. I reminded him that at the beginning of August, at the last inter-allied conference, there had been some discussion about a joint démarche by the ambassadors in Petrograd and that at the time I had been able, with Thomas' support, to convince the Allies that such a step would be both untimely and harmful. I reported this to you in telegram No. 620. I said I regretted I had not been informed beforehand about the present move. Balfour said there could be no question of making the Allied move public. He added in strict confidence that he had been personally opposed to the idea and regretted that it had fallen to the British Ambassador, as doyen of the diplomatic corps, to convey the joint statement to our government. You will understand that Balfour felt awkward about "shifting the blame," since he was thereby implicating the other Allies. I gathered from his carefully chosen words that the initiative had not come from here. I would suggest that the Allies have subsequently realized their mistake and feel that the sooner the whole regrettable incident is forgotten, the better . . .

Tereshchenko sent the Russian ambassador in Washington the following special message:

The British, French and Italian ambassadors were received today by the Prime Minister and on behalf of their governments informed him that steps had to be taken to restore the fighting efficiency of the army. This move could not but make a painful impression on the Provisional Government, especially since our Allies are aware of the unremitting efforts of the government to carry on the war against our common enemy. I would ask you to tell Lansing in strict confidence how much the Provisional Government appreciates the American ambassador's abstention from participation in this joint note.

Nabokov's certainty that the Allies had realized their mistake proved to be unfounded. There was no improvement in the Allied attitude to the new, democratic government in Russia. The Allies were determined not to maintain relations of friendship and trust with Russia until power had passed to a strong military dictator. The Americans, too, aligned themselves with this policy, which impelled Russia toward Brest-Litovsk and all the disasters that followed for Europe. The following description by an American scholar of the change in America's attitude needs no comment:

In August 1917, the United States decided to abandon the Russia of the March Revolution until the "normal process" of the upheaval came to an end and order was restored by an "unrestricted military authority." This policy, born of apathy and lacking in insight, was further strengthened by the belief that Kerensky was paying too much heed to the Radicals, the conviction that "we cannot do anything about it," and the conclusion that "some strong person will eventually put an end to it all."

Ignoring the numerous warnings from all sides as to the extreme danger of this policy to the interests of the United States, the Americans refused to alter their stand until, in November 1917, the Bolsheviks seized power.[42]

Our European allies knew full well that from the very beginning Russia had been subjected to an intense blockade,[43] and that the

---

[42] William Appleman Williams, *Russo-American Relations, 1791–1947* (New York, Reinhard, 1952), p. 91.

[43] Since Turkey entered the war, Russia had been cut off from the Mediterranean, and Russia now found herself completely blockaded. She was receiving only 2 percent of her former imports and exporting only 1 percent of the previous amount. Vladivostok was the only port open for contact with the outside world. Murmansk as a port did not begin functioning till November 1916. During these years of almost complete

February Revolution was the result of the unexpected collapse of the Monarchy. They knew that the disappearance of the former regime had been accompanied by the collapse of the whole of the administrative machinery. They knew that it had all come about at the height of a war in which they desperately needed Russian participation. They knew that to save herself from annihilation and to safeguard her future, Revolutionary Russia was steadfastly fighting on. They knew that Russia had only been able to surmount the extreme difficulties of the first few weeks of the anarchic collapse by the will of the people, and that by August the new, people's Russia was internally strong. They knew, as Winston Churchill has said in his *The Unknown War*,[44] that victory would have been impossible without Russia. They knew that, as a result of the failure of the Allied offensive under General Nivelle in the spring of 1917, the fighting capacity of the Anglo-French armies had been quite paralyzed. They knew that the summer and autumn operations of the Russian armies in that year had saved the Western Front and upset the plan of the German General Staff to crush the Allies before the arrival of help from the United States.

Yet, knowing *all* this, the Allied governments established contact with those who were conspiring to replace the legal Russian Government by a dictatorship. Why did they do this? I did not learn the answer until long after I had left Russia forever.

NOTE

Order Issued by General Krymov, in Command of the Third Cavalry Corps [45]

1.

I hereby make public a copy of the telegram from the Minister-President and Supreme Commander.

2.

A copy of the telegram from the Supreme Commander, General Kornilov.

---

blockade for Russia, England and France had, of course, been receiving considerable supplies from Canada, the U. S. A., Australia, India, and other countries.

[44] Winston Churchill, *The Unknown War* (New York, C. Scribner's Sons, 1931).

[45] *The Worker's Path*, No. 2 (September 5, 1917), p. 3.

3.

Having received Minister Kerensky's telegram, [I] ordered Maj. Gen. Dietrichs to proceed to Northern Front HQ to receive orders from Gen. Klembovsky, Commander-in-Chief of the Northern Front. Gen. Klembovsky told [him] to inform me that he had not taken supreme command of the armies because at this difficult time neither he nor any of the commanding officers recognized any other supreme commander than General Kornilov, whose orders are still all in effect. And the Cossacks decided some time ago that General Kornilov was irreplaceable, which I am making known to all for guidance.

4.

This evening I received a report from Supreme HQ and St. Petersburg to the effect that riots had broken out in the capital. The famine is being aggravated by the fact that people, panic-stricken at the sight of their own troops marching on St. Petersburg, have destroyed the railroad bridges and thereby prevented food supplies reaching the city. But which troops are they afraid of? Those who have sworn allegiance to the new regime; those who were loud in proclaiming at the Moscow Conference that they thought the best kind of rule for Russia was a republican system. The deliberately false rumors that some of the troops moving toward St. Petersburg are going there to change the regime are absurd. You can see from General Kornilov's telegram that he recognizes and considers that only a constituent assembly can have the last word on which state system we ought to have. It is for a different reason that we are being sent [there]. You have recently read in the papers of the terrible explosions at the munition plants at Kazan; information has now been received that there are plans afoot to blow up the munition plants near St. Petersburg, that disturbances have broken out, and all this at a time when the enemy is at the gates of our capital with its huge number of munition plants working for defense. Now, more than ever before, there must be order in the capital.

It is you we are sending there to maintain order. I firmly believe that no one among you wants to see the ruin and shame of his land.

22

The Allies and the Russian Government

Up to the moment that the Tsar was deposed, all the foreign diplomatic representatives in Russia behaved with the greatest decorum and in strict conformity with protocol. None of them ventured, certainly, to interfere in Russia's internal affairs. But no sooner had the upheaval begun than the situation took a drastic turn. Diplomatic practice was thrown to the winds. For the first time the *Corps Diplomatique* felt it was free to associate with anyone at all. Officially, of course, there was no reason why this should not have been possible before, but in practice foreign diplomats had mixed only in court circles and in high society. Now, in Free Russia, every one of them was able to go anywhere, attend any council, and sit in on any meeting. Some diplomats kept to their former custom and continued to visit their favorite salons, but others promptly sought the friendship of newly returned political exiles, the convicts of the day before.

Most of the Allied diplomats were critical of and even opposed to the Provisional Government. We were accused of weakness, spinelessness, indecision, and various other sins. The diplomats soon learned the art of abusing their new-found freedom just as adeptly as had the common soldiers and workers. Freedom of association naturally led to more intimate relations with persons whose sympathies were shared by certain embassies and individual Allied military attachés. In the long run this was not too far from encouraging the activities of persons who, in the eyes of the foreigners, were the true patriots. Thus, it is not so surprising that before long their own approach to the

393

situation plus their connections in the capital enabled nearly all the members of the Allied missions to find willing listeners among the rabid opponents of the Provisional Government, both in Petrograd and at Supreme Headquarters.

The extreme left-wing opposition found support in Berlin. The right wing found it in the embassies and on the Petrograd embankments. The most extraordinary thing about the situation was that we in the government were represented by the left-wing tub-thumpers to be the "hirelings of British capital," while the right-wing demagogues in the embassy ballrooms accused us of being slaves of the Soviet and semi-Bolsheviks.

I can quite understand the feelings of these diplomats and foreign military attachés. For them Russia was unthinkable without a tsar. An army that could not be run by the officers without the help of commissars from the War Ministry was for them no army. A government that was half made up of socialists and made no show of strength, as would have been the case in former times, was for them no government. All that is quite true. But it was not really the mentality of the local Allied representatives that was important—they had merely been influenced by the social set in which they mixed. There was something far more important at the bottom of it all.

The allied governments felt that the Revolution had, as it were, disqualified Russia from membership in the Entente, and although they were anxious to keep Russia fighting at the front, the Allies were forced to listen patiently to the diplomatic chatter of Russia's "inexperienced ministers." Therefore, they concluded, the Allies must pursue separate military and political policies and disregard Russian interests. That was how they reasoned.

It is usually claimed nowadays that the Russian offensive of July, 1917, was an adventure which the country was forced to undertake through Allied pressure. In reality the renewal of operations at the front was dictated by Russia's interests and followed from the very logic of the Revolution. Having grown partly out of a protest against a separate peace, the Revolution could only consolidate freedom and democracy if the outcome of the war was successful. Furthermore, as soon as we became aware of the Allied attitude toward us, it became plain that only the recovery of our fighting fitness and some show of strength would make them show a little more circumspection in deciding which of our diplomatic notes to ignore!

Why did the French and British Governments seize every opportunity to sabotage the Provisional Government? I have given this question a great deal of thought, but it was not until I began living abroad as an émigré that many things became clear to me. It was then for the first time in my life that I came into contact with the real Europe and its governing circles. The Allies' hostile reaction to Russia's new international policies was perfectly natural; after all, they were still thinking in terms of the old, pre-World War I Europe, while we had already left that world behind and were establishing (in our Manifesto of March 27) a new set of values in international relations.

The wording of the Provisional Government's statement would hardly seem so repugnant and unacceptable to anyone in Europe today.

Until the collapse of the Russian monarchy, the governments of Russia and the West were in complete harmony as to the common objectives of the war; after all, the great powers of the time were all imperialist in ideology. In both the enemy camps experts were busy haggling over which country would get what territory. At the Inter-Allied Conference in St. Petersburg in January, 1917, Gaston Doumergue, the French plenipotentiary and future president, and Pokrovsky, the Russian foreign minister who replaced Stürmer, were already negotiating the frontiers that France and Russia were to have when the war was finally won. In addition to Alsace-Lorraine and the Saar, the French planned to set up an independent protectorate on the left bank of the Rhine—on German territory—while the Russian Government was striving for agreement to the inclusion of the whole of Poland (that is to say, the Austrian, German, and Russian areas) into the Russian Empire as an autonomous province.

When the conference was over, Pokrovsky told Paléologue that Russia accepted the French demands regarding the demarcation of Germany's western borders.

On February 26, Izvolsky, the Russian ambassador to Paris, transmitted the text of a note from the Quai d'Orsay, in which France agreed that Russia should have a completely free hand to decide where her western frontier was to lie. His message, however, accidentally fell into the hands of the Provisional Government, which retaliated by promptly proclaiming the independence of Poland and the reunification of her Russian, German, and Austrian regions.[1]

This example will make it clear that the new Russia and her Western allies no longer shared the same ideology as regards the war aims as a whole.

However, the misunderstanding was cleared up at the first meetings between the new foreign minister and Allied representatives. Translated into diplomatic language we were saying: "The Provisional Government proposes that all the powers should jointly reconsider the aims of the war and, for its own part, states that Russia is ready to withdraw claim to her share of the booty in the interests of concluding peace as soon as possible, provided the other Allied powers do likewise."

We spent the whole summer trying to persuade the British and French governments to hold an immediate conference for this purpose. But the two governments spent that time trying to avoid doing so. It was not until after our offensive was launched that they finally gave way, but even then the talks, which they clearly found so boring and distasteful, dragged on for months. People in London and Paris simply refused to understand, or rather to recognize, that our revolution went much further than merely deposing the monarch; it was a long-drawn-out process of completely remolding the mentality of the people. Nowadays, after the spate of revolutions and counterrevolutions that Europe has witnessed, statesmen have a clearer idea of what it all means. But at that time, the Allies seemed to think that such a world-shaking event as the overthrow of the Russian monarchy could not possibly affect the country's foreign policy. And if by any chance it did, it was the fault of the weak, dithering men in power who were obviously under the thumb of the Bolsheviks.

After all, in 1917, Germany's position was critical, if not hopeless. Her military experts realized that the war could no longer be won by force of arms. Austria and Turkey had been virtually crushed, and

---

[1] *Collection of Secret Documents from the Archives of the Former Foreign Ministry* (Commissariat for Foreign Affairs, December, 1917), No. 42, Minister's Secret Archives.

were now millstones round the German neck. Since July there had been a joint move by the Catholic and Social Democrat groups in the Reichstag in favor of a prompt peace settlement. So why did the Entente stubbornly persist with their extreme and unrealizable demands?

I have already said that on the most uncertain day of the Kornilov revolt, August 28, among the host of "mediators" who urged the Provisional Government to come to terms with the rebel generals, were Russia's Western allies. Late that evening the doyen of the diplomatic corps, Sir George Buchanan, went to see Foreign Minister Tereshchenko and handed him the following note on behalf of the British, French, and Italian Governments:

> The representatives of the Allied powers met under the chairmanship of Sir George Buchanan to discuss the situation arising in connection with the conflict between the Provisional Government and General Kornilov. Acknowledging their obligation to remain at their posts in order to assist their fellow countrymen should the occasion arise, they consider it an important task at the same time to maintain the unity of all forces in Russia with a view to victorious continuation of the war, in consideration of which fact they unanimously declare that in the interests of humanity and anxious to avoid an irreparable misfortune they offer their good offices with the single desire to serve the interests of Russia and the Allied cause.

From the very outset of Kornilov's revolt rumors had gone round Petrograd that some of the Allied representatives were sympathetic to the general's cause. This gossip seemed all the more likely in that under the circumstances it was quite natural for them to have shared the feelings of their opposite numbers on the Russian General Staff. But the wagging city tongues inflated the rumors, and the right-wing press made no bones about the West's support for plans to reestablish a strong "national" regime in Russia.

At this juncture we had absolutely no palpable proof of that and obviously no official information to suggest that the Allied governments were deceiving the Provisional Government. To put a stop to the gossip and prevent the Allies losing face among the masses both at the front and at home, I instructed the War Minister's office to have a statement published in the press the very next morning, mentioning, among other things, that "General Kornilov cannot count on Allied support" and that the Allies "hoped for the liquidation of the revolt as soon as possible."

However, as Milyukov later said,[2] "it was in the interests of the Allies to prevent their name being used against General Kornilov."

This is why the verbal note was presented to the Provisional Government with the suggestion that the rebel general should be regarded as an equal partner in the state system, and that we should make peace with him through the mediation of foreign governments—I imagine, on their own terms!

Fortunately for the Allies, this rather cynical note was never published in its original form in Russia. On August 29, the Allied candidate for the dictatorship of Russia was politically out of the running, and on August 30, a colleague of his was sent by the Provisional Government to rid the Supreme Headquarters of conspirators. The next day, August 31, the memorable note appeared in the press, reworded to read as a fairly harmless message from "friends."

It was actually on the evening of August 28, just as Tereshchenko was being handed the "peacemaker's" note from the would-be mediators, that the commander of the British tank division in the southwest sector of the front received an order from Kornilov instructing him to render immediate assistance to his, Kornilov's troops, then advancing on Petrograd. On September 19, at the urgent request of the panicking British Ambassador, I instructed the publication of an official statement, after careful consultation with Tereshchenko. It ran as follows:

In connection with the current rumors that British armored vehicles are taking part in General Kornilov's advance, it is reported from authoritative sources that the rumors are a complete fabrication and that any information based on them is malicious slander aimed at sowing discord between ourselves and the Allies, and thereby weakening our might.

This one official statement, which denied what was obviously true, was not only published with my full consent, but on my instructions. It was motivated by considerations of extreme national importance.

Clearly enough, the Russian High Command could no more have

[2] *History of the Second Russian Revolution,* 2d ed., Vol. I, pp. 254–255.

ordered the British tank division to move on Petrograd, that is, against the Provisional Government, without preliminary consultations with the military authorities in London and with our headquarters, than the British Ambassador could have delivered the "collective" note to the government without the orders from the Cabinet in London and consent from the French and Italians.

The Breakup of the Democratic Parties

THE first news of the approach of General Kornilov's troops had much the same effect on the people of Petrograd as a lighted match on a powder keg. Soldiers, sailors, and workers were all seized with a sudden fit of paranoid suspicion. They fancied they saw counterrevolution everywhere. Panic-stricken that they might lose the rights they had only just gained, they vented their rage against all the generals, landed proprietors, bankers and other "bourgeois" groups.

Most of the Socialist leaders who had been in the coalition, fearing the possibility of a counterrevolutionary victory and subsequent reprisals, turned toward the Bolsheviks. During the first few hours of the hysteria, on August 27, they welcomed them back with loud acclaim, and side by side with them, set about "saving the revolution."

How could Lenin fail to take advantage of this? After the fiasco of his July uprising he had virtually acknowledged himself beaten, but with the change of mood wrought by Kornilov's mutiny, his prospects suddenly improved. The cautious "wait-and-see" tactics he had adopted after his escape to Finland could be abandoned now that General Kornilov had obligingly presented him with the opportunity of seizing power much sooner than he had planned, and, even more important, of doing so under the slogan "all power to the Soviets," which he had dropped after the July fiasco.

On August 30 Lenin sent a secret letter [1] to his Central Committee in Petrograd:

It is possible that these lines will come too late, for events are developing with a pace that is sometimes absolutely breathtaking. I am writing

---

[1] *Collected Works of V. I. Lenin,* Vol. XXI, Book I, pp. 137–139.

this on Wednesday, August 30, and the recipients will read it not earlier than Friday, September 15 [*sic*]. But in any case [on a chance] I consider it my duty to write the following:

Kornilov's revolt is a completely unexpected (at such a moment and in such a form) and almost incredible turn of events.

Like every sharp turn, it calls for a revision of tactics, and, as with every revision, one must be extremely cautious lest one lose sight of principles. . . .

We will fight, we are fighting against Kornilov, even as Kerensky's troops do, but we do not support Kerensky. On the contrary, we expose his weakness. There is a difference. It is a rather subtle difference, but it is essential and one must not forget it.

What change, then, is to be made in our tactics after Kornilov's revolt?

The change is in the form of our struggle against Kerensky. Without relaxing in the least our hostility toward him, without taking back a single word said against him, without renouncing the task of overthrowing Kerensky, we say: we must take into account the present moment; we shall not overthrow Kerensky right now; we shall approach the task of struggling against him in a different way. Namely, we shall point out to the people the weakness and vacillation of Kerensky. That has been done before. Now, however, it has become the main thing. Therein lies the change.

The change, further, consists in this, that the main thing is now to intensify our propaganda in favour of some kind of "partial demands" to be presented to Kerensky, demands saying: arrest Milyukov; arm the Petrograd workers; summon the Kronstadt, Vyborg, and Helsingfors troops to Petrograd; disperse the State Duma; arrest Rodzyanko; legalize the transfer of the landowners' lands to the peasants; introduce workers' control over bread and factories, etc., etc. With these demands we must address ourselves not only to Kerensky, and not so much to Kerensky, as to the workers, soldiers, and peasants who have been carried away by the course of the struggle against Kornilov. Keep up their enthusiasm; encourage them to beat up the generals and officers who express themselves in favour of Kornilov; urge them to demand the immediate transfer of the land to the peasants; give them the idea of the necessity of arresting Rodzyanko and Milyukov, dispersing the State Duma, shutting down the *Rech*,[2] and other bourgeois papers, and instituting investigations against them. The "left" Socialist Revolutionaries especially must be pushed in this direction.

It would be erroneous to think that we have moved away from the task of aiding the proletariat to conquer power. No! We have come much nearer to it, though not directly, but obliquely. This very minute we must conduct

[2] The Cadet newspaper, edited by Milyukov.

propaganda against Kerensky, not so much directly as indirectly, that is, by demanding an active and most energetic really revolutionary war against Kornilov. The developments of this war alone can lead us to power, and we must speak of this as little as possible in our propaganda (remembering very well that even tomorrow events may put power into our hands, and then we shall not relinquish it). It seems to me that this should have been transmitted to the propagandists in a letter (not in the press); it should have been transmitted to propagandist groups, to the members of the party in general. As to phrases about the defense of the country, about a united front of revolutionary democracy, about supporting the Provisional Government, etc., we must fight against them mercilessly, since these are merely phrases. What we must say is that now is the time for action; you, Messrs. Socialist Revolutionaries and Mensheviks, have long since worn these phrases threadbare. Now is the time for action; the war against Kornilov must be conducted in a revolutionary way by drawing in the masses, by arousing them, by inflaming them (as to Kerensky, he is afraid of the masses, *he is afraid of the people*). In the war against the Germans action is required right now; immediate and unconditional peace must be offered on definite terms. If we do this we can attain either a speedy peace or a transformation of the war into a revolutionary one; otherwise all the Mensheviks and Socialist-Revolutionaries remain lackeys of imperialism.

P.S. Having read six copies of the *Rabochi* [3] after this was written, I must say that there is perfect harmony in our views. I greet with all my heart the splendid editorials, press reviews and articles by V.M.——n and Vol——y. As to Volodarsky's speech, I have read his letter to the editors, which "liquidates" my reproaches as well. Once more, best greetings and wishes!

Lenin

But even before they had received Lenin's secret instructions, the Bolsheviks had joined forces with the Socialist Revolutionaries and Menshevik Social Democrats on August 27, organizing a worker's militia to "assist" the government and protect the working-class areas. Within days the "workers' militia" had become the Bolshevik "Red Guard," closely linked with the Bolshevik party apparatus.

On August 31, the Petrograd Soviet had virtually fallen into the hands of the Bolsheviks and adopted a resolution containing in brief the whole of the "October" revolt program. Nevertheless, in talking with other Socialists and in making joint statements with them, the

---

[3] I.e., *Rabochi i Soldat* (*Workers and Soldiers*), a Bolshevik newspaper coming out then in Petrograd in place of *Pravda,* which had been closed down.

Bolsheviks continued to hold forth on the "unity of the whole revolutionary democratic movement" in the struggle for a "truly democratic" regime, without the participation of the bourgeoisie, and especially of the Cadets.

This conciliatory policy on the part of the Bolsheviks toward the "petty-bourgeois" socialists was a brilliant success—and not just because of the impression made by their arguments on those Mensheviks and Socialist Revolutionaries who had always been opposed to collaborating with the "bourgeoisie." They, of course, were delighted that now, hand in hand with the Bolsheviks, they could save the Revolution from "counterrevolutionary trickery," and even take it a stage further.

But the real success of the new Bolshevik policy lay in its ability to bridge the gulf between the Bolsheviks and those Socialist Revolutionaries and Menshevik leaders who had hitherto taken part in the democratic coalition. These leaders, against all political logic, now felt it to be essential to restore the government coalition with Bolshevik participation, but without the Cadets.

Through my own political experience, I was well aware of the composition and mood of the Cadet organizations in the capital and in the provinces, and I knew many of their members. Like every other politician who had traveled extensively through Russia, I knew that the Cadet Party as a whole was an active, creative, and vital part of the forces engaged in building a democratic political system in Russia.

By preventing the Cadets from taking part with full rights in the formation of a new political, social, and economic organism, the government would be committing not only a crime against the country, but also a moral wrong. The Menshevik and Socialist Revolutionary leaders, who now condemned the entire Cadet Party because of the betrayal of democracy by Milyukov and his associates, had themselves done something even more unforgivable: they had made a rapprochement with Lenin and had taken the Bolshevik Party back into the fold of the "Revolutionary Democrats."

Milyukov and his group were a small minority in the party. The party itself did not recognize any form of dictatorship, and had taken just as large a part in the Revolution as any of the socialist parties. But as all the writings and actions of Lenin, Kamenev, Bukharin, Stalin, and others, make clear, the Bolsheviks from the very outset of the Revolution were out to replace the democratic system by the unlimited dictatorship of their party.

What was the sense of the expression "revolutionary democracy" if it embraced at one and the same time those fighting to establish it and those avowedly intending to destroy it?

Before World War I there had been no doubt about the meaning of the two words "revolution" and "counterrevolution." "Revolution" meant the forceful overthrow by the people of a state system which no longer met the requirements of the age and was incapable of evolution. "Counterrevolution" meant the restoration by force of the political system existing prior to the Revolution. Revolution was supposed to break out spontaneously, to have its roots deep among the people, and to bring about the establishment of democracy. Counterrevolution was usually the work of a particular group among the ruling classes, and was always followed by a period of "reaction."

I mention this elementary distinction because after World War I, in which millions of people throughout Europe were embroiled in a political maelstrom, *any* movement on a mass scale came to be termed a "revolution," no matter what aims its leaders were pursuing.

Many historians, sociologists, and political writers still take insufficient account of the profound change that has come about in political psychology—a change that is obscured by the use of traditional, but now wholly inapplicable terminology. They still take for granted Clemenceau's aphorism that "democracy has no enemies on the left." In the nineteenth century this maxim was true, for at that time all popular movements were aimed at social emancipation and the freedom of the personality. That was also the whole inspiration of the socialist movements. At that time the very idea that the "left" might produce obscurantists who, drawing support from the lowest social orders, would, in Dostoyevsky's words, "begin with complete freedom and finish with complete slavery," was considered to be political blasphemy. That was why Dostoyevsky, who in his novel *The Possessed* foresaw the sort of regime that Russia was to live through under Lenin and Stalin, was branded during his lifetime as a great "reactionary" by left-wing progressive and socialist circles. But now, after two world wars, it is impossible to deny the fact that reaction, masquerading as "revolution" and led by such demagogues as Lenin, Mussolini, and Hitler, who solicited support in their struggle for power from the lowest strata of society, can create totalitarian terrorist dictatorships which transgress all moral barriers. They have committed crimes of a sort and on a scale that would have horrified the reactionaries of former days.

There was a vast difference, from the point of view of the people's interests and the future of Russia, between the Kornilov movement, which had in any case been crushed, and Lenin's movement, which the Kornilov movement had revived.

The attempted military coup was only a futile rear-guard action of the privileged classes, a last, desperate effort to regain their power. There was no question of its being repeated, for the simple reason that the nonmilitary members of the plot, who had played on the wounded patriotic pride of a section of the Russian officers corps, had no political or social program to offer the masses of the people.

Lenin, however, was intent on climbing to power in the guise of a champion of political freedom and of the new social status gained by the people in the February Revolution.

Naturally, at the beginning of September, 1917, no one foresaw the kind of political sadism in which the Bolshevik dictatorship would indulge as soon as the democratic system had been annihilated. But all the leaders of the non-Bolshevik left-wing parties knew full well that Lenin and his henchmen were not aiming at rule by the people, but at a party dictatorship over the people. It is a pity that they were less concerned with the obvious nature of Lenin's ambitions than with the supposed untrustworthiness of the Cadet Party, which, whatever its faults, certainly had no dictatorial inclinations.

As I have said, on August 29 I was entrusted by the government with the delicate task of restoring the Coalition, including in it the same parties as before. I intended to do so as soon as possible.

Admittedly, the situation was a tricky one. For although I regarded the participation of the Cadets in the government as absolutely necessary, I knew that everything their leader, Milyukov, did—every article he wrote and every speech he made—would cause new waves of indignation, like those in March and April.

Then an unexpected event occurred. For a time it looked as though it might provide me with a way out of this dilemma. On August 30, a couple of hours before I was due to start my official appointments,

I was sitting in my private study on the top floor of the Winter Palace looking through hundreds of telegrams from different parts of the country congratulating us on our suppression of the Kornilov revolt.

Suddenly one of my aides came in and in great agitation told me that V. Lebedev [4] was insisting, despite the early hour, that I see him at once. A few moments later this honest, patriotic, and very excitable man burst into my study. Without greeting me, he waved a sheet of newspaper in the air, and gasped out several times, "There's your Milyukov for you!"

Noting his extreme agitation, I went over to him and said quietly, "what makes you think he's mine, and not yours? Tell me what the matter is. But first sit down and relax!"

He sat down obediently, like a child, and began to regain his composure. Then he asked me, "Have you seen today's *Rech?*"

"No," I said. "I haven't seen any of the papers today."

"Then take a look at this!" Again he began excitedly showing me the front page of the Cadet newspaper. On the sheet, which was dated August 30, there was a large blank where the leading article should have been. Still waving the sheet of newsprint, Lebedev went on to explain that the senior compositor from the *Rech* printing shop had come to see him and had told him that just as the newspaper was about to be printed, Milyukov's leading article had been withdrawn. According to the compositor, the chief editor of *Rech* had welcomed General Kornilov's victory and had demanded that the government come to terms with him at once.

Lebedev argued that this incident offered complete confirmation of the opinion of all genuine democrats that the Cadet Party supported General Kornilov and must not therefore continue to be part of the Coalition. I did not bother to listen to the rest of Lebedev's arguments. I knew exactly what I had to do, and as I said goodbye to him, I pointed out rather brusquely that the Cadets could not be held responsible for the actions of an individual member.

As soon as Lebedev had gone, I gave orders to have two of the most influential members of the Petrograd branch of the Cadet Central Committee—Nabokov and Vinaver—summoned to my office at once. Although it was not yet nine o'clock, they arrived almost imme-

4 One of the editors of *The People's Will,* the right-wing Socialist Revolutionary newspaper, and until shortly before, acting head of the Naval Ministry.

diately. When I told them why I had sent for them, Nabokov replied that they were themselves alarmed by what had happened. After a brief and candid discussion, all three of us reached the same conclusion, that if we were to form a new government coalition with representatives of all the democratic parties, Milyukov would have to relinquish his leadership of the party and his post as editor-in-chief of *Rech* for a while, and either go abroad or at least to the Crimea or the Caucasus. My visitors carried out this rather delicate mission very tactfully, and Milyukov left for the Crimea almost immediately after they had spoken to him.

That same day I told the Socialist ministers, Avksentiev and Skobelev, about my conversation with Nabokov and Vinaver, and asked them to report the gist of it to their respective Central Committees, hoping thereby to smooth the way for Cadet participation in the government.

At the same time Nekrasov and Tereshchenko also conferred about the Cadets with other prominent members of the Socialist parties, but without success.

At the meeting of *Vzik* (All-Russian Central Executive Committee) on August 30, at which the question of the organization of a new Cabinet came up for preliminary discussion, feelings against Cadet participation were so strong that Avksentiev and Skobelev decided to quit the government so as to have their hands free, as Skobelev put it, to defend government policy. The final decision of the Soviet on the makeup of the Coalition was to be taken on September 1.

After the fall of the Monarchy it had been agreed between the Provisional Committee of the Duma and the newly formed Soviet that Russia would remain without any definite political system pending a decision by the Constituent Assembly. By summer, however, Russia's ambiguous position as a state without a definite form of government was becoming intolerable. It was important to impress on everyone, by the express use of the word "Republic," that Russia was a democracy in name as well as deed. This was essential at a time when there were forces trying to establish a dictatorial regime in the country. Recognizing the danger of delay, on two separate occasions I had tried to effect the declaration of a republic in Russia. My first attempt was made just after the Bolshevik uprising of July 4, during my brief sojourn in Petrograd between visits to the front. On the night of July 6, at a conference with representatives of the socialist parties on a program for the new coalition government, I had insisted on the inclusion of two points in our forthcoming declaration: first, the proclamation of a republic; and, second, the dissolution of the State Council and the Duma. My points were adopted. Without waiting for the declaration to be published, I returned post-haste to the front, where I soon received a copy of the declaration as published. My two points had been omitted. This had been done without my consent, but times were so difficult that I did not deal with the matter as I should have done.

The second occasion arose at the Moscow State Conference,[5] when all the representatives of the various parties, classes, urban and *zemstvo* institutions, and so on, all declared themselves in favor of a republic. After the discussion, I asked the ministers present at the conference to allow me to declare Russia a republic, but they refused.

After the military revolt, however, no one in democratic circles had any further doubt as to the necessity for making formal acknowledgment of the existence of a republican form of government in Russia, and a meeting of the Council of Ministers on August 31, the final draft of a "Proclamation of a Republic" was adopted.

During the meeting I was informed that a delegation from the Central Committee of the Socialist Revolutionary Party wanted to see me at once.

I acceded to their request and went at once to my study where I found two members of this Central Committee, Zenzinov and Goetz. Recalling that the same two men had come to see me during the July crisis and had presented me with a kind of ultimatum from their Central Committee, I expected them to be bent upon the same sort of mission this time. I was right. They had come to tell me on behalf of their Central Committee that, if I dared to include a single Cadet in my government coalition, not one Socialist Revolutionary would take part in it. Suppressing my fury, I said: "Tell your Central Committee, first, that I will pass on its demand to the government; second, I personally consider it to be essential to include the Cadets in the government as well as all the other democratic parties; and third, that as

5 See Chapter 19.

head of a national government I cannot take orders from individual parties."

Zenzinov then tried to argue the point with me "off the record, as a friend," but I interrupted him and said that private conversations were out of place. "You have brought me an official resolution from your party's Central Committee," I said, "and I will pass it on immediately to the government." There the conversation ended.

Returning to the conference room, I reported on the meeting I had just had with the Socialist Revolutionary envoys. The reply I had given them was unanimously approved. None of us had the slightest doubt that the Socialist Revolutionary Party's resolution would delay for an indefinite period the restoration of a coalition government including all the democratic parties.

In the meantime we had to deal with the aftermath of the revolt as quickly as possible. Our main tasks were to set up a new Supreme Command, to restore discipline at the front, to put a stop to the lawlessness that had broken out again in the rear, and generally to get the country back to normal—or at any rate, as far as was actually possible under the circumstances. At the same time we had to resume important diplomatic talks with the Allies.

By now more than half the ministers had resigned for various reasons, and the exceptional powers with which I had been vested for the duration of the revolt were no longer mine.

Yet it was just at this point, when we were undergoing an awkward transitional period, that a concentration of administrative power and authority was absolutely essential to the conduct of both internal and foreign affairs.

As far as I recall, it was Tereshchenko who, after consultation with the Cadet and Socialist leaders, submitted a draft resolution in which he called for the formation of a committee of five ministers who would have full executive powers until a new Coalition was formed. The Foreign Minister's draft resolution was adopted, together with my proposal for a republic. The two proposals were then incorporated in the following official proclamation, which was published on September 1 under the signatures of myself and Zarudny, the minister of justice:

General Kornilov's revolt has been suppressed, but the sedition brought by him into the ranks of the army and the country is great. Once again a great danger threatens our native land and her freedom.

Considering it necessary to put an end to uncertainty as to the nature of the State, and remembering the wholehearted and enthusiastic acceptance of the republican idea at the Moscow State Conference, the Provisional Government announces that the state system by which the State of Russia is governed is republican, and hereby proclaims the Russian Republic.

The urgent necessity of adopting immediate and decisive measures for restoring order in the shattered organization of the state has induced the Provisional Government to transfer full power to five of its members,[6] headed by the Prime Minister.

The Provisional Government considers its principal task to be the restoration of state order and the fighting capacity of the army. Convinced that only through the concentrated efforts of all the vital forces of the country will it be possible to extricate our native land from the difficult position in which it finds itself, the Provisional Government will strive to expand its membership by inviting into its midst representatives of all those elements who place the permanent and common interests of our native land above the temporary and private interests of individual parties or classes.

The Provisional Government does not doubt that it will accomplish this task in the very near future.

On the evening of the same day, September 1, the second—and crucial—meeting of the *Vzik* (All-Russian Central Executive Committee of the Soviets) was held to discuss the crisis that had arisen over the Coalition.

The resolution adopted by the meeting [7] proved to be an amazing document, and it came as a complete surprise to both the government and the nation.

The preamble to the resolution proclaimed that "the tragic situation at the front and the state of civil war created by counterrevolutionaries (i.e., the followers and sympathizers of Kornilov) make it essential to have a single revolutionary authority able to carry out the program of 'revolutionary democracy,' and to offer active opposition to the counterrevolution and the enemy. A government of this kind,

---

[6] This special body, which came to be called the "Directory," was composed, apart from myself, of Tereshchenko, Foreign Minister; Nikitin, Minister of Posts and Telegraph, also in charge of the Ministry of Internal Affairs; Colonel Verkhovsky (now promoted to Major General); Rear Admiral Verderevsky, now War Minister, formerly in command of the Baltic Fleet. The military and naval representatives had first been brought into the government after I was appointed Supreme Commander.

[7] It was introduced by the Socialist Revolutionaries and Mensheviks.

formed by the democratic movement and responsible to its institutions, *must not enter into any agreement with the bourgeoisie.*"

In short, the highest body of the "revolutionary democracy," the All-Russian Executive Committee of the Soviet (*Vzik*), instead of dealing in a responsible way with the problem of a coalition capable of governing the republic, had decided to disqualify all representatives of the "bourgeois democracy" from participation in the government!

They further resolved to hold a conference of all the "democratic" —in their sense of the word—organizations as soon as possible to discuss the formation of a government able to keep the country going until the Constituent Assembly could be convened.

As for the existing government, they suggested it should remain in office pending this "democratic conference," but that it should act in close collaboration with the "People's Committee against Counter-revolution" (which came under the *Vzik*), in order to prevent the execution of any administrative measures that might give rise to trouble among the population.

This meant, in effect, that until it was replaced by a regime to be established by the proposed "democratic conference," the existing government was to submit all its administrative decisions to *Vzik* for approval.

Courageously opposing the resolution, Skobelev, who until the day before had been minister of labor, put forward the following arguments:

It has been said here that the very idea of a coalition with the bourgeoisie is not justified. I am of a different opinion. Regardless of the difficulty of the present situation, Russia still remains a democracy. Despite the severe tests to which the concept of a coalition has been put, it has nevertheless managed to preserve Russia and her freedom to the present day. And this idea must not die. . . .

Three kinds of government are possible: a coalition government, a purely bourgeois government, or a purely democratic [8] government. A purely bourgeois government cannot be justified. During the Kornilov conspiracy there was a conflict between two forces, one standing for autocracy, and the other standing for all of the people. The latter force won, and the situation could not have been otherwise. But it would be just as wrong to make sweeping accusations against the whole of the bourgeoisie, as it was then to say that the whole of the democratic movement participated in the street demon-

[8] It must be borne in mind that in this context "democratic" means "socialist."

strations of July 3–5.[9] Although certain bourgeois groups may have taken part in the Kornilov movement, the majority of them probably did not. We have no right, therefore, to exclude them all from the government.

Another concept of government is that power should be given entirely to the democratic movement. From the very outset of the revolution we have been told that the slogan "All Power to the Soviets" could save the country. During the past few days many of us have come to regard this slogan more favorably, and the number of people supporting it has increased.

But I have not been converted to it. I left the Provisional Government with the intention of freeing my hands so that I could put my ideas before you. The graver the situation at the front and here at home, the more imperative it is for us to rally all vital forces around us to defend the country.

Don't forget, Comrades, that Petrograd is not Russia; that is why we must first ask the opinion of the whole country.

I have been at the front twice, and I know that Petrograd does not enjoy complete confidence among the troops.

The reason for this is that we are too obsessed by the lust for power. Our eyes are on the Winter Palace, and we are overanxious to get into it. In the provinces they are not prey to the same ambitions, and they are, therefore, more sober-minded. . . .

Skobelev was a voice crying in the wilderness. He was supported only by Avksentiev, former minister and chairman of the Soviet of Peasant Deputies.

Everyone else, especially those who had been abroad for a number of years and those who had endured exile and forced labor in Siberia, showed extreme hostility toward the basic policies of the government. Completely ignoring all the difficult issues both abroad and at home, they felt they had the right (though heaven knows what it was based on) to set up a new regime of the "toiling masses."

Kamenev, Lenin's representative, made a speech which further convinced the advocates of a socialist government that their dream of permanent collaboration with the Bolsheviks was feasible. "We are all agreed on two requirements," Kamenev said. "First, that the government must be responsible to *us;* and second, that it must have the support of the revolutionary democratic movement. Neither of these requirements has been met. The government that has been announced to us here is a government that suits Kerensky, but a government that

[9] The Bolshevik uprising organized by Lenin.

suits Russia must be organized *here* with or without Kerensky, depending on what we decide."

Next to speak after Kamenev was Dan, a leading Menshevik, who also criticised the fact that my government was not accountable to the *Vzik*. Tsereteli, while supporting the Socialist Revolutionary and Menshevik resolution forbidding any contact with the bourgeoisie, attempted to dispute Kamenev's extreme interpretation of it. He argued that the resolution recognized the possibility of a coalition, as long as it was within the democratic movement itself. He did not enlarge on this rather vague notion, nor did he make it clear what precisely he meant by "democratic."

What the advocates of an all-socialist government actually had in mind was revealed by Chernov, the party chairman, in his address to the fourth congress of the Socialist Revolutionary Party in November, 1917.[10]

It was this sharp difference of opinion among the leaders of the revolutionary democracy, and the desire of many of them to put back the history of the Revolution half a year, that subsequently turned the Democratic Conference into the tragic farce—Lenin called it a comedy—that it was.

On September 3 *Vzik* sent out invitations to attend its Democratic Conference to a wide variety of political and civic bodies that it considered eligible. The Conference opened on September 14 with 1,492 delegates present. It is noteworthy that the balance of forces within the "revolutionary democratic" camp changed in between the sending out of the invitations and the actual conference.

On September 5 the Moscow Soviet had adopted a resolution iden-

---

[10] "The outburst of feeling against the risk of a military plot, and counterrevolution," Chernov said, "which for one moment restored the unity of the democratic revolutionary front against the largest party of the Russian privileged classes, a party which has continued to take an ambiguous stand, i.e., the Cadets—this surge of enthusiasm has strengthened the stand of socialist democracy and the somewhat shaken position of the Soviets. The Soviets, which swung to the right after the events of July 3–5, following the breach in the unity of the democratic front, have been enabled by this turn of events to straighten the line and bring about a new swing to the left. And it is no wonder, therefore, that many people, myself included, have been congratulating themselves on Kornilov's revolt as an act that, in reducing the swing to the right to an absurdity and carrying it through to its logical conclusion—a military plot—makes it possible, by utilizing the blunders and crimes of the right, to smooth over and put right what had been done through the blunders and folly of the left."

tical to the one passed in the Petrograd Soviet on August 31. The Menshevik and Socialist Revolutionary presidiums in both the Soviets resigned, and in both cities Bolsheviks and left-wing Socialist Revolutionaries and "internationalist" Mensheviks allied with them were elected instead. In all other large cities, workers' and soldiers' organizations were increasingly being dominated by the Bolsheviks and their sympathizers.[11] On September 6 the charter of the Red Guard was published in Moscow. The Bolshevik Red Guard had grown out of the workers' militia created by the Soviet on August 27 "to assist the government."

On September 10 the Central Committee of the Mensheviks was reelected, and the majority in it went over to the left-wing Menshevik "internationalists," headed by Martov. In the Central Committee of the Social Revolutionary Party a fierce struggle developed between those in favor of a wide democratic coalition and those demanding a socialist government.

The aim of the Conference was a very simple one. As formulated by Tsereteli on September 1, it was to demonstrate that the "revolutionary democratic" (i.e., socialist) movement was the only one that was sufficiently united and homogeneous to be able to set up the kind of government needed by the Revolution.

In fact, however, the "revolutionary democrats" were hopelessly disunited and contentious, and from the day the Conference opened, the same leaders of the socialist parties who had been at each other's throats on September 1 now continued to behave in exactly the same way for the whole five days of the conference, in full view of the attending delegates and, through them, of the whole country. The only difference was that the champions of a united socialist government were supported on this occasion by cohorts of rowdies who, with their constant heckling and threats, turned the Conference into a noisy free-for-all.

Naturally, apart from the speeches from the floor, which are not worth summarizing here, there were all kinds of back-room meetings at which the "loving enemies" strove to work out some sort of com-

---

[11] The organizers of the Democratic Conference allotted 446 seats, i.e., a third of the total, to workers' and soldiers' representatives, while the Soviet of Peasant Deputies, the spokesman of the great majority of the Russian population, only got 179 seats. Curious political arithmetic!

promise formula for a final resolution acceptable to all. At long last they found a wording to the effect that the Democratic Conference considered it necessary to organize a coalition government with the inclusion of certain bourgeois elements.

At 3:25 P.M. on September 19, the last day of the Conference, Chkheidze, who was in the chair, reconvened the meeting and proposed that the resolution be put to a vote. Immediately there were shouts from the left that they should first decide whether the voting was to be by secret ballot or by a roll call. The results were: 574 in favor of voting secretly, and 600 in favor of an open vote.

The roll-call vote on the resolution began at 4:30 and took five hours in all. The results were as follows: 766 in favor of a coalition and 688 against. Of the latter, 331, or almost a half, belonged to the delegates from the trade unions and the soviets of soldiers and workers, which were already in the hands of the Bolsheviks and their allies, the left-wing Socialist Revolutionaries and "internationalist" Mensheviks.

The announcement of these results was followed by a tremendous outburst from a crowd of Bolsheviks and left-wing Socialist Revolutionaries, who lost control of themselves and began shouting for a vote on their amendment. The chairman announced a lengthy recess. According to the next issue of *Izvestiya*,[12] the Presidium had not been able to decide, before taking the vote on the main resolution, in which order to vote on the two amendments. But according to my own more reliable information, the two amendments were introduced while voting on the main resolution was actually in progress. Their order of appearance is of no consequence, since, according to normal procedure in all civilized countries, amendments to a resolution are voted on before the resolution itself. But in the bedlam which reigned at that moment the Presidium was unable to cope with the situation. Reopening the meeting, the new chairman, Avksentiev, announced—rather nervously, according to eyewitnesses—that the two amendments would now be voted on—*after* the adoption of the main resolution. The first of these was submitted jointly by Bogdanov, a Menshevik, and Chernov, chairman of the Socialist Revolutionary Central Committee, who thereby violated his own party's ruling forbidding individual members to introduce any resolution at the Conference. This amendment ran:

[12] Published on September 20.

"Those members of the Cadet Party and other organizations who were implicated in the Kornilov conspiracy cannot be included in the coalition." It clearly rendered the main resolution meaningless. A large number of delegates were outraged by this move and refused to vote at all. But the amendment was finally passed by a majority of 798 votes—32 votes more than had been cast for the main resolution.

The second amendment, demanding the exclusion of *all* members of the Cadet Party, was moved jointly by the Bolsheviks and left-wing Socialist Revolutionaries and did not receive an absolute majority. Of the 595 votes obtained, 445 were cast by the Soviets and trade unions; in other words, every single one of the workers' and soldiers' delegates voted in favor of it.

After this another long recess was announced, and then the main resolution with the two amendments was put to the vote. But it was difficult to vote for such an absurdity, and it obtained only 183 votes.

Once more an adjournment was announced, this time amidst a dead silence.

The conference had ended in a total fiasco, but to save face the revolutionary democrats found a cunning, though transparent stratagem. After a further delay, Tsereteli, who, on September 1, had certainly been one of the chief initiators of the plan for a nonbourgeois government, read out the following statement:

The Presidium, having discussed the situation that has arisen as a result of the vote, has reached the conclusion that the voting has shown that there is among us no agreement or unity of will. . . .

The Presidium therefore proposes that the resolution should merely be regarded as an indication that the different groups and factions represented here were seeking to establish, through mutual agreements and concessions, a unity of purpose throughout the democratic movement.

Keeping this aim in view, the Presidium proposes that all groups should organize a conference with the Presidium that would be a step toward restoring unity within the movement.

The Presidium wishes to submit to you the following resolution, which it has itself already adopted unanimously:

"The All-Russian Democratic Conference resolves not to break up until such time as it has decided on the conditions under which the government is to be organized and the nature of its activities."

Once more I remind you that this resolution has been unanimously adopted by representatives of all political opinions and all groups in the Presidium.

I should point out here that the word "unanimously," twice stressed by Tsereteli, meant that the Bolsheviks and their satellites would continue to pursue a joint policy with the rest of the "revolutionary democrats."

The resolution and the Presidium's invitation to a conference the next day were adopted unanimously, without a vote, to the delighted applause of all present.

Since the amendment proposed by Chernov and the other supporters of an all-socialist government had been adopted by a greater majority of votes than the main resolution, and since Tsereteli's twice-stressed "unanimity" was enabling Kamenev to continue his game of "establishing unity of purpose in the democratic movement," I went the next day to the conference that the Presidium was holding for representatives of all parties.

I told them that, if the conference decided to form a government of socialist parties, I would hand over power peacefully, but I would not join the new government and neither would any other member of the government of the Republic. I added that, in view of the extremely serious situation in Russia at that moment, I was forced to insist that they give me an answer within three days. Kamenev replied at once that "in that case there's no point in even talking about an all-socialist government." Without Bolshevik participation, it would not have been possible for the Socialist Revolutionaries and Mensheviks to form the kind of government they wanted. They realized this themselves and had to capitulate.

But instead of simply and honestly admitting that they were courting disaster by aligning themselves with the Leninists and their supporters, they went on pretending to believe in the power and unity of "Revolutionary Democracy." They now proceeded to set up a so-called "Democratic Council." This fantastic council sent a delegation to present the government with a series of demands. However, when the delegates (Avksentiev, Rudnev, and Tsereteli) arrived to see me about reorganizing the government along the lines desired by the Democratic Council, they did not at all insist on their own plan. Instead, they agreed to attend a conference being held by the government for the purpose of restoring a democratic coalition along the old lines.

The conference was held on September 22, and I was in the chair. It was attended, apart from those mentioned, by Cadet representatives, members of the trade and industrial group, and the Central Union of Cooperatives.

Opening the proceedings, I announced our plan to restore a democratic coalition and to convene, pending the election of the Constituent Assembly, *a consultative body,* which was to be called the Provisional Council of the Republic.[13]

I pointed out that, at the crucial stage through which we were passing, we could not undertake any new programs, and ought rather to decide on the composition of the new Cabinet immediately, basing it on the balance of political forces in the country, and publish the names the next day.

After a lengthy and often stormy discussion, the plan was adopted. The new composition of the government was made public the next morning, September 23.

Apart from the members of parties who had been in the coalition up to August 27, the new Cabinet contained two representatives from the trade and industrial group.

In its statement on the institution of a republic and the formation of a directory, the government had declared that:

The Provisional Government will strive to expand its membership by inviting into its midst representatives of all those elements who place the interest of our native land above the temporary and private interests of individual parties or classes.

The Provisional Government does not doubt that it will accomplish this task in the very near future.

Because of the breakup of all the principal parties that had existed prior to August 27 and had been part of the Coalition, this "very near future" dragged on for almost a month. The obligation we undertook on September 1 was eventually fulfilled, but too late!

---

13 In practice, this came to be called the "pre-parliament."

24

The Final Struggle for My Russia

ALL legislative and political activity having come to a halt in the aftermath of the generals' revolt, I threw myself into the task of trying to save the foundations of democracy and attempting to secure for Russia a place among the victors at the forthcoming peace conference. In September, 1917 I no longer had any doubt that the next year, with the official entry of the United States into the war, Germany would be crushed. For not only would the effect of modern American weapons be overwhelming, but Germany would no longer be able to rely on her allies, Hungary and Turkey, since both had by 1917 lost their fighting capacity in battles with the Russian armies during the three preceding years.

Neither the setbacks suffered by the Russian front as the third year of the war drew to a close, nor any treachery within the country, could keep the Entente from winning or delete from the history of the war Russia's tremendous part in the approaching victory.

The German General Staff understood very well the significance of the operations on the Russian Front in 1917. As Major von der Busche [1] wrote:

In 1917, when Russian strength was totally exhausted and the Revolution had cast its shadow, there was still a threat of war on two fronts—this at a

[1] Von der Busche was General Ludendorff's closest associate. He was sent with instructions from the Supreme Command to organize the offensive of von Bothmer's army. Later, he was the representative of the War Ministry in Brest-Litovsk. During the last few months before Hitler's invasion of Russia, von der Busche published in the semi-official War Ministry Gazette *Militärische Woche* a strong protest against two-front war, basing his contention on Germany's unfortunate experience in the First World War. On March 2, 1941, the article was reproduced in full in *Pravda*. I quote here the part of it that deals with 1917. This excerpt is a very brief summary of everything written on the strategic position in the theater of war in 1917 by the German military authorities.

moment when things were going well for Germany, and the war on the Western Front could have been ended by one successful strike, at a moment when General Nivelle's French offensive had been crushed, against all expectations, with confusion and tremendous losses on the French side, and the French soldiers had begun to mutiny. . . .

It was under these circumstances that the few German reserves which could be gathered together at the time were moved back again to the Eastern Front so as to put an end first to the so-called Kerensky offensive in Galicia, and then to the Riga offensive, and finally, to secure the rear of our Western Front.

In 1917, from the standpoint of the soldiers, the real tragedy was the fact that the German Army on the Western Front was only able to mount an offensive against the real enemy, the British, at a time when it lacked the strength to break through Amiens and Abbéville to the Channel.[2]

We, the leaders of the Provisional Government, were very much aware of this, and certainty of victory was the basis of our entire policy at home and abroad up to the very last day of Free Russia's existence.

By the middle of September hostilities were already dying down following the fierce fighting near Riga. The Russian armies retreated to new defensive positions. On the Southwest and Rumanian fronts fighting of an inconclusive nature continued. After a spring and summer of inaction, the attempt of the British Army to advance in the north (Ypres) ended, like the spring offensive, in failure, but in September fighting on the Western Front flared up again, mainly in the Italian sector. Ludendorff was forced gradually to withdraw his crack divisions to the Western Front, but the move proved of no strategic value.

Having purged Supreme Headquarters in Mogilev and jailed the conspirators entrenched there, General Alekseyev remained chief of staff for only a few days more. He was replaced by a young, highly gifted officer of the General Staff, General Dukhonin, whom I had come to know well when he was chief of staff to the Commander-in-Chief of the Southwestern Front.

Dukhonin was a broad-minded man, straightforward, honest, and incapable of any political chicanery or tub-thumping. Unlike some of

2 See E. A. L. Buat, *L'Armeé allemande de 1914–18* (Paris, 1920), pp. 42, 51.

the older officers, he was not given to endless grumblings and growlings about the "new system," and he did not idealize the old army. He was not desperately afraid of the soldiers' committees and government commissars, since he recognized the need for them. Furthermore, his daily bulletins from Headquarters on the situation at the front were balanced and truthful, and he never tried to represent the active army as a band of undisciplined riffraff. There was nothing about him of the old military bureaucrat or martinet. He was one of those young officers who had learned "the art of winning" from the teachings of Suvorov and Peter the Great, which meant, among other things, that they did not treat their men as robots, but as human beings.

His great contribution was his rapid and smooth reorganization of the army in tune with the new ideals. After a number of conferences in Petrograd and Mogilev, attended not only by the minister of the army and navy but also by the civilian ministers of foreign affairs, finance, communications, and food, he compiled an itemized report showing the material and political state of the army. The report made one thing clear—the army would have to be cut down in size, reorganized internally, and purged of all disaffected elements among the officers and men. But once this had been done, the army would be able to guard Russia's frontiers and protect her basic interests, provided no major offensives were undertaken. The government and the High Command set themselves the task of securing the withdrawal of Turkey and Bulgaria from the war. This would make it possible to reestablish contact between Russia and her allies through the Dardanelles, thus putting an end to the blockade.

All summer long the ministers of food, internal affairs, and agriculture had been trying unsuccessfully to reach agreement with Headquarters on the demobilization of some of the older men. Now their demobilization began according to a fixed plan.

On September 29, as a further step in a policy that assumed the imminent end of the war, the Foreign Ministry set up a special interdepartmental commission whose task was to work out the first draft of a program for food and medical supplies during the demobilization period, and also for the return of refugees.

Toward the end of September, I sent a letter to Lloyd George informing him that our army was now undergoing reorganization and would be reduced in size. I emphasized, however, that an all-out military offensive by the Western Allies in 1918 would be given all necessary support on the Russian Front, but that Russia could not undertake a major offensive. The letter was sent on to London by the British Ambassador, and to this day it lies unpublished in some British Government archive.

The steps taken by the Provisional Government to reform the army were the only possible means of easing the burden of the war for both the army and the people without at the same time causing a breach with the Allies and thus forfeiting Russia's right to a decisive voice in the postwar settlement.

In the meantime, Tereshchenko's conscientious work in the diplomatic field was helping to improve the trend in favor of a just and democratic peace, and when the government conferred with the political parties on September 22, he was able to state that the Allied Conference on War Aims, which we had worked so hard to bring about, would be held at the end of October.

Disastrous as were the consequences of the military revolt, the six months of steady constructive work which had preceded it were not entirely wasted. Not for one moment in September, 1917 did the Russian army relapse into the state of paralysis that had overcome it during the first few weeks after the fall of the Monarchy. The overwhelming majority of the officers remained true to their duty. They kept their heads and did their best to deal with all the forces at work that were undermining the fighting spirit of the soldiers. The army committees and other organizations at the front, with the exception of a few hopeless cases, worked hard to overcome defeatist tendencies. At the Democratic Conference, representatives from the front-line organizations had been conspicuously opposed to the destructive moods which were rapidly growing among the intellectuals and workers in the capital. On the whole, it can be said that the government of the Republic had the firm backing of the army.

Nor did the Government lack support among the population, which, as in the days immediately following the February Revolution, was again plagued by widespread lawlessness and could look only to the government for protection. On August 27, panic-stricken by the Kornilov mutiny, the Socialist Revolutionaries and Mensheviks, without first consulting the government, had set up, in conjunction with the Bolsheviks, "People's Committees" against counterrevolution all over the country. These committees were at once taken over by the Bolsheviks and their sympathizers. The government immediately began receiving appeals for help from people unable to defend themselves from their self-appointed "protectors."

On September 4 a law (No. 479) ordering the dissolution of these committees was made public. But the all-Russian Executive Committee of the Soviet (*Vzik*), apparently considering itself an independent authority, ordered the committees to disregard the law.

This Bolshevik-sponsored "protection against counterrevolution" continued to be extended to the population, whether they liked it or not. Wherever they could, local authorities disbanded the committees, but they were unable to cope with all the disorders instigated by them. More and more frequently the minister of the interior had to resort to the aid of special organizations formed by local civic leaders, and in mid-October the war minister, General A. I. Verkhovsky, was compelled to send troops to assist the civil administration.

In September and October, despite the seriousness of the situation, the government passed a series of laws pertaining to the forthcoming elections to the Constituent Assembly. Given the state of the country at that stage, this was an extremely difficult and complex task for the local administration. In order to be able to hold the elections on the appointed date, November 12, simplifications had to be introduced in the electoral procedure. But the important thing is that the job was done, and despite all the obstacles created by the Bolsheviks, and all their attempts to cause trouble, the elections were duly held on the day fixed by the Provisional Government. The Bolsheviks, who were by then in power, received only a quarter of the votes.

I can still say, just as I did 48 years ago, that despite three years of war and blockade, despite Lenin's alliance with Ludendorff and the help given to Kornilov's supporters by our allies, the democratic government, which devoted itself to the service of the people and was obedient to their will, would never have been overthrown if the struggle against it had been waged by fair means and not by lies and slander.

The unrelenting campaign of defamation that was aimed both at the Provisional Government and at me personally in the wake of the

Kornilov affair was undoubtedly one of the major factors in the destruction of democracy in Russia.

My testimony before the Extraordinary Commission of Inquiry into the Kornilov Affair on October 8, 1917 ended with the words: "I have no doubt that Kornilov was backed by a group that not only masterminded the plot but also possessed substantial funds and bank credits." [3] My suspicions were only too well founded.

On December 12, 1917, *Izvestiya* published a letter that General Alekseyev had written to Milyukov on September 12 in which he said:

... Kornilov's venture was not instigated by a handful of adventurers. It had the sympathy and support of a large section of our intelligentsia. ... Its purpose was not to overthrow the present regime, but to replace certain persons in the government by men capable of saving Russia. ... Kornilov's plan was not a secret to the members of the government. The issue was discussed with Savinkov and Filonenko,[4] and through them with Kerensky. ... Only a primitive revolutionary court-martial would be able to ignore their participation in the preliminary negotiations and agreements ... Savinkov has already been made to confess in the press.

... The Third Cavalry Corps Division marched on Petrograd upon Kerensky's order, which had been transmitted by Savinkov.

... By then it was impossible to stop the deployment of these troops, as explained in General Lukomsky's telegram No. 6406 to Kerensky: "The arrival of Savinkov and Lvov, who on your behalf made a proposal to this effect to General Kornilov, has compelled General Kornilov to make a final decision, and in accordance with your proposal he issued final instructions, which it is now too late to withdraw."

... This refusal on the part of Kerensky, Savinkov, and Filonenko to participate in the plan devised to set up a government with a different membership, together with Kornilov's subsequent dismissal, was the cause of all the difficulties of August 27 to 31. The plan collapsed; its overt participants were branded as adventurers, traitors, and rebels. Its covert participants either remained the masters of our destinies or have completely withdrawn, exposing about 30 persons to dishonor, trial, and execution.

As you know, certain circles not only had full cognizance and were ideo-

[3] Alexander Kerensky in *Dyelo Kornilova* (*The Kornilov Affair;* Moscow, 1918), pp. 178–179.

[4] Commissar of Ministry of War attached to Headquarters. He went over to the conspirators. He was dismissed as soon as this became known to me. He was never a member of the government.

logical sympathizers, but even helped Kornilov to the utmost. . . . Why is it then that only 30 generals and officers, most of whom were not involved at all, have to pay the price?

. . . The time has come to launch a press campaign about this wretched business. Russia cannot tolerate a crime against her finest and most gallant sons. . . .

. . . Members of the Central Committee of the Officers' Union who did not participate in the undertaking are being prosecuted. Why have they been arrested and why are they threatened with a revolutionary court-martial?

. . . May I ask you for another favor? I do not know the addresses of Messrs. Vyshnegradsky, Putilov, and others. The families of the arrested men are near starvation. A sum of 300,000 rubles needs to be collected and passed on to the Officers' Union Committee in order to save them . . . We officers are more than interested in this matter.

If the more reputable press does not immediately start an all-out inquiry into the affair, our politicians will bring the case before the revolutionary court-martial in five to seven days, in order to reveal the truth and the real circumstances. Unless help comes immediately, Kornilov will have to give the court a detailed description of his preparations, negotiations with various individuals and groups, and will reveal to the people of Russia who it is he has been involved with, as well as the real goals he pursued, and how at the time of trial he was abandoned by all but a handful of officers who will now appear, together with him, before a court-martial.

Signed: Mikhail Alekseyev

It goes without saying that the implications of General Alekseyev's request were clearly understood by those afraid of "compromising themselves," as well as by Milyukov himself. The necessary funds were promptly raised by Putilov and other financiers who had masterminded the Kornilov affair. At the same time, a new publication *Obshcheye Delo* (*The Common Cause*) was launched as the vehicle of a press campaign on the lines suggested by Alekseyev. Its purpose was to discredit me as the head of the Provisional Government, and it printed material which was invaluable to Lenin in his campaign against me as a "traitor to the revolution" who had allegedly aided and abetted Kornilov!

The overall picture of the conspiracy emerged only after the Bolshevik seizure of power. General Alekseyev's name had never been mentioned in any documents pertaining to the conspiracy, and his complicity was, therefore, rather difficult to credit. I read his letter of September 12 after the October Revolution, while I was in hiding and working on my account of the Kornilov revolt. In addition to being an outstanding and farsighted strategist, General Alekseyev was an astute politician. He understood the reasons for Lenin's failure to seize power in July and for Kornilov's almost instant defeat nearly two months later. He realized that in order to stand any chance of success, a new aspirant to power would first have to break the close bond between the people and the army on the one hand, and the Provisional Government on the other, by undermining our ideals and by discrediting me personally. This was the purpose of the barrage of slander directed at me by the champions of Kornilov, who regarded their defeat as only a temporary setback. Needless to say, everything they said about me was grist to the mill of that other aspirant to dictatorial power—Lenin. General Alekseyev knew that these tactics would prompt the uneducated masses to seek guidance from the Left, but that did not worry him and his partisans. They were not at all alarmed by the prospect of the Bolsheviks coming to power. Lenin would overthrow Kerensky —so they reasoned—and would thus unwittingly prepare the way for a "sound government," which would inevitably follow three or four weeks later.[5]

During the slander campaign against the government, the "reputable" newspapers were sometimes induced to reproduce not only compromising rumors or hearsay, but also false evidence, such as Kornilov's, and fake documents. It was such "documents" that provided Lenin, Trotsky, Stalin, and the rest of them with the "evidence" they needed to misrepresent me as a pro-Kornilovite.

[5] I was told by Eugène Petit, a French government representative in Russia during World War I who lived through the whole of the February Revolution, that this was how Milyukov defined the tactics needed to pave the way for a military dictatorship. Petit was a man of impeccable truthfulness. He disapproved of a great deal that the Provisional Government was doing, but he was gravely alarmed by the policy pursued at that time by General Alekseyev, Rodzyanko, Milyukov, and some of the other right-wing opposition leaders. On his own initiative, or perhaps on instructions from the French Government, he had an earnest discussion on the subject with Milyukov, whom he had known personally for some time. At the end of the conversation, Milyukov told him of the tactics which I have outlined above. Milyukov and his friends were convinced—in the middle of October!—that Bolshevism was not a very serious threat and that Russia had only two parties: the "party of order," headed by Kornilov, and the "party of decay," led by me. Petit told me of this conversation with Milyukov some time after the event, when I was already an émigré.

In an interview in Moscow on October 4 with a journalist from the *Russkie Vedomosti* (*Russian Herald*), I. S. Shablovsky, chairman of the Extraordinary Commission of Inquiry, said that he had seen the material published on the Kornilov affair only when he got back to Moscow from Supreme Headquarters. In reply to the journalist's questions he said, *inter alia*:

"Although it can be admitted that General Kornilov's role stands out clearly and completely from the published memoranda, they nevertheless deal solely with the period before General Kornilov presented the Provisional Government with his ultimatum. Since that time the behavior and motives of the General have not been accounted for in the reports published by the press. Furthermore, the reports are in effect not entirely accurate. I could correct not only individual words and expressions, but the whole of General Alekseyev's evidence, which was published a few days ago. For a thorough investigation into all the circumstances preceding the famous ultimatum, the members of the Commission have crossexamined A. F. Kerensky, who himself volunteered to come and give the Commission his competent evidence. It is possible that within the next few days the Prime Minister will be crossexamined again." (The crossexamination took place on October 8, but my detailed and exhaustive account of the "ultimatum" did not, of course, appear in any of the papers.)

"As a whole," said Shablovsky at the end of the interview, "the furore caused by the publication of the memoranda is giving rise to false rumors disturbing the public and preventing the board of inquiry from calmly and objectively considering this burning question, which has already been given the historic name of 'Kornilovism.' "

On October 8, the papers printed an official statement by the Extraordinary Commission, which ran as follows:

Various organs of the press have of late published numerous reports dealing with facts pertaining to the Kornilov case as well as accounts given by persons crossexamined by the Commission. The Commission deems it necessary to state that the published reports originate neither from the Commission nor from any of its members.

Fully appreciating the legitimate interest in this matter on the part of the public, the Commission has nonetheless refrained from publishing the facts it has gathered for the purpose of conducting as full and objective an investigation as possible.

The work of the Commission in investigating most important aspects of the incident involving General Kornilov's actions against the Provisional Government will shortly be concluded, and on completion of its work, the Commission will make an appropriate statement to the press.

Signed: Chairman of the Commission
                          Shablovsky

But these two announcements by the chairman did not stop the flood of lies and slander. The "honest" press supporting General Alekseyev went on poisoning the minds of the public, representing me as a political charlatan and rogue, and the Leninist newspapers eagerly reproduced everything they said in *Rabochi Put* (*Workers' Path*) and various other Bolshevik papers.

I must admit that I was tried beyond endurance by this monstrous and evil campaign. I could do nothing but look on in silence [6] as this poison seeped into the minds of the intelligentsia, soldiers, and workers, undermining both my authority and that of the government. For a moment I lost my faith in human justice. On a visit to Supreme Headquarters I collapsed and remained in a critical condition for several days. I was brought to my senses by General Dukhonin's words: "Kerensky, you cannot, you dare not let yourself go at such a crucial moment. You are carrying too much responsibility on your shoulders." A day later I was back on my feet again, ready to go on fighting with the same determination.

During the September lull at the front, when the German Command saw that Lenin's operations inside Russia were still not producing results and that all of Germany's allies, led by Austria-Hungary, were seeking excuses to drop out of the war, Berlin decided as a last resort to move her entire fleet, with all the dreadnoughts, battleships, cruisers, destroyers, and submarines, and even air support, against Russia.

On September 27 (or 28) we received a signal that a huge German fleet was approaching Russian shores. Immediately after this, the commander of the Baltic Fleet informed us that operations had begun:

The battleships *Grazhdanin* (*Citizen*) and *Slava* (*Glory*), together with the cruiser *Bayan,* sailed into the Riga Straits to meet the enemy and drove

[6] To publish prematurely the facts brought to light by a preliminary investigation is considered a criminal act in all civilized countries and is punishable by law. As head of the government, I had no right to break the law.

off the enemy's vanguard with heavy fire. They then ascertained the whereabouts of the enemy's main force and engaged it in battle. Among the main force were two dreadnoughts, which during the unequal engagement that ensued tried to keep up their fire at maximum distance, which exceeded the range of the guns carried by our own obsolete battleships. Despite the obvious superiority of the enemy force, the Russian warships defended the entrance [to Monsund] for a considerable period, and it was only the severe damage inflicted by the dreadnoughts that forced us to retreat to the inner waters of Monsund. Heavy damage to the *Slava* below the water line caused her to sink. During the engagement our coastal batteries at the entrance to Monsund drove off the enemy destroyers that were attempting to get close to our battleships. At the end of the naval engagement, the German dreadnoughts turned their fire on the coastal batteries and obliterated them within a short time. Another group of Russian warships, actually in Monsund, withstood furious attacks by the enemy from the north. This maneuver was not successful. At the same time a large number of enemy aircraft heavily bombed our ships, the docks, and the island of Moon, which was occupied by Russian troops. Our observation posts, just as on the preceding days, spotted, in sight of the islands of Esel and Dago, a large number of enemy ships, including dreadnoughts, accompanied by a large number of destroyers and patrol boats. In this roadstead alone, at the farthest point visible to the observation posts, as many as 65 pennants could be seen.

The battle at sea for the Monsund defenses contributed a page of glory to the history of the Russian Navy. Like the fighting at Riga, it showed what Russians could do and what they could endure when their country was in danger.

On October 3 the German Navy carried out a landing operation on the island of Esel and the Monsund fortifications protecting the approaches to Kronstadt and Petrograd.

On October 12, the Bolsheviks set up a "military revolutionary committee" under the Petrograd Soviet. Officially this committee was supposed to protect the "capital of the revolution" from a German invasion, but in actual fact it was the headquarters for preparing an armed uprising against the government.

Obeying Lenin's directive, the Bolsheviks indignantly denied in all their public pronouncements that any such preparations were going on, but in a letter containing instructions sent from Finland Lenin wrote: "Only children could fail to realize that, in launching an armed uprising, we must shift not only the responsibility for it, but also the initiative, onto our adversaries."

Trotsky carried out the directive to the letter and bragged, in his writings, that the soldiers, workers, and sailors of Petrograd were certain that in destroying Russian democracy, they were really defending it against an impending counterrevolution by the "Kornilovites."

Lenin was later to resort to similar duplicity in his preparations for a separate peace, in the dispersion of the Constituent Assembly, in the abolition of all civil and political liberties, and in his merciless war against the peasantry.

Playing on their genuine patriotic feelings, Lenin, Trotsky, and the rest of them cynically asserted that the "procapitalist" Provisional Government headed by Kerensky was out to betray their homeland and the Revolution, the freedom and honor of their country, and was going to sell them to the Germans. Hence, so their line ran, it was up to the champions of the struggle for an "honorable, democratic peace for all peoples" to overthrow the supporters of a disgraceful separate peace so that "democratic revolutionary Russia" could make peace with the peoples on the other side over the heads of the "imperialist governments."

At meetings of workers the language used was different and somewhat more candid. Here they spoke of the "dictatorship of the proletariat." Only a dictatorship of that kind, they said, could safeguard the gains of the Revolution and the freedom that had been won. The proletariat was a stern and unrelenting guardian of the peace, and it demanded the overthrow of the Kerensky government in order to establish its dictatorship in the interests of the Revolution itself: that was the only means by which the peasants, workers, and soldiers could obtain a democratic peace, possession of the land, and complete freedom.

Many workers believed this and set off to destroy freedom and crucify the Revolution for the sake of an impending totalitarian dictatorship, certain that they were carrying out the "liberating mission of the proletariat."

Some foreigners might think that only politically immature, ignorant Russian soldiers, sailors, and workers could be taken in by Lenin's utter perversion of the truth. Nothing of the sort! There is a certain higher degree of falsehood which, by its very enormity, exercises a peculiar fascination for all human beings, whatever their intellectual level. There is a kind of psychological law according to which the more outrageous a lie is, the more likely it is to be believed. It was on this human failing that Lenin based his strategy for seizing power.

Lenin, Zinoviev, Kamenev, and Trotsky were all men who had spent many years abroad in the same émigré circles as other, non-Bolshevik socialists. From the point of view of the latter, Bolshevism was simply the most extreme wing of the general socialist and revolutionary movement. The average socialist could not bring himself to believe that Lenin, with the struggle for world revolution at heart, could possibly enter into a practical collaboration with the Germans. To them it was "filthy slander," clear and indisputable! Nor did it seem psychologically possible that Lenin and his general staff were getting ready to disperse the Constituent Assembly by force of arms.

Lenin remained in Finland right up to the outbreak of the October uprising, but he had two trusted agents—Trotsky and Kamenev—working for him in Petrograd. Trotsky was responsible for the technical side of the uprising and also for political agitation among the masses of soldiers, sailors, and workers. Kamenev had a different task, but a no less important one: In the period immediately preceding the uprising, he was to distract the attention of the central organizations of the socialist parties from Lenin's real aims, lull their suspicions, and make sure that when Trotsky attacked, the Provisional Government would get no active support from them.

Kamenev carried out his task to perfection. This mild, amiable man knew how to tell lies with incredible plausibility. He had a shrewd understanding of the people he was cheating, and he was able to do it with an almost childishly innocent expression on his face.

The decisive moment was rapidly approaching. November 12 was the date fixed for the elections to the Constituent Assembly. But Lenin could not afford to wait for them, because, as he himself admitted, they would not have brought him a majority.

The second All-Russian Congress of Soviets was due to open in Petrograd on November 7. According to Lenin, "it would have been a betrayal of the Revolution to make the childish and shameful pretense of formality by waiting for the Congress to begin, for although the Soviets were an excellent weapon with which to seize power, they would only be a *useless toy* after power had been seized."

The most important thing was to wrest power from the Provisional Government before the Austro-German-Turko-Bulgarian coalition disintegrated, that is, before the Provisional Government had had a chance to make an honorable peace together with the Allies. Here, once again, the interests of Lenin and the German General Staff coincided.

The Germans needed a coup d'état in Petrograd to stop Austria from signing a separate peace treaty. For Lenin, an immediate peace with Germany after his accession to power was the only way he could establish a dictatorship. Both the Germans and Lenin knew, of course, that on October 28 Foreign Minister Tereshchenko; General Golovin, the representative of Supreme Headquarters; Skobelev, the Social Democrat spokesman; and the British Ambassador, were due to leave for Paris to attend a conference of the Entente, scheduled for November 3, that might affect the course of the whole war.

In the socialist parties a great many people regarded rumors about a forthcoming Bolshevik uprising as "counterrevolutionary fabrications." Still shaken by the recent Kornilov revolt and under the spell of Kamenev's subtle propaganda, the left-wing parties were concerned only about the "danger from the right." As I have already shown, there was no such danger at all, and Lenin was well aware of this fact as early as August 30.

It will be remembered that in preparing to launch a blow at Petrograd, the right-wing conspirators had sought to "arrange" a Bolshevik revolt in that city. Now, in mid-October, all Kornilov supporters, both military and civilian, were instructed to sabotage government measures to suppress the Bolshevik uprising.

Thus, as before, the struggle was a three-way affair.

The Bolshevik and right-wing press, and the Bolshevik and right-wing agitators, were equally vehement in their attacks on me. There was, of course, a difference in the terminology of their abuse: The Bolsheviks called me a "Bonaparte," and the right wing called me a "semi-Bolshevik"; but for both camps alike my name was a symbol of democratic, revolutionary, free Russia that could not be destroyed without destroying the government that I headed.

Both the Bolsheviks and the Kornilovites knew full well that, by destroying the moral authority of those bearing the supreme authority in the Republic, they would paralyze all the democratic and popular forces in Russia for many years to come.

But, just as in the Time of Troubles three hundred years before, the political consciousness of many responsible statesmen and politicians was dulled. Their wills weakened and their patience failed them just at the moment when the destiny of Russia was at stake, when, as Churchill has so rightly pointed out, the Russian people held victory in their hands.

I am firmly convinced that the uprising of October 24–25 was deliberately timed to coincide with the serious crisis in Austro-German relations, just as Ludendorff's counterattack "coincided" with Lenin's attempted uprising in July.

By November 15, Turkey and Bulgaria were to have concluded a separate peace with Russia. Suddenly, on about October 20, we received a secret communication from Count Czernin, the foreign minister of the Austro-Hungarian Monarchy. The message, which came to us through Sweden, stated that Austria-Hungary was ready to make peace, unbeknown to Germany. It was arranged that representatives from Vienna would appear at the Conference on War Aims which was due to open in Paris on November 3.

Ludendorff and all the other advocates of fighting on to the bitter end probably knew all about this before we did. His aim was now to keep Austria from withdrawing from the war, and Lenin's plan was to seize power before the government could play this trump card, which would have robbed Lenin of any chance of seizing power.

On October 24 Lenin sent his Central Committee a hysterical letter in which he said:

Comrades:

I am writing these lines on the evening of the 6th [N. S.]. The situation is extremely critical. It is as clear as can be that delaying the uprising now really means death. . . .

We must not wait! We may lose everything! . . .

It would be disaster . . . to wait for the uncertain voting of November 7. . . .[7]

[7] The opening date of the Congress of Soviets.

On the night of October 23 Trotsky's "military-revolutionary committee" came out into the open and began to issue orders for the seizure of government offices and strategic points in the city.

Now having documentary proof of the incipient revolt, I went straight to the meeting of the Council of the Republic at 11 A.M. on October 24, and asked the chairman, Avksentiev, to allow me to speak at once.

After I had spoken for some time, Konovalov approached me and handed me a note. There was a long pause while I read it, and then I continued:

I have just been given a copy of the document which is now being illegally circulated to army units. It reads: "The Petrograd Soviet is in danger. You are to instruct the regiments to stand by for further orders. Delay or refusal to obey orders will be considered treachery to the Revolution. Signed, on behalf of the chairman [of the Revolutionary Committee], Podvoisky. Secretary Antonov." (Cries of "Traitors!" from the Right.) And so, at the present moment, the capital is in what is termed in legal language a state of revolt. We are faced with an attempt to incite the mob against the existing order, to thwart the plan for a Constituent Assembly (cries of "Hear, hear!" from the Center and Right), and to lay open the front lines to the armies of Kaiser Wilhelm. (Cries of "Hear, hear!" from the Right and Center; from the Left, jeering and shouts of "That's enough!") I use the term "mob" because the whole of the democratic movement and its Central Executive Committee, all the army organizations, and everything that Russia is justly proud of—the reason, conscience, and honor of the great Russian democracy—protest against it (stormy applause from all the benches, except the Menshevik Internationalists) . . . Let it be understood that the objective danger of this uprising lies not so much in the possibility that the movement, just as in July, may act as a signal for the Germans to launch a new attack against our frontiers and may result *in a new attempt, even more serious than Kornilov's* attempt. Let every one remember that Kalush and Tarnopol coincided with the July revolt. . . .

I have come here to appeal to your vigilance in defense of the freedom of the Russian people which has been won by many generations and much sacrifice of blood and lives. I have come here in the certainty that the Provisional Government, which at the present time is defending this newly won freedom, will receive the wholehearted support—not only of the Council, but of the whole nation. (Stormy applause from all but the Menshevik Internationalists.)

Here, on behalf of the government, I am able to state that the government has never violated the civil liberties of Russian citizens. Proceeding from a firm understanding of the present state of affairs, the Provisional Government has done its best not to cause any strong clashes of opinion prior to the Constituent Assembly. But the Provisional Government, fully aware of its responsibility to the country and to the future, now wishes to state that at the present time all elements in Russian society, all groups and parties that have dared to raise their hands against the free will of the Russian people, will immediately be put down with all possible firmness. (Stormy applause from the Center and part of the Left: laughter from the Internationalists.) Let the people of Petrograd know that they will be resolutely opposed, and that perhaps, at the last hour or minute, reason, conscience, and honor will prevail in the hearts of those who still possess them. (Applause from the Right and in the Center.)

On behalf of the country I ask and demand that, at today's meeting, you give the Provisional Government an answer to the question: Can it proceed with its duties strong in the certainty that it has the backing of this high assembly?"

Firmly convinced that the Council would give me the support I had demanded, I went back to the headquarters of the Petrograd Military District to attend to measures intended to nip the revolt in the bud. I felt sure that I would receive the reply I wanted within a couple of hours. But the rest of the day passed without any word. It was not until midnight that a delegation representing the majority in the Council came to see me and handed me a resolution adopted after long and stormy discussion in a variety of committees and subcommittees.

The resolution was completely useless. It was of no value to either the government or to any one else. It was so interminably long and so hopelessly muddled that it was barely intelligible. For anyone who looked hard enough it contained an expression of conditional confidence in the government, hedged around by many critical comments and reservations.

I told Dan (who led the delegation) somewhat curtly that the resolution was totally unacceptable. Dan replied calmly to my heated words. I shall never forget what he said. In his opinion, and evidently in that of the rest of the delegation, I was exaggerating the danger, under the influence of my "reactionary staff." He went on to say that the Council's resolution would be something of a blow to the *amour-*

propre of the government, but would be extremely useful in bringing about a "change of heart in the masses." He went on to say that the resolution would undoubtedly cause a decline in the effectiveness of Bolshevik propaganda. In fact, he said, according to an authoritative statement by the Bolshevik leaders, the revolt "had flared up against their wishes and without their sanction." They were ready "the very next day" to conform with the majority of the Council and take all necessary steps to halt the revolt. Gravely he advised me that the measures taken by the government to curb the uprising could only "irritate the masses." By its intervention, the government would merely "prevent those representing the majority in the Council from successfully negotiating with the Bolsheviks on a peaceful liquidation of the revolt." The results of Kamenev's handiwork were only too apparent: Without a word I went into the next room where a meeting of the government was in progress, and read aloud the resolution. Then I gave an account of my conversation with Dan. The reaction of my colleagues may be imagined. I went straight back to the delegation and returned the document to Dan with an appropriate comment on the absurd and criminal text.[8]

The delegation from the Council of the Republic came to me at a moment when armed detachments of Red Guards had already occupied some of the government offices and when one of the government ministers, Kartashov, had just been arrested on his way home from a meeting in the Winter Palace. He had been taken to the Smolny Institute, where his arrival coincided almost exactly with Dan's, the latter having gone there to continue his talks with Kamenev on ways

---

[8] A better comment has been made on this historical document, if it can be called such, by leading Communist historians in the introduction to the second volume of *The Revolution and Civil War as Described by the White Guards,* 2d ed., Vol. II (State Publishing House, 1926). The learned editors of this work write: "It must be admitted that speaking as they did on October 24, Dan and the Mensheviks fully deserved the title of 'Semi-Bolsheviks.' Indeed, all their demands matched the three basic pre-October Bolshevik demands, from which they were undoubtedly stolen. But they are as different from their prototype *as a bastard is from his 'left-wing' and 'right-wing' parents.* Hence the absurd gravity with which Dan, even in 1923, tells of the resolution adopted by the pre-parliament [i.e., the Council of the Republic] on the eve of October 25, as if it was an event of the first importance and likely to turn the Revolution in a different direction. Hence his *ridiculous attempt to convince Kerensky* that, at the moment of the uprising, salvation lay not in using armed force, but in posting up and circulating this remarkable resolution. . . ."

of "liquidating the uprising that had flared up" against the will of the Bolsheviks.

According to Dan, the gravest danger to the gains of the Revolution at that time was my "reactionary staff." In fact, however, in the Petrograd Military District three-quarters of the officers were engaged in sabotaging, along with Dan and his friends, all the government's efforts to deal with the uprising, which was fast gaining ground.

Kamenev, having spent the whole night of October 24 talking with the spokesmen of the other socialist parties, achieved his purpose; the Socialist Revolutionaries and the Mensheviks had their own military organizations, but they were not mobilized. In the barracks Bolshevik agitators operated in complete freedom, hardly meeting with any resistance at all from the representatives of the Menshevik and the Socialist Revolutionary parties.

The night of October 24–25 was a time of tense expectation. We were waiting for troops to arrive from the front. They had been summoned by me in good time and were due in Petrograd on the morning of October 25. But instead of the troops, all we got were telegrams and telephone messages saying that the railways were being sabotaged.

By morning (October 25) the troops had not yet arrived. The central telephone exchange, post office, and most of the government offices were occupied by detachments of Red Guards. The building that housed the Council of the Republic, which only the day before had been the scene of an endless and stupid discussion, had also been occupied by Red sentries.

The Winter Palace was cut off, and even telephone contact was broken. After a long meeting that had lasted into the early hours of the morning, most of the members of the government had gone home to get some rest. Left alone together, Konovalov and I walked over to the district military staff, which was a stone's throw away on the Palace Square. Another minister, Kishkin, one of Moscow's most popular Liberals, accompanied us.

After a brief discussion it was decided that I should drive out at once to meet the troops. We were all quite sure that the paralysis of will that had seized democratic Petrograd would pass as soon as it was recognized that Lenin's plot was by no means a "misunderstanding," but a perfidious blow that left Russia entirely at the mercy of the Germans.

Red Guard sentries had been posted in all the streets around the Winter Palace. Check points at the approaches to Petrograd along the road to Tsarskoye Selo, Gatchina and Pskov, were also occupied by armed Bolsheviks.

I decided to take a big risk and drive all the way across the city. This was part of my normal routine, to which everyone was accustomed. When the fast car I normally used arrived, we explained to the army driver what he was to do. At the last moment, just before the acting commander of the Petrograd military district, my adjutant, and I left, some officials from the British and U. S. embassies arrived on the scene and offered to drive us out of the city under the American flag. I thanked the Allies for their offer, but said that the head of the government could not drive through the Russian capital under the American flag. As I later learned, however, the car turned out to be useful for one of my officers who could not fit into my own car. It drove a distance behind us.

I said goodbye to Konovalov and Kishkin, who remained in Petrograd, and drove off. The driver and my adjutant were in front, and I sat in the back in my usual semimilitary uniform. Next to me sat Kuzmin, who was in command of the troops of the Petrograd District, and opposite us were two adjutants.[9]

The driver was told to maintain his usual speed along the main thoroughfares of the capital, which led to the checkpoints. This plan worked very well. My appearance in the streets of the city among the insurgents was so unexpected that they failed to react as they should have done. Many of the "revolutionary" sentries stood to attention! Once outside the city, my driver put his foot down on the accelerator, and we moved along at a hair-raising pace. He seemed to feel instinc-

[9] Lies and slander are often quite indestructible. Even to this day foreigners occasionally ask me, with some embarrassment, if it is true that I fled from the Winter Palace dressed as a nurse! That foreigners should believe this utter rubbish is perhaps forgivable. But it is quite extraordinary that this story is still put out for popular consumption in the Soviet Union. The more serious historical works published in Moscow give a factually accurate account of my departure from Petrograd to Gatchina, but in a vast number of popular histories the same story is repeated over and over again to fool the people of Russia, and also the people of other countries, that is, that I sneaked away dressed in a woman's skirt.

tively that someone must already have reported my departure to Lenin and Trotsky.

At the Moscow checkpoint our car was fired at, but we arrived safely at Gatchina. Despite an attempt to stop us here, we again got through unharmed.

By nighttime we had reached Pskov, headquarters of the commander-in-chief, Northern Front. To be on the safe side we were lodged in a private apartment belonging to my brother-in-law, Quartermaster General Baranovsky. General Cheremisov, the commander-in-chief, came to the apartment in obedience to my summons, but it turned out that he was already "flirting" with the Bolsheviks. The troops I had asked to have sent to Petrograd had been halted on his orders. After a very heated exchange, General Cheremisov left.

We had no doubt whatsoever that he would tell the new masters of the situation that I was there. We had to move on toward the front.

The Third Cossack Cavalry Corps was stationed in a little town called Ostrov. This was the same regiment that was supposed to have occupied the capital in September, under the command of General Krymov. In his conversation with me, Cheremisov had said that General Krasnov, the new commander of the Third Corps, had been in Pskov, trying to find me. I asked where he was and was told he had gone back to Ostrov.

We decided to go to Ostrov immediately, and if we did not find him, to go on to Mogilev and see General Dukhonin, chief of staff, at Supreme Headquarters. I learned later that Dukhonin had been trying to get me on the telephone, but that Cheremisov had refused to let him speak to me. Dukhonin had called up Northern Headquarters on the direct line, and the telephone had been answered by Lukirsky, Cheremisov's chief of staff. Lukirsky had told Dukhonin at the very beginning of the conversation that the commander-in-chief, Northern Front had rescinded his order for troops to be sent to Petrograd, but that he (Lukirsky) could give no explanation of this. Then Dukhonin asked Lukirsky if he could speak to Cheremisov personally, and the following conversation ensued:

Lukirsky: I'll go and tell the C.I.C. you're on the line.
Cheremisov: Hello, Nikolai Nikolayevich [Dukhonin]. You were about to say something just now.

Dukhonin: General Lukirsky has told me that it was you who gave the order canceling the dispatch of troops to Petrograd on instructions from the Supreme Commander. Why has that been done?

Cheremisov: It has been done with the consent of the Supreme Commander, which I received from him personally. . . .

Kerensky has stepped down and wishes to hand over his duties as Supreme Commander to me. The matter will be settled today. Please issue orders that the transfer of troops to Petrograd, if it is under way on other fronts, should be halted. The Supreme Commander is here with me. Do you have any message for him?

Dukhonin: Can he come to the telephone?

Cheremisov: It is not possible, in his own interest.

After a long conversation on the situation at the front and in Petrograd, about which the two generals took two decidedly different views, Dukhonin said to Cheremisov:

If Supreme Commander Kerensky intends handing over his duties to you, then in the name of your love for our country I implore you to let me tell this to the Provisional Government, with which I am in contact, and I implore you not to stop any instructions on the transfer of troops intended for Petrograd . . . As the future Supreme Commander, you will not have to reckon with the extremely grave—

Without letting Dukhonin finish, Cheremisov broke in with the words: "Sorry, . . . someone wants to talk to me. May I call you again in two hours' time?"

On the morning of October 26, General Dukhonin sent for General Lukirsky and was told by him that "yesterday, after the order canceling the movement of troops toward Petrograd, Kerensky arrived and stated that he did not share Cheremisov's opinion regarding the necessity for that cancellation. It was not possible, however, to pass on orders to continue the movement because special sentries had been posted at the telephones by the revolutionary committees set up in Pskov." [10]

General Cheremisov's statement that the movement of troops to Petrograd had been halted with my consent and that I had stepped down from the post of Supreme Commander and handed over my duties to him, was circulated to all the fronts without Dukhonin's knowl-

[10] *Archives of the Russian Revolution,* Vol. 7 (Berlin, 1920), pp. 297–299.

edge. The formation of detachments at the various fronts for Petrograd was halted, along with the movement of troop trains. On the morning of October 26 the truth came out, but by then several vital hours had been lost.

A few minutes before our departure for Ostrov, someone rang the front doorbell, and a moment later General Krasnov and Popov, his chief of staff, came into the room.

Cheremisov had been lying when he told me that General Krasnov had left Pskov. Fortunately, however, Krasnov had realized that the commander-in-chief of the Northern Front was trying to prevent his seeing me and had decided to come and find me himself, if he possibly could. Knowing that Baranovsky was my brother-in-law, he had decided to try his apartment.

By the morning of October 26 we were both at Third Corps Headquarters in Ostrov. The only troops there were a few hundred Cossacks (about 500–600). All the rest of the corps were deployed along the front and the approaches to the capital. We decided to make an immediate attempt to break through into Petrograd with our pitifully small force of men and artillery.

The hastily organized Bolshevik military committees and railroad workers had received orders from Lenin to prevent our detachment from getting back to the capital, but they failed to stop us.

That evening, in the train on the way back to Petrograd, we learned that the night before, the Bolsheviks had taken the Winter Palace and arrested the whole of the Provisional Government.

Overcoming a number of difficult obstacles en route, our detachment occupied Gatchina without a fight on the morning of October 27. The thousands of soldiers there, who were supposed to have joined the Bolsheviks, took to their heels, leaving their arms behind them.

The same morning in Gatchina I received a communication from Petrograd saying that the temporary paralysis had passed and that all the supporters of the Provisional Government in the various regiments and military schools were secretly mobilizing for battle. The fighting forces of the Socialist Revolutionary Party were also mobilized. General Dukhonin, together with the commanders-in-chief of all fronts except the Northern Front, had sent bodies of troops to assist us. Some 50 trainloads of soldiers were trying to get through to us from different parts of the front. Both at the front and in Moscow, fighting was breaking out between the defenders of the government and the Bolsheviks.

The Bolsheviks had by now captured the most powerful radio station in Russia, which was located at Tsarskoye Selo. They immediately launched a barrage of propaganda aimed at demoralizing the Russian front lines. At the same time, the Second Congress of Soviets issued its famous appeal for a universal democratic peace!

The forces we had in Gatchina were very small. There was nothing we could do to counteract the results of Lenin's propaganda at the front.

Krasnov agreed with me that we should try to take Tsarskoye Selo in an all-out attack, and from there move on immediately to Petrograd, where loyal army units, the officer cadets, and party fighting organizations would come to our aid.

At dawn on October 28, the government forces set out from Gatchina. General Krasnov was in excellent spirits and was quite confident of success. Our relationship was one of complete mutual confidence. Not wishing to interfere with Krasnov's orders, I remained at Gatchina and tried to help speed the arrival of the troop trains that had been sent to our assistance.

Several hours passed, but no word came through on Krasnov's progress. This puzzled me, for just before his detachment had set out, we had received quite encouraging news of the state of affairs at Tsarskoye Selo. The position could not have changed so drastically within a few hours. I ordered my car and set off after Krasnov.

Halfway between Tsarskoye Selo and Gatchina there was a meteorological observatory. From the top of it, through field glasses, I could make out the government troops camped in the fields. They appeared to be strangely inactive.

I drove on to find out what had happened. Krasnov gave me some sort of vague explanation, which made little sense. His attitude was formal and cautious.

Quite by chance I suddenly noticed that among those standing around General Krasnov were some familiar faces from the Soviet of the Cossack Troops. This soviet, one of the right-wing antidemocratic organizations, had been backing the policy of "using Lenin to overthrow Kerensky." I asked Krasnov why these people were present there. The General seemed greatly embarrassed, but declined to give any explanation. I realized then the reason for the sudden delay in the movement of the troops to Tsarskoye Selo and the change in Krasnov's behavior.

I had to use great pressure to get the detachment to move again. It was not until the early evening (instead of midday as originally expected), that we arrived at the outskirts of Tsarskoye Selo. Krasnov reported that he had decided to pull his troops back a little and take the town the next day. That was the last straw!

Just then someone prominent in political circles arrived from the capital and reported to me that everything was now ready in Petrograd for an armed uprising in support of the government forces, that the population and all the anti-Bolshevik parties were anxiously awaiting our arrival, and that it was vital to act without delay. I issued a written order to General Krasnov to occupy Tsarskoye Selo at once. He still hesitated. Then I drove up to the checkpoint at the entrance to the town, where there was a crowd of armed bedraggled soldiers, stood up in my car, took out my watch, and announced that I would give them three minutes to lay down their arms, after which the artillery would open fire on them. They obeyed at once.

Tsarskoye Selo was thus occupied without one shot being fired, but after a fatal delay of some twelve hours.

By the morning of the twenty-ninth we should have been in Petrograd, but we had only gotten as far as Tsarskoye Selo. That same day an anti-Bolshevik revolt broke out in the capital. At four in the afternoon I was called to the telephone. It was the Mikhailsky Castle calling from the very center of the city, where the headquarters of the government supporters was located. They begged me to send help, but we were unable to give it.

The final act in the tragedy of the Provisional Government's struggle for the freedom and honor of Russia was played out on October 30, near Pulkovo, the site of the famous observatory. Against us were arrayed 12,000 men variously armed. The so-called Pulkovo Heights were occupied by Kronstadt sailors. We had 700 Cossacks, one armored train, the first infantry regiment to reach us from the front, and a few field guns. Most of the troops of the Petrograd Garrison abandoned their positions as soon as our artillery began shelling them, and the Cossacks charged them on horseback. But the Bolshevik right flank, consisting of the Kronstadt sailors, held out.

Despite the tactical success at Pulkovo, we had to withdraw again to Gatchina. We simply did not have sufficient forces either to engage in pursuit or to consolidate our positions along the extensive battle line.

In Gatchina the morale of the government troops began to decline. General Krasnov and his staff officers were now urging me to open peace talks with the Bolsheviks. I was absolutely opposed to this, but on October 31 the Military Council decided to send a delegation to Petrograd. The reinforcements from the front were now approaching Gatchina. At Luga, the next town to Gatchina, the entire garrison was on the side of the government. I made up my mind to play for time. In Petrograd there was already a center of anti-Bolshevik forces—the "Committee for the Salvation of the Homeland and the Revolution." Using as a courier Stankevich, the commissar attached to Supreme Headquarters, I sent my terms, which were, of course, completely unacceptable to the Bolsheviks, direct to that committee. Stankevich left at once for the capital.

25

My Life Underground

Escape from Gatchina

O N October 31, 1917, General Krasnov authorized a Cossack delegation to go to Krasnoye Selo, near Petrograd, to open negotiations for a truce with the Bolsheviks. In the early morning hours of November 1, the Cossack delegation returned with a Bolshevik delegation headed by P. Dybenko.[1] The negotiations between the Bolsheviks and the Cossacks began on the ground floor of the Gatchina Palace in the presence of General Krasnov and Colonel Popov, his chief of staff.

I was waiting in my upper floor apartment for the outcome of the talks. All at once some friends came into my room with the alarming news that the negotiations were nearly over, and that the Cossacks had agreed to hand me over to Dybenko in exchange for a promise that they would be sent home to the Don and allowed to keep their horses and arms.

Gatchina Palace was deserted, except for a small group of loyal followers who were acting as intermediaries and keeping me informed on the development of the negotiations. We were aware of the demoralization of the Cossacks and the subversive activities going on all around us. But it still seemed incredible that General Krasnov or the commanding officers of the Cossack corps would stoop to plain treachery.

General Krasnov came to see me around 11 A.M. If before then I had had reason to suspect him, my suspicion became a certainty in

[1] A Red sailor who rose rapidly after the October Revolution, becoming commander-in-chief of the Red Army in Turkestan. He was executed in 1937 at the same time as Tukhachevsky.

the light of that conversation. He tried to persuade me to go to Petrograd and talk to Lenin. He assured me that I would be fully protected by a Cossack guard and that this was the only solution. I shall not go into the details of our last meeting.[2] In retrospect I realize how difficult the General's task had been, for he was not a traitor by nature.

Then my "observers" came running upstairs to report the final outcome of the negotiations. I was to be handed over to Dybenko, and the Cossacks were to return to the Don.

By then it was noon. The noise and shouting from downstairs grew louder. I kept urging everyone, except my personal aide, N. V. Vinner, to leave. Vinner and I were determined not to surrender alive. We intended to shoot ourselves in the back rooms while the Cossacks and sailors were searching for us in the front rooms. On the morning of November 14, 1917, this resolve of ours seemed quite logical and inevitable. As people were bidding me farewell, the door opened and two men appeared on the threshold, a civilian whom I knew, and a sailor I had never seen before. "There is no time to waste," they said. "Within half an hour an angry mob will storm your apartment. Take off your field jacket—hurry!" Seconds later I had become a rather grotesque-looking sailor: the sleeves of the jacket were too short, my tan shoes and the puttees did not match. My beribboned sailor's cap was far too small and perched precariously on the top of my head. My disguise was completed by a pair of automobile goggles. I embraced my aide, and he left through an adjoining room.

Gatchina Palace was built in the form of a medieval castle by the insane Emperor Paul I, and it was a real trap. It was surrounded by moats, and the only exit led across a drawbridge. We could only hope to bluff our way through the armed mob below to the car that was waiting for us in the forecourt. The sailor and I went out to the only staircase in the corridor. We walked like robots, our minds drained of thought and unconscious of danger.

We gained the forecourt without incident, but no car was to be seen. In despair we turned back without saying a word to each other. We must have looked very odd indeed. People in the crowd near the gateway were looking at us curiously, but fortunately some of them were on our side. Then a man came up to us and whispered: "The

[2] After World War II, General Krasnov was handed over to Stalin by the Allies and was executed in Moscow.

car is waiting at the Kitayskiye Vorota (Chinese Gate). Don't waste any time!" He spoke none too soon, for the crowd was already beginning to move in our direction and we felt very uncomfortable indeed. But just then a bandaged young officer suddenly "fainted," distracting the attention of the crowd and starting a commotion. We were quick to grasp the opportunity and dashed out of the palace yard. We headed straight toward the Chinese Gate, which gave on to the road to Luga. We walked slowly, chatting loudly to avoid suspicion.

My disappearance was discovered about 30 minutes later by the crowd of Cossacks and sailors as they burst into my upstairs apartment. Cars were sent out in all directions without delay, but once again we had a stroke of luck. For we suddenly saw a horse-cab moving slowly toward us down the deserted street. We hailed it and promised the cabbie a good tip to take us to the Chinese Gate. His jaw dropped when he finally got a 100-ruble tip from two sailors. The car was waiting for us there. I jumped into the seat next to the officer who was driving, while the sailor settled down in the back with four or five soldiers armed with hand grenades. The highway to Luga was superb, but we kept looking back, expecting at any moment to catch sight of our pursuers. In case of pursuit we had decided to use all the hand grenades stored in the back seat. Despite the strain, however, the officer appeared incredibly calm and even whistled a cheerful tune from Vertinsky as he drove on.

Owing to yet another stroke of luck our pursuers never caught up with us. My own driver, who had stayed behind in the Gatchina Palace, was loyal to me. He knew that we were heading for Luga, and when my disappearance was discovered he yelled that he had the fastest car and would catch up with the "scoundrel." Knowing that he would indeed have no difficulty catching up with us, he managed to feign a breakdown on the way.

Finally we reached a forest. The brakes shrieked. "Get out, Alexander Fyodorovich," the officer said. My sailor, whose name was Vanya, followed me. We were in the middle of nowhere—nothing but trees all around—and I wondered what it was all about. "Goodbye, sir. Vanya will explain everything. We must get going." Then he accelerated quickly and disappeared. "You see," said Vanya, "my uncle has a cottage here, in the middle of the forest. It's a quiet place. I haven't been here myself for two years. As long as there's no servant there, everything will be all right. Let's risk it, Alexander Fyodorovich!"

We followed an overgrown trail which led into the depths of the forest. We walked on, surrounded by dead stillness, without thinking, without wondering what would happen when we reached the cottage. I had boundless faith in these strangers who, for some reason, were risking their own lives so cheerfully in order to save me. Occasionally Vanya stopped to get his bearings. I had lost all sense of time, and the walk had begun to seem endless. Suddenly my companion said: "We're almost there." We reached a clearing and saw the cottage in front of us. "Just sit down awhile. I'll go and find out what's going on." Vanya disappeared into the cottage, but returned shortly to say "There's no servant. The maid left yesterday. My uncle and aunt are happy to welcome you. Let's go."

The Forest Cottage

That was the beginning of my life in the forest haven, where I was to spend 40 days.

The Bolotovs, an elderly couple, greeted me warmly. "Don't you worry. Everything will be all right," they consoled me. They offered me the shelter of their home wholeheartedly and generously, without even so much as hinting at what they were risking for my sake. They must have been fully aware of the danger they were running, for on October 27, *Izvestiya* had published the following announcement under the headline, *"Arrest of Former Ministers":* "The former ministers Konovalov, Kishkin, Tereshchenko, Malyantovich, Nikitin and others, have been arrested by the Revolutionary Committee. Kerensky has escaped. All army organizations will exert every effort to bring about Kerensky's immediate arrest and transfer to Petrograd. Any help or assistance given to Kerensky is punishable as high treason."

My pursuers looked for me high and low. It never occurred to them that I was not hiding somewhere on the Don or in Siberia, but was living almost under their noses, between Gatchina and Luga.

Meanwhile, there was nothing for me to do but to lie low and change my appearance as much as possible. I grew a beard and a moustache. The beard was a poor disguise, since it grew in a neat fringe around my cheeks, leaving the chin and the lower part of my face bare. Nevertheless, 40 days later, wearing glasses and a crop of untidy hair, I managed to look like a nihilist student of the 1860's.

The memory of those long November nights will never leave me. We were always on guard, and Vanya never left my side. We had kept a handful of grenades, and we were fully prepared to use them if we had to. In the daytime everything was peaceful and sunny, and the past seemed remote and unreal. But at night I was haunted by all that had happened, and the full horror of the *danse macabre* now going on in the country was borne in upon me. At all times I felt a gnawing fear, not so much for my own safety as for that of my good hosts. Whenever the night air came to life with the barking of the dogs in the neighboring village, we leaped from our beds to stand watch on the porch, hand grenades in readiness.

Sometimes in the early days of my stay at the friendly cottage I had fits of despair during the night and I wished that my pursuers would come and arrest me. Then, at least, I would be relieved of my thoughts and of my pain.

But gradually I began to feel that the Bolsheviks had been put off the scent and that the immediate danger had passed. Through Vanya I succeeded in establishing contact with Petrograd. News from the capital now began to reach me, and occasionally a trusted emissary came to see me. I knew it was my duty to fight on and serve Russia to the very end. I had traveled all over our vast country, and I knew that the people, without distinction of class, would not yield without a fight to the yoke of a dictatorship. I was sure that the poisonous effects of the unscrupulous Bolshevik propaganda in the capital would rapidly wear off as soon as Lenin and his accomplices had cast off their guise of democracy and patriotism.

The first to voice their alarm at Lenin's usurpation of power were the leaders of the Soviet of Peasants' Deputies, who, on October 26, issued the following statement:

Comrade Peasants!

All the liberties gained with the blood of your sons and brothers are now in terrible, mortal jeopardy.

The revolution is in danger! The homeland is in danger!

Again fraternal blood is being shed in the streets of Petrograd. Again the whole country is being thrown into an abyss of confusion and disintegration. Again a blow is being inflicted upon the army, which defends the homeland and the revolution from external defeat.

On October 26, the Bolshevik Party and the Petrograd Soviet of Workers' and Soldiers' Deputies, which is led by it, seized power in their hands. They have arrested and jailed in the Peter and Paul Fortress the Provisional Government and the socialist ministers, including the members of the Executive Committee of the Soviet of Peasants' Deputies, S. L. Maslov and S. S. Salaskin. They have dispersed by armed force the Provisional Council of the Russian Republic, elected for the supervision of the activity of the Provisional Government until [the convening of] the Constituent Assembly. Finally, they have declared the Prime Minister and Supreme Commander, A. F. Kerensky, a state criminal.

The calamities which these actions bring on Russia are incalculable; the crime against the people and the revolution of those who have raised the rebellion and spread confusion within the country is immeasurable. First, they divide the forces of the toiling people by bringing within their ranks confusion and discord and by making it easier for the external enemy to overwhelm our country.

The blow against the army is the first and the worst crime of the Bolshevik party!

Second, they have started a civil war and have seized power by violence at the very moment when the Provisional Government, by completing its work on the law regarding transfer of all land into the hands of the land committees, was taking a step desired by all the toiling peasantry, and when the election of the Constituent Assembly was imminent. They are deceiving the country by calling the Congress of the Soviets gathered in Petrograd the voice of the whole people, of the whole democratic movement, although all the representatives of the front, of the socialist parties, and of the Soviets of Peasants' Deputies, have withdrawn from it. Taking advantage of the presence of a few peasants who came to this Congress in spite of the decision of the Committee of the Soviet of Peasants' Deputies . . . they have the impudence to state that they have the support of the Soviets of Peasants' Deputies. Although they have no authority to do so, they speak in the name of the Soviets of Peasants' Deputies. Let all toiling Russia know that this is a lie and that all the toiling peasantry—the Executive Committee of the Soviet of Peasants' Deputies—indignantly rejects any kind of participation by the organized peasantry in this criminal violation of the will of all the toilers.

The Bolsheviks promise the people immediate peace, bread, land, and freedom. All these promises, by which advantage is taken of the exhaustion of the masses and their lack of [political] consciousness, are mere lies and bragging. They will be followed not by peace but by slavery. It is not bread, land, and liberty that they will bring, but, by increasing the confusion and by aiding evil forces to reestablish the accursed tsarist regime, they will bring civil war, blood, the same lack of land as before, and the triumph of the knout and of the nagaika.

Therefore, considering that the upheaval, which has taken place, threatens the army and the country with immediate defeat, that it delays the convening of the Constituent Assembly and cannot create a government which would enjoy the recognition of the whole nation, the Executive Committee of the Soviet of Peasants' Deputies deems it its sacred duty before its own conscience and before the whole country to declare that it *does not recognize the new Bolshevik power* as the government of the nation, and calls upon the local Soviets of Peasants' Deputies, upon the organs of local self-government, and upon the army not to obey this regime brought into being by violence, and at the same time to maintain order and defend the country against the external threat. The Executive Committee of the Soviet of Peasants' Deputies has set itself the following aims:

(1) The reestablishment of a government enjoying general recognition, one that can lead the country to the Constituent Assembly.

(2) The convening of the Constituent Assembly without any alteration of the electoral law.

(3) The transfer of all land to the jurisdiction of the land committees.

This historical document was published in the Socialist Revolutionary newspaper *Dyelo Naroda* (*The Cause of the People*) on October 28, 1917. I quote it in full because it categorically refutes the Bolshevik assertion that the Russian peasantry enthusiastically welcomed the Bolshevik revolution and became the support and bulwark of the new regime. Even today, of all the different sections of the Soviet population, the peasantry remains the most irreconcilable enemy of the totalitarian dictatorship, which deprived it of freedom, expropriated its land, and restored slave labor in a new form.

On November 8 or 9, two loyal friends brought me the Petrograd newspapers, among them Maxim Gorky's *Novaya Zhizn* (*New Life*) of November 7. The view of Lenin's regime that Gorky expressed was, for him, somewhat unusual, and it is particularly noteworthy for that reason:

Lenin, Trotsky, and their associates have already become intoxicated by the foul poison of power, as evidenced by their shameful attitude toward freedom of speech, the individual, and all the rights for which democracy has struggled. Blind fanatics and unscrupulous adventurers, they hurry at breakneck speed towards a supposed "social revolution" which, in reality, is a path that leads to anarchy and to disaster for the proletariat and the revolution. The working class must understand that Lenin is using them as guinea pigs in an attempt to take the revolutionary mood of the proletariat to extremes and find out what will happen as a result. The workers must prevent adventurers and madmen from involving the proletariat in shameful, senseless, and bloody crimes for which not Lenin but the proletariat will have to pay. It must be understood that Lenin is not an omnipotent magician but a callous juggler who does not spare the honor or the life of the proletariat.

There was also an article in *Dyelo Naroda,* which read:

... The elections to the Constituent Assembly were scheduled for next week. The bloody adventure is a terrible setback for that victory of Russian working-class democracy upon which such hopes had been placed ... The armed coup has created conditions and incited feelings quite incompatible with those which should prevail in the country during the forthcoming elections. A bullet is not a ballot, and a bayonet is not an election manifesto. What has happened to freedom of speech? And how about freedom of the press? Where is personal immunity? And the peaceful preelectoral campaign? Petrograd, Moscow, Kiev, Odessa, Kharkov, and Kazan have now experienced at first hand the "dictatorship of the proletariat." Machine guns, swords, and bayonets have been waging a rather eloquent pro-Bolshevik campaign. What will happen to the will of the people and those electoral districts where terror has left its bloody traces in streets and houses? ...

These articles prompted me to write an open letter on November 8, which my trusted friends took to the capital. It was subsequently published in *Dyelo Naroda* of November 22, 1917:

Come to our senses! Do you not see that you have been taken advantage of and deceived? You were promised peace with the Germans within three days and now those who plead for peace are branded as traitors. But Russian soil is soaked in the blood of your brothers. You have been turned into murderers. Nicholas II would have been proud. Truly, never have such

atrocities been committed. Malyuta Skuratov's [3] *oprichnina* has been out-
done by Leon Trotsky's men.

You were promised bread, but dreadful famine is beginning to spread
throughout our country.

You were promised the rule of freedom, the rule of the toiling masses.
Where then is that freedom? It has been trampled upon and disgraced.

A gang of madmen, scoundrels, and traitors has stifled freedom, betrayed
the revolution and is ruining our country. All those who have a conscience,
who are still human, come to your senses.

Fulfill your duty as citizens, do not join in the work of ruining your country and the revolution for which you have struggled for the last eight months.
Have nothing to do with the madmen and traitors! Return to the service of
your country and the revolution.

I, Kerensky, am speaking to you. Kerensky, whom your leaders brand as
a "counterrevolutionary" and a "Kornilov supporter" but whom Kornilov's
men were ready to hand over to the deserter Dybenko.

By the will of the revolution and of democracy I fought for the freedom
of the people and the future happiness of the toiling masses for eight long
months. I led you to the threshold of the Constituent Assembly. Now, in
these times of violence, Leninist terror and the Lenin-Trotsky dictatorship,
even a blind man can see that while I was in power there was true freedom
and genuine democracy, that the freedom of all citizens was respected, and
that equality and brotherhood was the goal.

Come to your senses! Soon it will be too late and our country will perish.
Hunger and unemployment will be the lot of our families and you will again
live under the yoke of slavery. Come to your senses!

I found life almost unbearable in those days. I knew that Russia
would suffer even crueler blows in the times to come. For the goal of
the Leninist revolt—a dictatorship through a separate peace treaty with
Germany—could only be attained by ruthless terror, the destruction
of the army, and the demolition of the democratic structure set up by
the February Revolution.

A Dictatorship in the Making

On October 24, 1917, at the last session of the Council of the Republic, I had pointed out that the two immediate objectives of the
Bolsheviks were: (1) to open the front to the Germans, and (2) to do
away with the Constituent Assembly.

[3] The head of Ivan the Terrible's *oprichnina* (an administrative and punitive body).

On Friday, October 27, *Izvestiya,* the official press organ of the All-Russian Executive Committee of the Soviets—by now, of course, completely Bolshevik-controlled—published the famous "Decree on Peace" signed by the Second Congress of Soviets. It aroused the enthusiasm of pacifists and wishful thinkers, who were deeply moved by this expression of a seeming desire to foster friendship between all the peoples of the world. In their message to "All Peoples and Governments of Belligerent Countries," the peace lovers in the Smolny Institute [4] called for "immediate peace talks in the true spirit of democracy, that is, immediate peace without annexations and indemnities . . ." The same issue of *Izvestiya* published the appeal of the Second Congress of Soviets to "Workers, Soldiers, and Peasants":

> The Congress of Soviets is convinced that the Russian army will be able to defend the revolution from all foreign imperialists until the new government succeeds in concluding an honest democratic peace, which it will offer to all peoples.

The meaning of this statement was clear enough: Should Germany reject a peace offer, the Soviet government would unleash a "revolutionary war" of the sort which had been constantly threatened by Lenin and Trotsky before the October Revolution.

Thus, the notorious campaign for a so-called "democratic peace" was launched.

This exalted and idealistic message of the "Decree on Peace" was sheer demagogy calculated to win the sympathies of the masses by raising their hopes for an imminent "peace among the peoples." More in the spirit of the real purpose of the decree, Lenin inserted into it a cryptic passage, which stood in direct contradiction to its intention and was obviously addressed to Berlin: ". . . the (Soviet) government wishes it to be known that it does not consider the above armistice terms as an ultimatum, and is willing to consider any other peace proposals, provided they are made speedily by any of the belligerent countries, are unambiguous, and contain no secret clauses. . . ."

As was to be expected, and as Lenin himself undoubtedly foresaw, there was no response from any quarter to the broadcast appeal to "All Peoples and Governments of Belligerent Countries." On November 8, Trotsky, in a circular note, invited the ambassadors of the

4 Lenin's headquarters.

Allied powers to regard the peace decree "as a formal offer for an immediate armistice on all fronts and the immediate initiation of peace negotiations."

Next, General Dukhonin, the commander-in-chief, was directed by the Council of People's Commissars to open direct peace negotiations with the enemy in the field. This order was transmitted by radio late on November 8, somewhat earlier than the memorandum to the ambassadors, and was received in army headquarters in the early morning hours of November 9.

Impatient to hear Dukhonin's reply, which had not come in by the evening of the eighth, Lenin, Stalin, and Krylenko called him on the direct line in the early morning hours of the next day. The conversation, which was fraught with tragic consequences for the General, lasted from 2 to 4 A.M. Pressed by Lenin for "a clear-cut answer" to his demand, the honest soldier and patriot declared: "As I understand it, direct negotiations are out of the question for you. But I cannot open peace talks on your behalf. Only a central government supported by the army and the people can have sufficient weight and significance in the eyes of the enemy to lend these negotiations the authority necessary for their success. I do believe, however, that a rapid general armistice would be in the interests of Russia."

But this straightforward reply only irritated Lenin, and the conversation went on as follows:

"Does this mean that you categorically refuse to give a clear-cut answer, and that you will not carry out our instructions?"

"I have already told you why I cannot carry out the instructions given in your telegram. Let me repeat: the peace, which is essential to Russia, can only be negotiated by a central government."

The reply to this, as preserved on tape, reads as follows: "In the name of the government of the Russian Republic, and on the orders of the Council of People's Commissars, you are dismissed from your post for noncompliance with government instructions and for behavior which threatens unprecedented calamity to the toiling masses in all countries, and particularly to the armed forces.

"You are herewith ordered, on pain of responsibility under wartime laws, to remain at your post of duty pending the arrival of the new commander-in-chief, or of his authorized representative, who will take over from you. Ensign Krylenko has been appointed commander-in-chief. Signed, Lenin, Stalin, Krylenko."

In the name of the Council of People's Commissars—though the Council knew nothing of the matter at the time—Lenin then wrote on a scrap of paper the order dismissing General Dukhonin and appointing Ensign Krylenko in his place.

Next, Lenin sent a radio message, signed by himself and Krylenko, to "All, repeat, all regiments, divisions, corps, army, and other committees, to all soldiers of the revolutionary army and the Baltic fleet . . ." It ended with the words:

> . . . Soldiers, the cause of peace is in your hands. Let not the counter-revolutionary generals hamper the great cause of peace . . . put the generals under guard to forestall lynching unworthy of the revolution and also to ensure that they are brought to justice. You must preserve the strictest revolutionary and military discipline. Let all front-line regiments appoint emissaries to initiate formal peace talks with the enemy. You are authorized to do so by the Council of People's Commissars. Keep us informed as much as possible on each phase of these negotiations. Only the Council of People's Commissars has the right to sign the final agreement. Soldiers! Peace is in your hands. Vigilance, discipline, energy and the cause of peace will win.

Most people were stunned by these events. Even within the Central Committee of the Bolshevik Party itself, great consternation was felt. Nevertheless, despite sporadic and belated protests, Lenin had achieved the first of his aims. He had inflicted a mortal wound on the Russian army and had virtually thrown the country upon the mercy of Kaiser Wilhelm.

But the German High Command was in no hurry to take advantage of the situation. It was saving all its strength for future battles on the Western Front and was content for the moment simply to look on as the Russian army disintegrated.

On November 14, when this process had become sufficiently advanced, the Austro-German High Command accepted Krylenko's offer for general armistice negotiations on the "democratic terms" offered by Lenin to all belligerents.

At the same time the Bolsheviks announced over the radio that the peace talks were being postponed for five days, until November 19, to enable Russia's allies to participate in the negotiations. That same day, however, a cease-fire agreement was in fact concluded between the Russians and the Austro-Germans. Also on November 14, a mixed detachment of soldiers and sailors led by Krylenko was sent to occupy Headquarters in Mogilev. This operation was successfully carried out on November 20. General Dukhonin, who had been arrested and put under guard on a train for Petrograd, was dragged out and murdered by Krylenko's drunken sailors and soldiers.

Negotiations for a separate peace between Russia and the Central Powers were opened that very day. It seemed to me at the time that the Germans and the Bolshevik leaders were reaching agreement with remarkable speed, and that a peace treaty would shortly be signed in Brest-Litovsk, the army headquarters of the German Eastern Front.

Nevertheless, the talks dragged on for three months before the treaty was finally signed on March 3, 1918.[5]

Preparations for a Separate Peace Treaty

Despite the genuine desire for peace that was prevalent in Russia, only fanatics of "world revolution," army deserters demoralized by defeatist propaganda, and the scum of the working masses, the *Lumpenproletariat,* found it easy to accept the idea of a humiliating peace treaty with Germany.

Lenin knew that there was strong opposition among all Russian democrats to a capitulation to Germany. Furthermore, his own party majority violently disagreed with him on this issue. He also realized that the Constituent Assembly would never sanction a separate peace.

The day after the October Revolution, *Pravda* had carried a banner headline saying: "Comrades! By shedding your blood you have assured the scheduled convocation of the All-Russian Constituent Assembly." Intended primarily for the sailors and soldiers of Russia, who were bemused by deliberately misleading propaganda, this message was a mockery. Lenin had wanted to suppress the Constituent Assembly in the early days after the October Revolution under the flimsy pretext of postponing the elections in order to adjust the electoral law to the radically changed political situation.

But Bukharin and others vehemently opposed a postponement, insisting that, after the Bolsheviks' fierce campaign against the "Kornilov-Kerensky" plans to "torpedo" the elections, the population would

[5] The Gregorian or New Style Calendar was adopted Feb. 14, 1918.

interpret any such step as an attempt to do away with the Constituent Assembly altogether.

Lenin had to give in. Furthermore, he saw the tactical advantages of encouraging people—for the time being at least—in the belief that the Bolsheviks would not dare raise their hands against an institution which was still regarded as sacred by public opinion.

The elections were duly held on the date that had been set by the Provisional Government, in the middle of November. The Bolsheviks won only 175 of the total of 707 seats. Furthermore, the Bolshevik faction in the Constituent Assembly was controlled, through its so-called "bureau," by "right wing" Bolsheviks—Kamenev, Larin, Rykov, and others—who were stubbornly opposed to the idea of dissolving the Constituent Assembly when this was proposed by the "Leninists" in the Central Committee at the beginning of December. The "bureau" insisted that a Party conference be held to decide the Party's attitude to the Constituent Assembly, and it hastily summoned to Petrograd all those members of the Party who had been elected to it. Seeing that the Bolshevik faction in the Assembly had the sympathetic support of a majority of the Party's rank and file—particularly in the provinces—Lenin decided to apply draconian measures to it.

At the Central Committee session of December 11, Lenin proposed: (1) to replace the bureau of the Bolshevik faction of the Constituent Assembly; (2) to put forth the views of the Central Committee on the issue in the form of theses; (3) to prepare an appeal to the faction recalling the statute of the Party on the submission of all representative institutions to the Central Committee; (4) to appoint a member of the Central Committee as faction leader; (5) to draft the statute of the faction. All these proposals were immediately accepted and put into effect.

On December 12 Lenin's *Theses on the Constituent Assembly* was published. The faction, having been "disciplined" the day before and put under the surveillance of a member of the Central Committee, had no alternative but to capitulate and accept the theses "unanimously." The theses were written clearly, and the warning was worded in no uncertain terms. I shall not quote the full text, but will confine myself to summarizing the gist of the argument by which Lenin settled the question of the Constituent Assembly.

Thesis 14 states quite rightly that the slogan "All power to the Constituent Assembly" means a "campaign for the abolition of the Soviet rule." Lenin then comments that in any case, the Constituent Assembly would be politically doomed if it were to come into conflict with Soviet rule.

Thesis 15 states: ". . . one of the burning issues of our times is that of peace." And Lenin concludes: ". . . a conflict between the members of the Constituent Assembly and the actual will of the people in the matter of ending the war is inevitable."

Thesis 18 is particularly revealing: "The only painless solution to the crisis created by the discrepancy between the elections to the Constituent Assembly and the popular will, and by the difference between the interests of the toilers and those of the exploiting classes, lies in letting the people exercise their right to reelect members of the Constituent Assembly, . . . in conducting these reelections in accordance with the [electoral] law of the *Vzik* (All-Russian Central Executive Committee of the Soviets), and in an unconditional declaration by the Constituent Assembly of its acceptance of Soviet power, the Soviet revolution, and its policies on questions of peace, land, and workers' control, thus indicating the firm adherence of the Constituent Assembly to the camp of those who oppose Cadet-Kaledin counterrevolutionaries."

The advocates of the Constituent Assembly were thus clearly told that they must either "submit or quit." The warning was given in an even more ominous form in Thesis 19: "The crisis in connection with the Constituent Assembly can only be solved by revolutionary means, by resolute, swift, firm, and unflinching revolutionary action on the part of the Soviet power. . . ."

Only after this subjugation of the Bolshevik faction of the Constituent Assembly was it possible to begin a campaign in favor of a separate peace treaty; but even so it was confined largely to Party circles, and was done rather cautiously.

Capitulation

On December 18 Krylenko reported to the Council of People's Commissars that the Russian army was no longer capable of fighting. The German High Command was, of course, well aware of this fact. In Berlin, in the meantime, the military party of irreconcilable imperialists, dazzled by the idea of world domination, had won the upper hand. The moderate foreign minister von Kühlmann, head of the German delegation in Brest-Litovsk, was soon replaced by General Max von Hoffmann. Other participants in the Brest-Litovsk Peace Conference, which opened on December 9, included the Austrian foreign minister Count Ottokar Czernin; the Turkish grand vizier Talsat Pasha; V. Radoslavov, prime minister of Bulgaria; and Prince Leopold of Bavaria, commander of the German Eastern Front, who presided over the conference on ceremonial occasions.

When the peace conference was resumed after a prolonged adjournment on January 2, 1918, the German delegation insisted on the right to maintain troops in Poland, Lithuania, Belorussia, and Latvia "for strategic reasons."

Public opinion in Russia was stunned. Many of the fiercest opponents of Lenin would have been willing to defend their country side by side with the hated Bolsheviks. The terms offered by the Germans threatened to split the Bolshevik Party. In Party committees, in the cities, in the Baltic Fleet, and in some Bolshevik regiments, protests and demands to break off negotiations with the "German imperialists" became louder and louder, and there was talk of waging a "revolutionary war." To Lenin it was quite clear that such a revolutionary war would certainly result in his downfall, and his dream of making Russia into a base for a future proletarian revolution in the West would never materialize. The patriotic feelings that had suddenly been aroused in the breasts of even the Party leaders had to be eradicated at all cost.

Immediately after the dissolution of the Constituent Assembly, a conference of Bolshevik leaders was convened in Petrograd on January 8, 1918. It was attended by 63 delegates from all parts of the country. Lenin decided to take the bull by the horns and read out his *Theses on the Question of a Separate and Annexationist Peace*,[6] which he had prepared for this meeting.

Unlike the theses on the Constituent Assembly, this document was nebulous, contradictory, and—what is even more unusual for Lenin—defensive in tone, as one can see from the following bizarre conclusion:

Those who say that they cannot sign a disgraceful and obscene peace treaty, betray Poland, and so forth, are unaware that by concluding peace

6 For the full text, see Lenin's *Collected Works*, vol. 22 (1929).

only on condition of liberating Poland, they strengthen *even more* German imperialism as directed against England, Belgium, Serbia, and other countries. A peace based on the liberation of Poland, Lithuania, and Kurland would indeed be a patriotic peace *from a Russian point of view,* but it would still be a peace with *annexationists,* with German imperialists [italics mine].

Lenin was defeated at the conference, and a motion in favor of revolutionary war was adopted by an absolute majority of 32. Trotsky's vague "no war—no peace" formula, which was also essentially anti-Leninist, was supported by 16 votes. Lenin, Zinoviev, and 13 followers were the only ones to vote in favor of a "shameful and obscene" capitulation. There was no other solution for Lenin but to take a "step backward" and play for time.

Trotsky now began an eloquent campaign against abject surrender and even made advances to the former Allies. But the Germans were growing impatient of Bolshevik procrastination, and to put an end to it they decided on a show of force. On February 10 they abruptly broke off the peace talks, and on February 18 the German High Command launched an offensive in the direction of Petrograd.

An extraordinary meeting of the Central Committee was convened at Smolny on February 18, but Lenin's motion for an "annexationist" peace was defeated by 6 to 7 votes. Later in the day, however, as the panic grew, Trotsky shifted his position and Lenin's proposal was finally carried with a 7 to 6 majority.

It was decided there and then to send a radiogram to Berlin agreeing to the original conditions and expressing willingness to negotiate on even harsher terms if necessary. The radiogram was signed by Lenin and Trotsky.

Only after the surrender to the Kaiser had been authorized by a majority vote of the Central Committee of the Bolshevik Party, and after the humiliating radiogram had been sent to Berlin, did Lenin dare to oppose publicly the champions of a "revolutionary war" and speak up in favor of a separate peace. Even now, however, he did so under a pseudonym. On February 21, 1918, *Pravda* carried an article entitled "Revolutionary Rhetoric" signed by "Karpov." On February 24, *Izvestiya* published the January *Theses on the Question of a Separate and Annexationist Peace.* On February 28 a new Bolshevik delegation arrived in Brest-Litovsk to accept unconditionally the harsh and merciless peace terms. Nevertheless, the triumphal advance of German armies on Petrograd continued until March 3, when the peace treaty was signed officially. On that day General Ludendorff's troops were just entering Narva on the border of Petrograd Province.

Thus, in order to conclude a separate peace treaty, Lenin had been obliged to conceal his plans even from his own supporters, to break down the resistance of the Bolshevik faction in the Constituent Assembly, and to abolish the latter before communicating his theses on the separate and annexationist peace to the Party elite.

It sometimes seems to me that it would have been better for Russia if Lenin had acted more quickly and accepted the terms offered by the more moderate von Kühlmann. But he did not have the courage to cast off his cloak of a fighter "for a general and just peace in the interests of the toilers" prematurely, and his double game only served to increase the appetite of the Berlin aspirants to world domination.

Return to Petrograd

Toward the end of my stay at the cottage I became obsessed by one idea: to try to make my way back to Petrograd so as to arrive there for the opening of the Constituent Assembly. I thought this might be my last chance to tell the country and the people what I thought of the situation.

In the early part of December two sledges drove up to the cottage. Several soldiers in fur caps emerged carrying hand grenades and rifles. They were trusted and courageous friends, who had come to take me to a forest hiding place on the way to Novgorod.

The forest estate belonged to Z. Belenky, a wealthy timber merchant. In the wintertime it was completely isolated from the outside world, and the dilapidated mansion was almost buried by snowdrifts. Belenky's son had served in the garrison at Luga, and it was he who had masterminded my escape from Gatchina. Now he had come to fetch me, as he had promised. My dear hosts were greatly frightened by his "Bolshevik" appearance until he explained the reasons for his visit.

I changed my clothes so as to look like my companions. As I said my farewells, my kind hostess burst into tears, and the old couple gave me a small icon to wear around my neck. This icon is the only possession I have brought out of Russia. My heart was heavy at the parting, and I had no way of repaying their kindness. They would not take money, and I was not even in a position to protect them from the possible consequences of their warm hospitality. My sailor companion Vanya had rejoined his ship.

Young Belenky and I and three or four soldiers set off in the first sledge, followed by a second, which carried five soldiers. No one paid any attention to us, for every place was now full of soldiers who had deserted from the front. We arrived at our destination late on a crisp, clear, winter night. Despite the threats of the Soviet government that anyone helping me would be severely punished, these people were in high spirits. They were particularly kind to me, as if trying to console and encourage me. After a whole week together, Belenky went to Petrograd for a few days and returned with the suggestion that we move closer to the capital. We set off again in our sledges, equipped with rifles and hand grenades, but singing army songs and laughing and joking.

We had a rather unpleasant experience when we reached the outskirts of Novgorod. Belenky had been given a wrong address, and we stopped at a house that turned out to be the headquarters of a local Soviet committee. We got away as quickly as we could and headed in the opposite direction until we found the right address, which turned out to be an insane asylum. We drove straight into the grounds and up to the female patients' wing, where the director was living. Belenky and I went in alone. We tried to look as respectable as possible. The director, who had been forewarned of my visit, welcomed us warmly and asked us both to stay, but Belenky was in a hurry to get back to his comrades, so the doctor and I were left alone. He started right out by telling me not to worry. When I asked whether there were any reasons for worry, he said: "You see, I am hardly ever here in the daytime, but the door is never locked. Occasionally, nurses and hospital personnel come in. But the way you look now nobody would recognize you. And, moreover, the hospital staff is not in sympathy with the Bolsheviks. They are good people."

For about six days I stayed in the hospital and had no trouble of any kind. The director had a good library and subscribed to all the newspapers. During the daytime I read, and in the evenings I talked with the director.

Soon my friends called again, as unexpectedly as before, to take me on the next stage of the journey. The director was not in when

Belenky appeared in the doorway and said curtly, "Let's go. The sledges are waiting."

"Where are we going now?" I asked.

He laughed. "We're moving closer to the capital. You can stay for a while on an estate near Bologoye." [7] It was a sunny winter morning. The horses trotted along gaily, and the sledge glided smoothly over the hard-packed snow.

At midday we decided to stop for a while in some quiet, secluded place. We noticed a coach house (*Postoyali Yvor*) on the outskirts of a village that looked all right. The old lady in charge showed us into her best room. It was warm and cozy, and over an old sofa there was a large lithograph of me. The situation was so comic that we burst out laughing and could not stop. The old woman looked at us in astonishment and seemed quite unaware of my identity, for when we finally stopped laughing she asked us from what front we had come. She gave us an excellent meal. Back in our sledge we roared with laughter again and someone said: "Just imagine, she didn't know what it was all about. She had no idea who you were, even though that's not much of a beard you've got!"

After they had brought me to the estate near Bologoye, my friends departed that same day. On their way back they stopped at the coach house again. The old woman was very glad to see them and asked one of them in a whisper: "Is he safe?"

"Yes, Grandma," he replied. She made the sign of the cross.

The estate was quite large, and the house was surrounded by dense forest. We stopped in front of a hunting lodge in a clearing from which we could see only the roof of the main building. There were two small rooms, the larger of which had an iron stove and a pile of logs in a corner. There were no beds, but there was plenty of straw. We were very grateful for these quarters, primitive though they were. We lit the fire, boiled water in a huge kettle, and made tea. Then we made ourselves comfortable on the straw. Next morning, Belenky went to the main house to see the owners, who were full of apologies. They had been expecting us a few days later, and as a result the lodge was not quite ready. They did not dare to invite us up to the house, because of the servants and the large number of guests they had invited for Christmas. But we were looked after lovingly, and we felt quite at

[7] A large railroad junction exactly halfway between Moscow and Petrograd.

home in the lodge. I was given a pair of skis, and I traveled many miles on them over forest tracks. The days were bitterly cold, but crystal clear and sunny.

Our hosts sent down lavish supplies for our Christmas Eve party. And on New Year's Eve—my last in Russia—we were finally invited up to the house; they had managed to get rid of all the servants for the day.

Next morning I had to leave for the capital. Belenky told me that we must get to Petrograd without delay. He also told me that an armed demonstration on the opening day of the Constituent Assembly had been prohibited by the central committees of the anti-Bolshevik socialist parties and that they had decided to stage only nonviolent demonstrations in support of the Constituent Assembly.

The situation was quite absurd. The slogan "All power to the Constituent Assembly" was now meaningless. It was clearly impossible for a truly elected Constituent Assembly to coexist with a dictatorship that rejected the very idea of popular sovereignty. A Constituent Assembly made sense only if it had the support of a government that was willing to recognize it as the supreme political authority.[8]

By the end of 1917, Russia no longer possessed such a government. The slogan "All power to the Constituent Assembly" now made sense only as a rallying cry for all the forces that were prepared to carry on the fight against the usurpers.

For reasons that I did not know at the time, the Union for the Defense of the Constituent Assembly failed to launch an effective struggle. But even so, I told myself, if the Constituent Assembly is doomed to perish, let it at least fulfill its duty toward the people and the country by going down proudly and in such a way as to keep alive the spirit of freedom.

The plan was that I should catch the Moscow night train that stopped at Bologoye at 11 P.M. The trains were overcrowded, dilapidated, and mostly without light, especially in the third-class compartments. I had been given the number of the coach in which my supporters were traveling, and I was to squeeze myself in a corner and make myself as inconspicuous as possible. We arrived at the station on time and walked up and down the platform as we waited for the

---

[8] I frequently expressed this view to people who came to see me while I was in hiding.

train, which was late. I still had my escort of men armed with hand grenades, but we had grown so used to this strange way of life that we scarcely took any precautions at all and talked loudly among ourselves. Suddenly one of my guards came up and said: "Be careful, some railroadmen on the other side are watching you. Look, they're following us." We fell silent. The group of railroad workers crossed from the Moscow platform to our side and came straight toward us. We were certain that all was lost. But the men removed their caps respectfully and said: "Alexander Fyodorovich, we recognized you by your voice. Don't worry, we won't give you away!" Thus my guard was doubled! After this, everything went smoothly. The train arrived and we were pushed into the right car, which was very dark. We arrived without incident in Petrograd, where a cab took us to a prearranged address.

The Constituent Assembly was scheduled to open on January 5, 1918, and it looked as though my plan was going very well. Within three days I expected to be in the Tauride Palace, where the Assembly was to convene.

On January 2, Zenzinov, a member of the Socialist Revolutionary faction of the Constituent Assembly, came to see me.

What was at first a very friendly conversation soon turned into a violent argument. Even now it is painful for me to remember that conversation. I told him that I felt it my duty to attend the opening of the Constituent Assembly. I had no admission ticket to the Tauride Palace, but I thought that, with my altered appearance, I could easily get in on a ticket made out to some unknown provincial deputy. I needed help to get a ticket, and I had assumed that my friends in the Constituent Assembly would see to this. But they flatly refused to do so. Zenzinov said that it was much too dangerous for me to appear at the opening session and that I had no right to run such a risk. He pointed out that I was the chief enemy of the Bolsheviks. I argued that my life was my own business, that he could not dissuade me from going, and that I was sure my decision was the right one. If I had been in the Peter and Paul Fortress, it would, of course, have been physically impossible for me to attend, but since I was free, it was my duty to do so. I reminded him of the article that had appeared in the Socialist Revolutionary publication *Dyelo Naroda* on November 22, 1917, under the title, "Kerensky's Fate":

The former head of the Russian Republic and leader of the revolution has had to go into hiding, and his very name has been virtually banned by order of those who have usurped the state power by armed force. Kerensky has momentarily withdrawn from political life, but he will return to it at the opening of the Constituent Assembly. At that time he will account for his activities to the people, who will be able to judge the positive, as well as the negative, aspects of A. F. Kerensky's political work during the eight months when he was a minister in, and subsequently the prime minister of, the Provisional Government of the Russian Revolution.

I told Zenzinov that I had come to do just that: to give an account of my work and activities. Zenzinov thought a moment, and said: "The situation in Petrograd has changed radically. If you appear at the Assembly, it will be the end of all of us." "No, it won't," I replied, "I have come to save you. I'll be the target of all the fury, and you will remain unnoticed." I immediately realized that this was a tactless argument, so I told him what I really wanted to do, on condition that he tell no one about it until after my death. He must have thought that the plan [9] unfolded to him was absolutely mad, but he was moved to tears by it, shook me by the hand, and said: "I'll talk it over with the others."

But this was only a friendly gesture on his part, and I did not cross the Rubicon of death. When he returned the following morning we talked much more calmly, and I no longer argued when he told me that the final answer was "No." I told him how upset I had been at the news that the armed demonstration had been called off and how important I thought it was that the Constituent Assembly should not give in without a fight. A strict party disciplinarian and a man of great integrity, Zenzinov agreed with me wholeheartedly and said that this was also the view of the party faction in the Assembly. I asked him who would be chosen as the president of the Constituent Assembly and was taken aback when he told me it would be Victor Chernov. All who knew that gifted and loyal party leader must have realized that he was unsuited as a spokesman for the whole of Russia. I pleaded with Zenzinov to exert every effort to prevent the appointment of Chernov to this crucial position. I implored him to find some candidate who, though perhaps less famous and less talented, possessed greater will power and was more fully aware that the tragedy we were living

[9] For purely personal reasons I cannot even now reveal my plan.

through was a betrayal of the aspirations and ideals of freedom for which generations of Russians had struggled and given their lives. I repeated this over and over again to the few visitors who came to see me during the two days before the opening of the Constituent Assembly.

The Tragedy of the Constituent Assembly

On the crucial day of January 5, the capital was like a besieged city. A so-called "Emergency Staff" had been set up by the Bolsheviks a few days before, and the entire Smolny area had been put under the jurisdiction of Lenin's henchman, Bonch-Bruyevich. The district around the Tauride Palace was being closely supervised by Blagonravov, the Bolshevik commandant. The Palace itself was surrounded by heavily armed troops, Kronstadt sailors, and Latvian riflemen, some of whom also took up positions inside the building. All streets leading to the Palace were cordoned off.

I do not need to describe this first and only session of the Constituent Assembly. The unspeakable treatment of the "elected representatives of the people" by Lenin's armed thugs has often been described by those who lived through the terrible hours of January 5–6. In the early morning hours of January 6 the Constituent Assembly was dispersed by brute force, and the doors of the Tauride Palace were locked. The peaceful crowds that had gathered to demonstrate in support of the Assembly were scattered by gunfire.

The easy victory of the Bolsheviks over the Constituent Assembly was followed almost at once by the murder of Shingarev and Kokoshkin, two former Cadet ministers of the Provisional Government, who had not attended the opening of the Assembly because they were under arrest in the Peter and Paul Fortress. Late on January 6 they had been transferred to the Mariinskaya Hospital, where they occupied a special ward guarded by soldiers. During the night of January 7 a band of Bolshevik soldiers and sailors came into the ward under the pretext of changing the guard, and the two Cadet statesmen, who had devoted their whole lives to the service of freedom and democracy, were bayoneted to death as they lay ill in bed.

On January 9, Maxim Gorky published an extraordinary article about these events which deserves to be quoted extensively.[10] After describing the events of "Bloody Sunday" (January 9, 1905), when the

[10] *Novaya Zhizn,* January 9, 1918.

Tsar's troops had fired on the crowds of peaceful, unarmed workers, Gorky went on to draw a comparison to the events that had just occurred:

On January 5, 1918, unarmed democratic workers and employees of Petrograd were peacefully demonstrating in favor of a Constituent Assembly.

For almost a hundred years the most enlightened Russians had lived in the hope of a Constituent Assembly—a political body that could give all democratic Russians the chance of freely expressing their will. Thousands of intellectuals, tens of thousands of workers and peasants had perished in prisons, in exile and in penal servitude, on the gallows and in front of firing squads, in the struggle for that ideal. Rivers of blood had flowed on the altar of sacrifice to that ideal, and now the People's Commissars had ordered the soldiers to fire on the democratic people as they demonstrated in favor of it. I will remind you that many of the People's Commissars had themselves through their political activity instilled in the soldiers the need to campaign for a Constituent Assembly. *Pravda* is telling lies when it says that the demonstration of January 5 was organized by the bourgeoisie, by bankers, and so on, and that it was the bourgeoisie that marched to the Tauride Palace.

Pravda is telling lies—it knows perfectly well that the bourgeoisie had no reason to welcome the opening of a Constituent Assembly; that they would have little to do among 246 Socialists of one party and 140 Bolsheviks.

Pravda knows that workers from the Obukhov, Patronny, and other plants took part in the demonstration, that it was workers from the Vassilievsky Island, Vyborg, and other districts who marched beneath the red banners of the Russian Social Democratic Party to the Tauride Palace.

And these were the workers who were shot down; no matter how many lies *Pravda* tells, it cannot hide the bitter truth.

The bourgeoisie may have been pleased to see the soldiers and Red Guards tear the revolutionary banners from the hands of the workers, trample on them and burn them on bonfires. But it is possible that this sight did not please all the bourgeoisie, for there are among them, after all, honest people who love their countrymen and their country.

One such man was Andrei Ivanovich Shingarev, foully murdered by savage brutes.

And so, on January 5, unarmed workers of Petrograd were shot down— shot down without warning, shot down from behind corners, through chinks in walls, in the cowardly fashion that assassins use.

And in exactly the same way as on January 9, 1905, people who had not lost their conscience and reason asked them: "What are you doing, you fools? These are our own people. Can't you see, they're carrying red banners, and there's not one placard that's anti-working-class, not one slogan that's hostile to us!"

And like the Tsarist soldiers they replied: "We have orders! We've been ordered to fire!"

And in just the same way as on January 9, 1905, the narrow-minded man-in-the-street, who is always a mere witness to the tragedies of life, cries with delight: "The bullets are certainly flying!" and shrewdly observes: "If they go on like this, they'll soon wipe each other out."

Yes, soon. There are rumors among the workers that the Red Guards from the Erickon factory have fired on workers from the Lensy factory, and that Lesny workers were shot at by the Red Guards from some other factory.

There are many such rumors. They may not be true, but that will not prevent their influencing the minds of the working masses in a drastic way.

I ask the People's Commissars, among whom there should be some decent and sensible people: Do they realize that by placing a noose around their own necks they will inevitably destroy Russian democracy and ruin all the gains of the revolution? Do they realize that? Or do they think, "As long as we stay in power, everyone and everything else can go to the devil"?

The opening of the Constituent Assembly ended as a tragic farce. Nothing happened to give it the quality of a memorable final stand in defense of freedom.

The best and bravest speech was made by Tsereteli, leader of the Mensheviks. But this speech was not in the style of the revolutionary Tsereteli denouncing Stolypin in the second Duma. It was critical, and it was delivered with feeling, but it was, nevertheless, only an expression of "loyal opposition." Indeed, in reading it, I was reminded of the style of "His Imperial Majesty's liberal opposition [Cadets]" in the peaceful days of the fourth Duma. The fact is that the Mensheviks had already, in the early part of November, renounced the idea of a revolutionary struggle against the Bolshevik "government of workers and peasants."

As for the speech of the chairman of the Assembly, Victor Chernov, I can only quote the words of Mark Vishniak, secretary of the Constituent Assembly and a fellow member of the Socialist Revolutionary Party:

It was couched in the language of internationalist and socialist ideas, with occasional undertones of demagogy. It was as though the speaker was deliberately seeking a common language with the Bolsheviks, and trying to persuade them of something instead of dissociating himself from them and standing up against them as a representative of Russian democracy. *It was not what it should have been* [italics mine]. There was nothing in it that could have impressed anyone, or satisfied the requirements of the historical moment even to a limited extent. It was a humdrum, cliché-ridden speech, and it was certainly not even Chernov at his best.

It is difficult to blame Chernov for the fiasco of the Constituent Assembly. He was a courageous man, and like many other people present, he was not intimidated by the guns trained on him by Lenin's drunken, hate-crazed soldiers and sailors. I believe that the apparent paralysis of will that contributed so much to the January 5 debacle had deep psychological causes that affected even the most steadfast democrats at that time. For one thing, there was a widespread fear of unleashing a civil war which could easily have resulted in a counter-revolutionary war against democracy in general. Then, too, one must not forget that the Bolsheviks were still considered to be nothing more than the extreme left wing of the Social Democrats. The idea that there were "no enemies on the left" was deeply ingrained. To most of the left wing it seemed inconceivable that freedom could be trampled underfoot by people claiming to represent the proletariat. Only the "bourgeoisie" was thought to be capable of this, and so the main danger appeared to many to be, not the Bolsheviks entrenched in the Smolny Institute, but the counterrevolutionaries now rallying around Ataman Kaledin in the Don country in the far south of Russia.

If the non-Bolshevik Socialist leaders had known the truth about Bolshevik-German contacts, they would no doubt have acted differently. But they could not believe this "slander" about a leader of the Russian working class.

Another powerful factor working in Lenin's favor was the mystic belief of many Socialist democrats, not to mention Kantian and Christian idealists, that a new age would arise from the boundless suffering and bloodshed of the "imperialist war" and that man would be "born anew." Many people saw Lenin as the midwife of this spiritual rebirth.

I have met refined and human people, such as Ivanov Razumnik, the outstanding Socialist Revolutionary, who sincerely believed this.

Boris Pasternak, who moved in Socialist Revolutionary circles, also knew Ivanov Razumnik, and in the following words from *Doctor Zhivago* we find an excellent expression of this belief:

What splendid surgery! You take a knife and with one masterful stroke you cut out all the stinking ulcers. Quite simply, without any nonsense, you take the old monster of injustice, which has been accustomed for centuries to being bowed and scraped and curtsied to, and you sentence it to death. This fearlessness, this way of seeing the thing through to the end, has a familiar national look about it. It has something of Pushkin's uncompromising clarity and of Tolstoy's unwavering faithfulness to the facts . . . And the real stroke of genius is this. If you charge someone with the task of creating a new world, of starting a new era, he would ask you first to clear the ground. He would wait for the old centuries to finish before undertaking to build the new ones . . . But here, they don't bother about anything like that. This new thing, this marvel of history, this revelation, is exploded right into the very thick of daily life without the slightest consideration for its course. It doesn't start at the beginning, it starts in the middle, without any schedule, on the first weekday that comes along, while the traffic in the street is at its height. That's real genius. Only real greatness can be unconcerned with timing and opportunity.

But it was not only in Russia that people were swept away by this kind of tragically misplaced enthusiasm.

In Finland

After the dissolution of the Constituent Assembly the atmosphere in Petrograd became unbearable, and it became pointless for me to stay there. It was therefore decided that I should go to Finland until the situation became clearer. Finland was on the threshold of an open civil war. Power was in the hands of the Finnish Social Democrat Party which was backed by Bolshevik soldiers and Baltic Fleet sailors. I was in contact with a group in Helsinki that had always been on friendly terms with the Socialist Revolutionaries, but in order to get there, I needed a travel permit from the Soviet authorities. We obtained a permit for two passengers without much difficulty, but surveillance of passengers at the railroad station was very strict. We had thought of using makeup, but fortunately we realized what it would look like after a trip to the station in the bitter cold and a subsequent journey in a heated compartment. We decided to take a chance and go without any disguise. V. Fabrikant, a bold and experienced conspirator, offered to accompany me to Helsinki. The absence of makeup saved our lives, because the train was overheated and my face would undoubtedly have turned into a pointillist painting. All went well, and as on many previous occasions we were completely unaware of any danger during the most dangerous moments. We passed the "Red checkpoint" at Helsinki station without incident. Soon we had arrived to stay in a small, cozy apartment belonging to a young Swede. It was quiet and peaceful, but it did not remain so for long. Responding to an appeal from General Mannerheim, many young men, irrespective of their political affiliations, abandoned their jobs and joined the anti-Bolshevik forces in the northern part of the country. Recalling the general helplessness and passivity of educated Petrograd society, as well as that of the revolutionary democratic circles, I was profoundly impressed by the inherent national consciousness of the Finnish intelligentsia. My host explained the developments in the seemingly peaceful Finnish capital. "I am going north soon, and then there will hardly be anyone left here. But we have made all the necessary arrangements for you. Friends will be waiting for you in the vicinity of Abo near the Gulf of Bothnia." That was my next stop.

I lived there in comfort, and I was kept well informed on developments in Russia and Europe, since my host, a gentleman dairy farmer, made frequent trips to Helsinki and knew what was going on. I had a feeling that he was actively involved in politics, and my assumption was soon confirmed in a rather extraordinary way.

Sometime toward the end of February, a few weeks before German troops came to Mannerheim's aid on April 3, my host approached me while I was alone and said: "Let's have a heart-to-heart talk, all right?"

"Of course."

"You see, we have been negotiating with Berlin to send us troops. Part of the German High Command will arrive ahead of time and stay here. It won't happen tomorrow, but we had to tell Berlin that you are here. Please don't worry. I am authorized to tell you that your safety is guaranteed and that no one will bother you."

"I am deeply appreciative of your hospitality," I replied, "but I cannot stay. I couldn't possibly accept German protection. Please ask

Mrs. U.[11] to come immediately. I'll ask her to go to Petrograd and arrange for my return to Russia."

My host was undoubtedly in touch with Mannerheim's headquarters, and he showed a full understanding of my request. "I won't argue with you. I'll send a wire to Mrs. U. immediately."

In due course Mrs. U. came to see me, and I described my situation. A few days later she returned from Petrograd with the following message: "Your friends have asked me to dissuade you from returning. It would serve no purpose at the moment."

"All right," I replied, "then I'll go on my own. Please have the trip arranged by your people and let me know when I can go. There is still plenty of time, but I cannot remain where I am. You must understand this as well as my host does."

She did what I asked her to do. I was convinced that anyone in my situation would have acted similarly.

Last Time in Petrograd

I took the train on March 9, 1918. This time, it was not even a second-class compartment, but a third-class car packed with drunken, vociferous soldiers. At the Finland Station in Petrograd, the snow had not been cleared away, and it was piled high on the platform. As I emerged from the train carrying a heavy suitcase, I slipped and fell flat on my face. A soldier and a sailor came running to help me to my feet. Laughing and joking, they retrieved my hat and the suitcase.

"Go ahead, pal, and watch out!" We shook hands.

There were no porters in sight, and no cabbies outside the station. The streetcars were not running. As I walked alone, lugging my suitcase, I was engulfed by a crowd of passengers with bags, bundles, baskets, and suitcases. In those troubled times, a pedestrian laden down with bundles or a suitcase did not seem out of place. It was the best way to go unnoticed. None of the militia men or agents could have noticed the bearded "enemy of the people No. 1" modestly strolling along Liteyny Prospekt carrying a heavy suitcase.

Without having any clear idea of where I was going, I followed Liteyny Prospekt, turned into Basseynaya Street, and emerged on the

[11] Mrs. U. was the daughter of a retired Finnish colonel in the Russian army. She was an active YWCA member and made frequent trips to Petrograd. At the same time, she acted as a liaison for me.

Ninth Rozhdestvenskaya. I was not even aware of the tremendous distance I had walked until I reached my mother-in-law's apartment. Fortunately, the street was deserted and the servants were out. But it would have been too risky to stay so near the street where the office of my faction in the Duma had been housed and where I was well known. It was arranged for me to go that night to a house on the remote Vassilyevsky Island.

There I lived for quite some time in the apartment of a woman doctor whose husband, also a physician, was in the army. She offered me her house unhesitatingly, although she was aware of the danger involved. And just like the old Bolotovs in the forest cottage, she took loving care of me. She never betrayed the slightest concern about the risk she was running. She always left early in the morning, and I remained alone in the empty apartment until late at night.

I do not recall the circumstances under which I obtained the record of my testimony before the Extraordinary Commission on the Kornilov Affair. This unexpected opportunity to write the truth about the case was overwhelming. Now, the truth has been admitted by the participants themselves (see Chapter 21), but at the time the true facts were unknown to the general public and in political circles. Reading over my own testimony, I relived the whole experience, and was able to reconstruct the affair and to throw further light on some aspects of it. My book, *The Kornilov Affair,* appeared in the summer of 1918, in Moscow.

My aim was not only to dissociate myself from the traitor Kornilov but also to neutralize the most potent weapon of Bolshevik propaganda, which had split the unity of democratic forces.

Once, while I was working on my manuscript and trying to recapture the flavor of Russia as it had been the summer before, when a new and better life had still seemed possible, I suddenly heard the sounds of a military band outside. A hum of voices reached me as I went up to the window and saw a rather pitiful sight. There was a sparse and gloomy crowd marching down the street in "celebration" of May Day. The workers carried banners, but there was no air of festivity about the demonstration. Nothing indicated the joy of a proletarian victory. The memory of April 18 (May 1), 1917, came back to me. The "capitalist government" had declared May 1 a national holiday. All plants, factories, government offices, and shops were closed. Thousands of workers, soldiers, sailors, white-collar workers, and professional men marched with banners and orchestras singing the Russian *Marseillaise*. Thousands of meetings were held throughout the city; it had been a joyful and festive occasion.

Shortly before my return from Finland, the Council of Peoples' Commissars had moved to the Kremlin (March 9, 1918). All central political committees, trade union headquarters, leading organs of peasant organizations, etc., had followed the government to Moscow. Petrograd had become deserted and politically dead.

After mailing my manuscript to my friends in Moscow, there was no point in hanging around empty Petrograd. All the more since a man in hiding should never remain in one place too long.

While I was staying quietly in Petrograd, a fierce civil war was being unleashed in Russia. In the winter of 1917–1918 fighting broke out between the Don Cossacks and the Volunteer army on the one hand, and the Red army on the other. Under the terms of the Brest-Litovsk Peace Treaty, German troops had occupied the Baltic states and the Ukraine. Bolshevik rule did not yet extend to Siberia. Peasant insurrections were the order of the day throughout Russia. The members of the dissolved Constituent Assembly met clandestinely in Samara to organize the overthrow of the local Soviet government, the formation of a Committee of the Constituent Assembly (*Komuch—Komitet uchreditel 'nogo sobraniya*), and the launching of armed struggle against the usurpers. I decided to go to Moscow and make contact with friends, in the hope of then traveling eastward, through the Bolshevik lines, to the Volga region or Siberia. It did not take me long to arrange my departure for Moscow.

Moscow

There were three of us at the Nikolaevsk Station waiting for the night train to Moscow. I was accompanied by V. Fabrikant, a friend, and a high official of the Ministry of Agriculture whom I had not met before. We had been promised a private compartment. But when we boarded the train, we found a respectable-looking man in our reserved compartment. The stranger did not participate in our conversation, but climbed onto the upper berth and presently began to snore. The three of us remained seated on the lower berth. We were discussing the events that had occurred in the Ministry of Agriculture during the summer and fall. Forgetting ourselves in the heat of the conversation, we raised our voices. It was not until late at night that we suddenly remembered that there was a fourth person traveling with us. Not a sound was heard from the upper berth. Reassured, we finally settled down for the rest of the night and fell asleep.

When we awoke, it was broad daylight and we were approaching Moscow. The upper berth was empty. We were very much alarmed, although our suspicions may have been unjustified. But to be on the safe side, Fabrikant and I decided to leave the train as it slowed down on the outskirts of the city, while our third companion continued on to the train terminal with our luggage. It took a long time to walk from the suburbs to the center of Moscow. After the emptiness of Petrograd the streets of Moscow seemed alive and crowded. It seemed almost incredible that we were not being followed. If our assumption was correct, and our traveling companion had indeed denounced us, the secret police would at that very moment be waiting to intercept us at the central station.

We strolled down the streets in a leisurely fashion so as to avoid attracting attention. Once, we even mingled with a small group of people to read a very interesting announcement of the first issue of an "interesting new political newspaper, *Vozrozhdenie,* due to come out on June 1." The list of the editorial staff and the contributors was full of familiar names. Most of them were Socialist Revolutionaries and belonged to the so-called rightist wing. There was also an annoucement that "A. F. Kerensky's memoirs will be published in *Vozrozhdeniye.*" I was relieved at the news that my manuscript had been received in time for publication.

I do not know whether it was because my short walks in Petrograd had always been taken at night and now it was a lovely spring morning, or whether it was because the city air was invigorating, but on that fine morning my constant feeling of tension suddenly left me. I felt relaxed and hopeful. Finally we reached our destination, the apartment of Ye. A. Nelidova, somewhere in the Arbat District near the Smolensk Market. Nelidova welcomed us like old friends, although we had never met before.

After lunch Nelidova and Fabrikant worked out a schedule for me, decided on my "visiting hours," and declared their willingness to establish the necessary contacts. Despite the seriousness of our purpose, our conversation was as completely relaxed as if we had been discussing some social function.

I could not help asking Nelidova if she were not afraid of the risks she was running. Her answer provided me with an explanation of my own changed mood. Apparently, life in Moscow was quite out of the ordinary. The Soviet Government had just finished moving to the Kremlin and was still in the process of reorganization. The notorious Lubyanka Prison had not as yet become an integral part of the system, and was operated primarily by volunteers. Even though arrests, raids, and executions were already fairly commonplace, it was all rather badly organized and haphazard in its operations.

The Germans were doing much to foster the prevalent confusion. Dzerzhinsky's Cheka existed side by side with a corresponding German agency, and they maintained close contact with each other. Lenin occupied the Kremlin, and Baron von Mirbach, the German ambassador, moved into a mansion on Denezhny Pereulok that was guarded day and night by a detachment of German soldiers. The average citizen was convinced that Mirbach was really in control of the proletarian regime. Complaints were lodged with him against the Kremlin, and monarchists of all political shades sought Mirbach's protection. Berlin had adopted a clever policy: The Kremlin leaders were being given financial aid while advances were simultaneously being made to the extreme monarchists, in case the Bolsheviks proved "unreliable." The monarchists were also being encouraged in Kiev, where the former General Skoropadsky had become hetman of an independent Ukraine by the grace of the German Kaiser. Under the aegis of the German high commissioner, Skoropadsky made a great show of his monarchist sympathies at every opportunity.

Also contributing to the confusion were the central committees of the most influential anti-Bolshevik and anti-German socialist, liberal, and conservative parties, which pursued their activities right under the nose of the Kremlin rulers.

The leaders of all these organizations held frequent meetings with various representatives of Russia's allies, the rank of the diplomat concerned depending on how much importance the "allies" attached to a given organization. It goes without saying that all these organizations were carrying on clandestine activities. But this was relatively easy at that time owing to the inefficiency of the Cheka system. Thus, even persons wanted by the Bolsheviks—including myself—met in secret. Needless to say, however, many adventurers and intelligence agents had infiltrated the endless committees, organizations, and "missions." This political chaos came to a sad end with the rising of the left-wing Socialist Revolutionaries, the assassination of Baron von Mirbach, the abortive attempt on Lenin's life, and the inhuman execution of thousands of hostages. But that was all still to come.

In my time, it was much easier to carry on underground activities in Moscow than in Petrograd, and neither the encounters in Nelidova's apartment, nor my attendance at other clandestine gatherings, were difficult to arrange. It seems quite incredible to me now that the "Grandmother of the Russian Revolution," as she was known, Catherine Breshkovska, a sworn enemy of the Kremlin, could come to visit me with impunity. One evening when I was seeing her home, we even passed Baron von Mirbach's house.

I told Breshko-Breshkovskaya what had brought me to Moscow and explained my plans to proceed to the Volga region. But she calmly replied: "They won't let you go." By "they" she meant the members of the Central Committee of the Socialist Revolutionary Party, with whom she had broken on my account. She was well acquainted with the mood of left-wing circles, and she told me in great detail about their internal dissensions, insecurity, and chaotic state of disorganization.

I do not recollect the exact date of that conversation, but I know that it took place after I met Boris Flekkel, my very young fellow worker from Petrograd, a fine and dedicated young man. He also intended to go to the Volga region, and he was delighted at the prospect of accompanying me there. He started the necessary negotiations, but a few days later he returned sad and taciturn. All he would tell me was that there were "difficulties." Evidently, some party leaders did not approve of me. Soon I was to learn the reasons for their disapproval of my trip to the Volga. At that time the "Union for the Resurrection of Russia" was engaged in important political work. I had already learned of the existence of the organization in Petrograd, but I had only a vague idea of its work and objectives. After the October Revolution and the peace treaty of Brest-Litovsk, all major political parties had split into a multitude of factions that were often hostile to each other. The "Union for the Resurrection of Russia" was not the usual coalition of democratic and socialist parties, but an organization *sui generis*. Some members belonged to the Popular Socialist Party, others to the Socialist Revolutionaries, the Cadets, the Plekhanov "Unity" group, the Cooperators, etc. They were united by a common approach to the fundamental problem and an awareness of the need for concerted action to solve it. They believed that a national government had to be created on democratic principles in the broadest possible sense, and that the front against Germany had to be restored in cooperation with Russia's western Allies. Not only was the restoration of the front strongly advocated by the political supporters of the Union, but it also received the wholehearted support of the parties to which the members belonged. The same trend was being followed by the National Center, an organization which included Cadets as well as moderate and even conservative groups that did not recognize the Brest-Litovsk Treaty and were willing to collaborate with the Union toward the common goal. The National Center was closely linked with the Volunteer Armies of Generals Alekseyev and Denikin. I was an ardent champion of an acceptable national government and an active military union with the Allies in conformity with the current circumstances, and I considered the work of the "Union for the Resurrection of Russia" to be of vital importance to the nation. I was determined not to hamper the activities of the Union or to give rise to dissension between the two patriotic organizations, which had their own ideological difficulties to cope with. This I believed: that after all the dreadful experiences both sides would overcome their difficulties and prejudices, uniting in their love for the people and fulfilling their duty to the state, and that men of the stature of General Alekseyev, Chaikovsky (a Popular Socialist), Astrov (a Cadet), Avksentiev (a Socialist Revolutionary) and others, would restore the real state power on the fundamental principles of spiritual and political freedom, equality and social justice, as pledged by the February Revolution.

For that reason I accepted the proposal made by the "Union for the Resurrection of Russia" that I should go abroad and negotiate with the Allies under the terms laid down by the Union.

Subsequently, the term "intervention" as used in the military clauses of the Union gave rise to misunderstanding. It was interpreted in foreign—and even some Russian—circles as an appeal for "intervention in internal Russian affairs." Under the provisions of clause 3, however, such intervention was inadmissible. In fact, it was an appeal to the Allies to continue the war on the Russian Front on a basis of equal partnership. At the request of France, Russian troops under the command of General Lokhvitsky had been sent to the Western Front, but this had not been regarded as Russian intervention in France. As a matter of fact, the front in Saloniki was composed of troops of every one of the major Allied countries, including Russia. If further justification is needed, let it be recalled that Austro-Hungarian and German prisoners of war were directed from Berlin and Vienna to give every possible armed assistance to the Bolsheviks in their struggle against the Volunteer Army in the south and the army of the Constituent Assembly in the Volga and the Ural areas. These foreign battalions were responsible for executions and reprisals, and they served on active duty in Moscow. This is the essential background to the appeal made to the Allies by the political and military men of the Union who, recalling Russia's contribution to victory, were the representatives of a Russia that did not recognize the Brest-Litovsk Treaty.

Before my departure all arrangements were made for me to maintain contact with Moscow.

I was scheduled to leave at the end of May via Murmansk, where British and French ships had been stationed to protect the vast stocks of military and other supplies in that port. This time I traveled in a so-called "extraterritorial" train for Serbian officers who were being repatriated. The head of the repatriation project, Colonel Iovanovich (a Serbian), was in charge of these special trains, and at the request of my friends he did not hesitate to issue documents for me in the name of a Serbian captain. A British visa was issued in my name by Robert Bruce Lockhart, the British consul general in Moscow, who had remained there as a special emissary after the departure of the Allied ambassadors. Lockhart granted the visa without cabling London for official approval. As he told me much later, he had had to act on his own because the visa application would have been rejected by the Foreign Office!

While arrangements for my departure were being made, I held final consultations with friends and followers in Moscow.

Departure for London

On the day of departure, Fabrikant and I arrived at the Arkhangelsk Station while it was still daylight. We had no difficulty in identifying two uniformed Serbian officers, and these led us unobtrusively to the right platform, where we mingled with a crowd of passengers. The train was filled to capacity, but we were assigned seats in a second-class compartment that was evidently reserved for officers. It was quite obvious that several of them became aware of my identity. The voyage seemed endless. The one-track Murmansk line had innumerable sidings. For no apparent reason we spent hours waiting at junctions. It seemed to us that the train hardly ever moved. But we did not complain. After all, there was no hurry, and outside was an intoxicating northern spring. We enjoyed the long stops at night, when the train came to a standstill in some clearing in the midst of a dense forest. It reminded me of the white nights in Petrograd. But here nature was more mysterious, the northern stillness and the pale light of the nights held a very special charm. Yesterday did not seem to exist, and we did not feel like speaking or thinking of the future. We were in complete harmony with the natural beauties around us, and we felt at one with the mysterious forest.

I have no exact recollection of how long it took, but the journey must have lasted about ten days. Finally we reached Murmansk, then a drab, deserted town. All the passengers went straight to the port, which was occupied by the Allies, although the town itself was under Soviet administration and we had to pass a Soviet checkpoint. The Soviet soldiers barely glanced at our documents. Then we filed past an Allied officer who checked our names against a list. My companion and I were met by two French naval officers who took us to their cruiser, *General Hobe*. On board, a Serbian officer handed our real documents and visas to the commander. Throughout our journey these papers had been kept by the head of the "extraterritorial" train. As I left my native land it did not even occur to me that I might never set foot on it again, and all my thoughts were for the future.

The French naval command welcomed us very warmly. It was a new experience to be completely relaxed. There was no longer any need to be constantly on the alert.

"You'd probably like to rest, wouldn't you?" asked one of the offcers.

"No, thanks. I'd like to go to the barber."

"What for?"

"I am sick and tired of my disguise. I want to be my own self again."

There was an outburst of laughter. A few minutes later I found myself in the skilled hands of a barber and my locks and beard were scattered all over the floor.

We spent three pleasant days on board. Fabrikant had spent a long time in emigration and had only recently returned to Russia from Paris, where his family was now expecting him. His French was perfect and he was an amusing *causeur,* and the officers obviously enjoyed listening to his stories about our adventures and the events in Russia.

Two days later a British officer came aboard, and presently we were asked to come to the commander's office. There we learned that our landing in England had been arranged for and that we were to leave the next morning on a small trawler.

The next morning the trawler was moored to our cruiser. It looked like a toy boat, and we wondered what the trip through the Arctic Ocean would be like.

On board the tiny ship the captain introduced us to the crew of 15 men, who all displayed curiosity about the mysterious strangers.

The Arctic waters were swarming with German submarines, and a small cannon had been set up on deck to defend the boat in case of attack. The Captain had been occupying the only private cabin, a small one located under the bridge, but now he offered it to me. He and Fabrikant settled in the forecastle.

We had a pleasant time on the tiny boat, and although we spoke no English we were on the best of terms with the captain and the crew. The weather was mild and clear. We were surprised to find the Arctic Ocean so calm. The translucence of the polar nights had a strange effect on us that kept us wide awake, and we spent hours on deck gazing at the skies and the water.

One afternoon Fabrikant told me that the barometer was falling. This meant that a storm was brewing. There was nothing unusual about the storm that raged for the next 48 hours, but to me it came as a sort of relief.

During one sleepless polar night about a week before the storm, my thoughts had wandered back to the year 1916. I was returning on a Volga steamer to Petrograd after giving a public report on the political situation and participating in endless political meetings in Saratov. It was a clear, crisp day in autumn, and as I paced the deck of the steamer enjoying the fresh air, I forgot all my political worries and surrendered myself to the feelings that the Volga always evoked in me. The happiness of my Simbirsk childhood revived in my memory, and the temptation to drop everything and climb again the Venetz hillside of my boyhood was almost overwhelming. I longed to see again the summit that had always left me breathless as a boy. I was completely absorbed in this nostalgia when suddenly I was struck by the ominous premonition that I would never again see my native Volga. It was with difficulty that I managed to suppress this unaccountable fear, which appeared utterly groundless at the time.

That sleepless night on board ship, the experience came back to me, and again I had an ominous feeling that I should never return to the Volga or to Simbirsk, and that I should never again set my foot on Russian soil.

The thought was intolerable, but it gripped me so strongly that I fell into a prolonged mood of despair. To awaken from this nightmare, to shake off my gloomy thoughts and pull myself together I needed a shock, and it was the storm that provided it.

The fiercer the raging of waves around us, the louder the roaring of the elements, the easier it was to forget the word "forever" and to convince myself that I was merely going on a special mission that would end after the capitulation of Germany.

With my fears dispelled and my sense of commitment reawakened, I disregarded the storm and prepared myself for my meeting with the rulers of Britain and France. I was, of course, well aware of their attitude toward the Provisional Government and toward me personally. But that did not bother me in the least. I had been delegated by the Russia that had refused to recognize a separate peace with Germany. My task consisted in obtaining immediate military aid from the Allies in order to restore the Russian front, thereby ensuring a place for Russia among the Allies in the forthcoming peace talks.

My innate optimism returned. I arrived at the conclusion that the strain of the last decisive battle with the enemy accounted for the ill will now shown toward Russia on the part of the Western Allies.

The fury of the storm subsided within two days. We were exhausted, but our spirits were high. In a few days we caught sight of the Orkney Islands, one of the main bases of the British fleet, and soon we landed at Thurso. There I stepped on non-Russian soil for the first time in my life. We stayed overnight in the peaceful town, which the war scarcely seemed to have affected.

Next evening we boarded a train, and in the morning of either June 20 or 21, 1918, I arrived in London.

A new phase in my life had begun, one that I believed would be very short, but which still remains to be completed.

The Turning Point
in World History

26

My Mission to London and Paris

London

THE next morning, June 20, we arrived at Charing Cross Station. Only Dr. Gavronsky, a representative of the Provisional Government in London, was there to meet us. It had been agreed beforehand that I should travel incognito and that my visit should remain unpublicized until I had met with British government officials.

Taking leave of the naval commander who had accompanied me, we went to Gavronsky's house, where I was to live during my stay in London. On the way there, the doctor told me that I would be seeing Lloyd George in a day or two and that in the meantime I could relax and take stock of my surroundings. I only needed a day or so of wandering around the streets, looking at the shops, and eating in the restaurants, to assure myself that despite the oppressive war Britain was still as strong, well organized, and determined as ever.

A policy based on the certainty that the Germans would collapse and on the conviction that Russia must continue to support the Allies until the war was ended was Russia's only way of salvation. That was my firm belief as I became acquainted with the atmosphere in London. I would have had no doubt that the imminent Allied victory would signal Russia's liberation and return to freedom—which was the firm conviction of those who had sent me on my mission—if the unity and patriotic spirit of the Russian people had not been so badly shaken.

On the third or fourth day of my stay, a well-dressed, pleasant-looking young man came to see me. It was Philip Kerr, the Prime

Minister's private secretary, who had come to invite me to visit Lloyd George the next morning. Promising to be there at the appointed time, I asked Kerr to tell the Prime Minister that I would bring Dr. Gavronsky as my interpreter, since I knew no English at all at that time.

I must confess that, much as I looked forward to it, the prospect of my meeting with Lloyd George made me nervous. I looked forward to it because I had always taken a keen interest in the career of the "Welsh Wizard," since he was known for his inimitable charm and his ability to make people do everything he wanted; but I was excited because I knew that he had tremendous influence on the policy of the Entente. I was worried because I did not know how accurately the policy professed to the Provisional Government by the Allied diplomats in Russia reflected the personal views of the British Prime Minister.

Shortly after Philip Kerr had left, I received a chance visit from K. D. Nabokov, the Russian chargé d'affaires, who knew of my presence in London. Nabokov was a shrewd diplomat with extensive government and society connections, and he was thoroughly versed in the political and diplomatic life of London. His dispatches to Milyukov and Tereshchenko, which I had had occasion to read from time to time, were always much to the point and full of intriguing and original comments on people and events.

His visit was very timely, for I was glad to be able to confer with him before meeting Lloyd George. On learning the purpose of my journey, he gave me a lengthy and detailed account of what the various officials thought about the Russian situation, but what he said was far from encouraging. The note of pessimism that had faintly echoed through his reports on Britain's attitude toward Russia was now clearly expressed in everything he said. Above all, he lacked all confidence in the successful outcome of my mission. So, for that matter, did Gavronsky, who had lived in London for a number of years and was also fully conversant with local opinion.

The next morning at nine o'clock, we arrived at No. 10 Downing Street and knocked at the door of a small house, hardly different in any way from the adjoining buildings. This short, narrow street was actually the hub of the British Empire, and No. 10 was probably as much mentioned in the political world then as the White House is today. It was the official residence of the British prime ministers, and for two centuries it had been the scene of historic decisions that had affected the destiny not only of Britain, but of the whole world.

As we went in, Philip Kerr came up to greet us and showed us into the Prime Minister's study. I found myself face to face with a short, stocky man with a shock of snow-white hair, a noble brow, and small, piercing, yet sparkling eyes that lit up the whole of his youthful, ruddy face. He welcomed us cordially, rather as if we had been old friends whom he had not seen for a long time. His manner immediately created a pleasant and relaxed atmosphere uninhibited by any formality.

I cannot give a verbatim account of our hour-long conversation, since it was conducted through an interpreter and no notes were taken. I shall, therefore, merely give the gist of what I said and of Lloyd George's totally unexpected response.

Having dealt briefly with the course of the war in Russia, the collapse of the Monarchy, the attempts to restore the state and the fighting fitness of the army, I said that all that was now in the past. At the present moment Russia's position could be summed up as follows: Central Russia had been seized by the Bolsheviks, who had now concluded a separate peace with Germany and were using German funds and military aid against their own countrymen, although neither the Treaty of Brest-Litovsk nor the Bolshevik dictatorship were recognized by the majority of the population.

In Siberia there were no Bolsheviks in power, and moreover a local democratic government had been formed in Tomsk. On the Volga members of the Constituent Assembly, mainly Socialist Revolutionaries, had set up a democratic anti-Bolshevik center and, assisted by the Czech legions,[1] had begun hostilities against the Bolsheviks. The Don and Kuban Cossacks were already fighting the Bolsheviks. The whole of the Volga as far as Samara and the Urals was free of Bolsheviks. In the south a volunteer army had been recruited through the joint effort of Generals Alekseyev and Denikin (Kornilov had been killed in April), and had already made contact with the advancing Bolsheviks. The Ukraine was still under German rule, but there, too, popular uprisings had sporadically broken out.

[1] Prisoners of war who had fought against Germany on the Russian Front and had then volunteered to fight the Germans on the Western Front and were on their way there via the Far East.

I told Lloyd George that at the time of my departure from Moscow there were two political centers in existence. Both bodies were trying to form a new coalition government and to recruit a volunteer army politically affiliated to the National Center.

It was the aim of the government now being formed, I went on, to continue the war alongside the Allies, to free Russia from Bolshevik tyranny, and to restore a democratic system. The representatives of the Allies in Russia had promised their support, and at the present moment it was vital for the Allied governments to maintain close relations with anti-Bolshevik and anti-German Russia. Furthermore, it was important to decide how national Russia could best contribute to the military operations of the Triple Alliance. But such a contribution could only be made if the Allies recognized (*de facto*) the new government and if there was unity of action among the Allied representatives in Russia.

I had surmised that Lloyd George would not be completely conversant with the fast-moving events in Russia and the policy of the British and French representatives on the spot. My impression was confirmed by a number of questions that the British Prime Minister put to me; I answered his questions accurately and candidly.

The moment arrived for him to leave for the House of Commons, and he said goodbye without having expressed any personal view regarding what I had told him. He suggested that I have a talk with his war minister, Lord Milner, as soon as possible. Then he suddenly added as an afterthought: "In a few days' time I am going to Paris for a session of the Supreme Allied Council in Versailles. Why don't you come too? You'll be invited to Versailles."

The same day, in a speech in the House of Commons, Lloyd George mentioned, among other things, that he had personally received good news from Russia that very morning.

We left No. 10 Downing Street in good spirits and with a feeling of achievement. My mission had gotten off to a flying start—in a few days' time all of the Great Five would have a first-hand account of the Russian situation.

It was a wonderful sunny morning. We decided to walk home, and on the way I dropped in at the Russian Embassy to ask Nabokov to arrange for a passport for me as soon as possible, since I had come to England without any papers and had no identification for travel outside the British Isles. Nabokov ironically congratulated me on the unexpected turn of events and promised to have a diplomatic passport ready for me the next day. When I returned home to Gavronsky's, I found that a telephone message had been left for me that Lord Milner was expecting me at six o'clock that evening.

I had a feeling that in sending me to see the War Minister Lloyd George was hoping to exert indirect influence on the military policy of my country. The disastrous fruits of this policy had already been reaped during the Kornilov affair, but I had no wish, nor any right, to mention those calamitous events to Lord Milner. After all, I had been sent for a specific purpose by political organizations which were striving to join forces for the sake of their homeland.

Lord Milner, a typical Victorian, received me with icy politeness. He listened carefully to what I had to say and put in a question from time to time, but he made no comment and gave no sign of what he was thinking. All the same, I knew exactly what he was thinking.

Several years later I met Lloyd George, then no longer in power, and we talked over former times. At the end of the conversation I asked him outright why the Entente had systematically encouraged all the military conspiracies aimed at establishing a dictatorship during the time of the Provisional Government. He evaded a direct answer, claiming he knew nothing about the matter. If that were true, he continued, then the British Ministry of Supply and the War Office must have been conducting their own private war.

Shortly after my visits to the Prime Minister and Lord Milner, the world press reported my arrival in London. The secret was out. It was most untimely, I might add, since there was no point in attracting public attention and arousing idle curiosity about my trip until the results of my talks in London and Paris were clear. However, it was too late.

Immediately after my arrival in London (June 20, 1918) Paul Painlevé, the brilliant French mathematician and statesman, came over to see me from Paris. In 1917, after the Nivelle disaster, he became minister of war in Ribot's cabinet, and later he was premier of France until the accession to power of Clemenceau. I had never met Painlevé before, but having greeted me, he went on to say, without wasting any words, that as soon as he heard of my arrival he felt he should come to see me right away and tell me personally how tremendously important the Russian offensive of the year before had been for the Western Allies' final victory. He stressed the point that not everyone in the West realized this.

He told me that General Alekseyev and most of the French military authorities and statesmen had tried to persuade General Nivelle to postpone his general offensive until the Russian army had recovered its fighting fitness [2] and that he himself, as war minister, had also insisted, with Ribot's consent, on postponing it. Nivelle, however, had refused point-blank to put off the offensive and threatened that he would resign if necessary.

Describing to me the whole tragedy of the French Front, Painlevé added in a quiet voice, though with feeling: "After Nivelle's risky venture, both our own and the British losses were so excessive that we could no longer dream of a decisive offensive on our front. I still shudder to think what the consequences of such an offensive might have been. . . ."

Painlevé suddenly jumped up from his chair, rushed over to me and embraced me warmly. From that moment on we were friends.

Paris

A few days after our meeting Lloyd George went to Paris, and as agreed, Dr. Gavronsky and I followed him. We took the night train and were careful not to let anyone know in advance of our arrival. However, hardly had I stepped into the apartment where I was to stay at the corner of Renoir and Cernovitz streets, when I received a visit from a representative of the French government, who told me that a car had been placed at my disposal and that for my protection I would be accompanied at all times by a police car.

When I asked in surprise why this was necessary, the security official explained that it was a normal courtesy extended to all persons of my rank. This well-intentioned move on the part of the police made it much easier for me to acquaint myself with the city, which I had never visited before, and to meet all sorts of people. During my brief stay in the capital I managed to see a tremendous number of people, both interesting and dull, from all walks of life.

Three days passed without a sign of an invitation to Versailles. I

[2] See Chapter 15.

decided that Lloyd George was either unable to contact the officials who were anxious for me to attend the Supreme Allied Council, or else that he had lost interest in the idea. Personally, I was just as keen to fulfill my mission as before, although I had heard one or two sinister facts regarding the invitation.

The Parisians were by no means as politically noncommittal and self-possessed as the Londoners, and in Paris it was considerably easier to gain an inkling of what the Allies really felt about the Russian events. In addition, the overall political setup in Paris was very different from that of London. Clemenceau, or the "Old Tiger," as he was nicknamed, had become head of the French government immediately after the Bolshevik coup in Russia, and his rule in France was a form of benevolent but firm dictatorship.

We had arrived in Paris ten days before the final German offensive, which swung the balance of the whole war. At last rid of Russian military pressure through the Bolshevik coup, the Germans had now concentrated all their fast-failing military strength in the West, and both Ludendorff and Hindenburg made several all-out attempts to break through the Allied defenses. But it was too late. The Germans now faced a new Anglo-French-American army under the joint command of General Foch—an army infinitely stronger in firepower and far better equipped with food, planes, and munitions than the German forces. The Germans, to all intents and purposes, were now fighting alone, for Austria and Turkey were by then literally *hors de combat*.

Speaking objectively, an Allied victory was certain, but for some reason the French were tormented by doubt and waited tensely to see how it would all end.

Paris was fascinating in those few days; it was a period when one felt, more than ever before, the deep devotion of the man in the street to his country, to its past, and to its greatness. From time to time the city was raided by German fighter planes, and every now and then, without the slightest warning, Big Bertha, the monstrous German gun some 30 or 40 miles away, would lob shells onto the Parisian buildings and boulevards.

At this point Clemenceau's behavior was giving rise to great panic within the government, even among his closest friends. The point was that he stood very much alone in the political world just then. Few of the French deputies could tolerate his "dictatorship," although the man in the street had great confidence that the Old Tiger would carry him through.

It goes without saying that the French government was well aware of my reason for coming to Paris, and during the first few days of my stay I received a visit from Georges Mandel, a close associate and confidant of Clemenceau, who brought me an invitation to visit the War Ministry the next day. Clemenceau usually received his visitors there.

Mandel made it quite clear that preparations were under way for a counterattack against the Germans and that although the "old man" was extremely busy, he had decided not to postpone seeing me. According to Mandel, Clemenceau had been following developments in Russia, and also my own activities, with great interest, and was very anxious to meet me. This was good news, though I still had grave misgivings as to the success of my mission in the light of what I had just learned.

I had my first meeting with Clemenceau on the morning of July 10. Also present were Stéphen Pichon, the French foreign minister, and V. Fabrikant, whom I had brought along in case my French failed me. Clemenceau, a thick-set man of advanced years with small, beady eyes beneath bushy eyebrows, was seated in a deep armchair behind a desk near the door. He rose as I entered, and gazing at me intently, offered me his hand across the desk with the words: "How nice to see you. Take a seat and tell me what I can do for you."

I liked very much the simplicity of his greeting, which was refreshingly unencumbered by flowery conventional phrases. It was obvious that the future *père de la victoire* had no time for mere formality.

Leaving out unnecessary details, I outlined the situation in Russia and told him the purpose of my visit. He listened quietly, tapping a paperweight in front of him with his artistic-looking fingers. However, as soon as I mentioned the French government's promises in Moscow —French support of the newly formed Russian government and help in the struggle against our common enemy, Germany—Clemenceau suddenly gave a start and said with a mixture of surprise and indignation that he knew nothing about the matter, and turning to Pichon, asked whether he did. Pichon hastily mumbled a negative reply.

Clemenceau paused for a moment and then turned to me with a smile and said reassuringly that there had probably been some misunderstanding. Of course the French government would assist the patriotic forces in Russia in every possible way, and he, for his part, was delighted to hear the news from me in person.

At the end of our conference we fixed a date for our next meeting. I also arranged to have my reports to Moscow transmitted in code, through the French Foreign Ministry, to the French consul general in Moscow, who would have them delivered to the proper person.

Unfortunately, this idyllic situation did not last very long. I think it was at my second meeting with Clemenceau, during a discussion of the latest dispatch to Moscow, that he showed me a cablegram from Lansing, the U.S. secretary of state. It said: "I consider a trip by Kerensky to the United States undesirable." Keeping my temper with difficulty, I said quietly to Clemenceau, "Monsieur le Premier, I have no intention of going there just at present." This was the truth—although my passport was valid for the United States, at that moment in 1918 I was certainly not planning to go to America, and as far as I knew no one had applied for a visa for me.

I was completely mystified by Lansing's cablegram, though not for long. A few days later the mystery was solved. My meetings with Clemenceau broke off soon afterward, though this fact was not in any way connected with the cablegram.

On July 14, the French national holiday, there was to be a ceremonial parade past the Arc de Triomphe, attended by members of the diplomatic corps. A detachment of Allied troops had been invited to march in it. The evening before the parade, the invitations which had been issued to the Russian chargé d'affaires, Sevastopulo, and the military attaché, Count Ignatyev, were suddenly withdrawn. The official who came to withdraw them explained that they had been sent through a misunderstanding. Then it came to light that General Lokhvitsky, commander of the Russian units in France, had not received a request to send a Russian detachment to take part in the parade. The military attaché went straight to the French chief of staff to find out what had happened. He was told that Russian representatives and army contingents were being excluded from the ceremonies, because "Russia had become a neutral country which had concluded peace with France's enemies, and that the friends of our enemies were our enemies." Count Ignatyev, who had been in France since the beginning of the war and had always been pro-French in his dealings with the Allies, returned at once to the Russian Embassy and insisted that Sevastopulo should go to see Pichon, the foreign minister, and get him to cancel the order, which, he said, was an open insult to the Russians. Sevastopulo flatly refused to go. Ignatyev then came to see me and told me what had happened. He felt certain that, as the former minister of war and supreme commander, I would be able to defend the honor of Russia.

It was the night of July 14—the zero hour for the final German advance, the subsequent failure of which signaled the start of the German collapse. In anticipation of my meeting with Clemenceau and Pichon, I was putting the finishing touches to a report to Moscow, but now, after Ignatyev's visit, the report had become pointless.

When I walked into Clemenceau's office the next day, I found him relaxed and smiling for the first time. He had just received news from the front that all German attacks had been repelled. He was now confident that victory would follow shortly.

"Right, let's see the report," he said gaily, stretching out his hand. I hesitated, looking disappointed. He noticed this and frowned.

"May I ask you a question, Monsieur le Premier?" I said.

"Yes, certainly."

"Why did your chief of staff tell the Russian military attaché that neither he nor any Russian troops were to be invited to the July 14 parade because Russia was a neutral country and had made peace with France's enemies? I hope you do not share this misguided view."

Clemenceau flushed scarlet and leaned back in his chair. Pichon became very still and almost fell off his seat. In the ensuing silence I heard Clemenceau's incisive voice say, *"La Russie est un pays neutre qui a conclu la paix séparée avec nos ennemis. Les amis de nos ennemis sont nos ennemis.*[3] Those were my words and my order."

Hardly able to contain myself, I rose, snapped my briefcase shut, and said: "In that case, M. le Premier, there is no point in my remaining in your office." I bowed, turned, and stalked out.

Rumors of the incident spread rapidly through all the government and political circles, giving rise to great excitement, speculation, and alarm.

The next day Deschanel, president of the Chamber of Deputies,

[3] "Russia is a neutral country which has concluded a separate peace with our enemies. The friends of our enemies are our enemies."

came to see me. Launching into an elegant but extremely long-winded speech, he spoke of the unbreakable ties between France and national Russia, France's loyalty to her ally, her great sacrifices for the common cause, and so on. Clemenceau's remark he explained as being the result of the tremendous strain which his superhuman efforts imposed upon him. A few days later I was invited to see Poincaré, president of the Republic, who repeated in his own rather frigid way what Deschanel had said, except that he did it more succinctly. Their words were empty phrases. Soon after, I returned to England.

The phrase "neutral country which has made a separate peace with our enemies," which the overworked and overstrained statesman had "let slip" during a discussion on military assistance for Russia, must have revealed some of Clemenceau's innermost thoughts and feelings, contrary to what Deschanel and Poincaré tried to make me believe. It was clear that, in their interviews with me, Lloyd George and Clemenceau had been keeping something up their sleeves. What was it?

It was simply that the Allies had begun to make plans for their own intervention in Russia for purposes that bore no relation to Russian interests and had little connection with the discussions that Allied representatives in Moscow had been holding with their Russian counterparts.

After a month abroad, I had reliable information, passed on from Russian officials, that two expeditionary forces were being formed and equipped at top speed. The first was to land in Vladivostok to pave the way for Admiral Kolchak, who was to replace the democratic authority there by a military dictatorship. The second, headed by the British General Poole, was to land at Archangel for the same purpose.

I also discovered that one of the men behind this Siberian venture was the notorious Zavoyko, Kornilov's "orderly," now living in Europe under the name of "Colonel Kurbatov" (the requisite identification papers had been issued by the British). "Colonel Kurbatov," as I was told rather ironically by a well-informed Englishman, had been invited to Versailles instead of me.

Further talks with the heads of the French and British governments were now pointless, and to me personally, rather distasteful. My mission to London and Paris was over. Now it was imperative that I return to Russia as soon as possible to report on everything I had seen, heard, and done in the West.

It was absolutely impossible to get to Russia from Britain in war-time without the aid of the British government. At the beginning of September, I wrote to Lloyd George and asked him to take steps immediately to enable me to return home. The following week I received a reply from Philip Kerr, in which, on behalf of the Prime Minister, he politely informed me that Lloyd George was unfortunately not in a position to help me since it would not be in keeping with British policy to interfere in the internal affairs of other countries.[4]

The meaning of the letter was clear. I would not be allowed to return to Russia because I might interfere with the British plans.

Philip Kerr's letter came at the exact moment that Admiral Kolchak reached Vladivostok on his way back from Singapore to Omsk. One month earlier the coup d'état in Archangel, led by Chaplin, a Russian naval officer, and assisted by General Poole, had overthrown the government which had just been formed (August 2) by local democratic circles under the leadership of N. V. Chaikovsky.[5]

In the middle of August I sent a long letter to Chaikovsky, who was by then merely a figurehead of the new "reformed" government, in which I said among other things: "The incident in which you have been involved in Archangel will be repeated in Ufa and Samara—this I state categorically."

As I have already said, the whole of Siberia was free of Bolsheviks. After a prolonged series of talks, a Directorate was set up at the state conference held in the city of Ufa on September 23, 1918. The Directorate was intended to be a national government, and had been created by agreement among all the parties that had not recognized the treaty of Brest-Litovsk, that is, the Socialist-Trudoviks and the Cadets, and in the South, the "White Command."

The Directorate was composed of Avksentiev (SR), and his deputy, Argunov (SR); Chaikovsky, a member of the Popular Socialist

---

[4] The original letter from Kerr was kept in my files in Paris, but it was removed, along with other documents, by the Germans during the occupation. Part of the text appears in my book, *From Afar,* published in Russian in Paris, in 1922, and I assume that a copy of it exists in the Foreign Office files in London.

[5] All facts relating to Admiral Kolchak are taken from the book, *The Interrogation of Kolchak,* published by the State Publishing House, Tsentrarkhiv (Moscow, 1925).

Party, and his deputy, Zenzinov (SR); N. Astrov, a member of the
Central Committee of the Cadet Party, and his deputy, V. Vinogra-
dov (Cadet); General Alekseyev and his deputy, General Boldyrev;
and the chairman of the Siberian Regional Government, Vologodsky
(Cadet).[6]

While the formation of the new government was actually in progress in Samara, and later in Ufa, contact with those of us who were
abroad was maintained. But when, in the face of the Bolshevik-
German advance, the Directorate was forced to move to Omsk, this
contact was almost entirely broken off.

In the autumn, the British and French governments were ostensibly
preparing to recognize the Directorate as the legal government of
Russia.

About the middle of October I received a telegram from Avksentiev
saying that they were awaiting reports from me. Apparently my letters to Omsk had not been getting through, just as theirs had not been
reaching me. I immediately took the message to Nabokov at the Embassy and asked him to let me send an answer to Avksentiev in the
Embassy code.

What transpired during our meeting is described by Nabokov himself in his book, *The Ordeal of a Diplomat,* from which I quote:

The British Government was inclining towards the official recognition of
the Directorate at Omsk. In order to enable me to establish relations with
this, the first serious effort at organised resistance to the Bolsheviks, approximately in the middle of October, 1918, the British Government granted
me once again the privilege of using cipher for telegrams to Omsk and to
my colleagues abroad. Kerensky apparently was in touch with some minor
officials in the Foreign Office and consequently became aware of this measure. He immediately addressed to me the request that he should be allowed
to use the Embassy cipher, or a cipher which he pretended to possess in
order to send "information" to Omsk. In support of this claim, he produced a telegram which he had received from his intimate friend, Mr. Avksentiev, the then President of the Directorate, informing him that his telegrams were expected. The letter by which the Foreign Office had notified
me that I was entitled henceforward to use cipher contained the definite
indication that this privilege was granted "as a token of special personal

---

[6] In the upshot, Astrov and General Alekseyev for certain reasons took no part in
the work of the Directorate.

confidence," and that the Foreign Office felt certain that the cipher would be used only for the transmission of *my* political and business telegrams. In view of this categorical declaration, and also bearing in mind that the transmission of political information emanating from irresponsible sources by means of the Embassy cipher was against elementary diplomatic ethics, and in practice detrimental, as it would inevitably result in contradictory information, I refused Kerensky's request. He did not seem to understand at the moment that his role as a politician had come to an end in Russia. He adopted a very haughty tone, invoked his "power," was very reproachful in regard to my "abetting British conspiracies," etc. It was a painful interview, as Kerensky displayed scant self-possession, great anger, and no wisdom whatsoever.

I promptly informed the President of the Directorate at Omsk of this incident. The reply was that "Kerensky is in London in a private capacity, that he has no mandate from the Union for the Regeneration," and that I was entirely justified in refusing to grant him the use of cipher. I forwarded to Kerensky a copy of this telegram—it occurred on or about October 25— and I have not seen him since.[7]

Nabokov, very sensibly from his point of view, barely mentions our second meeting, but it was a long and memorable one.

Gesturing to the telegram, I asked him: "What does this sentence mean: 'The refusal to give him the cipher is the right thing to do?' Did I ask you to give me your cipher? I only asked you to send my reports in the Embassy code and when you refused, I replied, 'If Pichon, the French foreign minister, offered to send my reports to Moscow in his code, then how can you, as the head of the Russian Embassy, refuse to do the same?' You know very well that I only asked you to send on my report in code to the head of the Directorate, and you saw the telegram he sent me. Surely it proves that I am carrying out a mission undertaken before I left Russia, and am not playing the impostor abroad." Nabokov was silent. "And where is Avksentiev's signature on the telegram you showed me?" I held out the telegram to Nabokov but he continued to say nothing. "You don't answer because you know as well as I do that this telegram was sent without the knowledge of the head of a government with which you are now associated. You don't answer because you know as well as I do that Avksentiev, a forthright and honest man, would not send a telegram of that kind,

[7] C. Nabokoff, *The Ordeal of a Diplomat* (London, 1921), pp. 258–259.

and that your original message did not reach him. You realize as well as I do that the false, unsigned answer you have received means that Avksentiev's position in the government he heads is shaky and that Admiral Kolchak is already in Omsk. But instead of being frank with me as you used to be, you have decided to pretend that the answer came directly from Avksentiev. Your reasons for doing this are clear to both of us . . ." I turned and left the room.

Immediately after this last meeting with Nabokov, I wrote to Avksentiev and described in detail the preparations for the coup d'état sponsored by General Knox. The letter ended: "I insist that you take steps to expose all the conspirators, for a repetition of the Kornilov affair may be the final nail in Russia's coffin." [8]

It happened that a day or so after this depressing interview with Nabokov, Albert Thomas came to see me, as he always did whenever he was in London.

Suddenly changing from the current affairs we were discussing, I asked him the one question that I had not been able to answer for myself, a question that seemed all the more perplexing in the light of my row with Nabokov: "Tell me," I said, "what is the aim of the Allied intervention in Russia? What is there about it that I seem unable to understand?"

Thomas looked at me hard for some moments; then in an obvious state of nervousness, he began to walk up and down the room. Finally he stopped in front of me and, after a heavy pause, said, *"Alors, écoutez!* You should know, but you alone." I promised that whatever he said would be treated with the strictest of confidence. He returned to his chair and began to speak in a clear, unemotional tone which made every word seem even more terrible . . . When at length he had finished, I knew the whole secret.

At the end of 1917, two months after the Bolshevik coup in Petrograd, representatives of the French and British governments (Lord Milner and Robert Cecil for Britain, Clemenceau, Foch, and Pichon for France) had signed a highly secret agreement on the division of the western regions of "the former Russian Empire," with their basically non-Russian population, into spheres of influence. Under this

---

[8] A copy of this letter was kept in my files in Paris but suffered the same fate as my other documents during the German occupation.

agreement, as soon as the war had been won, Britain was to set up protectorates in the Baltic provinces and neighboring islands, in the Caucasus, and in the Transcaspian regions, while France was to do the same in the Ukraine and Crimea.[9]

That was the gist of Thomas' terrible account of the Allies' intentions in Russia.

While I was listening to Thomas, I suddenly recalled what Clemenceau had said. Then I realized for the first time that even before the treaty of Brest-Litovsk, at the time of the truce between Germany and the Bolsheviks, the Allies had felt themselves to be no longer under any obligation to Russia.

In 1914, at the outset of the war, Russia, Britain, and France had made a formal agreement that none of them would sign a separate peace treaty with Germany. In violating this treaty, Russia had betrayed her Allies. She had thereby disqualified herself from the Alliance, which won the war without her help.

Since Russia had embarked upon a separate peace with the common enemy, which had capitulated after Russia's withdrawal from the Alliance, all Russian territories handed over to Germany in accordance with the treaty of Brest-Litovsk were to be considered the property of her former Allies by right of conquest.

Russia herself had forfeited the privilege of taking part in the Peace Conference, since she could be classed neither as a victorious power nor as a "liberated" nation.

Thus, the betrayal of Russia by Lenin and his associates enabled the Allies to treat Russia virtually as a defeated country and to turn the situation to their advantage in their schemes to rearrange the balance of power after Germany's capitulation. Russia's frontiers, as envisaged in these schemes, were to be those of pre-Petrine Muscovy, and she was to be separated from Western Europe by a belt of small and medium-sized national states under the protection of the victorious powers.

The Allied intervention in the "former Russian Empire" pursued these very aims. In the western provinces, detached under the Brest-Litovsk Treaty, they supported and strengthened the newly independ-

---

[9] The treaty was subsequently referred to in the *Large Soviet Encyclopedia*, Vol. 28, col. 641–642, published in 1937, and also in George Kennan's recent book, *Russia and the West Under Lenin and Stalin* (Boston, Little, Brown and Co., 1961), p. 46.

ent states, and in Russia proper they aimed at setting up a stable government that would be ready to accept the borders dictated to it.

After the capitulation at Brest-Litovsk and the conclusion of the
treacherous separate peace, Russia's allies had published an official
statement to the effect that they would never recognize it. The statement had been greeted with great jubilation by all Russians who had
similarly refused to recognize it. No one doubted the intention of this
Allied statement: everyone thought that, as soon as the war had been
won, the treaty would be completely annulled, together with all its consequences both for the West and for Russia herself.

It was indeed this firm belief in the eventual fate of the Brest-Litovsk
Treaty that had led the Allies, and those in Russia who did not recognize it, to set up the Directorate in Ufa so that they could help to end
the war and work side by side with the Allies for the establishment of
a new international order at the peace conference.

The sole purpose of my journey to London and Paris and of my
talks with British and French leaders had been to procure for national
Russia a rightful seat at the peace conference—or rather, in other
words, to speed up the Allied recognition of the new national government, without which Russia would never be allowed to participate in
the conference.

Nevertheless, recognition of the Directorate by the Western governments had been repeatedly postponed, until the situation, after my
conversation with Thomas, had become absolutely intolerable, especially because the final hour of the Central Powers was fast approaching. The arrival in Omsk of Admiral Kolchak and General Knox was
simply the last straw. I could no longer be silent . . .

Albert Thomas returned to Paris, and shortly thereafter I sent him
an article entitled "The Allied Peace and Russia," which was published in the very popular evening newspaper, *L'Information*. It read
in part:

The war is over. The representatives of the winning side have already
gathered to draft the peace terms and dictate them to Germany. Representatives of future governments and future states have been invited, quite rightly,
to the discussion. But where is Russia? Why has Russia's voice not been
heard?

Why is no one representing her interests at the Allied conference? Why is her name not even mentioned among the Allied nations? The Russian flag, which drips with the blood of those who fell fighting for the freedom of us all, does not flutter alongside the flags of the Allies. Why not? Because Russia is a neutral country that has concluded peace with our enemies—that was what Clemenceau told me on July 15, 1918 [10] . . . Surely this view cannot still prevail in the Allied attitude to Russia? Russia made peace with the enemy and now [according to the Allies] has to suffer the consequences of that act, including the right of the winning side to dispose of her territory as they please, without her consent.

The tragic misunderstanding between Russia and her allies goes on. It is extremely disturbing to all Russians. It may have a serious effect on the future of Europe and on the strength of "world peace." Many people feel that Russia no longer exists; that there is no longer a Russia which can be considered a power. No, Russia was, is, and—most important—will continue to exist. Although the Russians may lack strength at the present time, they are fully aware where their strength has gone. They know that it went into the struggle for truth and justice. Russians know that without the sacrifice of yesterday there would have been no victory today. The conscience and reason of the Russian people tell them that their duty in this war has been fulfilled.

It is with great alarm that we Russians look into the immediate future. At the height of the Bolshevik treachery, when the Germans tried to tell us that Russia had been wiped out, and that the old Muscovy, which really belongs in Asia, had been restored, we Russians were calmer than we are now. We believed that with the entry of the United States the war would be brought to a victorious conclusion. And we felt that the hour of victory would be the hour of Russia's renaissance . . . It is still not too late. Russia is impatiently waiting, and her people feel that they have an equal right to decide their own future at the peace conference. Though drunk with victory, you must not forget the rights of others.

At the end of the article I called for recognition of the Directorate as the legal government of Russia and for the invitation of Russian representatives to the peace conference. My appeal for recognition of the Directorate was in vain. On the night of October 17, four days after the publication of the first part of my article, the Socialist Revolu-

---

[10] *"Les amis de nos ennemis sont nos ennemis."* This sentence of Clemenceau's was deleted from my article despite protests on the part of Albert Thomas. The article was published in two instalments on November 14 and December 7.

tionary members of the Directorate (Avksentiev, Argunov, Zenzinov, and Rogovsky) were arrested and deported, and on October 18, Admiral Kolchak was declared the "Supreme Ruler of Russia."

The coup in Omsk took place a week after the final capitulation of the Central Powers, who signed the truce agreement on November 11. During this period the British government could have instructed General Knox to halt the planned coup d'état and at long last granted recognition to the Directorate. But it did not do so.

My conviction that the British government could have prevented the overthrow of the Directorate was further strengthened by an official statement made by Winston Churchill, then minister of war in Lloyd George's cabinet. On June 6, 1919, Churchill declared in the House of Commons: "We created Kolchak." [11]

However, having replaced the Directorate by a one-man military dictatorship, no one seemed unduly anxious to recognize it as the legal government in Russia.

The aim had been attained; there was no place for Russia in the Council of Ten, nor at the conference itself. And for a very good reason—Russia had no government that was recognized by the winning powers. My mission had ended in total failure.

It appeared that implementation of the secret Anglo-French agreement of December 22, 1917, had been blocked by a serious obstacle, namely, President Wilson's peace program, which he had outlined in a message to Congress on January 8, 1918.

The difficulty was that Point Six of the program stated that all troops should be withdrawn from Russian territory and that Russia should have the right to determine her own political and national policy.

However, Point Six did not stop the British and French from putting into effect their agreement on the division of the former Russian Empire into spheres of influence. In December, 1918, French troops landed in Odessa to provide support for the separatist Ukrainian Central Rada (Council), headed by Petlyura. British troops appeared on both sides of the Caucasus to aid the independent governments of the local minorities that had been formed during the German occupation. [12]

---

[11] See Notes at end of chapter.

[12] On December 30, advance units of the Japanese Expeditionary Force landed in the Far East Maritime Region, occupied Vladivostok, and began advancing along the Trans-Siberian Railroad. Under the Franco-British agreement the Japanese were sup-

In the meantime the peace conference was due to open in January, and it was imperative that the Russian question be settled while Wilson was actually there.

The peoples of Europe, ravished and exhausted by the long-drawn-out war, were eagerly awaiting the President's arrival, and they based great hopes on his leadership. He was thought of as an all-powerful figure who had been able to break the fighting spirit of the German people by his Fourteen Points, and thereby bring the war to an end.

His program was based on strictly democratic principles, which showed him to be opposed to all the imperialist war aims that, a year and a half before, the Provisional Government in Russia had also opposed.

The Fourteen Points called for an open discussion between the victors and the losers and the adoption of peace terms. They promised a new international order based on the principle that "right is might" and not "might is right." They also stipulated that all international disputes should be settled, not by war, but by "decisions of an alliance of nations which should be set up to ensure mutual political independence and territorial immunity on an equal footing for both larger and smaller states."

As is well known, on October 4, 1918, the new liberal German chancellor, Prince Max of Baden, sent a message to the Supreme Allied Council at Versailles on behalf of Germany and Austria-Hungary, in which he proposed the conclusion of a truce and then of a peace treaty based on the Fourteen Points.

Lloyd George replied that the Austro-German troops would have to give up all territories they had occupied, and that the Western Allies would only make peace with a democratic government.

On November 5, when the Central Powers had complied with these demands, the Supreme Council solemnly promised to make peace as agreed on the basis of the Fourteen Points.

President Wilson finally arrived at the end of December.

---

posed to guard this railroad, so that the Allied forces could proceed toward Russia's western borders without impediment and establish a front against Germany there. The crass absurdity and impracticability of this plan is obvious to all and the Japanese staff must also have known it. The Japanese took their time in moving into Siberia and attempted to expropriate Russian territory in the Far East which they were not entitled to do under the agreement. It was not until 1922 that, under pressure from the U. S. government, they finally gave up the territory they had taken over.

In London and Paris he was greeted by crowds of joyful people from all classes, who hailed him as the conquering hero. Everyone was sure that now there would be world peace and that the terrible and devastating war had been a "war to end all war." They were certain, too, that in its wake the last traces of traditional absolutism would be swept away. After all, that had been the promise given to the millions of young men as they left for the trenches.

The day the President arrived in London I was among the hundreds of thousands of enthusiastic people who welcomed him. They were not just ordinary people of the kind who gather in the streets to watch crowned heads or visiting dignitaries go by. They were people who had been shocked by what they had lived through in four years of war, people who were aware that "this kind of war" must not happen again, and who believed that the only man who could make their dream come true had now arrived.

I could not help being thrilled by the enthusiasm of these crowds, although I could see that their cherished hopes for a transformation of the world would be pitilessly shattered. The plans and intentions of the ruling circles in Europe were too far removed from the idealistic aims of the fourteen-point peace program.

NOTE I

Kolchak's Rise to Power [13]

The appearance of Kolchak in Omsk in mid-October in the wake of the new All-Russian Government (Directorate) was totally unexpected. From the end of July, 1917, until just before his arrival, he had been living abroad.

Kolchak was an outstanding sailor widely known both in Russia and abroad. Shortly before the collapse of the Monarchy he had been appointed commander-in-chief of the Black Sea Fleet. Like most of the senior naval officers, he had first been much in favor of the coup d'état. He had always maintained very good relations with the naval personnel and after the coup readily collaborated with the Central Committee of the Black Sea Fleet and Sebastopol Garrison. But in character Kolchak was impatient, capricious, and easily influenced.

[13] This brief outline of Kolchak's rise to power is taken from the evidence he himself gave the Bolsheviks in Irkutsk prior to his execution by a firing squad on the night of February 6–7, 1920. *The Interrogation of Kolchak* (Moscow, Gosizdat Tsentrarkhiv, 1925).

His first verbal report to the Provisional Government when he arrived in Petrograd on April 20 was very optimistic. But not long afterward—the beginning of May—he had his first clash with the naval authorities and I had to go to Sebastopol to make peace, as they called it, between the Admiral and the Central Committee. In June there was another difference of opinion, this time a more serious one. The Admiral lost all patience, threw up his post, and departed from Sebastopol, taking Smirnov, his chief of staff, with him.

In the train going to Petrograd he found himself traveling with an American admiral named Glenon, who offered him the chance of going to the United States as an instructor to the navy in the latest techniques of submarine warfare. Admiral Kolchak accepted the invitation.

Although he had never been involved in politics before, Kolchak was soon drawn into the secret "Republican Center" (see Chapter 21) and even at that stage was singled out as a candidate for the planned dictatorship. Meanwhile the Provisional Government received an official request from the government of the United States to send Kolchak to America to work on the staff of the commander-in-chief of the U.S. Navy. Permission was granted and at the end of July he made his way to Washington, stopping off in London on the way. But he was wasting his time. When he arrived in Washington, there was no job waiting for him. At the beginning of 1918, this time without the permission of the Provisional Government, he joined the British navy and was sent to Singapore, where he was at the disposal of the commander-in-chief of the Pacific Fleet.

In March he received a telegram from the British authorities in London instructing him to proceed at once to Peking and report to the Russian envoy, Prince Kudashev.

At the end of March or beginning of April he had a meeting in Peking with the Cossack leader, Semenov, and then left for Harbin, from where he went on to Chita to join Semenov. He immediately broke off relations with Semenov, however, as soon as he found out that the latter was working in close collaboration with the Japanese General Staff. He returned to Harbin and in July went to Tokyo. The Japanese, on agreement with the British and French (dating from December, 1917), had occupied Vladivostok and then gone on to seize a great deal of the Russian Far East.

As soon as the Japanese had been driven out of these territories, the Admiral left for Vladivostok with the British general, Knox, who had come to the public eye earlier in connection with the Kornilov affair. According to Kolchak's own statement, he handed the General a memorandum on the formation of an iron-fisted regime.

The next move in the game was the arrival of the Czech general, Hayda, in Vladivostok, and subsequent discussion of the question of a dictatorship in Siberia.

Kolchak and Knox reached Omsk in mid-October shortly after the arrival of the Directorate. A few weeks later the Admiral met with representatives of General Denikin, who had come there especially to meet him. Kolchak then began corresponding with the General through General Lebedev, who had arrived from Yekaterinodar.

At the insistence of the Siberian government and with the consent of General Boldyrev, a member of the Directorate, Kolchak was appointed minister of war. On November 7, he left for the front, and returned on November 16. On the night of November 18–19, a coup d'état took place during which several members of the Directorate were arrested and others were forced to resign, and the same day Admiral Kolchak was proclaimed the "Supreme Ruler" of Russia.

The men who carried out the coup, the Cossack colonels Volkov, Krasilnikov and Katanayev, immediately informed the Admiral, who obviously already knew about it, and were promptly arrested and tried, but acquitted on November 21. The members of the Directorate arrested—Avksentiev, chairman of the Directorate; Argunov, his deputy; Chaikovsky's deputy, Zenzinov; and their police chief, Rogovsky—all four of whom were right-wing Socialist Revolutionaries, were later deported via China.

The Tragedy of Versailles

Russia Ostracized

AFTER my summer trip to Paris for talks with Clemenceau I remained in England until the spring of 1920, living part of the time in London and part of the time in the country. At the very height of the peace conference I traveled again to Paris. I had been asked to come by members of the deposed Directorate, who had finally reached Paris via China and the United States, after having been exiled as the result of the Kolchak coup d'état.

At that time Lloyd George was considered one of the most powerful statesmen in Europe, and London was the hub of the political world. My status in England was rather ambiguous. Officially I was a private citizen and had no formal relations at all with the British authorities, but in actual practice I was still the representative of a free and democratic Russia in the eyes of the majority of the population. I was on friendly terms with a number of extremely well-informed statesmen and politicians among our former allies. Neither the negative attitude of the semiofficial press in Britain and France toward the February Revolution, the Provisional Government, and myself in particular, nor my harassment by the émigré supporters of the White dictatorships, had any effect on the way I was treated by liberal-minded Europeans or by many of my compatriots.

It was from the latter that I learned some very interesting facts. It seems that at the beginning of December, 1918 some Bolshevik political scouts had arrived in London from Moscow entirely unannounced. The Kremlin had evidently received word of the dissension within the British Cabinet regarding British policy toward Russia and had discovered that neither Lloyd George nor his aides were entirely sympathetic—to put it mildly—to Northcliffe's policy of setting up a military dictatorship. These Russian scouts had been instructed to try to gain direct access to Lloyd George, or, failing that, to contact his aides. In either case they were to try to persuade them that good relations with the "only true government" in Russia were perfectly possible, and that Russia had absolutely no ambitions regarding world revolution, but rather hoped for an immediate resumption of former relations with the Allies—especially Britain. Finally, they were to plead for British aid in restoring the war-ravaged economy. Shortly afterward, I received a visit from these political scouts (Krysin and Polovtzeva) "just over from Moscow," who confirmed the rumors of what had been going on.

Lloyd George obviously had an ulterior motive in trying to straighten out British relations with an economically and politically devastated Russia just before the peace conference with Germany. There can be no doubt, however, that he was influenced by these overtures from the Bolsheviks—who did indeed need world support, This was amply demonstrated during the first few days of the preliminary sessions of the Council of Ten, at which the problem of Russia was discussed.

I found out later, during a visit from Bernard Baruch, who occasionally carried out personal missions for the President of the United States, that the White House had been receiving similar approaches since the beginning of the Bolshevik regime. These two facts are of some historical importance and are directly linked with William Bullitt's secret trip to Russia early in the spring of 1919.

As I have already mentioned, even before the peace conference opened, Russia's fate had been settled once and for all by the Supreme Council (the Big Five).[1] When the joint delegation from the Denikin and Kolchak governments finally arrived, it was not admitted to the conference room. Nor were the delegates at any time received by the Council or any member of it.

Russia was in a paradoxical position unprecedented in history.

---

[1] The Supreme Council, which became known as the Big Ten and later as the Big Five, was composed of President Wilson and the prime ministers of the chief powers (United States, Great Britain, France, Italy, and Japan) and their foreign ministers (Wilson, Lansing; Lloyd George, Balfour; Clemenceau, Pichon; Orlando, Sonnino; Saionji, Makino).

Her name was not on the list of participants in the conference for the simple reason that only the winning side was eligible; the war had been won after Russia had become "a neutral country which had concluded peace with the enemy."

Since she had not been conquered by her former Allies, her name was not on the list of losers either. In fact, but for Russia, they would never have won at all.

The Allied nations, then rulers of the world, hoped that by their actions they could strike Russia off the list of world powers, force her back behind the boundaries of pre-Petrine Russia, and cordon her off from Europe by a chain of small, independent states.

To keep Russia from attending the peace conference was an easy matter, but deliberately to ignore her while attempting to rearrange the balance of power in Europe and Asia was utterly impossible. Russia's rightful chair in the conference room remained empty, but her specter hovered above it.

The day after the decision was made to exclude the Russian delegation, the Big Five continued discussion of the "Russian question."

"Russia is an enormous country covering much of eastern Europe and a considerable part of Asia," said Lloyd George. "Now that we have decided her fate, we must find a government there that will accept our decision."

Several days of heated arguments were needed to decide which government to approach. Some of the speakers, including Lloyd George himself, were in favor of coming to terms with Moscow, while others, Clemenceau for instance, would not hear of it and pressed for talks with Kolchak and Denikin. At long last, on January 22, tempers died down and a compromise was reached: All the *de facto* governments of territories previously part of the Russian empire would be called to a meeting on the Isle of Principo, where, presumably, the necessary agreement would be reached. It need hardly be said that the idea of holding a conciliatory meeting at the height of a bitter civil war was both psychologically unacceptable and politically impossible.

That was what I said at the Reform Club in London, where I had been invited to give a talk on why anti-Bolshevik Russia (not just the "White" generals but all the democratically minded people in the country) had refused to accept the "remarkably impartial" decision of the Big Five, when Moscow had accepted it readily, thereby showing its eagerness to restore peace in Russia as soon as possible.

It soon became known, however, that Moscow had only agreed on condition that all Anglo-French and other Allied troops be withdrawn from the territory they occupied before the conciliatory conference opened. This condition proved to be totally unacceptable to the Big Five, and the conference was canceled.

The day after the failure of this project, U. S. Secretary of State Lansing sent William Bullitt [2] to Moscow for a secret conference with Lenin.

His mission was to find out whether or not it would be possible for Lloyd George and President Wilson to reach an agreement with the Soviet government that would provide a *modus vivendi*.

Bullitt returned in the middle of March with good news for those who had been clamoring for direct talks with the Soviets. Or at least that is what I was told by people in the know, and it is probably true. But it caused a storm in the Allied Council, and the mission soon turned out to have been a failure. The reason was that events had been developing at a furious pace during the month that Bullitt had spent scurrying between Paris, Moscow, and Washington, and any possibility there might have been for talks with the Soviets disappeared completely.

It was exactly at the time of these approaches from the West that the Communist International (Comintern) suddenly sprang into action (March 2, 1919) with frantic appeals to all European workers and demobilized soldiers to oppose their "imperialist warmongering governments."

And the fact that the Red Army marched into the Ukraine at the end of March, coupled with the collapse of French intervention in support of the separatist Ukrainian movement led by Petlyura, left no doubt that the Bolsheviks had no intention of leaving their revolution a "localized occurrence" or of keeping to the articles of the Brest-Litovsk Treaty.

By the end of May, 1919, the whole of the Ukraine was in Bolshevik hands.

[2] Bullitt later became the first U. S. ambassador to Moscow after resumption of diplomatic relations.

The fact that the French intervention failed was not due to any tactical errors on the part of the French High Command; it was the result of a profound change in the British and French way of thinking.

In France public opinion was obsessed with internal politics; the millions of war-weary demobilized servicemen were only interested in staying in "civvy street" and had no wish to fight again in foreign parts for ideals they neither understood nor cared about.

In Britain, however, these feelings were stronger and more marked than in France. It grew more and more difficult to find volunteers for the British expeditionary forces, spread out at that time from the Black Sea to Central Asia. An unsuccessful attempt was made to replace the British troops in Georgia by Italians.

I learned of this incident from Francesco Nitti, prime minister of Italy from June 19, 1919, to June 9, 1920. He had left Italy at the time of Mussolini's accession to power and had settled in Paris, where I made his acquaintance. He was a quick-witted, observant, and rather cynical politician and diplomat of the classical Italian school.

One day when we were talking, the subject came around to Mussolini. To my surprise, although he spoke of Il Duce with some irony and made many jokes at his expense, his remarks showed no malice. I asked him why he had left his country if he believed in Mussolini. He replied that he was *persona non grata* with Il Duce, and then he told me the following story: In the spring of 1919, Lloyd George suggested to Orlando and Sonnino, the Italian delegates to the peace conference, that the British troops occupying Georgia should be replaced by Italians, who should also occupy the Crimea. The offer was accepted. The Italians began top-speed preparations in Rome for the fitting out of an expeditionary force of two divisions. In the meantime, however, relations between President Wilson and the Italian delegates were fast deteriorating, and in June they finally broke off altogether after a stormy scene in the Council of Five. Orlando and Sonnino returned to Rome in a huff, and the entire Italian cabinet resigned. They were replaced by Nitti and Tittoni, his foreign minister, who promptly canceled the preparations for this misguided venture. "Mussolini and his group never forgave me for my refusal to carry out the plan," said Nitti in conclusion.

The dispatch of troops to the former Russian territories merely increased the effectiveness of Communist propaganda among the demobilized soldiers and workers in the West.

What could be done? Clearly, if militant Communism was to be defeated, Moscow, as the hot-bed of the movement, had to be destroyed. To achieve this, there would have to be an anti-Communist government inside Russia to act in concert with the Allies, and it would have to be a government that the Allies could recognize.

Pressure on the Allies increased when, at the beginning of May, the first draft of the German peace treaty was handed to the German delegation in Paris. Quite naturally the Big Five wanted to settle the Russian question before the signing of the treaty, and, of course, they wanted to settle it in accordance with their own international plans.

Finally, when Kolchak's army made an apparently successful push toward Moscow in the spring of 1919, the Big Five recognized Admiral Kolchak's government.

On May 23, the Big Five reached unanimous agreement on the text of the note to be sent to Kolchak [3] with their terms for the recognition of his government, and the note was despatched to Omsk three days later.

Admiral Kolchak's reply reached Paris on June 4.

Both documents are of exceptional historical importance, although they were known only to very few at the time and have since been completely forgotten.

The terms contained in the Big Five note specified the internal policy Kolchak's government was to pursue and the nature of the relations he was to establish with the newly formed states on the territory of the former Russian Empire.

The note directed Kolchak to hold elections to a constituent assembly as soon as he had occupied Moscow, on the basis of universal suffrage and the secret ballot. If the elections could not be held at once, the Constituent Assembly elected in 1917 was to be revived. Further, in all regions occupied at present by Kolchak's men a democratic form of administration was to be restored.

All the points concerning internal policy, except the one regarding the Constituent Assembly, were accepted by Kolchak, who stressed that he had already decided to hold immediate elections to a Constituent Assembly after the Bolshevik dictatorship had been finally

[3] See Note I at end of chapter.

smashed, and that Russia both now and in the future could never be anything but a democracy.

In short, his views on internal policy seemed to be in exact agreement with the Big Five, and in equally exact disagreement with his subordinates.

The note went on to demand the independence of Finland and Poland, and a speedy solution to the question of relations between Russia and Estonia, Latvia, Lithuania, and the Caucasus and trans-Caspian territories, all disagreements to be subject to the arbitration of the League of Nations.

Wilson's consent to the demand that Kolchak give up the western territories of the former Russian Empire came as an unpleasant shock to me, for it was in complete contradiction to the true meaning of Point Six of the President's peace program. I felt that he had made a grave error in allowing himself to be swayed by the other members of the Big Five, all of whom were involved in secret agreements to which he himself was not a party.

This point had been published at a moment when the Brest-Litovsk Conference was broken off, following the Bolshevik refusal to agree to the dismemberment of Russia.

At that moment the meaning of Point Six was clear and unequivocal. It referred to the whole of Russia as she was on the day the Bolsheviks seized power, with the exception of Poland, whose independence had been proclaimed by the Provisional Government in complete harmony with public opinion in Russia. Polish independence had also been recognized by the Entente and the United States, and that is why President Wilson had dealt with Poland separately in Point Thirteen.

It was not until many years later, when I read the commentary drafted on Point Six at the request of the President in October, 1918,[4] that I realized that it is actually Point Thirteen that should now be construed to mean that all the western provinces split off from Russia under the Brest-Litovsk agreement were to be made independent.

And so, in his commentary, President Wilson provided the Anglo-French agreement with a fully democratic basis—the right of peoples to self-determination—and justified, albeit unwittingly, the territorial concessions hoped for by the German extremists at Brest-Litovsk. The

[4] See Note II at end of Chapter 25.

latter, in fact, had faithfully carried out the very program that Kolchak was supposed to agree to in exchange for his recognition.

In answer to the note from the Big Five, Kolchak recognized the independence of Poland, which had already been proclaimed by the Provisional Government. For the rest, he agreed to arbitration by the League of Nations, but added:

> The Russian Government believes, however, that it should recall the fact that the final sanction of any decisions that may be taken on behalf of Russia will belong to the Constituent Assembly. Russia cannot now or in the future be anything but a democratic state, in which all questions pertaining to territorial frontiers and external relations must be ratified by a representative body, as the natural expression of a nation's sovereignty.

It must be admitted that there was nothing to which the Western powers could take exception in Kolchak's reply; there was not the slightest hint of "Russian imperialism" or of a desire to restore the old, centralized government. His sole stipulation was that the final settlement of all territorial problems concerning Russia must be sanctioned by the free will of the people—and from a democratic point of view, he was completely in the right.

Nevertheless, the coming talks between the Russian government, the new states, and the League of Nations were of little interest just then to the Big Five. They were in urgent need of Kolchak's recognition of the new states and of an agreement that he would not impede direct relations between the Big Five and the *de facto* governments of those states. No such undertaking was forthcoming.

A brief reply was sent to Admiral Kolchak in response to his letter. It said that the Council of Five welcomed the tone of the reply, which seemed ". . . to contain satisfactory assurance for the freedom, self-government, and peace of the Russian people."

And with this elegant and diplomatic phrase the problem of recognizing Admiral Kolchak as the legitimate ruler of Russia was promptly "settled."

Obviously, Kolchak had come to power with the aid of Russia's former allies, but he was certainly no hireling of theirs, despite what the Bolsheviks said about him. He was a sincerely patriotic Russian who firmly believed that he could restore his country to her former power. It was with this conviction that he had refused to give the signature they demanded, thus thwarting the Big Five's attempt to secure the dismemberment of Russia.

A Peace That Continued the War

After my arrival in the West in 1918, it did not take me long to realize that the leaders of Western democracy, the average citizen, and even the socialists, were all hopelessly oversimplifying the Bolshevik revolution. They were convinced—and even tried to prove to me—that the collapse of the democratic system in Russia could never have occurred in the West. They explained away Russia's unprecedented catastrophe as a "local development" that was the logical outcome of the history of a Russian people who had never known freedom and did not even understand the concept.

I can still remember a conversation I had with an erudite economist named Helferding,[5] during the course of a visit to Berlin in 1923. Our discussion turned to the Russian Revolution, and after listening to me for several minutes, Helferding suddenly exclaimed: "But how could you have lost power when you held it all in your hands? That could not possibly happen here!" Then, realizing the tactlessness of his words and not wishing to offend me, he quickly added in a condescending tone: "Anyway, your people are not capable of living in freedom."

Eleven years later he was in exile in Paris and no better off than myself. Then, in my very presence, he had occasion to hear the same thing said about the Germans by a leading French socialist.

This kind of national rivalry struck me as being very childish. I knew the true history of Russia and the true facts of Lenin's ascent to power, and, even as I watched, the process of political and moral rot in our country began to spread throughout the whole of Western Europe.

No one in the West knew for sure exactly what was happening in Russia after the October victory. But the completely cynical and impudent propaganda that came pouring out of Moscow, while it frightened the rulers of the West, had a magnetic attraction for their subjects and was avidly absorbed by soldiers, workers, peasants, and

[5] A prominent leader of the German Social Democrats and a member of the Weimar Government.

leftist socialists and radical intellectuals. They wanted to believe it because they were anxious to forget the past. They fell for it because something akin to it had been promised by their own governments in 1914, and they realized that in their own countries there were no major social changes in the offing.

Naturally, the optimists found a very simple explanation for these sinister symptoms of incipient spiritual degeneration: After every prolonged and onerous war, people do not return at once to their peacetime routine, and political and social upheavals are characteristic of a transitional period.

But I could not share this optimism about the aftermath of a war which had absorbed the entire male population, a war in which millions of people had been killed, a war in which millions of others were uprooted from their normal surroundings and turned into homeless vagrants, a war which had, in fact, been unprecedented in history.

Fulfilling the predictions of military strategists and scholars made in the 1890's, the First World War was not a war fought by armies alone but by whole nations, and it brought social, political, and psychological devastation to all the belligerent countries. The peace conference began at a moment when the old mentality and the old social and political structures were already rotting away. But this fact was not noticed by the heads of the victorious countries, and the danger signals were ignored by the all-powerful Three at the Conference. President Wilson, Lloyd George, and Clemenceau, drunk with victory, boldly snipped at the political map of Europe and changed the whole of the eastern hemisphere with a total disregard for history and for the mentality of the different peoples involved.

After the Russian disaster of October, 1917, there was only one member of the ruling class in the British Empire who understood that the balance of power between the two coalitions had changed and that the time of secret agreements and pacts concluded before the war had passed.

I learned of this man quite unexpectedly, during a visit from D. V. Soskice [6] shortly after my return to London from Paris after my talks

---

[6] D. V. Soskice participated in the Russian revolutionary movement of the 1880's and 1890's. He became a political émigré in London, contributed to the *Observer* and the *Manchester Guardian*. I met him in Russia before 1914. In 1917 he became a member of my personal secretariat and prepared summaries from the British press

with Clemenceau. Soskice told me that Scott, owner and editor of the *Manchester Guardian,* was in London and had asked him to arrange a conversation with me. Two days later I met Scott, with Soskice acting as interpreter. Scott was resolutely opposed to the postwar policy of our former allies.

When I told him why I was in London, Scott said calmly: "Your mission has no chance of succeeding. Right now, Lloyd George's government is debating its policy toward Russia, but Russia is not even being mentioned as an ally of the Western powers." He believed that the superimperialistic plan of reshaping the political map was impractical, and he referred me to Lord Lansdowne's "Open Letter" in the *Daily Telegraph* of November 29, 1917. Naturally, I had not known about this letter, and Scott promised to mail it to me. Lord Lansdowne, who started his career under Gladstone, had been a member of various British cabinets until a ripe old age. An expert in European history in the fifty years preceding World War I, he knew that the peace plans of the Triple Entente were divorced from reality and that the restoration of Western Europe, including an equal reconstruction of Germany and Austria-Hungary, was a priority task. He contended that peace in the West should be reinforced by a sound political and economic order, created by the joint efforts of all Europe. ". . . To end the war honorably would be a great achievement," he wrote. "To prevent the same curse falling upon our children would be a greater achievement still. This is our avowed aim, and the magnitude of the issue cannot be exaggerated. *For, just as this war has been more dreadful than any in history, so we may be sure the next war would be even more dreadful than this. The prostitution of science for purposes of pure destruction is not likely to stop short . . ."* [Italics mine].

Scott was right when he called Lord Lansdowne's letter "prophetic." But the policymakers of the world paid no heed to the warning.

In December of 1917 Russia was thrown out of the Councils of Europe. Now the victors had deprived Germany of all her rights. Now, at the opening of the Paris Peace Conference, Wilson's famous

---

for me. I have enjoyed a lifelong friendship with him and his son, Sir Frank Soskice, who became a leading member of the Labour Party under Attlee.

Fourteen Points were no longer in force. Germany's fate had been decided although the Germans were excluded from the negotiations. The peace "dictate" drafted in the various commissions of the victorious Allies and adopted by the Council of Five was a watered-down version of the peace treaty signed by Lenin's representatives in Brest-Litovsk.

The treaty was submitted to the German delegation on May 7. A few days later, Count Brockdorff-Rantzau, the coauthor of Parvus' "master plan" to destroy Russia, vigorously objected to the terms of the treaty, which he declared to be not only in violation of the conditions on which Germany had laid down her arms, but also, in many cases, impossible of fulfillment.

In his brilliant book on World War I, *The Gathering Storm,* Winston Churchill contends that the 1939–1945 war was "useless," but that after the Versailles Peace Treaty, it was inevitable. Robert Lansing, secretary of state under President Wilson, writes in his unpublished papers: [7]

May 5, 1919: The conditions of peace are to my mind unrighteous since they are based on selfish desire rather than justice . . . they will certainly cause new wars and new social upheavals.

May 7, 1919: If I have read correctly the minds of the European statesmen assembled now in Paris, the treaty which they desire to be drafted will contain the germs of future wars . . .

May 8, 1919: The terms of peace appear immeasurably harsh and humiliating . . . We have a treaty of peace but it will not bring permanent peace, because it is founded on the shifting sands of self-interest.

May 19, 1919: The consensus was that the treaty was unwise and unworkable, that it was conceived in intrigue and fashioned in cupidity, and that it would produce rather than prevent future wars.

The peaceful interval was over almost before it had begun. The disintegration of the old world, which began in 1914, not only continued after the Versailles Treaty but actually proceeded even more rapidly.

[7] Confidential memoranda books, papers of Robert Lansing in the Library of Congress, Manuscripts Division.

NOTE I

Paris Peace Conference
Dispatch to Admiral Kolchak

Paris, May 26th, 1919.

The Allied and Associated Powers feel that . . . the[ir] policy . . . [should be] . . . to avoid interference in the internal affairs of Russia . . .

They are prepared however to continue their assistance . . . [and] help the Russian people to liberty.

The Allied and Associated Government now wish to declare . . . [that] the object of their policy is to restore peace. . . .

1. In the first place, that, as soon as they reach Moscow they will summon a Constituent Assembly elected by a free, secret and democratic franchise as the Supreme Legislature for Russia to which the Government of Russia must be responsible or if at that time order is not sufficiently restored they will summon the Constituent Assembly elected in 1917, to sit until such time as new elections are possible.

2. Secondly, that throughout the areas which they at present control they will permit free elections in the normal course for all local and legally constituted assemblies such as municipalities, zemstvos, etc.

3. Thirdly, that they will countenance no attempt to revive the special privileges of any class or order in Russia. The Allied and Associated Powers have noted with satisfaction the solemn declaration made by Admiral Kolchak and his associates that they have no intention of restoring the former land system. They feel that the principles to be followed in the solution of this and other internal questions must be left to the free decision of the Russian Constituent Assembly but they wish to be assured that those whom they are prepared to assist stand for the civil and religious liberty of all Russian citizens and will make no attempt to reintroduce the regime which the revolution destroyed.

4. Fourthly, that the independence of Finland and Poland be recognized and that in the event of the frontiers and other relations between Russia and these countries not being settled by agreement, they will be referred to the arbitration of the League of Nations.

5. Fifthly, that if a solution of the relations between Estonia, Latvia, Lithuania, Ukraine and the Caucasus and Trans-Caspian territories and Russia is not speedily reached by agreement the settlement will be made in consultation and cooperation with the League of Nations and that until such settlement is made the government of Russia agrees to recognize these terri-

tories as autonomous and to confine the relations which may exist between their defacto governments and the Allied and Associated governments.

6. Sixthly, the right of the Peace Conference to determine the future of the Rumanian part of Bessarabia, be recognized.

7. Seventhly, that as soon as a government for Russia has been constituted on a democratic basis, Russia should join the League of Nations and cooperate with the other members in the limitations of armaments and of a military organization throughout the world.

Finally, that they abide by the declaration made by Admiral Kolchak on November 27, 1918, in regard to Russia's national debts.

NOTE II

The French Chargé at Omsk (De Martel) to the French Ministry of Foreign Affairs.

Omsk, June 4, 1919.

Admiral Kolchak requests me to communicate the following reply to Mr. Clemenceau.

1. ... my first thought at the moment when the Bolsheviks are definitely crushed will be to fix the date for the elections of the Constituent Assembly. ...

... the Government, however, does not consider itself authorized to substitute for the inalienable right of free and legal elections the mere re-establishment of the Assembly of 1917, which was elected under a regime of Bolshevik. ...

It is to the legally elected Constituent Assembly alone, which my Government will do its utmost to convoke promptly that there will belong the sovereign rights of deciding the problems of the Russian State.

2. We gladly consent to discuss ...

The Russian Government thinks however, that it should recall the fact that the final sanction of the decisions which may be taken in the name of Russia, will belong to the Constituent Assembly. Russia cannot now and cannot in future ever be anything but a democratic State where all questions involving modifications of the territorial frontiers and of external relations must be ratified by a representative body which is the natural expression of the people's sovereignty.

3. Consider the creation of a unified Polish State to be one of the chief just consequences of the World War ... confirming the independence of Poland proclaimed by the Provisional Government 1917.

The final solution of the frontiers of Poland be postponed till the meeting of the Constituent Assembly.

. . . final solution [for] Finland be postponed till the meeting of the Constituent Assembly.

4. Baltic countries . . . prompt settlement will be made, seeing that the government is assuring as from the present time, the autonomy of the various nationalities will be settled separately . . .

The Government is ready to have recourse to . . . good office of the League of Nations.

5. The above principle implying the ratification of the agreement by the Constituent Assembly should be applied to Bessarabia.

6. The Russian Government . . . accepted the burden of the national debt of Russia.

7. As regards the question of internal politics . . . there cannot be a return to the regime which existed in Russia before February 1917. The provisional solution which my Government has adopted in regard to the agrarian question aims at satisfying the interests of the great mass of the population and is inspired by the conviction that Russia can only be flourishing and strong when the millions of Russian peasants receive all guarantees for the possession of the land. Similarly as regards the regime to be applied to the liberated territories, the Government far from placing obstacles in the way of the free election of local assemblies, municipalities and zemstvos, regards the activities of these bodies and also the development of the principle of self-government as the necessary conditions for the reconstruction of the country and is already actually giving them its support and help.

8. Having set about . . . re-establishing order and justice ensuring individual security to the persecuted population . . . affirms equality before the law of all classes and all citizens . . . without distinction of origin or of religion. . . .

Signature

Kolchak

Reply to Kolchak

The Allied and Associated Powers . . . welcome the tone of that reply which seems . . . to contain satisfactory assurance for the freedom, self-government and peace of the Russian people.

NOTE III

Official American Commentary on the Fourteen Points

October, 1918.

VI. The evacuation of all Russian territory and such a settlement of all questions affecting Russia as will secure the best and freest cooperation of the other nations of the world in obtaining for her an unhampered and unembarrassed opportunity for the independent determination of her own political society of free nations under institutions of her own choosing; and, more than a welcome, assistance also of every kind that she may need and may herself desire. The treatment accorded Russia by her sister nations in the months to come will be the acid test of their good will, of their comprehension of her needs as distinguished from their own interests, and of their intelligent and unselfish sympathy.

The first question is whether Russian territory is synonymous with territory belonging to the former Russian Empire. This is clearly not so, because Proposition XIII stipulates an independent Poland, a proposal which excludes the territorial reestablishment of the Empire. What is recognized as valid for the Poles will certainly have to be recognized for the Finns, the Lithuanians, the Letts and perhaps also for the Ukrainians.

. . . .

This can mean nothing less than the recognition by the Peace Conference of a series of *de facto* Governments representing Finns, Esths, Lithuanians, Ukrainians. This primary act of recognition should be conditional upon the calling of National Assemblies for the creation of *de jure* Governments, as soon as the Peace Conference has drawn frontiers for these new states.

. . . .

Provision should also be made by which Great Russia can federate with these states on the same terms.

As for Great Russia and Siberia, the Peace Conference might well send a message asking for the creation of a government sufficiently representative to speak for these territories. It should be understood that economic rehabilitation is offered, provided a government carrying sufficient credentials can appear at the Peace Conference.

. . . .

The essence of the Russian problem then in the immediate future would seem to be:

1. The recognition of Provisional Governments.
2. Assistance extended to and through these Governments.

The Caucasus should probably be treated as part of the problem of the Turkish Empire. No information exists justifying an opinion on the proper policy in regard to Mohammedan Russia—that is, briefly, Central Asia. It may well be that some power will have to be given a limited mandate to act as protector.

In any case the treaties of Brest-Litovsk and Bucharest must by cancelled as palpably fraudulent. Provision must be made for the withdrawal of all German troops in Russia and the Peace Conference will have a clean slate on which to write a policy for all the Russian peoples.

28

At the Juncture of Two Eras

The Breakup of Europe

ROBERT LANSING'S harsh judgments on the Treaty of Versailles have never been previously published.[1] Nevertheless, many close and keen observers of the Versailles tragedy and its consequences had arrived at the same conclusion. I was one of those observers [2] when I visited Paris in 1919 during the peace conference. Moreover, in 1920 I left London to establish my residence in Paris, where I had occasion to meet outstanding statesmen, political figures, and journalists from many countries. When I recall what I saw, heard, and experienced during those years, and when I compare my impressions and conclusions with those of Robert Lansing, I cannot help noting a certain identity of views in our evaluation of the peace treaty.

It was on June 28, 1919, that the Germans finally signed the Treaty of Versailles, but by the end of 1920 the coalition of powers which had dictated the conditions of peace had ceased to exist. In the first place, the United States, which had replaced Russia in the Entente, never signed the treaty at all.

One of the main reasons for the United States' failure to sign was that, by the Treaty of Versailles, Japan was to inherit all the former German islands in the Pacific. Both the more conservative elements and the military in the United States were irritated by the emergence of Japan as a first-class military and naval power in the Pacific, now straddling the ocean highway between the United States and China.

---

[1] See Chapter 27.

[2] See my article *Evropa na uscherbe* (*Europe in Decline*), June–July 1921, which was first printed in *Volya Rosii* and then in my Russian book *Izdaleka* (*From Afar*) (Paris, Povolotzky, 1922).

At this time the United States also declined to join the League of Nations, although President Wilson had been its originator.

At the conference of the naval powers in Washington in 1922, Great Britain was obliged to renounce the renewal of her alliance with Japan. The balance of power had now changed radically, and the inevitability of a clash between Washington and Tokyo may be dated from that time.

In France the situation had changed too. After the victory, Clemenceau, who had been the idol of the French nation during the war, became an object of hatred in French nationalist circles.

France had expected to receive the left bank of the Rhine from Germany. But President Wilson and Lloyd George had persuaded the "Old Tiger" to give up his demand and to accept in its place a guarantee of Anglo-American aid to France in case Germany should ever renew hostilities. However, after heated debates in the United States Senate, the President had been unable to sign this guarantee pact. In the years that followed, it was painful for me to watch the growth of mistrust and the intensification of anger and irritation in France, as well as the rebirth of the notion that "perfidious Albion" was again the chief and hereditary enemy of France.

From conversations with many French and English members of the government and the press, it became clear to me that the aims of France and England in their war with Germany had been basically different—and even contradictory. England and France had been able to fight their enemy in unity, but they could have no unified plan for building and maintaining peace in Europe after the war.

Until Admiral von Tirpitz had built up a powerful German navy, Great Britain in her European policy was satisfied to let the balance of power rest on the confrontation of the Triple Alliance (Germany, Austria, and Italy) and the Dual Alliance (France and Russia). After the building up of the German fleet, however, the situation changed radically, and British policy altered accordingly. It now became Britain's aim to destroy Germany as an oceanic naval power and to arrest Germany's advance through Turkey and Baghdad to the Persian Gulf. In this aim Great Britain succeeded. Germany's advance to the Persian Gulf was stopped, and the menace of the German Fleet disappeared. According to the peace treaties of Versailles, the German battle fleet was to be surrendered to Britain. It was while carrying out these provisions that the German fleet committed suicide by scuttling itself at Scapa Flow. England, unlike France, was not disturbed by Germany —even a strong Germany—as an exclusively continental power. As such, Germany was even considered necessary to the maintenance of the balance of power in Europe.

For France, on the other hand, a strong and eventually rearmed Germany represented a deadly menace. A great feeling of insecurity began to prevail among the French leadership, and the victory seemed incomplete. New provisions for safety had to be made. The hatred for Germany that had been accumulating since Sedan, as well as the new ties established between Berlin and Moscow, now prompted French statesmen to devise stronger security guarantees.

The French delegation at the Versailles Conference had pressed for the maximum military provisions, humiliating "sanctions," territorial and economic sacrifices on the part of Germany, and even her dismemberment.

Russia had now withdrawn from Germany's eastern frontiers and in her place a chain of smaller states was set up, a chain composed of the fragments of the former empires of Russia and Austria-Hungary. It was on these states, and especially on Poland, that France began to rely as buffers between Berlin and Moscow. Italy, France's southern neighbor, also broke with her former allies, after Mussolini came to power in 1922.

Thus, the coalition of powers which had dictated the peace treaty had virtually evaporated. As had been the case before 1914, Europe fell apart and split into two irreconcilable camps. A new arms race had begun. Although numerous disarmament conferences were held in the 1920's and 1930's, they all came to naught.

It was strange for me to observe that in the West the men who were in power and who directed public opinion were firmly convinced in the early postwar years that the Peace of Versailles could be the foundation of a new and stable Europe. These men were also convinced that in order to consolidate postwar Europe they must "paralyze" Russia for a decade or two. They thought that the *cordon sanitaire* between Europe and Russia, upon which Clemenceau had insisted, would also help to sever the ties between Berlin and Moscow.

They thought that the German people would become reconciled, without protesting or resisting, to those conditions of bondage.

In this they were cruelly mistaken.

On April 10, 1922, an international conference was called in Genoa. Germany and Russia were officially present. The purpose of this conference was to consider the Russian situation, general economic questions, and the problem of reparations.

Simultaneously, Germany and Russia were negotiating on questions of mutual interest. On April 16, they signed the Treaty of Rapallo, by which the two countries became allies and renounced any claims to reparations.

After this event, the Genoa Conference dragged on until May 19, when it finally broke down, mainly as a result of Rapallo and Russia's absolute refusal at Genoa to pay her prewar debts to France. In openly declaring their close political collaboration at Rapallo, the representatives of Germany and Soviet Russia had passed over in silence the most important and significant fact—that of their military cooperation.

I happened to learn of this cooperation a year later when I was on the editorial staff of the Russian newspaper *Dni* (Days), which was temporarily being published in Berlin. One day in the autumn of 1923, three German foremen called at the editorial offices. They had just returned from Russia, where they had been working at a gas and explosive plant near Samara on the Volga. According to them, the plant in question had been constructed by the German Ministry of War, which had been granted extraterritorial privileges by the Soviet Government. The plant was on the secret list, and no one was admitted without a permit from the German authorities. At first we were skeptical, but then one of the foremen produced a document bearing an official stamp. It stated that a certain worker had undertaken, under penalty of treason, not to disclose that he was working in Russia, or what he was doing there.

We learned later that the Soviet Government had granted the German High Command a similar but rather more extensive extraterritorial concession in the vicinity of Lipetsk, a town in the province of Tambov. This concession took the form of a proving ground for heavy artillery, an airfield for training pilots, and a plant for manufacturing bomber and fighting planes. In a word, all the types of armament that had been prohibited to Germany by the Treaty of Versailles were now being manufactured in small quantities in Soviet Russia.

These facts were kept strictly secret, as Leon Trotsky stated in his New York Times articles of March 4 and 5, 1938, at the time of the Bukharin trial. In his article of March 5, Trotsky threw some direct light on this German-Soviet military cooperation:

The Military Commissariat, which I headed, was planning in 1921 the reorganization and rearmament of the Red Army in line with its passing from a state of war to one of peace. Vitally concerned to improve military technique, we could then get cooperation only from Germany. At the same time the Reichswehr, deprived by the Versailles Treaty of opportunities for development, especially in fields of heavy artillery, aviation, and chemical warfare, naturally aimed to make use of the Soviet military industry as a test field. The beginnings of German concessions in Soviet Russia took place at a time when I was still immersed in the civil war. The most important of these in its potentialities, or more accurately, in its expectations, was the concession granted to the Junkers aircraft concern. This concession involved a certain number of German officers coming to Soviet Russia. In turn, several representatives of the Red Army visited Germany, where they became acquainted with the Reichswehr and those German military "secrets" which were graciously shown them. All this work was, of course, conducted under the cover of secrecy . . .

In 1923 Eduard Bernstein, one of the leaders of the German Social Democratic Party and the first revisionist of the Marxist doctrine, asked me to call on him. In the conversation that followed, Bernstein informed me that he was investigating the links between the agents of the German government and the Lenin group of Bolsheviks. He asked me what data the Russian government may have had relative to this matter, and I told him all I knew. All our information had pointed to Stockholm and to the activities there of Lucius, the German ambassador, and his agents. But, I added, we had no direct information as to what had been going on in Berlin. Nor did we know how the links between the German government and the Bolsheviks had been forged. Bernstein, in his turn, revealed everything he had discovered about this matter from the secret archives of the various ministries.[3] Bernstein told me further that he had been unable to complete his investigation. In the previous year, he had published his first article

[3] Some of these documents have since been published.

on the connection between Lenin and Berlin. President Ebert had immediately summoned him to his office, where the minister of foreign affairs and other high officials and representatives of the army were also present. Bernstein was warned that he would be charged with treason if he published any further articles on the subject.

By themselves, all these military preparations would not have led to a second world war if the allies, and France in particular, had not obstinately refused to reconsider and lighten in good time the intolerable conditions of the "peace that continued the war."

The impossibility of resolving this psychological impasse encouraged the spread of hatred, and eventually helped to bring Hitler to power. It can even be said that Hitler was born of the Peace Treaty of Versailles.

In 1923, after the French had occupied the Ruhr and while Germany was undergoing a grave financial crisis as a result of the fantastic reparations she had been paying the Allies, Adolf Hitler and General Erich Ludendorff attempted to seize state power in Bavaria. This so-called "Beer Hall Putsch" in Munich failed within three days. Hitler himself was given a five-year prison sentence, but was reprieved within a year and came out of prison after writing his *Mein Kampf*. Hatred of the Allies was rapidly gathering force, and Hitler soon became convinced that he could carry through his National Socialist program. He had briefly summed up his program when he declared during his trial in the Leipzig court: "Yes, I am using all my rights as a citizen under the democratic Weimar Constitution to destroy the democracy I detest." Within ten years Hitler had become chancellor of the Reich.

The governing circles in the West realized how instable and artificial was the character of the political structure in postwar Europe. There were an endless number of conferences on a high level concerned with questions of disarmament and reparation, but nothing came of any of them. And indeed, nothing could have come of them. Even Aristide Briand, one of the most farsighted statesmen at the time, did not dare to face the issue squarely and to reexamine the situation while the Weimar Republic was still in existence. Now, almost half a century after the emergence of the Europe of Versailles, it is superfluous to attempt to demonstrate that the peace did, indeed, continue the war. The twenty years since 1919 were a mere interlude, a truce rather than a more permanent peace settlement.

I shall not deal here with the fruitless attempts to consolidate peace in Europe, attempts that did little to cure anything beyond the external symptoms of a grave illness. One would have to devote a separate volume to the consequences of Versailles. Nor is it necessary to do so, because there already exists a whole library of volumes on the subject.

Before the outbreak of World War I, the leaders of Western democracy had solemnly proclaimed that the war against German imperialism would be the last of all wars, a war to put an end to all wars, and that all vestiges of absolutism would be swept away. According to them, a new world of solidarity would arise, based upon the principles of democracy and equality of all peoples. Tens of millions of people had given enthusiastic credence to the words of their political leaders. They had gone to the front and suffered through years of trial and privation, both in the trenches and at home. But when, after the victory of the democracies, these people returned home, they saw that everything was the same as before. The blatant contradiction between what had been promised, namely, a new, transfigured world, and the return to the harsh realities of the old world and its set forms, now proved intolerable to many people. For them, this was a psychological catastrophe. This discontent became the arena in which there began a struggle between Communism, on the one hand, and Fascism and Nazism, on the other, for the allegiance of the masses.

But after their victory, the democratic powers began to insist with special fervor on the necessity of preserving their prewar mode of life. That is, in an age of rapid change, they tended to become a conservative force in Europe. The overconservative attitudes of the powers at this time helped to promote the emotional collaboration between Stalinism and Fascism, both of which in many ways reflected the psychology of the new postwar world. The now unexpectedly sobered and peaceful Europe was suddenly seen to be activated also by irrational and insane forces. With my own eyes I saw this struggle develop. I realized the source of the strength of these new doctrines, which, though they aimed at very contradictory goals, were all of them filled with a like hatred for free men. In the psychology of both Communism and Fascism there was undoubtedly something that answered the mood of those who had fought in the war. Their faith was savage; their goals were aimless, that is, utopian; their creative energy was destructive; and their will was perverted.

But where now were the faith, the emotion, the will, and the enthusiasm of the democracies? They seemed to be missing. Internally, a sort of paralysis of the will had set in. Externally, the new postwar democracies found themselves under attack from two sides. There is a parallel between what was now happening to the democratic parties in the West, and in France in particular, and what had happened to the democratic forces in Russia after the Kornilov rebellion. A split developed in both the bourgeois and the Socialist parties. In the West, a section of these parties began to look toward Moscow, and another section toward Rome and Berlin. With the coming to power of the *Front Populaire* government in France, this split reached its nadir. In the parliamentary elections of 1936—the year that also saw the outbreak of the civil war in Spain, which was the prelude to World War II—the French Socialist Party under Léon Blum won at the polls with the help of the French Communist Party, directed by Thorez and Cachin. I warned Léon Blum of the possible consequences of such a collaboration.[4]

Up to our day, Western democrats have found it difficult to grasp that the war of 1914, which had destroyed all the foundations of normal life among all classes of society, gave birth to a hitherto unparalleled reaction—a reaction which had its main effect not on the aristocratic and capitalist milieu but on that of the working class and middle class.

In Russia, during the most difficult months of the February Revolution and the war, democracy had also been attacked on two sides: by the Communists on the one hand; and by the generals, egged on by top-level capitalists, on the other. And it was the generals who also received support from the Allies. In Germany, too, democracy was crushed between the Communists and the Nazis. And in Italy this had been done by the Communists and the Fascists.

At the beginning of World War II, when the French people tem-

---

[4] At this time I also hastened to publish my *L'Expérience Kerenski* (Paris, Payot, 1936).

porarily lost their capacity for fighting, it was because, deep down, they believed that only Stalin could save them from the legions of Hitler. But within three weeks of the German attack on Poland, Stalin had thrown off his mask as the defender of liberty and had publicly admitted the conclusion of the Soviet-German pact, which had been signed in his presence by Molotov and Ribbentrop.

From that time on, the chauvinist circles in France acted openly on the side of Mussolini and Hitler. On May 10, 1940, Hitler launched his panzer divisions under the command of General Guderian, and on June 22, at Compiègne, France was obliged to sign an armistice.

After the capitulation of France, all of continental Europe (with the exception of Sweden and Switzerland) found itself under the heel of the Hitler dictatorship. But despite Hitler's mad, lightning success, the war was far from over. Britain was still stubbornly resisting, and beyond the ocean, there was the menacing might of the United States.

On June 22, 1941, Hitler's armies burst into Russia, proving that the Moscow-Berlin pact had been an unnatural one. On December 7 of the same year, Japan destroyed an important part of the United States fleet at Pearl Harbor. On December 8 the United States officially entered the war.

Within four years Germany, Italy, and Japan had ceased to exist as political and military powers. But Western Europe had also ceased to be the ruling center of the world. The world's destinies were now in the hands of a new, all-powerful triumvirate. Before the end of the war, this triumvirate (Roosevelt, Stalin, Churchill) were already meting out punishment to the conquered, reorganizing democracy, and reestablishing order and peace in the world. Indeed, as is clear from the provisions of Yalta, this triumvirate laid the foundations of the post-1945 world.

At the time of Yalta, Hopkins is reported to have made the following statement to Robert E. Sherwood:

We really believed in our hearts that this was the dawn of the new day we had all been praying for and talking about for so many years. We were absolutely certain that we had won the first, great victory of the peace—and by "we," I mean *all* of us, the whole civilized human race. The Russians had proved that they could be reasonable and farseeing, and there wasn't any doubt in the mind of the President or any of us that we could live with them and get along with them peacefully for as far into the future as any of us could imagine. But I have to make one amendment to that—I think we all had in our minds the reservation that we could not foretell what the results would be if anything should happen to Stalin. We felt sure that we could count on him to be reasonable and sensible and understanding—but we never could be sure who or what might be in back of him there in the Kremlin . . ." [5]

In the light of our experience after Yalta, this statement of Hopkins' strikes us as so idyllic that it is difficult to believe it was made by one who took part in the Yalta Conference. In this sense it may serve as a key to our understanding of the reason why, instead of a new era of peace, the end of the war immediately ushered in the Cold War.

The Birth of a New Era

On September 17, 1919, Lloyd George made a speech in the House of Commons in which he explained as follows his policy for weakening Russia in every way and for preventing an imaginary Russian invasion of India:

> Let us really face our difficulties. Here you have got the Baltic States . . . Then there is Finland . . . Poland . . . the Caucasus . . . Georgia, Azerbaijan, the Russian Armenians. Then you have Kolchak and Petliura, all those forces anti-bolshevist. Why are they not united? Why cannot you get them united? Because their objects in one fundamental respect are incompatible. Denikin and Kolchak are fighting for two main objects. The first is the destruction of bolshevism and the restoration of good government in Russia. Upon that they could get complete unanimity among all the forces, but the second is that they are fighting for a re-united Russia. Well, it is not for me to say whether that is a policy which suits the British Empire. There was a very great statesman . . . Lord Beaconsfield, who regarded a great, gigantic, colossal, growing Russia rolling onwards like a glacier towards Persia and the borders of Afghanistan and India as the greatest menace the British Empire could be confronted with.

But Lloyd George was hopelessly behind the times as regards India and the maintenance of the British Empire. By this time the struggle for the liberation of India was already well on its way and was gather-

[5] Robert E. Sherwood, *Roosevelt and Hopkins* (New York, Harper & Bros., 1948), p. 870.

ing increasing momentum, as the Amritsar Massacre was soon to show. Besides, by the end of March, 1919, Ghandi had already launched his campaign of passive resistance, a long and stubborn fight, which was to culminate in Indian independence a quarter of a century later. At the same time, Ireland was already on the verge of gaining her freedom.

In 1881, Dostoyevsky had foreseen the inevitability of an all-European war. He thought that this war would be Europe's way of paying for the centuries of domination which she had exercised over Asiatic and African peoples.

The aim of the European powers in 1914 was certainly not that of freeing the colored peoples from their colonial bonds; it was, rather, that of redistricting colonial and semicolonial territories among the victors. However, the slogans under which the Allies had fought proclaimed the freedom of all peoples in the free and democratic world of the future. These slogans penetrated into every corner of the then embattled world and became, as it were, the emblems of the hopes and aspirations of the oppressed peoples. Soon the striving for freedom from foreign domination was no longer characteristic of Ireland and India alone, but had spread all through Asia and all over the world. Thus the movement for independence and national rebirth rapidly developed into a world phenomenon. This movement could not be arrested, but it might be contained. It could also be accelerated.

It was the avowed purpose of Lenin and his fellow Bolsheviks to accelerate this process, for their revolutionary activity and their propagation of world revolution had met with resistance even among the working classes in the Western countries. At the second and third congresses of the Comintern in Moscow in 1920 and 1921, two resolutions of Lenin's were adopted; these encouraged the struggle for national independence in the Asiatic countries. To the slogan of "proletarians of all lands unite" were added the words, "and the oppressed peoples." Some years later these resolutions were excellently summed up by Stalin in his interview with the Japanese correspondent of *Nichi-Nichi*. In 1925, a diplomatic flirtation had developed between Moscow and Tokyo, for Stalin had decided to draw Japan into the anticolonial struggle. According to *Pravda* of July 4, 1925, Stalin, when interviewed by the correspondent of *Nichi-Nichi,* made the following statement:

... The colonial countries are the main base of imperialism. The revolutionization of this base cannot help but undermine imperialism, not only in the sense that imperialism will be deprived of its base, but also in the sense that the revolutionized East must provide a decisive impetus in order to sharpen the crisis in the West. *Attacked on both sides—from the front and the rear—imperialism will have to admit itself vanquished.*

But the Japanese had their own plans for the future and Stalin received no reply. In the meantime, Communists from France, Russia, and the United States were sent to China to lend support to the nascent Communist movement being organized there by Mao Tse-tung, while a special university at Baku was turning out agitators and propagandists for action in the Middle and Far East.

Upon her entry into the war in 1941, Japan began to bring strenuous pressure against the British and American possessions in the Pacific and to make effective use of the slogan "Asia for the Asians." As a result of her brilliant initial victories, Japan succeeded in a short space of time in establishing under her protectorate a number of local national governments (in the Philippines, Indochina, Dutch East Indies, Singapore, Burma). In the end, Japan was defeated, but the countries that Japan had overrun during the war insisted on proclaiming their independence.

In my opinion, the "antiwhite" policy of the Japanese and their slogan of "Asia for the Asians" played a no less important part in this process of liberation than did the Communists through their work of propaganda and subversive organization. The Communist approach was a very different one. It aimed "to uproot Anglo-American imperialism in the colonial countries in order to ensure the success of the proletarian revolution in the West." The Japanese, on the other hand, had striven to establish and consolidate their own national dominion in China and South Asia. In any case, the situation after the fall of Japan was such that Communism was able to advance rapidly and surely under more favorable conditions. However, the national liberation movement in these countries was made up not only of Communists. National-democratic slogans also played an important part in the postwar upsurge of national sentiments.

On April 18, 1955, a conference of 29 Asian and African states opened at Bandung in Indonesia. Among the countries represented there were China (Chou En-lai), India (Nehru), Vietnam (Ho Chi Minh), Indonesia (Sukarno), and the Congo (Lumumba). This conference proved a landmark of historic significance. Here, for the first time, former colonial and semicolonial peoples proclaimed themselves to be sovereign and independent states. The Bandung Conference may be said to mark the end of white hegemony in the world. A new era had begun, a new era in the history of mankind. Man had now entered upon a period of really universal history—until then the vast majority of mankind had been the object of history; their fate had depended on the will of others. Now, after centuries of political paralysis, they had become the subjects of history, the masters of their own destiny.

The world had taken a new turn, a turn which Vladimir Soloviev, the famous Russian philosopher, had foreseen when, at the beginning of the century, at the height of the Boxer Rebellion (1900–1901) against the "white devils," he had with extraordinary perspicacity predicted in general terms the state of the world as we now find it sixty years later. In the August issue of *Problems of Philosophy and Psychology*,[6] Soloviev had published a letter about the Boxer Rebellion in which, among other things, he had stated:

Who has really grasped that the old world has ceased to exist, the former history has indeed come to an end, though it may still persist by force of inertia, as a sort of play of marionettes on the historical scene? Who understands that the historical period now beginning is as far—nay, much farther —removed from all our previous historical problems and questions as the time of the Great Revolution and the Napoleonic wars was removed in its interests from the War of the Spanish Succession; or as the age of Peter the Great and Catherine the Great with us in Russia had vastly outstripped the days of the princes of Muscovy? That the scene of universal history has of late expanded to terrifying proportions, and embraces the whole of the terrestrial globe—is now an obvious fact.

Soloviev foresaw not only the end of a whole age of European domination, but was also keenly aware of the determining role China would play in the history of Asian peoples. Indeed, if we consider the past of China and everything she has lived through in the last dec-

6 *Voprozy Philosophii i Psychologii* (St. Petersburg, August, 1900).

ades of the nineteenth century and the first decades of the twentieth, we can perhaps discover the deep psychological source of Mao Tse-tung's international policy—a policy which, under the cover of Communism, is striving to reassert the former might of the Celestial Empire.

In the years following Bandung the number of "liberated peoples" has greatly multiplied. Within a short time, native populations in Asia and Africa had followed the example and had been transformed into independent states.

Yet today the new generations of mankind are faced with tasks of almost superhuman proportions—those of creating a new order of life in freedom and peace for all "equal" nations. This is a most urgent task demanding willpower, determination, and awareness of the dangerous pitfalls of history. For, looking back at the world some twenty years after Yalta and some ten years after Bandung, we still see a world entangled in problems of the gravest consequence, problems old and new. The world is still confronted by the continuing and intensified menace of power politics and rearmament. Now, as before 1914 and 1939, we are witnessing a rearmament race. We are again living under the hypnosis of a possible new world catastrophe. Only fear of the monstrous might of the H-bomb and of new forms of aerial weapons seems able to halt the trend of disaster and to save the world from a new explosion of death-carrying hatred. At present, not only in Europe but in the world at large, we are divided into two camps where hatred is proliferating.

At the end of my long life, which has been entirely passed in the critical years of our present historical turning point, I can clearly see that no one gets away with anything and that one has to pay for everything. No one can get away with Machiavellian policy, which teaches that politics and morality do not mix and that what is regarded as unethical and criminal in the life of an individual is permissible and even essential for the good and the power of the state. It has always been so, but it must not be so any longer. But should it continue to be so, then the destructive forces which have accumulated in the depths of the soulless mechanical civilization of the contemporary world will burst out. Man must learn to live not by hatred and revenge, but by love and forgiveness.

The time has come when people should remember above all the words of Leo Tolstoy, whose moral authority was once acknowledged by the whole cultured world with no distinction of race or color: "How hopelessly morally blind and spiritually deaf is the man who, after the terrible cultural and spiritual collapse of the contemporary world, nevertheless believes that by means of material progress man's life in human society can be ennobled. For, in order to overcome present-day barbarism, it is essential that *man be transfigured.*"

Index